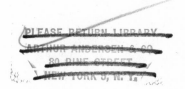

THE AICPA
INJUNCTION CASE

Re: ARB No. 44 (Revised)

AMERICAN INSTITUTE of CertiFied Public Accounts, "' et. al., Defendants

CASES IN
PUBLIC ACCOUNTING PRACTICE

Volume 1

ARTHUR ANDERSEN & CO.
1960

510151

COPIES OF THIS BOOK MAY BE
OBTAINED FROM THE PUBLISHER.

Library of Congress
Catalog Card Number: 60-10746

PREFACE

———

This is the first volume in a series of Cases in Public Accounting Practice. There has long been a need for a source to which practitioners, professors and students could turn for the record of the principal cases that have established important precedents in the practice of public accounting.

It is our hope in undertaking this series to compile the available material on many of these cases in a form suitable for reference, research and educational purposes. There will be no editorial comment in these volumes. The record will be factual. For instance, this first volume consists entirely of court documents, except for the first eight pages giving a brief factual resume.

This case is of particular interest because, as stated in an editorial in The Journal of Accountancy (August, 1959), it "established an important precedent upholding the authority of an Institute committee to express opinions on accounting principles."

A copy of each volume will be furnished without charge to the libraries of colleges or universities that offer any courses in accounting. Additional copies may be obtained from the publisher, at cost.

ARTHUR ANDERSEN & CO.

TABLE OF CONTENTS

INJUNCTION PROCEEDINGS REGARDING INTERPRETATION OF
ACCOUNTING RESEARCH BULLETIN NO. 44 (REVISED)
BY THE COMMITTEE ON ACCOUNTING PROCEDURE OF THE
AMERICAN INSTITUTE OF CERTIFIED PUBLIC ACCOUNTANTS

RESUMÉ

This is a case in which three utility companies were the plaintiffs, Appalachian Power Company, Ohio Power Company and Indiana & Michigan Electric Company.

The defendants were the American Institute of Certified Public Accountants, L. H. Penney (its president), William W. Werntz (chairman of its Committee on Accounting Procedures) and Carman G. Blough (its Director of Research).

The plaintiffs sought an injunction to restrain the defendants from issuing a certain proposed letter interpreting Accounting Research Bulletin No. 44 (Revised) (to the effect that credits arising from provisions for deferred income taxes may not in accordance with generally accepted accounting principles be included in the stockholders' equity section of the balance sheet) unless it followed the usual "exposure" procedure, allowed a waiting period of at least 60 days, and otherwise complied with the practices and procedures of the Institute and the Committee with respect to the publication of Accounting Research Bulletins.

The background of the litigation is as follows: In July, 1958, the Committee on Accounting Procedure of the American Institute of Certified Public Accountants (AICPA) had issued Accounting Research Bulletin No. 44 (Revised), which related to the accounting treatment of liberalized depreciation for tax purposes. This bulletin is reproduced on page 33. This bulletin took no definite position as to the proper treatment of accounts for deferred taxes on corporate balance sheets. On December 30, 1958, the Securities and Exchange Commission (SEC) issued a "Notice of Intention to Announce Interpretation of Administrative Policy" (SEC Release No. 4010, page 56), which read, in part as follows:

"Notice is hereby given that any financial statement which designates as earned surplus or its equivalent or includes as a part of equity capital (even though accompanied by words of limitation such as 'restricted' or 'appropriated') the accumulated credit arising from accounting for reductions in income taxes for various items including those under sections 167 and 168 of the Internal Revenue Code of 1954, filed with this Commission dated as of December 31, 1958, or thereafter, will pursuant to the administrative policy announced in Accounting Series Release No. 4 be presumed by the Commission 'to be misleading or inaccurate despite disclosure contained in the certificate of the accountant or in footnotes to the statements provided the matters involved are material.'"

"The Commission considers that the action thus taken is necessary or appropriate in the public interest or for the protection of investors and is consistent with the intent of Congress as expressed in section 167 (liberalized depreciation) and section 168 (accelerated amortization) of the Internal Revenue Code of 1954." The SEC requested and received written comments on this proposal by interested persons.

At public hearings subsequently held by the SEC early in April, 1959, pursuant to this notice, the Director of Research of AICPA testified that an opinion letter on this same subject had been approved by the Committee on Accounting Procedure and was being prepared for distribution. He read into the public record the significant portion of the letter. The entire letter reads as follows:

"American Institute of Certified
    Public Accountants
        270 Madison Avenue,
        New York 16, N.Y.

                                                      "April 15, 1959

"To the Members of the American
 Institute of Certified Public Accountants

"Gentlemen:

"Question has been raised with respect to the intent of the committee on accounting procedure in using the phrase 'a deferred tax account' in Accounting Research Bulletin No. 44 (revised), Declining-balance Depreciation, to indicate the account to be credited for the amount of the deferred income tax (see paragraphs 4 and 5).

"The committee used the phrase in its ordinary connotation of an account to be shown in the balance sheet as a liability or a deferred credit. A provision in recognition of the deferral of income taxes, being required for the proper determination of net income, should not at the same time result in a credit to earned surplus or to any other account included in the stockholders' equity section of the balance sheet.

"Three of the twenty-one members of the committee, Messrs. Jennings, Powell and Staub, dissented to the issuance at this time of any letter interpreting Accounting Research Bulletin No. 44 (revised).

                        "Committee on Accounting Procedure

                            By William W. Werntz, Chairman"

Appalachian Power Company, Ohio Power Company and Indiana & Michigan Electric Company, subsidiaries of American Electric Power Company, were among the public utility companies which had opposed the proposed issuance by the SEC of its "Interpretation of Administrative Policy" previously referred to. These three companies carried an aggregate of more than $65,000,000 in accounts for deferred Federal income taxes in the stockholders' equity section of their balance sheets. As it appeared that the proposed letter dated April 15, 1959, was about to be issued by the Committee on Accounting Procedure of AICPA, these companies filed a complaint on April 15, 1959, in the United States District Court for the Southern District of New York, against the American Institute of Certified Public Accountants and L.H. Penney, William W. Werntz and Carman G. Blough.

The complaint, which should be read in full (page 9) alleged, among other things:

That the Committee on Accounting Procedure of the AICPA publishes, from time to time, Accounting Research Bulletins, which are generally accepted by the members of the accounting profession as establishing the accounting principles to be followed.

That the Securities and Exchange Commission, in passing on the form and content of financial statements to be distributed to the public in connection with the sale of securities, permits financial statements to be prepared on the basis of the accounts prescribed by state regulatory commissions, only if the accounting principles reflected in such statements are in accordance with generally accepted accounting principles, and opinions of the Committee on Accounting Procedure are accepted by the SEC as persuasive authority in determining whether principles of accounting are generally accepted.

That, aware of the importance of its opinions, it has been the practice of the Committee to circulate an "exposure draft" of any proposed opinion to a considerable group and to give consideration to the views of this group before the opinion is adopted in its final form and published as an Accounting Research Bulletin.

That the actual purpose of the Committee in issuing the proposed letter without previously circulating an exposure draft is not to specify any prior intent, but to promulgate a new accounting rule without permitting interested parties a reasonable opportunity to be heard.

The final paragraphs of the complaint are quoted in their entirety as follows:

"29. The distribution to the 33,000 members of the Institute, and to others, of the proposed opinion will, because of the aforesaid prestige and authority of the Institute and the Committee, cause substantial numbers of accountants, financial institutions, investment banking concerns, rating services, financial analysts and government agencies to question the continued inclusion of credits for deferred taxes in the earned surplus accounts of plaintiffs with the result that plaintiffs will be seriously interfered with in their dealings and relationships with such persons and institutions. The question which will be raised as to the propriety of including $65,784,398 as a part of earned surplus will raise additional questions as to the validity of the announced debt ratios of the plaintiffs which are the basis upon which plaintiffs have in the past, and propose in the future, to borrow funds and sell securities to finance their respective current construction programs for which there has been budgeted more than $100,000,000 for the year 1959 alone.

"30. The Institute and the Committee know that the foregoing will result from the publication of the opinion expressed in the proposed letter, that irreparable injury, loss and damage will result to plaintiffs therefrom and intend that such irreparable injury, loss and damage shall occur.   The actions of the defendants in connection with the proposed distribution of the said letter and the opinion contained therein are in wanton, reckless and willful disregard of the said consequences of their proposed action.

"31. Plaintiffs have no adequate remedy at law.

"WHEREFORE plaintiffs demand judgment against the defendants:

"1. Pending the hearing and final determination of this Court and permanently, restraining and enjoining the defendants, their agents, servants and employees and other persons acting in concert with or on behalf of the said defendants, from adopting, issuing, promulgating, circulating, printing or in any manner publishing to the members of the Institute or to any members of the accounting profession, the aforesaid proposed letter or any utterance, opinion, recommendation, promulgation or statement to the effect that the Institute or the Committee is of the opinion or recommends that charges made to income in recognition of the deferral of income taxes should not or may not in accordance with generally accepted accounting principles be credited to earned surplus or to any other account included in the stockholders' equity section of the balance sheet, until such time as the Institute and the Committee have:

"(a) Submitted a draft of the proposed letter to the persons to whom the exposure draft of Accounting Research Bulletin No. 44 was submitted.

"(b) Permitted such reasonable period of time, not less than 60 days, to have elapsed subsequent to said submission in order that such persons may have the opportunity of submitting for the consideration of the Committee their views and opinions.

"(c) Otherwise complied with the Institute's and the Committee's practices and procedures with respect to the publication of Accounting Research Bulletins.

"2. Granting such other, further and different relief as to this Court may seem just and proper in the premises, together with the costs and disbursements of this action."

On the basis of the complaint and an accompanying affidavit the plaintiff obtained from the District Court a temporary order restraining the circulation of the letter pending hearing and determination of an order to show cause why a preliminary injunction should not be issued. The defendants filed a cross-motion to dismiss for failure to state a claim on which relief could be granted. On May 6, 1959, the defendants served affidavits of William W. Werntz, F. Merrill Beatty and George C. Christie in opposition to the application for an injunction, the parties exchanged briefs and the plaintiffs served a reply affidavit of Donald C. Cook.

On May 20, 1959, the District Court filed an opinion (page 134) in which it concluded that, because of the submission of matters beyond the pleadings, the motion to dismiss was to be treated as a motion for summary judgment.

The Court said, among other things,

"There is no allegation that the method of accounting proposed by defendants is inherently false or fraudulent. On the contrary, it is supported by respectable authority. Neither is there any allegation of special damages, except in the most general and speculative terms.

"This action is not to prevent interference with plaintiffs' contracts, their sales or their property. It seeks to delay the distribution of an adverse opinion relative to accounting procedures. True, it may ultimately affect plaintiffs' application for credit. However, such a result is collateral, not direct, an effect which incidentally flows from a justifiable act. The plaintiffs may have grievances, but they relate to the distribution of honest opinions, not facts. No threat of intentional, unjustifiable harm to plaintiffs' business rights or property exists.

"This court has been unable to find any precedent under the doctrine of prima facie tort or otherwise for a preliminary or final injunction forbidding a group from publishing and distributing opinions under circumstances equivalent or even similar to these.

"Accordingly, the application for preliminary injunction must be denied and the complaint dismissed and summary judgment granted."

Plaintiffs thereupon filed a notice of appeal to the United States Court of Appeals and were granted a stay until the United States Court of Appeals could hear a motion for an injunction pending appeal. Affidavits were filed by Whitney North Seymour as attorney for the plaintiffs and by John L. Carey, Executive Director of the American Institute of Certified Public Accountants, in opposition to the motion for injunction pending appeal. Briefs were exchanged and oral arguments were heard by the United States Court of Appeals, Second Circuit. This court handed down its decision on June 17, 1959 (page 202), affirming the decision of the District Court and vacating the stay.

The following paragraph, taken from the Appeal Court's opinion, is of interest:

"On the merits we agree with Judge Levet's reasoned opinion below, D.C.S.D. N.Y., May 20, 1959. We think the courts may not dictate or control the procedures by which a private organization expresses its honestly held views. Defendants' action involves no breach of duty owed by them to the plaintiffs. On the contrary every professional body accepts a public obligation for unfettered expression of views and loses all right to professional consideration, as well as all utility, if its views are controlled by other criteria than the intellectual conclusions of the persons acting. Absent a showing of actual malice or its equivalent the courts would be making a great mistake, contrary indeed to their own ideals and professions, if they assumed to restrict and denigrate this widely recognized and assumed professional duty."

The plaintiffs obtained a further stay on June 19, 1959, pending the hearing of an application to a Justice of the Supreme Court of the United States not later than July 9, 1959, for a restraining order pending action by the Supreme Court on a proposed petition for a writ of certiorari. On July 7, 1959, Mr. Justice Brennan denied this application on the ground that, in his judgment, none of the three questions proposed to be presented in the petition for certiorari had the prospect of commanding four votes for review.

Soon after Mr. Justice Brennan's decision (reproduced on page 238) the letter in question was mailed to the members of the American Institute of Certified Public Accountants under its original date of April 15, 1959, together with a transmittal letter of June 18, 1959, and a memorandum of July 9, 1959, from L. H. Penney, President of AICPA, explaining the delay. The transmittal letter and the memorandum read as follows:

"AMERICAN INSTITUTE OF CERTIFIED PUBLIC ACCOUNTANTS
270 Madison Avenue, New York, N.Y.

"June 18, 1959

TO THE MEMBERS OF THE AMERICAN INSTITUTE
OF CERTIFIED PUBLIC ACCOUNTANTS

Gentlemen:

"I am sending you herewith a letter from the Committee on Accounting Procedure, dated April 15, 1959, in regard to balance sheet treatment of the credit for deferred income taxes arising from accounting recognition of the use of the liberalized methods of depreciation authorized by Section 167 of the Internal Revenue Code for income tax purposes but not for accounting purposes.

"On April 8, 1959, the Institute's Research Director, Mr. Carman G. Blough, appeared as a witness at a Securities and Exchange Commission rule-making hearing--a public hearing of which a transcript is available to any member of the public. At that hearing he testified, among other things, that the letter dated April 15, a copy of which is sent you herewith, had been approved by the Committee on Accounting Procedure and was about to be sent out. Also he read into the public record of that hearing the significant portion of the letter.

"Mailing of this letter has been delayed because of a injunction originally obtained on April 15 of this year, without notice and without a hearing, by Appalachian Power Company, Ohio Power Company, and Indiana & Michigan Electric Company from the United States District Court for the Southern District of of New York.

"The injunction forbade the mailing of the letter without first exposing it for comment to those to whom the exposure draft of Accounting Research Bulletin No. 44 (revised) was submitted and deferring its mailing until at least sixty days after such exposure.

"Later a hearing was held by the District Court on May 7. On May 20, that Court filed an opinion deciding that the injunction should be dissolved and the suit dismissed and advising counsel to submit on notice, an appropriate order to put the decision in effect. On May 25 an order was entered to the effect that the suit should be dismissed. However, the District Court at that time enjoined the mailing of the letter pending a hearing by the Court of Appeals on a motion for an injunction, provided such a motion were filed in the Court of Appeals no later than June 1. Such a motion was duly filed and on June 17 that Court affirmed the ruling of the lower Court that the suit should be dismissed and dissolved the injunction.

"Thus, although the significant portions of the letter of April 15 have been a matter of public record since April 8, we have been unable to send you a copy of the letter until now because of the injunction proceeding.

Very truly yours,

L. H. Penney
President"

"AMERICAN INSTITUTE OF CERTIFIED PUBLIC ACCOUNTANTS
270 Madison Avenue   New York 16, N. Y.

"July 9, 1959

"Before the enclosures could be mailed, on June 19th Judge Lumbard of the Court of Appeals reinstated the injunction, pending a hearing by a Justice of the United States Supreme Court on or before July 9th of an application for a further injunction. Such an application was heard and denied by Justice Brennan of that Court on July 6th.*

L.H.P."

*Should read, July 7th.

On September 9, 1959, the plaintiffs filed a petition for a writ of certiorari in the Supreme Court of the United States (October Term, 1959), which may be found in pages 240 through 285. The following is quoted from the petition (case references omitted):

"Subsequent to the said denial by Mr. Justice Brennan, the proposed letter was distributed. In their brief and argument on said application, respondents pointed out to Mr. Justice Brennan, and it is therefore conceded, that the denial of the restraint and the subsequent issuance of the letter would not eliminate the controversy and would not render the case moot even in so far as equitable relief is concerned. Petitioners had sought, in addition to an injunction, such other relief as the Court might deem proper. Respondents pointed out, for example, that petitioners might obtain a declaratory judgment that respondents' acts in issuing the letter were tortious and that petitioners could still recover damages even though the later event had made the granting of injunctive relief nugatory."

During September, 1959, the defendants filed a brief in opposition which is reproduced on pages 286 through 304.

On November 9, 1959, the Supreme Court denied the petition for a writ of certiorari and the case is, therefore, closed.

END OF RESUME

UNITED STATES DISTRICT COURT
For the Southern District of New York

Appalachian Power Company,
Ohio Power Company and
Indiana & Michigan Electric Company,

Plaintiffs,

against

American Institute of Certified Public
Accountants, L. H. Penney, William W.
Werntz and Carman G. Blough,

Defendants.

VERIFIED COMPLAINT

Plaintiffs, by Messrs. SIMPSON THACHER & BARTLETT, their attorneys, complaining of the defendants, allege that:

1. Jurisdiction of this action is based upon diversity of citizenship. The amount in controversy exceeds, exclusive of interest and costs, the sum of $10,000.

2. Plaintiff Appalachian Power Company (hereinafter "Appalachian") is, and at all times mentioned in this complaint has been, a corporation duly organized and existing under and by virtue of the laws of the Commonwealth of Virginia, with its principal place of business in Roanoke, Virginia.

3. Plaintiff Ohio Power Company (hereinafter "Ohio") is, and at all times mentioned in this complaint has been, a corporation duly organized and existing under and by virtue of the laws of the State of Ohio, with its principal place of business in Canton, Ohio.

4. Plaintiff Indiana & Michigan Electric Company (hereinafter "Indiana") is, and at all times mentioned in this complaint has been, a corporation duly organized and existing under and by virtue of the laws of the State of Indiana, with its principal place of business in Fort Wayne, Indiana.

5. Upon information and belief, defendant American Institute of Certified Public Accountants (hereinafter "the Institute") is, and at all times mentioned in this complaint has been, a corporation duly organized and existing under and by virtue of the laws of the District of Columbia, with its principal place of business in New York City, New York.

6. Upon information and belief, the Institute is an organization of certified public accountants formed for the purpose of uniting the accountancy pro-

fession in the United States and, among other things, to advance accounting research; it is the only national organization of certified public accountants; the Institute's Committee on Accounting Procedure (hereinafter "the Committee") has as its objective the narrowing of areas of difference and inconsistency in accounting practices and the furthering of the development and recognition of generally accepted accounting principles, through the issuance of opinions and recommendations which serve as the criteria for determining the suitability of accounting practices; there are more than 33,000 certified public accountants who are members of the Institute, including every well known and reputable accounting firm experienced and active in electric public utility accounting.

7. Upon information and belief, defendant L. H. Penney is the President of the Institute; defendant William W. Werntz is the Chairman of the Committee; defendant Carman G. Blough is Director of Research of the Institute; none of the individuals named as defendants are citizens of Virginia, Ohio or Indiana.

8. Appalachian, Ohio and Indiana are all operating electric public utility companies.

9. Appalachian, as of December 31, 1958, had recorded on books of account maintained by it pursuant to requirements of the State Corporation Commission of Virginia and the Public Service Commission of West Virginia a total capitalization of $425,012,331, including a common stock equity of $152,089,098, of which $22,622,432 was recorded in an account designated as "earned surplus restricted for future federal income taxes".

10. Ohio, as of December 31, 1958, had recorded on books of account maintained by it pursuant to the requirements of the Public Utility Commission of Ohio a total capitalization of $447,921,130, of which $26,107,537 was recorded in an account designated as "earned surplus restricted for future federal income taxes".

11. Indiana, as of December 31, 1958, had recorded on books of account maintained by it pursuant to the requirements of certain orders of the Public Service Commission of Indiana and the Michigan Public Service Commission a total capitalization of $266,689,187, including a total common stock equity of $98,504,027, and an earned surplus of $35,389,162, of which $17,054,429 was recorded in an account designated as "earned surplus restricted for future federal income taxes".

12. The amounts recorded in such restricted earned surplus accounts of Appalachian, Ohio and Indiana, totaling $65,784,398, have been accrued in accordance with generally accepted accounting principles over a period of years and represent credits to such balance sheet accounts arising from charges made in the income statement (normalization charges) to provide for federal income taxes which may have to be paid in the future but which are currently deferred,

measured by the difference between actual income taxes and the amount such taxes would have been if such companies had not elected to take for tax purposes accelerated amortization deductions under Section 168 and liberalized depreciation deductions under Section 167 of the Internal Revenue Code. Said accounting principles have been used by the plaintiffs, as well as by many, if not all, electric public utility companies, for a number of years, and financial statements prepared on the basis of said accounting principles have been certified by all of the certified public accounting firms experienced in electric public utility accounting as being in accordance with generally accepted accounting principles.

13. The Committee publishes, from time to time, Accounting Research Bulletins. Upon information and belief, opinions, recommendations and pronouncements of the Committee, as published in its Accounting Research Bulletins, are generally accepted by the members of the accountancy profession as establishing the accounting principles to be followed by the accountancy profession.

14. The form and content of financial statements of plaintiffs which are distributed to the public in connection with the sale of securities for capital purposes is prescribed by the Securities and Exchange Commission under the various statutes administered by said Commission. Said Commission permits financial statements to be prepared on the basis of the accounts prescribed by state regulatory authorities having jurisdiction over plaintiffs, only if the accounting principles reflected in such statements be in accordance with generally accepted accounting principles. Opinions of the Committee are accepted by the Securities and Exchange Commission as persuasive authority in determining whether principles of accounting are generally accepted.

15. The Institute, recognizing the aforesaid results of the opinions, recommendations and pronouncements of the Committee, has had adopted certain procedures prerequisite to the publication of such an opinion, including the following:

(a) Any opinion or recommendation before issuance must be submitted in final form to all members of the Committee either at a meeting or by mail.

(b) No such opinion or recommendation is to be issued unless it has the approval of two-thirds of the entire Committee.

(c) Any member of the Committee dissenting from an opinion or recommendation issued under the preceding rule is entitled to have the fact of his dissent and his reasons therefor recorded in the document in which the opinion or recommendation is presented.

(d) Before reaching any conclusion, the Committee must give consideration to prior opinions, to prevailing practices, and to the views of professional and other bodies concerned with accounting procedures.

Upon information and belief, the practice of the said Committee has been at all times and is to circulate to a very considerable group what is known as an "exposure draft" of any proposed opinion, recommendation or pronouncement and to give consideration to the views of said group before such an opinion, recommendation or pronouncement is adopted in final form and published in the Accounting Research Bulletin.

16. In November, 1952, the Committee issued Accounting Research Bulletin No. 42 and in June, 1953, issued Accounting Research Bulletin No. 43.

17. Said Accounting Research Bulletin No. 42 contained, and said Accounting Research Bulletin No. 43 adopted without change, an opinion of the Committee with respect to the practice of normalization of income in connection with the tax aspects of accelerated amortization of capital expenditures. The Committee, at all times mentioned herein, has recognized such treatment of the income account, i.e., normalization of income by charges to the income account resulting from accelerated amortization or liberalized depreciation, as in accordance with generally accepted accounting principles. With respect to the credit resulting from such treatment of the income account, the Committee, in said Accounting Research Bulletin No. 43, recognized that the credit in such cases should properly be made to "an account for deferred income taxes". The said restricted earned surplus accounts of the plaintiffs, totaling $65,774,398, are accounts which reflect such credits and for balance sheet purposes are and have been treated as part of common stock equity.

18. Upon information and belief:

(a) In 1957 the Committee determined that it would be desirable to formulate and distribute an opinion with respect to accounting for the income tax effect of the liberalized depreciation provisions which had been contained, for the first time, in the Internal Revenue Act of 1954. An exposure draft of a proposed opinion was prepared and distributed to members of the Committee and other interested persons for comment. The exposure draft indicated, with respect to liberalized depreciation, that accounting recognition should be given in the income account to the deferral of federal income taxes. No mention was made in the exposure draft of any required credit to a balance sheet account.

(b) In June, 1958, after consideration of comments which had been received with respect to the proposed opinion and after rejection of an attempt by certain members of the Committee specifically to prescribe a balance sheet account for such a credit, a ballot draft of the proposed opinion to be published as Accounting Research Bulletin No. 44 was prepared and distributed to members of the Committee for formal action. This draft again contained no reference to any required balance sheet treatment of the credit resulting from the said normalization of income.

(c) In July, 1958, Accounting Research Bulletin No. 44 was published and distributed to the entire membership of the Institute. Accounting Research Bulletin No. 44, as distributed, contained for the first time, a provision that under certain circumstances it would be alternatively appropriate, "instead of crediting a deferred tax account" to recognize the taxes deferred as additional amortization or depreciation. Neither the members of the Committee as it was then constituted, nor the members of the Institute, had an opportunity to vote upon, or to express an opinion as to the desirability of adopting, the quoted phrase. Accounting Research Bulletin No. 44 did not, even with the unauthorized insertion of the quoted phrase, specify any required balance sheet treatment of the normalization credit.

19. It was not the intention of the Committee in adopting its Accounting Research Bulletin No. 44 to specify the proper balance sheet account for recording the credit arising from a charge for deferred taxes.

20. At the time of the adoption and publication of Accounting Research Bulletins Nos. 43 and 44, the Institute and the Committee knew that the plaintiffs, other electric public utility companies, and the certified public accounting firms experienced and active in electric public utility company accounting were and for some time had been recording the credits arising from normalization charges as restricted earned surplus and, therefore, as a part of common stock equity.

21. On information and belief, the Chairman of the Committee and the Director of Research of the Institute defendants Werntz and Blough, are about to mail to the 33,000 members of the Institute under the purported authority of the Institute and the Committee, a letter to the effect that:

"The committee used the phrase (deferred tax account) in its ordinary connotation of an account to be shown in the balance sheet as a liability or a deferred credit. A provision in recognition of the deferral of income taxes, being required for the proper determination of net income, should not at the same time result in a credit to earned surplus or to any other account included in the stockholders' equity section of the balance sheet."

22. On information and belief, the purported purpose of the publication of said proposed letter is to state the intent of the Committee in using the phrase "deferred tax account" in Accounting Research Bulletin No. 44. Said purported purpose is false and is not the true purpose of issuing said proposed letter. The

members of the Committee, as aforesaid, never had the opportunity to consider or pass upon the inclusion of that phrase in Accounting Research Bulletin No. 44 and therefore could have had no intent in connection with its unauthorized insertion therein.

23. Upon information and belief, the actual purpose of the proposed letter is not to specify any prior intent of the Committee but to promulgate a new accounting rule without permitting interested parties, including plaintiffs and members of the Institute who have requested it, a reasonable opportunity to be heard. There is no justification for such unreasonable procedures and haste.

24. The distribution of the proposed letter would result in arbitrary, unreasonable and unjustifiable distinction between accounting for deferred taxes with respect to accelerated amortization and liberalized depreciation since the letter does not purport to modify or otherwise act with respect to Accounting Research Bulletin No. 43

25. On information and belief, the Committee's own aforesaid procedures prerequisite to the issuance of an opinion or the publication of such an opinion in an Accounting Research Bulletin have not been complied with in connection with the proposed letter, nor has the Committee taken any other steps reasonably designed to ascertain the propriety of adopting the opinions contained in the proposed letter; no exposure draft of said letter has been submitted to the members of the Institute, and the Committee has not given proper consideration to its own prior opinions, to prevailing generally accepted accounting practices and to the views of professional bodies concerned with accounting procedures.

26. The said proposed letter purports to be for universal application in the accountancy profession and contains no exception for businesses in which the adoption of such a practice would conflict with generally accepted accounting principles in said industry. The proposed practice of treating such deferred income tax credits as liabilities or deferred credits for balance sheet purposes rather than as part of earned surplus is in conflict with the generally accepted accounting principles which the plaintiffs have been specifically authorized to employ by state regulatory agencies and which are employed by many electric public utility companies and accounting firms specializing in such work for many years up to the present.

27. Upon information and belief, a majority of the members of the Committee have no experience in electric public utility company accounting as such.

28. The members of the Committee have been informed and are on notice that the adoption and publication of the proposed opinion will cause great, immediate and irreparable injury, loss and damage to the plaintiffs and other electric public utility companies.

29. The distribution to the 33,000 members of the Institute, and to others, of the proposed opinion will, because of the aforesaid prestige and authority of the Institute and the Committee, cause substantial numbers of accountants, financial institutions, investment banking concerns, rating services, financial analysts and governmental agencies to question the continued inclusion of credits for deferred taxes in the earned surplus accounts of plaintiffs with the result that plaintiffs will be seriously interfered with in their dealings and relationships with such persons and institutions. The question which will be raised as to the propriety of including $65,784,398 as a part of earned surplus will raise additional questions as to the validity of the announced debt ratios of the plaintiffs which are the basis upon which plaintiffs have in the past, and propose in the future, to borrow funds and sell securities to finance their respective current construction programs for which there has been budgeted more than $100,000,000 for the year 1959 alone.

30. The Institute and the Committee know that the foregoing will result from the publication of the opinion expressed in the proposed letter, that irreparable injury, loss and damage will result to plaintiffs therefrom and intend that such irreparable injury, loss and damage shall occur. The actions of the defendants in connection with the proposed distribution of the said letter and the opinion contained therein are in wanton, reckless and wilful disregard of the said consequences of their proposed action.

31. Plaintiffs have no adequate remedy at law.

WHEREFORE plaintiffs demand judgment against the defendants:

1. Pending the hearing and final determination of this Court and permanently, restraining and enjoining the defendants, their agents, servants and employees and any other persons acting in concert with or on behalf of any of the said defendants, from adopting, issuing, promulgating, circulating, printing or in any manner publishing to the members of the Institute or to any members of the accountancy profession, the aforesaid proposed letter or any utterance, opinion, recommendation, promulgation or statement to the effect that the Institute or the Committee is of the opinion or recommends that charges made to income in recognition of the deferral of income taxes should not or may not in accordance with generally accepted accounting principles be credited to earned surplus or to any other account included in the stockholders' equity section of the balance sheet, until such time as the Institute and the Committee have:

(a) Submitted a draft of the proposed letter to the persons to whom the exposure draft of Accounting Research Bulletin No. 44 was submitted.

(b) Permitted such reasonable period of time, not less than 60 days, to have elapsed subsequent to said submission in order that such persons may have the opportunity of submitting for the consideration of the Committee their views and opinions.

(c) Otherwise complied with the Institute's and the Committee's practices and procedures with respect to the publication of Accounting Research Bulletins.

2. Granting such other, further and different relief as to this Court may seem just and proper in the premises, together with the costs and disbursements of this action.

SIMPSON THACHER & BARTLETT

By /s/ RICHARD M. DICKE
A Member of the Firm

Attorneys for Plaintiffs,
Office and Post Office Address,
120 Broadway,
New York 5, New York.

STATE OF NEW YORK $\}$ ss.:
COUNTY OF NEW YORK $\}$

    ROBERT O. WHITMAN, being duly sworn, deposes and says, that:

    I am the Treasurer of Appalachian Power Company, Ohio Power Company and Indiana & Michigan Electric Company, the plaintiffs in the above-entitled action; I have read the foregoing Complaint and know the contents thereof; the same is true to my own knowledge and belief, except as to the matters therein stated to have been alleged upon information and belief and as to those matters, I believe it to be true; the reason that this verification is made by me rather than by plaintiffs is that the plaintiffs are corporations.

Sworn to before me this $\}$
15th day of April, 1959 $\}$

        /s/ ROBERT O. WHITMAN

/s/ STEPHEN E. DAVIS
    Notary Public

UNITED STATES DISTRICT COURT
For the Southern District of New York

Appalachian Power Company,
Ohio Power Company and
Indiana & Michigan Electric Company,

Plaintiffs,

against

American Institute of Certified Public
Accountants, L. H. Penney, William W.
Werntz and Carman G. Blough,

Defendants.

AFFIDAVIT

STATE OF NEW YORK
COUNTY OF NEW YORK } ss.

ROBERT O. WHITMAN, being duly sworn deposes and says that:

1. I reside at 35 Riverview Road, Irvington-on-Hudson, New York. I am the Treasurer of each of the plaintiff corporations and am fully familiar with all the facts and matters hereinafter stated.

2. This affidavit is submitted in support of plaintiffs' application, pursuant to Rule 65 of the Federal Rules of Civil Procedure, for an order granting a preliminary injunction herein and in support of plaintiffs' application for an order to show cause bringing on the plaintiffs' said application for a preliminary injunction and in support of plaintiffs' application for a temporary restraining order pending the hearing and determination of said application for a preliminary injunction.

3. I have since 1940 been a certified public accountant, have had more than twenty years' experience concentrated in accounting in the electric public utility field, and for sixteen and a half years was associated with Niles & Niles, a certified public accounting firm, a substantial portion of whose practice was devoted to the public utility field. I have been a member of the defendant American Institute of Certified Public Accountants since 1942. I am also a member of the New York State Society of Certified Public Accountants.

4. Annexed as Exhibit "A" hereto and made a part hereof is a true copy of the verified complaint in this action. Said complaint was verified by me and I hereby adopt and incorporate in this affidavit each and every statement and allegation contained in said verified complaint as if such allegation were repeated in full herein. I have personal knowledge of all of the matters alleged in the com-

plaint, except those alleged to have been made on information and belief. The sources of my information and belief with respect to such allegations are transcripts of testimony given at official proceedings of Federal and State administrative bodies, examination of official publications and statements of the defendant American Institute of Certified Public Accountants and its Committee on Accounting Procedure, correspondence with members of the said Committee on Accounting Procedure and examination of records of the plaintiff corporations.

5. The reason that this application for a preliminary injunction is sought to be brought on by order to show cause and the reason for the application for a temporary restraining order pending the hearing on said application is that the plaintiffs, as more fully appears hereinafter, will suffer immediately all of the irreparable injuries more fully alleged in the verified complaint herein unless the defendants are immediately restrained from effecting the proposed acts complained of in the complaint.

6. The Director of Research of the defendant Institute of Certified Public Accountants, the defendant Carman G. Blough, publicly stated on April 8, 1959, that the proposed letter and opinion complained of in the complaint was at that time being prepared for distribution to the thirty-three thousand members of the defendant Institute of Certified Public Accountants. Its distribution is, therefore, imminent. The fact is that during the course of a meeting held between representatives of the plaintiffs and defendants Werntz and Blough immediately prior to the execution of this affidavit, plaintiffs were unable to secure from defendants Werntz and Blough any commitment to delay the distribution of the said proposed letter and opinion.

7. Unless this Court grants plaintiffs' application for a temporary restraining order prohibiting the defendants from the distribution of said proposed letter and opinion, it will forthwith be distributed to the membership of the defendant Institute of Certified Public Accountants and immediately upon said distribution, the irreparable harm alleged in the verified complaint and incorporated in this affidavit will ensue. Once the said distribution has occurred, this application and indeed, this action for equitable relief, will have been rendered moot, and plaintiffs will be unable to secure from this Court, or any other court, the relief necessary to protect them from the consequences of the said distribution.

8. No harm, damage, loss or injury can occur to the defendants from the granting of the relief sought herein, which will at most delay the challenged activity until such time as defendants have justified their conduct. There is no reason why the defendants must distribute their letter and opinion with such undue haste. No benefits will accrue to defendants or anyone else by reason of an early distribution and no harm by reason of a later distribution if the same is determined to be justifiable. The sole interests affected one way or the other are those of the plaintiffs.

9. The summons and verified complaint herein are being filed in this Court simultaneously with the presentation of this application for an order to show cause, and it is the intention of the plaintiffs to cause the service of the summons and complaint herein simultaneously with the service of the order to show cause and temporary restraining order sought herein.

10. No previous application has been made to any Court or Judge for the relief sought herein.

11. By reason of the foregoing, plaintiffs respectfully request that an order to show cause be signed herein bringing on plaintiffs' application for a preliminary injunction and that, pending the hearing and determination of said application for a preliminary injunction, a temporary restraining order be granted, restraining and enjoining the defendants, their agents, servants and employees and any other persons acting in concert with or on behalf of any of the said defendants, from adopting, issuing, promulgating, circulating, printing or in any manner publishing to the members of the defendant American Institute of Certified Public Accountants, or to any members of the accountancy profession, the aforesaid proposed letter or any utterance, opinion, recommendation, promulgation or statement to the effect that the defendant American Institute of Certified Public Accountants or its Committee on Accounting Procedure is of the opinion or recommends that charges made to income in recognition of the deferral of income taxes should not or may not, in accordance with generally accepted accounting principles, be credited to earned surplus or to any other account included in the stockholders' equity section of the balance sheet, until such time as the defendant American Institute of Certified Public Accountants and its Committee on Accounting Procedure have:

(a) Submitted a draft of the proposed letter to the persons to whom the exposure draft of Accounting Research Bulletin No. 44 was submitted.

(b) Permitted such reasonable period of time, not less than 60 days, to have elapsed subsequently to said submission in order that such persons may have the opportunity of submitting for the consideration of the Committee on Accounting Procedure their views and opinions.

(c) Otherwise complied with the defendant American Institute of Certified Public Accountants' and its Committee on Accounting Procedure's practices and procedures with respect to the publication of Accounting Research Bulletins.

/s/ ROBERT O. WHITMAN
Robert O. Whitman

Sworn to before me this

15th day of April, 1959

/s/ STEPHEN E. DAVIS
Stephen E. Davis
Notary Public, State of New York
Qualified in Bronx County
Cert. filed in New York County
No. 03–5941025
Commission Expires March 30, 1960

UNITED STATES DISTRICT COURT
For the Southern District of New York

Appalachian Power Company,
Ohio Power Company and
Indiana & Michigan Electric Company,

Plaintiffs,

against

American Institute of Certified Public
Accountants, L. H. Penney, William W.
Werntz and Carman G. Blough,

Defendants.

ORDER TO SHOW CAUSE
Civ. 145-161

Upon the verified complaint herein and the annexed affidavit of ROBERT O. WHITMAN, duly sworn to on April 15, 1959,

LET the defendants herein, or their attorneys, show cause, at a Motion Term of this Court, to be held at Room 506 of the United States Court House, Foley Square, New York, N.Y., on the 17 day of April, 1959, at 3 o'clock in the afternoon of that day, or as soon thereafter as counsel can be heard, why an order, pursuant to Rule 65 of the Federal Rules of Civil Procedure, should not be made and entered herein, granting a preliminary injunction enjoining the defendants as requested in the prayer for relief in the verified complaint herein and in the said moving affidavit of Robert O. Whitman annexed hereto, and why the plaintiffs should not have such other, further and different relief as to the Court may seem just and proper in the premises.

It appearing from the verified complaint herein and the said affidavit of Robert O. Whitman that plaintiff has no adequate remedy at law, and it appearing therefrom that the distribution of the letter and opinion proposed to be distributed by the defendants to the members of the defendant American Institute of Certified Public Accountants, to the effect that the defendant American Institute of Certified Public Accountants or its Committee on Accounting Procedure is of the opinion or recommends that charges made to income in recognition of the deferral of income taxes should not or may not, in accordance with generally accepted accounting principles be credited to earned surplus or to any other account included in the stockholders' equity section of the balance sheet, will cause substantial numbers of accountants, financial institutions, investment banking concerns, rating services, financial analysts and governmental agencies to question the continued inclusion of credits for deferred taxes in the earned surplus accounts of plaintiffs and will seriously interfere with plaintiffs in their dealings and relationships with such persons and institutions and will raise questions as to the validity of the announced debt ratios of the plaintiffs which are the basis upon which plaintiffs have in the past, and propose in the future, to borrow funds and sell securities to finance their respective current construction programs, and it appearing that such irreparable injury, loss and damage will result to the plaintiffs herein before notice can be served and a hearing had herein, unless the defendants are restrained from the acts hereinafter set forth, and the plaintiffs having given and filed the undertaking required by law in the sum of Five Hundred Dollars,

IT IS ORDERED that, pending the hearing and determination of plaintiffs' application for a preliminary injunction herein, the defendants, their agents, servants and employees and any other persons acting in concert with or on behalf of any of the said defendants, be and they hereby are enjoined and restrained from adopting, issuing, promulgating, circulating, printing or in any manner publishing to the members of the defendant American Institute of Certified Public Accountants or to any members of the accountancy profession, the aforesaid proposed letter or any utterance, opinion, recommendation, promulgation or statement to the effect that the defendant American Institute of Certified Public Accountants or its Committee on Accounting Procedure is of the opinion or recommends that charges made to income in recognition of the deferral of income taxes should not or may not, in accordance with generally accepted accounting principles, be credited to earned surplus or to any other account included in the stockholders' equity section of the balance sheet, until such time as the defendant American Institute of Certified Public Accountants and its Committee on Accounting Procedure have:

(a) Submitted a draft of the proposed letter to the persons to whom the exposure draft of Accounting Research Bulletin No. 44 was submitted.

(b) Permitted such reasonable period of time, not less than 60 days, to have elapsed subsequent to said submission in order that such persons may have the opportunity of submitting for the consideration of the Committee on Accounting Procedure their views and opinions.

(c) Otherwise complied with the defendant American Institute of Certified Public Accountants' and its Committee on Accounting Procedure's practices and procedures with respect to the publication of Accounting Research Bulletins.

Sufficient reason appearing therefor, let service of a copy of this order, together with a copy of the papers upon which it is based, upon the defendants, at or before 5:30 o'clock on the   *   day of April, 1959, be deemed good and sufficient service thereof.

Dated, April 15th, 1959

at 4:30 PM

/s/ EDWARD L. PALMIERI

U.S.D.J.

*Not shown on copy in U.S.D.C. file.

UNITED STATES DISTRICT COURT
For the Southern District of New York

Appalachian Power Company,
Ohio Power Company and
Indiana & Michigan Electric Company,

Plaintiffs,

against

American Institute of Certified Public
Accountants, L. H. Penney, William W.
Werntz and Carman G. Blough.

Defendants.

NOTICE OF CROSS-MOTION

Civil Action File No. 145–161

PLEASE TAKE NOTICE that upon the complaint herein, the undersigned will move this Court at a motion term thereof to be held at Room 506, United States Court House, Foley Square, New York 7, N.Y., on May 7, 1959, at ten o'clock in the forenoon, or as soon thereafter as counsel can be heard, for an order pursuant to Federal Rule of Civil Procedure 12(b), dismissing the complaint on the ground that it fails to state a claim against defendants upon which relief can be granted.

Yours, etc.

Dated: New York, N.Y.,
      May 1, 1959

/s/ HOWARD C. WESTWOOD
Howard C. Westwood

/s/ FONTAINE C. BRADLEY
Fontaine C. Bradley

/s/ STANLEY L. TEMKO
Stanley L. Temko

Attorneys for Defendants

Office & P.O. Address:
c/o American Institute of
    Certified Public Accountants
270 Madison Avenue
New York 16, New York
    - and -
Covington & Burling
701 Union Trust Building
Washington 5, D. C.

TO:
SIMPSON, THACHER & BARTLETT
120 Broadway
New York 5, New York
Attorneys for Plaintiffs

UNITED STATES DISTRICT COURT

For the Southern District of New York

Appalachian Power Company, Ohio Power Company and Indiana & Michigan Electric Company, *Plaintiffs*, against American Institute of Certified Public Accountants, L. H. Penney, William W. Werntz and Carman G. Blough, *Defendants*	MEMORANDUM OF POINTS TO BE RAISED ON CROSS–MOTION TO DISMISS Civil No. 145–161

Defendants intend to raise and rely on the following points in urging dismissal of the complaint herein:

1. The complaint seeks to restrain the freedom of expression of opinion of the Committee on Accounting Procedure of the defendant, American Institute of Certified Public Accountants, on a matter of public concern and interest, in violation of the rules of the common law and of the First Amendment to the United States Constitution and Article 1, Section 8 of the Constitution of New York State.

2. The complaint does not allege facts showing that the said Committee lacks the power to issue the proposed letter and alleges no violation of the charter or by-laws of the Institute.

3. The decision to proceed with the issuance of said letter appears from the face of the complaint to be a matter which the plaintiffs have no standing to challenge because it is part of the internal affairs of a private nonprofit corporation of which none of the plaintiffs is or has ever been a member, and with which none of the plaintiffs has any contractual relationship or is in any way in privity.

4. The complaint does not allege that the defendants are motivated by any malicious desire to injure the plaintiffs.

5. The complaint does not allege that the defendants contemplate the use of unlawful means in expressing their opinions on accounting questions.

6. The opinions of the Committee on Accounting Procedure, which appear from the complaint to be published to the public at large, are not alleged to bind anyone or to depend for their authority on anything other than the strength of

their reasoning; the complaint shows that they are not determinative of rights, liabilities or duties in any sense and it is open to plaintiffs to counteract whatever authority the committee's opinions may carry.

7. The complaint does not allege any acts or proposed acts of the defendants which can be the legal cause of injury or damage, if in fact there be any, to the plaintiffs.

8. The complaint alleges no actual damage or injury or threat thereof, and contains no more than a conclusory assertion of injury or damage which is supported by no allegation of fact and is, on its face, too speculative and remote to state a claim for any relief.

9. In any event, even if any injury or loss should materialize, there would be an adequate remedy at law by way of a claim for money damages, which precludes any relief in equity.

Dated: New York, N.Y.   Respectfully submitted,
      May 1, 1959

    /s/ HOWARD C. WESTWOOD
         Howard C. Westwood

    /s/ FONTAINE C. BRADLEY
         Fontaine C. Bradley

    /s/ STANLEY L. TEMKO
         Stanley L. Temko

      Attorneys for Defendants

UNITED STATES DISTRICT COURT
For the Southern District of New York

Appalachian Power Company,
Ohio Power Company and
Indiana & Michigan Electric Company,

Plaintiffs,

against

American Institute of Certified Public
Accountants, L. H. Penney, William W.
Werntz and Carman G. Blough,

Defendants.

Civil Action No. 145-161

AFFIDAVIT IN OPPOSITION
TO PLAINTIFFS' APPLICATION
FOR PRELIMINARY INJUNCTION

WILLIAM W. WERNTZ, being first duly sworn deposes and says:

1. He is one of the defendants herein and he resides at Glen Ridge, New Jersey.

2. He is presently a partner in the accounting firm of Touche, Niven, Bailey & Smart; a firm of independent public accountants with 22 offices in the United States. He is a Certified Public Accountant licensed by the states of New Jersey and Michigan, being first licensed to practice in New Jersey in 1950. He has been a member of the American Institute of Certified Public Accountants since 1950.

3. The said American Institute of Certified Public Accountants is a non-profit corporation organized under the laws of the District of Columbia. All certified public accountants licensed as such by any state are eligible for election to membership, provided they:

1. have passed an examination in accounting and related subjects satisfactory to its Committee on Admissions, and

2. have been in the public accounting practice on their own account or in the employ of a practicing public accountant for not less than two years or have had experience which in the opinion of its Committee on Admissions is equivalent to two years' public accounting practice, and at the date of application for membership are engaged in work related to accounting.

The examination now used by all states in connection with licensing certified public accountants is a uniform examination prepared by the Institute and which consequently is an examination satisfactory to it.

4. He is presently Chairman of the Committee on Accounting Procedure of the American Institute of Certified Public Accountants. He has been Chairman of the said Committee continually since 1956 and he has been a member of the said Committee continually since 1950.

5. This affidavit is made in opposition to plaintiffs' application for a preliminary injuction.

6. The Accounting Research Bulletins issued by the Committee on Accounting Procedure neither have nor purport to have an official status. As stated at p. 9 of the introduction to Accounting Research Bulletin No. 43 (1953), a copy of which is attached hereto as Exhibit A., except in cases in which adoption by the Institute membership has been asked and secured, the authority of opinions reached by the Committee rests upon their general acceptability by members of the profession and upon no other basis.

7. The letter which the Committee on Accounting Procedure proposed to send out to the members of the Institute is an interpretation of the phrase "deferred tax account" which is used in Accounting Research Bulletin No. 44 (revised) issued in July 1958, a copy of which is attached hereto as Exhibit B. The said phrase is used as a general description to refer to the credit in the balance sheet arising from a charge against income for deferred taxes in order to properly reflect net income when the liberalized depreciation methods allowed by Section 167 of the Internal Revenue Code are used for tax purposes, but not for accounting purposes.

8. The issuance of the said Accounting Research Bulletin No. 44 (revised) was in complete accord with the procedures adopted by the Committee as set forth therein and as set forth more completely in the Introduction to Accounting Research Bulletin No. 43. A draft of the said Accounting Research Bulletin No. 44 (revised) was circulated among various interested parties, but the exposure of drafts of proposed Bulletins is not required by any rule of the Committee on Accounting Procedure. The decision as to the extent to which exposure of drafts of bulletins for comments shall be made has been recognized to lie within the discretion of the Committee, as illustrated by the Report of the Subcommittee of the Executive Committee on the Technical Committees, submitted to, and approved by, the Council of the Institute, which is the Institute's governing body, at its meeting of May 2, 1949, a copy of which Report is attached hereto as Exhibit C. Several recent Bulletins have been issued by the Committee on Accounting Procedure without any advance exposure to persons other than members of the Committee and of the staff of the Institute. Among such Bulletins was the original Accounting Research Bulletin No. 44, issued in October 1954, which is the predecessor of Accounting Research Bulletin No. 44 (revised).

9. The phrase "deferred tax account" was inserted in Accounting Research Bulletin No. 44 (revised), after the return of the ballot draft sent to the

members of the Committee, by the technical staff, in response to suggestions from members of the Committee, and with the permission of the Chairman in order to clarify the meaning of the said Accounting Research Bulletin No.44 (revised). Said action by the technical staff was in complete accordance with the terms of the ballot submitted to the members of the Committee, a copy of which ballot is attached hereto as Exhibit D, which ballot stated that changes in language not affecting substance could be made by the technical staff, with the approval of the Chairman. The insertion of the phrase "deferred tax account" in Accounting Research Bulletin No. 44 (revised) made no substantive change in the said Bulletin. Advance copies of the said Bulletin containing the phrase in question, were circulated to the members of the Committee one week before final distribution of the Bulletin to the members of the Institute, but no member of the Committee objected to the insertion of the said phrase as making a substantive change in meaning, or otherwise objected, at that time, to the Bulletin in any manner.

10. The use of the phrase "deferred tax account" in Accounting Research Bulletin No. 44 (revised) is in accordance with the treatment recommended by the Committee on Accounting Procedure in Accounting Research Bulletin No. 42, issued in November, 1952, a copy of which is attached hereto as Exhibit E, in paragraph 12 of which the Committee recommended that the deferred tax credit arising from the use of accelerated amortization as authorized under Section 124 A of the 1939 Internal Revenue Code (now section 168 of the 1954 Internal Revenue Code) for tax purposes but not for accounting purposes be carried in an "account for deferred income taxes." The text of Accounting Research Bulletin No. 42 has been carried over into and adopted as Chapter 9(c) of Accounting Research Bulletin No. 43, Exhibit A attached hereto, and is still in full force and effect as the recommendation of the Committee on this subject. The objective of achieving substantial uniformity in mode of expression between Accounting Research Bulletin No. 44 (revised) and Accounting Research Bulletin No. 43 was one of the chief reasons the phrase "deferred tax account" was inserted in Accounting Research Bulletin No. 44 (revised).

11. The proposed issuance of the letter interpreting the said words "deferred tax account" in Accounting Research Bulletin No. 44 (revised) is in accordance with the accepted procedures of the Committee in that before the decision to issue the said letter was made the affirmative vote of over two-thirds of the Committee which, at that time, and at all times since then, has consisted of 21 members, was obtained as required by the Committee's rules. The said interpretive letter does not purport to change nor does it change the substance of Accounting Research Bulletin No. 44 (revised). 18 of the 21 members of the Committee have so indicated that the said interpretive letter does not vary the meaning of Accounting Research Bulletin No. 44 (revised), and 16 of the said 18 were members of the Committee at the time the said Accounting Research Bulletin No. 44 (revised) was issued and constitute more than two-thirds of the entire Committee as it was then constituted and as now constituted.

12. The said interpretive letter which the Committee on Accounting Procedure proposed to issue is in accordance with general accounting principles. The said letter is also in accordance with accounting principles used in the electric public utility field, as is indicated by the following facts, which deponent states on information and belief:

1. Before Accounting Research Bulletin No. 44 (revised) was issued in July, 1958, the Federal Power Commission, in Orders No. 203 and 204, issued May 29, 1958, reported in the Federal Register for June 12, 1958 (23 Fed. Reg. 4160-4167 (1958)), ordered that all public utility companies and all natural gas companies subject to its regulation shall not include the credit arising from the accounting recognition of deferred Federal income taxes in a surplus account, but shall treat it in an account for "accumulated deferred taxes on income," a method substantially identical with that subsequently recommended by the Committee on Accounting Procedure.

2. In December, 1957, the Public Service Commission of the State of Indiana ordered all companies subject to its regulation, among which is the plaintiff, Indiana & Michigan Electric Company, to cease treating the credit for deferred income taxes as a surplus account. In the Matter of Accounting Procedures to be Followed by Utilities (issued December 24, 1957), Par. 17,794.01 CCH Pub. Utilities L. Rep. (1958). In its latest Annual Report to stockholders the said plaintiff, Indiana & Michigan Electric Company, has stated that it is appealing the validity of the said order by the Public Service Commission for the State of Indiana to the courts, but, as of the present date, said appeal from the said order of the Public Service Commission of the State of Indiana is still pending.

In addition it should be noted that the Securities and Exchange Commission has issued a proposed interpretation of administrative policy which would characterize as misleading the handling of the credit for deferred income taxes in the manner adopted by the plaintiffs herein by all companies required to file financial statements with the Commission, including Public Utility Holding Companies. (Securities Act of 1933 Release No. 4010 (December 30, 1958)).

13. The proposal to issue the said letter interpreting the meaning of Accounting Research Bulletin No. 44 (revised) was not made with the intent of injuring the plaintiffs herein nor in wanton disregard of the plaintiffs' rights. Said

proposal was made in order to inform the members of the American Institute of Certified Public Accountants what the Committee has always considered to be generally accepted accounting principles in this area.

/s/ WILLIAM W. WERNTZ
William W. Werntz

Subscribed and sworn to before me
this 4th day of May, 1959.

/s/ ELLEN M. HARDEN
Notary Public

My Commission Expires:
3/30/1960

EXHIBIT A

Only page 9, paragraph 8, (referred to in parapraph 6 of Mr. Werntz's affidavit) is quoted below. Accounting Research Bulletin No. 43, a document of 159 pages, may be obtained from the American Institute of Certified Public Accountants, 270 Madison Avenue, New York 16, New York.

A. R. B. 43, page 9, paragraph 8:

8. Except in cases in which formal adoption by the Institute membership has been asked and secured, the authority of opinions reached by the committee rests upon their general acceptability. The committee recognizes that in extraordinary cases fair presentation and justice to all parties at interest may require exceptional treatment. But the burden of justifying departure from accepted procedures, to the extent that they are evidenced in committee opinions, must be assumed by those who adopt another treatment.

Chapter 9 (c) of A. R. B. 43, referred to in parapraph 10 of Mr. Werntz's affidavit, is identical with A. R. B. 42, which appears as Exhibit E of this affidavit.

Accounting Research BULLETINS

★

Issued by the
Committee on Accounting Procedure
American Institute of
Certified Public Accountants
270 Madison Avenue, New York 16, N. Y.
Copyright 1958 by
American Institute of Certified Public Accountants

July, 1958

No. 44
(Revised)

Declining-balance Depreciation

(Supersedes Accounting Research
Bulletin No. 44 issued in October 1954)

1. The declining-balance method of estimating periodic depreciation has a long history of use in England and in other countries including, to a limited extent, the United States. Interest in this method has been increased by its specific recognition for income-tax purposes in the Internal Revenue Code of 1954.

2. The declining-balance method is one of those which meets the requirements of being "systematic and rational." [1] In those cases where the expected productivity or revenue-earning power of the asset is relatively greater during the earlier years of its life, or where maintenance charges tend to increase during the later years, the declining-balance method may well provide the most satisfactory allocation of cost. The conclusions of this bulletin also apply to other methods, including the "sum-of-the-years-digits" method, which produce substantially similar results.

3. When a change to the declining-balance method is made for general accounting purposes, and depreciation is a significant factor in the determination of net income, the change in method, including the effect thereof, should be disclosed in the year in which the change is made.

4. There may be situations in which the declining-balance method is adopted for income-tax purposes but other appropriate methods are used for financial accounting purposes. In such cases, accounting rec-

---

[1] Accounting Terminology Bulletin No. 1, par. 56.

ognition should be given to deferred income taxes if the amounts thereof are material, except in those rare cases, such as are mentioned in paragraph 8, where there are special circumstances which may make such procedure inappropriate. The foregoing provision as to accounting recognition of deferred income taxes applies to a single asset, or to a group of assets which are expected to be retired from service at about the same time; in this case an excess of depreciation taken for income-tax purposes during the earlier years would be followed by the opposite condition in later years, and there would be a tax deferment for a definite period. It applies also to a group of assets consisting of numerous units which may be of differing lengths of life and which are expected to be continually replaced; in this case an excess of depreciation taken for income-tax purposes during the earlier years would be followed in later years by substantial equality between the annual depreciation for income-tax purposes and that for accounting purposes, and a tax deferment would be built up during the earlier years which would tend to remain relatively constant thereafter. It applies further to a gradually expanding plant; in this case an excess of depreciation taken for income-tax purposes may exist each year during the period of expansion in which event there would be a tax deferment which might increase as long as the period of expansion continued.

5. Where it may reasonably be presumed that the accumulative difference between taxable income and financial income will continue for a long or indefinite period, it is alternatively appropriate, instead of crediting a deferred tax account, to recognize the related tax effect as additional amortization or depreciation applicable to such assets in recognition of the loss of future deductibility for income-tax purposes.

DISCUSSION

6. Following the passage of the Internal Revenue Act of 1954 in August of that year, permitting the use of declining-balance and similar accelerated depreciation methods for federal income-tax purposes, the committee anticipated that many companies would be considering whether such methods should be adopted for general accounting purposes. In October of that year, Accounting Research Bulletin No. 44 was issued in which the committee stated that such accelerated methods met the requirement of being "systematic and rational." The

committee also stated that when such methods were adopted for general accounting purposes, appropriate disclosure of the change should be made whenever depreciation was a significant factor in the determination of net income.

7. Since the issuance of Accounting Research Bulletin No. 44, the committee has been observing and studying cases involving the application of the bulletin. Studies of published reports and other source material have indicated that, where material amounts are involved, recognition of deferred income taxes in the general accounts is needed to obtain an equitable matching of costs and revenues and to avoid income distortion, even in those cases in which the payment of taxes is deferred for a relatively long periqd. This conclusion is borne out by the committee's studies which indicate that where accelerated depreciation methods are used for income-tax purposes only, most companies do give recognition to the resultant deferment of income taxes or, alternatively, recognize the loss of future deductibility for income-tax purposes of the cost of fixed assets by an appropriate credit to an accumulated amortization or depreciation account applicable to such assets.

8. Many regulatory authorities permit recognition of deferred income taxes for accounting and/or rate-making purposes, whereas some do not. The committee believes that they should permit the recognition of deferred income taxes for both purposes. However, where charges for deferred income taxes are not allowed for rate-making purposes, accounting recognition need not be given to the deferment of taxes if it may reasonably be expected that increased future income taxes, resulting from the earlier deduction of declining-balance depreciation for income-tax purposes only, will be allowed in future rate determinations.

9. In those rare situations in which accounting for deferred income taxes is not appropriate, full disclosure should be made of the amount of deferred income taxes arising out of the difference between the financial statements and the tax returns when the declining-balance method is adopted for income-tax purposes but other appropriate methods are used for financial accounting purposes.

10. The committee believes that, in applying the provisions of this bulletin to cases where there was no accounting recognition of deferred income taxes for the years since 1953, the entries made for periods

subsequent to the issuance of this bulletin should be based upon all assets acquired after 1953 as to which the declining-balance method has been elected for tax purposes. As is indicated in the "Notes" to each Accounting Research Bulletin, opinions of the committee are not intended to be retroactive unless they contain a statement of such intention. If a retroactive adjustment is made for prior periods, the adjustment may be made in a lump sum, or the deficiency may be systematically accumulated over a reasonable future period of time.

The statement entitled "Declining-balance Depreciation" (July 1958) was adopted unanimously by the twenty-one members of the committee, of whom five, Messrs. Burns, Graham, Halvorson, Jennings, and Powell, assented with qualification.

Mr. Burns objects to the exceptions mentioned in paragraph 4 and discussed in paragraphs 8 and 9. He believes that accounting principles apply equally to all companies operated for profit and that the exceptions referred to are wholly inconsistent with the basic principles stated in paragraph 4; further, that the last sentence of paragraph 8 is based upon an untenable concept, namely, that accounting resulting from the application of an accounting rule prescribed by a regulatory commission may properly be approved by public accountants notwithstanding the fact that the rule is clearly contrary to generally accepted accounting principles.

Mr. Graham objects to the exceptions mentioned in the second sentence of paragraph 4 and discussed in the last sentence of paragraph 8 and in paragraph 9. He believes that accepted accounting principles should be applied uniformly to all corporations, including regulated companies. He does not believe that rate-making rules which are in conflict with these accepted principles constitute a sound basis for sanctioning a departure from these principles in financial reporting. Furthermore, he disagrees with the validity of the assumption which, by implication, forms the basis for this exception; he does not believe that public utility rates will always be adjusted automatically to compensate fully, or even substantially, for increases in future income taxes; he believes that this assumption is not in accord with the known realities of rate regulation and is not, therefore, a proper basis for the anticipation of future revenues.

Mr. Halvorson dissents from the recommendations of paragraph 4 because he believes its requirements for accounting recognition of deferred income taxes should be limited to a requirement for compliance with the recommendations of chapter 10(b) of Accounting Research Bulletin No. 43; he believes that paragraph 4 is effectively a revision of chapter 10(b) and that it is improper thus to make a substantive change in the committee's existing recommendations for tax allocation in the guise of a revision of a bulletin on depreciation.

Messrs. Jennings and Powell dissent from the conclusion (expressed in paragraph 4 and implied in the related discussion) that where the declining-balance method is adopted for income-tax purposes but other appropriate methods are used for financial accounting purposes, there should be accounting recognition of deferred income taxes, except for certain rare cases. They believe this calls for more extensive allocation of income taxes among periods of time than is necessary or desirable, especially where the situation is such that the so-called tax deferment is in effect a permanent tax reduction. Further, they object to the use of a bulletin on depreciation incidentally as a vehicle for making an important change in the committee's views, as set forth in previous bulletins, on accounting for income taxes.

NOTES

(See Introduction to *Accounting Research Bulletin No. 43.*)

1. Accounting Research Bulletins represent the considered opinion of at least two-thirds of the members of the committee on accounting procedure, reached on a formal vote after examination of the subject matter by the committee, the technical services department, and the director of research. Except in cases in which formal adoption by the Institute membership has been asked and secured, the authority of the bulletins rests upon the general acceptability of opinions so reached.

2. Opinions of the committee are not intended to be retroactive unless they contain a statement of such intention. They should not be considered applicable to the accounting for transactions arising prior to the publication of the opinions. However, the committee does not wish to discourage the revision of past accounts in an individual case if the accountant thinks it desirable in the circumstances. Opinions of the committee should be considered as applicable only to items which are material and significant in the relative circumstances.

3. It is recognized also that any general rules may be subject to exception; it is felt, however, that the burden of justifying departure from accepted procedures must be assumed by those who adopt other treatment. Except where there is a specific statement of a different intent by the committee, its opinions and recommendations are directed primarily to business enterprises organized for profit.

EXHIBIT C

REPORT OF THE SUBCOMMITTEE OF THE EXECUTIVE COMMITTEE ON THE TECHNICAL COMMITTEES

This subcommittee was appointed by the President pursuant to a resolution of Council at its meeting September 23, 1948 that the basic organization question of the issuance of pronouncements by committees of the Institute be referred to the Executive Committee with instructions to report fully on the matter at the spring 1949 Council meeting.

The only committees which have or may have authority to issue technical pronouncements appear to be the Committee on Accounting Procedure, the Committee on Auditing Procedure, and the Income Study Group. The position of the latter is not clear but it is included in this report partly because the President at the Council meeting asked that the resolution be broadened to include it, and partly because our subcommittee believes its position also should be clarified.

COMMITTEE ON ACCOUNTING PROCEDURE

Your subcommittee has directed its first attention to the Committee on Accounting Procedure. We have reviewed the resolutions of the Council and of the Executive Committee at the various meetings in which authority was granted to the Committee, or its activities were approved or limited, or its organization fixed. We have considered the rules established by the Committee for its own guidance as well as its body of practice which may be said to constitute its unwritten rules. We are familiar with and have considered the events immediately prior to and leading up to the Council meeting in September, 1948. We have written to a number of representative accountants in various parts of the country, and have noted written comments received from others. The testing of opinion by letter was not extensive and was not intended to be a complete testing of professional accountants. Our report, accordingly, represents our own opinion rather than a consensus.

Our subcommittee believes that there should be no basic change in the authority granted to the Committee. We do believe, however, that it is advisable to review herein the present Committee structure and rules, unwritten and written, imposed by Council or self-imposed by the Committee. These constitute the current "charter" of the committee. We propose also to review and express our opinion upon the points raised in our considerations.

The Committee has authority to issue pronouncements. This authority has been considered and reaffirmed in various explicit and implicit actions at dates subsequent to the original grant. At such times, the rules of the Committee and the limitations on its authority were known and considered, so that certain rules of the Committee appear to be just as binding as if included in the original grant of authority. These are:

1. A requirement that bulletins or pronouncements cannot be issued without approval of two-thirds of the Committee.

2. A position that bulletins shall not be retroactive.

3. A disclaimer of any authority beyond that of the Committee itself and the strength of its own reasoning.

4. Bulletins shall disclose the names of dissenting members and, when requested by them, carry brief explanations of such dissents.

5. There is to be maximum exposure possible and practicable in the circumstances of the thinking of the Committee prior to final Committee action and the issuance of a bulletin, but the amount of such exposure that is practicable in the circumstances is in the discretion of the Committee. This rule does not require or even imply that the bulletins need to be approved by other organizations or by state societies or by Council or by membership or otherwise.

6. Effort is to be made to complete accounting research bulletins in the summer so that they might be issued in the fall when they would be most useful to the membership.

7. While not a rule of the Committee, it nevertheless was enunciated at the authorization of the Committee that its membership should be large (21 members), representative of all sections of the country, of all types of accounting firms, and of teachers of accounting. That general structure has been adhered to, and it is believed it should continue to be the basis of the appointment of the Committee.

8. There has grown up a precedent for giving a chairman an opportunity to serve more than one year in order to provide continuity, but, fortuitously or otherwise, the appointments have never run beyond three years. This limitation should be continued.

9. Turnover in the Committee has been held down deliberately because it was believed necessary to permit new members to orient themselves and familiarize themselves with the efforts of the Committee and one year is hardly long enough for that need. Nevertheless, there should be a policy of bringing in new members to the Committee each year. A core of seasoned veterans is necessary to the functioning of the Committee provided these do not come to dominate the Committee. History shows that the seasoned members disagree among themselves and that danger of domination is remote. Continual rotation of geographical members has proved beneficial to the profession.

10. A strong research staff has been developed and has been a prominent factor in the work of the Committee. The maintenance of such a staff should be considered as a necessary part of the Committee's charter.

* * * * * * * *

With the foregoing background your subcommittee considered suggestions that have been made for additional restrictions or basic changes. No one of these appears to have numerous supporters, and some are counter-balanced by specific opposite comments or suggestions. The principal suggestions follow:

1. Should the pronouncements or bulletins require the approval of a super committee such as the Executive committee or the Council or the membership? The authority of the committee has been considered more than once by the Executive Committee or the Council and each time the Committee's status has been overwhelmingly approved. The reasons against changing the Committee's status appear to us to be quite convincing. First, it would be difficult, if not impossible, to get a top group of men to work as it is necessary to work on this Committee if their conclusions were to be issued only after approval by some other, and perhaps less qualified, group. There is at present no other group adequately set up to pass upon such pronouncements. The Executive Committee, for instance, is and should be selected for ability in overall direction of Institute policies and administration. The Council today consists of a large number of men, many of whom are members ex-officio, and its members could not be expected to take the time to inform themselves adequately on the subject matter of bulletins. Approval by vote of the Institute membership seems even more impracticable.

Another phase of the same problem is whether there should be advance approval by state societies before bulletins are issued. Most societies would not want such responsibility and not many would assume it seriously. If it would be difficult to inform Council members, how much more difficult would it be to inform adequately members of the state societies on the problems inherent in decisions upon committee bulletins. Perhaps most of the state societies are not so organized as to be able to discharge such a responsibility, nor do some of them meet frequently enough to deal with it. (See, however, the discussion about advance disclosure).

It is interesting to note that the suggestion for approval by a higher authority comes not only from those who believe the Committee has too much authority, is occasionally high-handed, and who believe that a requirement for approval would cut down committee activity and reduce its importance, but the same suggestion comes also from those who believe the Committee does not have enough authority and that approval by an offical body of the Institute would force compliance with such bulletins.

We believe the present situation constitutes a satisfactory middle ground and it is our conclusion that requirements for super approval would so restrict the issue of bulletins as to impede seriously the progress of accounting and would transfer the leadership in the development of accounting principles away from the Institute to other groups.

2. <u>Are the members adequately advised about bulletins in advance?</u> The desirability of advance notice of committee activities is well recognized in the Committee. It has, by articles, by notes in the Journal, by its Committee reports and by speeches of members, told of the problems which are before the Committee. In most cases it submits a preliminary draft bulletin, not yet voted upon, to various organizations, including the state societies, for comment. It asks in many ways for comment on projects before the Committee or on draft bulletins. It has tried pro-and-con presentations, but some of these proved more confusing than helpful. There have been research memos on many subjects. It is the experience of the Committee that the comments which have been elicited by advance disclosure of draft bulletins have seldom presented valid arguments not already considered by the Committee. We recommend that the Committee on Accounting Procedure should continue its efforts to expose its projects, its thinking, and its drafts of proposed bulletins.

3. Some criticism is voiced that the Committee issues too many bulletins or too few bulletins. Some also that the Committee is too arrogant or too wishy-washy. These points of view do not appear to be widely held and appear to balance each other out. Some other criticism is made on the conclusions the Committee has reached on individual bulletins. All of these criticisms are primarily criticisms of the way in which the Committee is functioning. If at any time it should become apparent that the Committee is not representative, then the remedy lies not in new rules at this time but in the ability of the President of the Institute to name a new Committee Chairman and new members of the Committee.

4. <u>Timing.</u> This has been a recurring problem. The Executive Committee in 1946 asked that releases not be made at the end of the calendar year, but that they be issued in the fall when they would be most useful to members and their clients. The Committee has accepted this as desirable, but no rigid rule to that effect was put into effect, nor was one believed to be necessary.

The practical operating difficulties have been such, however, that for each year since that date some bulletins have been issued in October and November and one (in 1947) in December. That has resulted in the issuance by an outgoing committee of a bulletin dated after the beginning of the new administration and the appointment of the new committee. Generally speaking, the bulletins were issued early enough, or the position of the Committee was known early enough, to be timely for the use of the profession in planning the treatment of problems at the year end closings, and thus be in accord with the desirable procedure and timing mentioned above.

In 1948, however, a most unusual set of circumstances concentrated attention on the timing of bulletins, this time in relation to the annual meeting. While it is the opinion of our subcommittee that the circumstances of that case were so unusual that it does not need study for itself, that case has pointed up the problems of earlier release and the issuance of bulletins by an outgoing committee after the new one has been appointed.

Our subcommittee does not believe it to be advisable to prohibit the publication of bulletins by the outgoing committee after the annual meeting, provided all necessary committee action has been taken before that time, and nothing remains but the readying of the bulletin for printing in the area within the powers of the chairman, such as working out the wording of any dissents. We believe that the program of the annual meeting should provide a session wherein the Committee can report fully on any positions agreed upon, but not published, and present other problems that are before the Committee.

Our subcommittee, however, does believe it to be desirable to relate the work of the Committee more closely to the fiscal year of the Institute than has been the case. This is a matter of emphasis and of administrative procedure, rather than rule. It is complicated by the fact that the Annual Meeting of the Institute may be held as early as September 20th, or as late as November 4th. It is complicated also by the necessity of exposing the thinking of the Committee to state societies and to other organizations, by the busy season, and by the fact that some of the most important and pressing problems have not been apparent until there is a scrutiny of annual reports available in the spring of a year. Some bulletins, too, are suggested definitions, or are on points on which there is not widespread interest or controversy.

Our subcommittee suggests that the Committee be appointed immediately after the election of the new president, by telegraph if necessary, and that the organization and planning meeting be held within a few days after the annual meeting. This would be helpful in utilizing the fall months for committee activity. Emphasis should be placed on an attempt to obtain committee action in June rather than September. Emphasis should also be placed on cutting down the time between final Committee approval and actual publication. Such emphasis might make action at a September meeting satisfactory in years when the annual meeting takes place in November, but not satisfactory in those cases when the annual meeting is in September. We suggest this to the Committee, but believe no rigid restrictions or controls in this respect are desirable.

We suggest also that more information be included in the Journal as to the Committee reports and activities.

5. <u>Press Releases.</u> There has been objection to the use of a press release in advance of the mailing of the bulletins. There seemed to be adequate reasons

for such action this year, particularly since no new position was being taken. Nevertheless, while it seems unwise to us to ask that prior press releases be banned, it is pertinent to commend the decision of the Committee to issue press releases only after the mailing of a bulletin, and to suggest that any departures from that practice have the approval of the President.

* * * * * * *

In summary, we believe that with the essential codification of rules and practices into a Charter as herein stated, and with emphasis on certain difficulties and dangers inherent in the latitude that must be given the Committee, as herein pointed out, the activity of the Committee can be continued, with the thanks of the entire profession for the unstinted service which has been given.

COMMITTEE ON AUDITING PROCEDURE

This Committee has a grant of authority similar to that given to the Committee on Accounting Procedure, though it was given some years later. Its work on the whole has been to prepare and issue studies of various kinds that have not been controversial. Its bulletins 23 and 24 were pronouncements rather than studies and these have provoked much comment and considerable objection. Bulletin 23 changes a position previously approved by vote of the membership, and, accordingly, needed to be referred to membership. Its difficult progress, and the necessity for very extensive education adequately demonstrates the problem of getting an informed and critical membership vote on a technical matter.

Also, because of the nature of its releases it had not exposed its thinking in advance. With Bulletins 23 and 24 this was necessary and was done.

It is suggested that the "Charter" of the Committee on Accounting Procedure be adopted for the Committe on Auditing Procedure where and when applicable.

* * * * * * *

CONCLUSION

Your subcommittee suggests that perhaps the greatest assurance of the reasonableness of the activity of the various technical committees is that the criticisms seem to be somewhat balanced between those who wish them to have less authority and those who wish them to have more; between those who think the committees are too active and those who think they are not active enough; between those who think that bulletins have received too wide an acceptance and those who think there is too much lack of acceptance. We point out that if these committees are to help accounting move forward to meet changing needs of the times, there will always be cases where the change will be objected to by many people.   In our opinion this need not cause alarm.

It is the considered opinion of your subcommittee that the bulletins of the technical committees have had an inestimably important part in the development of the prestige of the accounting profession over the last ten years.

Respectfully submitted,

GEORGE E. PERRIN
J. HAROLD STEWART
GEORGE D. BAILEY
Chairman

BALLOT

EXHIBIT D

Letter to Institute membership interpreting "a deferred tax account" in Accounting Research Bulletin No. 44 (revised).

(Please return by April 10, 1959 to the Technical Service Department, American Institute of Certified Public Accountants, 270 Madison Avenue, New York 16, N. Y.)

_____ 1. I assent to the letter and approve its distribution to the membership of the Institute.

_____ 2. I dissent from the issuance of the letter.

      (If your ballot records a dissent, please indicate whether or not you wish to have the fact of your dissent shown in the letter, and, if so, also send a brief statement of the basis of your dissent which may be used in the letter.)

Without qualifying my assent, I make the following suggestions for changes:

Date _____ Name _____

    By resolution of the committee, June 26, 1939, the assent of two-thirds of the entire committee is necessary before a statement may be published.

    The technical services department will regard itself as free, with the approval of the chairman of the committee, to make in its discretion minor changes in the text not affecting its substance, which may be suggested by members. If members suggest changes in substance and approve the issue only subject to such changes being made, the department will either treat them as dissenting from the issue or re-submit the document with the suggestions to the entire membership of the committee.

EXHIBIT E

Accounting Research BULLETINS

★

Issued by the
Committee on Accounting Procedure,
American Institute of Accountants,
270 Madison Avenue, New York 16, N. Y.
Copyright 1952 by American Institute of Accountants

November, 1952   No. 42

**Emergency Facilities —
Depreciation, Amortization,
and Income Taxes**

CERTIFICATES OF NECESSITY

1. Section 124A of the Internal Revenue Code, which was added by the Revenue Act of 1950, provides for the issuance of certificates of necessity under which all or part of the cost of so-called *emergency facilities* may be amortized over a period of 60 months for income tax purposes. In many cases, the amounts involved are material, and companies are faced with the problem of deciding whether to adopt the 60-month period over which the portions of the cost of the facilities covered by certificates of necessity may be amortized for income tax purposes as the period over which they are to be depreciated in the accounts.

2. Thinking on this question apparently has become confused because many so-called *percentage certificates* have been issued covering less than the entire cost of the facility. This fact, together with the fact that the probable economic usefulness of the facility after the close of the five-year amortization period is considered by the certifying authority in determining the percentage covered by these certificates, has led many to believe that the percentage used represents the Government's conclusion as to the proportion of the cost of the facility that is not expected to have usefulness at the end of five years.

3. In some cases, it is apparent that the probable lack of economic usefulness of the facility after the close of the amortization period must constitute the principal if not the sole basis for determining the percentage to be included in the certificate. However, it must be recognized that the certifying authority has acted under orders to give consideration also to a variety of other factors to the end that the amount certified may be the minimum amount necessary to secure expansion of industrial capacity in the interest of national defense during the emergency period. Among the factors required to be considered in the issuance of these certificates, in addition to loss of useful value, are (a) character of business, (b) extent of risk assumed (including the amount and source of capital employed, and the potentiality of recovering capital or retiring debt through tax savings or pricing),

(c) assistance to small business and promotion of competition, (d) compliance with Government policies (e.g., dispersal for security), and (e) other types of incentives provided by Government, such as direct Government loans, guaranties and contractual arrangements.

DEPRECIATION CONSIDERATIONS

4. The argument has been advanced from time to time that, since the portion of the cost of properties covered by certificates of necessity is amortized over a five-year period for income tax purposes, it is necessary to follow the same procedure in the accounts. Sound financial accounting procedures do not necessarily coincide with the rules as to what shall be included in "gross income," or allowed as a deduction therefrom, in arriving at taxable net income. It is well recognized that such rules should not be followed for financial accounting purposes if they do not conform to generally accepted accounting principles. However, where the results obtained from following income tax procedures do not materially differ from those obtained where generally accepted accounting principles are followed, there are practical advantages in keeping the accounts in agreement with the income tax returns.

5. The cost of a productive facility is one of the costs of the services it renders during its useful economic life. Generally accepted accounting principles require that this cost be spread over the expected useful life of the facility in such a way as to allocate it as equitably as possible to the periods during which services are obtained from the use of the facility. This procedure is known as depreciation accounting, "a system of accounting which aims to distribute the cost or other basic value of tangible capital assets, less salvage (if any), over the estimated useful life of the unit (which may be a group of assets) in a systematic and rational manner. It is a process of allocation, not of valuation."[1]

6. The committee is of the opinion that from an accounting standpoint there is nothing inherent in the nature of emergency facilities which requires the depreciation or amortization of their cost for financial accounting purposes over either a shorter or a longer period than would be proper if no certificate of necessity had been issued. Estimates of the probable useful life of a facility by those best informed in the matter may indicate either a shorter or a longer life than the statutory 60-month period over which the certified portion of its cost is deductible for income tax purposes.

7. In determining the proper amount of annual depreciation with respect to emergency facilities for financial accounting purposes, it must be recognized that a great many of these facilities are being

---

[1] *Accounting Research Bulletins* Nos. 16, 20, and 22.

Emergency Facilities

acquired primarily for what they can produce during the emergency period. To whatever extent it is reasonable to expect the useful economic life of a facility to end with the close of the amortization period the cost of the facility is a proper cost of operation during that period.

8. In determining the prospective usefulness of such facilities it will be necessary to consider their adaptability to post-emergency use, the effect of their use upon economic utilization of other facilities, the possibility of excessive costs due to expedited construction or emergency conditions, and the fact that no deductions for depreciation of the certified portion will be allowable for income tax purposes in the post-amortization years if the company elects to claim the amortization deduction. The purposes for which emergency facilities are acquired in a great many cases are such as to leave major uncertainties as to the extent of their use during the amortization period and as to their subsequent usefulness—uncertainties which are not normally encountered in the acquisition and use of operating facilities.

9. Consideration of these factors, the committee believes, will in many cases result in the determination of depreciation charges during the amortization period in excess of the depreciation that would be appropriate if these factors were not involved. Frequently they will be so compelling as to indicate the need for recording depreciation of the cost of emergency facilities in the accounts in conformity with the amortization deductions allowable for income tax purposes. However, the committee believes that when the amount allowed as amortization for income tax purposes is materially different from the amount of the estimated depreciation, the latter should be used for financial accounting purposes.

10. In some cases, certificates of necessity cover facilities which the owner expects to use after the emergency period in lieu of older facilities. As a result the older facilities may become unproductive and obsolete before they are fully depreciated on the basis of their previously expected life. In such situations, the committee believes depreciation charges to income should be determined in relation to the total properties, to the end that sound depreciation accounting may be applied to the property accounts as a whole.

RECOGNITION OF INCOME TAX EFFECTS

11. In those cases in which the amount of depreciation charged in the accounts on that portion of the cost of the facilities for which certificates of necessity have been obtained is materially less than the amount of amortization deducted for income tax purposes, the amount of income taxes payable annually during the amortization period may be significantly less than it would be on the basis of the income reflected in the financial statements. In such cases, after the

Accounting Research Bulletins

close of the amortization period the income taxes will exceed the amount that would be appropriate on the basis of the income reported in the statements. Accordingly, the committee believes that during the amortization period, where this difference is material, a charge should be made in the income statement to recognize the income tax to be paid in the future on the amount by which amortization for income tax purposes exceeds the depreciation that would be allowable if certificates of necessity had not been issued. The amount of the charge should be equal to the estimated amount by which the income tax expected to be payable after the amortization period exceeds what would be so expected if amortization had not been claimed for income tax purposes in the amortization period. The estimated amount should be based upon normal and surtax rates in effect during the period covered by the income statement with such changes therein as can be reasonably anticipated at the time the estimate is made.

12. In accounting for this deferment of income taxes, the committee believes it desirable to treat the charge as being for additional income taxes. The related credit in such cases would properly be made to an account for deferred income taxes. Under this method, during the life of the facility following the amortization period the annual charges for income taxes will be reduced by charging to the account for deferred income taxes that part of the income tax in excess of what would have been payable had the amortization deduction not been claimed for income tax purposes in the amortization period. By this procedure the net income will more nearly reflect the results of a proper matching of costs and revenues.

13. There are those who similarly recognize the necessity for giving effect to the amount of the deferred income taxes but who believe this should be accomplished by making a charge in the income account for additional amortization or depreciation. They would carry the related credit to an accumulated amortization or depreciation account as a practical means of recognizing the loss of future deductibility of the cost of the facility for income tax purposes. If this procedure is followed the annual charges for depreciation will be correspondingly reduced throughout the useful life of the facility following the amortization period. Although this procedure will result in the same amount of net income as the procedure outlined in paragraph 12, and therefore may be considered as acceptable, the committee regards the paragraph 12 procedure as preferable. In any circumstances, there should be disclosure of the procedures followed

The statement entitled "Emergency Facilities—
Depreciation, Amortization, and Income Taxes"
was adopted unanimously by the twenty members
of the committee.

Emergency Facilities

NOTES

1. Accounting Research Bulletins represent the considered opinion of at least two-thirds of the members of the committee on accounting procedure, reached on a formal vote after examination of the subject matter by the committee and the research department. Except in cases in which formal adoption by the Institute membership has been asked and secured, the authority of the bulletins rests upon the general acceptability of opinions so reached. (See Report of Committee on Accounting Procedure to Council, dated September 18, 1939.)

2. Opinions of the committee are not intended to be retroactive unless they contain a statement of such intention. They should not be considered applicable to the accounting for transactions arising prior to the publication of the opinions. However, the committee does not wish to discourage the revision of past accounts in an individual case if the accountant thinks it desirable in the circumstances. Opinions of the committee should be considered as applicable only to items which are material and significant in the relative circumstances.

3. It is recognized also that any general rules may be subject to exception; it is felt, however, that the burden of justifying departure from accepted procedures must be assumed by those who adopt other treatment. (See Bulletin No. 1, page 3.)

COMMITTEE ON ACCOUNTING PROCEDURE (1952-1953)

PAUL K. KNIGHT, *Chairman*
FREDERICK B. ANDREWS
FRANK S. CALKINS
H. A. FINNEY
ROY GODFREY
THOMAS G. HIGGINS
JOHN A. LINDQUIST
PERRY MASON

EDWARD F. McCORMACK
JOHN PEOPLES
MAURICE E. PELOUBET
JOHN W. QUEENAN
WALTER L. SCHAFFER
C. AUBREY SMITH
C. OLIVER WELLINGTON
WILLIAM W. WERNTZ

EDWARD B. WILCOX
RAYMOND D. WILLARD
ROBERT W. WILLIAMS
KARL R. ZIMMERMANN

CARMAN G. BLOUGH
Director of Research

UNITED STATES DISTRICT COURT
For the Southern District of New York

Appalachian Power Company, Ohio Power Company and Indiana & Michigan Electric Company, *Plaintiffs,* *against* American Institute of Certified Public Accountants, L. H. Penney, William W. Werntz and Carman G. Blough, *Defendants.*	AFFIDAVIT IN OPPOSITION TO PLAINTIFFS' APPLICATION FOR PRELIMINARY INJUNCTION ——————————— Civil Action No. 145-161

F. MERRILL BEATTY, being first duly sworn, deposes and says:

1. He resides in Montclair, New Jersey.

2. He is presently in charge of the public utility division of the firm of Arthur Andersen & Co., a firm of independent Public Accountants with 26 offices in the United States and 13 offices in other countries. He is a Certified Public Accountant, licensed by the states of California, Indiana, Iowa, Louisiana, Michigan, Minnesota, Missouri, New York, Pennsylvania, Texas, Washington, Wisconsin, and New Jersey, being first licensed to practice in 1924, in Illinois.

3. He has been a member of the American Institute of Certified Public Accountants since 1936.

4. The said firm of Arthur Andersen & Co. of which he is a member, has made a survey of the manner in which utility companies account for the treatment of the accumulated credit arising from the use of the liberalized depreciation methods available under Section 167 of the 1954 Internal Revenue Code. In the course of this survey the 1957 published stockholders' reports of 353 utilities were reviewed. Of these companies, 127 either did not take liberalized depreciation or made no reference to it in their reports. Of the 226 utility companies which reported an accumulated credit arising from the use of the said liberalized depreciation methods under Section 167 of the 1954 Internal Revenue Code, 176 treated the credit outside of the equity-capital section of the balance sheet; 30 companies allowed the tax reduction to flow through income into earned surplus; and 20 companies included this credit in equity-capital as appropriated or restricted surplus.

5. The accounting firm of Arthur Andersen & Co., of which he is a member, examines the financial statements of roughly one third of all the electric and gas

utility companies in the United States, both in number and dollar amount of total assets. It is the opinion of the said Arthur Andersen & Co. that the credit for deferred income taxes arising from the accounting recognition of the effect of the use of liberalized depreciation under Section 167 of the Internal Revenue Code of 1954 for tax purposes, but not for accounting purposes, should not be included in the equity-capital section of the balance sheet, and that should the amount of the credit for deferred taxes be material, the said Arthur Andersen & Co. would take exception in their auditors' certificate to the treatment of the said credit for deferred taxes in the equity-capital section if it is unable to persuade the client to remove the credit from the equity-capital section.

/s/ F. MERRILL BEATTY

F. Merrill Beatty

Sworn and subscribed to before me
this 4th day of May, 1959.

/s/ MARGARET C. BEAVIS

Notary Public

My Commission Expires:
3/30/1960

UNITED STATES DISTRICT COURT
For the Southern District of New York

Appalachian Power Company,
Ohio Power Company and
Indiana & Michigan Electric Company,

Plaintiffs,

against

American Institute of Certified Public
Accountants, L. H. Penney, William W.
Werntz and Carman G. Blough,

Defendants.

AFFIDAVIT OF
GEORGE C. CHRISTIE
IN OPPOSITION TO
APPLICATION FOR
PRELIMINARY INJUNCTION

Civil Action No. 145-161

GEORGE C. CHRISTIE, being first duly sworn, deposes and says:

1. That he resides at 1819 G Street, N.W., Washington, D.C.

2. That he is an attorney at law, having been admitted to practice by the Court of Appeals for the State of New York on December 9, 1957, and by the District Court for the District of Columbia on July 9, 1958.

3. That he is employed as an associate by the law firm of Covington & Burling, 701 Union Trust Building, Washington 5, D. C., which firm is counsel to the defendants herein.

4. That he has examined the public files of the Securities and Exchange Commission and that the facts stated herein are based on his personal examination of the said public files of the said Securities and Exchange Commission, and that the copies of all documents attached to this affidavit are true and correct copies of documents in the public files of the said Securities and Exchange Commission.

5. That on April 8th and 10th, 1959, the Securities and Exchange Commission conducted public hearings to receive comments on the proposed adoption of an administrative policy under which the treatment of the deferred tax credit arising from the accounting recognition of the deferral of Federal income taxes resulting from the use of liberalized depreciation and accelerated amortization as part of surplus, would be regarded as misleading, regardless of whether such surplus is marked as "Restricted" or "Appropriated" or whether any other disclosure of the underlying facts is made (SEC Release No. 4010 dated December 30, 1958 - Exhibit T attached).

6. That many public utility and other companies indicated their support for the proposed policy issued by the Securities and Exchange Commission, which policy is in accord with Accounting Research Bulletin No. 44 (Revised) and the proposed letter interpreting the words "deferred tax account" in said Bulletin, which letter is the subject of this suit. That among such companies submitting such comments in support of the principles therein enunciated are:

1. The Commonwealth Edison Company (Exhibit U attached)

2. The Illinois Power Company (Exhibit V attached)

3. The Columbia Gas System (Exhibit W attached)

7. That the utility companies listed in paragraph 6 have constructed the financial statements contained in their latest annual reports available for public inspection at the Securities and Exchange Commission in a manner consistent with said Commission's proposed policy and inconsistent with the method adopted by plaintiffs.

8. That the said proposal of the Securities and Exchange Commission has also been supported by, among other companies and organizations, American Telephone & Telegraph Co., the National Federation of Financial Analysts Society, and the Harris Trust and Savings Bank of Chicago in letters submitted to the Commission, copies of which are attached hereto as Exhibits X, Y and Z, respectively.

/s/ GEORGE C. CHRISTIE
George C. Christie

Sworn to and subscribed to before me
on this 6th day of May, 1959.

/s/ SERAFINA R. Di PRETA
Notary Public

EXHIBIT T

For IMMEDIATE Release, Tuesday, December 30, 1958

SECURITIES AND EXCHANGE COMMISSION
Washington 25, D. C.

SECURITIES ACT OF 1933
Release No. 4010
SECURITIES EXCHANGE ACT OF 1934
Release No. 5844
PUBLIC UTILITY HOLDING COMPANY ACT OF 1935
Release No. 13894
INVESTMENT COMPANY ACT OF 1940
Release No. 2814

NOTICE OF INTENTION TO ANNOUNCE
INTERPRETATION OF ADMINISTRATIVE POLICY

Notice is hereby given that the Securities and Exchange Commission has under consideration the announcement of an interpretation of administrative policy on financial statements regarding balance sheet treatment of credits equivalent to the reductions in income taxes. In view of the importance of the amounts involved, any interested person may on or before January 31, 1959, file in triplicate with the Secretary of the Commission written views and comments to be considered in this matter. Except where it is requested that such views and comments not be disclosed, they will be considered available for public inspection.

The proposed announcement follows:

Interpretation of administrative policy on financial statements regarding balance sheet treatment of credit equivalent to reduction of income taxes.

Notice is hereby given that any financial statement which designates as earned surplus or its equivalent or includes as a part of equity capital (even though accompanied by words of limitation such as "restricted" or "appropriated") the accumulated credit arising from accounting for reductions in income taxes for various items including those under sections 167 and 168 of the Internal Revenue Code of 1954, filed with this Commission dated as of December 31, 1958 or thereafter, will pursuant to the administrative policy on financial statements announced in Accounting Series Release No. 4, be presumed by this Commission "to be misleading or inaccurate despite disclosure contained in the certificate of the accountant or in footnotes to the statements provided the matters involved are material."

The Commission considers that the action thus taken is necessary or appropriate in the public interest or for the protection of investors and is consistent with the intent of Congress, as expressed in section 167 (liberalized depreciation) and section 168 (accelerated amortization) of the Internal Revenue Code of 1954. The effect of these sections is to permit the tax-free recovery from operations of capital invested in plant at a faster rate than would be possible by depreciation methods previously permitted for income tax purposes.[1] The cash working capital is thus temporarily increased by an amount equal to the current tax reduction resulting from the excess depreciation deductions taken for tax purposes in earlier years. This procedure will result in reduced depreciation deductions in future years for tax purposes on the related plant with a resulting increase in income taxes over the amount of taxes which otherwise would be payable.

In order that the net income from operations of a corporation which deducts liberalized depreciation or accelerated amortization for tax purposes but only normal depreciation in its books of account be not overstated in the earlier years and understated in the later years, it is necessary, except in rare cases, to charge current income with an amount equal to the tax reduction.[2] The exception to this procedure is found in those cases described in paragraph 8 of Accounting Research Bulletin No. 44 (Revised), Declining-Balance Depreciation, issued in July 1958 by the Committee on Accounting Procedure of the American Institute of Certified Public Accountants.[3] The contra credit should

---

[1] That this was the intent of these sections of the Code is disclosed by the Report of the House Committee on Ways and Means and the Report of the Senate Committee on Finance. See H. Rep. No. 1337 (83rd Cong., 2nd Sess.), p. 24, and Sen. Rep. No. 1622 (83rd Cong., 2nd Sess.), p. 26.

[2] This charge to income is not necessary where the corporation treats the related tax effect in its books of account as additional amortization or depreciation applicable to the asset in question in recognition of the loss of future deductibility for income tax purposes, or charges liberalized depreciation or accelerated amortization in its books of account.

[3] "Many regulatory authorities permit recognition of deferred income taxes for accounting and/or rate-making purposes, whereas some do not. The Committee believes that they should permit the recognition of deferred income taxes for both purposes. However, where charges for deferred income taxes are not allowed for rate-making purposes, accounting recognition need not be given to the deferment of taxes if it may reasonably be expected that increased future income taxes, resulting from the earlier deduction of declining-balance depreciation for income tax purposes only, will be allowed in future rate determinations."

be accumulated in an appropriately captioned balance sheet account[4] and returned to income proportionately in later years when the depreciation then allowed for tax purposes is less than the normal depreciation charged to income in the books of account.

It is not contemplated that the portion returned to income will offset exactly the actual tax to be paid in future years, as it is made only for the purpose of allocating to future periods the effect on income of the tax reduction taken. These tax reductions therefore enter into the determination of income and to the increase of equity capital only through the passage of time.

By the Commission.

ORVAL L. DuBOIS
Secretary

---

4   Companies required to comply with a uniform system of accounts of the Federal Power Commission shall use the balance sheet captions and classification of deferred taxes prescribed by that Commission in its Orders No. 203 and 204, Dockets No. R-158 and R-159, respectively, issued May 29, 1958. Other companies may use the same or other appropriate captions and classification provided they avoid any implication that the credit balance in question is a part of earned surplus or of equity capital

EXHIBIT U

COMMONWEALTH EDISON COMPANY

72 WEST ADAMS STREET * CHICAGO 90 ILLINOIS

January 23, 1959

Securities and Exchange Commission
Washington 25, D. C.

Attention: Mr. Orval L. DuBois
Secretary

Gentlemen:

Commonwealth Edison Company favors the adoption of the announced interpretation of administrative policy on financial statements regarding balance sheet treatment of credits equivalent to the reduction in income taxes as outlined in your Notice of Intention dated December 30, 1958.

The proposed interpretation of administrative policy is in accord with our view that a company which deducts liberalized depreciation or accelerated amortization for tax purposes but records only normal depreciation on its books of account should charge current income with an amount equal to the resulting tax reduction and concurrently credit a balance sheet account which clearly indicates by its title and balance sheet position that the accumulated credit is an accrued liability of the company. Consequently, we believe that this credit should not be shown as earned surplus or equity capital.

Yours very truly,

/s/ GRANT H. WIER

Grant H. Wier
Comptroller

EXHIBIT V

ILLINOIS POWER COMPANY

500 SOUTH 27TH STREET

DECATUR, ILLINOIS

February 26, 1959

Securities and Exchange Commission
425 Second St., N. W.
Washington, D. C.

Attention: Mr. Orval L. DuBois, Secretary

Subject: SECURITIES ACT OF 1933
        Release No. 4010
        SECURITIES EXCHANGE ACT OF 1934
        Release No. 5844
        PUBLIC UTILITY HOLDING COMPANY ACT OF 1935
        Release No. 13894
        INVESTMENT COMPANY ACT OF 1940
        Release No. 2814

Dear Sirs:

We have been informed that the Edison Electric Institute is considering appearing by counsel at the public hearing to be held March 25, 1959 with respect to above-named Releases of the Securities and Exchange Commission, for the purpose of making a presentation which, in effect, will be in opposition to the proposed interpretation of administrative policy set forth in such Releases. In order that the record may be clear, we advise you that neither Edison Electric Institute nor its counsel is authorized to represent Illinois Power Company in the proceedings with respect to the above-named Releases or to make any presentation on its behalf. The position of Illinois Power Company with respect to the matters involved in the proceedings is as follows:

1. It seems essential, in order to prevent financial statements from being misleading, that uniform accounting principles be established which will not permit reporting companies to vary net income or earned surplus merely by the election of a particular accounting presentation. This is true even though some accounting presentation, other than that required by the above Releases, is adopted as the standard.

2. The fact that different accounting presentations are authorized or required by different State regulatory bodies for rate-making or other regulatory purposes does not justify refraining from establishing a uniform accounting standard. The fact that a particular accounting presentation is authorized by a State regulatory body does not in itself prevent such presentation from being misleading.

3. Illinois Power Company is in favor of the accounting presentation required by the proposed interpretation of administrative policy set forth in the above-named Releases.

4. Our examination of many electric operating utility annual reports discloses that many (probably a majority in number) of electric operating utilities in the United States follow the accounting presentation required by the proposed interpretation of administrative policy set forth in above-named Releases.

We request that this letter be read into the record at the public hearing to be held with respect to the above Releases.

Very truly yours,

ILLINOIS POWER COMPANY

By /s/ ALLEN VAN WYCK
Allen Van Wyck
President

EXHIBIT W

THE COLUMBIA GAS SYSTEM, INC.

CHARLES H. MANN
TREASURER

ADDRESS REPLY TO
120 EAST 41ST STREET
NEW YORK 17, N. Y.

March 24, 1959

Securities and Exchange Commission
Washington 25, D. C.

Attention: Mr. Orval L. DuBois, Secretary

Gentlemen:

This letter is in reference to Release No. 4010, Securities Act of 1933, titled "Notice of Intention to Announce Interpretation of Administrative Policy." By the issuance of Releases 4023 and 4038, the Commission extended the time for submitting views and comments to March 25, 1959, and announced a public hearing on April 8, 1959.

For the reasons clearly set forth in your announcement, the companies comprising the Columbia Gas System are in complete agreement with the theory of deferred tax accounting where liberalized depreciation is claimed for income tax purposes, but only normal depreciation is recorded on the books of account.

We think that this accounting treatment is particularly applicable to regulated public utilities and have successfully advocated this treatment before the Federal Power Commission and several State regulatory commissions (see FPC Opinion at Docket No. G–6358 re Amere Gas Utilities Company, et al). Attached hereto and made a part of our comments is the statement of the Columbia Gas System Companies filed on September 6, 1957 at FPC Docket No. R–158, which sets forth in greater detail our position with respect to this accounting treatment.

Our Companies also desire to have time allotted to them at the public hearing on this matter to be held April 8, 1959.

Very truly yours,

/s/ C. H. MANN

Enclosure

EXHIBIT X

AMERICAN TELEPHONE AND TELEGRAPH COMPANY
195 BROADWAY, NEW YORK 7, N. Y.

ALEXANDER L. STOTT
COMPTROLLER

February 26, 1959

Mr. Orval L. DuBois, Secretary
Securities and Exchange Commission
Washington 25, D. C.

Dear Mr. DuBois:

This is in reference to the Notice of Intention to Announce Interpretation of Administrative Policy released by the Commission on December 30, 1958, relative to "interpretation of administrative policy on financial statements regarding balance sheet treatment of credits equivalent to reductions of income taxes".

While none of the Bell System telephone companies in the United States have adopted the provisions of Sections 167 and 168 of the Code in preparing their Federal income tax returns, and do not plan to do so, the American Telephone Company as an interested party submits the following comments on behalf of the Bell System telephone companies.

The proposed announcement deals with financial statements of companies which have adopted the liberalized depreciation or accelerated amortization procedures set forth in Sections 167 and 168, respectively, of the Internal Revenue Code of 1954. It states that, except in rare cases, it is necessary for a corporation which deducts liberalized depreciation or accelerated amortization for tax purposes but only normal depreciation in its books of account, to charge current income with an amount equal to the tax reduction in order that its net income be not overstated in the earlier years and understated in the later years. The exception to this procedure is found, according to the Notice, in those cases described in paragraph 8 of Accounting Research Bulletin No. 44 (Revised) which provides that where charges for deferred income taxes are not allowed for rate-making purposes, accounting recognition need not be given to the deferment of taxes if it may reasonably be expected that increased income taxes will be allowed in the future.

We are in complete agreement with the general rule that where normal depreciation is used in the books of account it is essential to give deferred tax treatment to the differentials arising from the use of accelerated depreciation or amortization for tax purposes. Our belief is based on the following reasons:

When straight line depreciation (which communication carriers are required to use under the Federal Communications Commission's Uniform Systems of Accounts) is used for both the books of account and tax purposes, the net cost of depreciation after taxes is distrubuted equitably over the service life of the property and, in the case of a utility, over the generations of ratepayers. However, use of straight line depreciation for the books of account and accelerated depreciation for tax purposes, as permitted under the Internal Revenue Code, has the effect of borrowing tax deductions from the future to reduce current taxes. If a tax deduction, arising from use of depreciation accruals applicable to future years, is used in the current year, the benefit of the right to such deduction, which is a valuable right granted by Congress, is lost for the future. Under such conditions if deferred tax accounting is not used the reduction in taxes in the early years of the life of the property would flow through to net income and result in an overstatement of earnings during that period. If deferred tax treatment is used, there is synchronization in the accounts of the depreciation expense shown and the related tax deduction over the life of the related plant with no distortion of net income at any time.

Deferred tax treatment also provides protection against the possibility that the Internal Revenue Code may change. At some time the Code may not permit any tax deductions arising from the use of accelerated depreciation or may limit the deductions to a greater extent than is now the case. If such deductions are no longer permitted or are limited, and deferred tax treatment has not been used, it becomes apparent immediately that net income has been overstated in the interim and that a company is then faced with carrying the burden of taxes properly applicable to past periods, in addition to the burden of current taxes.

Deferred tax treatment permits public utilities to obtain the benefits intended by Congress for all corporations as clearly stated in the Notice of Intention. Public utilities which adopt accelerated depreciation can obtain such benefits only if they are permitted to charge as an expense for rate-making purposes the difference between normal taxes and taxes currently paid. If such utilities are allowed only taxes currently paid, the entire benefit of Sections 167 and 168 will be passed on to present ratepayers and the tax deferment will not be available to aid the utilities in their expansion programs, as intended by Congress. The benefit to present ratepayers would require future ratepayers to bear the burden of higher taxes if taxes currently paid are also allowed in the future.

For these reasons, and others set forth in your announcement, we strongly advocate use of the deferred tax treatment where normal depreciation is used in the accounts and, except for the reference to paragraph 8 of Accounting Research Bulletin No. 44 (Revised), we are in agreement with the principles and proposed accounting treatment of material matters of this nature as presented in your announcement.

With respect to paragraph 8 of Bulletin 44 (Revised), we concur in the belief expressed in the second sentence of that paragraph to the effect that regulatory authorities should permit the recognition of deferred income taxes for both book and rate-making purposes, inasmuch as both accounting and rate-making concepts are concerned with reflecting true costs in any period of operation. However, we cannot concur with respect to the third sentence of that paragraph which states that where charges for deferred income taxes are not allowed for rate-making purposes, accounting recognition need not be given to the deferment of taxes if it may reasonably be expected that increased future income taxes, resulting from the earlier deduction of declining-balance depreciation for income tax purposes only, will be allowed in future rate determinations. First, we have not been able to understand why regulatory policy with respect to rate-making should determine generally accepted accounting principles. Furthermore, we doubt that any regulatory authority can give reasonable assurance of increased future taxes being allowed in subsequent rate-making procedures by the regulatory authority as constituted at a future date. Despite the often repeated statement that commission will allow taxes actually paid, it has been our experience that, in situations unrelated to accelerated depreciation, many regulatory authorities have made disallowances of current income taxes actually paid. Also, other utilities have experienced commission disallowances of depreciation accruals to amortize past deficiencies in depreciation caused by the application of depreciation theories accepted by the same commission at a previous time. Accordingly, we do not see any practical means for implementing the treatment referred to in paragraph 8 of Bulletin 44 (Revised).

As required by the Notice, two additional copies of this letter are enclosed.

Very truly yours,

/s/ A. L. STOTT
Comptroller

Enclosures

EXHIBIT Y

THE NATIONAL FEDERATION OF FINANCIAL ANALYSTS SOCIETIES

February 2, 1959

Mr. Orval L. DuBois
Secretary
Securities and Exchange Commission
Washington, 25, D. C.

      Re: SECURITIES ACT OF 1933
             Release No. 1010
             SECURITIES EXCHANGE ACT OF 1934
             Release No. 5844
             PUBLIC UTILITY HOLDING COMPANY ACT OF 1935
             Release No. 13894
             INVESTMENT COMPANY ACT OF 1940
             Release No. 2814

NOTICE OF INTENTION TO ANNOUNCE
INTERPRETATION OF ADMINISTRATIVE POLICY

To the Commission:

    The National Federation of Financial Analysts Societies consists of autonomous societies of financial analysts in twenty cities in the United States and two in Canada with a membership of over six thousand. The nature of our work in appraising the relative investment value of securities is such that we believe our membership more nearly represents the interests of the investor than other groups in the accounting and securities industry whose interests are often more closely identified with corporate management than with that of the individual investor.

    While the following comments cannot be said to represent the views of all analysts, they do represent the opinion of our Standing Committee empowered to deal with such matters and of the Executive Committee of the Federation. As such, the views presented herein can be said to be representative of the general thinking of the financial analysts, and hence of the individual investor.

    In general, we are in hearty accord with the proposed announcement of an interpretation of administrative policy on financial statements regarding balance sheet treatment of credits equivalent to the reduction in income taxes. We believe, however:

1.) That the amount of credits or debits to the deferred balance sheet item for the period should be set forth in the income statements.

2.) That all companies subject to the Security and Exchange Commission's jurisdiction should be required to charge income and credit to a deferred income account the amount of estimated tax savings without regard to the exceptions noted in Paragraph 8 of Accounting Research Bulletin No. 44.

3.) That the amount of deferred taxes for the year and changes in the reserve be required to be shown in the financial statements.

We believe that a lack of uniformity in income and balance sheet accounting is misleading to the investor. The National Federation of Financial Analysts, therefore, as a matter of general principle, is in favor of measures such as that now being proposed by the Commission leading in the direction of uniform accounting practice.

Respectfully submitted,

/s/ M. DUTTON MOREHOUSE

M. Dutton Morehouse
Chairman—Government
Relations Committee
NATIONAL FEDERATION
OF FINANCIAL
ANALYSTS SOCIETIES

EXHIBIT Z

HARRIS TRUST AND SAVINGS BANK
ORGANIZED AS N.W. HARRIS & CO. 1882. INCORPORATED 1907

115 WEST MONROE STREET   TELEPHONE: STATE 2-8200

CHICAGO 90, ILLINOIS

SECURITIES ANALYSIS
DEPARTMENT   January 29, 1959

<u>Air Mail</u>

Mr. Orval L. DuBois, Secretary
Securities and Exchange Commission ,
Washington 25, D. C.

Dear Mr. DuBois:

Accounting for Accelerated Depreciation
and Deferred Income Taxes

In response to your release dated December 30, 1958, we are writing to say that we favor your proposed rule regarding balance sheet treatment of deferred tax provisions. We would not be in favor of any exceptions, however, since our interest lies in uniformity of financial statements for ready analysis and comparison, regardless of varying regulatory policies for the regulated companies.

It is our understanding from your release that companies would also, in effect, be required to make a provision for deferred taxes on the income statement.

As you pointed out in your release, the rule is not required for those concerns which charge additional depreciation in the amount of the tax saving. We concur with this view, and also add that it is not required in cases where the depreciation charge is equivalent to tax depreciation.

Yours very truly,

/s/ WILLIAM C. NORBY
Vice President

UNITED STATES DISTRICT COURT
For the Southern District of New York

Appalachian Power Company
Ohio Power Company and
Indiana & Michigan Electric Company,

Plaintiffs,

against

American Institute of Certified Public
Accountants, L. H. Penney, William W.
Werntz and Carman G. Blough,

Defendants.

REPLY
AFFIDAVIT

State of New York
County of New York

ss.:

DONALD C. COOK, being duly sworn, deposes and says that:

1. I am a Vice President of each of the plaintiff corporations and am fully familiar with all of the facts and matters hereinafter stated.

2. This affidavit is submitted in support of plaintiffs' application, pursuant to Rule 65 of the Federal Rules of Civil Procedure, for an order granting a preliminary injunction herein and in reply.to the affidavits submitted in opposition to said motion.

3. I have been since 1941 a certified public accountant, have had twenty-four years experience in accounting and have been a member of the defendant American Institute of Certified Public Accountants for more than fifteen years.

4. I was a Commissioner of the Securities and Exchange Commission from 1949 to 1953, during which period I served as Vice Chairman from 1950 to 1952 and as Chairman of the Commission from 1952 to 1953. I previously had served for approximately ten years (1935-1945) as a member of the staff of the Securities and Exchange Commission, during which period I was employed for approximately five years (1937-1942) as a utilities analyst and for approximately two years (1943-1945) as Assistant Director of the Public Utilities Division of the Commission.

5. I have had, as a result of the above experience, a unique opportunity to ascertain how accounting principles are developed and applied in the public utility and regulatory fields. I also had an opportunity to familiarize myself with the identity of the accounting firms which, during the period when I was employed by the Securities and Exchange Commission, certified the financial statements of public utility companies filed with the Commission under the various statutes which the Commission administers. I have since ascertained from official publications of defendant Institute the current composition of its Committee on Accounting Procedure and have noted that, of the twenty-one members of that Committee, fifteen members are from accounting firms which, during the period I was associated with the Securities and Exchange Commission, did little, if any, public utility accounting work before said Commission.

6. It is my responsibility as Vice President of each of the plaintiff corporations to supervise all financial and accounting matters affecting such corporations. I have, since the early 1940's, studied the accounting principles followed by utility companies in accounting for the amortization of emergency facilities and, since 1954, have studied the principles followed by utility companies in accounting for liberalized depreciation where charges are made in the income statement (normalization charges) to provide for federal income taxes which may have to be paid in the future but which are currently deferred, measured by the difference between actual income taxes and the amount such taxes would have been if such companies had not elected to take for tax purposes accelerated amortization deductions under Section 168 and liberalized depreciation deductions under Section 167 of the Internal Revenue Code. My studies indicate that, where utilities normalize provisions for federal income taxes in the income account, two definite alternatives exist with respect to balance sheet treatment of the credit resulting from the charge against income as a provision for deferred taxes. One such alternative involves crediting a restricted earned surplus account, the other involves crediting a reserve or other account outside the stockholders equity section of the balance sheet. Each of these alternatives has been considered to be a generally accepted method of accounting. Although accounting periodicals have contained arguments in favor of and against which of these alternatives is preferable, my examinations of annual reports and prospectuses of utility companies indicate that the recordation of the deferred tax credit in restricted earned surplus is an accounting principle not only accepted by a majority of the nationally recognized accounting firms having experience in the utility field, but also that balance sheets reflecting the credit to a restricted earned surplus account have been certified by each of such accounting firms.

7. The balance sheets of the plaintiff corporations which have been and are contained in annual reports to stockholders and in prospectuses used in connection with the sale of securities, have been and are prepared in accordance with the orders of the state regulatory commissions having jurisdiction over plaintiffs, which require, except with respect to accounting for liberalized de-

preciation in the case of Ohio Power Company, that provisions for deferred taxes be credited to restricted earned surplus accounts. These balance sheets have been and are now certified by Niles & Niles, the independent certified public accounting firm which audits the financial statements of the plaintiff corporations, as being in accordance with generally accepted accounting principles.

8. In July, 1958, I received Accounting Research Bulletin No. 44 (Revised) upon its publication and distribution by the Committee on Accounting Procedure of the defendant American Institute of Certified Public Accountants. Upon receipt of said Bulletin I examined the same and ascertained that the same dealt with the accounting to be followed in an income statement with respect to the income tax effect of the use of the liberalized depreciation provisions which were inserted by the Internal Revenue Act of 1954.

9. My examination of said Bulletin failed to disclose any evidence that the Committee intended, by promulgating said Bulletin, to define and prescribe any required balance sheet treatment of the credit arising from the charge which said Bulletin required to be made against income as a provision for deferred income taxes. As a matter of fact, said Bulletin did not, with one exception, even mention the balance sheet. The one exception was in paragraph 5 of said Bulletin where it was stated that under certain circumstances it would be alternatively appropriate "instead of crediting a deferred tax account" to recognize deferred taxes in the income account as additional amortization or depreciation. Although it was obvious that this phrase did not attempt to specify any particular balance sheet account for the credit arising from a normalization charge, I concluded that it would be prudent to ascertain with precision whether the Committee on Accounting Procedure could possibly have intended to deal with the question of the balance sheet treatment of the normalization credit.

10. Accordingly, I requested Mr. William Meglaughlin of Niles & Niles to communicate with the research department of the defendant Institute and ascertain whether the quoted phrase was intended to have any particular significance. Mr. Meglaughlin informed me that he had communicated with the research department of the Institute and been advised that the Committee on Accounting Procedure did not intend to deal in the Bulletin with the proper balance sheet treatment of deferred tax provisions, and that while Committee members had discussed the matter it had been decided to side-step the question and not include any required balance sheet treatment in the Bulletin.

11. In the latter part of 1958, however, I participated in a financing program of plaintiff Indiana & Michigan Electric Company involving the proposed issue and sale at competitive bidding of $20,000,000 aggregate principal amount of First Mortgage Bonds to finance the 1959 construction program of said Company. In connection therewith Indiana & Michigan prepared a registration statement under the Securities Act of 1933 and caused the same to be filed with the Secu-

rities and Exchange Commission. Said registration statement contained financial statements of Indiana & Michigan Electric Company as at June 30, 1958 and included a balance sheet which disclosed that more than $15,000,000 had been recorded by said Indiana & Michigan Electric Company as provisions for deferred income taxes in a restricted earned surplus account pursuant to orders of regulatory commissions of Indiana and of Michigan. While said registration statement was pending before the Securities and Exchange Commission, Mr. W. J. Rose, Secretary of plaintiff Indiana & Michigan Electric Company, informed me that he had received a telephone call from a member of the staff of the Commission on October 15, 1958 and had been advised that the staff of the Commission proposed to deliver a letter to said Company to the effect that it was the opinion of the Commission that in accordance with accepted accounting principles the amounts recorded in the restricted earned surplus account on the balance sheet should be excluded from the equity section of the balance sheet and shown separately.

12. Upon being advised by Mr. Rose of his telephone conversation with the staff member of the Commission I immediately communicated by telephone with the office of the Chief Accountant of the Commission, and arranged for a conference at the offices of the Commission in Washington, D. C. On October 20, 1958 I participated in the scheduled conference with representatives of plaintiff Indiana & Michigan Electric Company, Mr. Andrew Barr, the Chief Accountant of the Commission and other members of the staff of the Commission.

13. I requested Mr. Barr to inform me why the staff of the Commission had concluded that it was no longer in accordance with sound accounting principles that normalization credits be recorded in restricted earned surplus accounts as required by state regulatory agencies. Mr. Barr replied that he had discussed Accounting Research Bulletin No. 44 (Revised) with defendant Werntz, the Chairman of the Committee on Accounting Procedure of the defendant Institute; that Mr. Barr understood defendant Werntz to have stated that said Committee, in issuing Accounting Research Bulletin No. 44 (Revised), had intended to prescribe a required balance sheet treatment of normalization credits, and that the Committee had specified in the Bulletin that such amounts should not be recorded in a restricted earned surplus account.

14. I replied that Mr. Barr must be mistaken; that the text of Accounting Research Bulletin No. 44 (Revised) did not contain any language which specified any required balance sheet treatment, and that I had the matter checked with the research department of the Institute. Mr. Barr stated that he was not mistaken; that he had had his discussion with defendant Werntz shortly before our conference and that he understood that defendant Werntz had testified or proposed to testify before the Public Utilities Commission of California in accordance with Mr. Barr's understanding.

15. I responded that I had not only had the matter checked with the research department of the Institute but that I had also asked Mr. Weldon Powell, a member of the defendant Institute's Committee on Accounting Procedure, in a telephone conversation whether the Committee had intended to specify a required balance sheet account and that he had stated that the Committee had specifically intended not to deal with the matter at that time. I also stated to Mr. Barr that all the nationally recognized accounting firms had certified, and the Securities and Exchange Commission had accepted, since the issuance of Accounting Research Bulletin No. 44 (Revised) in July, 1958, financial statements which contained provisions for deferred taxes resulting from normalization charges in restricted earned surplus accounts and that that was strong evidence that no change in accounting principles as to such balance sheet treatment was intended in the Bulletin. Mr. Barr replied that he had cleared the sending of the proposed deficiency letter with the Securities and Exchange Commission.

16. I then requested, in view of Mr. Barr's statements, that representatives of Indiana & Michigan Electric Company be permitted to appear before the Commission itself to explain what appeared to me to be a misunderstanding upon the part of the Chief Accountant of the Commission. This request was granted and, on the same day, I participated in an administrative conference with the members of the Securities and Exchange Commission. During the course of such conference I advised the Commission, among other things, that I had communicated with a member of the Committee on Accounting Procedure of the Institute and that I had been advised by such member that it was not the intention of the Committee on Accounting Procedure to specify any required balance sheet treatment of the normalization credit resulting from deferred tax accounting. The Commission indicated that it would consider the matter further.

17. I was advised on the following day in a telephone conversation with a member of the staff of the Commission that the proposed deficiency would be withdrawn and that it would not be necessary for Indiana & Michigan Electric Company to designate the provisions for deferred taxes in any manner other than as restricted earned surplus and common stock equity. The Commission, within the next few days, permitted the registration statement to become effective and the securities were subsequently issued and sold pursuant to the authorization of the Commission.

18. It is my belief that the proposed issuance of a deficiency letter by the Securities and Exchange Commission in connection with the aforesaid financing was based upon the mistaken belief of the Chief Accountant and the Commission that the intention of the Institute's Committee on Accounting Procedure in promulgating Accounting Research Bulletin No. 44 (Revised) was to specify a balance sheet treatment of the credit for deferred taxes and to disapprove the inclusion of such credits in restricted earned surplus accounts. The above facts thus demonstrate clearly the authority which is given by regulatory agencies con-

cerned with accounting principles to pronouncements by the defendants. The effect which the distribution of the proposed letter would have on plaintiffs is thus also an established fact. With respect to the authority of defendants' pronouncements, the official transcript of a current proceeding before the Securities and Exchange Commission indicates that defendant Blough himself stated to the Securities and Exchange Commission that:

> "These bulletins are widely recognized as authoritative by the accounting profession and they carry a great deal of weight in the business community generally."

During the period in which I served the Securities and Exchange Commission in the above-mentioned capacities, it was my experience that the Commission generally considered promulgations by the Institute's Committee on Accounting Procedure as correctly representing applicable accounting principles.

19. The damaging effects which the distribution of the proposed letter would have on plaintiffs are forcibly illustrated by reference to the fact that the purported basis for the issuance of the proposed letter is the same incorrect statement which influenced the Securities and Exchange Commission and its Chief Accountant to consider sending a deficiency letter, namely, the mistaken idea that it was the intention of the Institute's Committee on Accounting Procedure in issuing Accounting Research Bulletin No. 44 (Revised) to disapprove of the inclusion of credits for deferred taxes in restricted earned surplus accounts. In support of the allegations of the complaint and my prior statements herein to that effect, there is documentary proof that the Institute's Committee on Accounting Procedure had no such intention and that the avowed purpose for distributing the proposed letter has no basis in fact. Attached hereto as Exhibit A is a copy of the "Exposure Draft" of Accounting Research Bulletin No. 44 (Revised) which was distributed by the Committee on Accounting Procedure for consideration by Institute members and others in the latter part of 1957. No reference to any required balance sheet treatment appears therein nor is there any reference therein to the phrase "a deferred tax account." Attached hereto as Exhibit B is a copy of the "Ballot Draft" of Accounting Research Bulletin No. 44 (Revised) which was distributed by the Committee on Accounting Procedure to its members for formal vote in June, 1958. This Ballot Draft did not refer to any required balance sheet treatment nor did it contain the phrase "a deferred tax account". Attached hereto as Exhibit C* is a copy of Accounting Research Bulletin No. 44 (Revised) as published in July, 1958. The Bulletin was distributed in this form to the membership of defendant Institute and contained for the first time in paragraph 5 thereof a provision that under certain circumstances it would be alternatively appropriate "instead of crediting

---

* ARB No. 44 (Revised) has been printed as Exhibit B to the Werntz affidavit and is omitted here.

a deferred tax account" to recognize the taxes deferred as additional amortization or depreciation. I am informed by Mr. Meglaughlin of Niles & Niles that Mr. Meglaughlin was advised by the research department of defendant Institute that the research staff of the Institute, after the formal vote by the Committee on Accounting Procedure on the Ballot Draft of the Bulletin, inserted, with the acquiescence of defendant Werntz, the quoted phrase and that the members of the Committee never voted on the inclusion of this phrase. Even with the insertion of this phrase, Accounting Research Bulletin No. 44 (Revised) did not specify any required balance sheet treatment of the normalization credits. This documentary proof, however, establishes that, contrary to the statement in the proposed letter, since the Committee did not vote on the inclusion of the phrase "deferred tax account", it could not have been the intention of the Committee by the use of such phrase to designate a balance sheet treatment for such credits or to establish any accounting principles with respect thereto.

20. Indeed defendant Werntz admitted in his testimony during an official proceeding before the Public Utilities Commission of the State of California on October 9, 1958 that the Institute's Committee on Accounting Procedure had no such intention in promulgating Accounting Research Bulletin No. 44 (Revised). Mr. Werntz testified as follows:

"MR. WRIGHT: Would it be fair to say then that your Committee and the American Institute has not designated the proper account for the deferral - -

MR. WERNTZ: We have not designated the classification, that is correct." (Page 1173 of official transcript of proceedings)

The official transcript of a current proceeding before the Securities and Exchange Commission indicates that defendant Blough also has publicly made the same admission. Mr. Blough there said:

"The disposition of the credit resulting from this charge to income was not specifically dealt with by the Committee in the Bulletin." (Page 6 of official transcript, April 8, 1959)

The record in the same proceeding before the Securities and Exchange Commission contains a copy of a letter, dated March 30, 1959, addressed by Mr. Walter Staub, a member of the Institute's Committee on Accounting Procedure and a member of the accounting firm of Lybrand, Ross Bros. & Montgomery, to the defendant Institute, which states in part as follows:

"At the time ARB 44 (Revised) was under consideration the suggestion was made that it include a statement that the deferred tax credit should not be carried to a restricted surplus account, but our committee * * * decided not to include such a statement in the revised bulletin."

21. In my opinion the issuance of the proposed letter, because of the authority of such a pronouncement, will inflict immediate and irreparable injury, loss and damage on the plaintiffs. The removal of more than $65,000,000 from the common stock equity of the plaintiffs would, in the first instance, have the effect of limiting the short term borrowing power of plaintiffs under applicable statutes so as to decrease the amounts which plaintiffs can borrow from banks by $6,500,000. Since plaintiffs currently and regularly utilize short term bank borrowings to finance their respective construction expenditures pending permanent financing, the effect of such a decrease in short term borrowing power will be (i) to seriously impair plaintiffs' financial flexibility and, among other things, accelerate the necessity for permanent financing, and (ii) to effect an increase in capital charges on said $6,500,000 of approximately a quarter of a million dollars a year. The replacement of the $65,000,000 now in restricted earned surplus accounts by the issuance of common stock would result in net increased capital charges to the plaintiffs aggregating approximately $4,400,000 each year, or an additional amount of approximately $4,150,000 a year.

22. During the year 1958, moreover, the plaintiffs sold approximately 20.4 billion kilowatt hours of electric energy. If plaintiffs are to incur additional annual capital charges of more than $4,400,000, the effect of such charges upon the cost per kilowatt hour of the electric energy sold in 1958 would be to increase the cost of such energy by approximately 2/100ths of a cent per kilowatt hour. Plaintiffs' ability to develop sales of electric energy and to increase their respective businesses depends in large measure upon their ability to offer substantial quantities of electric energy to consumers at reasonable costs which are competitive with those of other areas of the United States. In many cases customers are attracted to the service areas of the plaintiffs by differentials in the cost per kilowatt hour of electric energy amounting to as little as 9/1000 of a cent per kilowatt hour. For example, in a recent case, one of the plaintiffs failed to secure as a customer a substantial aluminum reduction operation because it could not further cut its rate on power by 9/1000ths of a cent per kilowatt hour. An increase of 2/100ths of a cent per kilowatt hour would have increased the annual cost of an existing aluminum customer consuming 3.2 billion kilowatt hours annually by $640,000. The effect of such an increase would impel such a customer to decide to locate new facilities in some other location thus restricting the development by plaintiffs of their respective service areas.

23. The foregoing injuries, since they adversely affect the development by plaintiffs of their respective businesses in a manner and to an extent which is not subject to calculation, are irreparable and not compensable by money damages.

24. With respect to the merits of the subject matter of defendants' proposed action, my professional opinion is that, as an accounting matter, the preferable and more logically correct method of accounting for the tax effect of ac-

celerated amortization and liberalized depreciation is to reflect the credit resulting from current tax reductions in an earned surplus account which is restricted against the payment of cash dividends on the capital stock of the accounting utility.   This method of accounting is preferable because the process of normalizing income is concerned solely with the timing of the recognition of income in the income statement and not with the question of whether income has in fact been received. Normalizing an income account neither creates nor destroys income; it merely fixes the time when income that has actually been received is recognized in the income account. Therefore, the normalizing charge cannot be a current cost and cannot measure a liability; it can only serve to channel earnings, which otherwise would have appeared as net income after taxes, directly into surplus and therefore into common stock equity. No effort has been made in the letter which it is proposed will be published by defendants on behalf of the Committee on Accounting Procedure to refute the above principles and no effort has been made to explain why it is considered that it follows that a charge which affects only the timing of the recognition of income, but not the fact of its receipt, should not be recorded as a part of the surplus and hence common stock equity.

25. That the accounting principles followed by plaintiffs are sound and generally accepted accounting principles, is attested to by the facts that financial statements which included credits arising from normalization charges in restricted earned surplus accounts have been certified by every major accounting firm active in utility accounting, have been accepted by both state and federal regulatory agencies including the Securities and Exchange Commission, and, moreover, by the fact that the regulatory commissions of at least 24 states have authorized or required the use of restricted earned surplus for the contra-credit in respect of deferred tax accounting for accelerated amortization and at least 13 state regulatory commissions have authorized or required such treatment in respect of liberalized depreciation.

26. Not only is the proposed letter based on a false premise in purporting to describe the Committee's intention in using a phrase which was inserted by the staff of the Institute and not voted upon by the Committee, but also the procedures followed by the defendants in connection with the preparation of the proposed letter are in violation of their previous practices and their own rules of conduct with respect to accounting research bulletins as set forth in the complaint and in Mr. Whitman's affidavit, and the issuance of the proposed letter would conflict with a basic policy which the defendant Institute has adopted since the temporary restraining order in this action was signed on April 15, 1959. On April 22, 1959 defendant Institute issued a press release, a copy of which is attached hereto as Exhibit D, in which it was announced that a new procedure would thereafter be followed in enunciating accounting principles. The new procedure contemplates that there will be a public announcement each time the Institute's research staff begins a study of some aspect of accounting

principles; that interested groups will be invited at that time to submit their views; that later, after the researchers have completed their study, a formal report, containing pro and con arguments on controversial points, will be given the widest possible distribution and exposure to the public and the accounting profession with a request for further comments; that only after such publication of a formal report containing such pro and con arguments would it be reviewed by a newly created Accounting Priciples Board of the Institute which will, in the light of the comments received from interested groups, decide whether to adopt or to reject the proposed accounting principle. The procedure so adopted by the defendant Institute is exactly the procedure which the plaintiffs have requested, without success, be employed by the defendants in respect of the letter, the distribution of which has been restrained by the Court until defendants follow the procedures which the Institute has itself adopted for the future.

27. Not only would the distribution of the proposed letter be directly injurious to the plaintiffs to the knowledge of the defendants, but the reckless procedures followed by them have deprived others interested in and affected by it of the opportunity of expressing their views in opposition. For example, I am annexing as Exhibits E and F hereto copies of letters sent by the Accounting Section of the American Gas Association, representing the gas industry in the United States, and by the Accounting Division of the Edison Electric Institute, representing the electric industry in the United States, which letters request that the distribution of the proposed letter be withheld until an opportunity is afforded for the submission of views. I have been advised that comparable letters have been sent to defendant Institute by or on behalf of several other organizations, Institute members and public utilities, each requesting that the Institute defer the publication of the proposed letter until an opportunity is afforded to such interested parties to present their views thereon.

28. The foregoing facts, I submit, demonstrate the many inaccuracies and distortions contained in the affidavits of F. Merrill Beatty, George C. Christie and defendant Werntz submitted in opposition to plaintiffs' application for a preliminary injunction. Specifically, however, I wish to point out to the Court that:

> (a) No attempt has been made in any of said affidavits to deny that immediate and irreparable injury, loss and damage to plaintiffs will occur as a result of the publication of the proposed letter. Nor is any attempt made to justify defendants' haste in insisting on the immediate publication of the proposed letter prior to the receipt and consideration of comments on proposed action from Institute members and other interested parties.

> (b) With respect to the affidavit of F. Merrill Beatty, which states that, should the amount of the credit for deferred taxes be material, Arthur Andersen & Co. would take exception in their auditors' certificate to the

treatment of said credit in the equity capital section if it is unable to persuade the client to remove the credit from the equity capital section, it is the fact that Arthur Andersen & Co. have certified financial statements in which such credits appeared in restricted earned surplus accounts.

Arthur Andersen & Co. must have concluded that $13,000,000 is an insignificant and immaterial amount, for a prospectus, dated March 8, 1958, of Ohio Edison Company relating to its First Mortgage Bonds, which I have examined, contains consolidated financial statements of said Company and its subsidiaries as of December 31, 1957, which set forth in the common stock equity section of the balance sheet an amount of $13,812,000 classified as earned surplus restricted for deferred taxes. These financial statements were certified without exception by Arthur Andersen & Co. as having been prepared in conformity with generally accepted accounting principles consistently applied. I have examined several other such financial statements certified by Arthur Andersen & Co. as having been prepared in accordance with generally accepted accounting principles.

(c) With respect to the affidavit of George C. Christie, Esq., the Securities and Exchange Commission is considering whether it would be desirable to adopt an administrative policy relating to financial statements filed with said Commission under the various statutes which it administers. It has completed its hearings but has reached no decision as yet. Since there have been two alternatives, each considered to be a generally accepted method of accounting, for the treatment of the contra-credit relating to a normalization charge for deferred taxes, it is only natural that certain companies, currently following the alternative which does not involve the recordation of the credit in restricted earned surplus, should favor the accounting principles followed by them, just as companies using the restricted surplus account should favor the accounting principles followed by them.

At the hearing before the Securities and Exchange Commission on April 8 and April 10, 1959, oral arguments were made on behalf of three public utility holding company systems and ten operating public utility companies. All but two of these companies urged the Commission not to adopt the proposed administrative policy. In addition, representatives of the Washington and the Idaho regulatory commissions appeared before the Securities and Exchange Commission and opposed the adoption of such an administrative policy. The Federal Power Commission also urged the Securities and Exchange Commission not to adopt the administrative policy as it had been proposed for consideration.

Unlike the hasty action proposed by defendants, the Securities and Exchange Commission first gave notice of its proposed action in December, 1958, held hearings in April, 1959, and has not yet issued its decision.

(d) With respect to the affidavit of defendant Werntz:

(1) Paragraph 6 of said affidavit of defendant Werntz states that Accounting Research Bulletins neither have nor purport to have an official status. The question of whether the status of such bulletins is "official" is irrelevant in view of the allegation, not denied in the answering affidavits, that opinions, recommendations and pronouncements of the Committee, as published in its Accounting Research Bulletins, are generally accepted by the members of the accounting profession as establishing the accounting principles to be followed by the accountancy profession. The fact is that the publication on behalf of the Institute of the proposed letter will, because of its authority, inflict the injury, loss and damage described in the complaint and in the foregoing paragraphs 21 and 22 of this affidavit.

(2) It is alleged in paragraph 7 of the affidavit of defendant Werntz that the proposed letter is "an interpretation" of the phrase "deferred tax account". This statement is in conflict with the statement of defendant Blough to the Securities and Exchange Commission that the purpose of the letter was to state the intention of the Committee in using said phrase. As indicated in paragraph 19 of this affidavit, the Committee on Accounting Procedure of defendant Institute could not have had any intention with respect to the phrase since the members of the Committee never voted on the inclusion of the phrase.

(3) Paragraph 8 of the affidavit of defendant Werntz states that the issuance of Accounting Research Bulletin No. 44 (Revised) was in complete accord with the procedures adopted by the Committee as set forth in said Bulletin and as set forth more completely in the Introduction to Accounting Research Bulletin No. 43, attached as Exhibit A to said affidavit. Defendant Werntz, however, fails to state that the proposed letter purports to state an accounting principle, and the manner in which it has been prepared for issuance did not, in any respect, comply with the usual policies and practices of the Institute and its Committee on Accounting Procedure with respect to the issuance of important promulgations as to substantive matters of accounting principles. Defendant Werntz also fails in said paragraph 8 to refer in any way to the new policy which the Institute adopted as recently as April 23, 1959 and which is described in paragraph 26 of this affidavit or to state why the new procedures are not being followed in this instance.

(4) It is stated in paragraph 9 of the affidavit of defendant Werntz that the phrase "deferred tax account" was inserted in Ac-

counting Research Bulletin No. 44 (Revised) by the technical staff, and that such action was in complete accordance with the terms of the ballot submitted to the members of the Committee on Accounting Procedure. Exhibit D to the affidavit of defendant Werntz, which purports to support that statement, indicates on its face that it could not have been used as a ballot for the formal vote of the Committee on Accounting Procedure on Accounting Research Bulletin No. 44 (Revised). No ballot is before this Court, or has otherwise come to the attention of the affiant, which indicates that the Chairman of the Committee, or the technical staff, had any authority to make any changes whatsoever in the text of the ballot draft of the Bulletin after it had been voted upon.

(5) Paragraph 10 of the affidavit of defendant Werntz states that the use of the phrase "deferred tax account" in Accounting Research Bulletin No. 44 (Revised) is in accordance with the treatment recommended by the Committee in Chapter 9(c) of Accounting Research Bulletin No. 43 which was originally adopted in 1952 as Accounting Research Bulletin No. 42. The clause "account for deferred taxes", which appeared in Accounting Research Bulletin No. 42, had been interpreted by accounting firms of nationally recognized standing since 1952 to permit the recordation of the normalization credit in a restricted earned surplus account. No attempt is made in the proposed letter to describe the "intent" of the Committee in using this clause in Accounting Research Bulletin No. 42. No attempt is made, on the other hand, to indicate that the clause has one meaning in Accounting Research Bulletin No. 43 and another meaning in Accounting Research Bulletin No. 44 (Revised).

(6) It is stated in paragraph 11 of the affidavit of defendant Werntz that the proposed letter does not purport to change, nor does it change, the substance of Accounting Research Bulletin No. 44 (Revised). This statement is clearly wrong in that Accounting Research Bulletin No. 44 (Revised) did not, as testified to by defendant Werntz, purport to prescribe any required balance sheet treatment for a normalization credit for deferred taxes and the proposed letter specifically does attempt to achieve such a result. That others have so construed the proposed letter is demonstrated by the letter, a copy of which is attached hereto as Exhibit G, dated May 4, 1959, from General Public Utilities Corporation to defendant Penney.

(7) Reference is made in paragraph 12 of the affidavit of defendant Werntz to action taken by the Federal Power Commission in 1958. Defendant Werntz fails to state, however, that the action taken by the Federal Power Commission was for the purpose of prescribing reporting requirements for the purposes of that Commission and that

Order No. 204, issued May 29, 1958, by the Federal Power Commission specifically stated that accounting utilities which were required to report deferred taxes to a state regulatory commission in a surplus account might classify the deferred taxes in accordance with state requirements for state purposes and use the treatment specified in the Order for the purposes of the Federal Power Commission. The Order also stated that the action taken by the Federal Power Commission would not foreclose financial analysts, investors and others from considering such amounts as part of equity capital if they think proper, with such consequential benefits to the rating of the Company's securities and costs of financing as may result therefrom.

(8) Reference is made in paragraph 12 of the affidavit of defendant Werntz to an Order, issued in December, 1957, by the Public Service Commission of Indiana, and to statements in the Annual Report to Stockholders of plaintiff Indiana & Michigan Electric Company. Defendant Werntz failed to state in his affidavit that said Annual Report of plaintiff, Indiana & Michigan Electric Company, indicates that it has been advised by its counsel that the Order, which was issued without notice of or opportunity for hearing, is invalid. Defendant Werntz also appears to be unaware of the fact that since December, 1957, plaintiff, Indiana & Michigan Electric Company, has presented to the Public Service Commission of Indiana two separate financing programs involving the sale of debt securities aggregating $45,000,000; that such financing programs involved the submission to the Public Service Commission of Indiana of financing statements reflecting Indiana & Michigan Electric Company's provision for deferred taxes as restricted earned surplus, and that in the light of such circumstances the Public Service Commission of Indiana authorized plaintiff, Indiana & Michigan Electric Company, on both such occasions to proceed with the issuance and sale of such securities.

(9) It is stated in paragraph 13 of the affidavit of defendant Werntz that the proposal to issue the proposed letter was made in order to inform the members of defendant Institute what the Committee has always considered to be generally accepted accounting principles in this area. Defendant Werntz does not state, however, that he relies upon documentation of any sort to establish that the Committee on Accounting Procedure and its constantly changing personnel has recorded a view which defendant Werntz states has always prevailed. Nor does defendant Werntz state what process he employed to establish the subjective intent of each member of the Institute who has from time to time been a member of the Committee of which defendant Werntz is Chairman. The only evidence which has been available to me, i.e. the statements of defendant Werntz and Blough

that the Committee did not as a Committee intend to specify a required balance sheet treatment, tends to establish that the Committee has not, prior to the preparation of the proposed inaccurate letter, formulated any official view on the matter.

29. I believe that defendants, being three individuals and a professional organization having no substantial assets, would be unable fully to respond in money damages even if the amounts of damage to plaintiffs could be precisely calculated.

/s/ DONALD C. COOK

Sworn to before me
this 6th day of May, 1959.

/s/ THOMAS W. EVANS
Notary Public

EXHIBIT A

Exposure Draft 12/17/57

Accounting Research Bulletin No. 44 (Revised)

DECLINING-BALANCE DEPRECIATION

(Superseded Accounting Research Bulletin No. 44 Issued in October 1954)

1. The declining-balance method of estimating periodic depreciation has a long history of use in England and in other countries including, to a limited extent, the United States. Interest in this method has been increased by its specific recognition for income-tax purposes in the Internal Revenue Code of 1954.

2. The declining-balance method is one of those which meets the requirements of being "systematic and rational."[1] In those cases where the expected productivity or revenue-earning power of the asset is relatively greater during the earlier years of its life, or where maintenance charges tend to increase during the later years, the declining-balance method may well provide the most satisfactory allocation of cost. The conclusions of this bulletin also apply to other methods, including the "sum-of-the-years-digits" method, which produce substantially similar results.

3. When a change to the declining-balance method is made for general accounting purposes, and depreciation is a significant factor in the determination of net income, the change in method, including the effect thereof, should be disclosed in the year in which the change is made.

4. There may be situations in which the declining-balance method is adopted for income-tax purposes but other appropriate methods are used for financial accounting purposes. In such cases, accounting recognition should be given to deferred income taxes in accordance with the general principles expressed in Chapters 9(c) and 10(b) of Accounting Research Bulletin No. 43 if the amounts thereof are material. This applies to a single asset, or to a group of assets which are expected to be retired from service at about the same time; in this case an excess of depreciation taken for tax purposes during the earlier years would be followed by the opposite condition in later years, and there would be a tax deferment for a definite period. It applies also to a group of assets consisting of numerous units which may be of differing lengths of life and which are expected to be continually replaced; in this case an excess of depreciation taken for tax purposes during the earlier years would be followed in later years

---

(1) Accounting Terminology Bulletin No. 1, par. 56.

by substantial equality between the annual depreciation for tax purposes and that for accounting purposes, and a tax deferment would be built up during the earlier years which would tend to remain relatively constant thereafter. It applies further to a gradually expanding plant; in this case an excess of depreciation taken for tax purposes may exist each year during the period of expansion in which event there would be a tax deferment which might increase as long as the period of expansion continued.

5. Where it may reasonably be presumed that the accumulative difference between taxable income and financial income will continue for a long or indefinite period, it may be preferable to recognize the related tax effect as additional depreciation rather than to carry it forward indefinitely as a deferred tax account in the balance sheet.

EXHIBIT B

Ballot draft 6/7/58

Accounting Research Bulletin No. 44 (Revised)

DECLINING-BALANCE DEPRECIATION

(Supersedes Accounting Research Bulletin No. 44 issued in October 1954)

1. The declining-balance method of estimating periodic depreciation has a long history of use in England and in other countries including, to a limited extent, the United States. Interest in this method has been increased by its specific recognition for income-tax purposes in the Internal Revenue Code of 1954.

2. The declining-balance method is one of those which meets the requirements of being "systematic and rational."[1] In those cases where the expected productivity or revenue-earning power of the asset is relatively greater during the earlier years of its life, or where maintenance charges tend to increase during the later years, the declining-balance method may well provide the most satisfactory allocation of cost. The conclusions of this bulletin also apply to other methods, including the "sum-of-the-years-digits" method, which produce substantially similar results.

3. When a change to the declining-balance method is made for general accounting purposes, and depreciation is a significant factor in the determination of net income, the change in method, including the effect thereof, should be disclosed in the year in which the change is made.

4. There may be situations in which the declining-balance method is adopted for income-tax purposes but other appropriate methods are used for financial accounting purposes. In such cases, accounting recognition should be given to deferred income taxes if the amounts thereof are material, except in those rare cases, such as are mentioned in paragraph 8, where there are special circumstances which make such procedure inappropriate. The foregoing applies to a single asset, or to a group of assets which are expected to be retired from service at about the same time; in this case an excess of depreciation taken for income-tax purposes during the earlier years would be followed by the opposite condition in later years, and there would be a tax deferment for a definite period. It applies also to a group of assets consisting of numerous units which may be of differing lengths of life and which are expected to be continually replaced; in this case an excess of depreciation taken for income-tax purposes during the earlier years would be followed in later years by substantial equality be-

---

(1) Accounting Terminology Bulletin No. 1, par. 56.

tween the annual depreciation for income-tax purposes and that for accounting purposes, and a tax deferment would be built up during the earlier years which would tend to remain relatively constant thereafter. It applies further to a gradually expanding plant; in this case an excess of depreciation taken for income-tax purposes may exist each year during the period of expansion in which event there would be a tax deferment which might increase as long as the period of of expansion continued.

5. Where it may reasonably be presumed that the accumulative difference between taxable income and financial income will continue for a long or indefinite period, it is also appropriate to recognize the related tax effect as additional amortization or depreciation applicable to such assets in recognition of the loss of future deductibility for income-tax purposes.

DISCUSSION

6. Following the passage of the Internal Revenue Act of 1954 in August of that year, permitting the use of declining-balance and similar accelerated depreciation methods for federal income-tax purposes, the committee anticipated that many companies would be considering whether such methods should be adopted for general accounting purposes. In October of that year, Accounting Research Bulletin No. 44 was issued in which the committee stated that such accelerated methods met the requirement of being "systematic and rational." The committee also stated that when such methods were adopted for general accounting purposes, appropriate disclosure of the change should be made whenever depreciation was a significant factor in the determination of net income.

7. Since the issuance of Accounting Research Bulletin No. 44, the committee has been observing and studying cases involving the application of the bulletin as they arose. Based on studies of published reports and other source material, it appears that instances of companies adopting the declining-balance method for income-tax purposes only are considerably more widespread than the committee anticipated in 1954. Experience has also indicated that, where material amounts are involved, recognition of deferred income taxes in the general accounts is needed to obtain an equitable matching of costs and revenues and to avoid income distortion, even in those cases in which the payment of taxes is deferred for a relatively long period. This conclusion is borne out by the committee's studies which indicate that where accelerated depreciation methods are used for income-tax purposes only, most companies do give recognition to the resultant deferment of income taxes or, alternatively, recognize the loss of future deductibility for income-tax purposes of the cost of fixed assets by an appropriate credit to an accumulated amortization or depreciation account applicable to such assets.

8. Many regulatory authorities permit recognition of deferred income taxes for accounting and rate-making purposes, whereas some do not. The committee believes that they should permit the recognition of deferred income taxes for both purposes. However, where charges for deferred income taxes are not allowed for rate-making purposes, accounting recognition need not be given to the deferment of taxes if it may reasonably be expected that increased future income taxes, resulting from the earlier deduction of declining-balance depreciation for income-tax purposes only, will be allowed in future rate determinations.

9. In those rare situations in which accounting for deferred income taxes is not appropriate, full disclosure should be made of the amount of deferred income taxes arising out of the difference between the financial statements and the tax returns when the declining-balance method is adopted for income-tax purposes but other appropriate methods are used for financial accounting purposes.

10. The committee believes that, in applying the provisions of this bulletin to cases where there was no accounting recognition of deferred income taxes for the years since 1953, the entries made for periods subsequent to the issuance of this bulletin should be based upon all assets acquired after 1953. As is indicated in the "Notes" to each Accounting Research Bulletin, opinions of the committee are not intended to be retroactive unless they contain a statement of such intention. If a retroactive adjustment is made for prior periods, the adjustment may be made in a lump sum, or the deficiency may be accumulated over a reasonable future period of time.

EXHIBIT C

Accounting Research Bulletin No. 44 (Revised)

The bulletin as issued (see Exhibit B of Werntz affidavit on page 33).

EXHIBIT D

NEWS FROM AMERICAN INSTITUTE OF CERTIFIED PUBLIC ACCOUNTANTS
270 MADISON AVENUE   NEW YORK 16, N.Y.
DEPARTMENT OF PUBLIC RELATIONS

FOR RELEASE: Thursday, April 23, 1959

Belleair, Florida -- April 22 -- The governing council of the American Institute of Certified Public Accountants today voted to expand its accounting
research program to narrow the inconsistencies in financial reporting.

In announcing the council's action, Louis H. Penney, CPA, president of the
Institute, explained that the main purpose of the program will be to advance the
statement of "generally accepted accounting principles" -- standards which
CPAs use as guides in determining whether financial statements are fairly presented. The new program may cost $250,000 a year when it gets going as planned.

"The public thinks we accountants operate under an authoritative code of
accounting, which produces precise and comparable results," Mr. Penney pointed
out. "This is not true. Generally accepted accounting principles at this time
are not a clearly defined, comprehensive set of rules. Like common law, they
develop by the evolutionary process, and their development will probably never
be completed."

The president of the 34,000-member national professional society went on
to say that some of the major accounting principles have been formally defined
or clarified in recommendations issued over the past 20 years by the Institute.
He added, however, that there are still some areas in which the use of alternative but equally acceptable accounting principles or procedures could result
in widely varying reports of net income or earnings-per-share. These are the
areas that are to receive top priority in the new research program.

Mr. Penney said that the principal products of the new program will be a
series of studies prepared by a staff of AICPA researchers and recommendations
on generally accepted accounting principles by an eighteen-man Accounting
Principles Board made up of Institute members. He emphasized that industry,
stock exchanges, governmental agencies, various accounting groups, and other
interested organizations will be given ample opportunity to present their views.

There will be a public announcement each time the Institute's accounting
research staff begins a study of some aspect of accounting principles. Interested
individuals or groups will be invited at that time to submit their views. Later,

after the researchers have completed their study, a formal report will be published and given the widest possible exposure to the public and accounting profession with a request for further comments.

"This is the only way to stimulate and crystallize thinking on the accounting principles which are so vital to the reporting of corporate profits to the public," Mr. Penney said. "The published studies will give pro and con arguments on controversial points, offer conclusions, and where possible illustrate the applications of the principles. They will be strictly informative reports to the public, the tentative basis for any official pronouncements which might come later."

Following the publication of an accounting research study, it will be reviewed by the newly created AICPA Accounting Principles Board. This group could then either accept the study as the basis for a statement on generally accepted accounting principles, reject it with a public explanation for the rejection, or lay it aside for future attention.

If two-thirds of the board members agreed with the findings of the study, the board would then issue a statement which it is expected would be regarded as an authoritative expression of the application of generally accepted accounting principles to the problem under study.

The Institute would rely on persuasion rather than compulsion, Mr. Penney said, to encourage adoption of some of its more controversial pronouncements. "We feel that the best method of enforcing most of the board's pronouncements would be to secure their acceptance as high authority by certified public accountants in advising their clients and preparing reports on financial statements."

EXHIBIT E

AMERICAN GAS ASSOCIATION
120 LEXINGTON AVENUE   NEW YORK 17, N.Y.

J. GORDON ROSS, CHAIRMAN
ACCOUNTING SECTION

May 1, 1959

Mr. L. H. Penney, President
American Institute of Certified Public Accountants
L. H. Penney & Company
San Francisco, California

Dear Mr. Penney:

The American Gas Association Committee on Application of Accounting Principles has reviewed the official report of proceedings before the Securities and Exchange Commission (April 8 and 10, 1959) in the matter of Notice of Intention to Announce Interpretation of Administrative Policy on Financial Statements Regarding Balance Sheet Treatment of Credit Equivalent to Reduction in Income Taxes.

We note that Mr. Carman G. Blough, as Director of Research of the American Institute of Certified Public Accountants, testified with respect to the Institute's Accounting Bulletin 44 Revised; and to the Institute Committee on Accounting Procedure intent of the phrase "a deferred tax account" as contained in that bulletin. Also, that the Committee on Accounting Procedure had approved by a vote of 18 to 3 the issuance of a letter to the effect that:

> "The committee used the phrase (deferred tax account) in its ordinary connotation of an account to be shown in the balance sheet as a liability or a deferred credit. A provision in recognition of the deferral of income taxes, being required for the proper determination of net income, should not at the same time result in a credit to earned surplus or to any other account included in the stockholders' equity section of the balance sheet."

The American Gas Association committee has reported that the phrase "deferred tax account" was not included in the Exposure Draft (12/17/57) of Accounting Research Bulletin 44 Revised upon which the committee and many members of our Association had submitted extensive and detailed comments. It must be pointed out that this proposed letter of intent represents a substantial change in Bulletin 44 Revised which was not considered by the Committee at the time the revised bulletin was adopted.

The appearance in the above referred to Proceedings indicate quite clearly that the accounting problems arising from tax reductions of accelerated amortization and rapid depreciation principally concern the regulated gas and electric public utilities.

We wish to call to your attention that prior to the issuance of original Bulletin 44, the Chairman of the Accounting Section of the American Gas Association forwarded a communication to the then President of the American Institute under date of November 8, 1954 requesting opportunity to review an accounting research bulletin dealing with liberalized depreciation prior to the issuance of such bulletin, and that on December 20, 1954, after the issuance of the bulletin, the Chairman again wrote expressing disappointment at the breakdown of the usual review procedure resulting in a premature release of an accounting research bulletin and urging that review be established for all proposed bulletins without exception. The last paragraph of the reply by Mr. Maurice E. Stans, President, under date of January 7, 1955, is significant:

> "On behalf of the Institute, I appreciate your giving your point of view. On the other hand I must say, in all fairness, that I think there may be occasions in which, under pressure of circumstances, the Committee will again decide to issue a Bulletin, on a relatively simple subject, without advance circulation. I am sure that you would agree that securing advice and counsel on a Bulletin, valuable as that is, may nevertheless, under unusual conditions, have to be subordinated to the needs of the accounting profession, and accountants generally, for a prompt statement of principle on a timely matter. With this exception, I believe I can assure you that the Institute has not, in any way, altered its basic policy of submitting proposed bulletins of its Accounting Research Committee for thorough exposure to criticism and suggestions of the cooperating groups." (underlining supplied)

It is ironic in view of subsequent developments to have referred to the issuance of original Bulletin 44 as a decision on a relatively simple matter, but it does emphasize the danger that results from hasty action and the damage which may be caused by action taken without full realization of the practical effects of the Institute pronouncements on the operations of our regulated industries.

The importance of full and complete consideration of all viewpoints prior to the issuance of an accounting research bulletin is further emphasized in the action taken by the Institute Council at its recent meeting, April 20-23, 1959, to reorganize the procedure for the issuance of Institute pronouncements on accounting principles and to give formal recognition to expressions and opinions of industry groups.

In view of the adoption of this new program, we believe that our Committee on Application of Accounting Principles should be given the opportunity to submit comments on the proposed interpretation of Bulletin 44 Revised. We earnestly hope that you can prevail upon the Committee on Accounting Procedure to withhold the issuance of this letter interpreting Bulletin 44 Revised for a reasonable period of time so that our committee and the members of our industry may have the opportunity to review it.

We are addressing this letter to you as President of the American Institute because we believe that the Institute Committee on Accounting Procedure has not been giving sufficient consideration to the problems of regulated public utility industries and to the damaging consequences which may result therefrom. The Institute Committee on Accounting Procedure has consistently maintained that accounting principles must be made uniformly applicable to all industries and without regard to the effect of the application of broad accounting principles upon regulated gas and electric utility companies. So strong has been the conviction of the Institute Committee in this respect that all offers to discuss the special problems of our industries with them have been consistently ignored.

Our committee representatives are anxious to discuss this proposed letter of interpretation with representatives of the Institute at the time and place which you may designate.

Very truly yours,

/s/ J. GORDON ROSS

Chairman Accounting Section
American Gas Association

EXHIBIT F

EDISON ELECTRIC INSTITUTE
750 THIRD AVENUE   .   NEW YORK 17

BEACH J. MCMILLEN, CHAIRMAN
ACCOUNTING DIVISION EXECUTIVE COMMITTEE

May 4, 1959

Mr. L. H. Penney, President
American Institute of Certified Public Accountants
270 Madison Avenue
New York 16, New York

Dear Mr. Penney:

The testimony of Mr. Carman Blough on April 8, 1959 before the Securities and Exchange Commission indicated the AICPA was ready to issue a letter to its members interpreting the phrase "deferred tax account" as used in paragraph 5 of your Institute's Bulletin No. 44 Revised. Also, that the proposed interpretation had been approved by a vote of eighteen to three by your Institute's Committee on Accounting Procedure.

Following the Exposure Draft of December 17, 1957 on Bulletin 44 Revised, the Edison Electric Institute submitted its comments and suggestions to the AICPA on March 13, 1958. The bulletin was released in July 1958 after changes had been made which obviously resulted from the suggestions and comments submitted to Mr. Blough and reconsideration by the Committee on Accounting Procedure.

As stated in paragraph 8 of such bulletin, "Many regulatory authorities permit recognition of deferred income taxes for accounting and/or rate-making purposes, whereas some do not." There is also a difference of opinion among regulatory authorities and utility companies as to the proper classification in the balance sheet of accumulated provisions for deferred income taxes.

The E.E.I. is very appreciative of having been given the opportunity to comment on Bulletin No. 44 and other Bulletins prior to issuance by the AICPA. It also was interested in and pleased with the announcement by your Governing Council's April 23 release in which it announced the expansion of its accounting research program and its intention to give industry, stock exchanges, government agencies, various accounting groups and other interested organizations ample opportunity to present their views.

Since the proposed letter of interpretation deals with a matter that is of great importance to public utility companies, it would be greatly appreciated by many of them and, in our opinion, also helpful to the AICPA if they had an opportunity to submit their suggestions and comments relative to the proposed interpretation.

We earnestly hope that you will prevail upon the Committee on Accounting Procedure to withhold issuance of their letter of interpretation until we have had an opportunity to submit our views.

Sincerely,

/s/ B. J. McMILLEN

EXHIBIT G

GENERAL PUBLIC UTILITIES CORPORATION

May 4, 1959

Mr. Louis H. Penney, President
American Institute of Certified Public Accountants
270 Madison Avenue
New York 16, New York

Dear Mr. Penney:

As you may know, General Public Utilities Corporation ("GPU") is a public utility holding company registered as such under the Public Utility Holding Company Act of 1935. Its domestic public utility subsidiaries operate in the states of Pennsylvania and New Jersey. For several years GPU and its subsidiaries have been closely following the various actions taken or considered by the American Institute of Certified Public Accountants relating to accelerated amortization and liberalized depreciation and it is in this context that this letter is being sent to you.

Representatives of GPU and its subsidiaries participated in the hearings before the Securities and Exchange Commission on Securities Act Release No. 4010 and heard Mr. Carman Blough state at the hearing that the Committee on Accounting Procedure proposed to issue a letter which he read purporting to interpret Accounting Research Bulletin No. 44 (Revised), and also heard the comments of Messrs. Cook, Spacek and Powell with respect to Mr. Blough's statement.

It is our understanding that the letter which Mr. Blough thus stated was to be sent to the membership of the American Institute of Certified Public Accountants had not, in fact, been sent but that the Committee still has the matter under consideration. We strongly urge, in the interests of procedural due process and fair play, that the letter referred to by Mr. Blough not be issued unless and until the Committee on Accounting Procedure has followed the procedural safeguards customarily employed before any new Accounting Research Bulletin is issued.

The letter mentioned by Mr. Blough purports to interpret the phrase "deferred tax account" as it appears in paragraph 3 of Accounting Research Bulletin No. 44 (Revised) as precluding reflection of the accumulated credits therein referred to in the equity section of the balance sheet. We are not herein addressing ourselves to the merits of the position thus proposed to be taken in that letter. Nor are we addressing ourselves to the question raised by Mr. Cook of whether the Committee on Accounting Procedure can reasonably be represented as construing its own language in view of the fact that the phrase "deferred tax account" was added to Accounting Research Bulletin No. 44 (Revised) after the Committee had voted on the previous ballot draft of that Bulletin which did not contain that language. Instead, what we are concerned about is the basic question of the propriety and wisdom of the issuance by the Committee of what amounts to a new Accounting Research Bulletin without the opportunity for consideration and comment that has usually been followed in the formulation of new Bulletins.

Specifically, the proposed letter in question purports merely to interpret Bulletin No. 44 (Revised) rather than add anything to it. Certainly, however, this is disingenuous if nothing more. In paragraph 12 of Section C, Chapter 9 of Accounting Bulletin 43 (page 78) the Committee stated that the related credits growing out of the employment of accelerated amortization should be to "an account for deferred income taxes." That phrase appeared in exactly the same context in paragraph 12 of Accounting Research Bulletin 42, issued in November 1952. Thus for a period of more than six years the phrase "account for deferred income taxes" has been employed to describe the proper lodging place of the credits attributable to the use of accelerated amortization. So far as we are aware, no reputable firm of certified public accountants has refused an unqualified certificate if the accumulated credits attributable to accelerated amortization were classified in the equity section of the balance sheet. In other words, when the Committee on Accounting Procedure came to write Accounting Research Bulletin No. 44 (Revised), it well knew that the phrase "account for deferred income taxes" which had been employed in Bulletins 42 and 43, in connection with accelerated amortization, had been construed by the accounting profession, including those firms which are represented on the Committee, as permitting reflection of the subject credits in the equity section of the balance sheet. Moreover, it is our understanding that the question of where in the balance sheet the accumulated credits attributable to the employment of liberalized depreciation should be reflected was the subject of some consideration by the Committee prior to the issuance of Bulletin 44 (Revised), and that the failure of that Bulletin to specify such lodging place reflects in part, at least, the inability of the Committee to reach agreement.

Against this background, it seems to us there can be no questions but that the proposed letter described by Mr. Blough in effect would make, in the guise of interpretation, a substantive addition to Bulletin 44 (Revised). Regardless of the merits of the "interpretation" now proposed to be given, the fact is that by this process a document akin to a new Bulletin would be adopted by the Committee without any opportunity for comment thereon by any interested or affected party.

In large measure the respect which the Accounting Research Bulletins have commanded in the past has been attributable not only to the capabilities of the personnel comprising the Committee and the Institute's research staff, but also to the fact that the Bulletins did not receive final approval by the Committee until after they had been exposed to the light of day and there had been opportunity for the submission of comments thereon and careful consideration by the Committee. The wisdom of this course of action on the part of the Institute was again confirmed by the action taken by the Governing Council of the Institute concerning the procedures to be followed in the activities of the Accounting Principles Board. The emphasis given in your press release dated April 23, 1959 on the procedures to be followed by the Accounting Principles Board, and to the fact that there would be ample opportunity for presentation and consideration of all views, reflects the significance attributed by all parties to the concept that no pronouncement of the Institute or an Institute agency should be formulated and adopted hastily and without ample opportunity for the submission of comments by interested groups and persons. Moreover, we have noted that the procedures described in the press release closely followed those described in the December 1958 issue of The Journal of Accountancy and commented on in the editorial in that issue.

In our view, the issuance of the proposed letter is inconsistent with the procedural safeguards the necessity of which has thus been confirmed by the Institute in December and again in April and may well result in compromising seriously the possibility of the Accounting Principles Board achieving the objectives for which it is being established.

We therefore repeat our strong recommendation to you that this proposed letter not be issued at the present time or without compliance with the procedural safeguards heretofore employed by the Committee on Accounting Procedure.

Very truly yours,

GENERAL PUBLIC UTILITIES CORPORATION

By /s/ E. W. MOREHOUSE

E. W. Morehouse
Vice President

UNITED STATES DISTRICT COURT
For the Southern District of New York

Appalachian Power Company,
Ohio Power Company and
Indiana & Michigan Electric Company

          Plaintiffs,

    against

American Institute of Certified Public
Accountants, L. H. Penney, William W.
Werntz and Carman G. Blough,

          Defendants.

PLAINTIFFS' MEMORANDUM IN SUPPORT OF
APPLICATION FOR PRELIMINARY INJUNCTION AND
IN OPPOSITION TO MOTION TO DISMISS COMPLAINT

(MAY 6, 1959)

SIMPSON THACHER & BARTLETT,
Attorneys for Plaintiffs,
120 Broadway,
New York 5, N. Y.

WHITNEY NORTH SEYMOUR
RICHARD M. DICKE
WILLIAM J. MANNING

    Of Counsel.

UNITED STATES DISTRICT COURT
For the Southern District of New York

Appalachian Power Company,
Ohio Power Company and
Indiana & Michigan Electric Company,

Plaintiffs,

against

American Institute of Certified Public
Accountants, L. H. Penney, William W.
Werntz and Carman G. Blough,

Defendants.

PLAINTIFFS' MEMORANDUM IN SUPPORT OF
APPLICATION FOR PRELIMINARY INJUNCTION AND
IN OPPOSITION TO MOTION TO DISMISS COMPLAINT

Statement

This memorandum is submitted in support of plaintiffs' motion for an order granting a preliminary injunction herein enjoining the defendants as requested in the prayer for relief in the verified complaint, and in opposition to defendants' motion to dismiss the complaint on the ground that it fails to state a claim against defendants on which relief can be granted.

The Complaint and Affidavits

This is an action for an injunction. It seeks on the basis of the doctrine of prima facie tort to enjoin reckless, wanton and intentional conduct by the defendants, which if not restrained immediately will irreparably harm plaintiffs. The doctrine of prima facie tort and the appropriateness of the remedy of injunction are well recognized both in this Court and in the courts of the State of New York.

Plaintiffs are three operating electric utility companies. The defendant American Institute of Certified Public Accountants (the "Institute") is a national organization of Certified Public Accountants; the individual defendants are the President of the Institute, the Chairman of its Committee on Accounting Procedure (the "Committee"), and its Director of Research.

In summary the complaint alleges and the affidavits establish that:

The plaintiffs have recorded on their books of account, pursuant to applicable requirements of State regulatory agencies, an aggregate of more than

$65,000,000 in accounts designated as "earned surplus restricted for future federal income taxes". These amounts have been accrued by plaintiffs in accordance with accounting principles which have been generally accepted over a period of years by all of the major well known accounting firms experienced in utility accounting, including members of the Institute and its Committee. (Detailed explanation of these accounting principles is set forth in the complaint and in the affidavits submitted in support of plaintiffs' motion.)

The institute, through its Committee, from time to time, publishes Accounting Research Bulletins, which are accepted by State and Federal regulatory agencies, including the Securities and Exchange Commission, members of the accountancy profession and interested members of the business community as establishing the accounting principles which must be followed by the accountancy profession.

Prior to the acts complained of in the complaint, the Institute had recognized the authority attached by such persons and groups to its opinions and recommendations as published in its Accounting Research Bulletins and had adopted procedures prerequisite to the publication of such opinions and recommendations. Such procedures were designed to insure that its opinions and recommendations were correct and reflected the consensus of opinion of those expert and experienced in accountancy. Such procedures included, among other things, the circulation to a very considerable group of what was known as an "exposure draft" of any proposed opinion or recommendation so that the Institute and its Committee could give consideration to the views of the members of that group before final publication, and the submission of a so-called "ballot draft" to the members of the Committee so that they could vote upon the proposed opinion and recommendation.

The Committee had twice before 1957 considered certain aspects of the accounting principles here involved, but had never considered the balance sheet treatment thereof. In 1957 it again determined to formulate and distribute in an Accounting Research Bulletin its opinion with respect to certain aspects of such accounting principles. It complied with all of its procedures and practices, including the submission to a large group of an "exposure draft" and the submission of a "ballot draft" to the members of the Committee. Neither the "exposure draft" nor the "ballot draft" contained any mention of the balance sheet treatment of accounts arising from the application of such accounting principles. After the "ballot draft" had been acted upon by the Committee, and without giving even the members of the Committee any genuine opportunity to vote or comment thereon, however, there was added a reference in said Accounting Research Bulletin to making a credit to "a deferred tax account" in applying said accounting principles. Even that comment, however, made no reference to any balance sheet treatment.

The defendants have at all times known that it has been the practice of plaintiffs to make said credits to restricted surplus accounts and have had full knowledge that plaintiffs have accumulated more than $65,000,000 in such accounts. The defendants have at all material times known that all of the major accounting firms have certified statements of plaintiffs and other public utilities which include such credits in "restricted earned surplus accounts".

In a public proceeding before the Securities and Exchange Commission, the Chairman of the Committee and the Director of Research stated that they were about to mail under the authority of the Institute and the Committee to the members of the Institute and presumably to all those who had received copies of the prior Accounting Research Bulletin on the subject, a letter to the effect that:

> "The committee used the phrase (deferred tax account) in its ordinary connotation of an account to be shown in the balance sheet as a liability or a deferred credit. A provision in recognition of the deferral of income taxes, being required for the proper determination of net income, should not at the same time result in a credit to earned surplus or to any other account included in the stockholders' equity section of the balance sheet."

The defendants have followed none of their own procedures and practices with respect to the publication of Accounting Research Bulletins or the rendering of an opinion or recommendation on accounting principles and have taken no steps whatever to permit either members of the Institute or any other interested parties or any members of the accountancy profession in general to express their opinion either in agreement or disagreement with the contents of the proposed letter.

The purported purpose of sending said letter is to state that the intent of the Committee in using the phrase "deferred tax account" in its prior Accounting Research Bulletin was to specify a balance sheet treatment for the credits involved and to disapprove of the inclusion of such credits in restricted earned surplus accounts or any other accounts included in the stockholders' equity section of the balance sheet. The facts are that this purported purpose has no basis in fact, that the Committee could have had no such intent since its members never even had the opportunity to vote or comment on the use of the quoted words, and further that both defendants Blough and Werntz have admitted in official public proceedings that the Committee had no such intention. Another member of the Committee, moreover, is on record in proceedings before a public body to the same effect, and documentary proof of the falsity of the purported purpose is annexed to the affidavits herein.

The actions of the defendants in preparing and in intending to publish the proposed letter are without legal justification and bear no reasonable relationship to any benefits which the defendants may be seeking or to any legitimate purpose. The failure to take any steps whatever which are reasonably designed to ascertain the propriety of the opinion contained in the proposed letter, coupled with the defendants' actual knowledge of the damage which will be caused plaintiffs by its distribution, demonstrates that the defendants' actions have been taken in wanton, reckless and wilful disregard of the consequences of their actions.

Defendants have knowledge of, and at least one of them ha s publicly acknowledged, the weight of authority which is attached to their opinions and recommendations as set forth in their Accounting Research Bulletins. For example, on one occasion, a communication from one of the defendants to the Securities and Exchange Commission to the effect that the Committee had intended to disapprove of the inclusion of such credits in restricted earned surplus accounts, caused the Securities and Exchange Commission to prepare a deficiency letter in connection with a proposed financing by one of the defendants, which letter was held up only when the fact that the Committee had had no such intention was demonstrated to the Securities and Exchange Commission.

The sending of the proposed letter will, because of the force and authority accorded such a document by accountants, regulatory agents, financial institutions, investment banking concerns, rating services and financial analysts, cause great and irreparable injury, loss and damage to the plaintiffs, and defendants intend to inflict such damages. (See complaint, paragraph 29, and Cook affidavit, paragraphs   *   ). No denial that such damages will ensue is contained in any of defendants' affidavits herein.

POINT I
THE COMPLAINT STATES, AND THE MOVING AFFIDAVITS MAKE OUT, A CLAIM FOR RELIEF BY WAY OF INJUNCTION

The complaint herein is bottomed upon the doctrine of prima facie tort, that is, that otherwise lawful conduct is actionable if it is done intentionally and is calculated to damage, unless the actor can show legal justification. This doctrine finds its genesis in Keeble v. Hickeringill, 11 Easts' Rep. 574 (1809), and a classic statement of it appears in Mogul Steamship Co. v. McGregor, Gow & Co., 23 Q.B.D. 598, 613 (1889), aff'd [1892] A.C. 25, where the court said:

> "Now, intentionally to do that, which is calculated in the ordinary course of events to damage, and which does, in fact, damage another in that person's property or trade, is actionable if done without just cause or excuse."

Perhaps the most often quoted enunciation of the doctrine is that of Mr. Justice Holmes in Aikens v. Wisconsin, 195 U.S. 194, 204 (1904), where he said:

*Not shown on copy in U.S.D.C. file.

"* * * prima facie, the intentional infliction of temporal damage is a cause of action, which, as a matter of substantive law * * * requires a justification if the defendant is to escape."

The leading New York case in this field decided by a unanimous Court of Appeals is controlling in the instant case. In Advance Music Corporation v. American Tobacco Co., · 296 N.Y. 79 (1946), the complaint, in an action for damages and an injunction, alleged that plaintiff was engaged in the business of publishing musical compositions and derived its revenue chiefly from sales of sheet music to the public and from royalties for the use of its compositions in the entertainment field. It spent large sums of money advertising that its songs were among the most popular of the day, for plaintiff's customers normally purchased those compositions which they thought were the most popular. Defendants, a tobacco company and an advertising concern, sponsored and produced a well-known weekly coast-to-coast radio program, the Hit Parade, which had a listening audience estimated to be in excess of 15,000,000 per week. On said program defendants listed and had performed 9 or 10 songs, claiming that they were in fact the most popular songs of the week and claiming further that these popularity ratings were based upon an extensive and accurate nationwide survey.

The complaint further alleged that the defendants' ratings and listings of songs were in fact the result of caprice or other considerations foreign to a selection based on an accurate and extensive nationwide survey; that in fact, some of plaintiff's songs which were among the most popular 9 or 10 songs of the day were either completely ignored by the defendants or given an improper rating. The complaint alleged that by reason of these acts of the defendants in improperly rating or ignoring plaintiff's songs, it was suffering damages in that dealers prematurely returned plaintiff's compositions, thus preventing distribution thereof to retail outlets for sale to the public, that retail purchasers, entertainers and other customers and potential promoters of the songs, influenced by defendants' inaccurate ratings, failed to purchase plaintiff's compositions, and that plaintiff's business prestige was impaired. The complaint further alleged that the acts and representations of the defendant were made wantonly, in bad faith and with intent to injure plaintiff.

The Court of Appeals reversed a dismissal of the complaint and held that the facts pleaded stated a cause of action. The Court said:

"The foregoing * * * [allegations] * * * are there followed by the further allegation that 'the aforesaid acts and representations on the part of the defendants are made with intent to injure the plaintiff'. Thus in sum and substance the second cause of action constitutes a statement to this effect: The defendants are wantonly causing damage to the plaintiff by a system of conduct on their part which warrants an inference that they intend harm of that type. So read, the second cause of action is, we think, adequate in its office as a plaintiff's pleading." (Emphasis added.)

"In Skinner & Co. v. Shaw & Co. [1893], 1 Ch. 413, 422, Lord Justice
BOWEN said: 'At Common Law there was a cause of action whenever one
person did damage to another wilfully and intentionally, and without just
cause or excuse.' * * * These broad propositions were approved by Sir
FREDERICK POLLOCK as authority for his doctrine that all willful harm
is actionable unless the defendant justify or excuse his conduct. Pollock,
The Law of Torts, 14th ed. 17–18." (296 N.Y. at pp. 83–84).

* * *

"The justification that is required in a case like this must, of course, be
one which the law will recognize." (296 N.Y. at p. 85)

The Court also cited its earlier opinions in Opera on Tour, Inc. v. Weber, 285
N.Y. 348 (1941) and American Guild of Musical Artists v. Petrillo, 286 N.Y. 226
(1941), in concluding that the complaint stated a cause of action "for relief
either at law or in equity".

In Opera On Tour, Inc. v. Weber, supra, the Court of Appeals had reversed
the dismissal of a complaint for an injunction restraining labor unions from interfering with plaintiff's business by inducing its members not to work for plaintiff, although it recognized the rights of the defendants' members to refuse to
work for any legitimate reason. The Court held that the complaint made out a
cause of action in prima facie tort since there was no legal justification for the
acts performed in that the defendants' acts had no reasonable connection with
any legitimate or lawful labor objective sought to be gained by defendant from
its acts. It was said that the self-interest of labor, like the self-interest of any
other person or organization, receives immunity only for those of its actions
which have a legitimate and reasonable relationship to benefits which that party
is seeking.

"Harm done to another or to the public may be countenanced only if
the purpose, in the eye of the law, is sufficient to justify such harm."
(285 N.Y. at p. 356)

In American Guild of Musical Artists v. Petrillo, supra, plaintiffs, a
membership corporation of musical artists and certain members thereof, sought to
enjoin the defendant labor union and its president from notifying prospective employers that plaintiffs were not recognized as members of the union and that
members of the union would not be permitted to render services at any functions
at which plaintiffs were to perform. The Appellate Division had held that the
complaint failed to state a cause of action since it was not shown that the defendants maliciously or illegally interfered with plaintiff's members but rather
that the defendant union was acting in its legitimate self-interest. The Court of
Appeals reversed and reinstated the judgment of the lower court granting the in-

junction, stating that its holding in the Opera on Tour case established the broad doctrine that harm intentionally done is actionable if not justified, and holding that a labor union, like any one else, could be enjoined from the intentional infliction of harm unless the acts performed were justified as in pursuance of a lawful labor objective and that " * * * no sign of such a justification reveals itself on the face of the complaint * * * ." It went on to say that malice in law does not mean ill will against a person but merely intentional action without justification.

And the prima facie tort doctrine as enunciated by the New York courts is not peculiar to them. In the time-honored case of American Bank & Trust Company v. Federal Reserve Bank, 256 U.S. 350 (1921), the Supreme Court, in an opinion written by Mr. Justice Holmes, unanimously reversed the dismissal of an action to enjoin the defendant Federal Reserve Bank, from committing acts calculated to compel the plaintiff banks, which had too small a capital to make it profitable for them to join the Federal Reserve System, either to face financial ruin or to become members of the Federal Reserve System or at least to open non-member clearing accounts with it, thereby making it necessary for the plaintiffs to maintain much larger reserves than they needed in their existing operations. The Court stated:

> "A man has a right to give advice, but advice given for the sole purpose of injuring another's business and effective on a large scale, might create a cause of action. * * * If without a word of falsehood but acting from what we have called disinterested malevolence a man by persuasion should organize and carry into effect a run upon a bank and ruin it, we cannot doubt that an action would lie. * * *"(256 U.S. at pp. 358–59)

Both this Court and the Court of Appeals for this Circuit have had no hesitation in giving full recognition to the prima facie tort doctrine as enunciated in the Advance Music case. See:

Original Ballet Russe v. Ballet Theatre, 133 F. 2d 187, 189 (2nd Cir. 1943)

U.S. Aluminum Siding Corp. v. Dun & Bradstreet, Inc. 163 F. Supp. 906 (S.D.N.Y.1958)

Davis Electronics Co. v. Channel Master Corp., 166 F. Supp. 919 (S.D.N.Y. 1953) (complaint held to state a claim for injunctive relief)

The applicability of the doctrine of prima facie tort to the instant action cannot be gainsaid. The Advance Music case is itself dispositive of most of the points raised by defendants in support of their motion to dismiss the complaint. In essence, the complaint alleges that the defendants, without lawful justification, are pursuing a course of conduct calculated in the ordinary course of events to damage plaintiffs in their business and that they are intentionally following that course of conduct with specific knowledge that it will damage plaintiffs. Each element of the tort is present in the pleading and is established by the affidavits.

Of course, the complaint must be examined upon defendants' motion to dismiss, in light of the well established rule that a "complaint should not be dismissed for insufficiency unless it appears to a certainty that plaintiff is entitled to no relief under any state of facts which could be proved in support of the claim." 2 Moore, Federal Practice P 12.08, at 2245 (2d ed. 1948). Bearing in mind the state of facts set forth in the affidavits, which certainly can be proved in support of the allegations of the complaint, we shall now address ourselves seriatim to the points raised by defendants.

A

The defendants' contention that the complaint seeks to restrain freedom of speech in violation of applicable constitutional provisions is unsound. In the Advance Music case, the Court held that the complaint stated a cause of action "for relief either at law or in equity", and the only prayer for equitable relief was a prayer for an injunction against the continuance of the expression by defendant of its opinion that the songs performed on its program were the most popular and that its ratings of songs were based upon extensive and accurate surveys. Indeed, examination of the briefs and record in the Advance Music case discloses that the constitutional objection was expressly raised and overruled by the Court of Appeals.

Nor did the New York Court of Appeals see any constitutional objection in granting injunctions in the Opera on Tour and American Guild cases. The effect of these New York decisions is to overrule, at least with respect to actions based upon the doctrine of prima facie tort, the dictum which did appear in an older New York case, Marlin Fire Arms Co. v. Shields, 171 N.Y. 384(1902), to the effect that equity had no jurisdiction to restrain a publication. The actual holding in the Marlin case was that an injunction should be denied when the publication is not of such a character as would support an action at law for damages. The Marlin case, moreover, had been severely criticized by Dean Pound in his article in 29 Harvard Law Review 640, "Equitable Relief against Defamation and Injuries to Personality", and in an article by Professor Nims in 19 Cornell Law Quarterly 63. Both Pound and Nims, after reviewing the authorities and precedents, were firmly of the opinion that equity not only had, but should exercise, the power to enjoin tortious acts when necessary to prevent irreparable harm to one's business or property.

Chief Judge Cardozo cited Dean Pound's article in <u>Nann v. Raimist</u>, 255 N.Y. 307, 317 (1931) where he discussed the power of equity to enjoin publications as follows:

"* * * Equity does not intervene to restrain the publication of words on a mere showing of their falsity. * * * It intervenes in those cases where restraint becomes essential to the preservation of a business or of other property interests threatened with impairment by illegal combinations <u>or by other tortious acts,</u> the publication of the words being merely an instrument and incident * * *. (citations omitted)" (Emphasis added.)

Perhaps the leading case in which constitutional objection was raised to the granting of an injunction to restrain tortious conduct is <u>Black & Yates v. Mahogany Ass'n.</u> 129 F. 2d 227 (3rd Cir. 1941). There, in reversing the denial of injunctive relief and restraining statements by defendant which tended to injure plaintiff's business, the Court cited Dean Pound's article and said:

"In view of this critic's eminence, it is not necessary to add much to his demolition of the reasons advanced for the Chancellor's hesitations. Later commentators have discussed them and have greeted with enthusiasm each decision which edges away from the traditional doctrine of negation. The irrelevance of 'free speech' and of 'a libel is for a jury' are patent. Freedom of discussion of public issues does not demand lack of 'previous restraint' for injury to private individuals. Disparagement of goods presents no confusing or complicated matter of personality requiring the sympathetic attention of one's peers.

"We are quite willing to repudiate the 'waning doctrine that equity will not restrain the trade libel'. We are further willing to do so directly and without hiding behind the other equitable principles put forward in some of the cases." (129 F. 2d at p. 231)

Nor do any of the opinions of the United States Supreme Court on the subject of prior restraints on freedom of expression in any way impair the foregoing authorities. The Supreme Court cases deal in the main, with State action, not disputes between private individuals, and with blanket restraints rather than with restraints against specific and limited tortious acts. Indeed, in the leading case of <u>Near v. Minnesota,</u> 283 U.S. 697 (1931) the Supreme Court specifically said:

"* * * Nor are we now concerned with questions as to the extent of authority to prevent publications in order to protect private rights according to the principles governing the exercise of the jurisdiction of courts of equity." (Citing Dean Pound's article) (283 U.S. at p. 716)

The Near case and in particular a later case, <u>Chaplinsky v. New Hampshire,</u> 315 U.S. 568 (1941) both point out that there are well defined classes of speech, the prevention of which have never been thought to raise any constitutional problem. These include the lewd and obscene, the profane, libelous and insulting and all utterances which "* * * are no essential part of any exposition of ideas, and are of such slight social value as a step to truth that any benefit that may be derived from them is clearly outweighed* * *." To the same effect see Kingsley Books, Inc., v. Brown, 354 U.S. 436 (1957) and Beauharnais v. Illinois, 343 U.S. 250 (1952).

The above quotation from Mr. Justice Holmes opinion in American Bank & Trust Company v. Federal Bank, supra, indicates that he saw no constitutional objection to granting an injunction against the publication of tortious words, and this Court held the complaint in U.S. Aluminum Siding Corp. v. Dun & Bradstreet, Inc., supra, to state a claim for injunctive relief.

B

Defendants' second challenge to the complaint is that it fails to allege facts showing that defendants lack the power to issue the proposed letter and that it alleges no violation of the Charter or By-Laws of the defendant Institute. The power or lack of power to commit the acts complained of is an irrelevant consideration. Neither the Advance Music case nor the other New York cases cited above contained any allegation with respect to the power of defendants therein to commit the acts complained of. Such an objection to the complaint was specifically disposed of in American Bank & Trust Company v. Federal Reserve Bank, supra, where the Court said:

"We lay on one side as not necessary to our decision the question of the defendants' powers, and assuming that they act within them consider only whether the use that according.to the bill they intend to make of them will infringe the plaintiffs' rights." (256 U.S. at p. 357).

C

The next point relied upon by defendants is that the plaintiffs lack standing to challenge the issuance of the proposed letter because it relates to the internal affairs of defendant Institute with which none of the plaintiffs is in privity. But it could not be the law that one being injured by tortious conduct of another must be in privity with the tort feasor in order to recover. In none of the above cited cases in which injunctions were granted were the plaintiffs either members of the defendant organizations or in any way in privity with the defendants. Plaintiffs herein have no concern with the internal affairs of the defendant Institute, but do have a concern with the effect that defendants' actions will have on their business.

D

The contention by defendants that the complaint is defective for failing to allege that defendants are motivated by a malicious desire to injure the defendants is both factually and legally unsupportable. The complaint does allege in paragraph 30 that the defendants have actual knowledge of the damages which will befall plaintiffs by reason of the distribution of the proposed letter and that they intend to inflict such damage, and further that their actions are in wanton, reckless and willful disregard of the consequences of their proposed action. That allegation brings the complaint squarely within the rule of the Advance Music case where the Court of Appeals held that the allegation that the acts of the defendant were made with the intent to injure the plaintiff constituted an allegation that they were wanton causing damage to the plaintiff "* * * by a system of conduct on their part which warrants an inference that they intend harm of that type", and that so read the complaint stated a cause of action. The complaint herein is, therefore, more specific in its allegations of intent than was the complaint in the Advance Music case, and the facts which plaintiffs intend to prove under those allegations are set forth in the affidavits. Certainly if such allegations constitute a cause of action under the more stringent rules of pleading in the New York Courts, they constitute a claim for relief under the more liberal rules of pleading in this Court.

The defendants' contention, moreover, is legally unsound in that "malice" is no element of a claim for relief based on the prima facie tort doctrine and indeed is meaningless in such an action. In American Guild of Musical Artists v. Petrillo, supra, the Appellate Division had at least in part based its dismissal of the complaint on the fact that the complaint failed to allege "that the defendant maliciously or illegally interfered" with the plaintiff. The Court of Appeals, in reversing, said:

> "The averments which impute malice to the defendant-union do not imply more than is elsewhere stated in the complaint. 'Malice' in common acceptance means ill-will against a person, but in its legal sense it means a wrongful act done intentionally without just cause or excuse." (286 N. Y. at 226).

And in Kelite Products v. Binzel, 224 F. 2d 131 (5th Cir. 1955), the Court of Appeals held that malice, in the sense of actual ill-will, is not an essential element of the tort and that the cases referring to malice mean only that a harmful act has been done intentionally without justification.

Such has long been the rule in New York and indeed the New York Court of Appeals in Campbell v. Gates, 236 N.Y. 457, 460 (1923) said that a malicious act is:

"* * * a wrongful act, done intentionally, without just cause or excuse, and from this a malicious motive is to be inferred. This does not necessarily mean actual malice or ill-will, but the intentional doing of a wrongful act without legal or social justification."

In none of the New York cases cited above were allegations of maliciousness held to be necessary elements of the cause of action. See also Note, "The Prima Facie Tort Doctrine", 52 Columbia Law Review 503, 505–7 for cases holding that not even a specific intent to cause damage is an essential element of the tort - that intent to do the act complained of is sufficient.

E

The contention that "the complaint does not allege that the defendants contemplate the use of unlawful means" is without merit and indeed begs the question. The American Guild case, supra, specifically disposed of this very argument. The very basis of the doctrine of prima facie tort, moreover is that the conduct of the defendants is otherwise lawful and is made actionable only by their intention that it harm plaintiffs and by their lack of justification. There is thus no issue as to whether the means used are lawful or unlawful, the sole questions being whether the acts of defendants will harm plaintiffs, whether defendants intend to harm and whether the defendants have legal justification. The Advance Music case and others cited above are dispositive of defendants' contention.

F

The next contention of defendants in support of their motion is that the complaint is defective in that it fails to allege that defendants' opinions are binding on anyone or definitive of rights, liabilities or duties. The complaint, however, does specifically allege that the pronouncement of the defendants are generally accepted by the members of the accountancy profession as establishing the accounting principles to be followed by the accountancy profession (par. 13), that they are accepted by the Securities Exchange Commission and other government agencies as persuasive authority in determining whether principles of accounting are generally accepted (par. 14), that the publication of the proposed letter, because of the authority of the opinions and recommendations of defendants would cause accountants, financial institutions, investment banking concerns, rating services, financial analysts and governmental agencies to question plaintiffs' financial statements and would cause irreparable injury to plaintiffs (pars. 28 and 29).

In support of these allegations, the affidavit of Donald C. Cook establishes that the opinions and recommendations of the defendant are accepted by the Securities and Exchange Commission as authoritative and that in at least one instance even an oral advice by a member of the defendant Institute as to the intention of the defendants was relied upon by the Securities and Exchange Commission, that defendant Blough himself stated in a public hearing that such opinions and recommendations are accepted as authoritative by the accounting profession and carry a great deal of weight in the business community generally, and finally that the issuance of the proposed letter would, based upon his experience, immediately cause harm to the plaintiffs. The foregoing clearly shows that the actions of defendants have the power to harm and will in fact harm plaintiffs.

In the Advance Music case, moreover, there were no allegations in the complaint that the public or anyone else were bound to accept the ratings accorded musical compositions by the defendants, but the complaint was nevertheless held to state a cause of action. Analysis of that case and the other New York cases reveals that it is essential only that the defendants' actions have the power and the likely effect of inflicting harm on plaintiffs. Whether those actions are binding on anyone is clearly irrelevant.

G

Defendants' contention that the complaint fails to allege any acts of the defendants which can be the legal cause of injury to plaintiffs is factually and legally unsupportable. The complaint alleges that the defendants, without justification, and with intent to injure plaintiffs are about to issue a publication which will in fact injure plaintiffs. The complaint alleges all of the elements of a prima facie tort and upon the authority of the Advance Music and other cases cited above, therefore, alleges facts which are actionable.

H

The contention that the complaint fails to allege actual damage or injury or threat thereof and is on its face too speculative and remote is unsupportable. No more need be added to the statement of damages than appears in paragraph 29 of the complaint and in paragraphs 21 et seq. of Mr. Cook's affidavit, where Mr. Cook explains both the immediate and long range effect which defendants' action will necessarily have on plaintiffs' business. The damages alleged are far more specific than those alleged in the Advance Music case where the damage to plaintiff was contingent upon the failure of the buying public to purchase the plaintiff's musical compositions. Similarly in the American Guild case any damage to the plaintiffs depended upon the compliance or non-compliance of disinterested third parties with the demand being made by the defendants in that case.

And in U.S. Aluminum Siding Corp. v. Dun & Bradstreet, Inc., supra, the damage alleged was strikingly similar to some of the allegations of damage alleged in the complaint herein. There it was alleged that the defendants' conduct would prevent the plaintiff "* * * from procuring credit upon the easiest and most economical terms" and would "impair its normal growth and expansion, and that plaintiff's credit standing would be impaired." The complaint alleges and Mr. Cook's affidavit specifies the damage which will occur to the plaintiffs' ability to secure short term borrowings, the detrimental effect on plaintiffs' normal growth and expansion and the damage to plaintiffs' credit rating. The complaint alleges and Mr. Cook's affidavit demonstrates, moreover, that additional irreparable harm will befall plaintiffs in that capital charges aggregating $4,000,000 annually will have to be incurred when plaintiffs replace the $65,000,000 now in earned surplus with other equity securities.

I

To the allegation that there is an adequate remedy at law by way of a claim for money damages also, no more reply is needed than a reference to the complaint and Mr. Cook's affidavit. The damages to plaintiffs by way of decreased credit ratings and the necessity for permanent financing, the increase in borrowing rates, the necessity of increasing charges to consumers and the ultimate stultification of the growth of the plaintiffs' business by their own nature cannot be compensated for in money damages. The damages involved amount to more than $4,000,000 per annum and it is clear that the defendants would be unable to respond in money damages even if said amounts could be precisely calculated, for the defendants are three individuals and a professional organization. By no stretch of the imagination would they be financially able to respond in money damages for the amounts alleged in the complaint and affidavits. Whenever damages are so large in amount that a successful plaintiff would be unable to recover money judgments it obtained against the defendants, the remedy at law is inadequate, and a case is made out for the interposition of a court of equity. See Mulford v. Smith, 307 U.S. 38, 46–47 (1939).

POINT II
PLAINTIFFS' RIGHTS CAN ONLY BE PROTECTED
BY THE ISSUANCE OF A PRELIMINARY INJUNCTION

The verified complaint and the affidavits submitted in support of this motion demonstrate beyond cavil that immediate and irreparable harm will befall plaintiffs immediately upon the distribution of the proposed letter.

That equitable relief, including the granting of an injunction, is a proper remedy in an action based upon the prima facie tort doctrine is made clear by the Advance Music, Opera on Tour, American Guild, Davis Electronics, and other cases cited above, and in Williams v. McCarthy, 67 N.Y.S. 2d 763 (Sup. Ct., N.Y.Co. 1946, not officially reported), an action founded on the prima facie tort doctrine and which cited the Advance Music case, plaintiff's motion for a temporary injunction was granted. In that case, the Court was strongly influenced by the fact that any burden imposed upon the defendants by the granting of the temporary injunction was incidental and heavily over-balanced by the potential harm to the plaintiff.

Upon applications for preliminary injunctions, this Court and the Court of Appeals for this Circuit have applied this doctrine of weighing the relative harms that will ensue to the parties from the grant or denial of a preliminary injunction.

In Douds v. Milk Drivers and Dairy Employees Union Local 584, 154 F. Supp. 222, 234 (S.D. N.Y.), aff'd 248 F. 2d 534 (2d Cir. 1957), this Court said:

"Even where grave and difficult questions of law are involved and where an answer might disclose disputed issues of fact, preliminary injunctions * * * will be granted where injury to the plaintiffs would be certain and irreparable if the application were denied, while granting of the application would not seriously damage and inconvenience defendants."

Similarly, in Hamilton Watch Co. v. Benrus Watch Co., 206 F. 2d 738 (2d Cir. 1953), the Court of Appeals said:

"To justify a temporary injunction it is not necessary that the plaintiff's right to a final decision, after a trial, be absolutely certain, wholly without doubt; if the other elements are present (i.e., the balance of hardships tips decidedly toward plaintiff), it will ordinarily be enough that the plaintiff has raised questions going to the merits so serious, substantial, difficult and doubtful, as to make them a fair ground for litigation and thus for more deliberate investigation." (206 F. 2d 740).

* * *

"[A] preliminary injunction —— as indicated by the numerous more or less synonymous adjectives used to label it —— is, by its very nature, inter-locutory, tentative, provisional, * * *. It serves as an equitable policing measure to prevent the parties from harming one another during the litiga-tion; to keep the parties, while the suit goes on, as far as possible in the respective positions they occupied when the suit began." (206 F 2d 742)

The Court of Appeals in that case also quoted with approval Restatement, Torts, §941, comment f, as follows:*

"The 'hardship plaintiff will suffer * * * may make interlocutory relief imperative where the same showing at a final hearing would not outweigh the hardship the defendant would suffer from a permanent injunction. Thus

---

*Through an apparent typographical error, the Court's citation is to §94, rather than §941, of the Restatement.

in view of the character and extent of the emergency presented, of the provisional and temporary character of the relief sought, of the probable period of its duration, and of the court's tentative opinion on the substantive issues involved, the factor of relative hardship is measured, on an application for interlocutory injunction, with a different yardstick from that used at final hearing.' '' (206 F. 2d 743).

The irreparable nature of the harm which will befall plaintiff immediately upon the publication and distribution of the proposed letter alone makes imperative the issuance of the preliminary injunction sought. The denial of the injunction and the consequent publication and distribution of the letter would render moot this entire action. On the other hand, there is not even the possibility that defendants would even be inconvenienced, much less damaged, by the granting of the preliminary injunction and the maintenance of the status quo pending trial. Indeed, the granting of the relief sought will delay defendants in the distribution of the proposed letter, in the event that it is finally determined that they have the right to distribute the same, for no longer a period of time than would have been consumed had they, in the first instance, followed their own procedures and practices, and for a lesser period of time than if they were to follow their newly promulgated rules of practice and procedure.

CONCLUSION

A preliminary injunction should be granted herein enjoining the defendants as requested in the prayer for relief in the verified complaint herein, and defendants' motion to dismiss the complaint should be denied in its entirety.

Respectfully submitted,

SIMPSON THACHER & BARTLETT,
Attorneys for Plaintiffs,
Office and Post Office Address,
120 Broadway,
New York 5, N.Y.

(May 6, 1959)

WHITNEY NORTH SEYMOUR
RICHARD M. DICKE
WILLIAM J. MANNING

Of Counsel.

UNITED STATES DISTRICT COURT
For the Southern District of New York

Appalachian Power Company, Ohio Power Company and Indiana & Michigan Electric Company, *Plaintiffs,* against American Institute of Certified Public Accountants, L. H. Penney, William W. Werntz and Carman G. Blough, *Defendants.*	Civil Action No. 145-161

MEMORANDUM OF DEFENDANTS IN OPPOSITION TO
PLAINTIFFS' ORDER TO SHOW CAUSE AND IN
SUPPORT OF CROSS-MOTION TO DISMISS THE COMPLAINT

(MAY 6, 1959)

Howard C. Westwood
Fontaine C. Bradley
Stanley L. Temko

Attorneys for Defendants

Rinaldo L. Bianchi
George C. Christie
Phil R. Stansbury

Of Counsel

Covington & Burling
Union Trust Building
Washington, D. C.

UNITED STATES DISTRICT COURT
For the Southern District of New York

Appalachian Power Company,
Ohio Power Company and
Indiana & Michigan Electric Company,

Plaintiffs,

against

American Institute of Certified Public
Accountants, L. H. Penney, William W.
Werntz and Carman G. Blough,

Defendants.

Civil Action No. 145-161

MEMORANDUM OF DEFENDANTS IN OPPOSITION TO
PLAINTIFFS' ORDER TO SHOW CAUSE AND IN
SUPPORT OF CROSS-MOTION TO DISMISS THE COMPLAINT

This memorandum is submitted on behalf of defendants, The American Institute of Certified Public Accountants (hereinafter "Institute") and three of its officials, in opposition to the order to show cause why a preliminary injunction should not be granted and in support of defendants' cross-motion to dismiss the complaint. A temporary restraining order was issued ex parte on April 15, 1959 to remain in effect until hearing and determination of the application for preliminary injunction. By stipulation, this hearing was postponed from April 17, 1959, to May 7, 1959.

The plaintiffs are three electric utility companies none of which is a member of the Institute. Their complaint and their order to show cause seek an injunction to prevent the publication by the Institute's Committee on Accounting Procedure of a letter setting forth the views of said Committee on certain accounting questions relating to the balance sheet treatment of deferred income taxes resulting from fast depreciation.

By cross-motion defendants have moved to dismiss the complaint on the ground that it fails to state a claim upon which relief can be granted. Point II of this memorandum, in support of the motion to dismiss, sets forth several grounds each of which is sufficient in itself to compel dismissal of the complaint. As there shown, the suit is completely without legal foundation and is no more than an unwarranted attempt to interfere with the practices and activities of the Institute, a nonprofit membership organization which is dedicated solely to advancing the profession of accountancy and to the public service.

At the outset, however, it is clear that, on the grounds set forth in Point I below, the temporary restraining order should be dissolved immediately and injunctive relief refused.

I

NO BASIS EXISTS FOR AN INJUNCTION AGAINST DEFENDANTS' PUBLICATION AND CIRCULATION OF THE VIEWS OF THE COMMITTEE ON ACCOUNTING PROCEDURE

A. There Is No Desire to Injure Plaintiffs,
    No Use of Improper Means and No Showing
    of Damage, Let Alone Threat of Irreparable
    Injury.

This case arises from the fact that plaintiffs do not agree with the position of the Institute's Committee on Accounting Procedure that deferred tax credits cannot, under sound accounting procedure, be credited to a surplus account or to any other account in the stockholders' equity portion of the balance sheet. They therefore seek to enjoin the circulation by the Committee of a letter confirming that this is the Committee's view.

The complaint itself reveals, and the affidavits in opposition confirm, that no injunctive relief is justified. It is axiomatic that, before an injunction is granted, there must be an immediate threat of irreparable injury. There is none here. Moreover, both the common law and the Federal and State Constitutions prevent interference by injunction with the defendants' right to free speech. This would be true, even if there were a desire by defendants to injure the plaintiffs. But here there is no such motivation and no unlawful means are employed. All that the Committee seeks to do is to circulate its own views, adopted in conformity with Committee procedures. In such circumstances, there is no basis for interference by injunction with the proper activities of a non-profit public service organization such as the Institute.

The complaint shows that the proposed letter indicates on its face that it is intended "for universal application in the accounting profession" (par. 26) and thus concerns the accounting practices of the plaintiff utilities only to the extent that it concerns the accounting practices of all enterprises. As for the defendants' intent, the plaintiffs allege no more than the claim that the defendants know that general acceptance of their views may damage the plaintiffs (par. 30). Plaintiffs carefully and necessarily avoid making the claim that defendants are motivated by any positive desire to injure the plaintiffs or anyone else. Nowhere does the complaint allege that the defendants have any private interest to serve by promulgating the statement complained of. On the contrary, it appears from the allegations that the corporate defendant is a professional society and that its committee is concerned only with upholding and raising the standards of the accounting profession.

Of what do the plaintiffs complain? They complain that the purported purpose of publishing the letter in question, to interpret a previous Accounting Research Bulletin issued by the Committee, is "false" (par. 22) and that "the actual purpose of the proposed letter is not to specify any prior intent of the Committee but to promulgate a new accounting rule" without permitting interested parties an opportunity to be heard (par. 23).

As for damages, the complaint is limited to vague and conclusory statements that distribution of the Committee's letter will injure plaintiffs in that it will cause accountants, financial institutions, investment banking concerns, rating services, financial analysts and governmental agencies to question the accounting practices followed by plaintiffs (par. 29).

Defendants have presented the following three affidavits in opposition to the application for preliminary injunction: by defendant William W. Werntz, Chairman of the Committee on Accounting Procedure; by F. Merrill Beatty, partner in and head of the Public Utility Division of Arthur Andersen & Co., independent public accountants; and by George C. Christie, a lawyer who has reviewed various pertinent files in the Securities and Exchange Commission.

These affidavits establish that:

1. The letter, the issuance of which plaintiffs attack, was adopted by the Committee in conformity with its established procedures. It was specifically approved by 18 of the 21 members of the Committee. Sixteen of the 18 members voting for the proposed letter of interpretation were members of the Committee at the time it voted in favor of the adoption of Accounting Research Bulletin #44 (Revised). Under the Committee's procedures, a 2/3 vote - 14 of the 21 members - is sufficient to adopt an opinion or recommendation. In short, what plaintiffs attack here is a formal vote by more than 2/3 of the Committee, stating their own understanding and view of an accounting question.

2. The opinions of the Committee have no official standing to bind anyone, and depend for their authority solely on their general acceptability.

3. Although plaintiffs claim that the letter should be "exposed" in draft form, Committee procedures do not require such exposure of bulletins or opinions and several bulletins have been issued by the Committee without any advance exposure to persons other than the members of the Committee and of the staff of the Institute. Among such bulletins was the original Accounting Research Bulletin #44, issued in October 1954, which is the predecessor of Accounting Research Bulletin #44 (Revised).

4. Contrary to the complaint's inference that the Committee's view is contrary to sound accounting practice, the facts are (a) the Committee's position is followed by Arthur Andersen & Co., which audits the accounts of 1/3 of the utility companies in the country; (b) based on a survey of the 1957 published stockholders reports of 353 utilities, of 226 reporting an accumulated credit resulting from the use of liberalized depreciation under Section 167 of the Internal Revenue Code, 176 treated the credit outside the equity-capital section of the balance sheet and only 50 companies treated the credit as either earned surplus or restricted surplus; (c) the Public Service Commission of the State of Indiana has ordered all companies subject to its regulations, including plaintiff Indiana & Michigan Electric Company, to cease treating the credit for deferred income taxes as a surplus account; (d) the Federal Power Commission issued on May 29, 1958, an order that all public utility companies subject to its regulation shall not include credit for deferred income taxes in a surplus account; (e) the SEC has promulgated a proposed policy in accord with the Committee's views; and (f) many public utility and other companies have endorsed the SEC proposal.

Whether the purpose of the Committee is to issue a letter of interpretation or a new recommendation, the Committee is not overstepping its powers and the plaintiffs seek to force the Committee to abide by a practice which it is under no compulsion to respect. The complaint (par. 15) enumerates the alleged "procedures" of the Institute prerequisite to the publication of an opinion by the Committee. By the plaintiff's own admission the so-called exposure "practice" is not within these procedures, and the affidavits demonstrate that such exposure is not required.* The short answer to the request for injunction is that the facts show that all the Committee has done is act within its rights in proposing to express its views.

Also fatal is the absence of any legal damage and certainly the absence of threatened irreparable injury. The circulation of the Committee letter cannot result in legal injury to the plaintiffs. Insofar as the form and content of their financial statements is prescribed by the Securities and Exchange Commission, it is open to plaintiffs to attack the Committee's letter and its view before the Commission. Plaintiffs can present to the Commission the same criticisms

---

*Plaintiffs seem to contend that the failure to hear the opinions of many persons interested in the subject before issuing the proposed letter amounts to a misrepresentation of the amount of well-informed consideration which has gone into the formulation of what actually is a new recommendation. But this contention founders upon the very fact that the proposed letter, as quoted in paragraph 21 of the complaint, purports to interpret what the committee meant in a previous bulletin and thus reveals to every reader of the letter that the statement of accounting principle, as clarified, would not have been exposed to outsiders for their comments.

It is impossible to see how the plaintiffs could be harmed by any alleged misrepresentation that the letter was an interpretation of an old rule, when that very "misrepresentation" makes it clear to all readers of the letter that the accounting principle, as fully and clearly stated therein, has not been "exposed."

they allege here. So too, the plaintiffs are free to differ from, to belittle, criticize or attack in any way they desire the Committee's position before any other governmental agency. The same is true in plaintiffs' dealings with financial institutions, accountants, or any other governmental or private body. Insofar as the plaintiffs differ with the Committee view, they are completely free to persuade any agency, institution or person to accept their views rather than the Committee's position. If plaintiffs are successful in securing acceptance of their views, there is no conceivable damage. If they are unsuccessful, there is still no damage, and certainly no legal injury, in being required to follow sound accounting procedures.

There is no ground for injunctive relief on such a showing. Clearly, this is so where the injunction sought would throttle a public service organization in expressing its views on a matter of public concern.

B. The Injunction Sought Runs Afoul of the Policy
   of Our Courts Not to Interfere in the Internal
   Affairs of an Organization Performing Volunteer
   Public Service.

As the complaint itself indicates and the defendants' affidavits confirm, the Institute is a private, non-profit organization, devoted to the performance of public service. This litigation is concerned solely with the decision of a Committee of the Institute as to whether, when, and how it will issue the proposed letter setting forth the Committee's views on an accounting question. This decision is in no sense determinative of the civil or property rights of any of the plaintiffs or any other person, but is merely an internal decision related to the fulfillment of the Committee's duties. Even as to members of an organization such as the Institute, the rule is uniform that a court will not interfere in this type of question. As stated in Carey v. International Brotherhood of Paper Makers, 123 Misc. 680, 206 N.Y.S. 73, 83 (Sup. Ct. 1924):

"The court will intervene in the affairs of voluntary associations when civil or property rights are involved, but where such rights are involved and are determined according to the rules and regulations of the associations (there being no question of public policy involved) the court will not intervene, on the theory that the constitution and by-laws of the association constitute the contract between the association and members of it, and that until their provisions are violated there is no ground upon which to invoke the jurisdiction of the court." (Emphasis added.)

See also Dusing v. Nuzzo, 177 Misc. 35, 29 N.Y.S. 2d 882 (Sup. Ct. 1941), aff'd, 263 App. Div. 59, 31 N.Y.S. 2d 849 (3d Dept. 1941); Bianco v. Eisen, 190 Misc. 609, 75 N.Y.S. 2d 914 (Sup. Ct. 1944).

Though no procedural irregularity has been alleged, it is well to remember that, as unequivocally pointed out in Weinstock v. Ladisky, 197 Misc. 859, 98 N.Y.S. 2d 85 (Sup.Ct. 1950), voluntary associations have inherent power to provide for the welfare of their members and to regulate their affairs so as to attain the objects and purposes for which they were constituted. The courts, in interpreting the rules governing these bodies, "will accept the interpretations placed on such provisions by the organization itself through its officers and authorized tribunals." (98 N.Y.S. 2d at 101) A contrary holding would violate one of the most precious prerogatives of private associations: "The right of a voluntary association to interpret and administer its own rules and regulations is as sacred as is the right to make them." State ex rel. Smith v. Kanawha County, 78 W. Va. 168, 88 S.E. 662, 664, 20 A.L.R. 1030, 1033 (1916); McNulty v. Higginbotham, 40 So. 2d 414 (Ala. 1944), 4 Am. Jur., Associations & Clubs, Sec. 6.

This salutary rule, founded in judicial respect for the autonomy of nonprofit organizations, applies with even more force here where plaintiffs are strangers who can claim no privity whatsoever with the Institute. There is no basis for their enlisting the aid of our courts to impede the exercise of the functions of a public service organization.

The wisdom of this judicial rule is apparent once we realize its contribution to the furtherance of the public interest involved. Mindful of the importance to society of the public services performed by voluntary associations, the courts have not hesitated to uphold the validity of certain official acts even where procedural irregularities have been alleged and proved in a suit brought by a member of the association. In United States ex rel. Noel v. Carmody, 80 App. D.C. 58, 60, 148 F. 2d 684, 686 (1945), the Court of Appeals stated:

> "It is idle to expect that voluntary public or community service, not involving the administration of property or money, will ever be carried on with the meticulous observance of charters and by-laws required in the administration of property or money. The interest that holds community service organizations together is not property but the unselfish spirit of those willing to sacrifice their time and energy to a public cause. That interest would not be protected but destroyed by strict judicial supervision of elections in such agencies on complaint of their members. The court would find itself a constant intermeddler in community affairs serving no purpose other than to disrupt the morale and good will of voluntary organizations. To make community service as technical as business dealings would be to destroy the spirit which sustains it."

The same principle was succinctly put by Professor Chafee in his landmark article "The Internal Affairs of Associations Not For Profit," 43 Harv. L. Rev. 993, 1027 (1930):

> "The value of autonomy is a final reason which may incline the courts to leave associations alone. The health of society will usually

be promoted if the groups within it which serve the industrial, mental and spiritual needs of citizens are genuinely alive. Like individuals, they will usually do most for the community if they are free to determine their own lives for the present and the future. A due regard for the corresponding interests of others is desirable, but must be somewhat enforced by public opinion. Legal supervision must often be withheld for fear that it may do more harm than good."

In the present case, no allegation is made that the Committee lacks the power to issue the proposed letter of clarification. It is only claimed that, because certain procedural steps which plaintiffs desire were not taken, the Committee's issuance of the letter would be premature. Since the Committee has been empowered to use its discretion as regards the adoption of the "exposure" procedure, no transgression can be found in the Committee's application of its rules.

No injunctive relief could be granted on such grounds even if it could be proved that the Committee had departed from its own rules. It is settled that any group can modify or waive their own rules of procedure. See, e.g., Rutherford v. City of Nashville, 168 Tenn. 499, 79 S.W. 2d 581, 584 (1935). Where there has been no express suspension of the rules, it is "inferable from action in violation of such rules even though there was no formal vote to that effect." Coleman v. Louison, 296 Mass. 210, 5 N.E. 2d 46 (1936).

C. The Injunction Sought Would Violate Constitutional Guarantees of Free Expression.

Equally determinative of the fact that an injunction is not in order, are both the Federal and New York State constitutional guarantees of free expression. The proposed letter of the Committee on Accounting Procedure is an expression of opinion on a matter of public concern. Its publication, therefore, is protected by both the Federal and State constitutions, and cannot be enjoined. The scope of the constitutional protection against prior restraint was set forth in Near v. Minnesota ex rel. Olson, 283 U.S. 697, 716 (1931):

"[T] he protection even as to previous restraint is not absolutely unlimited. But the limitation has been recognized only in exceptional cases . . . No one would question but that a government might prevent actual obstruction to its recruiting service or the publication of the sailing dates of transports or the number and location of troops. On similar grounds, the primary requirements of decency may be enforced against obscene publications. The security of community life may be protected against incitements to violence and the overthrow by force of orderly government . . . These limitations are not applicable here."

Perhaps the best discussion of the law on this matter is to be found in the recent case of Krebiozen. Research Foundation v. Beacon Press, Inc., 334 Mass. 86, 134 N.E. 2d 1, cert. denied, 352 U.S. 848 (1956), in which a cancer research foundation and physicians brought suit to enjoin a publisher from publishing a book allegedly containing false statements unfavorable to the research methods used in establishing the value of the drug Krebiozen in cancer treatment. The complaint alleged not only that the book in question would hurt the reputations of the plaintiff doctors but also that it would destroy the commercial value and trade name of Krebiozen. (134 N.E. 2d at 3.) The court affirmed the lower court's dismissal of the complaint on the ground that the book in question contained discussion on a matter of public concern which is protected by the United States Constitution under the doctrine of the Near case. The court said:

> "The establishment of the truth about Krebiozen as soon as possible is critically important to the public. . . It is axiomatic in our society that full information and free discussion are important in the search for wise decisions and best courses of action. In a particular case, to be sure, new discovery may be impeded by a false and unjust attack. . . But basing a rule on that possibility would end or at least effectively emasculate discussion in the very controversial fields where it is most important. . .

> "Mr. Chafee has answered the plaintiffs' question (Government and Mass Communications, pages 91-92); 'One may ask, "What is the value of letting people read false statements?" That is not quite the whole story. In the first place, the matter in question may not be wholly false. Along with the lies and distortions may go a good deal of truth, which the public ought to read and will never read if the publication be prohibited. An injunction cannot very well discriminate in such cases; it must root up the wheat with the tares. . . Furthermore, we cannot safely assume that the statements are really false. All we know is that the plaintiff and the judge call them false. . . One man's judgment is not to be trusted to determine what people can read. . . So our law thinks it better to let the defamed plaintiff take his damages for what they are worth than to intrust a single judge (or even a jury) with the power to put a sharp check on the spread of possible truth.' " 134 N.E. 2d at 7.

As to the fact that the plaintiffs were private parties rather than the state, the court said:

> "While in that case [the Near case] the complainant was the State and here the complainants are those whose private property and personal rights are affected, the Minnesota officials who were libelled had of course private rights at stake, and the fact that a public interest against the pub-

lication of a scandalous newspaper could be shown was an argument in
the Near case against the decision of the court." 134 N.E. 2d at 8.

The doctrine of the Krebiozen case is itself dispositive of plaintiffs' claim
for injunction here. Moreover, the law in New York as well as other jurisdictions
is even more emphatic in its protection of speech against injunctive relief.
Courts have persistently refused on constitutional grounds to allow injunction
even against trade libels of a wholly private significance where, as in the present case, only speech was complained of and not a course of oppressive conduct to which speech was merely incidental. See Marlin Firearms Co. v. Shields,
171 N.Y. 384, 64 N.E. 163 (1902); Donnely v. United Fruit Co., 4 A.D. 2d 855,
166 N.Y.S. 2d 392 (1st Dept. 1957); Dartmore Corp. v. Columbia Products Corp.,
18 N.Y.S. 2d 366 (Sup. Ct. 1939); Eversharp, Inc. v. Pal Blade Co., 182 F. 2d
779, 781 (2d Cir. 1950); Kuhn v. Warner Bros. Pictures, Inc., 29 F. Supp. 800,
801 (S.D.N.Y. 1939); Montgomery Ward & Co. v. United R., W. & D. Store Emp.,
400 Ill. 38, 79 N.E. 2d 46 (1948); Lindsay & Co. v. Montana Federation of Labor,
37 Mont. 264, 96 Pac. 127 (1908); Mark & Haas Jeans Clothing Co. v. Watson,
168 Mo. 133, 67 S.W. 391 (1902); Annotation, Injunction as remedy in case of
trade libel, 148 A.L.R. 853 (1944).

In the leading case of Marlin Firearms Co., supra, which involved an attempt to enjoin disparagement of the plaintiff's product, the New York Court of
Appeals sustained a demurrer to the complaint and stated:

"The constitutional guaranty of freedom of speech and press, which in
terms provides that 'every citizen may freely speak, write, and publish
his sentiments on all subjects being responsible for the abuse of that
right; and no law shall be passed to restrain or abridge the liberty of
speech or of the press' (Const. N.Y. art. 1, § 8), has for its only limitations the law of slander and libel. . . [T] he precedent which the plaintiff seeks to establish would open the door for a judge sitting in equity to
establish a censorship not only over the past and present conduct of a
publisher of a magazine or newspaper, but would authorize such judge by
decree to lay down a chart for future guidance in so far as a plaintiff's
property rights might seem to require, and, in the case of the violation of
the provisions of such a decree, the usual course and practice of equity
would necessarily be invoked, which would authorize the court to determine whether such published articles were contrary to the prohibitions
of the decree, and, if so found, punishment as for a contempt might follow. Thus a party could be punished for an article which was not libelous,
and that, too, without a trial by jury." 64 N.E. at 165.

The guaranty of freedom of expression in Article 1, § 8 of the New York
Constitution protects even statements of a private nature, such as product dis-
paragements or other trade libels, from interference by injunction. Clearly, a

statement by the Institute's Committee on Accounting Procedure on a matter of public concern - the proper accounting treatment to be given credits for deferred income taxes - must be protected.

II

THE COMPLAINT SHOULD BE DISMISSED BECAUSE IT FAILS TO STATE A CLAIM UPON WHICH RELIEF CAN BE GRANTED

The complaint fails to state a claim upon which relief can be granted because of incurably insufficient allegations on the questions of wrongful intent and the wrongfulness of the means which the defendants propose to use in carrying out their purposes. As is stated in Prosser, Torts § 107 (2d ed. 1955), at page 748, "No case has been found in which intended but purely incidental interference resulting from the pursuit of the defendant's own ends by proper means has been held to be actionable."

The Court of Appeals of New York State has clearly delineated the requirements which must be present before even an intentional infliction of damages can be said to state a cause of action. The action complained of must be motivated solely by the malicious purpose of causing injury to the plaintiffs, as can be seen from the recent decision of Reinforce, Inc. v. Birney, 308 N.Y. 164, 124 N.E. 2d 104 (1954):

> "The Presiding Justice . . . did not agree that the element of malice was immaterial. Defendants' acts, he pointed out, were concerted and so, if prompted by malice alone, would cast defendants in damages. But the evidence here, as he saw it, was insufficient to show that malice was the only spur to the union's activity, or that damage to plaintiffs was the union's sole purpose. We agree with the Presiding Justice's analysis of the proof and with his statement of the law." 124 N.E. 2d at 105.

> "If the doers, by means not in themselves unlawful, of acts not in themselves unlawful, have any proper purpose to serve, they are not liable for the damage they cause [citing cases]. Unions as well as everyone else, may claim the benefit of the settled rule that 'the genesis which will make a lawful act unlawful must be a malicious one unmixed with any other and exclusively directed to injury and damage of another' [citing cases]." 124 N.E. 2d at 106.

See also Benton v. Kennedy-Van Saun Mfg. & Eng. Corp., 2 A.D. 2d 27, 152 N.Y. S. 2d 955 (1st Dept. 1956).

Here plaintiffs do not allege - and it cannot be seriously suggested that they could allege - that the defendants were activated by malice toward the plaintiffs. As for alleging that the action was prompted solely by malice as is required under the decisions, this would be beyond the pale.

Absent an intent that is solely malicious, that is, that the defendants were prompted "by malice alone," a plaintiff might have a cause of action if he could allege and prove that unlawful means - fraud or intimidation or breach of fiduciary duty - were used to deprive him of advantageous business relations. See Duane Jones Co. v. Burke, 306 N.Y. 172, 117 N.E. 2d 237 (1954).

Here no such unlawful means are alleged. Plaintiffs do not claim that the Committee or any of the other defendants plan to do anything that will affect or injure the plaintiffs other than publishing the proposed letter. The Committee's alleged departure from its usual practice cannot be considered to be unlawful means. The alleged failure to "expose" the letter in the way desired by the plaintiffs is not fraud, is not intimidation, and is not a breach of fiduciary duty. It cannot be actionable. Furthermore, the allegation that the letter's purported character as an interpretation of a prior accounting research bulletin is a misrepresentation (Compl., Par. 22) does not show any way in which such alleged misrepresentation could mislead third parties and eventually hurt the plaintiffs. On the contrary, the letter's purported character as a statement of what the Committee previously meant would indicate to readers thereof that the accounting principle as clarified therein has not been "exposed" for the opinions of persons other than the Committee's members.

The complaint should also be dismissed because it shows on its face that the proposed letter of the Committee could not be the legal cause of damage to the plaintiffs. The complaint, in stating that the Committee's pronouncements "are generally accepted by the members of the accountancy profession" (par. 13) and "are accepted by the Securities and Exchange Commission as persuasive authority in determining whether principles of accounting are generally accepted" (par. 14) makes it clear that such pronouncements bind no one and could not harm any companies except to the degree that government agencies and others influenced by such agencies take action upon being convinced that such pronouncements are based upon sound reasoning.

In this connection the very recent holding of the New York Court of Appeals in Brandt v. Winchell, 3 N.Y. 2d 628, 148 N.E. 2d 160 (1958) is conclusive on the subject of causation.. In that case the defendant Walter Winchell succeeded in persuading government agencies to put the plaintiff's cancer foundation out of business. The court held for defendant Winchell despite its assumption that his actions were motivated by an improper desire to injure the plaintiff:

> "In the case now before us, the . . . items of temporal damages . . . are a direct result of action taken against plaintiff by public authori-

ties. Assuming, as we must, that such action was properly taken against plaintiff, we are confronted with a situation where there was no infliction of temporal damages by defendants - a situation where the plaintiff is suffering from the consequences of some conduct inimical to the public interest committed by plaintiff himself. Are the defendants to be cast in damaged for setting the official agencies in motion merely because in so doing they may have taken advantage of the opportunity to gratify a vindictive spirit? We think the answer to that question is obvious. The best interests of the public are advanced by the exposure of those guilty of offenses against the public and by the unfettered dissemination of the truth about such wrongdoers. Such a person is entitled to immunity from civil suit at the hands of the one exposed, for the truth is not to be shackled by fear of a civil action for damages. If the one who sets the agencies in motion is actuated by an evil motive he may perhaps be subject to judgment in the form of morals but he is free from liability in a court of law." 148 N.E. 2d at 164.

An independent but related ground upon which the complaint should be dismissed is that the expression of opinion complained of is privileged under the common law, apart from the strictly constitutional considerations outlined in Part I, supra. As is said in Prosser, Torts § 106 (2d ed. 1955), at page 720, even interference with existing contracts

"may be privileged if its purpose is the protection of a sufficient interest of the defendant, or of others. In general, any disinterested motive of a socially desirable kind will serve as a justification."

It is difficult to conceive of a clearer example of such privilege. As the complaint itself shows, all that is involved here is the desire by a committee of the Institute to express its views on a question of accounting principle, an issue of interest to all accountants and to the business community at large. This by its nature is both privileged and protected from any prior restraint, such as the complaint here seeks, by both the Federal and State Constitutions. Any difference of opinion which plaintiffs have with the views of the Committee do not state a cause of action for this Court; they are views which the plaintiffs should present to those interested, be they government agencies or persons in the business community, and seek their acceptance in the market place.

CONCLUSION

For the foregoing reasons, defendants pray that the Court deny the application for a preliminary injunction and dismiss the complaint for failure to state a claim upon which relief can be granted.

Respectfully submitted,

Howard C. Westwood
Fontaine C. Bradley
Stanley L. Temko

Attorneys for Defendants
(May 6, 1959)

Rinaldo L. Bianchi
George C. Christie
Phil R. Stansbury

Of Counsel

UNITED STATES DISTRICT COURT
For the Southern District of New York

Appalachian Power Company,
Ohio Power Company and
Indiana & Michigan Electric Company,

Plaintiffs,

against

American Institute of Certified Public
Accountants, L. H. Penney, William W.
Werntz and Carman G. Blough,

Defendants.

PLAINTIFFS' REPLY MEMORANDUM
(MAY 6, 1959)

Simpson Thacher & Bartlett,

Attorneys for Plaintiffs,
120 Broadway
New York 5, N.Y.

Whitney North Seymour
Richard M. Dicke
William J. Manning

Of Counsel

UNITED STATES DISTRICT COURT
For the Southern District of New York

Appalachian Power Company,
Ohio Power Company and
Indiana & Michigan Electric Company,

Plaintiffs,

    against

American Institute of Certified Public
Accountants, L. H. Penney, William W.
Werntz and Carman G. Blough,

Defendants.

PLAINTIFFS' REPLY MEMORANDUM

We do not intend in this reply memorandum to take issue with the many assertions of fact contained in defendants' memorandum in opposition to the motion for a temporary injunction and in support of the motion to dismiss, which are unsupported by the affidavits, nor to discuss again their distortions of the allegations of the complaint. Rather this reply memorandum shall be limited to comments upon a few of the cases cited in defendants' memorandum.

A. Interference With Internal Affairs

We believe that our memorandum in chief disposes of this contention but point out that Carey v. International Brotherhood of Paper Makers, 123 Misc. 680 (Sup. Ct. 1924) which is cited by defendants actually supports the plaintiffs' contention. The very portion of that case quoted in defendants' memorandum states that "The court will intervene in the affairs of voluntary associations when civil or property rights are involved * * *".

Such is exactly the case now before this court.

B. Constitutional Objections

We have already met this point in our memorandum in chief and have already discussed therein most of the cases cited by defendants. Defendants main reliance is on Krebiozen Research Foundation v. Beacon Press Co., Inc., 334 Mass. 86 134 NE 2d 1 (1956). That case is clearly distinguishable on the ground that it sought to enjoin a publisher of a book from carrying on his business of publishing books. The rationale of the holding was that the publisher could show a legal justification in that he had an economic interest in the publication of the book, controversial as it was. For that reason alone it is not controlling in this case, but moreover with respect to the free speech issue the court therein said:

> "But later cases have held that equity will take jurisdiction where there is a continuing course of unjustified and wrongful attack upon the plaintiff motivated by actual malice, and causing damage to property rights as distinguished from 'injury to the personality affecting feelings, sensibility and honor' * * *". (134 NE 2d at page 5)

Defendants' reliance on that case for the proposition that equity may not enjoin tortious conduct is therefore misplaced.

The cases cited on page 16 of defendants' memorandum have for the most part either been previously discussed or are from other jurisdictions. Donnelley v. United Fruit Company, 4 A.D. 2d 855 (1st Dept. 1957), however, held merely that since the relationship of master and servant between the parties had terminated, there was no necessity to resort to a declaratory judgment as to their rights; and Eversharp Inc. v. Pal Blade Co., 182 F. 2d 779 (2nd Cir. 1950) was decided solely on the ground that the allegations and proof of special damage necessary to sustain an action for trade libel had not been pleaded.

C. Prima Facie Tort

The absence of any reference whatever in defendants' memorandum to the Advance Music case and other cases cited in plaintiffs' memorandum is conspicuous. The cases cited by defendants in no way dilute or impair the force of the holdings of the cases cited in plaintiffs' memorandum.

Reinforce Inc. v. Birney, 308 NY 164 (1954) was decided solely on the basis that the plaintiff had failed to sustain its burden of proof that the defendants' actions were done with the intent to injure plaintiff and without justification. Indeed, the case cites favorably the holding in the Opera on Tour, Inc. case relied upon by plaintiffs herein.

Benton v. Kennedy-Van Saun Mfg. Corp., 2 A.D. 2d 27 (1st Dept. 1956) specifically supports plaintiffs' contention that malice is no element of a complaint based upon prima facie tort and that an improper motive may be inferred from the intentional doing of an act calculated to damage without just cause or excuse. The case quotes from Campbell v. Gates, 236 NY 457 (1923) cited in plaintiffs' memorandum, and also cites the Advance Music case. The actual holding moreover was that the defendant had a sufficient economic justification for its actions.

Duane Jones Co. v. Burke, 306 NY 172 (1954) actually held for the plaintiff and stated moreover that injury done to another's business is actionable not only if done through unlawful means but also if "done without justifiable cause". (306 NY at 190)

Brandt v. Winchell, 3 NY 2d 628 (1958) was an action to recover damages for setting in motion public authorities whose acts caused plaintiff damages. The court specifically recognized the existence of causes of action based upon prima facie tort but said that the court must analyze and weigh the conflicting interests of the parties and the public in such cases and held that as a matter of public policy the instigation of official action is an exception to the doctrine and is actionable only upon proof of all of the elements of the tort of malicious prosecution.

CONCLUSION

Plaintiffs' application for a preliminary injunction should be granted and defendants' motion to dismiss the complaint should be denied.

Respectfully submitted,

SIMPSON THACHER & BARTLETT
Attorneys for Plaintiffs,
Office and Post Office Address,
120 Broadway,
New York 5, N. Y.

(May 6, 1959)

WHITNEY NORTH SEYMOUR
RICHARD M. DICKE
WILLIAM J. MANNING

Of Counsel.

UNITED STATES DISTRICT COURT
Southern District of New York

Appalachian Power Company, Ohio Power Company and Indiana & Michigan Electric Company, *Plaintiffs,* *against* American Institute of Certified Public Accountants, L. H. Penney, William W. Werntz and Carman G. Blough, *Defendants*	OPINION NO. 25150 Civil 145-161

APPEARANCES:

Simpson Thacher & Bartlett
Attorneys for Plaintiffs
120 Broadway, New York, N.Y.
  Whitney North Seymour, Richard M. Dicke,
  William J. Manning,
    Of Counsel

Howard C. Westwood, Fontaine C. Bradley,
Stanley L. Temko
Attorneys for the Defendants
c/o American Institute of Certified Public Accountants
270 Madison Avenue, New York, N.Y.
                and
Covington & Burling
Union Trust Building
Washington, D. C.
  Rinaldo L. Bianchi, George C. Christie,
  Phil R. Stansbury
    Of Counsel.

LEVET, D. J.

This is a motion for preliminary injunction to restrain defendants from the promulgation or distribution of certain opinions recommending certain accounting practices which allegedly affect plaintiff's financial statements, unless a waiting period of 60 days elapses, and certain other prerequisites are complied with.

The above-named plaintiffs, public utility companies, engaged in the sale of power, seek a preliminary injunction to enjoin the defendant American Institute of Certified Public Accountants (hereinafter called "Institute") and the individual defendants, certain officers or Committeemen of said Institute, from adopting, issuing, promulgating, circulating, printing or in any manner publishing to the members of the defendant Institute or to any members of the accountancy profession a certain proposed letter. This letter is to the effect that the said defendant Institute or its Committee on Accounting Procedure (hereinafter called "Committee") is of the opinion or recommends that charges made to income in recognition of the deferral of income taxes should not, in accordance with generally accepted accounting principles, be credited to earned surplus or to any other account included in the stockholders' equity section of the balance sheet. The plaintiffs seek to enjoin the distribution of said letter until such time as the defendants and the Committee shall have submitted a draft thereof to certain persons; a period of not less than 60 days shall thereafter have elapsed, and the Institute's and its Committee's practices and procedures with respect to the publication of accounting research bulletins shall otherwise have been complied with.

The letter in dispute is as follows:

"AMERICAN INSTITUTE OF CERTIFIED PUBLIC ACCOUNTANTS
"270 Madison Avenune, New York 16, N.Y.

"April 15, 1959

"To the Members of the American
Institute of Certified Public Accountants

"Gentlemen:

"Question has been raised with respect to the intent of the committee on accounting procedure in using the phrase 'a deferred tax account' in Accounting Research Bulletin No. 44 (revised), Declining-balance Depreciation, to indicate the account to be credited for the amount of the deferred income tax (see paragraphs 4 and 5).

"The committee used the phrase in its ordinary connotation of an account to be shown in the balance sheet as a liability or a deferred credit. A provision in recognition of the deferral of income taxes, being required for the proper determination of net income, should not at the same time result in a credit to earned surplus or to any other account included in the stockholders' equity section of the balance sheet.

"Three of the twenty-one members of the committee, Messrs. Jennings, Powell and Staub, dissented to the issuance at this time of any letter interpreting Accounting Research Bulletin No. 44 (revised).

"COMMITTEE ON ACCOUNTING PROCEDURE

"By William W. Werntz, Chairman"

By cross-motion the defendants have moved for an order pursuant to Rule 12(b) of the Federal Rules of Civil Procedure dismissing the complaint on the ground that it fails to state a claim against them upon which relief can be granted. Since matters outside the pleadings have been presented to the court, and since the parties have submitted such proof, I am treating this motion as one for summary judgment as provided in Rule 56 of the Federal Rules of Civil Procedure.

The complaint herein, seeking permanent injunctive relief, was filed on April 15, 1959. This application apparently is based upon the following assertions of the plaintiffs:

(1) Plaintiffs, three operating electric utility companies, have recorded on their books of account, pursuant to certain alleged applicable requirements of state regulatory agencies, an aggregate of more than $65,000,000 in accounts designated as "Earned Surplus Restricted for Future Federal Income Taxes." In this connection plaintiffs contend that these amounts have been so accrued by them in accordance with accounting principles which heretofore have been generally accepted over a period of years by all of the well-known accounting firms experienced in utility accounting.

(2) The defendant Institute, through its Committee, from time to time publishes accounting research bulletins which are allegedly "accepted" by state and federal regulatory agencies, including the Securities and Exchange Commission, members of the accounting profession and interested members of the business community as establishing the accounting principles which must be followed by the accounting profession.

(3) Prior to the present dispute in reference to pertinent accounting procedures, it is said that the Institute had adopted procedures prerequisite to the publication of such opinions and recommendations. These procedures included, it is said, the circulation of so-called "exposure drafts of any proposed opinion" to a certain group so that the members might comment thereon, and a further procedure involving the submission of a so-called "ballot draft" to members of the Committee so that they could vote upon the proposed opinion.

(4) Plaintiffs aver that the defendants have known accounting practices of plaintiffs in reference to these matters and have had full knowledge that plaintiffs have accumulated more than $65,000,000 in these accounts.

(5) It appears that in a proceeding before the Securities and Exchange Commission the Chairman of defendant's Committee and its Director of Research stated that they were about to mail under the authority of the Institute and the Committee to members of the Institute and other recipients of bulletins a letter with respect to the deferred tax account to the effect that "a provision in recognition of the deferral of income taxes, being required for the proper determination of net income, should not at the same time result in a credit to earned surplus or to any other account included in the stockholders' equity section of the balance sheet."

(6) Plaintiffs claim that the defendants in preparing and intending to publish this letter are "without legal justification," that their acts "bear no reasonable relationship to any benefits which the defendants may be seeking or to any legitimate purpose," and that the actions of the defendants in connection with the proposed distribution of the said letter and the opinion contained therein are "in wanton, reckless, and wilful disregard of the said consequences of their proposed action."

(7) As a result, plaintiffs assert that substantial numbers of accountants, financial institutions, etc., will question the plaintiffs' continued inclusion of credits for deferred taxes in earned surplus and as a result plaintiffs "will be seriously interfered with in their dealings," etc., and, as stated by Donald Cook, a vice-president of each of the plaintiff corporations:

> "*** The removal of more than $65,000,000 from the common stock equity of the plaintiffs would, in the first instance, have the effect of limiting the short term borrowing power of plaintiffs under applicable statutes so as to decrease the amounts which plaintiffs can borrow from banks by $6,500,000. ***" (Affidavit sworn to May 6, 1959, item 21, p. 13)

The defendants in their opposing papers point out that:

(1) The letter, the issuance of which, without certain preliminaries, plaintiffs oppose, was adopted by the Committee in conformity with its established procedures; was specifically approved by over two-thirds of the 21 members of the Committee; that under the Committee's procedure, a two-third vote -- that is, 14 out of 21 members -- is sufficient to adopt an opinion or recommendation.

(2) The opinions of the Committee have no official effect.

(3) The Committee procedures do not require the so-called "exposure" in draft form of the proposed letter, though on occasion in the past, this "exposure" procedure has been employed.

(4) a. The Committee's position as to the accounting practice in question is followed by Arthur Andersen & Co., public accountants, who audit the accounts of one-third of the utility companies in the country;

b. Based on a survey of the 1957 published stockholders' reports of 353 utility companies, of 226 companies reporting an accumulated credit resulting from the use of the liberalized depreciation under Sec. 167 of the Internal Revenue Code, 176 treated the credit outside the equity-capital section of the balance sheet and only 50 treated the credit as either earned surplus or restricted surplus;

c. The Public Service Commission of the State of Indiana has ordered all companies subject to its regulations, including plaintiff Indiana and Michigan Electric Company, to cease treating the credit for deferred income taxes as a surplus account;

d. The Federal Power Commission on May 29, 1958, issued an order to the effect that all public utility companies subject to its regulations shall not include credit for deferred income taxes in a surplus account;

e. The Securities and Exchange Commission has promulgated a proposed policy in accord with the Committee's views.

Jurisdiction herein is based upon diversity of citizenship. Hence, the law of the State of New York is applicable. The plaintiffs predicate the validity of their complaint upon the doctrine of "prima facie tort." They rely upon the New York cases of Advance Music Corporation v. American Tobacco Co., 296 N.Y. 79 (1946); Opera on Tour, Inc. v. Weber 285 N.Y. 348 (1941); American Guild of Musical Artists v. Petrillo, 286 N.Y. 226 (1941).

Subsequently, in other decisions New York courts have discussed this doctrine of so-called "prima facie tort." Among these are Brandt v. Winchell, 283 App. Div. 333 (1st Dept., 1954); Brandt v. Winchell, 286 App. Div. 249 (1st Dept. 1955), affirmed 3 N.Y. 2d 628 (1958); Ruza v. Ruza, 286 App. Div. 767 (1st Dept., 1955); Knapp Engraving Co. Inc. v. Keystone Photo Engraving Corp., 1 App. Div. 2d 170 (1st Dept., 1956). See also Benton v. Kennedy-Van Saun Mfg. & Eng. Corporation, 2 App. Div. 2d 27 (1st Dept., 1956); Travelers Indemnity Company v. Unger, 4 Miss. 2d 955 (S. Ct., Queens Co., 1956); Green v. Time, Inc., 147 N.Y.S. 2d 828 (S. Ct., N.Y. Co., 1955), affirmed 1 App. Div. 2d 665 (1st Dept., 1955), affirmed 3 N.Y. 2d 732 (1957).

The essential elements of "prima facie tort" include the following:

(1) There must be an intent to injure plaintiff, at least to the extent of infliction of wrongful harm upon plaintiff without just cause or excuse. Beardsley v. Kilmer, 236 N.Y. 80 (1923); Ruza v. Ruza 286 App. Div. 767 (1st Dept. 1955); Advance Music Corporation v. American Tobacco Co., 296 N.Y. 79 (1946).

In Ruza v. Ruza, supra, Mr. Justice Breitel wrote:

"The key to the prima facie tort is the infliction of intentional harm, resulting in damage, without excuse or justification, by an act or a series of acts which would otherwise be lawful. The need for the doctrine of prima facie tort arises only because the specific acts relied upon -- and which it is asserted caused the injury -- are not, in the absence of the intention to harm, tortious, unlawful, and therefore, actionable. The remedy is invoked when the intention to harm, as distinguished from the intention merely to commit the act, is present, has motivated the action, and has caused the injury to plaintiff, all without excuse or justification." (p. 769)

In Knapp Engraving Co. Inc. v. Keystone Photo Engraving Corp., 1 App. Div. 2d 170 (1st Dept., 1956), Mr. Justice Botein, now Presiding Justice of the First Department Appellate Division, wrote of prima facie tort:

"It attempts to justify the ommission of these conventional tort requirements on the ground that the counterclaim should be regarded as a 'prima facie tort'. A cause of action, however, must be judged by its allegations, not its label. A prima facie tort derives from the ancient form of action on the case, covering those situations where intentional harm has been inflicted, resulting in damage, by an act or series of acts which might otherwise be lawful and which do not fall within the categories of traditional tort actions (Aikens v. Wisconsin, 195 U.S., 194; Opera on Tour v. Weber, 285 N.Y. 348; American Guild of Musical Artists v. Petrillo, 286 N.Y. 226; Advance Music Corp. v. American Tobacco Co., 296 N.Y. 79; Brandt v. Winchell 283 App. Div. 338, amended complaint dismissed 286 App. Div. 249)." (p. 172)

(2) Justification may be viewed as a neutralizing factor that overrides the intent to injure. What constitutes justification is a policy consideration.[1] In Reinforce, Inc. v. Birney, 308 N.Y. 164 (1954), Desmond J., wrote:

"***If the doers, by means not in themselves unlawful, of acts not in themselves unlawful, have any proper purpose to serve, they are not liable for the damage they cause (Peabody, Jr., & Co. v. Travelers Ins. Co., 240 N.Y. 511, 519; Al Raschid v. News Syndicate Co., 265 N.Y. 1) ***" (p. 169)

---

(1) Recent developments in the New York Law of Prima Facie Tort, 32 St. John's Law Review, 282, 288.

In Beardsley v. Kilmer, 236 N.Y. 80 (1932) the concept of justification was expressed as follows:

"*** The question how far one individual shall be restrained from doing acts which are inherently proper out of respect for the rights of others is bound to be a delicate one. The proposition that a man may not dig a well upon his own land or enter upon a lawful business is one to be advanced with considerable caution and the cases seem firmly to establish the rule that if he digs a well because he really wants the water or starts the business for personal advantage or gain his neighbor is without remedy however much he suffers, and even though the act may also have been tinged with animosity and malice." (pp. 89-90)

In Brandt v. Winchell, 3 N.Y. 2d 629 (1958) Chief Judge Conway stated:

"***The law is now settled in this State that, 'Even a lawful act done solely out of malice and ill will to injure another may be actionable.' (Al Raschid v. News Syndicate Co., 265 N.Y. 1, 4 emphasis supplied; see, also Beardsley v. Kilmer, 236 N.Y. 80). This is not to say that the present state of the law is that an act not otherwise tortious will, without exception become actionable when it is done with the blameworthy purpose of injuring another and such other is in fact injured. There are situations where for one of several reasons a court is constrained to ignore the wrongful motive of the actor. For example, a court may be prompted to disregard the actor's motive by reason of the paramount consideration of the public welfare. Accordingly, it may fairly be said that whenever the gist of an alleged cause of action (as here) is that an otherwise lawful act has become unlawful because the actor's motives were malevolent, the court is called upon to analyze and weigh the conflicting interests of the parties and of the public in order to determine which shall prevail." (pp. 634-635)

(3) Damages, which must be specially pleaded. Rager v. McCloskey, 305 N.Y. 75 (1953); Brandt v. Winchell, 286 App. Div. 249 (1st Dept. 1955), affirmed 3 N.Y. 2d 628 (1958); Faulk v. Aware Inc., 3 Misc. 2d 833,839 (S. Ct. N.Y. Co., 1956) affirmed without opinion 3 App. Div. 2d 703 (1st Dept. 1957).

In Brandt v. Winchell, supra, the Appellate Division, 1st Department, in a per curiam opinion stated:

"***The amended complaint proceeds solely on the theory of prima facie tort. As we previously noted, damage is an essential element in a cause of action for prima facie tort and must be pleaded specially, for it consists of injury due to loss in plaintiff's occupation or business (see 283 App. Div. 338, 342)." (p. 250)

Although "the most conspicuous use of the prima facie tort doctrine has been to create new causes of action where the plaintiff's claim does not fall within a traditional tort category."[2]   as Mr. Justice Breitel said in Ruza v. Ruza, 286 App. Div. 767 (1st Dept., 1955): "A bad complaint is not made good by the blanket assertion that it relies on the doctrine of 'prima facie tort.'" (p. 769)

Plaintiffs, although not members of the Institute, seek to force it to follow certain prerequisites to publication of opinions of the Institute's Committee. Plaintiffs, having adhered to certain accounting procedures for several years, have recorded in "restricted earned surplus accounts" some $65,000,000, representing credits for payment of federal income taxes which may have to be paid in the future. Now, urge the plaintiffs, the Institute's Committee's opinion will or may be accepted by the Securities and Exchange Commission in rulings on financial statements.

The facts in the case of Advance Music Corporation v. American Tobacco Co., 296 N.Y. 79 (1946) are basically different from those in the present case:

(1) There, the defendant misrepresented the nature of the survey of the popularity of the songs presented based on sales -- a fact not an opinion.

(2) The defendant's acts and representations definitely and directly affected plaintiff's sales. A business interference resulted.

(3) Damages naturally flowing from the acts and misrepresentations of the defendant and causally affecting the sales of the plaintiff were set forth.

(4) No justification for the defendant's acts appeared.

Here, the communications, which defendants intend to promulgate do not mention plaintiffs. The plaintiffs, like other business enterprises which may be affected, may, if they so elect, appear before the appropriate governmental body to sustain their own contentions. There is no misrepresentation, no fraud. The acts of the defendants can hardly be termed wanton. The purposes of the defendant Institute are adequate justification, if justification, indeed, be required, to permit the proposed communications. There is no adequate proof (even if the plaintiffs had any right to insist on the Committee procedures they mention) that the Institute's rules have been or are about to be violated. In fact, the contrary appears.

There is no allegation that the method of accounting proposed by defendants is inherently false or fraudulent. On the contrary, it is supported by respectable authority. Neither is there any allegation of special damages, except in the most general and speculative terms.

---

(2) The Prima Facie Tort Doctrine, 52 Columbia Law Review 503, 512.

This action is not to prevent interference with plaintiffs' contracts, their sales or their property. It seeks to delay the distribution of an adverse opinion relative to accounting procedures. True, it may ultimately affect plaintiffs' application for credit. However, such a result is collateral, not direct, an effect which incidentally flows from a justifiable act. The plaintiffs may have grievances, but they relate to the distribution of honest opinions, not facts. No threat of intentional, unjustifiable harm to plaintiffs' business rights or property exists.

This court has been unable to find any precedent under the doctrine of prima facie tort or otherwise for a preliminary or final injunction forbidding a group from publishing and distributing opinions under circumstances equivalent or even similar to these.

Accordingly, the application for preliminary injunction must be denied and the complaint dismissed and summary judgment granted.

Settle order on notice.

Dated: New York, N.Y.
May 20, 1959   /s/ RICHARD H. LEVET

United States District Judge

UNITED STATES DISTRICT COURT
For the Southern District of New York

Appalachian Power Company,
Ohio Power Company and
Indiana & Michigan Electric Company,

Plaintiffs,

against

American Institute of Certified Public
Accountants, L. H. Penney, William W.
Werntz and Carman G. Blough,

Defendants.

JUDGMENT

Civil Action No. 145-161

This cause having come on to be heard on application of plaintiffs for a preliminary injunction and on the cross-motion of defendants to dismiss the complaint on the ground that it fails to state a claim upon which relief can be granted, and the Court having considered the pleadings in the action, the affidavits of Robert O. Whitman and Donald C. Cook submitted on behalf of plaintiffs and the affidavits of William W. Werntz, F. Merrill Beatty and George C. Christie submitted on behalf of defendants, and having heard oral argument, and having determined to treat the cross-motion to dismiss the complaint as one for summary judgment pursuant to Rule 56 of the Federal Rules of Civil Procedure, and the Court having found that there is no genuine issue as to any material fact and that defendants American Institute of Certified Public Accountants, L. H. Penney, William W. Werntz and Carman G. Blough are entitled to judgment as a matter of law, it is

ORDERED, ADJUDGED AND DECREED, that plaintiffs are entitled to no injunctive or other relief and the application for preliminary injunction be, and the same hereby is, denied; and it is further

ORDERED, ADJUDGED AND DECREED, that summary judgment, be and the same hereby is, granted in favor of defendants dismissing the complaint on the merits.

Dated: New York, New York
    May 25, 1959   /s/ RICHARD H. LEVET

                                       U. S. D. J.

Judgment entered: May 25, 1959
/s/ HERBERT A. CHARLSON
        Clerk

UNITED STATES DISTRICT COURT
For the Southern District of New York

Appalachian Power Company,
Ohio Power Company and
Indiana & Michigan Electric Company

Plaintiffs,

against

American Institute of Certified Public
Accountants, L. H. Penney, William W.
Werntz and Carman G. Blough,

Defendants.

NOTICE OF APPEAL

Civil Action No. 145-161

S I R S :

PLEASE TAKE NOTICE that the plaintiffs hereby appeal to the United States Court of Appeals for the Second Circuit from the order and judgment of this Court duly entered on May 25, 1959, denying the motion of the plaintiffs for a temporary injunction and granting summary judgment in favor of the defendants dismissing the complaint herein and from each and every part of said order and judgment and the whole thereof.

Dated, New York, N.Y.
May 25, 1949

TO:
MESSRS. HOWARD C. WESTWOOD,
FONTAINE C. BRADLEY and
STANLEY L. TEMKO,
Attorneys for Defendants,
c/o American Institute of
  Certified Public Accountants,
270 Madison Avenue,
New York, N.Y.
    and
MESSRS. COVINGTON & BURLING,
Union Trust Building,
Washington, D.C.

Yours, etc.,

SIMPSON THACHER & BARTLETT

/s/ By WHITNEY NORTH SEYMOUR

Member of the Firm

Attorneys for Plaintiffs,
Office and Post Office Address,
120 Broadway
New York 5, N.Y.

See page 307 for notice of settlement, by plaintiffs, and page 308 for order of Richard H. Levet, United States District Judge, restraining defendants from distributing proposed letter dated April 15, 1959, (quoted on page 2 herein).

UNITED STATES COURT OF APPEALS
For the First Circuit

Appalachian Power Company,
Ohio Power Company and
Indiana & Michigan Electric Company,

Appellants,

against

American Institute of Certified Public
Accountants, L. H. Penney, William W.
Werntz and Carman G. Blough,

Appellees.

NOTICE OF MOTION

SIRS:

PLEASE TAKE NOTICE that upon the notice of appeal herein, dated May 25, 1959, the annexed affidavit of Whitney North Seymour, duly sworn to on May 26, 1959, the order and judgment of the United States District Court for the Southern District of New York, Hon. Richard H. Levet, Judge, duly entered on May 25, 1959, in the above-entitled action, denying the motion of the appellants for a temporary injunction, granting appellees' motion to dismiss the complaint and granting summary judgment in favor of appellees, and upon all the papers upon which said motions were heard, including the complaint, duly verified on April 15, 1959, the order to show cause signed by Hon. Edward L. Pulmieri, Judge of the United States District Court for the Southern District of New York, on April 15, 1959, the affidavits of Robert O. Whitman and Donald C. Cook, duly sworn to on April 15 and May 6, 1959, respectively, submitted in support of appellants' said motion, the affidavits of F. Merrill Beatty and William W. Werntz, both duly sworn to on May 4, 1959, and the affidavit of George C. Christie, duly sworn to on May 6, 1959, all submitted in opposition to appellants' said motion, and appellees' notice of motion to dismiss the complaint dated May 1, 1959, the undersigned will move this Court at a Motion Term thereof, to be held at Room 1705 of the United States Court House, Foley Square, New York, N.Y., on the 1st day of June, 1959, at 10:30 o'clock in the forenoon of said day, or as soon thereafter as counsel can be heard, for an order restraining and enjoining the appellees, during the pendency of the appeal herein, from distributing to the members of the appellee American Institute of Certified Public Accountants or to any members of the accountancy profession, the proposed letter referred to in the complaint herein or distributing to the aforesaid any like statement to to the effect that the appellee American Institute of Certified Public Accountants or its Committee on Accounting Procedure is of the opinion or recommends that charges made to income in recognition of the deferral of income taxes should not or may not, in accordance with generally accepted accounting principles, be credited to earned surplus or to any other account included in the stockholders' equity section of the balance sheet, and for an order granting such other further and different relief as to the Court may seem just and proper in the premises.

Dated, New York, N. Y.
    May 26, 1959

                Yours, etc.

                SIMPSON THACHER & BARTLETT

/s/ By WHITNEY NORTH SEYMOUR
                A Member of the Firm

                Attorneys for Appellants,
                Office & P.O. Address,
                120 Broadway,
                New York 5, N.Y.

TO:

MESSRS. HOWARD C. WESTWOOD,
FONTAINE C. BRADLEY and
STANLEY L. TEMKO,
Attorneys for Appellees,
c/o American Institute of Certified Public Accountants,
270 Madison Avenue,
New York, N.Y.
    and
COVINGTON & BURLING,
Union Trust Building,
Washington, D. C.

UNITED STATES COURT OF APPEALS
For the Second Circuit

Appalachian Power Company, Ohio Power Company and Indiana & Michigan Electric Company, <div align=center>*Appellants,*</div><div align=center>*against*</div>American Institute of Certified Public Accountants, L. H. Penney, William W. Werntz and Carman G. Blough, <div align=center>*Appellees.*</div>	**AFFIDAVIT**

STATE OF NEW YORK } ss.:
COUNTY OF NEW YORK }

WHITNEY NORTH SEYMOUR, being duly sworn, deposes and says that:

1. I am an attorney and a member of the firm of Simpson Thacher & Bartlett, attorneys for the appellants herein.

2. This affidavit is submitted in support of appellants' motion for an injunction pending the appeal herein and for an order to show cause bringing on said motion and restraining defendants as requested therein pending the hearing and determination of said motion.

3. This is an action for an injunction. The action was commenced by the filing of a verified complaint on April 15, 1959. Simultaneously therewith, Hon. Edward L. Palmieri, Judge of the United States District Court for the Southern District of New York, signed an order to show cause bringing on a motion by appellants for a preliminary injunction for hearing on April 17, 1959, and restraining the appellees from committing the acts complained of pending the hearing and determination of said motion. By stipulation of the parties, the hearing of appellants' said motion was adjourned to May 7, 1959, and the provisions of the said restraining order continued.

4. On May 1, 1959, appellees served a notice of cross-motion to dismiss the complaint for failure to state a claim upon which relief could be granted, returnable on said adjourned date. Both motions were heard together on that date before Hon. Richard H. Levet.

5. Copies of all of the papers upon which said motions were heard will be submitted to the Court upon this motion and are incorporated by reference as exhibits to this affidavit.

148

6. On May 21, 1959, Judge Levet filed his opinion holding that appellants' motion for a preliminary injunction must be denied, and, having treated appellees' motion as one for summary judgment, that judgment must be entered for appellees dismissing the complaint. An order and judgment to that effect was duly signed and entered on May 25, 1959. An appeal was taken therefrom on the same date.

7. The primary relief sought herein is an injunction preventing appellees from distributing a certain proposed letter, which distribution will, as alleged in the verified complaint, cause irreparable injury to appellants. I am informed and believe that said letter is now ready for distribution. Indeed, a printed copy of said letter, dated April 15, 1959, was handed to the Court below upon the argument of the motions.

8. Accordingly, unless an order is entered restraining the distribution of said letter, this appeal will be rendered moot insofar as it seeks review of the denial of appellants' motion for a temporary injunction and insofar as any equitable relief is concerned, and the irreparable injury to the appellants alleged in the complaint and, I submit, established by the moving affidavits below, will immediately befall appellants.

9. Application for the relief requested herein was made to Judge Levet on May 25, 1959, and granted only to the extent that the appellees have been so enjoined until the hearing of this motion by this Court. No other such application has been made to any Court or Judge thereof.

10. For the foregoing reasons, it is respectfully requested that an order be entered herein, granting the injunction sought pending the hearing and determination of this appeal.

Sworn to before me this
26th day of May, 1959   /s/ WHITNEY NORTH SEYMOUR
/s/ ALBERT X. BADER
    Notary Public

UNITED STATES COURT OF APPEALS
For the Second Circuit

Appalachian Power Company,
Ohio Power Company and
Indiana & Michigan Electric Company,

Appellants,

against

American Institute of Certified Public
Accountants, L. H. Penney, William W.
Werntz and Carman G. Blough,

Appellees.

AFFIDAVIT OF JOHN L. CAREY
IN OPPOSITION TO MOTION
FOR INJUNCTION PENDING APPEAL

JOHN L. CAREY, being first duly sworn deposes and says:

1. He resides in Cold Spring Harbor, New York.

2. He is the Executive Director of the American Institute of Certified Public Accountants, a defendant-appellee, herein.

3. This affidavit is prepared in response to the allegations contained in paragraph 26 of the affidavit of Donald C. Cook, which affidavit was served on defendants-appellees the evening before the hearing on defendants-appellees' motion to dismiss in the District Court. In the said paragraph 26 of the said affidavit of the said Donald C. Cook the new research organization of the said American Institute of Certified Public Accountants is described in such a manner as to be capable of creating some uncertainty as to what has in fact been done by the said American Institute of Certified Public Accountants.

4. After many months of consideration and study, the said American Institute of Certified Public Accountants recently decided to initiate an expanded program of accounting research and, to that end, has decided to organize an Accounting Principles Board, and an Accounting Research Staff under the administrative direction of a Director of Accounting Research. The said Accounting Research Staff shall, subject to the supervision of the said Accounting Principles Board, institute research studies, and will have complete authority to publish reports on accounting procedures and principles based on the said research studies. The new organizational framework will take over in the fall of 1959 the functions presently being performed by the Committee on Accounting Procedure of the American Institute of Certified Public Accountants. The said Accounting Principles Board will have the power to adopt the conclusions of the Accounting Research Staff as statements of generally accepted accounting principles similar to the pronouncements of the Accounting Research Bulletins issued by the present

Committee on Accounting Procedure. The Accounting Principles Board will not, however, be confined merely to accepting or rejecting the conclusions of the said Accounting Research Staff, insofar as the said conclusions of the said Accounting Research Staff purport to involve questions of accounting principles. On the contrary, the said Accounting Principles Board will have the same power and discretion as the present Committee on Accounting Procedure with regard to the formulation and publication, and to the method of formulation and publication, of what the said Accounting Principles Board shall consider generally accepted accounting principles.

5. As indicated in the preceding paragraph of this affidavit the new organizational framework for research into, and for the publication of statements concerning, generally accepted accounting principles will take over the functions presently being performed by the said Committee on Accounting Procedure, and will begin to function at the start of the said American Institute of Certified Public Accountants' next fiscal year, which fiscal year commences on September 1, 1959. The said Committee on Accounting Procedure has been advised that it will go out of existence at the end of the said American Institute of Certified Public Accountants' present fiscal year, which fiscal year ends on August 31, 1959, and that the said Committee should proceed to wind up its affairs.

State of New York
County of New York

/s/ JOHN L. CAREY
John L. Carey

Sworn to before me this
1st day of June, 1959

/s/ EUNICE G. MERRITT
Notary Public

Commission Expires March 30, 1961

UNITED STATES COURT OF APPEALS
For the Second Circuit

Appalachian Power Company,
Ohio Power Company and
Indiana & Michigan Electric Company,

Appellants,

against

American Institute of Certified Public
Accountants, L. H. Penney, William W.
Werntz and Carman G. Blough,

Appellees.

APPELLANTS' MEMORANDUM IN SUPPORT OF
MOTION FOR INJUNCTION PENDING APPEAL

(June 3, 1959)

SIMPSON THACHER & BARTLETT,
Attorneys for Appellants,
Office & Post Office Address,
120 Broadway,
New York 5, N.Y.

WHITNEY NORTH SEYMOUR
RICHARD M. DICKE
WILLIAM J. MANNING
Of Counsel.

UNITED STATES COURT OF APPEALS
For the Second Circuit

Appalachian Power Company,
Ohio Power Company and
Indiana & Michigan Electric Company,

Appellants,

against

American Institute of Certified Public
Accountants, L. H. Penney, William W.
Werntz and Carman G. Blough,

Appellees.

APPELLANTS' MEMORANDUM IN SUPPORT OF
MOTION FOR INJUNCTION PENDING APPEAL

Statement

This memorandum is submitted in support of appellees' motion for an order granting an injunction pending the appeal taken by them herein from the order and judgment of the United States District Court for the Southern District of New York, Hon. Richard H. Levet, Judge, entered on June 25, 1959, (sic)* denying appellants' motion for a preliminary injunction and granting summary judgment in favor of appellees dismissing the complaint.

Appellants are three operating electric public utility companies. Appellee American Institute of Certified Public Accountants (the "Institute") is a national organization of certified public accountants with more than 33,000 members. The individual appellees are the President of the Institute, the Chairman of its 21-member Committee on Accounting Procedure (the "Committee") and its Director of Research.

Appellants seek in this action to restrain the distribution by the Committee to the 33,000 members of the Institute and others of a proposed letter to the effect that the accounting procedures followed by appellants and others and heretofore recognized as generally accepted accounting principles are now improper. That pronouncement, because of the authority of the appellees in the accounting profession and in the business community, will cause immediate and irreparable harm to appellants by impairing their credit and limiting their growth.

We submit that the appellees, before issuing a pronouncement which they know will harm others, are under a duty and responsibility to use some minimum standards of care in ascertaining the propriety and correctness of their pronouncement. It is noteworthy that the appellee President of the Institute has

* Should read May 25, 1959.

recognized the existence of such a duty and responsibility. Mr. Penney said on April 22, 1959, in reporting on procedures hereafter to be followed by the Institute, that making a public announcement when a study of any accounting principle is commenced, giving "* * * industry, stock exchanges, governmental agencies, various accounting groups and other interested parties * * * ample opportunity to present their views" and issuing, before an "official pronouncement" is made, "a formal report * * * given the widest possible exposure * * * with a request for further comments" are "* * * the only way to stimulate and crystallize thinking on the accounting principles which are so vital to the reporting of corporate profits to the public" (Exhibit D to affidavit of Donald C. Cook).

The complaint alleges that the appellees have utterly disregarded this responsibility and failed in this duty as well as having inserted a false statement as to the purported purpose for issuing the proposed letter, to wit, attributing an intention with respect to the use of certain words in a prior publication which intention did not and could not have existed.

It is appellants' position that the facts presented in the verified complaint establish all of the elements of a tort in that the stated purpose for distributing the proposed letter is false, appellees are acting wilfully, wantonly and recklessly in preparing to distribute the letter, appellees intend thereby to injure appellants and can show no legal justification for so doing, and the distribution of that letter will cause the immediate and irreparable harm to appellants which is alleged in the complaint and established by the moving papers. The fact is, therefore, that unless an injunction is granted pending the appeal herein, enjoining the distribution of that letter, appellants' appeal from the denial of its motion for a temporary injunction and indeed the entire appeal, and the action itself, in so far as equitable relief is concerned, will become moot.

The authority of this Court to grant the relief requested is clear. Rule 62(g) of the Federal Rules of Civil Procedure makes plain that other provisions of that Rule recognizing the authority of the District Courts to grant relief pending appeal:

"* * * do not limit any power of an appellate court * * * to suspend, modify, restore, or grant an injunction during the pendency of an appeal or to make any order appropriate to preserve the status quo * * * ".

Rule 62(g), read together with 28 U.S.C. Section 1651, the "All Writs Statute", amply supports this Court's authority to grant relief sought herein. Public Utilities Com'n. v. Capital Transit Co., 214 F. 2d, 242 (D.C. Cir. 1954). The wisdom and justice of the exercise of that authority was well expressed in Scripps-Howard Radio v. Federal Communications Comm., 316 U.S. 4 (1941) where the Court said:

"No court can make time stand still. The circumstances surrounding a controversy may change irrevocably during the pendency of an appeal, despite anything a court can do. But within these limits it is reasonable that an appellate court should be able to prevent irreparable injury to the parties or to the public resulting from the premature enforcement of a determination which may later be found to have been wrong. It has always been held, therefore, that as part of its traditional equipment for the administration of justice, a federal court can stay the enforcement of a judgment pending the outcome of an appeal." (316 U.S. at 9-10).

This very Court said in Masses Pub. Co. v. Patten, 245 Fed. 102 (2d Cir. 1917), on a motion to stay an injunction pending appeal:

"* * * Such stays, granted by the trial judge, are not uncommon; I have, myself, awarded not a few. They rest on the belief that doubtful questions of law, or difficult contests of fact (or both) are presented by the record, and that the relations of the parties, or exigencies of business are such that (perhaps by the giving of security) no injury will result from letting matters remain in status quo (except for opinion filed) until decisive action can be had in the Court of Appeals.

There can be no difference in principle, between such an application to the trial judge, and a similar one addressed to a member of the appellate court. * * *

* * *

Defendant's situation, however, is quite different. The order appealed from, if complied with, fulfills the whole object of suit. If reversed, no restitution or restoration of status quo is possible; and in my judgment the appeal becomes a futility, presenting to the appellate court nothing but an interesting moot point. * * * I * * * strongly incline to the view that this is the rare instance in which an appeal without a stay is not only futile, but legally impossible; yet the statute gives the absolute right of appeal." (245 Fed. at 103-105)

The Proceedings Below

This action was commenced by the filing of a verified complaint on April 15, 1959. Simultaneously therewith, Hon. Edward L. Palmieri, Judge of the United States District Court for the Southern District of New York, signed an order to show cause bringing on for hearing on April 17, 1959, a motion by appellants for a preliminary injunction and containing a temporary restraining order enjoining the appellees as requested in the prayer for relief in the complaint.

Appellees requested an adjournment of the hearing on said motion, and it was adjourned to May 7, 1959, the temporary restraining order being continued by consent.

On May 1, 1959, appellees served a notice of cross-motion, pursuant to Rule 12(b) of the Federal Rules of Civil Procedure, for an order dismissing the complaint on the ground that it failed to state a claim upon which relief could be granted.

Both motions were heard by Judge Levet on May 7, 1959, and his opinion thereon was filed on May 21, 1959. That opinion held that appellants' motion for a temporary injunction must be denied, that appellees' motion had been treated as one for summary judgment pursuant to Rule 56 of the Federal Rules of Civil Procedure and that summary judgment must be entered dismissing the complaint.

An order and judgment in accordance with Judge Levet's opinion was duly signed and entered on May 25, 1959, and at the same time Judge Levet signed an order enjoining the distribution of the said letter until this motion could be heard.

The Grounds upon Which Appellants Rely

On this motion appellants rely upon the following facts:

1. Unless the relief sought is granted, appellants' appeal from the denial of their motion for a temporary injunction will become moot, and they will in effect be denied their absolute right of appeal from the determination and will be forever precluded from the equitable relief which they seek even if this Court should later determine that the lower Court erred. To that extent the very jurisdiction of this Court will have been thwarted.

2. An examination of the record and opinion below will, we submit, provide this Court with a substantial indication of probable success by appellants on this appeal.

3. Absent the intervention of this Court to maintain the status quo pending this appeal, irreparable injury will immediately befall appellants.

4. The granting of the relief requested will neither damage nor even inconvenience appellees.

5. Since appellants are public utilities, which will be irreparably harmed with resulting damage to the public, the public interest favors the granting of this relief.

The Complaint

The facts alleged in the verified complaint, which we submit should have been accepted as established at least for the purposes of appellees' motion to dismiss, are as follows:

The appellant electric utility companies have recorded on their books more than $65,000,000 in the aggregate in accounts designated as "earned surplus restricted for future federal income taxes." These amounts have been accrued by the appellants over a period of years in books of account maintained by them pursuant to requirements of the State regulatory agencies having jurisdiction over them, and have been accrued in accordance with generally accepted accounting principles.

These amounts represent credits to such balance sheet accounts, which credits arise from charges made against income ("normalization charges") to provide for federal income taxes which may have to be paid in the future but which are currently deferred. The amounts so accrued represent the difference between the actual income taxes paid by appellants and the amount of such taxes that would have been paid if the appellants had not elected to take for tax purposes accelerated amortization deductions and liberalized depreciation deductions under Sections 167 and 168 of the Internal Revenue Code.

Financial statements prepared on the same basis as appellants have been certified without exception by all of the certified public accountant firms experienced in electric public utility accounting as being in accordance with generally accepted accounting principles.

The Institute, through its Committee, from time to time, publishes Accounting Research Bulletins. The opinions, recommendations and pronouncements of the Institute and its Committee, as published in the Accounting Research Bulletins, are generally accepted by members of the accountancy profession, governmental regulatory agencies, financial institutions, investment banking concerns, rating services and financial analysts as establishing the accounting principles to be followed by the accountancy profession.

Prior to the acts complained of, the Institute had recognized the general acceptance of, and the authority attached by such persons and groups to, its opinions and recommendations as published in the Accounting Research Bulletins. It had, therefore, adopted certain procedures and practices prerequisite to the publication of such an opinion in order to ensure the reasonableness, correctness, propriety and utility of such opinions. These included the giving of consideration to prior opinions of the Institute and its Committee, to prevailing accounting practices and to the views of professional and other bodies concerned with accounting procedures. It was also the practice of the Committee to circulate to a very considerable group what is known as "an exposure draft" of any proposed opinion or recommendation, and to give consideration to the views of that group before any such opinion or recommendation was adopted in final form and published in an Accounting Research Bulletin.

In Accounting Research Bulletins Nos. 42 and 43 issued in 1952 and 1953, the Committee had recognized the practice of making normalization charges to income in connection with accounting for accelerated amortization as in accordance with generally accepted accounting principles. In Accounting Research Bulletin No. 43, although the Committee did not specifically discuss the balance sheet treatment of the credit arising from such charges, it was recognized that such a credit should properly be made to an "account for deferred income taxes".

In 1957, the Committee again considered the making of normalization charges, this time in connection with accounting for liberalized depreciation, and in Accounting Research Bulletin No. 44 (Revised), it recognized this procedure as being in accordance with sound accounting procedures.

Prior to the publication of Accounting Research Bulletin No. 44 (Revised), and in accordance with its persistently followed practices and procedures, an exposure draft of the proposed opinion set forth therein was prepared and distributed, and after the receipt of comments thereon, a ballot draft was prepared and submitted to the members of the Committee for formal action. Neither of these drafts contained any reference to any required balance sheet treatment of the credits arising from normalization charges.

When Accounting Research Bulletin No. 44 (Revised) was published, it did not prescribe or specify any required balance sheet treatment of such credits but there had been added to the opinion a provision, which had not appeared in the exposure and ballot drafts, that under certain circumstances it would be appropriate "instead of crediting a deferred tax account" to treat the credit in another manner.

It was not the intention of the Committee in adopting Accounting Research Bulletin No. 44 (sic)* to specify any balance sheet treatment for recording the credit arising from normalization charges. Neither the members of the Institute or the Committee, nor other interested parties, nor those to whom the exposure draft had been sent, had the opportunity to express any opinion as to the desirability of adopting even the above-quoted phrase, which in any event did not specify any required balance sheet treatment. The Committee in fact had turned down the suggestion by one of its members that the Committee consider and take a position on the balance sheet treatment of such credits.

The appellees, however, under the pretext of stating the intention of the Committee in using the phrase "a deferred tax account" in Accounting Research Bulletin No. 44 (Revised), are about to mail to the members of the Institute a

---

* Should be "No. 44 (Revised)."

letter to the effect that:

> "The committee used the phrase (deferred tax account) in its ordinary connotation of an account to be shown in the balance sheet as a liability or a deferred credit. A provision in recognition of the deferral of income taxes, being required for the proper determination of net income, should not at the same time result in a credit to earned surplus or to any other account included in the stockholders'equity section of the balance sheet."

The distribution of the proposed letter is wholly unjustified on any ground. For one thing, it would result in an arbitrary and unreasonable distinction between accounting for the credits arising from normalization charges when made for accelerated amortization and accounting for such charges when made for liberalized depreciation since the letter does not purport to read upon Accounting Research Bulletin No. 43.

The proposed letter is being sent without the Committee or any of the appellees having taken any steps reasonably designed to ascertain the propriety or correctness of the opinion expressed therein. A vast majority of the Committee members have no experience in public utility accounting and hence none in the subject matter at hand. The Committee, indeed, has not even complied with its own well-established practices and procedures, for no exposure draft or ballot draft of the proposed opinion has been prepared and distributed, no consideration has been given to their own prior opinions and no consideration has been given either to prevailing generally accepted accounting practices or to the views of other professional bodies concerned with accounting procedures. The accounting procedure proposed in the letter, moreover, is in direct conflict with the heretofore generally accepted accounting principles which the appellants have used and have been specifically authorized to use by State regulatory bodies and which have been employed by many other public utility companies and by all of the public accounting firms specializing in such work.

The appellees have been specifically informed and put on notice that the adoption and publication of the proposed opinion would cause great immediate and irreparable injury, loss and damage to the appellants. Appellees were on specific notice that the distribution of the proposed opinion would, because of the prestige and authority attached to any such opinion, cause accountants, financial institutions, investment banking concerns, financial analysts and governmental agencies to question the continued inclusion of the $65,000,000 in the restricted earned surplus accounts of appellants with the result that appellants would be seriously interfered with in their dealings and relationships with such persons and institutions, and that the doubts raised as to the propriety of including that $65,000,000 as part of restricted earned surplus would raise additional questions as to the validity of the announced debt ratios of the appellants, which are the basis upon which appellants have in the past and propose in the future to borrow funds and sell securities to finance their current construction programs budgeted at more than $100,000,000 for the year 1959 alone. The appellees intend that such injuries, losses and damages shall befall the appellants. The proposed distribution of the letter by appellees is in wanton, reckless and wilful disregard of the consequences thereof.

* * * * *

With the above allegations of the complaint in mind, we turn to a demonstration of the reasonable probability of success on this appeal.

POINT I

THE LOWER COURT ERRED IN TREATING
APPELLEES' MOTION TO DISMISS AS A
MOTION FOR SUMMARY JUDGMENT AND IN
GRANTING SUMMARY JUDGMENT

The District Court, in its opinion said that:

> "Since matters outside the pleadings have been presented to the court, and since the parties have submitted such proof, I am treating this motion as one for summary judgment as provided in Rule 56 of the Federal Rules of Civil Procedure." (Opinion, pp. 3-4)

In this the Court erred. The only authority for treating a motion to dismiss as one for summary judgment is found in Rule 12(b) of the Federal Rules of Civil Procedure, where it is said that:

> "* * * If, on a motion asserting the defense numbered (6) to dismiss for failure of the pleading to state a claim upon which relief can be granted, matters outside the pleading are presented to and not excluded by the court, the motion shall be treated as one for summary judgment and disposed of as provided in Rule 56, and all parties shall be given reasonable opportunity to present all material made pertinent to such a motion by Rule 56." (Emphasis added)

The fact is that no matters outside the pleadings were presented to the Court on the motion to dismiss by either party. The only affidavits before the Court were there on the motion for a temporary injunction solely. They were not intended by appellants for consideration on the motion to dismiss, and we believe that appellees likewise had no such intention. The main papers upon which appellants relied below even with respect to the motion for an injunction were the verified complaint and the affidavit of Robert O. Whitman, which were prepared, served and filed at a time prior to the making of appellees' motion to dismiss. The sole other document submitted to the Court by appellants was the reply affidavit of Donald C. Cook, which was limited to a refutation of the matters set forth in the affidavits submitted in opposition to the motion for a temporary injunction.

Appellants had no knowledge at any time up to the date of the filing of the opinion that the Court was treating the motion as one for summary judgment, and, accordingly, did not have any opportunity to prepare and submit the affidavits it would have prepared and submitted had it known that the motion was being considered as one for summary judgment. This denial to the appellants of the opportunity to prepare and submit matters appropriate on a motion for summary judgment is in direct conflict with the specific provision of Rule 12(b) that when the Court treats a motion to dismiss as one for summary judgment:

> "* * * all parties shall be given a reasonable opportunity to present all matters made pertinent to such a motion by Rule 56."

This sentence was added to Rule 12 by a 1946 amendment. The revisors said:

> "* * * It will also be observed that if a motion under Rule 12(b)(6) is thus converted into a summary judgment motion, the amendment insures that both parties shall be given a reasonable opportunity to submit affidavits and extraneous proofs to avoid taking a party by surprise through the conversion of the motion into a motion for summary judgment.* * * "
> (Report of Proposed Amendments, Advisory Committee on Rules for Civil Procedure, June 1946, p. 14, 15)

No such reasonable opportunity was given to appellants.

The treatment of a motion to dismiss as one for summary judgment without affording an opportunity to present all matters pertinent to such a motion was held to be ground for reversal in Pacific American Fisheries v. Mullaney, 191 F. 2d 137 (9th Cir. 1951). There too the lower Court had denied a motion for a preliminary injunction and granted summary judgment. In reversing, the Court of Appeals said:

> "Upon hearing on this motion the court determined to treat the motion as one for a summary judgment, and ordered that such judgment be entered for the defendant. It does not appear that either party was afforded an opportunity to make any further showing by way of affidavit or otherwise after the court determined to treat the motion as one for summary judgment. . . .

* * *

Appeal was taken both from the order denying a temporary injunction and from the summary judgment. With respect to the summary judgment, appellant contends that irrespective of all other considerations, it was error for the court to undertake to treat the motion for judgment on the pleadings as a motion for summary judgment and then proceed to grant that judgment without giving the appellant an opportunity to present evidence on the questions of fact involved. . . .

* * *

We think that the contention that the entry of a summary judgment was erroneous under the circumstances is sound. . . .''

See also Herron v. Herron, 255 F. 2d 590 (5th Cir. 1958).

More basic even than this denial of the due process provided for by the Federal Rules is the error of the Court below, when in treating the motion as one for summary judgment, it chose to disregard uncontroverted matters set forth in the verified complaint and in appellants' affidavits, to accept as true statements set forth in appellees' affidavits which were in conflict with those in appellants' affidavits and to decide issues of fact on the affidavits. No citation of authority seems necessary to support the proposition that jurisdiction to grant summary judgment should be exercised with caution and only in the clearest of cases and that on a motion for summary judgment the Court may not decide issues of fact, but is limited to the inquiry as to whether any such questions exist.

For example, the Court found as a fact that the proposed letter "* * * was adopted by the Committee in conformity with its established procedures." (Op. p. 6) The verified complaint and the moving affidavits specifically allege that the Committee did not follow its established procedures and practices, pointing out that there were no exposure or ballot drafts submitted, that no opportunity was given to interested parties to express their opinion, and no consideration given to the prior opinions of the appellees themselves. Surely this conflict in the affidavits raised an issue of fact that could not and should not have been determined on affidavits.

The Court also found that "The opinions of the Committee have no official effect." (Op. p. 7). Whether the effect of the opinions of the Committee is official or unofficial, is, of course, irrelevant, the only pertinent inquiry being what their effect is. But in any event there is at least an issue of fact as to whether or not the opinions of the appellees have the effect and are accorded the authority alleged in the complaint, for the appellees' papers may be searched in vain for any denial of those allegations and averments.

Similarly the Court found that the Committee's procedures:

"Do not require the so-called 'exposure' in draft form of the proposed letter, though on occasion in the past this 'exposure' procedure has been adopted." (Op. p. 7)

Here too there was at least a question of fact raised as to the practice of using exposure drafts. And, moreover, the Court's finding is not even supported by appellees' papers, for the most that was alleged by appellees was that there were a few previous occasions on which exposure drafts had not been circulated, a quite different thing from the finding that only on occasion had exposure drafts been used.

The Court also specifically found that:

"The Committee's position as to the accounting practice in question is followed by Arthur Andersen & Co., public accountants, who audit the accounts of one-third of the utility companies in the country." (Op. p. 7)

This finding ignores the sharp issue of fact concerning Arthur Andersen & Co.'s accounting practices. Although the affidavit by a member of the Arthur Andersen firm states that it is of the opinion that credits arising from normalization charges should not be included in the equity section of a balance sheet, and that "Arthur Andersen & Co would take exception in their auditors certificate" to such treatment, Mr. Cook's affidavit cites specific instances in which Arthur Andersen & Co. have certified statements without exception as having been prepared in conformity with generally accepted accounting principles, where as much as $13,000,000 in credits arising from normalization charges was included in restricted earned surplus accounts. Certainly there was at least an issue of fact as to Arthur Andersen & Co.'s practices. The above finding also ignores the allegation of the complaint and the statement in the affidavit of Donald C. Cook, former Chairman of the Securities and Exchange Commission, that the practice followed by appellants and about to be condemned by the appellees, had always been considered to be no less a generally accepted accounting principle than that now espoused by the appellees.

The Court also found and apparently was influenced by the assertion that the Public Service Commission of the State of Indiana had ordered one of the appellants to cease recording credits for deferred income taxes in its surplus account. But it overlooked the facts set forth in Mr. Cook's affidavit where he points out first of all that there is a real issue as to the validity of the order referred to and that because thereof the Public Service Commission of Indiana has since the date of the order in question accepted financial statements of that appellant in which such credits were included in restricted earned surplus accounts.

The entire opinion is pregnant, moreover, with the suggestion of disbelief of the statements contained in the moving papers and in the verified complaint, even though they were not contradicted by appellees' affidavits, whereas every statement made in appellees' affidavit has been accepted as a fact even though controverted and in many cases shown to be without merit on the basis of documentary evidence.

We submit, therefore, that the dismissal of the complaint must eventually be reversed on this appeal by reason of the above errors.

POINT II

THE COMPLAINT STATES A CAUSE OF ACTION
FOR RELIEF AT LAW OR IN EQUITY

The complaint herein is bottomed upon the doctrine of prima facie tort, that is, that otherwise lawful conduct is actionable if it is done intentionally and is calculated to damage, unless the actor can show legal justification. This doctrine finds its genesis in Keeble v. Hickeringill, 11 Easts' Rep. 574 (1809), and a classic statement of it appears in Mogul Steamship Co. v. McGregor, Gow & Co., 23 Q.B.D. 598, 613 (1889), aff'd [1892] A.C. 25, where the court said:

> "Now, intentionally to do that which is calculated in the ordinary course of events to damage, and which does, in fact, damage another in that person's property or trade, is actionable if done without just cause or excuse."

Perhaps the most often quoted enunciation of the doctrine is that of Mr. Justice Holmes in Aikens v. Wisconsin, 195 U.S. 194, 204 (1904), where he said:

> "* * * prima facie, the intentional infliction of temporal damage is a cause of action, which, as a matter of substantive law * * * requires a justification if the defendant is to escape."

Prima facie tort has been for some time an integral part of the law of the State of New York, and recognizing its obligation so to do under the Erie v. Thompson doctrine, the lower Court quite properly held the law of the State of New York to be applicable herein. But while thus stating that the validity of the complaint was predicated upon the doctrine of prima facie tort as enunciated by the New York courts and citing the cases relied on by appellants, the lower Court, we submit, had a misconception of a basic principle of the doctrine as it is applied by the New York Courts. The lower Court said (Op. p. 9) that "[T]here must be an intent to injure plaintiff, at least to the extent of infliction of wrongful harm upon plaintiff without just cause or excuse." But the New York cases are clear that the harm inflicted need not be "wrongful" in itself. Indeed, the very basis of the doctrine is that the acts complained of are otherwise lawful and are actionable only because done intentionally and without justification.   Were this not so there would be no need to resort to the doctrine of prima facie tort, for acts wrongful in themselves are actionable independent of intent and justification.

The leading New York case in this field, decided by a unanimous Court of Appeals, is Advance Music Corporation v. American Tobacco Co., 296 N.Y. 79 (1946). That case is strikingly similar to the instant one and should have been treated by the Court below as controlling. It reached the New York Court of Appeals after the Appellate Division had dismissed the complaint for failure to state a cause of action. The complaint, in an action for damages and for an injunction, alleged that plaintiff was engaged in the business of publishing musical compositions and derived its revenue chiefly from sales of sheet music to the public and from royalties for the use of its compositions in the entertainment field. It spent large sums of money advertising that its songs were among the most popular of the day, for plaintiff's customers normally purchased those compositions which they thought were the most popular. Defendants, a tobacco company and an advertising concern, sponsored and produced a well-known weekly coast-to-coast radio program, the Hit Parade, which had a listening audience estimated to be in excess of 15,000,000 per week. On said program defendants listed and had performed the supposedly 9 or 10 most popular songs of the week, claiming that these popularity ratings were based upon an extensive and accurate nationwide survey.

The complaint further alleged that the defendants' ratings and listings of songs were in fact the result of caprice or other considerations foreign to a selection based on an accurate and extensive nationwide survey; that in fact, some of plaintiff's songs which were among the most popular of the day were either completely ignored by the defendants or given an improper rating.

The complaint alleged that by reason of these acts of the defendants in improperly rating or ignoring plaintiff's songs, it was suffering damages in that dealers prematurely returned plaintiff's compositions, thus preventing distribution thereof to retail outlets for sale to the public, that retail purchasers, entertainers and other customers and potential promoters of the songs, influenced by defendants' inaccurate ratings, failed to purchase plaintiff's compositions, and that plaintiff's business prestige was impaired.

The complaint further alleged that the acts and representations of the defendant were made wantonly, in bad faith and with intent to injure plaintiff.

The Court of Appeals reversed a dismissal of the complaint and held that the facts pleaded stated a cause of action. The Court said:

"The foregoing * * * [allegations]* * * are there followed by the further allegation that 'the aforesaid acts and representations on the part

of the defendants are made with intent to injure the plaintiff.' Thus in
sum and substance the second cause of action constitutes a statement to
this effect: The defendants are wantonly causing damage to the plaintiff
by a system of conduct on their part which warrants an inference that they
intend harm of that type. So read, the second cause of action is, we think,
adequate in its office as a plaintiff's pleading." (Emphasis added.)

"In Skinner & Co. v. Shew & Co. [1893], 1 Ch. 413, 422, Lord Justice BOWEN said: 'At Common Law there was a cause of action whenever
one person did damage to another wilfully and intentionally, and without
just cause or excuse.' * * * These broad propositions were approved by
Sir FREDERICK POLLOCK as authority for his doctrine that all willful
harm is actionable unless the defendant justify or excuse his conduct.
Pollock, The Law of Torts, 14th ed. 17-18." (296 N.Y. at pp. 83-84).

* * *

"The justification that is required in a case like this must, of course,
be one which the law will recognize." (296 N.Y. at p. 85)

The Court also cited its earlier opinions in Opera on Tour, Inc. v. Weber, 285
N.Y. 348 (1941) and American Guild of Musical Artists v. Petrillo, 286 N.Y.
226 (1941), in concluding that the complaint stated a cause of action "for relief either at law or in equity".

Analysis of the complaint and the Court of Appeals' opinion in the Advance
Music case indicates that there is no basis whatever for the lower Court's statement that it is "basically different" from the instant case.   The alleged distinctions found by the Court below simply do not exist.

In the Advance Music case, the defendants were representing that they had
made an extensive and accurate survey and that based thereon they were presenting the most popular songs of the day. Here the appellees are representing
that it was the intention of the Committee in using certain words in Accounting
Research Bulletin 44 (Revised) to disapprove of the accounting procedures now
followed by appellants, whereas the complaint alleges that the Committee in
promulgating Accounting Research Bulletin No. 44 (sic)* not only did not have,
but could not have had, such an intention, for the problem was not considered and,
indeed, the suggestion that it be considered had been specifically rejected.
This element of the falsity and wilfulness of the appellees' proposed action is
not even mentioned in the opinion below, although it is a fact uncontroverted on
this record and which squarely shows the similarity of the challenged activity in
this case to that in the Advance Music case.

Even apart from this particular instance of falsity, however, the complaint
alleges that appellees, in preparing the proposed letter for publication, have

* Should be "No. 44 (Revised)."

taken no steps whatever reasonably designed to ensure the propriety thereof, and moreover, that the appellees have failed even to take the steps recognized by them not only as proper but as the only way to stimulate and crystallize thinking on this important accounting issue. Those who receive the proposed letter, on the other hand, will logically assume that the Committee has acted in accordance with its theretofore followed practices and procedures and will accord the letter the persuasiveness and authority accorded to opinions arrived at in accordance with regular practices and procedures. These allegations, we submit, are quite apposite to the allegations that the purportedly extensive and accurate survey was in fact based on whim and caprice.

In the Advance Music case, it was alleged that the representations made by the defendants therein were accepted by the buying public and others as establishing the more popular songs and that thereby the buying public and others were influenced not to purchase the plaintiff's songs. Here the uncontroverted allegation of the complaint is that the opinions of the appellees are accepted by accountants and others with whom appellants must deal in connection with their business and that the effect of the proposed opinion will be to impair appellants' credit and otherwise irreparably harm appellants. Allegations of impairment of credit and growth were held sufficient to resist a motion to dismiss in U. S. Aluminum Siding Corp. v. Dun & Bradstreet, Inc., 163 F. Supp. 906 (S.D.N.Y. 1958).

The distinction attempted to be made between the nature of the damages in this case and in Advance Music is equally unsupported by the record. The lower Court here said that appellants could appear before any governmental body or any other person and attempt to convince them to accept appellants' accounting procedures and to reject those espoused by the appellees in their proposed opinion and for that reason were remote. On this record, however, it is established that as a matter of fact the appellees' position will be accepted by others. But the more important factor is that in the Advance Music case, the plaintiffs were as free as appellants here would be, by advertising or other means of persuasion, to convince those with whom they dealt that their songs were the most popular and that they should disregard the ratings announced by the defendants in that case. The Court of Appeals nevertheless found that the damages alleged were sufficient to sustain a complaint at law or in equity. That controlling statement of the New York law should have been applied in this case.

And appellees here cannot, and have not even attempted to point out any more justification for their proposed actions than could the defendant in the Advance Music case. At least in that case the appellants had somewhat of a business justification in that they were trying to encourage the public to listen to their radio programs and buy cigarettes. The appellees have no such economic interest. It affirmatively appears, moreover, that the only justification asserted by appellees for their acts, that is, the expression of the intention of the Committee in using certain words in Accounting Research Bulletin No. 44 is false.

The appellees' affidavits are devoid of any other statement of any reason for so precipitously issuing an opinion which will be accorded such authority and will cause such damage.* Nowhere in their papers do the appellees offer any justification for departing from their own practices and procedures or for failing to give any interested parties or any other professional bodies the chance to comment upon the proposed opinion. Nor is any excuse offered for promulgating an accounting practice which will result in an inconsistency in accounting for the twin deductions of liberalized depreciation and accelerated amortization.

We disagree most strenuously with the statement of the lower Court that: "The purposes of defendant Institute are adequate justification, if justification, indeed, be required, to permit the proposed communications" (Op. p. 14). Even though it may be one of the purposes of the Institute to narrow areas of differ- ence and inconsistency in accounting practices, such a purpose we submit must be accomplished in a responsible fashion. The mere fact that one is in the busi- ness of giving opinions does not relieve him of the responsibility of seeing to it that those opinions are arrived at and given only when there is some basis therefor and only after some rational and reasonable consideration has been given to them, when the opinion giver knows that it is within his power to damage others by giving an opinion.

And on the element of intent to inflict injury, we submit that appellants herein have a much stronger case than did the plaintiff in the Advance Music case. There the Court of Appeals held that the allegations that the defendants' ratings of songs were not in fact based on inaccurate survey, but upon caprice or other considerations foreign to an accurate survey, gave rise to an inference that they intended harm and that such an inference was sufficient in law. There was nothing in the Advance Music complaint to indicate that the defendants even knew of the existence of the plaintiff or of the harm they were causing the plaintiff. Here the complaint alleges that the appellees were on notice that appellants followed the practice of putting credits arising from normalization charges in restricted earned surplus accounts, knew that appellants had $65,000,000 in such accounts, knew that the effect of their opinion will be to cause irreparable harm to appellants and nevertheless have in violation of their own practices and of any standards by which to judge the correctness of their opinion, nevertheless, wilfully and wantonly determined to issue the proposed opinion in reckless disregard of its consequences.

The Court below also attempted to distinguish this case from the Advance Music case by the statement (Op. p. 13) that the proposed letter does not mention the appellants. But it clearly appears that the defendants in the Advance Music case similarly made no mention of the plaintiff therein.

---

* In American Guild of Musical Artists v. Petrillo, 286 N.Y. 226 (1941), moreover, the law of New York was held to be that a complaint based on prima facie tort is sufficient unless "* * * such a justification reveals itself on the face of the complaint * * * ."

We submit that under the law of New York as enunciated in the Advance Music case, the complaint herein states a claim for relief. And the Advance Music case is not the only New York case to which appellants can point in support of this complaint. In Opera on Tour, Inc. v. Weber, supra, the Court of Appeals reversed the dismissal of a complaint seeking an injunction restraining labor unions from interfering with plaintiff's business by inducing its members not to work for plaintiff, although it recognized the rights of the defendants' members to refuse to work for any legitimate reason. The Court held that the complaint made out a cause of action in prima facie tort since there was no legal justification for the acts performed in that the defendants' acts had no reasonable connection with any legitimate or lawful labor objective sought to be gained by defendant from its acts. It was said that the self-interest of labor, like the self-interest of any other person or organization, receives immunity only for those of its actions which have a legitimate and reasonable relationship to benefits which that party is seeking. In the instant case, we submit, appellees' proposed letter could bear a reasonable relationship to the legitimate objectives of appellees only if the appellees had first taken reasonable steps to stimulate and crystallize thinking by accountants on the subject of the proposed letter. Since in this case no steps whatever have been taken to ascertain the views of the profession which the Institute represents appellees are therefore not immune from liability for their proposed action.

"Harm done to another or to the public may be countenanced only if the purpose, in the eye of the law, is sufficient to justify such harm." (285 N.Y. at p. 356)

Similarly, in American Guild of Musical Artists v. Petrillo, supra, plaintiffs, a membership corporation of musical artists and certain members thereof, sought to enjoin the defendant labor union and its president from notifying prospective employers that plaintiffs were not recognized as members of the union and that members of the union would not be permitted to render services at any functions at which plaintiffs were to perform. The Appellate Division had held that the complaint failed to state a cause of action since it was not shown that the defendants maliciously or illegally interfered with plaintiff's members but rather that the defendant union was acting in its legitimate self-interest. The Court of Appeals reversed and reinstated the judgment of the lower court granting the injunction, stating that its holding in the Opera on Tour case established the broad doctrine that harm intentionally done is actionable if not justified, and holding that a labor union, like any one else, could be enjoined from the intentional infliction of harm unless the acts performed were justified as in pursuance of a lawful labor objective and that "* * * no sign of such a justification reveals itself on the face of the complaint * * *." It went on to say that malice in law does not mean ill will against a person but merely intentional action without justification.

Thus while we do not disagree with any of the quotations set forth in the opinion from various New York cases, we do submit that the Advance Music case and above cited cases are the controlling authorities, and that it is clear from those cases that the complaint herein states a claim for relief.

And although on the record herein we dispute the lower Court's statement (Op. p. 14) that the appellants' grievances relate to the "distribution of honest opinions not facts", that statement gives occasion to refer to a leading and time-honored case in this field, although not decided by the Courts of the State of New York. Mr. Justice Holmes, whose opinions in this field are most often quoted, in American Bank & Trust Company v. Federal Reserve Bank, 256 U.S. 350 (1921), wrote that:

"A man has a right to give advice, but advice given for the sole purpose of injuring another's business and effective on a large scale, might create a cause of action. * * * If without a word of falsehood but acting from what we have called disinterested malevolence a man by persuasion should organize and carry into effect a run upon a bank and ruin it, we cannot doubt that an action would lie. * * *" (256 U.S. at pp. 358-59)

In that case the Supreme Court unanimously reversed the dismissal of an action which sought to enjoin the defendant Federal Reserve Bank from committing acts calculated to compel the plaintiff banks, which had too small a capital to make it profitable for them to join the Federal Reserve System either to face financial ruin or become members of the Federal Reserve System or at least to open non-member clearing accounts with it, thereby making it necessary for the plaintiffs to maintain much larger reserves than they needed in their existing operations.

The sufficiency of the complaint herein should have been determined in light of the well-established rule that a "complaint should not be dismissed for insufficiency unless it appears to a certainty that plaintiff is entitled to no relief under any state of facts which could be proved in support of the claim." 2 Moore, Federal Practice, p. 2245 (2d ed. 1948). Bearing that rule in mind we submit that the complaint herein sets forth the elements of a prima facie tort, to wit, intentional infliction of damage without legal justification, for the appellees with full knowledge and intent and in reckless disregard of the consequences of their action are pursuing a course of conduct and are about to issue an opinion letter calculated in the ordinary course of events to damage appellants and have no legal justification for acting in such a reckless and wanton fashion.

The pleading alone of each of these elements of prima facie tort raised issues of fact which could not be decided on motion. In Miller v. Shell Oil Co., 161 F. Supp. 373 (N.D.N.Y. 1958), in denying summary judgment the Court said:

"The third claim, based upon inducement of breach of contract or 'prima facie tort' seems well-established in the law of New York if it can be proved factually, and has been recently pointed out again as settled law in the State. * * * The questions of excuse, justification, malice, wilfullness and intention to harm entail facts and circumstances, acts and statements of people, and should not be decided on depositions or affidavits. Colby v. Klune, supra, 178 F. 2d at page 874; Arnstein v. Porter, supra, 154 F. 2d at page 471.''

POINT III

APPELLANTS MADE OUT A CASE FOR
THE GRANTING OF A PRELIMINARY
INJUNCTION

That equitable relief included the granting of an injunction is a proper remedy in an action based upon the prima facie tort doctrine is made clear by the Advance Music, Opera on Tour and American Guild cases, supra.

We have already pointed out that nowhere in the affidavits submitted in opposition to appellants' motion for a preliminary injunction did the appellees deny either the authority and acceptance of their pronouncements or that the effect of the proposed opinion would be irreparably to harm appellants. The only effort made in this direction was the statement that the appellees' opinions were without "official" effect, and of course it is the conceded nature of the "effect" that is controlling whether it be official or non-official.

But in any event the reply affidavit of Donald C. Cook, a certified public accountant, a member of the Institute, a former Commissioner and Chairman of the Securities and Exchange Commission, a utilities analyst and a man experienced for over fifteen years in the accounting methods of utility companies is completely dispositive of appellees' contentions and clearly satisfies the burden of appellants on their motion for a preliminary injunction of showing facts in support of the allegations of the complaint and the threat of immediate and irreparable harm. That affidavit points out, among other things, the following:

(a) In accounting for the credits arising from normalization charges two alternate and at least equally generally accepted accounting methods have developed over the years, one of which was to place the credits in a restricted earned surplus account as the appellants have done, and that although there are arguments in favor of and against each of the alternatives, Mr. Cook's examination of the annual reports and statements of utility companies indicated that the recordation of such credits in restricted earned surplus accounts was not only a generally accepted accounting principle, but was accepted by a majority of the recognized public accounting firms having experience in the utility field.

(b) Mr. Cook had made specific inquiry of the Institute and the Committee as to its intention in using the words "a deferred tax account" in Accounting

Research Bulletin No. 44 (Revised), when he noticed that those words had been inserted, and had been informed that there was no intention to deal with the balance sheet treatment of credits arising from normalization charges and indeed that the Committee had decided to side step that question; that the quoted phrase had been inserted by the Research Staff of the Institute after the members of the Committee had voted so that they never had the chance to vote on the inclusion of that phrase; and that appellees Werntz and Blough had both specifically stated in their testimony in official proceedings before regulatory bodies that the Committee had not intended to specify any balance sheet treatment when promulgating Accounting Research Bulletin No. 44 (Revised). It is thus clear and undisputed on the record that the purported purpose for issuing the proposed letter is false in fact.

(c) Defendant Blough himself, again in testimony in an official proceeding before a regulatory body, had admitted that the opinions of the appellees are recognized as authoritative in the accounting profession and carry a great deal of weight in the business world, and that Mr. Cook knew from his experience with the Securities and Exchange Commission that the appellees' opinions are considered as clearly representing the correct and applicable accounting principles. The effect of appellees' pronouncements on accounting matters is thus clear.

(d) Mr. Cook also added to the allegations of the verified complaint as to the immediate and irreparable damage which will befall appellants upon the issuance of the proposed letter, by demonstrating that the immediate effect will be to impair appellants' credit to the extent of $6,500,000 and in the long run to increase appellants' capital charges by about $4,400,000 annually, as well as affecting the expansion of appellants' business and the rates charged the public.

This showing of immediate and irreparable harm clearly entitled appellants to a preliminary injunction by the Court below and we submit should move this Court in its discretion to grant such an injunction pending appeal. Even apart from the irreparable nature of the injuries, the amounts involved alone make clear that there is no adequate remedy at law, for the appellees would be unable to respond in damages even if such amounts could be precisely calculated. It has been held that when damages are so large in amount that a successful plaintiff would be unable to recover any judgment obtained, the remedy at law is inadequate. Mulford v. Smith, 307 U.S. 38, 46-47 (1939).

Upon application for preliminary injunctions this Court has consistently applied the doctrine of weighing the relative harms that will ensue to the parties from the grant or denial of the application. In Douds v. Milk Drivers and Dairy Employees Union Local 548, 154 F. Supp. 222, 234 (S.D.N.Y.), aff'd 248 F. 2d 534 (2d Cir. 1957), the lower Court had said:

"Even where grave and difficult questions of law are involved and where an answer might disclose disputed issues of fact, preliminary injunctions * * * will be granted where injury to the plaintiffs would be certain and irreparable if the application were denied, while granting of the application would not seriously damage and inconvenience defendants."

And in <u>Hamilton Watch Co</u>. v. <u>Benrus Watch Co</u>., 206 F. 2d 738 (2d Cir. 1953), this Court said:

"To justify a temporary injunction it is not necessary that the plaintiff's right to a final decision, after a trial, be absolutely certain, wholly without doubt; if the other elements are present (i.e., the balance of hardships tips decidedly toward plaintiff), it will ordinarily be enough that the plaintiff has raised questions going to the merits so serious, substantial, difficult and doubtful, as to make them a fair ground or litigation and thus for more deliberate investigation." (206 F. 2d 740).

* * *

"[A] preliminary injunction - as indicated by the numerous more or less synonymous adjectives used to label it - is, by its very nature, interlocutory, tentative, provisional, * * *. It serves as an equitable policing measure to prevent the parties from harming one another during the litigation; to keep the parties, while the suit goes on, as far as possible in the respective positions they occupied when the suit began." (206 F. 2d 742).

In that same opinion this Court quoted with approval from the <u>Restatement</u>, <u>Torts</u>, §941, comment f. as follows:

"The 'hardship plaintiff will suffer * * * may make interlocutory relief imperative where the same showing at a final hearing would not outweigh the hardship the defendant would suffer from a permanent injunction. Thus in view of the character and extent of the emergency presented, of the provisional and temporary character of the relief sought, of the probable period of its duration, and of the court's tentative opinion on the substantive issues involved, the factor of relative hardship is measured, on an application for interlocutory injunction, with a different yardstick from that used at final hearing.' " (206 F. 2d 743).

The irreparable nature of the harm which will befall appellants immediately upon the publication and distribution of the proposed letter makes imperative the issuance of the injunction pending appeal which is sought on this motion. The denial of such relief and the consequent publication and distribution of the proposed letter, moreover, would render moot the appeal from the denial of the injunction and frustrate the jurisdiction of this Court should it - as we submit it will - subsequently determine that the Court below erred. On the other hand, there is not even the possibility that appellees would be inconvenienced, much less damaged, by the granting of this relief and the maintaining of the status quo pending the review of the lower Court's decision, to which appellants are entitled as a matter of law.

CONCLUSION

An order should be entered herein restraining and enjoining the appellees, pending the determination of the appeal herein, from distributing the proposed letter or any similar statement.

Respectfully submitted,

SIMPSON THACHER & BARTLETT,
Attorneys for Appellants,
Office & Post Office Address,
120 Broadway,
New York 5, N. Y.
(June 3, 1959)

WHITNEY NORTH SEYMOUR
RICHARD M. DICKE
WILLIAM J. MANNING
        Of Counsel.

UNITED STATES COURT OF APPEALS
For the Second Circuit

Appalachian Power Company
Ohio Power Company and
Indiana & Michigan Electric Company

Appellants,

against

CIVIL ACTION NO. 145–161

American Institute of Certified Public
Accountants, L. H. Penney, William W.
Werntz and Carman G. Blough,

Appellees.

MEMORANDUM ON BEHALF OF APPELLEES
IN OPPOSITION TO APPELLANTS' MOTION FOR
INJUNCTION PENDING APPEAL

(JUNE 3, 1959)

Howard C. Westwood
Fontaine C. Bradley
Stanley L. Temko

Attorneys for Appellees

George C. Christie
Phil R. Stansbury

Of Counsel

Covington & Burling
Union Trust Building
Washington, D. C.

TABLE OF CONTENTS

TABLE OF AUTHORITIES

PAGE

MEMORANDUM ON BEHALF OF APPELLEES IN
OPPOSITION TO APPELLANTS' MOTION FOR
INJUNCTION PENDING APPEAL

QUESTION PRESENTED

Shall this Court enjoin the expression of an opinion to the members of a private voluntary organization of professional accountants by a committee of that organization on a question of the proper balance sheet treatment in corporate financial statements of charges to income on account of deferred income taxes, the injunction to be in force pending the determination of an appeal from a summary judgment dismissing a complaint by non-members of the organization in question which sought to require that the organization follow certain preliminary steps before its committee might express any such opinion?

STATEMENT OF THE CASE

The parties

The appellants, plaintiffs below, are three interrelated electric utility companies.

The appellees, defendants below, are the American Institute of Certified Public Accountants, and three of its officials. The Institute, an incorporated body, is a nonprofit, nation-wide membership organization, membership in which is open to all properly qualified certified public accountants, and the purpose of which is the furtherance of the ideals and principles of the accounting profession. It

— 2 —

is like bar associations, medical associations, and other professional associations which play such an important part in the professional life of the nation, and which are dependent upon the public spirit of their members who contribute extensively in their time and energy to the attainment of professional aims.

The three individual appellees are the President of the Institute (Mr. L.H. Penney), the Chairman of the Institute's Committee on Accounting Procedure (Mr. William W. Werntz), and a member of the Institute's relatively small paid staff, the Institute's Director of Research (Mr. Carman G. Blough).

The appellants are not members of the Institute. Membership is confined to individual accountants.

The relief sought by the complaint

The appellants' complaint seeks a judgment temporarily and permanently enjoining the appellees and anyone acting on their behalf from circulating "to the members of the Institute or to any members of the accountancy profession" a certain letter from the Institute's Committee on Accounting Procedure (hereinafter termed "Committee"), without first having taken certain preliminary procedural steps referred to below. (Complaint, pp. 12–13) The letter in question is as follows:

– 3 –

"AMERICAN INSTITUTE OF CERTIFIED PUBLIC ACCOUNTANTS
"270 Madison Avenue, New York 16, N.Y.

"April 15, 1959

"To the Members of the American Institute of Certified Public Accountants

"Gentlemen:

"Question has been raised with respect to the intent of the committee on accounting procedure in using the phrase 'a deferred tax account' in Accounting Research Bulletin No. 44 (revised), Declining-balance Depreciation, to indicate the account to be credited for the amount of the deferred income tax (see paragraph 4 and 5).

"The committee used the phrase in its ordinary connotation of an account to be shown in the balance sheet as a liability or a deferred credit. A provision in recognition of the deferral of income taxes, being required for the proper determination of net income, should not at the same time result in a credit to earned surplus or to any other account included in the stockholders' equity section of the balance sheet.

"Three of the twenty-one members of the committee, Messrs. Jennings, Powell and Staub, dissented to the issuance at this time of any letter interpreting Accounting Research Bulletin No. 44 (revised).

"COMMITTEE ON ACCOUNTING PROCEDURE
"By William W. Werntz, Chairman"

The complaint also seeks to enjoin the appellees and anyone acting on their behalf

"from adopting, issuing, promulgating, circulating, printing or in any manner publishing to the members of the Institute or to any members of the accountancy profession . . . any utterance, opinion, recommendation, promulgation or statement to

– 4 –

the effect that the Institute or the Committee is of the opinion or recommends that charges made to income in recognition of the deferral of income taxes should not or may not in accordance with generally accepted accounting principles be credited to earned surplus or to any other account included in the stockholders' equity section of the balance sheet, until such time as the Institute and the Committee . . . "

have first taken the procedural steps referred to. (Complaint, pp. 12–13).

The preliminary procedural steps which the appellants thus seek to have the Court require the appellees to follow are that the Institute and Committee must have

"(a) Submitted a draft of the proposed letter to the persons to whom the exposure draft of Accounting Research Bulletin No. 44 was submitted.

"(b) Permitted such reasonable period of time, not less than 60 days, to have elapsed subsequent to said submission in order that such persons may have the opportunity of submitting for the consideration of the Committee their views and opinions.

"(c) Otherwise complied with the Institute's and the Committee's practices and procedures with respect to the publication of Accounting Research Bulletins."

The complaint likewise seeks "such other, further and different relief" as may seem just and proper.

The proceedings below

The opinion letter in question was about to be sent by the Committee to the Institute's members when, without notice, the appellants secured a temporary restraining order

– 5 –

on April 15, 1959, from Judge Palmieri of the District Court, and an order to show cause why a preliminary injunction should not be issued, returnable on April 17. For the convenience of counsel for both sides, the return date was postponed to May 7, at which time there were brought on for hearing before Judge Levet the appellants' motion for preliminary injunction and the appellees' motion to dismiss for failure to state a claim. Affidavits were filed by both sides together with extensive briefs, and the case was argued orally. In view of the submission of matters beyond the pleadings the Court, acting under Rule 12(b) of the Federal Rules of Civil Procedure, treated the motion to dismiss as a motion for summary judgment.

On May 20 Judge Levet filed a full opinion holding that summary judgment should be granted for the appellees and that the motion for preliminary injunction should be denied. An order to that effect was entered on May 25. On the same date the appellants requested Judge Levet to issue an injunction pending disposition of their appeal. The Judge refused to grant such an injunction, continuing restraint only until the hearing of appellants' motion to this Court for an injunction pending their appeal, provided such a motion were made on or before June 1. The appellants immediately perfected their appeal.

Judge Levet's opinion is reproduced in an Appendix to this Memorandum. (Omitted here as it has already been reproduced herein.)

– 6 –

The jurisdiction of the lower court and the
theory of the alleged cause of action.

The appellants are citizens of Virginia, Ohio, and Indiana, respectively. The appellees are citizens of different states. Jurisdiction is based on diversity and an alleged amount in controversy exceeding the statutory minimum. (Complaint, paragraphs 1–5, 7.)

The theory of the appellants' complaint, as explained in their written and oral argument below, is that the issuance of the letter or of a similar statement of opinion would be a tort under the so-called doctrine of prima facie tort as that doctrine is applied by New York state courts, in that it would result in financial injury to the appellants and that the appellees know that it would result in such injury and therefore "intend" such injury. The injury, it is alleged, would be irreparable; the alleged irreparability of the injury is supported by an affidavit of Mr. Donald C. Cook, a vice president of each of the appellants, stating that the appellees would be financially unable to satisfy a claim for damages sufficient to compensate the appellants for the damage which they allegedly would suffer from the issuance of the letter, even if the amount of damage "could be precisely calculated." (Affidavit of Mr. Cook, paragraph 29; see also paragraph 23.)

– 7 –

The facts

The Institute has some 33,000 members. Like other similar professional organizations, it functions to a large extent through committees of its membership. There is also a "Council" (the governing board), a relatively small paid headquarters staff, and the usual elected officers.

One of the Institute's committees is the Committee on Accounting Procedure. That Committee from time to time issues, to the members of the Institute, Accounting Research Bulletins, which are in printed form and which set forth the Committee's opinions as to what is required by sound accounting principles on various matters arising in the work of certified public accountants, notably the proper treatment of items in corporate financial statements. (Complaint, paragraph 13.)

These Bulletins make clear that they represent only the opinions of the Committee, unless they have been specifically adopted by the Institute's membership. (Affidavit of Mr. William W. Werntz, paragraph 6.)

The Committee is composed of 21 members of the Institute, one of whom is chairman. For an opinion to be adopted it must receive the favorable vote of two-thirds of the members of the Committee. Dissenters are privileged to have their dissents, and reason therefor if they desire, included with the opinions. (Affidavit of Mr. Werntz, paragraph 11, and Exhibit A, pp. 8–9.)

– 8 –

Except for the requirement that the Committee act by two-thirds vote, with the privilege of expression of dissent, and that, unless adopted by the Institute, the Bulletins reflect only the Committee's own opinion, the Committee's discretion determines its procedure. (Affidavit of Mr. Werntz.)

The Director of Research and others on the Institute's headquarters staff assist the Committee in its work.

Often the Committee will circulate a draft of a proposed Bulletin to persons both within and without the Institute's membership to get the benefit of their comments. This process is known as "exposure." (Affidavit of Mr. Werntz, paragraph 8.)

The draft finally proposed for adoption by the Committee is sent to each Committee member with a ballot for his vote. After a vote, the Institute's staff, with the approval of the Chairman of the Committee, may make non-substantive alterations in the "ballot" draft after the vote and before issuance of the Bulletin. (Affidavit of Mr. Werntz, paragraph 9.)

Neither by any law nor under the Institute's own regime do the statements of the Committee have any effectiveness or force save as expressions of opinion by the Committee. (Affidavit of Mr. Werntz, paragraph 6, and Exhibit A, p. 9.)

It is a fact, however, that in the accountancy profession the Committee's opinions are given great weight by

– 9 –

virtue of the professional prestige of the Committee and of the members of the Committee. In the selection of the Committee's members an effort is made to enlist the services of professional men of high standing and conscientiousness.

By virtue of the accelerated amortization provision of section 168 and of the liberalized depreciation provision of section 167 of the Internal Revenue Code, taxpayers, for federal income tax purposes, are permitted in certain circumstances to write off assets (i.e. to take a deduction from income for income tax purposes) at a rate faster than would be permitted under normal rates of depreciation. These are relatively recent tax provisions and as experience with them has been accumulated certified public accountants have become increasingly concerned with problems respecting corporate financial statements arising when such fast write-offs are adopted for tax purposes but when, for other purposes, normal rates of depreciation are retained. The problems stem largely from the fact that, theoretically at least, fast write-offs will diminish taxes payable in earlier years but increase taxes payable in later years--in effect "deferring" from earlier to later years the payment of a portion of "normal" taxes.

State and federal government agencies having regulatory powers with respect to various accounting matters as well as with other matters such as the fixing of reasonable

– 10 –

rates to be charged consumers of goods or services have also become concerned with various problems stemming from the same phenomenon.

In November 1952 the Committee issued its Bulletin No. 42 dealing with the matter of accelerated amortization. This Bulletin, as originally issued, appears as Exhibit E to the affidavit of Mr. Werntz. This Bulletin without changes now appears in codified form as Chapter 9, Section c, of Accounting Research Bulletin No. 43, which appears as Exhibit A to the affidavit of Mr. Werntz. Paragraph 12 of that Section (see p. 78 of the Bulletin) opens with the statement:

> "In accounting for this deferment of income taxes, the committee believes it desirable to treat the charge as being for additiohal income taxes. The related credit in such cases would properly be made to an account for deferred income taxes." (Emphasis added.)

In July 1958 the Committee issued a revision of another of its bulletins, Bulletin No. 44. (The original Bulletin No. 44 had not been "exposed" but the revision was "exposed." [Affidavit of Mr. Werntz, paragraph 8.]) The revision was designed to deal with the matter of liberalized depreciation--generally along the same lines as the treatment of the accelerated amortization matter in the previous Bulletin No. 42 just referred to. As issued, this Bulletin No. 44 (revised) appears as Exhibit B to Mr. Werntz's affidavit. Neither the "exposure" nor the "ballot" draft of this Bulletin, although stating that "recognition should be given to deferred income taxes if the amounts thereof are material" (see second sentence of paragraph 4 of the Bulletin), made any reference to crediting a deferred tax account such as appeared in the underlined portion of the above quotation from the previous Bulletin No. 42 on the related problem. (Affidavit of Mr. Werntz, paragraph 9.)

Accordingly, with the approval of the Chairman of the Committee, the Institute's staff inserted in the final draft, after the vote, a reference to "crediting a deferred tax account"--that phrase appears in paragraph 5 of Bulletin No. 44 (revised). The insertion was made in the interest of consistency of expression as between the two Bulletins and was not deemed to be a substantive change. Advance copies of the Bulletin were sent to the members of the Committee, with the staff's revision, and no member of the Committee objected. (Affidavit of Mr. Werntz, paragraphs 9 and 10.)

It will be observed that neither of these Bulletins specifically stated where the "deferred tax account" should appear in the balance sheet.

Just prior to the issuance of Bulletin No. 44(revised) the Federal Power Commission had promulgated an order applicable to utilities under its jurisdiction which forbade the inclusion of such a deferred tax account in the stockholders' equity section of a balance sheet, as restricted surplus or otherwise, stating that

"it is evident that classification of tax deferrals as surplus, even though restricted, tends to disregard their essential character as provisions from income committed to the single purpose of providing for future taxes. . . . [W] hat is called for, in our judgment, is a separate balance sheet classification for accumulated deferred taxes. This will assure clear disclosure of this important item and lessen the possibilities of misunderstanding and misinterpretation of the nature and purposes of accumulated tax deferrals." 23 Federal Register, p. 4161 (June 12, 1958). *]

In December 1958, some five months after issuance of Bulletin No. 44 (revised), the Securities and Exchange Commission issued a "Notice of Intention to Announce Interpretation of Administrative Policy", which, like the Federal Power Commission regulation, would forbid inclusion of the deferred tax account in the stockholders' equity section of a balance sheet on the ground that such treatment would be deceptive to investors. (The SEC proposal appears as Exhibit T to the affidavit of Mr. George C. Christie.)

A public hearing was held by the SEC on its proposal during April 1959.

---

*   The Commission stated that even if a State regulatory commission should require restricted surplus treatment for its own purposes, the utility involved must nevertheless use the treatment specified by this order for the purposes of the Federal Power Commission. 23 Fed. Reg. 4162 (1958).

– 13 –

Shortly prior thereto the Committee's interpretive letter which has led to the present suit was drafted. The draft of the letter was sent to the Committee members and was voted on. No "exposure" procedure was followed. The Committee members approved the letter, and its circulation to the members of the Institute, by a vote of 18 to 3. Of the 18 members favorably voting, 16 had been members of the Committee when Bulletin No. 44 (revised) was issued a few months before during the previous year. They constitute more than two-thirds of the members of the Committee in office at that time. (Affidavit of Mr. Werntz, paragraph 11.)

On April 8, 1959, the appellee Mr. Blough, as the Institute's Director of Research, appeared as a witness at the SEC's rule-making hearing--a public hearing of which a transcript is available to any member of the public--and testified, among other things, that the Institute's Committee had adopted and was about to send out the letter in question, and read into the record the significant portion of the letter. (See affidavits of Mr. Robert O. Whitman, paragraph 6; and of Mr. Cook, paragraph 18.)

Thereupon this suit was filed and at the same time the restraining order was issued without notice.

It would appear from the affidavit of Mr. Cook that he and his companies are opposing, before the SEC, the adoption of the SEC's proposed statement.

– 14 –

It also appears from Mr. Cook's affidavit (paragraph 28(d)(8)) and from Mr. Werntz's affidavit (paragraph 12(2)) that Indiana & Michigan Electric Company, one of the appellants, has been ordered by the Indiana State Public Service Commission to eliminate from the stockholders' equity section of its balance sheet its account for deferred taxes and has appealed that order to the Indiana courts.

The alleged damage to the appellants

The appellants' complaint and affidavits allege that if the letter is issued the appellants will be injured as follows:

Each of the companies carries in its balance sheet large sums (totaling for the three $65,000,000) in an account for deferred federal income taxes which account appears in a restricted surplus account in the stockholders' equity section of the balance sheet.

It is said that if the letter is distributed then because of the "prestige and authority of the Committee" it will "cause substantial numbers of accountants, financial institutions, investment banking concerns, rating services, financial analysts and governmental agencies to question the continued inclusion of credits for deferred taxes in the earned surplus accounts" of appellants so that appellants "will be seriously interfered with in their dealings and relationships with such persons and institutions." (Complaint, paragraph 29; affidavit of Mr. Cook, paragraph 21.)

– 15 –

As we have noted, supra, p. 6, it is also alleged that the appellees would not be financially able to pay amounts sufficient to meet the damages that the appellants might thus suffer, so that equity should enjoin the letter unless the Committee first follows the procedures which the appellants ask and which are specified supra at p. 4.

The alleged intent to injure appellants

The complaint alleges that:

"30. The Institute and the Committee know that the foregoing [damage] will result . . . and intend that such . . . injury . . . shall occur. . . . The actions of the defendants . . . are in wanton, reckless and wilful disregard of the said consequences of their proposed action."

The only basis for the allegation that the Institute and the Committee know of the alleged injury to the appellants and "intend" that it shall occur appears in the affidavit of Mr. Whitman, at paragraph 6, wherein it is stated that just before the execution of that affidavit representatives of the appellants met with the Committee Chairman and with the Director of Research but were unable to secure a commitment "to delay the distribution" of the opinion letter.

There is neither allegation nor suggestion that the opinion letter was aimed at the appellants or that it was intended to deal with the appellants except as the appellants, like all other corporations issuing financial statements, might come within the general purview of the letter.

– 16 –

ARGUMENT

The appellants rely on the doctrine of "prima facie tort."

The lower Court's opinion states:

"This court has been unable to find any precedent under the doctrine of prima facie tort or otherwise for a preliminary or final injunction forbidding a group from publishing and distributing opinions under circumstances equivalent or even similar to these."

This statement was made by the Court although distinguished counsel for the appellants had submitted an exhaustive legal memorandum of 31 pages, and a further memorandum of 5 pages in reply to the appellees' memorandum, although counsel had fully argued his cause, and although the Court itself, as its elaborate opinion makes clear, had carefully and independently researched the cases.

Both authority and reason point to the entirely insubstantial nature of the appellants' claim.

I

We agree that New York law applies. But, as Mr. Justice Botein has said so aptly of the prima facie tort doctrine, a cause of action "must be judged by its allegations, not its label." Knapp Engraving Co. v. Keystone Photo Engraving Corp., 1 A.D. 2d 170, 172, 148 N.Y.S. 2d 635, 637 (1st Dept. 1956). Prima facie tort does not make

— 17 —

actionable every conscious or deliberate act or utterance which has consequences damaging to someone. At most the doctrine makes actionable damaging conduct--otherwise lawful--

> "when the intention to harm, as distinguished from the intention merely to commit the act, is present, has motivated the action, and has caused the injury to plaintiff, all without excuse or justification." See Mr. Justice Breitel in Ruza v. Ruza, 286 App. Div. 767, 769, 146 N.Y.S. 2d 808, 811 (1st Dept. 1955).

Thorough combing of precedents has led the appellants to pitch their case on the decision of the New York Court of Appeals in Advance Music Corp. v. American Tobacco Co., 296 N.Y. 79, 70 N.E. 2d 401 (1946).

As the Court below made clear, that case is wide of the mark.

There the Court of Appeals reversed a decision dismissing a complaint brought by a publisher of popular songs against the sponsor, and its advertising agent, of a radio program known as "Your Hit Parade." The complaint alleged that the program falsely represented to its large audience that it had ascertained, on the basis of volume of sales, the nine or ten most popular songs each week, and the order of their sales popularity; that in fact no such ascertainment was made at all; that the plaintiff's songs were consistently excluded from the hits, without justification, or were given an unjustifiably low ranking; that this was done with

— 18 —

intent to injure the plaintiff; and that the plaintiff had, indeed, been injured by a refusal of jobbers and others to distribute plaintiff's songs to dealers because of their omission or low ranking on "Your Hit Parade."

The Advance Music case was thus a perfectly clear case of wanton misrepresentation of fact, and came very close to a case of common law unfair competition. The present case is completely different. As pointed out in the opinion
of the District Court, the proposed letter of the Committee on Accounting Procedure is simply an expression of opinion on a general accounting question. Moreover, it is not alleged that the opinion is not honestly held by the members of
the Committee who voted to issue the letter. In fact, as found by the lower Court,
the Committee's view is supported by most respectable authority. *

- 19 -

The Advance Music case relied for support primarily upon Aikens v. Wisconsin, 195 U.S. 194 (1904), a case in which Mr. Justice Holmes held that "maliciously injuring"-- the basis for prima facie tort--means "doing a harm malevolently for the sake of the harm as an end in itself, and not merely as a means
to another end legitimately desired." (195 U.S. at 203). The New York Court
of Appeals itself has taken the same position in the recent decision of Reinforce, Inc. v. Birney, 308 N.Y. 164, 124 N.E. 2d 104 (1954):

> "If the doers, by means not in themselves unlawful, of acts not in
> themselves unlawful, have any proper purpose to serve, they are not liable
> for the damage they cause [citing cases]. Unions, as well as everyone
> else, may claim the benefit of the settled rule that 'the genesis which will
> make a lawful act unlawful must be a malicious one unmixed with any other
> and exclusively directed to injury and damage of another' [citing cases]."
> 308 N.Y. at_____, 124 N.E. 2d at 106.

In the present case there is no semblance of an allegation that the Committee has reached its view of the proper treatment of deferred income taxes, of

---

* The Committee's position is followed by Arthur Andersen & Co., which audits the accounts of one-third of the electric and gas utility companies in the country; based on a
survey of the 1957 published stockholders reports of 353 utilities, of 226 reporting an accumulated credit resulting from the use of liberalized depreciation under Section 167 of the
Internal Revenue Code, 176 treated the credit outside the equity-capital section of the
balance sheet and only 50 companies treated the credit as either earned surplus or restricted surplus. (Affidavit of Mr. F. Merrill Beatty, passim). Also, the Public Service
Commission of the State of Indiana has ordered all companies subject to its regulations,
including plaintiff Indiana & Michigan Electric Company, to cease treating the credit for
deferred income taxes as a surplus account; the Federal Power Commission issued on May
29, 1958, an order that all public utility companies subject to its regulation shall not include credit for deferred income taxes in a surplus account. (Affidavit of Mr. William W.
Werntz, paragraph 12). The SEC has promulgated a proposed policy in accord with the
Committee's views and many public utility and other companies have endorsed the SEC
proposal. (Affidavit of Mr. George C. Christie, passim).

universal application in the business world, with the aim of effecting injury to the plaintiffs.*

– 20 –

II

Apart from the question of intent to injure, the plaintiff in a prima facie tort case can get no relief where there is "justification" for the defendant's act, as was recognized by the court in the Advance Music case. (296 N.Y. at_____, 70 N.E. 2d at 403). In the present case the District Court said, "The purposes of the defendant Institute are adequate justification, if justification, indeed, be required, to permit the proposed communications." As is said in Prosser, Torts § 106 (2d ed. 1955), at page 720, "In general, any disinterested motive of a socially desirable kind will serve as a justification." That the proposed letter is an expression of opinion on a matter of great public concern is conclusively shown by the current interest taken in this matter by the Securities and Exchange Commission and the Federal Power Commission. It is difficult to conceive of a matter on which it would be more appropriate for a committee of accountants to express their professional opinion.

– 21 –

III

Particularly when a plaintiff requests drastic equitable relief, a court will not recognize merely speculative or incidental injury.

The appellants do not claim that anything forces accountants to agree with the position taken by the Committee on Accounting Procedure; Mr. Donald C. Cook, or other officers of the appellants, are free to persuade accountants who review appellants' books that the Committee is wrong. When the Federal Power Commission adopted a rule along the lines of the Committee's opinion it made the point that exclusion of provision for deferred taxes from surplus accounts

---

* Appellants have also invoked a case in which defendant made a false statement of fact concerning plaintiff in a credit rating of the plaintiff, U.S. Aluminum Siding Corp. v. Dun & Bradstreet, Inc., 163 F. Supp. 906 (S.D.N.Y. 1958), and two labor cases in which the New York Court of Appeals, found, respectively, that persuading members not to work for plaintiff employer or with members of a rival plaintiff organization were not justified by a lawful labor objective. Opera on Tour, Inc. v. Weber, 285 N.Y. 348, 34 N.E. 2d 349 (1941); American Guild of Musical Artists, Inc. v. Petrillo, 286 N.Y. 226, 36 N.E. 2d 123 (1941). For out-of-state support, appellants rely primarily on Mr. Justice Holmes' opinion in American Bank & Trust Co. v. Federal Reserve Bank, 256 U.S. 350, 358 (1921), in which defendant Federal Reserve Bank, motivated by "disinterested malevolence," was pursuing a course of action which, in effect, amounted to a run on plaintiff banks. We need not elaborate upon the point that all these cases, involving words and action specifically aimed solely at the plaintiffs concerned, have nothing to do with the present case.

190

"will not foreclose financial analysts, investors and others from considering these amounts as part of equity capital if they think proper, with such consequential benefits to the rating of the company's securities and costs of financing as may result therefrom." 23 Federal Register, page 4161 (June 12, 1958).

Mr. Cook has already argued to the Securities and Exchange Commission concerning the matter; in the future he may or may not be able to persuade that Commission, and other regulatory bodies, that the Committee's view is ill-considered. If he fails he cannot complain that the appellees' acts are the legal cause of appellants' difficulties. The New York Court of Appeals has very recently ruled out any such complaint

– 22 –

in a case far more appealing than the appellants'. Brandt v. Winchell, 3 N.Y. 2d 628, 148 N.E. 2d 160 (1958).*

IV

A special reason why a court of equity should not grant relief in this case is that the court is being asked to interfere with the internal procedure of a private, voluntary, professional organization at the behest of persons who are not even members of that association.

The District Court found, "There is no adequate proof (even if the plaintiffs had any right to insist on the Committee procedures they mention) that the Institute's rules have been or are about to be violated. In fact, the contrary appears."

The fact of the matter is that when the appellees pointed out, in their motion to dismiss, that the appellants had not alleged that the Committee was violating the rules of the Institute the appellants replied in their legal memorandum to the District Court that, "The power or lack of power to commit the acts complained of is an irrelevant consideration." (See Plaintiffs' Memorandum in Support of Application for Preliminary Injunction and in Opposition to Motion to Dismiss

– 23 –

Complaint filed with the District Court, at page 19.) In other words, the appellants are attempting to persuade the courts to determine how a committee of a private association should run its affairs. This the courts will not do: the cases

---

* In that case the Court assumed that defendant acted with an "evil motive." (3 N.Y. 2d at_____ , 148 N.E. 2d at 164).

to that effect are legion.* Even where a bar association admittedly had failed to follow its own organic law, and even at the suit of a member, a Court of Appeals would not entertain an effort to have it supervise the association's procedures, because--

> "It is idle to expect that voluntary public or community service, not involving the administration of property or money, will ever be carried on with the meticulous observance of charters and by-laws required in the administration of property or money. The interest that holds community service organizations together is not property but the unselfish spirit of those willing to sacrifice their time and energy to a public cause. That interest would not be protected but destroyed by strict judicial supervision of elections in such agencies on complaint of their members. The court would find itself a constant intermeddler in community affairs serving no purpose other than to disrupt the morale and good will of voluntary organizations. To make community service as technical as business dealings would be to destroy the spirit which sustains it." United States ex rel. Noel v. Carmody, 80 App. D.C. 58, 60, 148 F. 2d 684, 686 (1945); and see Chafee, The Internal Affairs of Associations Not for Profit, 43 Harv. L. Rev. 993, 1027 (1930).

– 24 –

Not only do appellants ask the Court to prescribe what procedures this professional organization shall follow, but a grant of their request would dictate how the opinions of such an organization on matters of public interest should be formulated. A strong reason why appellants should not be granted an injunction pending this appeal is that injunctive relief under these circumstances would violate the Federal and State constitutional guarantees of free expression.

In the leading case of Marlin Firearms Co. v. Shields, 171 N.Y. 384, 64 N.E. 163 (1902), which involved an attempt to enjoin disparagement, by clearly false statements, of the quality and safety of guns manufactured by the plaintiff, the New York Court of Appeals sustained a demurrer to the complaint on the ground that the relief requested would be a prior restraint in violation of the freedom of speech provisions of the New York Constitution. Marlin was a far more persuasive case for injunctive relief than the present one in that there defendant's statements did not concern all enterprises, or even all gun-makers, but were specifically directed at the plaintiff and its products and were deliberately untrue and spiteful fabrications. Nevertheless, the Marlin case states the law not only in New York but in the vast majority of other jurisdictions. See Annotation, Injunction as Remedy in Case of Trade Libel, 148 A.L.R. 854 (1944).

---

* E.g., Weinstock v. Ladisky, 197 Misc. 859, 98 N.Y.S. 2d 85, 101 (Sup. Ct. 1950); McNulty v. Higginbotham, 40 So. 2d 414 (Ala. 1944); State ex rel. Smith v. Kanawha County, 78 W. Va. 168, 88 S.E. 662, 664, 20 A.L.R. 1030, 1033 (1916); 4 Am. Jur., Associations & Clubs, §6.

25

Appellants relied, below, on Chief Judge Cardozo's opinion in Nann v. Raimist, 255 N.Y. 307, 174 N.E. 690(1930), to belittle the authority of the Marlin case. The Nann case involved a dispute between two competing unions. The Court of Appeals approved an injunction against defendant's picketing, because of a history of violence in connection with previous picketing, but expressly refused to enjoin the defendants' distribution of circulars and handbills which specifically attached the plaintiff union. In explaining this refusal the eminent Chief Judge said: "Equity does not intervene to restrain the publication of words on a mere showing of their falsity."--citing the Marlin case. (255 N.Y. at_____ , 174 N.E. at 694). He went on to explain that equity will act only where essential to preserve a property interest--

"threatened with impairment by illegal combinations or by other tortious acts, the publication of words being merely an instrument and incident. . . . Courts have enough to do in restraining physical disorder without busying themselves with logomachies in which the embattled words are the expression of the opinion of the writer or speaker. If there is redress for such a wrong, unassociated with wrongful acts, the remedy is not in equity." Ibid. "What is wrong must be so clearly wrong that only 'disinterested malevolence' (American Bank & Trust Co. v. Federal Reserve Bank of Atlanta, 256 U.S. 350, 358, 41 S. Ct. 499, 500, 65 L. Ed. 983), or something close akin thereto, can have supplied the motive power (Steinert & Sons Co. v. Tagen, 207 Mass. 394, 397, 93 N.E. 584, 32 L.R.A. (N.S.) 1013). If less than this appears, a court of equity will stand aside." (255 N.Y. at_____ , 174 N.E. at 695.)

26

The appellants have also suggested that the Marlin case was overruled sub silentio by the Advance Music case, where the New York Court of Appeals sustained a cause of action based upon false representations over the radio. The appellants invoke the court's statement in that case that the complaint disclosed "a case for relief either at law or in equity." 296 N.Y. at_____ , 70 N.E. 2d at 403. But the very sentence containing that statement referred to the second cause of action in the complaint, and that cause of action was one only for damages. See the opinion of the Appellate Division, 268 App. Div. 707,_____ , 53 N.Y.S. 2d 337, 339-40 (1st Dept. 1945). And in the sentence preceding the one quoted, the Court of Appeals had said that it was not deciding "anything in respect of the nature of the judgment to which the plaintiff may be entitled." In short, the court decided only the abstract proposition that a cause of action had been alleged--not that a case for equitable relief had been stated. And in at least two authoritative decisions since the Advance Music case the Marlin case is recognized as still stating the law of New York. Donnelly v. United Fruit Co.,

4 App. Div. 2d 855, 166 N.Y.S. 2d 392 (1st Dept. 1957); Everharp, Inc. v. Pal Blade Co., 182 F. 2d 779, 781 (2d Cir. 1950).*

– 27 –
V

This Court has repeatedly held that a party requesting a stay pending appeal, or any preliminary injunctive relief, has the burden of showing that he is likely to prevail on the merits. See, e.g., Eastern Air Lines v. Civil Aeronautics Board, 261 F. 2d 830 (2d Cir. 1958); Hall Signal Co. v. General Ry. Signal Co., 153 Fed. 907, 908 (2d Cir. 1907). The appellants fail to meet any such condition. As the District Court stated, there is no "precedent under the doctrine of prima facie tort or otherwise for a preliminary or final injunction forbidding a group from publishing and distributing opinions under circumstances equivalent or even similar to these." Supra, p. 16.

Appellants claim that, without an injunction, their appeal will become moot insofar as injunctive relief is concerned. This is not so. The appellants pray for an injunction not only against the circulation of the Committee's opinion letter to the members of the Institute but also

– 28 –

against any adoption by the Institute of the Committee's letter or of any other opinion to the same effect. See supra, pp. 3 – 4; Complaint, pp. 12–13.

Therefore the sending of the Committee's letter does not eliminate the controversy which the appellants have posed. And even if no further action were ever to be threatened by the Committee or the Institute, the appellants would still have their argument for a declaratory judgment that the appellees' acts in the promulgation of their opinion were tortious. In addition to injunctive relief the complaint seeks "such other, further and different relief" as may seem just and proper; and declaratory relief may be granted regardless of whether such has been specifically requested in the complaint. See Rule 54 (c), F.R.C.P.; Becker v. Buder, 88 F. Supp. 609, 611 (E.D.Mo. 1949), affirmed, 185 F. 2d 311 (8th Cir. 1950), cf., Truth Seeker Co., Inc. v. Durning, 147 F. 2d 54 (2d Cir. 1945); Carmichael v. Mills Music, Inc., 121 F. Supp. 43 (S.D.N.Y. 1954). Indeed, as a practical matter, such a declaration would have virtually the same value to the ap-

---

* Equity's refusal to interfere with the expression of opinion is emphasized by a recent decision of the Supreme Court of Massachusetts in Krebiozen Research Foundation v. Beacon Press, Inc. 334 Mass. 86, 134 N.E. 2d 1, cert. denied, 352 U.S. 848 (1956). Although Massachusetts has been readier than any other American jurisdiction to enjoin trade libels, the Krebiozen case held that allegedly false statements concerning a drug for use in cancer treatment would not be enjoined, though severely damaging to plaintiff physicians and a cancer foundation, because equity should not attempt to determine what shall and shall not be said on matters of public concern.

pellants as the injunction they seek -- in that it could be used to effective purposes in connection with any questions that might be raised by accountants, financial institutions, or otherwise with respect to the appellants' balance sheets
or even in connection with the position the appellants have taken at the SEC.
Also, either under

– 29 –

a declaratory judgment or otherwise, a court still could grant damages in this lawsuit even after events had made the granting of injunctive relief nugatory. Subin
v. Goldsmith, 224 F. 2d 753, 761–62 (2d Cir.), cert. denied, 350 U.S. 883 (1955).*

But even if mootness were threatened, an injunction is not issuable as of
right. In Jimenez v. Barber, 252 F. 2d 550 (9th Cir.), application for stay of deportation denied, 355 U.S. 943 (1958), an injunction against a deportation order,
pending an appeal, was sought; absent the injunction the case obviously would be
mooted for the appellant would be physically deported from the country. But the
court refused to enjoin because of the lack of merit in the appellant's case.

Here, it is submitted, the appellants' case is wholly devoid of merit. Nowhere in the books is there the slightest basis for the contention that a court of
equity should or can impose a gag upon a committee of professional men as to
their opinion on a matter of obvious public concern. That the gag is to be imposed as an incident to

– 30 –

prescribing for a private, voluntary association a course of procedure as to how
its committee is to arrive at an opinion makes it all the more unprecedented and
obnoxious to elementary conceptions of chancery jurisdiction.

Finally, as the affidavit of Mr. John L. Carey, Executive Director of the
Institute, filed by the appellees with this Court shows, the Committee is to go
out of existence as of September 1, 1959, as a result of the adoption by the Institute of a new program which has long been under study. The Institute, understandably, proposes that the Committee wind up its affairs before the new program
goes into effect. An injunction pending appeal would be an obvious impediment
to the completion of this transition and could even lead to such confusion and delay in the Institute's processes as to accomplish the appellants' aim without ever
being brought to a final determination on the appeal.

---

* "It is suggested that, as apparently the transfer of . . . assets . . . was
completed after denial of the preliminary injunction, a final injunction will serve no
purpose, and therefore plaintiff, if he wins, can obtain no relief. . . . The complaint asks 'for such other and further relief as may be just and proper.' Accordingly, the court can award damages if they will afford adequate relief. See F.R.C.P. 54
(c)." 224 F.2d at 761–62.

Issuance of the injunction would create the spectacle of the SEC's having been advised of the Committee's opinion in a public hearing but the Institute's own members being deprived of that same knowledge unless they happen to read the advance sheets reporting the lower Court's opinion in which the letter is quoted in full. It is unthinkable that equity should create any such state of affairs.

— 31 —

CONCLUSION

The injunction should be denied. Indeed, on its own motion, this Court should dismiss the appeal as insubstantial as did the court in Jimenez v. Barber (252 F. 2d at 554).

Respectfully submitted,

HOWARD C. WESTWOOD
FONTAINE C. BRADLEY
STANLEY L. TEMKO

Attorneys for Appellees

GEORGE C. CHRISTIE
PHIL R. STANSBURY

(June 3, 1959)

Of Counsel

UNITED STATES COURT OF APPEALS
For the Second Circuit

Appalachian Power Company,
Ohio Power Company and
Indiana & Michigan Electric Company,

Appellants,

against

American Institute of Certified Public
Accountants, L. H. Penney, William W.
Werntz and Carman G. Blough,

Appellees.

APPELLANTS' REPLY MEMORANDUM
IN SUPPORT OF MOTION FOR AN
INJUNCTION PENDING AN APPEAL

(June 3, 1959)

SIMPSON THACHER & BARTLETT,
Attorneys for Appellants,
Office & Post Office Address,
120 Broadway,
New York 5, N.Y.

WHITNEY NORTH SEYMOUR
RICHARD M. DICKE
WILLIAM J. MANNING
Of Counsel.

UNITED STATES COURT OF APPEALS
For the Second Circuit

Appalachian Power Company,
Ohio Power Company and
Indiana & Michigan Electric Company,

Appellants,

against

American Institute of Certified Public
Accountants, L. H. Penney, William W.
Werntz and Carman G. Blough,

Appellees.

APPELLANTS' REPLY MEMORANDUM
IN SUPPORT OF MOTION FOR AN
INJUNCTION PENDING AN APPEAL

Statement

Appellees' memorandum in opposition to this motion is eloquent in its silence with respect to the false statement set forth in the proposed letter as to the purported purpose for its issuance. It is profound in its failure to point to any justification for the issuance of the proposed letter under the circumstances or in any way to point to any steps taken by the appellees to insure the propriety and correctness of the opinion set forth in the proposed letter. For example, no effort is made therein to explain how appellee Werntz, the chairman of the Committee, could testify under oath in an official proceeding that the Committee had not intended to designate the correct balance sheet treatment of credits arising from normalization charges in issuing Accounting Research Bulletin No. 44 (Revised) and a short time later in the proposed letter state to the members of the Institute that the Committee had a specific intent. And it may be searched in vain for any hint of harm to appellees from the issuance of the injunction sought herein.

We therefore would not burden this Court with a further memorandum but for the necessity of answering the contentions made with respect to interference with internal affairs and freedom of speech.

The Issue of Interference
With the Internal Affairs
of the Appellees

Appellants stand upon the statement made in their brief below and quoted by appellants that the power or lack of power of the appellees to commit the acts complained of is an irrelevant consideration. The doctrine of noninterference by courts with the internal affairs of corporations generally or the affairs of any other private organization is a doctrine of corporate law and has no application in the field of tort. It simply could not be the law that a corporation or other organization is immune from liability for its tortious conduct merely because its own private rules and regulations do not prohibit it from committing the acts complained of by another. Just such an objection was put to one side by Mr. Justice Holmes in American Bank & Trust Company v. Federal Reserve Bank, 256 U.S. 350 (1921) where, in reversing the dismissal of an action to enjoin tortious conduct by the defendant bank, the Court wrote:

"We lay on one side as not necessary to our decision the question of the defendants' powers, and assuming that they act within them consider only whether the use that according to the bill they intend to make of them will infringe the plaintiffs' rights." (256 U.S. at p. 357).

Appellees' entire argument in this regard fails, moreover, for it is based upon a misconception or misstatement of the relief sought by appellants in this action. Appellants do not seek in any way to regulate the manner in which appellees conduct their affairs nor to impose any specific standards of conduct upon them, but appellants only insist upon their fundamental right to be free from the consequences of tortious conduct upon the part of appellees. The court below also seemed to be laboring under this misapprehension that appellants are seeking to force the appellees to follow either the procedures heretofore followed by them or any other specific set of procedures. What appellants seek is merely that they be held harmless from the consequences of intentional irresponsible conduct by appellees.

The Issue of Freedom of Speech

The appellees' contention that the complaint seeks to restrain freedom of speech in violation of applicable constitutional provisions is equally unsound. The hard fact is that the Advance Music case did hold that the second cause of action therein stated a cause of action "for relief either at law or in equity", and that the prayer for relief in that action contained a prayer for an injunction against the continuance of the expression by the defendants therein of their opinions that the songs performed on the radio program were the most popular songs of the day. And no matter how the appellees characterize the holding of that case, the fact is that an examination of the record and the briefs in the Court of Appeals discloses that the constitutional objection was expressly raised and argued in the Court of Appeals and rejected by it. The Court of Appeals likewise saw no constitutional objection in granting injunctions in the <u>Opera On Tour</u> and the <u>American Guild</u> cases. Examination of <u>Nann v. Raimist</u>, 255 N.Y. 307 (1930) reveals no support for the distinctions attempted to be drawn by appellees in order to avoid the impact of Judge Cardozo's flat statement that equity "* * * intervenes in those cases where restraint becomes essential to the preservation of a business or of other property interests threatened with impairment by illegal combinations <u>or by other tortious acts</u> * * *." (255 N.Y. at 317, emphasis added).

These cases did in fact overrule the dictum which appeared in the <u>Marlin Fire Arms</u> case relied upon by appellees. The actual holding in the <u>Marlin Fire Arms</u> case was that equity would not assume jurisdiction to restrain the publication of criticisms of a product "* * * when such publication will not support an action at law * * *". (171 N.Y. at 392) The <u>Marlin</u> case stands for no more than the proposition that when one "* * * has no remedy at law because of his inability to prove special damage * * * (171 N.Y. at 391) equity will not intervene."

The <u>Marlin</u> case, moreover, had been severely criticized by Dean Pound in his article in 29 Harvard Law Review 640 "Equitable Relief Against Defamation and Injuries to Personalty". Dean Pound, after reviewing the authorities and precedents was firmly of the opinion that equity not only had, but should exercise, the power to enjoin tortious acts when necessary to prevent irreparable harm to one's business or property.

Appellees' memorandum is noteworthy for its failure even to cite what is perhaps the leading case in which constitutional objection was raised to the granting of an injunction to restrain tortious conduct. In <u>Black & Yates v. Mahogany Ass'n.</u>, 129 F. 2d 227 (3rd Cir. 1941), in reversing the denial of injunctive relief and restraining statements by a defendant which tended to injure plaintiff's business, the Court cited Dean Pound's article and said:

"In view of this critic's eminence, it is not necessary to add much to his demolition of the reasons advanced for the Chancellor's hesitations. Later commentators have discussed them and have greeted with enthusiasm each decision which edges away from the traditional doctrine of negation. The irrelevance of 'free speech' and of 'a libel is for a jury' are patent. Freedom of discussion of public issues does not demand lack of 'previous restraint' for injury to private individuals. Disparagement of goods presents no confusing or complicated matter of personality requiring the sympathetic attention of one's peers.

"We are quite willing to repudiate the 'waning doctrine that equity will not restrain the trade libel'. We are further willing to do so directly

and without hiding behind the other equitable principles put forward in some
of the cases." (129 F.2d at p. 231)

Nor do any of the opinions of the United States Supreme Court on the subject of prior restraints on freedom of expression in any way impair the foregoing
authorities. The Supreme Court cases deal in the main, with State action, not
disputes between private individuals, and with blanket restraints rather than with
restraints against specific and limited tortious acts. Indeed, in the leading case
of Near v. Minnesota, 283 U.S. 697 (1931) the Supreme Court specifically said:

"* * * Nor are we now concerned with questions as to the extent of authority to prevent publications in order to protect private rights according to
the principles governing the exercise of the jurisdiction of courts of equity."
(Citing Dean Pound's article) (283 U.S. at p. 716)

The Near case and in particular a later case, Chaplinsky v. New Hampshire,
315 U.S. 568 (1941) both point out that there are well defined classes of speech,
the prevention of which have never been thought to raise any constitutional problem. These include the lewd and obscene, the profane, libelous and insulting
and all utterances which "* * * are no essential part of any exposition of ideas,
and are of such slight social value as a step to truth that any benefit that may be
derived from them is clearly outweighed * * *." To the same effect see Kingsley
Books, Inc. v. Brown, 354 U.S. 436 (1957) and Beauharnais v. Illinois, 343 U.S.
250 (1952).

The opinion of Mr. Justice Holmes in American Bank & Trust Company v.
Federal Reserve Bank. supra, indicates that he saw no consitutional objection
to granting an injunction against the publication of tortious words.

The other cases relied upon by appellees do not stand for the proposition
for which they are cited. Krebiozen Research Foundation v. Beacon Press Co.,
Inc., 334 Mass. 86, 134 N.E. 2d 1 (1956) is clearly distinguishable on the ground
that it sought to enjoin a publisher of a book from carrying on his business of
publishing books. The rationale of the holding was that the publisher could show
a legal justification in that he had an economic interest in the publication of the
book, controversial as it was. For that reason alone it is not controlling in this
case, but moreover with respect to the free speech issue the court therein said:

"But later cases have held that equity will take jurisdiction where there is
a continuing course of unjustified and wrongful attack upon the plaintiff
motivated by actual malice, and causing damage to property rights as distinguished from 'injury to the personality affecting feelings, sensibility
and honor' * * *." (134 N.E. 2d at p. 5)

Donnelley v. United Fruit Company, 4 A. D. 2d 855 (1st Dept. 1957), moreover, held merely that since the relationship of master and servant between the parties had terminated, there was no necessity to resort to a declaratory judgment as to their rights; and Eversharp Inc. v. Pal Blade Co., 182 F. 2d 779 (2nd Cir. 1950) was decided solely on the ground that the allegations and proof of special damage necessary to sustain an action for trade libel had not been pleaded.

The utterance of words intended and calculated in the ordinary course to harm another, when no legal justification for their utterance appears, is well within those classes of speech which are without constitutional protection.

CONCLUSION

An order should be entered herein restraining and enjoining the appellees pending the determination of the appeal herein from distributing the proposed letter or any similar statement.

Respectfully submitted,

SIMPSON THACHER & BARTLETT,
Attorneys for Appellants,
Office and Post Office Address,
120 Broadway,
New York 5, N.Y.

(June 3, 1959)

WHITNEY NORTH SEYMOUR
RICHARD M. DICKE
WILLIAM J. MANNING
    Of Counsel.

UNITED STATES COURT OF APPEALS
SECOND CIRCUIT
UNITED STATES COURTHOUSE
FOLEY SQUARE
NEW YORK 7

A. DANIEL FUSARO
CLERK

June 17, 1959

Appalachian Power Company

vs.

American Institute of CPA's

Dear Sirs:

The Court has today handed down a decision in the above-entitled cause affirming the decision of the District Court, and stay vacated.

Copies of opinions may be obtained in the Clerk's office in the afternoon of the day following decision, in accordance with Rule 18(5) of this Court.

Judgment has been entered today and a mandate will issue in accordance with Rule 28 of this Court.

Very truly yours,

A. DANIEL FUSARO
Clerk

(Before Clark, Chief Judge, and Lumbard and Waterman, Circuit Judges)

OPINION

PER CURIAM

On a theory of prima facie tort plaintiffs seek to enjoin defendants, a professional association of accountants, and several of its officers from distributing to its members and others a letter to the effect that the Institute considers certain accounting procedures improper. Plaintiffs allege that in the preparation of this letter the Institute disregarded its usual practice of circulating proposed opinions for comment prior to their issuance, and that the promulgation of the views contained in the letter, because of the Institute's authority in the accounting profession and in the business community will impair plaintiffs' credit and limit their growth.

The court below properly considered this action as on a motion for summary judgment once both parties had filed supporting affidavits to their motion. F.R. C.P. 12(b) specifically authorizes this procedure and we do not see that plaintiffs were denied the opportunity to present materials pertinent to summary judgment which the rule provides.

On the merits we agree with Judge Levet's reasoned opinion below, D.C. S.D.N.Y., May 20, 1959. We think the courts may not dictate or control the procedures by which a private organization expresses its honestly held views. Defendants' action involves no breach of duty owed by them to the plaintiffs. On the contrary, every professional body accepts a public obligation for unfettered expression of views and loses all right to professional consideration as well as all utility if its views are controlled by other criteria than the intellectual conclusions of the persons acting. Absent a showing of actual malice or its equivalent the courts would be making a great mistake, contrary indeed to their own ideals and professions, if they assumed to restrict and denigrate this widely recognized and assumed professional duty.

By stipulation of the parties this appeal was heard both upon the appellants' motion for a stay and upon the merits. Our order must therefore be that the stay heretofore granted is vacated and the judgment below is affirmed.

UNITED STATES COURT OF APPEALS
For the Second Circuit

Appalachian Power Company,
Ohio Power Company and
Indiana & Michigan Electric Company,
 	
             Appellants,
 	
     against
 	
American Institute of Certified Public
Accountants, L. H. Penney, William W.
Werntz and Carman G. Blough,
 	
             Appellees.
	NOTICE OF MOTION
	Docket No. 25715

S I R S :

PLEASE TAKE NOTICE that upon the annexed affidavit of Whitney North Seymour, duly sworn to on June 19, 1959, and upon all the papers and proceedings heretofore had herein, the undersigned will make an application before Hon. J. Edward Lumbard, Judge of the United States Court of Appeals for the Second Circuit, at his Chambers in the United States Courthouse, Foley Square, New York, N.Y., on June 19, 1959, at 9:45 A.M. in the forenoon of said day, for an order restraining and enjoining the appellees until July 9, 1959 from distributing to the members of the appellee American Institute of Certified Public Accountants or to any members of the accountancy profession, the proposed letter referred to in the complaint herein or distributing to the aforesaid any like statement to the effect that the appellee American Institute of Certified Public Accountants or its Committee on Accounting Procedure is of the opinion or recommends that charges made to income in recognition of the deferral of income taxes should not or may not, in accordance with generally accepted accounting principles, be credited to earned surplus or to any other account included in the stockholders' equity section of the balance sheet, and for an order granting such other, further and different relief as to the Court may seem just and proper in the premises.

Yours, etc.,

Dated, New York, N.Y.
     June 19, 1959

SIMPSON THACHER & BARTLETT

By /s/ <u>WHITNEY NORTH SEYMOUR</u>
                 Member of the Firm

Attorneys for Appellants,
Office and P.O. Address,
120 Broadway,
New York 5, N.Y.

TO:

MESSRS. HOWARD C. WESTWOOD, FONTAINE
C. BRADLEY and STANLEY L. TEMKO,
Attorneys for Appellees,
c/o American Institute of Certified Public Accountants,
270 Madison Avenue,
New York, N.Y.
        and
COVINGTON & BURLING,
Union Trust Building,
Washington, D. C.

UNITED STATES COURT OF APPEALS
For the Second Circuit

Appalachian Power Company,
Ohio Power Company and
Indiana & Michigan Electric Company,

Appellants,

against

American Institute of Certified Public
Accountants, L. H. Penney, William W.
Werntz and Carman G. Blough,

Appellees.

AFFIDAVIT
Docket No. 25715

STATE OF NEW YORK

COUNTY OF NEW YORK } ss.:

WHITNEY NORTH SEYMOUR, being duly sworn deposes and says, that:

1. I am an attorney and a member of the firm of Simpson Thacher & Bartlett, attorneys for the appellants herein.

2. This affidavit is submitted in support of appellants' application for an order restraining and enjoining the appellees as requested in said motion.

3. The appeal herein was argued on June 4, 1959 and on that day this Court granted an injunction, pending the determination of said appeal, restraining the appellees from distributing a certain proposed letter. The primary relief sought in this action was an injunction restraining the appellees from distributing that letter.

4. On June 18, 1959 appellants first learned that this Court had filed its decision and order, dated June 17, 1959, affirming the District Court's dismissal of the complaint and vacating the injunction previously granted pending the appeal. Appellants are now considering the filing of petition for review on writ of certiorari of the decision and order of this Court, but time has not permitted a determination to be made as to whether or not to proceed in that manner. In connection with said petition, appellants would apply to a Justice of the United States Supreme Court for an injunction pending determination by the United States Supreme Court of such a petition for review on writ of certiorari.

5. Unless an order is entered herein restraining the distribution of the proposed letter pending such an application to a Justice of the United States Supreme

Court, however, this appeal would be rendered moot by the distribution of the proposed letter, in so far as appellants' right to equitable relief is concerned. I am informed and believe that the proposed letter is now ready for distribution.

6. Accordingly, it is respectfully requested that this Court enter an order restraining the distribution of the proposed letter for a period of twenty (20) days, that is, until July 9, 1959, in order that appellants may have such reasonable period in which to determine whether to seek review by the United States Supreme Court and to make application to a Justice thereof for an injunction pending its determination upon such a petition for review.

Sworn to before me this

19th day of June, 1959. /s/ WHITNEY NORTH SEYMOUR

/s/ VINCENT GERACI

    Notary Public
    State of New York
No. 36-6490400
Qualified in Orange County
Certificate filed in New York County
Commission Expires March 30, 1960

UNITED STATES COURT OF APPEALS
For the Second Circuit

Appalachian Power Company,
Ohio Power Company and
Indiana & Michigan Electric Company,

Appellants,

against

American Institute of Certified Public
Accountants, L. H. Penney, William W.
Werntz and Carman G. Blough,

Appellees.

ORDER
───────
Docket No. 25715

A decision and final order having béen entered herein on June 17, 1959, affirming the judgment of the United States District Court for the Southern District of New York entered therein on May 25, 1959, denying appellants' motion for an order granting a preliminary injunction and granting summary judgment in favor of appellees dismissing the complaint on the ground that it failed to stay (sic)* a claim upon which relief could be granted, and vacating the injunction pending appeal granted herein on June 4, 1959.

And appellants having made application for an order granting an injunction pending the application on or before July 9, 1959, to a Justice of the United States Supreme Court for an injunction pending a determination of a petition by appellants for review upon writ of certiorari of the said decision and order of this Court.

NOW, upon the decision and order of this Court filed and entered on June 17, 1959, the notice of appeal herein, the aforesaid order and judgment of the United States District Court for the Southern District of New York, and upon the complaint herein, duly verified on April 15, 1959, the affidavits of Robert O. Whitman and Donald C. Cook, duly sworn to on April 15 and May 6, 1959, respectively, submitted in support of appellants' motion for a temporary injunction, the affidavits of F. Merrill Beatty and William W. Werntz, both duly sworn to on May 4, 1959, and the affidavit of George C. Christie, duly sworn to on May 6, 1959, all submitted in opposition to appellants' said motion, and it appearing from the foregoing that the distribution of the letter and opinion proposed to be distributed by the appellees to the members of the appellee American Institute of Certified Public Accountants, or any other communication, to the effect that the appellee American Institute of Certified Public Accountants or its Committee on Accounting Procedure is of the opinion or recommends that charges made to income in recognition of the deferral of income taxes should not or may not, in accordance with generally accepted accounting principles, be credited to earned surplus or

───────────
* Should read "state a claim".

to any other account included in the stockholders' equity section of the balance sheet, would cause a petition for review on writ of certiorari herein to become moot insofar as review is sought of the affirmance of the denial of appellants' application for a preliminary injunction,

IT IS ORDERED THAT, pending the hearing of an application to be made by appellants to a Justice of the United States Supreme Court not later than July 9, 1959, for an injunction pending the determination of a petition by appellants for review on writ of certiorari of the decision and order of this Court entered and filed on June 17, 1959, the appellees be and they hereby are enjoined and restrained from distributing to the members of the appellee American Institute of Certified Public Accountants or to any members of the accountancy profession, the aforesaid proposed letter or distributing any like statement to the aforesaid to the effect that the appellee American Institute of Certified Public Accountants or its Committee on Accounting Procedure is of the opinion or recommends that charges made to income in recognition of the deferral of income taxes should not or may not, in accordance with generally accepted accounting principles, be credited to earned surplus or to any other account included in the stockholders' equity section of the balance sheet.

It is further ordered that in no event shall this injunction extend beyond July 9, 1959.

Dated, June 19, 1959

/s/ J. EDWARD LUMBARD
Judge of the United States Court
of Appeals for the Second Circuit

IN THE SUPREME COURT OF THE UNITED STATES
OCTOBER TERM, 1959

NO._____

Appalachian Power Company
Ohio Power Company and
Indiana & Michigan Electric Company,

Petitioners,

against

American Institute of Certified Public
Accountants, L. H. Penney, William W.
Werntz and Carman G. Blough,

Respondents.

APPLICATION BY PETITIONERS FOR AN ORDER
STAYING THE MANDATE OF THE COURT BELOW
AND RESTRAINING THE RESPONDENTS
PENDING THE FINAL DETERMINATION OF THIS
ACTION BY THE SUPREME COURT
OF THE UNITED STATES

(JUNE 30, 1959)

Petitioners herein respectfully pray that the mandate of the United States Court of Appeals for the Second Circuit on the judgment entered by said court in this action on June 17, 1959 be stayed and that the respondents be restrained, pending the final determination of this action by the Supreme Court of the United States, from distributing to the members of the respondent American Institute of Certified Public Accountants or to any members of the accountancy profession, the proposed letter referred to in the verified complaint and set forth in the record herein.

Oral argument on this application is respectfully requested.

Jurisdiction

The jurisdiction of the Supreme Court of the United States to review this case on petition for certiorari rests upon 28 U.S.C. § 1254(1). Jurisdiction to grant the stay and injunctive relief requested rests upon 28 U.S.C. § 2101 (f) and 28 U.S.C. § 1651. This application is made pursuant to Rules 27, 31, 35,

50 and 51 of the Revised Rules of the Supreme Court of the United States. Federal jurisdiction in the first instance was based upon diversity of citizenship.

Nature of the Case

This is an action for an injunction. Petitioners are three operating electric public utility companies. Respondent American Institute of Certified Public Accountants (the "Institute") is a national organization of certified public accountants with more than 33,000 members. The individual respondents are the President of the Institute, the Chairman of its Committee on Accounting Procedure (the "Committee") and its Director of Research.

Petitioners seek in this action to restrain the distribution by the Committee to the 33,000 members of the Institute and other accountants and members of the business community of a proposed letter to the effect that certain accounting practices and procedures followed by petitioners and some other electric public utility companies and heretofore recognized as generally accepted accounting principles are now improper. The distribution of that letter, because of the authority of the respondent Institute and its Committee in the accounting profession and in the business community, will cause immediate and irreparable harm to petitioners by impairing their credit, increasing their financing charges and limiting their growth.

The amount involved in this action is substantial. The petitioners have recorded on their books in the aggregate more than $65,000,000 in accounts designated as "Earned Surplus Restricted for Future Federal Income Taxes." The effect of the proposed letter to be sent by the respondents would be to remove those amounts not only from the earned surplus section but from any other account included in the stockholders' equity section of the balance sheet. The question is of general importance, for many other utilities and other businesses employ the very accounting methods now challenged by respondents. It is important also because it involves the question of whether a professional organization may be held responsible for damage caused by its tortious conduct in intentionally using its persuasive authority to harm others.

It is petitioners' position that the facts presented in the verified complaint establish all of the elements of a prima facie tort under settled principles of New York law and call for the exercise of the injunctive power of a court of equity, to protect petitioners from immediate and irreparable harm. First of all, it is alleged in the verified complaint that the stated purpose for distributing the proposed letter, to wit, to express the intent of the Committee in using certain words in a prior publication by it, is spurious and that the Committee did not and could not have had the intent claimed in the proposed letter. The record incontrovertibly shows that before the letter was prepared, representatives of the

Institute, including several of the named respondents, expressly disclaimed an intention to deal with the matter which the letter pretends was a part of such earlier intention.

It is further alleged in the verified complaint that the respondents have full knowledge of the harm which the proposed letter will cause petitioners and intend to cause that harm, that they have no legal justification for causing such harm to petitioners and that they are acting wilfully, wantonly and recklessly in preparing to distribute the proposed letter. For example, it is alleged that the respondents completely abdicated their responsibility to use some minimum standards of care in formulating this pronouncement which they know will harm others and have taken no steps whatever reasonably designed to ascertain its propriety or correctness and, indeed, that they have also failed to follow their own well established practices and procedures heretofore used by them in connection with the distribution of opinions upon accounting matters. This is not an attack upon their failure to follow established procedure. It is an attack on the issuance of a false ukase, which also neglected the internal due process contemplated by the usual procedure of the Institute.

Prior Proceedings

This action was commenced by the filing of a verified complaint on April 15, 1959. Simultaneously therewith, Hon. Edward L. Palmieri, Judge of the United States District Court for the Southern District of New York, signed an order to show cause bringing on for hearing on April 17, 1959 a motion by petitioners for a preliminary injunction and containing a temporary restraining order enjoining the respondents from distributing the proposed letter pending a hearing on that motion. Respondents requested an adjournment of the hearing on said motion and it was adjourned to May 7, 1959, the temporary restraining order being continued by consent.

On May 1, 1959 respondents served a notice of cross-motion for an order, pursuant to Rule 12(b) (6) of the Federal Rules of Civil Procedure, dismissing the complaint on the ground that it failed to state a claim upon which relief could be granted. No affidavits or other materials were served with that motion, and no motion for summary judgment was made.

On May 6, 1959 respondents served three affidavits in opposition to petitioners' motion for a preliminary injunction, and on May 7, 1959 petitioners served an affidavit in reply to respondents' said affidavits. Examination of the affidavits shows that neither party considered them to be submitted on the motion to dismiss--they were all submitted on the motion for injunction.

Both motions were heard before Hon. Richard H. Levet on May 7, 1959, who continued the restraining order pending his decision. The District Court's opinion was filed on May 21, 1959, holding that petitioners' motion for a temporary injunction must be denied, that respondents' motion had been treated as one for summary judgment pursuant to Rule 56 of the Federal Rules of Civil Procedure and that summary judgment must be entered dismissing the complaint. An order and judgment to that effect was signed and entered on May 25, 1959. At no time, on the argument or otherwise, was there any suggestion that the motion was to be regarded as one for summary judgment. Petitioners were thus given no opportunity to submit the affidavits in support of their claim which the record shows would have been readily available and forthcoming.

Also on May 25, 1959, Judge Levet signed an order enjoining the distribution of the proposed letter pending the making of an application by petitioners to the Court of Appeals for the Second Circuit for an order restraining the distribution of that letter pending an appeal to that Court.

Petitioners' motion for an injunction pending appeal was argued before the Court of Appeals on June 4, 1959. That motion was granted from the bench, and Judge Levet's restraining order was continued pending decision by the Court of Appeals. On consent of the parties the briefs and argument on petitioners' motion for a restraining order pending appeal were considered as the briefs and argument on the appeal on the merits.

On June 17, 1959 the Court of Appeals filed its decision, holding that the judgment below must be affirmed and the stay vacated.

On June 19, 1959 application was made by petitioners to Hon. J. Edward Lumbard, Judge of the United States Court of Appeals for the Second Circuit, for a stay order restraining the distribution of the proposed letter until July 9, 1959 in order that petitioners would have time to prepare this application for a stay pending action by this Court on petitioners' petition for review on writ of certiorari. An order to that effect was signed and entered on that date. Counsel for respondents urged that no stay should be granted by the Court of Appeals but that any application for a stay should be made to a Justice of this Court, but Judge Lumbard granted the stay requested so that an application might be made here.

The verified complaint, the order to show cause, the temporary restraining order, the affidavits in support of and in opposition to the motion for a preliminary injunction, the notice of motion to dismiss the complaint, the opinions of the District Court and the Court of Appeals and the above-mentioned stay orders will be handed to the Court together with this application.

The Opinions Below

The essence of the District Court's opinion was that:

"*** the purposes of the defendant Institute are adequate justification, if justification, indeed, be required, to permit the proposed communications. *** This Court has been unable to find any precedent under

the doctrine of prima facie tort or otherwise for a preliminary or final injunction forbidding a group from publishing and distributing opinions under
circumstances equivalent or even similar to these."

The Court of Appeals agreed with Judge Levet and went on to say:

"*** We think the courts may not dictate or control the procedures
by which a private organization expresses its honestly held views.***
Absent a showing of actual malice or its equivalent the courts would be
making a great mistake, contrary indeed to their own ideals and professions, if they assumed to restrict and denigrate this widely recognized and
assumed professional duty."

The Reasons for Certiorari

The principal reasons for granting a writ of certiorari, which petitioners
will rely on in their petition, are as follows:

I

The action of the court below in treating respondents' motion to dismiss
the complaint pursuant to Rule 12(b) (6) of the Federal Rules of Civil Procedure
as a motion for summary judgment and the approval thereof by the Court of Appeals for the Second Circuit is in direct conflict with the decision of the Court
of Appeals for the Ninth Circuit in Pacific American Fisheries v. Mullaney, 191
F. 2d 137 (9th Cir. 1951), and in conflict with the principle of the decision of
the Court of Appeals for the Fifth Circuit in Herron v. Herron, 255 F. 2d 590 (5th
Cir. 1958).

The District Court, in its opinion herein said that:

"Since matters outside the pleadings have been presented to the
court, and since the parties have submitted such proof, I am treating this
motion as one for summary judgment as provided in Rule 56 of the Federal
Rules of Civil Procedure." (Opinion, pp. 3–4)

The Court of Appeals said in its opinion that:

"The court below properly considered this action as on a motion for
summary judgment once both parties had filed supporting affidavits to their
motions. Fed. R. Civ. F. 12(b) specifically authorized this procedure, and
we do not see that plaintiffs were denied the opportunity to present materials pertinent to summary judgment which the rule provides." (Opinion, p.
1486)

The only authority for treating a motion to dismiss as one for summary
judgment is found in Rule 12(b) of the Federal Rules of Civil Procedure, where
it is said that:

"*** If, on a motion asserting the defense numbered (6) to dismiss for failure of the pleading to state a claim upon which relief can be granted, matters outside the pleading are presented to and not excluded by the court, the motion shall be treated as one for summary judgment and disposed of as provided in Rule 56, and all parties shall be given reasonable opportunity to present all material made pertinent to such a motion by Rule 56."

It is entirely clear that no matters outside the pleadings were presented to the Court by either party on the motion to dismiss. The only affidavits before the Court were there on the motion for a temporary injunction solely. They were not intended by either side for consideration on the motion to dismiss. The three affidavits submitted on behalf of respondents were each entitled "Affidavit in Opposition to Plaintiffs' Application for Preliminary Injunction." The main papers upon which petitioners relied below, the verified complaint and the affidavit of Robert O. Whitman, were prepared, served and filed at a time prior to the making of respondents' motion to dismiss. The only other document submitted to the Court by petitioners was the affidavit of Donald C. Cook, which was on its face "*** submitted in support of plaintiffs' application *** for an order granting a preliminary injunction herein and in reply to the affidavits submitted in opposition to said motion." None of these papers were submitted on the motion to dismiss.

Petitioners had no knowledge at any time up to the date of the filing of the opinion that the Court was treating the motion as one for summary judgment, and, accordingly, did not have any opportunity to prepare and submit the affidavits and other proofs of the allegations of the complaint, which would have been prepared and submitted had it been known that the motion was being considered as one for summary judgment. This denial to the petitioners of the opportunity to prepare and submit matters appropriate on a motion for summary judgment is in direct conflict with the specific provision of Rule 12(b) that when the Court treats a motion to dismiss as one for summary judgment:

"*** all parties shall be given reasonable opportunity to present all matters made pertinent to such a motion by Rule 56."

This sentence was added to Rule 12 by a 1946 amendment. The revisors said:

"*** It will also be observed that if a motion under Rule 12(b)(6) is thus converted into a summary judgment motion, the amendment insures that both parties shall be given a reasonable opportunity to submit affidavits and extraneous proofs to avoid taking a party by surprise through the conversion of the motion into a motion for summary judgment.***" (Report of Proposed Amendments, Advisory Committee on Rules for Civil Procedure, June 1946, p. 14,15)

No such reasonable opportunity was given to petitioners. This deprived them of of substantial rights and of the due process required by the Rule and principles of fairness. Summary judgment is a useful device for avoiding trials where there are no issues of fact, but is a dangerous snare when used to preclude the presentation and identification of issues of fact.

The approval by the Court of Appeals of the action of the District Court in treating the motion to dismiss as one for summary judgment when no materials outside the pleadings were presented thereon and without affording petitioners the opportunity to submit additional affidavits or without extraneous proofs not only conflicts with the plain requirements of Rule 12(b) but directly conflicts with Pacific American Fisheries v. Mullaney, 191 F. 2d 137 (9th Cir. 1951). In that case such a treatment of a motion to dismiss by the trial court was held to be ground for reversal. The court in that case said:

> "Upon hearing on this motion the court determined to treat the motion as one for a summary judgment, and ordered that such judgment be entered for the defendant. It does not appear that either party was afforded an opportunity to make any further showing by way of affidavit or otherwise after the court determined to treat the motion as one for summary judgment.***

*****

> "Appeal was taken both from the order denying a temporary injunction and from the summary judgment. With respect to the summary judgment, appellant contends that irrespective of all other considerations, it was error for the court to undertake to treat the motion for judgment on the pleadings as a motion for summary judgment and the proceed to grant that judgment without giving the appellant an opportunity to present evidence on the questions of fact involved.***

*****

> "We think that the contention that the entry of a summary judgment was erroneous under the circumstances is sound.***"

This action thus presents a clear conflict between the Circuits with respect to the question of the proper interpretation to be given to Rule 12(b) and as to the proper procedures to be followed on motions to dismiss. This is an important question of Federal procedural due process which merits the attention of this Court because of its far reaching effect on all litigants in the Federal courts.

II

The District Court was able to reach its decision only by deciding issues of fact as to which there were conflicting statements in the verified complaint and the affidavits submitted by the parties. The Court of Appeals has thus sanctioned such a departure from the accepted and usual course of judicial proceeding as to call for an exercise of this Court's power of supervision. Indeed, this action of the courts below is in direct conflict with the decisions of this Court and of the Courts of Appeal for each of the Circuits holding that jurisdiction to grant summary judgment should be exercised with caution and only in the clearest of cases and that on a motion for summary judgment the court may not decide such conflicts, but is limited to inquiry as to whether any such questions exist. Kennedy v. Silas Mason Co., 334 U.S. 249 (1948); Elgin, J. & E. R. Co. v. Burley, 325 U.S. 711, 719, 744 (1945), adhered to on rehearing, 327 U.S. 661 (1946); Arenas v. United States, 322 U.S. 419, 431 (1944); Sarter v. Arkansas Gas Corp. 321 U.S. 620 (1944); for decisions from the Courts of Appeal for each Circuit, see 6 Moore, Federal Practice 2107 et seq.

The District Court itself recognized that the elements of the tort alleged consisted of intention to injure, lack of legal justification and damages. The Court of Appeals added the element of actual malice. Each of these elements, we submit, entails facts, circumstances, actions and statements of people, and is a question of fact which should not and cannot be decided on the basis of conflicting affidavits.

For example, the District Court found that as a fact the proposed letter "was adopted by the Committee in conformity with its established procedures" (Opinion, p. 6), whereas the verified complaint and the moving affidavit on the motion for a preliminary injunction specifically allege that the Committee did not follow its established procedures and practices, pointing out that there was a departure from the Committee's previous practices and procedures of giving wide circulation to so-called exposure or ballot drafts, of giving opportunity to interested parties to express their views on the subject in issue and giving consideration to the prior opinions of the respondents themselves. The District Court also found that there was no intent to harm petitioners whereas such an intent was specifically pleaded, and petitioners are now denied the right to prove that allegation of fact. The District Court did not so much as mention the allegation of falsity in the statement in the proposed letter as to the intent of the Committee, which is documented in the record, but must have resolved even this issue of fact against petitioners. The District Court also found that "The opinions of the Committee have no official effect" (Opinion p. 7). Whether the effect of the opinions of the Committee is official or unofficial, is, of course, irrelevant, the only pertinent inquiry being what their effect is. But in any event there was at least an issue of fact as to whether or not the opinions of the respondents have the effect and are accorded the authority alleged in the complaint, for the record may be searched in vain for any denial of these allegations and averments.

The entire opinion is pregnant with the suggestion of disbelief of the statements contained in the verified complaint and petitioners' affidavits, many of which are not even controverted by respondents' affidavits, whereas the statements made in the affidavits submitted on behalf of respondents are accepted in the opinion as facts even though controverted.

We submit that the disposition of an important action involving large sums of money on the basis of accepting as established fact, statements contained in affidavits which are controverted by the opposing party is such a departure from the established rules of law with respect to motions for summary judgment, so in conflict with the decisions of this Court and other Federal courts, and such a departure from the accepted and usual course of judicial proceedings as to call for the exercise of this Court's power of supervision.

III

The doctrine of prima facie tort has been for some time an important and integral part of the law of the State of New York, which law is controlling in this case under the Erie v. Tompkins doctrine. The decision of the lower court in dismissing the complaint herein is in conflict with the applicable decisions of the New York Court of Appeals. The leading New York case in the field of prima facie tort is Advance Music Corporation v. American Tobacco Co., 296 N.Y. 79 (1946). That case is strikingly similar to the instant one and should have been treated by the court below as controlling. Other apposite New York opinions in this field are Opera on Tour, Inc. v. Weber, 285 N.Y. 348 (1941) and American Guild of Musical Artists v. Petrillo, 286, N.Y. 226 (1941).

Analysis of the complaint and the opinion of the New York Court of Appeals in the Advance Music case indicates that there is no basis whatever for the District Court's statement that it is "basically different" from the instant case. The complaint in that case alleged that plaintiff was engaged in the business of publishing musical compositions. It spent large sums of money advertising that its songs were among the most popular of the day, for its customers normally purchased those compositions which they thought were the most popular. Defendants sponsored and produced a well known weekly coast-to-coast radio program, the Hit Parade. On said program defendants listed and had performed the supposedly nine or ten most popular songs of the week, claiming that these popularity ratings were based upon an extensive and accurate nationwide survey.

The complaint further alleged that the defendants' ratings and listings of songs were in fact the result of caprice or other considerations foreign to a selection based on an accurate and extensive nationwide survey; that in fact, some of plaintiff's songs which were among the most popular of the day were either completely ignored by the defendants or given an improper rating.

The complaint alleged that by reason of these acts of improperly rating or ignoring plaintiff's songs, it was suffering damages in that retail purchasers, entertainers and other customers and potential promoters of the songs, influenced by defendants' inaccurate ratings, failed to purchase plaintiff's compositions, and that plaintiff's business prestige was impaired.

The complaint further alleged that the acts and representations of the defendant were made wantonly, in bad faith and with intent to injure plaintiff.

The New York Court of Appeals reversed a dismissal of the complaint and held that the facts pleaded stated a cause of action. The court said:

"The foregoing (allegations) *** are there followed by the further allegation that 'the aforesaid acts and representations on the part of the defendants are made with intent to injure the plaintiff.' Thus in sum and substance the second cause of action constitutes a statement to this effect: The defendants are wantonly causing damage to the plaintiff by a system of conduct on their part which warrants an inference that they intend harm of that type. So read, the second cause of action is, we think, adequate in its office as a plaintiff's pleading. (Emphasis added.)

"In Skinner & Company v. Show & Company (1893), (1 Ch. 413, 422) Lord Justice BOWEN said: 'At Common Law there was a cause of action whenever one person did damage to another wilfully and intentionally, and without just cause or excuse.' *** These broad propositions were approved by Sir FREDERICK POLLOCK as authority for his doctrine that all willful harm is actionable unless the defendant justify or excuse his conduct. (Pollock, The Law of Torts (14th ed.) 17–18). (296 N.Y. at pp. 83–84)

"The justification that is required in a case like this must, of course, be one which the law will recognize.***" (Citations omitted. 296 N.Y. at p. 85)

The Court of Appeals for the Second Circuit, in its per curiam opinion on this important issue of state law, refused to treat this decision as controlling and, moreover, added to the elements of prima facie tort as enunciated by the New York courts the requirement of a showing of "actual malice." In the Advance Music case, the Court of Appeals said that an allegation that a party was wantonly causing damage warranted an inference that they intended such harm and that such an allegation was sufficient. In the American Guild of Musical Artists case, the Court of Appeals specifically held that actual malice was an unnecessary allegation since malice in the law of New York does not mean ill-will against a person but merely intentional action without justification. In Campbell v. Gates, 236 N.Y. 457, 460 (1923), it was said that a malicious act is one "*** done intentionally, without just cause or excuse, and from this a malicious motive is to be inferred. This does not necessarily mean actual malice or ill-will, but the intentional doing of a wrongful act without legal or social justification."

We submit that the opinions below in this action constitute holdings in conflict with the applicable and controlling decisions of the New York Court of Appeals on this important issue of law.

IV

An important federal question concerning the equity powers of the federal judiciary is here involved on which there is no controlling decision of this Court. On this question, moreover, the decisions below conflict in principle with decisions by this Court and by the Court of Appeals for the Third Circuit and are in direct conflict with the decisions of the New York Court of Appeals on this issue.

In respondents' motion to dismiss the complaint the first point raised and relied upon by them in urging dismissal was that "*** The complaint seeks to restrain the freedom of expression of opinion of the *** (respondents) on a matter of public concern and interest, in violation of the rules of the common law and of the First Amendment to the United States Constitution *** " This point was fully briefed and argued both in the District Court and in the Court of Appeals and holding that a court of equity has no power to enjoin tortious speech and that there is no limitation upon the right of a professional organization to express its views are implicit in the District Court's opinion and explicit in the Court of Appeals' per curiam opinion.

This important question was expressly left open by this Court in Near v. Minnesota, 283 U.S. 697 (1931) where the Court said:

> "*** Nor are we now concerned with questions as to the extent of authority to prevent publications in order to protect private rights according to the principles governing the exercise of the jurisdiction of courts of equity." (283 U.S. at p. 716)

But both the Near case and a later case, Chaplinsky v. New Hampshire, 315 U.S. 568, 572 (1941), point out that there are well defined classes of speech, "the prevention and punishment of which have never been thought to raise any Constitutional problem." These include all "*** utterances which are no essential part of any exposition of ideas, and are of such slight social value as a step to truth that any benefit that may be derived from them is clearly outweighed by the social interest in order and morality."

The New York Court of Appeals has long since ruled that there is no limitation on the power of its courts of equity to enjoin tortious speech. This is made clear not only by the Advance Music and other cases cited above but was specifically pointed out by Chief Judge Cardozo in Nann v. Raimist, 255 N.Y. 307, 317 (1931), where, in discussing the power of a court of equity to enjoin publications, he wrote:

> "*** Equity does not intervene to restrain the publication of words on a mere showing of their falsity. *** It intervenes in those cases where restraint becomes essential to the preservation of a business or of other

property interests threatened with impairment by illegal combinations <u>or</u> <u>by other tortious acts,</u> the publication of the words being merely an instrument and incident ***. (Citations omitted.)" (Emphasis added.)

And this Court, through Mr. Justice Holmes in <u>American Bank & Trust</u> <u>Company v. Federal Reserve Bank</u>, 256 U.S. 350 (1921), reversed the dismissal of a complaint in an action for an injunction and said:

> "A man has a right to give advice, but advice given for the sole purpose of injuring another's business and effective on a large scale, might create a cause of action. *** If without a word of falsehood but acting from what we have called disinterested malevolence a man by persuasion should organize and carry into effect a run upon a bank and ruin it, we cannot doubt that an action would lie. ***" (256 U.S. at 358)

A leading decision by a federal court in an action in which objection was raised to the granting of an injunction to restrain tortious conduct is <u>Black &</u> <u>Yates v. Mahogany Ass'n</u>. 129 F. 2d 227 (3d Cir. 1941). It is with the principle upon which that case was decided that the opinions below are in conflict. There, in reversing the denial of injunctive relief and restraining statements by the defendant which tended to injure the plaintiff's business, the court said:

> "The irrelevance of 'free speech' and of 'a libel is for a jury' are patent. Freedom of discussion of public issues does not demand lack of 'previous restraint' for injury to private individuals. Disparagement of goods presents no confusing or complicated matter of personality requiring the sympathetic attention of one's peers.

> "We are quite willing to repudiate the 'waning doctrine that equity will not restrain the trade libel.' We are further willing to do so directly and without hiding behind the other equitable principles put forward in some of the cases." (129 F. 2d at p. 231)

This action thus presents important issues of law concerning the power of a court of equity to compel obedience to law and prevent injury, on which this Court has not directly ruled and as to which the decisions below are in conflict with an opinion of another Federal Court of Appeals as well as with those of the New York Court of Appeals.

V

The importance of this action, even apart from the above specific issues, is indicated by the amount of money involved and by the very nature of the holdings that a professional organization is immune from responsibility for damage caused by its irresponsible conduct. And it must be pointed at that not only will these petitioners be irreparably harmed and lose the benefits of retaining $65,000,000 in the equity sections of their balance sheet, but there are many other electric public utility companies similarly situated and which will be similarly damaged by the distribution of the proposed letter by the respondents. The effect, moreover, will be felt and the damages ultimately shouldered, as appears in the record, by the consuming public served by the petitioners.

Reason for Requesting the Stay

The proposed letter is dated April 15, 1959. A printed copy thereof is part of the record in this proceeding. It is now ready for distribution. Unless appropriate relief, is granted restraining the distribution of that letter pending action by this Court, the letter will be distributed, petitioners will suffer the irreparable harm alleged in the verified complaint and the petition for review on writ of certiorari will be rendered moot insofar as petitioners' request for equitable relief is concerned. It is only by the granting of the relief requested that the status quo can be maintained until this Court acts. On the other hand, there is no possibility of any damage whatever to the respondents. It is in such a set of facts and circumstances that this Court has in the past been moved to exercise its discretionary power to grant the relief requested herein. Cf. Tuscarora Nation of Indians v. Power Authority, 79 Sup. Ct. 4 (1958); Breswick & Co. v. United States, 75 Sup. Ct. 912 (1955); see also International Boxing Club v. United States, 78 Sup. Ct. 4 (1957).

WHEREFORE, petitioners respectfully pray that an order be entered herein staying the mandate of the court below and restraining the respondents, pending final determination of this cause by this Court, from distributing to the members of the respondent American Institute of Certified Public Accountants or to any members of the accountancy profession, the proposed letter referred to in the complaint herein or distributing to the aforesaid any like statement to the effect that the respondent American Institute of Certified Public Accountants or its Committee on Accounting Procedure is of the opinion or recommends that charges made to income in recognition of the deferral of income taxes should not or may not, in accordance with generally accepted accounting principles, be credited to earned surplus or to any other account included in the stockholders' equity section of the balance sheet.

/s/ WHITNEY NORTH SEYMOUR

Whitney North Seymour,
Counsel for Petitioners,
Office & Post Office Address,
120 Broadway,
New York 5, New York.

(June 30, 1959)

In The
SUPREME COURT OF THE UNITED STATES
OCTOBER TERM, 1959

No. ____

*Appalachian Power Company, Ohio Power Company and
Indiana & Michigan Electric Company,*

Petitioners,

v.

*American Institute of Certified Public Accountants
L. H. Penney, William W. Werntz and Carman G. Blough,*

Respondents.

MEMORANDUM IN OPPOSITION TO APPLICATION
FOR ORDER STAYING MANDATE AND ENJOINING
RESPONDENTS PENDING FINAL DETERMINATION
BY THIS COURT

(July 3, 1959)

This case, in which federal jurisdiction rests solely on diversity of citizenship, involves an attempt by petitioners, three interrelated electric utility companies, to persuade the federal courts to interpret New York state law to justify enjoining the Committee on Accounting Procedure of the American Institute of Certified Public Accountants from transmitting to the Institute's members a letter expressing the Committee's views on an accounting question of general application and general interest.

The District Court granted summary judgment in favor of respondents. After examining in detail the applicable New York law, the District Court stated that it had:

". . . been unable to find any precedent under the doctrine of prima facie tort or otherwise for a preliminary or final injunction forbidding a group from publishing and distributing opinions under circumstances equivalent or even similar to these."

The Court of Appeals for the Second Circuit affirmed the judgment dismissing the complaint on the merits. It explicitly held that it agreed with the District Court's interpretation of the applicable law and concluded:

"We think the courts may not dictate or control the procedures by which a private organization expresses its honestly held views. Defendants' action involves no breach of duty owed by them to the plaintiffs. On the contrary every professional body accepts a public obligation for unfettered expression of views and loses all right to professional consideration, as well as all utility, if its views are controlled by other criteria than the intellectual conclusions of the persons acting. Absent a showing of actual malice or its equivalent the courts would be making a great mistake, contrary indeed to their own ideals and professions, if they assumed to restrict and denigrate this widely recognized and assumed professional duty."

Copies of the opinions of the District Court and the Court of Appeals are filed with this memorandum.

Petitioners, by their application here, now seek to enjoin respondents from transmitting the letter expressing the Committee's views to the Institute's members until final determination of the case by this Court. In the normal course of events, action on a petition for a writ of certiorari could not be taken until October at the earliest. To grant petitioners' application would mean that petitioners, by filing a petition for certiorari in a case which we respectfully submit does not present any issue meriting review by this Court, would have effectively enjoined respondents for an additional period of at least three months. The result would be that respondents would be hamstrung in the exercise of the rights which both the District Court and the Court of Appeals, after extensive briefing and oral argument, have fully sustained.

Petitioners have been heard in two courts below and have no right to a hearing, let alone an injunction pending the filing of a request for hearing, in this Court. As Mr. Chief Justice Taft stated:

"No litigant is entitled to more than two chances, namely, to the original trial and to a review, and the intermediate courts of review are provided for that purpose. When a case goes beyond that, it is not primarily to preserve the rights of the litigants. The Supreme Court's function is for the purpose of expounding and stabilizing principles of law for the benefit of the people of the country, passing upon constitutional questions and other important questions of law for the public benefit. It is to preserve uniformity of decision among the intermediate courts of appeal." Hearings before the Committee on the Judiciary of the House of Representatives on H.R. 10479, 67th Cong., 2d Sess. 2 (1925).

In this situation the basic rule that a stay should not be granted absent a substantial likelihood of obtaining review is particularly pertinent. As Mr. Justice Harlan pointed out in Breswick & Co. v. United States, 100 L.Ed. 1510, 1513 (1955):

"It goes without saying that a single Justice's stay powers in a case such as this should be exercised most sparingly, both in fairness to the prevailing parties below and out of deference to the Court."

This case presents no issue which would warrant the Court's exercising its discretion to grant review by certiorari and consequently presents no basis for granting a stay which will, despite the considered rejection of the petitioners' claims by both courts below, enable them to continue their unjustified interference with respondents' activities. Petitioners' application advances two main grounds as those upon which they will rely as reasons for granting a writ of certiorari: one is the Court of Appeals' approval of the District Court's granting of summary judgment and the other is the claimed misapplication of the law of New York State in the holdings of both courts below that respondents' proposed conduct is not tortious.

Neither point presents any question meriting this Court's review. The short answer to petitioners' claim of error in treating the case as a proper one for summary judgment is that, as the Court of Appeals found, plaintiffs were not denied the opportunity to present all relevant materials. Petitioners presented extensive affidavits, and at no time in the proceedings in two courts below have they indicated any specific fact not set out in their affidavits, which could change the decision that they were entitled to no injunctive or other relief against respondents. Moreover, there is no conflict with the decision of any other circuit.

It is also clear that the alleged misapplication of the law of New York State presents no question meriting review here. Petitioners' claims as to the meaning of the New York law were fully considered by both courts and resolved against petitioners. As this Court has frequently indicated, in this situation it would defer to the judgment of the lower federal courts, both of which sit in New York and are, as this Court has stated, in a position which gives them particular skill in the law of the State involved. See, e.g., County of Allegheny v. Mashuda Co., No. 347, O.T. 1958, decided June 8, 1959; Propper v. Clark, 337 U.S. 472 486-87 (1949); Estate of Spiegel v. Commissioner, 335 U.S. 701, 707-708 (1949).

Finally, petitioners seek to inject as a reason which would justify review by this Court a contention that the decisions below raised the question whether a court of equity has the power to enjoin tortious speech. There is not a word in the opinion of either the District Court or the Court of Appeals which presents this question. The flat and explicit holding of both courts below is that as a matter of New York law the proposed conduct of respondents is not tortious and that accordingly petitioners have no right to relief of any kind.

STATEMENT OF THE CASE

The Parties.

Respondents, defendants below, are the American Institute of Certified Public Accountants and three of its officials. The Institute, an incorporated body, is a nonprofit, nation-wide professional society, membership in which is open to all properly qualified certified public accountants and the purpose of which is the furtherance of the ideals and principles of the accounting profession. The three individual respondents are the President of the Institute (Mr. L. H. Penney), the Chairman of the Institute's Committee on Accounting Procedure (Mr. William W. Werntz), and the Institute's Director of Research (Mr. Carman G. Blough).

The petitioner utility companies are not members of the Institute, in which membership is confined to individual accountants.

The Relief Sought by the Complaint

The complaint seeks a judgment temporarily and permanently enjoining the respondents and anyone acting on their behalf from circulating "to the members of the Institute or to any members of the accountancy profession" a certain letter from the Institute's Committee on Accounting Procedure without first having taken certain preliminary procedural steps set out below. (Complaint, pp. 12-13.) The letter in question is as follows:

"AMERICAN INSTITUTE OF CERTIFIED PUBLIC ACCOUNTANTS
"270 Madison Avenue, New York 16, N.Y.

"April 15, 1959

"To the Members of the American
    Institute of Certified Public Accountants

"Gentlemen:

"Question has been raised with respect to the intent of the committee on accounting procedure in using the phrase 'a deferred tax account' in Accounting Research Bulletin No. 44 (revised), Declining-balance Depreciation, to indicate the account to be credited for the amount of the deferred income tax (see paragraphs 4 and 5).

"The committee used the phrase in its ordinary connotation of an account to be shown in the balance sheet as a liability or a deferred credit. A provision in recognition of the deferral of income taxes, being required for the proper determination of net income, should not at the same time result in a credit to earned surplus or to any other account included in the stockholders' equity section of the balance sheet.

"Three of the twenty-one members of the committee, Messrs. Jennings, Powell and Staub, dissented to the issuance at this time of any letter interpreting Accounting Research Bulletin No. 44 (revised).

"COMMITTEE ON ACCOUNTING PROCEDURE

"By William W. Werntz, Chairman"

The complaint also seeks to enjoin the respondents from adopting or issuing any other statements to the same effect (Complaint, pp. 12-13), and seeks "such other, further and different relief" as may seem just and proper.

The preliminary procedural steps which the petitioners seek to impose upon the respondents are that the Institute and Committee must have

"(a) Submitted a draft of the proposed letter to the persons to whom the exposure draft of Accounting Research Bulletin No. 44 was submitted.

"(b) Permitted such reasonable period of time, not less than 60 days, to have elapsed subsequent to said submission in order that such persons may have the opportunity of submitting for the consideration of the Committee their views and opinions.

"(c) Otherwise complied with the Institute's and the Committee's practices and procedures with respect to the publication of Accounting Research Bulletins."

The Theory of the Alleged Cause of Action

Each of the petitioner companies carries in its balance sheet large sums (totalling for the three $65,000,000) in an account for deferred federal income taxes, which account appears in a restricted surplus account in the stockholders' equity section of the balance sheet.

It is said that if the letter is distributed then because of the "prestige and authority of the Committee" it will "cause substantial numbers of accountants, financial institutions, investment banking concerns, rating services, financial analysts and governmental agencies to question the continued inclusion of credits for deferred taxes in the earned surplus accounts" of petitioners so that petitioners "will be seriously interfered with in their dealings and relationships with such persons and institutions." (Complaint, paragraph 29; affidavit of Mr. Donald C. Cook, a vice president of each of the petitioners, at paragraph 21).

As to the intent to injure, the complaint alleges the following:

"30. The Institute and the Committee know that the foregoing [damage] will result . . . and intend that such . . . injury . . . shall occur. The actions of the defendants . . . are in wanton, reckless and wilful disregard of the said consequences of their proposed action."

There has been no suggestion by petitioners, in pleadings, on brief or in oral argument, that the opinion letter was aimed at the petitioners or that it was intended to deal with them except as they, like all other corporations, might come within the general purview of the letter.

The Proceedings Below

The opinion letter in question was about to be sent by the Committee to the members of the Institute when, without notice, the petitioners secured a temporary restraining order on April 15, 1959 from Judge Palmieri of the District Court for the Southern District of New York, and also an order to show cause why a preliminary injunction should not be issued, returnable on April 17. For convenience of counsel for both sides, the return date was postponed to May 7. On May 1, respondents filed a cross-motion to dismiss the complaint for failure to state a claim upon which relief can be granted. On the morning of May 6 the respondents served affidavits in opposition to the petitioners' application for an injunction, and that day the parties exchanged briefs. A reply affidavit by Mr. Cook, 28 pages in length with seven exhibits, was served upon the respondents late in the evening of May 6. On the morning of May 7, the District Court held a hearing on the petitioners' motion for preliminary injunction and the respondents' motion to dismiss. The petitioners' brief relied on Mr. Cook's affidavit in opposing the motion to dismiss; and in their argument on both motions petitioners did not differentiate between facts which came from the complaint and facts which came from affidavits.

On May 20 the District Court filed a full opinion holding that the motion for preliminary injunction should be denied and that summary judgment should be granted for respondents because, in view of the submission and consideration of matters beyond the pleadings, the motion to dismiss should be treated as a motion for summary judgment under Rule 12(b) of the Federal Rules of Civil Procedure.

On May 25 counsel appeared before the District Court to settle the terms of the order. At no time during this hearing, which was approximately an hour-and-one-half in length, did petitioners suggest that they had any further material to offer in connection with summary judgment. The Judge refused to grant petitioners' request for an injunction pending disposition of their appeal, but granted an injunction only until the hearing of petitioners' motion to the Court of Appeals for an injunction pending appeal, provided such motion was made on or before June 1.

The petitioners immediately appealed to the Court of Appeals for the Second Circuit and moved therein for an injunction pending appeal. This motion was set for argument on June 4. On the preceding day, June 3, the parties exchanged voluminous briefs. Petitioners' brief raised for the first time the claim that they were prejudiced by the District Court's treating the case as being ripe for summary judgment. At the hearing on June 4 the Court of Appeals determined, with the consent of the parties, that it would decide the appeal on the merits on the basis of the oral argument and the briefs which had been submitted and extended the stay restraining respondents from circulating the Committee's letter until its decision was handed down.

On June 17 the Court of Appeals, in a unanimous per curiam decision, affirmed the judgment of the District Court and vacated its stay.

On June 19 petitioners applied to Circuit Judge Lumbard for an order enjoining respondents until July 9, 1959 from distributing the Committee's proposed letter or any similar statement. By order of the same date Judge Lumbard granted such injunction pending the hearing of an application to be made by petitioners to a Justice of the Supreme Court not later than July 9, 1959, for an injunction pending the determination of a petition for review on writ of certiorari. The Circuit Judge's order stated that in no event was the injunction to extend beyond July 9, 1959.

The Facts

The petitioners contend that the Committee owes them a legal duty to "expose" its views tentatively before making any final decisions. The Accounting Research Bulletins published by the Committee on Accounting Procedure make clear that they represent only the opinions of the Committee, unless they have been specifically adopted by the Institute's membership. Neither by any law nor under the Institute's own rules do the statements of the Committee have any authority beyond the force of their own reasoning. (Affidavit of Mr. William W. Werntz, Chairman of the Committee, at paragraph 6 and Exhibit A, p. 9.)

Furthermore, the Committee has discretion to work out its own procedure, except for a requirement that it act by a two-thirds majority of its 21 members, with the privilege of publication of dissent with reasons therefor along with the majority opinion, and a requirement that the Committee may only presume to speak for itself. (Affidavit of Mr. Werntz, especially at paragraph 11, and Exhibit A, pp. 8-9.)

The proposed opinion letter purports to clarify the Committee's intent as expressed in the phrase "a deferred tax account" in Accounting Research Bulletin No. 44 (revised). This is impossible, the petitioners claim, because the phrase in question did not appear in the version of the Bulletin voted upon by the Committee but was inserted afterwards.

After a vote the Institute's staff, with the approval of the Chairman of the Committee, may make nonsubstantive alterations in the "ballot" draft before issuance of the Bulletin. (Affidavit of Mr. Werntz, paragraph 9.) Accordingly, with the approval of the Chairman of the Committee, the Institute's staff inserted in the final draft, after the vote, a reference to "crediting a deferred tax account" in the interest of consistency of expression as between that Bulletin and Chapter 9, Section c, of Accounting Research Bulletin No. 43 -- an earlier Bulletin dealing with the matter of accelerated amortization under Section 168 of the Internal Revenue Code.* The change was not deemed to be substantive; neither of these Bulletins specifically stated where the "deferred tax account" should appear in the balance sheet. Advance copies of Bulletin No. 44 (revised) were sent to members of the Committee, with the staff's revision, and no member of the Committee objected. (Affidavit of Mr. Werntz, paragraphs 9 and 10.)

The Committee members approved the interpretive letter and its circulation to the members of the Institute, by a vote of 18 to 3. Of the 18 members favorably voting 16 had been members of the Committee when the Bulletin interpreted was issued a few months before, during the previous year. They constituted more than two-thirds of the members of the Committee in office at that time. (Affidavit of Mr. Werntz, paragraph 11.)

It should briefly be noted here that the Committee's view is supported by most respectable authority, as the District Court found. For example, on May 29, 1958, the Federal Power Commission promulgated an order forbidding utilities under its jurisdiction from including such a deferred tax account in the stockholders' equity section of balance sheets. (23 Fed. Reg. 4161 (June 12, 1958).) Indiana & Michigan Electric Company, one of the petitioners, has been ordered by the Indiana State Public Service Commission to eliminate from the stockholders' equity section of its balance sheet its account for deferred taxes and has appealed that order to the Indiana courts. (Affidavit of Mr. Cook, paragraph 28(d)(8), and affidavit of Mr. Werntz, paragraph 12(2).) The Securities and Exchange Commission has tentatively announced a policy similar to that of the Federal Power Commission. (Affidavit of Mr. George C. Christie, Exhibit T.)

Many utilities follow the Committee's position in their accounting practices. The Committee's position is followed by Arthur Andersen & Co., which audits the accounts of one-third of the electric and gas utility companies in the country; based on a survey of the 1957 published stockholders' reports of 353 utilities, of 226 reporting an accumulated credit resulting from the use of liberalized depreciation under Section 167 of the Internal Revenue Code, 176 treated the credit

---

* This Bulletin was originally issued in 1952 as Accounting Research Bulletin No. 42 and appears as Exhibit E to the affidavit of Mr. Werntz. As codified without change in Bulletin No. 43, it appears in Exhibit A to the affidavit of Mr. Werntz. The reference to deferred income taxes appears in paragraph 12 of this Bulletin.

outside the equity-capital section of the balance sheet and only 50 companies treated the credit as either earned surplus or restricted surplus. (Affidavit of Mr. F. Merrill Beatty, passim.)

I.

THE DECISION OF THE DISTRICT COURT ON A QUESTION OF NEW YORK LAW, UNANIMOUSLY AFFIRMED BY THE COURT OF APPEALS, PRESENTS NO QUESTION WHICH WOULD MERIT REVIEW BY THIS COURT

Petitioners' case from the outset has been predicated upon the doctrine of "prima facie tort," and they have relied principally upon the New York case of Advance Music Corp. v. American Tobacco Co., 296 N.Y. 79, 70 N.E. 2d 401 (1946).* The District Court concluded, after an extensive review of the New York law, that neither the Advance Music case nor any other precedent would justify any injunctive or other relief against the respondents for their seeking to publish and distribute the views of the Institute Committee. Before the Court of Appeals, petitioners again fully briefed and presented their claims under the New York law. The Court of Appeals, in its opinion affirming the judgment in favor of respondents, stated that it agreed with the District Court's decision on the substantive law.

A question of state law does not warrant review by this Court. As the Court has indicated on many occasions, in this area it defers to the decisions of the lower federal courts -- skilled in the law of particular states -- unless their conclusions are shown to be unreasonable. Far from being unreasonable, the decision on the merits here has been fully considered by two federal courts, which have uniformly concluded that petitioners simply have no claim against respondents.

With respect to the Advance Music case, as the District Court made clear, it, like the other decisions advanced by petitioners is wide of the mark. In the Advance Music case the New York Court of Appeals reviewed a decision dismissing a complaint brought by a publisher of popular songs against the sponsor, and its advertising agent, of a radio program known as "Your Hit Parade." The complaint alleged that the program falsely represented to its large audience that it had ascertained, on the basis of volume of sales, the nine or ten most popular

---

* Petitioners also rely on two labor cases in which the New York Court of Appeals found respectively, that persuading members not to work for plaintiff employer or with members of a rival plaintiff organization were not justified as a lawful labor objective. Opera on Tour, Inc. v. Weber, 285 N.Y. 348, 34 N.E. 2d 349 (1941); American Guild of Musical Artists, Inc. v. Petrillo, 286 N.Y. 226, 36 N.E. 2d 123 (1941). We need not elaborate upon the point that these cases, involving words and action specifically aimed solely at the plaintiffs concerned, having nothing to do with the present case.

songs each week, and the order of their sales popularity; that in fact no such ascertainment was made at all; that the plaintiff's songs were consistently excluded from the list, without justification, or were given an unjustifiably low ranking; that this was done with intent to injure the plaintiff; and that the plaintiff had, indeed, been injured by a refusal of jobbers and others to distribute plaintiff's songs to dealers because of their omission or low ranking on "Your Hit Parade."

The Advance Music case was thus a perfectly clear case of wanton misrepresentation of fact and came very close to a case of common-law unfair competition. The present case is completely different. As pointed out in the opinion of the District Court, the proposed letter of the Committee on Accounting Procedure is simply an expression of opinion on a general accounting question. Moreover, it is not alleged that the opinion is not honestly held by the members of the Committee who voted to issue the letter. In fact, as found by the District Court, the Committee's view is supported by most respectable authority.

The simple fact is that petitioners have ignored here, in their application for a stay, as they have sought to do below, the fact that the basis of prima facie tort is malicious injury -- doing a harm malevolently for the sake of the harm as an end in itself and not merely as a means to another end legitimately desired. The limitations of the doctrine have been recently stated by the New York Court of Appeals in Reinforce, Inc. v. Birney, 308 N.Y. 164, 124 N.E. 2d 104 (1954), a case which is not mentioned by petitioners. In that case the Court held:

> "If the doers, by means not in themselves unlawful, of acts not in themselves unlawful, have any proper purpose to serve, they are not liable for the damage they cause [citing cases]. Unions, as well as everyone else, may claim the benefit of the settled rule that 'the genesis which will make a lawful act unlawful must be a malicious one unmixed with any other and exclusively directed to injury and damage of another' [citing cases]." 308 N.Y. at _____ , 124 N.E. 2d at 106.

Moreover, as was recognized by the New York Court in Advance Music (296 N.Y. at _____ , 70, N.E. 2d at 403) and other cases, the plaintiff in a prima facie tort case can get no relief where there is "justification" for the defendant's act. Here the purposes of the defendant Institute -- those of a voluntary, professional association -- are adequate justification, if justification be required, for the proposed communication.

In short, what petitioners seek to thwart here by the application for a further injunction is the effectiveness of a decision based on state law on which they have been heard in two federal courts versed in that law -- a decision which does not in any sense fall within the criteria for granting certiorari.

II.

THE DISTRICT COURT'S TREATMENT OF THE CASE AS ONE FOR SUMMARY JUDGMENT WAS PROPER AND PRESENTS NO ISSUE FOR THIS COURT'S REVIEW.

Rule 12(b) of the Federal Rules of Civil Procedure permits a District Court to treat a motion to dismiss for failure to state a claim as a motion for summary judgment where matters outside the pleadings are before the court. It requires that in such circumstances all parties be given reasonable opportunity to present material pertinent to a motion for summary judgment.

In this case the District Court, having before it affidavits submitted on behalf of both petitioners and respondents, treated respondents' motion to dismiss as one for summary judgment. In the Court of Appeals petitioners briefed and argued at length a claim that the District Court erred in so doing. The Court of Appeals concluded unanimously that the District Court's treatment of the case was proper and that petitioners were not denied the opportunity to present material pertinent to summary judgment which Rule 12(b) guarantees.

In the Court of Appeals petitioners relied upon Pacific American Fisheries, Inc. v. Mullaney, 191 F. 2d 137 (9th Cir. 1951), and in their present application they assert a conflict between the decision below and that case. There is no conflict. Both the Second Circuit here and the Ninth Circuit there read Rule 12(b) in the only way in which it can be read, i.e., as requiring that all parties be given an opportunity to present pertinent material.

The Pacific American Fisheries case involved the validity of an Alaskan license tax imposing a higher levy on nonresident than on resident fishermen. Defendant, the Alaskan Tax Commissioner, moved for judgment on the pleadings on the grounds: (1) a recent decision of the same court holding the tax valid and (2) an asserted lack of power to enjoin a criminal prosecution. The District Court treated this motion as a motion for summary judgment and entered summary judgment for the defendant, apparently on the second ground, saying it had considered matters outside the pleadings and "there is no issue of fact in view of the lack of power to grant injunctive relief." 191 F.2d at 139-40. The Court of Appeals reversed, holding, inter alia, that the District Court was mistaken in its view that plaintiff could not obtain injunctive relief and that summary judgment was improper in part because the plaintiff was not given the opportunity to support the allegation in its complaint, controverted by an affidavit on behalf of defendant, that there was no such additional cost or burden of enforcing the statute against nonresident fishermen as to justify the discriminatory tax rate. Clearly, then, this was a case in which facts which were immaterial on the District Court's view of the law were rendered material by the Court of Appeals' different opinion and therefore became pertinent to summary judgment.

The present case is quite different.   Neither in the District Court nor in their application to this Court have petitioners pointed to any facts not covered by the extensive affidavits of Mr. Whitman and Mr. Cook submitted on their behalf which they would wish to present to the District Court. Accordingly, the Court of Appeals was clearly correct in its conclusion that "we do not see that plaintiffs were denied the opportunity to present materials pertinent to summary judgment which the rule provides."

In addition, it is to be noted that in the Pacific American Fisheries, Inc. case, the motion for judgment on the pleadings was considered some time after the hearing on preliminary injunction in connection with which the affidavits were filed. In the instant case the application for preliminary injunction and the cross-motion to dismiss were briefed and argued together. Petitioners, both in their oral argument and in their memorandum, relied heavily on the materials in their affidavits in arguing that the complaint should not be dismissed for failure to state a claim. There is not and scarcely could be any conflict between this case and the Pacific American Fisheries case.*

In a slight variation of their claim, petitioners here contend that the District Court in granting summary judgment decided controverted issues of material fact.   They are vague as to precisely what issues of fact they consider both material and controverted.   As we have shown in our discussion of the interpretation of the relevant state law by the courts below, there were no controverted issues of material fact.

Thus, petitioners claim that the District Court decided against them issues concerning respondents' intent in publishing the Committee's letter; concerning whether the characterization of the letter as interpretive of a prior bulletin was false, and concerning the actual effect of the Committee's opinions. The District Court's opinion makes plain that on its view of New York law the allegations of petitioners on their side of these issues were insufficient in law to sustain their claim. Therefore, they are not material facts.

The Court of Appeals has not misread Rule 12(b). It has not rendered a decision in conflict with that of any other Court of Appeals, and it has not sanctioned the use by the Court of Appeals of the summary judgment procedure to decide material issues of fact.

---

* In Herron v. Herron, 255 F. 2d 589 (5th Cir. 1958), with the "principle" of which petitioners assert this case conflicts, the complaint sought to establish a trust. An answer denied the existence of a trust and raised other material issues of fact. Plaintiff moved for production and inspection of documents; the motion came on for hearing, and at the hearing the District Judge put plaintiff on the stand; he was cross-examined, and the court then ruled that there was no trust and granted summary judgment for defendant. The Court of Appeals reversed on the ground that "without notice, without an opportunity to produce witnesses or to examine books and records of obvious bearing on the issue, without realizing what was happening to him -- it happened: the case was disposed of on the merits." 255 F.2d at 594.

III.

GRANTING OF THE INJUNCTION HERE SOUGHT BY PETITIONERS WOULD EFFECTIVELY DENY RESPONDENTS THEIR RIGHTS AS UPHELD BY BOTH COURTS BELOW, A RESULT INJURIOUS TO RESPONDENTS AND CONTRARY TO THE PUBLIC INTEREST

Petitioners baldly assert that, if their application for an injunction be granted, there is no possibility of any damage whatever to respondents. This position apparently reflects a view that damage can mean nothing except financial damage and unless the Institute can show financial injury, respondents and the public have no rights which merit consideration. This of course ignores the important function which non-profit public service organizations such as the Institute perform and the damage and injury which can result to them if their rights to select their internal procedures and to conduct their public service activities can be disrupted in the manner which petitioners have attempted in this litigation. The basic public interest involved can be put no better than it was by the Court of Appeals in its succinct opinion pointing out the public obligation accepted by every professional body for unfettered expression of its views.

As a result of this proceeding, respondents have been prevented since April 15 from functioning in accordance with the Institute's own procedures. During this period petitioners' claims have been considered by both the District Court and the Court of Appeals. After full consideration, they were rejected by both courts. There is no justification for granting to petitioners, after their contentions have been fully aired and determined adversely to them, an injunction which prevents the Committee from performing its functions. There is no issue which petitioners can present to this Court which would justify the exercise of a power which is to be used sparingly.

Moreover, it must be pointed out once again that the views of the Committee, as expressed in the proposed letter or otherwise, are not binding on anyone. For example, insofar as the form and content of petitioners' financial statements are prescribed by the Securities and Exchange Commission, it is open to them to attack the Committee's letter and its views before the Commission. Petitioners can present to the Commission the same criticisms they make here. They can tell the Commission that they disagree not only with the letter but with the decisions of the two lower courts and that they intend to petition this Court for an adjudication vindicating their position that the procedures followed in adopting and issuing the letter were not satisfactory.

So, too, petitioners are free to differ from, to belittle, criticize or attack in any way they desire the Committee's position before any other governmental agency. The same is true in petitioners' dealings with financial institutions, accountants or any other governmental or private party. Insofar as the petitioners differ with the Committee's view, they are completely free to persuade any agency, institution, or person to accept their views rather than the Committee's position. If petitioners are successful in securing acceptance of their views there is no conceivable damage. If they are unsuccessful, there is still no damage and certainly no legal injury, in being required to follow sound accounting procedures.

On April 8, 1959, respondent Blough, as the Institute's Director of Research, appeared as a witness at an SEC rule-making hearing -- a public hearing of which a transcript is available to any member of the public -- and testified, among other things, that the Institute's Committee had adopted and was about to send out the letter in question, and read into the record the significant portion of the letter. (See affidavits of Mr. Robert O. Whitman, par. 6; and of Mr. Cook, par. 18.) Consequently, issuance of the injunction here sought would create the spectacle of the SEC's having been advised of the Committee's opinion in a public hearing but the Institute's own members being deprived of that same knowledge unless they happen to read the advance sheets reporting the District Court's opinion, in which the letter is quoted in full. It is unthinkable that equity should create any such state of affairs.

Finally, as the affidavit of Mr. John L. Carey, Executive Director of the Institute, shows, the Committee on Accounting Procedure is to go out of existence as of August 31, 1959, as a result of the adoption by the Institute of a new program which has been under study since long before this litigation began. The Institute, understandably, proposes that the Committee wind up its affairs before the new program goes into effect. An injunction would be an obvious impediment to the completion of this transition and could even lead to such confusion and delay in the Institute's processes as to accomplish the petitioners' aim even though they lose their case.

Petitioners contend that denial of the injunction applied for would render the case moot insofar as their request for equitable relief is concerned. This is not so. Petitioners' complaint prays for an injunction not only against the circulation of the Committee's opinion letter to the members of the Institute but also against any adoption by the Institute of the Committee's letter or of any other opinion to the same effect. (See Complaint, pp. 12-13).

Therefore the sending of the Committee's letter does not eliminate the controversy which petitioners have posed. If it be assumed that review would be granted on petition for certiorari -- an assumption for which, we believe, there is no basis -- and the decision below reversed, petitioners could still, for example, seek a declaratory judgment that respondents' acts in the promulgation of their opinion were tortious. In addition to injunctive relief the complaint seeks "such other, further and different relief" as may be granted regardless of whether such has been specifically requested in the complaint. See Rule 54(c), F.R.C.P.; Becker v. Buder, 88 F.Supp. 609, 613 (E.D. Mo. 1949), affirmed, 185 F.2d 311 (8th Cir. 1950), cf. Truth Seeker Co., Inc. v. Durning, 147 F.2d 54 (2d Cir. 1945); Carmichael v. Mills Music, Inc., 121 F.Supp. 43 (S.D.N.Y. 1954).

As a practical matter, such a declaration would have virtually the same value to the petitioners as the injunction they seek -- in that it could be used to effective purposes in connection with any questions that might be raised by accountants, financial institutions, or otherwise with respect to the petitioners' balance sheets or even in connection with the position the petitioners have taken at the SEC. Also, either under a declaratory judgment or otherwise, a court still could grant damages in this lawsuit even after events had made the granting of injunctive relief nugatory. Subin v. Goldsmith, 224 F.2d 753, 761-62 (2d Cir.), cert. denied, 350 U.S. 883 (1955):

> "It is suggested that, as apparently the transfer of . . . assets . . . was completed after denial of the preliminary injunction, a final injunction will serve no purpose, and therefore plaintiff, if he wins, can obtain no relief. . . . The complaint asks 'for such other and further relief as may be just and proper.' Accordingly the court can award damages if they will afford adequate relief. See F.R.C.P. 54(c)."

But even if mootness were threatened, an injunction is not issuable as of right. See Edwards v. New York, 76 S.Ct. 1058, 1059 (1956), in which Mr. Justice Harlan denied a stay of execution of a death sentence pending certiorari proceedings:

> "[W] hat I must determine is whether any of these matters is sufficiently debatable to lead to the belief that at least four members of the Court would vote to grant certiorari."

See also Jimenez v. Barber, 252 F. 2d 559 (9th Cir.), application for stay of deportation denied. 335 U.S. 943 (1958).

CONCLUSION

For the foregoing reasons, respondents submit that no further stay of any kind is justified and petitioners' application should be denied.

Respectfully submitted,

HOWARD C. WESTWOOD
FONTAINE C. BRADLEY
STANLEY L. TEMKO
PHIL R. STANSBURY

COVINGTON & BURLING
Of Counsel

July 3, 1959

Attorneys for Respondents

SUPREME COURT OF THE UNITED STATES

OCTOBER TERM, 1959.

Appalachian Power Company, Ohio Power Company and
Indiana & Michigan Electric Company, Petitioners,
v.
American Institute of Certified Public Accountants, L. H.
Penney, William W. Werntz and Carman G. Blough.

(July 7, 1959)

MR. JUSTICE BRENNAN, Circuit Justice (temporarily assigned).

The petitioners apply for an order (1) staying the Mandate of the United States Court of Appeals for the Second Circuit on its judgment of June 17, 1959, affirming a summary judgment for respondents entered by the District Court for the Southern District of New York, and (2) restraining the respondents, pending the final determination of this action by this Court, from distributing to the members of the respondent American Institute of Certified Public Accountants or to any other members of the accounting profession a proposed letter dated April 15, 1959, or any other communication, to the effect that the respondent American Institute of Certified Public Accountants or its Committee on Accounting Procedure is of the opinion or recommends that a deferred tax account set up in recognition of the deferral of income taxes should not be credited to earned surplus or to any other account included in the stockholders' equity section of the balance sheet.

The petitioners, public utility companies which account for deferred taxes in the stockholders equity section of their balance sheets, brought this diversity suit in the District Court. They sought, in addition to other relief, an injunction against respondents promulgating or distributing said letter except upon compliance with certain specified procedures. An interim restraint was granted pending hearing on a motion for preliminary injunction. Respondents made a motion to dismiss the complaint under Rule 12 (b) of the Federal Rules of Civil Procedure. Affidavits were filed by both sides. The District Court heard the motions together, denied the motion for a preliminary injunction and, treating the motion to dismiss, since affidavits of both sides were filed, as a motion for summary judgment under Rule 56 of the Federal Rules of Civil Procedure, entered summary judgment for the respondents. The District Court found that the letter of April 15 reflected the Committee's "honest opinions," that it was not "false or fraudulent" and that it could "hardly be termed wanton." The District Court held that, under such circumstances, the law of New York, which governs in this diversity case, does not provide a cause of action. The Court of Appeals unanimously affirmed.

The stay and temporary restraining order are sought by the petitioners upon allegations that respondents will distribute the letter, unless restrained, and this will cause petitioners irreparable injury and also render moot their proposed petition for certiorari, at least insofar as concerns their prayers for injunctive relief against such a distribution. Even assuming, however, the possibilities of irreparable injury and mootness, as claimed by the petitioners, I do not feel at liberty to grant their application unless in my judgment there is a prospect that the petition for certiorari which they propose to file will appear to at least four members of the Court to present questions which warrant our review.

I heard oral argument on this application and after consideration of the arguments made and the briefs filed, it is my judgment that the questions proposed to be presented in the petition for certiorari will not command four votes for review. The petitioners state that three contentions will be presented. One is that the District Court and the Court of Appeals erred in their conclusion as to the relevant state law. But this Court ordinarily accepts the determination of state law as found by the Court of Appeals, particularly when, as here, the same finding is made by the District Court, and no showing has been made to persuade me that such would not be the case here. The second contention is that the District Court, in treating respondent's motion to dismiss as a motion for summary judgment, erred in not following the requirement of Rule 12 (b) that "all parties shall be given reasonable opportunity to present all material made pertinent to such motion (for summary judgment) by Rule 56." But ordinarily an application by a District Court of the Rules of Civil Procedure when affirmed by the Court of appeals will not be reviewed by this Court. This is particularly true where, as here, the question is one that concerns the judgment of the District Judge in relation to a particular set of facts. And I do not find the conflict suggested by petitioners between the decision below and *Pacific American Fisheries v. Mullaney,* 191 F. 2d 137. That decision simply held that the District Court was incorrect in its conclusion as to the pertinent law, and that under the Court of Appeals' view of the law certain relevant facts were in dispute, so that the grant of summary judgment was improper. Finally, the petitioners suggest they will present in their petition for certiorari the question whether federal courts, in light of the First Amendment, are empowered to enjoin tortious communications. But the holdings below are that in the circumstances of this case the distribution by respondents of the proposed letter would not constitute a tortious act under New York law; therefore no First Amendment problem is involved.

The application is denied, since, in my judgment, none of the questions proposed to be presented in the petition for certiorari has the prospect of commanding four votes for review.

IN THE

Supreme Court of the United States

OCTOBER TERM, 1959

No. 388

APPALACHIAN POWER COMPANY, OHIO
POWER COMPANY and INDIANA & MICHIGAN
ELECTRIC COMPANY,

Petitioners.

—*against*—

AMERICAN INSTITUTE OF CERTIFIED PUBLIC
ACCOUNTANTS, L. H. PENNEY, WILLIAM W.
WERNTZ and CARMAN G. BLOUGH,

Respondents.

**PETITION FOR A WRIT OF CERTIORARI TO THE
UNITED STATES COURT OF APPEALS FOR THE
SECOND CIRCUIT**

WHITNEY NORTH SEYMOUR
Counsel for Petitioners
120 Broadway
New York 5, New York

RICHARD M. DICKE,
WILLIAM J. MANNING,
SIMPSON THACHER & BARTLETT,
Of Counsel

September 9, 1959

TABLE OF CONTENTS

ii

AUTHORITIES CITED

Cases

iii

Federal Rules of Civil Procedure

iv

Miscellaneous

———

IN THE

Supreme Court of the United States

OCTOBER TERM, 1959

APPALACHIAN POWER COMPANY, OHIO
  POWER COMPANY and INDIANA &
  MICHIGAN ELECTRIC COMPANY,

                              Petitioners,

—*against*—

AMERICAN INSTITUTE OF CERTIFIED PUB-
  LIC ACCOUNTANTS, L. H. PENNEY,
  WILLIAM W. WERNTZ and CARMAN G.
  BLOUGH,

                              Respondents.

No. 388

PETITION FOR A WRIT OF CERTIORARI TO THE UNITED STATES COURT OF APPEALS FOR THE SECOND CIRCUIT

Petitioners respectfully pray that a writ of certiorari issue to review the judgment of the United States Court of Appeals for the Second Circuit entered in the above-entitled action on June 17, 1959.

OPINIONS BELOW

The opinion of the United States District Court for the Southern District of New York, Levet, *J.*, is unreported as yet and is printed in Appendix A hereto. The opinion of the Court of Appeals is likewise unreported as yet and is printed in Appendix B hereto.

2

JURISDICTION

The judgment of the Court of Appeals was entered on June 17, 1959. The jurisdiction of this Court is invoked under 28 U. S. C. § 1254(1). Federal jurisdiction in the first instance was based upon diversity of citizenship.

QUESTIONS PRESENTED

1. Was it not error, and in conflict with a decision of the Court of Appeals for the Ninth Circuit, to treat respondents' motion to dismiss the complaint for failure to state a claim upon which relief could be granted as a motion for summary judgment (a) when no matters outside the pleading were presented to the Court on said motion, and (b) without affording petitioners a reasonable opportunity to present all material pertinent to a motion for summary judgment?

2. Was it not error, and in conflict with decisions of this Court and other Federal Courts, to fail to accept as facts, on respondents' motion to dismiss, matters well pleaded in the complaint and to grant summary judgment in the face of issues of fact revealed by the record before the Court?

3. Did not the decision below depart from the New York rule that it is an actionable tort intentionally to inflict harm on another without legal justification?

4. Do the District Courts, sitting as courts of equity, lack power to enjoin the publication of tortious words by a professional organization?

3

FEDERAL RULES OF CIVIL PROCEDURE INVOLVED

The Federal Rules of Civil Procedure here involved are Rules 12 and 56, the pertinent portions of which are printed in Appendix C hereto.

STATEMENT OF THE CASE

Petitioners are three operating electric public utility companies. Respondent American Institute of Certified Public Accountants (the "Institute") is a national organization of certified public accountants with more than 33,000 members. The individual respondents are the President of the Institute, the Chairman of its Committee on Accounting Procedure (the "Committee") and its Director of Research (Complaint, pars. 2-5, 7).[1]

Petitioners sought in this action to restrain the distribution by respondents to the 33,000 members of the Institute and other accountants and members of the business community of a proposed letter opinion to the effect that certain accounting practices and procedures with respect to accounting for credits for deferred taxes (followed by petitioners and some other electric public utility companies) heretofore recognized by all as generally accepted accounting principles are now to be regarded as improper. The proposed letter is set forth in full in the opinion of the District Court (D. C. Opinion, p. 3).

The petitioners have recorded on their books, in accordance with orders of the state regulatory agencies having

---

[1]There is no printed record herein. When petitioners moved for an injunction pending appeal to the Court of Appeals, said motion was heard on the original record from the District Court. The argument on said motion was then, with the consent of the parties, considered to be the argument of the appeal. The original record, duly certified, has been submitted to the Clerk of this Court together with nine photostatic copies of the pertinent portions thereof. The numbered pages of the certified record from the District Court will be referred to as "D. C. p.   ", and those from that of the Court of Appeals as "C. A. p.   ".

4

jurisdiction over them, more than $65,000,000 in accounts designated as "Earned Surplus Restricted for Future Federal Income Taxes". The complaint alleged that, by reason of the prestige and authority of the respondents in the accounting profession and the business community, the distribution of the proposed opinion would cause substantial numbers of accountants, financial institutions, investment banking concerns, rating services, financial analysts and governmental agencies to question the continued inclusion of that $65,000,000, which represents credits for deferred taxes, in the above described accounts or in any other part of the stockholders equity section of the balance sheet, with the result that petitioners would be seriously interfered with in their dealings and relationships with such persons and institutions, and that a further question would be raised as to the validity of the announced debt ratios of the petitioners, which were the bases upon which they had in the past, and proposed in the future, to borrow and sell securities to finance current construction programs which had been budgeted at more than $100,000,000 for the year 1959 alone (Complaint, pars. 6, 9-30).

It is petitioners' position that the facts presented in the verified complaint established all of the elements of a prima facie tort under settled principles of New York law and called for the exercise of the injunctive power of a court of equity to protect the petitioners from immediate and irreparable harm—in short, that the respondents were, without justification and with intent to injure, about to inflict irreparable harm upon petitioners.

The complaint alleged, first of all, that the stated purpose for distributing the proposed letter was spurious and that the Committee did not have, and could not have had, the intent claimed in the proposed letter. It further alleged that the respondents with full knowledge of the harm which would be caused to petitioners thereby, intended to cause that harm, that respondents had no legal justification for

5

causing such harm, and that they were acting wilfully, wantonly and recklessly in preparing to distribute the letter. It was also alleged that the respondents had completely abdicated their responsibility and duty to use some minimum standards of care in formulating this pronouncement which they knew would harm others, that they had taken no steps whatever reasonably designed to ascertain its propriety or correctness and, indeed, that they even had failed to follow their own well established practices and procedures heretofore used by them in connection with the distribution of opinions upon accounting matters (Complaint, pars. 18-30).

The action was commenced by the filing of the verified complaint on April 15, 1959 (D. C. pp. 1-14). Simultaneously therewith, Hon. Edward L. Palmieri, Judge of the United States District Court, signed an order to show cause bringing on a motion by petitioners for a preliminary injunction and containing a temporary restraining order enjoining the respondents from distributing the proposed letter pending a hearing on that motion (D. C. pp. 17-40). The preliminary injunction and temporary restraining order were sought because petitioners were unable to secure from respondents any commitment to delay the distribution of the proposed letter (Whitman aff., par. 6).

On May 1, 1959 respondents served a Notice of Cross-motion for an order, pursuant to Rule 12(b)(6) of the Federal Rules of Civil Procedure, dismissing the complaint on the ground that it failed to state a claim upon which relief could be granted (D. C. pp. 49-51). No affidavits or other materials were served in support of that motion, and no motion for summary judgment was made then or later.

On May 6, 1959 respondents served three affidavits in opposition to petitioners' motion for a preliminary injunction, and on May 7, 1959 petitioners served an affidavit in reply thereto. Examination of the captions and substance of these affidavits shows that neither party considered them to be submitted on the motion to dismiss but that they were

6

all submitted on the motion for a temporary injunction (Werntz, Beatty, Christie and Cook affs.).

Both the motion for a temporary injunction and the motion to dismiss for failure to state a claim were heard before Hon. Richard H. Levet on May 7, 1959. From the bench, the restraining order was continued pending decision. The District Court's opinion was filed on May 21, 1959 (D. C. pp. 222-36). It held that petitioners' motion for a temporary injunction must be denied, that respondents' motion had been treated as one for summary judgment pursuant to Rule 56 of the Federal Rules of Civil Procedure and that summary judgment must be entered dismissing the complaint.

At no time, however, on the argument or otherwise, had there been any suggestion that the motion to dismiss was to be treated as one for summary judgment, and petitioners were given no opportunity to take depositions or to submit affidavits in support of the well-pleaded allegations of the verified complaint. Examination of the record reveals that such proofs would have been readily available and forthcoming.

Judge Levet did, however, sign an order enjoining the distribution of the proposed letter pending the making of an application to the Court of Appeals for the Second Circuit for an order restraining its distribution pending appeal (D. C. pp. 237-40). Such an application was made (C. A. pp. 3-9) and argued before the Court of Appeals on June 4, 1959. The Court of Appeals granted that application from the bench (C. A. pp. 1-2), and on consent of the parties the briefs and argument on that motion were considered as the briefs and argument on the appeal on the merits (C. A. p. 16).

On June 17, 1959 the Court of Appeals filed its decision affirming the judgment below and vacating the stay (C. A. pp. 14-16).

7

On June 19, 1959 Hon. J. Edward Lumbard, *J.* of the Court of Appeals, signed an order restraining the distribution of the proposed letter pending an application to a Justice of this Court for a stay pending action on this petition for review on writ of certiorari (C. A. pp. 24-27). Said application was duly made before Mr. Justice Brennan (in the absence of Mr. Justice Harlan) and was denied by him in a memorandum dated July 7, 1959, a copy of which is printed in appendix D hereto.[2]

REASONS FOR GRANTING THE WRIT

I.

THE DECISION OF THE COURT OF APPEALS IS IN CONFLICT WITH THE DECISION OF THE COURT OF APPEALS FOR THE NINTH CIRCUIT IN *PACIFIC AMERICAN FISHERIES* v. *MULLANEY*, 191 F. 2d 137 (9th CIR. 1951) IN SO FAR AS IT APPROVED THE TREATING OF RESPONDENTS' MOTION TO DISMISS THE COMPLAINT FOR FAILURE TO STATE A CLAIM UNON WHICH RELIEF COULD BE GRANTED AS A MOTION FOR SUMMARY JUDGMENT.

The only authority for treating a motion to dismiss as one for summary judgment is found in Rule 12(b) of the Federal Rules of Civil Procedure which states:

---

[2]Subsequent to the said denial by Mr. Justice Brennan, the proposed letter was distributed. In their brief and argument on said application, respondents pointed out to Mr. Justice Brennan, and it is therefore conceded, that the denial of the restraint and the subsequent issuance of the letter would not eliminate the controversy and would not render the case moot even in so far as equitable relief is concerned. Petitioners had sought, in addition to an injunction, such other relief as the Court might deem proper. Respondents pointed out, for example, that petitioners might obtain a declaratory judgment that respondents' acts in issuing the letter were tortious (Rule 54(c) of the Federal Rules of Civil Procedure; *Becker* v. *Buder,* 88 F. Supp. 609, 613 (E. D. Mo. 1949) aff'd, 185 F. 2d 311 (8th Cir. 1950)) and that petitioners could still recover damages even though the later event had made the granting of injunctive relief nugatory (*Subin* v. *Goldsmith,* 224 F. 2d 753, 761-2 (2d Cir. 1955)).

8

"* * * If, on a motion asserting the defense numbered (6) to dismiss for failure of the pleading to state a claim upon which relief can be granted, matters outside the pleading are presented to and not excluded by the court, the motion shall be treated as one for summary judgment and disposed of as provided in Rule 56, and all parties shall be given reasonable opportunity to present all material made pertinent to such a motion by Rule 56."

On the face of the above-quoted Rule, two things are prerequisite to the power of the District Court to convert a motion to dismiss into a motion for summary judgment, to wit, (a) matters outside the pleading must be presented to the court on the motion to dismiss, and (b) all parties must be given reasonable opportunity to present all material pertinent to a motion for summary judgment. It is entirely clear that neither of these prerequisites was satisfied in the instant case.

No matters outside the pleading were presented to the court on the motion to dismiss. The only affidavits before the court were there only on the motion for a temporary injunction, and were not intended by either side for consideration on the motion to dismiss. The three affidavits submitted on behalf of respondents were each entitled "Affidavit in Opposition to Plaintiffs' Application for Preliminary Injunction" (Werntz, Beatty and Christie Affs.). The affidavit of Robert O. Whitman, submitted by the petitioners, stated that it was "* * * submitted in support of plaintiffs' application * * * for a preliminary injunction and * * * temporary restraining order" and the affidavit of Donald C. Cook likewise stated that it was "* * * submitted in support of plaintiffs' application * * * for an order granting a preliminary injunction herein and in reply to the affidavits submitted in opposition to said motion." (Whitman aff., par. 2; Cook aff. par. 2).

9

Petitioners, moreover, had no intimation at any time up to the date of the filing of the District Court's opinion that the motion to dismiss would be treated as a motion for summary judgment. Accordingly, petitioners were deprived of their important right under Rule 12 to have an opportunity to prepare and submit affidavits and other proofs or to request permission to take depositions or to have discovery in accordance with the provisions of Rule 56.[8]

The importance of this latter right is underscored by the statement of the revisers made at the time of the 1946 amendment to Rule 12 that:

> "* * * It will also be observed that if a motion under rule 12(b)(6) is thus converted into a summary judgment motion, the amendment insures that both parties shall be given a reasonable opportunity to submit affidavits and extraneous proofs to avoid taking a party by surprise through the conversion of the motion into a motion for summary judgment. * * *" (Report of Proposed Amendments, Advisory Committee on Rules for Civil Procedure, June 1946, pp. 14-15)

The denial of this opportunity was a denial of substantial rights of the petitioners and of the due process required by the Federal Rules and by principles of fairness. Summary judgment is a useful device for avoiding trials where there are no issues of fact or when the complaint is frivolous, but it can be a dangerous snare when used to preclude the identification and presentation of issues of fact.

The record thus incontrovertibly shows that the District Court and the Court of Appeals were mistaken in stating

---

[8]Respondents' counsel suggested in argument before Mr. Justice Brennan that, since, after the decision by the District Court and when counsel were before that Court on the question of a stay, no objection was made to the disposition of this matter as on summary judgment, some kind of estoppel should be applied. Of course, at that stage, protest was quite futile in face of an existing adverse decision. In our view, appeal and not re-argument is the proper, and indeed, usually the only effective method of correcting error.

10

that "* * * matters outside the pleadings have been presented to the court, and since the parties have submitted such proof * * *" (D. C. Opinion, pp. 3-4) and that "both parties had filed supporting affidavits to their motions. * * *" (C. A. Opinion, p. 2). It is clear that even if such were the case, the only proper and fair procedure is that followed in *Huke* v. *Ancilla Domini Sisters,* 267 F. 2d 96 (7th Cir. 1959), where, in sharp contrast to this case, the Rule was properly applied. There the District Court notified the parties that it was going to consider the motion to dismiss as one for summary judgment since the parties had submitted affidavits and gave them ten days to submit "all material pertinent to such motion." To the same effect see *Herron* v. *Herron,* 255 F. 2d 589 (5th Cir. 1958) ; *Mantin* v. *Broadcast Music,* 248 F. 2d 530 (9th Cir. 1957) ; and *Slagle* v. *United States,* 228 F. 2d 673 (5th Cir. 1956), all of which emphasize the importance of giving opportunity to present all pertinent matter when a motion to dismiss is converted to one for summary judgment.

The action of the Courts below in this regard conflicts not only with the plain requirements of Rules 12(b) and 56, but with the decision in *Pacific American Fisheries* v. *Mullaney,* 191 F. 2d 137 (9th Cir. 1951). In that case similar treatment of a motion to dismiss by the trial court was held to be ground for reversal. The Court in that case said :

> "Upon hearing on this motion the court determined to treat the motion as one for a summary judgment, and ordered that such judgment be entered for the defendant. It does not appear that either party was afforded an opportunity to make any further showing by way of affidavit or otherwise after the court determined to treat the motion as one for summary judgment. * * *

* * * * *

11

Appeal was taken both from the order denying a temporary injunction and from the summary judgment. With respect to the summary judgment, appellant contends that irrespective of all other considerations, it was error for the court to undertake to treat the motion for judgment on the pleadings as a motion for summary judgment and then proceed to grant that judgment without giving the appellant an opportunity to present evidence on the questions of fact involved. * * *

* * * * *

We think that the contention that the entry of a summary judgment was erroneous under the circumstances is sound. * * *

* * * * *

When we turn to those portions of the complaint directed to appellant's claim for an injunction, it would appear that if the allegations of the complaint were true, appellant was without an adequate remedy at law and threatened with irreparable injury. * * *

* * * * *

* * * The genuineness of the issue and the materiality of the facts were not disproven by the fact that the appellee denied the allegations of the complaint * * *.

* * * * *

Because of the importance of the issues presented in this suit, we think that it was not one to be disposed of by summary judgment, even if proper motion for such judgment had been made or proper opportunity afforded for appropriate showing by affidavit or otherwise. * * *" (191 F. 2d at 139-141)

This action thus presents a conflict between Circuits with respect to the proper interpretation to be given to Rule 12(b) and as to the proper procedures to be followed on motions to dismiss. This is an important question of fed-

12

eral procedural due process which merits the attention of this Court because of its far reaching effect on litigants in the federal courts.

While errors in interpretation of the Rules may sometimes not be sufficiently important to call for this Court's review, here departure from the plain language of the Rule has caused the kind of unfairness which this Court has been alert to prevent and has raised an important question as to the proper application of the Rules. Cf. *Societe Internationale* v. *Rogers*, 357 U. S. 197 (1958); *Johnson* v. *New York, N. H. & H. R. Co.*, 344 U. S. 48 (1952); *Globe Liquor Co.* v. *San Roman*, 332 U. S 571 (1948); *Anderson* v. *Yungkan*, 329 U. S. 482 (1946); *Arenas* v. *United States*, 322 U. S. 419 (1944); *Sartor* v. *Arkansas Gas Corp.*, 321 U. S. 620 (1944).

II.

THE COURT OF APPEALS, IN APPROVING THE DISTRICT COURT'S ACTION IN DECIDING CONTESTED ISSUES OF FACT ON RESPONDENTS' MOTION TO DISMISS, HAS SANCTIONED SUCH A DEPARTURE FROM THE ACCEPTED AND USUAL COURSE OF JUDICIAL PROCEDURE AND FROM THE HOLDINGS OF THIS COURT AND THE COURTS OF APPEALS FOR THE OTHER CIRCUITS AS TO CALL FOR AN EXERCISE OF THIS COURT'S POWER OF SUPERVISION.

The District Court was able to reach its decision only by deciding issues of fact as to which there were conflicting statements in the verified complaint and in the affidavits submitted by the parties on the injunction motion. Of course, had the court not erroneously treated the motion to dismiss as one for summary judgment, judgment could not have been entered for the respondents, for all matters well pleaded in the verified complaint would have had to be treated as true and established, and the applicable test would

13

have been the rule that no complaint can be dismissed "unless it appears beyond doubt that the plaintiff can prove no set of facts in support of his claim which would entitle him to relief." *Conley* v. *Gibson,* 355 U. S. 41, 45-46 (1957); 2 Moore, *Federal Practice,* p. 2245 (2d ed. 1948). Neither Court below held, nor could it have held, that the verified complaint on its face did not state a claim upon which relief could be granted.

But apart from this error in converting the motion to dismiss into one for summary judgment, the District Court clearly erred in making findings of fact rather than limiting itself to an inquiry as to whether any issues of fact existed. This Court and the Courts of Appeals for each of the Circuits have long since held that jurisdiction to grant summary judgment should be exercised with caution and only in the clearest of cases and that no power exists to determine issues of fact upon motion. *Kennedy* v. *Silas Mason Co.,* 334 U. S. 249 (1948); *Elgin, J. & E. R. Co.* v. *Burley,* 325 U. S. 711, 719, 744 (1945), *adhered to on re-hearing,* 327 U. S. 661 (1946); *Arenas* v. *United States,* 322 U. S. 419, 431 (1944); *Sartor* v. *Arkansas Gas Corp.,* 321 U. S. 620 (1944); for decisions from the Courts of Appeals for each Circuit, see 6 Moore, *Federal Practice,* p. 2107 *et seq.* (2d ed. 1953).

The District Court itself recognized that the elements of the tort alleged consisted of intention to injure, lack of legal justification and damage (D. C. Opinion, pp. 9-12). The Court of Appeals added the element of actual malice (C. A. Opinion, p. 3). Each of these elements entails facts, circumstances, actions and statements of people, and is a question of fact which should not and cannot be decided on the basis of conflicting affidavits and which precludes the entry of summary judgment.

As to the specific issues, for example, the District Court found as a fact that the proposed letter "was adopted

14

by the Committee in conformity with its established procedures" (D. C. Opinion, p. 6), whereas the verified complaint and the reply affidavit in support of the motion for a preliminary injunction specifically alleged that the Committe did not follow its established procedures and practices, pointing out that there was a departure from the Committee's previous practices and procedures of giving wide circulation to so-called exposure or ballot drafts, of giving opportunity to interested parties to express their views on the subject in issue and giving consideration to the prior opinions of the respondents themselves (Complaint, pars. 15, 18, 22, 25; Cook aff. pars. 26, 27).

The District Court also found that there was no intent to harm petitioners, whereas such an intent was pleaded (Complaint, par. 30), and petitioners have been denied the right to prove that allegation of fact, which, of course, could be proved only by examination and cross-examination and is incapable of determination on affidavit.

The District Court did not even mention the allegation of the complaint as to the falsity of the statement in the proposed letter with respect to the intent of the Committee in issuing it, although the facts, including admissions of the respondents, in support of this allegation, are documented in the record (Complaint, pars. 18, 19, 22 and 23; Cook aff. pars. 19-20). This issue of fact must have been resolved against petitioners for the Court referred to "honest opinions" (D. C. Opinion, p. 14). The Court of Appeals likewise failed even to give recognition to this issue, but nevertheless stated that the proposed opinion was "honestly held" (C. A. Opinion, p. 3).

And the Court of Appeals, having held (erroneously, we submit) that a showing of actual malice or its equivalent was necessary to support the relief requested, (C. A. Opinion, p. 3) must have determined that respondents were acting without actual malice, and this without giving peti-

15

tioners the opportunity to prove the allegation of the complaint that respondents were acting in wanton, reckless and wilfull disregard of petitioners' rights and with intent to injure petitioners (Complaint, par. 30).

We submit that the disposition of an important action, involving large sums of money and affecting the consuming public, by determining issues of fact on the basis of conflicting statements contained in affidavits, is such a departure from the established rules of law with respect to motions for summary judgment, so in conflict with the basic requirements of decisions of this Court and other federal courts, and such a departure from the accepted and usual course of judicial procedure as to call for the exercise of this Court's power of supervision.

III.

THE DECISION OF THE COURT OF APPEALS IN THIS ACTION IS AN UNJUSTIFIED DEPARTURE FROM THE LAW OF THE STATE OF NEW YORK WHICH IS HERE CONTROLLING.

The doctrine of prima facie tort has been for some time an important part of the law of the State of New York, which law is controlling in this case under the *Erie* v. *Tompkins* doctrine. The decision in this action departs from and thus essentially disregards the applicable decisions of the New York Court of Appeals. The leading New York case in the field of prima facie tort is *Advance Music Corporation* v. *American Tobacco Co.,* 296 N. Y. 79 (1946). That case is strikingly similar to the instant one and should have been treated as controlling. Other apposite New York opinions in this field are *Opera on Tour, Inc.* v. *Weber,* 285 N. Y. 348 (1941) and *American Guild of Musical Artists* v. *Petrillo,* 286 N. Y. 226 (1941).

16

Analysis of the complaint and the opinion of the New York Court of Appeals in the *Advance Music* case indicates that the District Court's statement that it is "basically different" from the instant case is erroneous (D. C. Opinion, p. 13). The complaint in that case alleged that plaintiff was engaged in the business of publishing musical compositions; that defendants sponsored and produced a well known weekly coast-to-coast radio program, the Hit Parade; that on said program defendants listed and had performed the supposedly nine or ten most popular songs of the week, claiming that these popularity ratings were based upon an extensive and accurate nationwide survey; that the defendants' ratings and listings of songs were in fact the result of caprice or other considerations foreign to a selection based on an accurate and extensive nationwide survey; and that some of plaintiff's songs which were actually among the most popular of the day were either completely ignored by the defendants or given an improper rating.

The complaint went on to allege that plaintiff was suffering damages in that retail purchasers, entertainers and other customers and potential promoters of songs, influenced by defendants' inaccurate ratings, failed to purchase plaintiff's compositions, and that the acts and representations of the defendant were made wantonly, in bad faith and with intent to injure plaintiff.

The Court of Appeals reversed a dismissal of the complaint and held that the facts pleaded stated a cause of action. The Court said:

> "The foregoing [allegations] * * * are there followed by the further allegation that 'the aforesaid acts and representations on the part of the defendants are made with intent to injure the plaintiff'. Thus in sum and substance the second cause of action constitutes a statement to this effect: *The defendants are wantonly causing damage to the plaintiff by a system of conduct on their part which*

17

warrants an inference that they intend harm of that type. So read, the second cause of action is, we think, adequate in its office as a plaintiff's pleading. (Emphasis added.)

In *Skinner & Company* v. *Shew & Company* [1893], (1 Ch. 413, 422) Lord Justice BOWEN said: 'At Common Law there was a cause of action whenever one person did damage to another wilfully and intentionally, and without just cause or excuse'. * * * These broad propositions were approved by Sir FREDERICK POLLACK as authority for his doctrine that all willful harm is actionable unless the defendant justify or excuse his conduct. (Pollack, The Law of Torts [14th ed.], 17-18.)" (296 N. Y. at pp. 83-84)

* * *

"The justification that is required in a case like this must, of course, be one which the law will recognize. * * *" (citations omitted, 296 N. Y. at p. 85)

The court below, in its *per curiam* opinion on this important question of state law, in effect refused to treat this decision as controlling and, instead, struck out on its own and added to the elements of prima facie tort as enunciated by the New York Court of Appeals the requirement of a showing of "actual malice" (C. A. Opinion, p. 3). But in the *Advance Music* case, the Court of Appeals had said that an allegation that a party was wantonly causing damage warranted an inference that they intended such harm and that such an allegation was sufficient. And in the *American Guild of Musical Artists* case, the Court of Appeals specifically held that actual malice was an unnecessary allegation, since malice in the law of New York does not mean ill-will against a person but merely intentional action without justification. In *Campbell* v. *Gates,* 236 N. Y. 457, 460 (1923), moreover, it was said that a malicious act is one "* * * done

18

intentionally, without just cause or excuse, and from this a malicious motive is to be inferred. This does not necessarily mean actual malice or ill-will, but the intentional doing of a wrongful act without legal or social justification."

The opinions below in this action depart from and therefore conflict with and give inadequate weight to the applicable and controlling decisions of the New York Court of Appeals on this important question of New York law.

IV.

THIS ACTION RAISES AN IMPORTANT QUESTION CON-CERNING THE EQUITY POWERS OF THE FEDERAL JUDI-CIARY ON WHICH THERE IS NO CONTROLLING DECISION OF THIS COURT AND ON WHICH THERE IS AT LEAST IM-PLICITLY A CONFLICT BETWEEN THE DECISION BELOW AND DECISIONS OF THIS COURT AND THE COURT OF APPEALS FOR THE THIRD CIRCUIT.

The Court of Appeals said:

"* * * We think the courts may not dictate or control the procedures by which a private organization expresses its honestly held views. Defendants' action involves no breach of duty owed by them to the plaintiffs. On the contrary every professional body accepts a public obligation for unfettered expression of views and loses all right to professional consideration, as well as all utility, if its views are controlled by other criteria than the intellectual conclusions of the persons acting.* * *" (C. A. Opinion, p. 3)

The record will show that the above quotation from the Court of Appeals decision resulted from the respondents' contention, fully briefed and argued below, that the complaint should be dismissed on the ground that it "* * * seeks to restrain the freedom of expression of opinion of the * * * [respondents'] on a matter of public concern and interest,

19

in violation of the rules of the common law and of the First Amendment to the United States Constitution.* * *" (D. C. pp. 49-51). It was thus an acceptance of limitation on the equity power of Federal courts, which we believe was erroneous and presents a grave question warranting this Court's review.

That part of the decision seems clearly to be a holding that a Federal court of equity may not enjoin tortious speech by a professional organization and that there is no limitation upon the right of such a body to express itself, for it is in substance an approval of the District Court's holding that the purposes alone of a professional organization are "* * * adequate justification, if justification, indeed, be required * * *" of such a body (D. C. Opinion, p. 14). But this creates a classification of private organizations above the law, who may express themselves with impunity and not be answerable for their torts as all other are. There is no basis for conferring such immunity. We submit, on the contrary, that a professional organization, like any other individual or body corporate, may be enjoined from the intentional infliction of harm without justification, that the fact that the organization uttering the words is professional in nature is irrelevant, and that a federal court sitting as a court of equity has the power and duty to enjoin tortious words. No principle of law, or requirement of the Constitution, binds the hands of a federal equity court from restraining a private wrongdoer in such circumstances as are presented here.

This important question was expressly left open by this Court in *Near* v. *Minnesota*, 283 U. S. 697 (1931) where the Court said:

> "* * * Nor are we now concerned with questions as to the extent of authority to prevent publications in order to protect private rights according to the principles governing the exercise of the jurisdiction of courts of equity." (283 U. S. at p. 716)

20

The New York Court of Appeals has long since ruled that there is no limitation on the power of courts of equity to enjoin tortious speech. This is made clear not only by the cases cited above but was specifically pointed out by Chief Judge Cardozo in *Nann* v. *Raimist,* 255 N. Y. 307, 317 (1931), where, in discussing the power of a court of equity to enjoin publications, he wrote:

> "* * * Equity does not intervene to restrain the publication of words on a mere showing of their falsity. * * * It intervenes in those cases where restraint becomes essential to the preservation of a business or of other property interests threatened with impairment by illegal combinations or by other tortious acts, the publication of the words being merely an instrument and incident * * *. (Citations omitted.)"

This Court, through Mr. Justice Holmes in *American Bank & Trust Company* v. *Federal Reserve Bank,* 256 U. S. 350 (1921), reversed the dismissal of a complaint in an action for an injunction and said:

> "* * * A man has a right to give advice, but advice given for the sole purpose of injuring another's business and effective on a large scale, might create a cause of action. * * * If without a word of falsehood but acting from what we have called disinterested malevolence a man by persuasion should organize and carry into effect a run upon a bank and ruin it, we cannot doubt that an action would lie. * * *" (256 U. S. at 358)

A leading decision by a federal court in an action in which objection was raised to the granting of an injunction to restrain tortious conduct is *Black & Yates* v. *Mahogany Ass'n,* 129 F. 2d 227 (3d Cir. 1941). There, in reversing the denial of injunctive relief and restraining statements by the defendant which tended to injure the plaintiff's business, the court said:

21

"* * * The irrevelance of 'free speech' and of 'a libel is for a jury' are patent. Freedom of discussion of public issues does not demand lack of 'previous restraint' for injury to private individuals.* * *

We are quite willing to repudiate the 'waning doctrine that equity will not restrain the trade libel'. We are further willing to do so directly and without hiding behind the other equitable principles put forward in some of the cases." (129 F. 2d at p. 231)

This action thus presents important issues of law concerning the power of a court of equity to compel obedience to law and prevent injury, on which this Court has not directly ruled and as to which the decision below appears to conflict in principle with opinions of this Court, of the Third Circuit and of the New York Court of Appeals.

CONCLUSION

For the foregoing reasons, this petition for a writ of certiorari should be granted.

Respectfully submitted,

WHITNEY NORTH SEYMOUR
Counsel for Petitioners
120 Broadway
New York 5, New York

RICHARD M. DICKE,
WILLIAM J. MANNING,
SIMPSON THACHER & BARTLETT,
Of Counsel

1a

APPENDIX A

UNITED STATES COURT OF APPEALS

For the Second Circuit

October Term, 1958.

(Argued June 4, 1959   Decided June 17, 1959.)

Docket No. 25715

Appalachian Power Company, Ohio Power Company
and Indiana & Michigan Electric Company,

Plaintiffs-Appellants,

—v.—

American Institute of Certified Public Accountants, L. H. Penny, William W. Werntz and Carman
G. Blough,

Defendants-Appellees.

Before:

Clark, *Chief Judge,* and
Lumbard and Waterman, *Circuit Judges.*

Appeal from the United States District Court for the
Southern District of New York, Richard H. Levet, *Judge.*

Appalachian Power Company and others appeal from a
decision of Judge Levet, D. C. S. D. N. Y., May 20, 1959,
denying a temporary injunction and granting summary
judgment dismissing their complaint on defendants' motion
under Fed. R. Civ. P. 12.

2a

WHITNEY NORTH SEYMOUR of Simpson
Thacher & Bartlett, New York City (Richard
M. Dicke and William J. Manning, of Simpson Thacher & Bartlett, New York City, on
the brief), *for plaintiffs-appellants*.

HOWARD C. WESTWOOD, of Covington & Burling, Washington, D. C. (Fontaine C. Bradley, Stanley L. Temko, George C. Christie,
and Phil R. Stansbury, of Covington &
Burling, Washington, D. C., on the brief),
for defendants-appellees.

PER CURIAM:

On a theory of prima facie tort, plaintiffs seek to enjoin
defendants, a professional association of accountants and
several of its officers, from distributing to its members and
others a letter to the effect that the Institute considers
certain accounting procedures improper. Plaintiffs allege
that in the preparation of this letter the Institute disregarded its usual practice of circulating proposed opinions
for comment prior to their issuance and that the promulgation of the views contained in the letter, because of the
Institute's authority in the accounting profession and in
the business community, will impair plaintiffs' credit and
limit their growth.

The court below properly considered this action as on a
motion for summary judgment once both parties had filed
supporting affidavits to their motions. Fed. R. Civ. P. 12(b)
specifically authorizes this procedure, and we do not see
that plaintiffs were denied the opportunity to present
materials pertinent to summary judgment which the rule
provides.

On the merits we agree with Judge Levet's reasoned
opinion below, D. C. S. D. N Y., May 20, 1959. We think
the courts may not dictate or control the procedures by
which a private organization expresses its honestly held
views. Defendants' action involves no breach of duty owed
by them to the plaintiffs. On the contrary every profes-

3a

sional body accepts a public obligation for unfettered expression of views and loses all right to professional consideration, as well as all utility, if its views are controlled by other criteria than the intellectual conclusions of the persons acting. Absent a showing of actual malice or its equivalent the courts would be making a great mistake, contrary indeed to their own ideals and professions, if they assumed to restrict and denigrate this widely recognized and assumed professional duty.

By stipulation of the parties this appeal was heard both upon the appellants' motion for a stay and upon the merits. Our order must therefore be that the stay heretofore granted is vacated and the judgment below is affirmed.

1b

APPENDIX B

UNITED STATES DISTRICT COURT
Southern District of New York

APPALACHIAN POWER COMPANY, OHIO
POWER COMPANY and INDIANA &
MICHIGAN ELECTRIC COMPANY,

Plaintiffs,

—against—

AMERICAN INSTITUTE OF CERTIFIED PUB-
LIC ACCOUNTANTS, L. H. PENNEY,
WILLIAM W. WERNTZ and CARMAN G.
BLOUGH,

Defendants.

Civil 145-161

OPINION

APPEARANCES:

Simpson Thacher & Bartlett
Attorneys for Plaintiffs
120 Broadway, New York, N. Y.
    Whitney North Seymour, Richard M. Dicke,
    William J. Manning,
        Of Counsel.

Howard C. Westwood, Fontaine C. Bradley,
Stanley L. Temko
Attorneys for Defendants
c/o American Institute of Certified Public Accountants
270 Madison Avenue, New York, N. Y.
    —and—
Covington & Burling
Union Trust Building
Washington, D. C.
    Rinaldo L. Bianchi, George C. Christie,
    Phil R. Stansbury,
        Of Counsel.

2b

LEVET, *D. J.*

This is a motion for preliminary injunction to restrain the defendants from the promulgation or distribution of certain opinions recommending certain accounting practices which allegedly affect plaintiffs' financial statements, unless a waiting period of 60 days elapses, and certain other prerequisites are complied with.

The above-named plaintiffs, public utility companies, engaged in the sale of power, seek a preliminary injunction to enjoin the defendant American Institute of Certified Public Accountants (hereinafter called "Institute") and the individual defendants, certain officers or Committeemen of said Institute, from adopting, issuing, promulgating, circulating, printing or in any manner publishing to the members of the defendant Institute or to any members of the accountancy profession a certain proposed letter. This letter is to the effect that the said defendant Institute or its Committee on Accounting Procedure (hereinafter called "Committee") is of the opinion or recommends that charges made to income in recognition of the deferral of income taxes should not, in accordance with generally accepted accounting principles, be credited to earned surplus or to any other account included in the stockholders' equity section of the balance sheet. The plaintiffs seek to enjoin the distribution of said letter until such time as the defendants and the Committee shall have submitted a draft thereof to certain persons; a period of not less than 60 days shall thereafter have elapsed, and the Institute's and its Committee's practices and procedures with respect to the publication of accounting research bulletins shall otherwise have been complied with.

3b

This letter in dispute is as follows:

"AMERICAN INSTITUTE OF CERTIFIED
PUBLIC ACCOUNTANTS

"270 Madison Avenue,
New York, 16, N. Y.

"April 15, 1959

"To the Members of the American
Institute of Certified Public Accountants

"Gentlemen:

"Question has been raised with respect to the intent of the committee on accounting procedure in using the phrase 'a deferred tax account' in Accounting Research Bulletin No. 44 (revised), *Declining-balance Depreciation,* to indicate the account to be credited for the amount of the deferred income tax (see paragraphs 4 and 5).

"The committee used the phrase in its ordinary connotation of an account to be shown in the balance sheet as a liability or a deferred credit. A provision in recognition of the deferral of income taxes, being required for the proper determination of net income, should not at the same time result in a credit to earned surplus or to any other account included in the stockholders' equity section of the balance sheet.

"Three of the twenty-one members of the committee, Messrs. Jennings, Powell and Staub, dissented to the issuance at this time of any letter interpreting Accounting Research Bulletin No. 44 (revised).

"COMMITTEE ON ACCOUNTING PROCEDURE
"By William W. Werntz, Chairman"

By cross-motion the defendants have moved for an order pursuant to Rule 12(b) of the Federal Rules of Civil Procedure dismissing the complaint on the ground that it fails

4b

to state a claim against them upon which relief can be granted. Since matters outside the pleadings have been presented to the court, and since the parties have submitted such proof, I am treating this motion as one for summary judgment as provided in Rule 56 of the Federal Rules of Civil Procedure.

The compliment herein, seeking permanent injunctive relief, was filed on April 15, 1958. This application apparently is based upon the following assertions of the plaintiffs:

(1) Plaintiffs, three operating electric utility companies, have recorded on their books of account, pursuant to certain alleged applicable requirements of state regulatory agencies, an aggregate of more than $65,000,000 in accounts designated as "Earned Surplus Restricted for Future Federal Income Taxes." In this connection plaintiffs contend that these amounts have been so accrued by them in accordance with accounting principles which heretofore have been generally accepted over a period of years by all of the well-known accounting firms experienced in utility accounting.

(2) The defendant Institute, through its Committee, from time to time publishes accounting research bulletins which are allegedly "accepted" by state and federal regulatory agencies, including the Securities and Exchange Commission, members of the accounting profession and interested members of the business community as establishing the accounting principles which must be followed by the accounting profession.

(3) Prior to the present dispute in reference to pertinent accounting procedures, it is said that the Institute had adopted procedures prerequisite to the publication of such opinions and recommendations. The procedures included, it is said, the circulation of so-called "exposure drafts of any proposed opinion" to a certain group so that the members might comment thereon, and a further procedure involving the submission of a so-called "ballot draft" to members of the Committee so that they could vote upon the proposed opinion.

(4) Plaintiffs aver that the defendants have known accounting practices of plaintiffs in reference to these matters

5b

and have had full knowledge that plaintiffs have accumulated more than $65,000,000 in these accounts.

(5) It appears that in a proceeding before the Securities and Exchange Commission the Chairman of defendant's Committee and its Director of Research stated that they were about to mail under the authority of the Institute and the Committee to members of the Institute and other recipients of bulletins a letter with respect to the deferred tax account to the effect that "a provision in recognition of the deferral of income taxes, being required for the proper determination of net income, should not at the same time result in a credit to earned surplus or to any other account included in the stockholders' equity section of the balance sheet."

(6) Plaintiffs claim that the defendants in preparing and intending to publish this letter are "without legal justification," that their acts "bear no reasonable relationship to any benefits which the defendants may be seeking or to any legitimate purpose," and that the actions of the defendants in connection with the proposed distribution of the said letter and the opinion contained therein are "in wanton, reckless and wilful disregard of the said consequences of their proposed action."

(7) As a result, plaintiffs assert that substantial numbers of accountants, financial institutions, etc. will question the plaintiffs' continued inclusion of credits for deferred taxes in earned surplus and as a result plaintiffs "will be seriously interfered with in their dealings," etc. and, as stated by Donald C. Cook, a vice-president of each of the plaintiff corporations:

"* * * The removal of more than $65,000,000 from the common stock equity of the plaintiffs would, in the first instance, have the effect of limiting the short term borrowing power of plaintiffs under applicable statutes so as to decrease the amounts which plaintiffs can borrow from banks by $6,500,000. * * *" (Affidavit sworn to May 6, 1959, item 21, p. 13)

6b

The defendants in their opposing papers point out that:

(1) The letter, the issuance of which, without certain preliminaries, plaintiffs oppose, was adopted by the Committee in conformity with its established procedures; was specifically approved by over two-thirds of the 21 members of the Committee; that under the Committee's procedure a two-third vote—that is, 14 out of 21 members—is sufficient to adopt an opinion or recommendation.

(2) The opinions of the Committee have no official effect.

(3) The Committee procedures do not require the so-called "exposure" in draft form of the proposed letter, though on occasion in the past, this "exposure" procedure has been employed.

(4) a. The Committee's position as to the accounting practice in question is followed by Arthur Andersen & Co., public accountants, who audit the accounts of one-third of the utility companies in the country;

b. Based on a survey of the 1957 published stockholders' reports of 353 utility companies, of 226 companies reporting an accumulated credit resulting from the use of the liberalized depreciation under § 167 of the Internal Revenue Code, 176 treated the credit outside the equity-capital section of the balance sheet and only 50 treated the credit as either earned surplus or restricted surplus;

c. The Public Service Commission of the State of Indiana has ordered all companies subject to its regluations, including plaintiff Indiana & Michigan Electric Company, to cease treating the credit for deferred income taxes as a surplus account;

d. The Federal Power Commission on May 29, 1958, issued an order to the effect that all public utility companies subject to its regulations shall not include credit for deferred income taxes in a surplus account;

e. The Securities and Exchange Commission has promulgated a proposed policy in accord with the Committee's views.

7b

Jurisdiction herein is based upon diversity of citizenship. Hence, the law of the State of New York is applicable. The plaintiffs predicate the validity of their complaint upon the doctrine of "prima facie tort." They rely upon the New York cases of *Advance Music Corporation* v. *American Tobacco Co.*, 296 N. Y. 79 (1946); *Opera on Tour, Inc.* v. *Weber*, 285 N. Y. 348 (1941); *American Guild of Musical Artists* v. *Petrillo*, 286 N. Y. 226 (1941).

Subsequently, in other decisions New York courts have discussed this doctrine of so-called "prima facie tort." Among these are *Brandt* v. *Winchell*, 283 App. Div. 338 (1st Dept., 1954); *Brandt* v. *Winchell*, 286 App. Div. 249 (1st Dept., 1955), affirmed 3 N. Y. 2d 628 (1958); *Ruza* v. *Ruza*, 286 App. Div. 767 (1st Dept., 1955); *Knapp Engraving Co., Inc.* v. *Keystone Photo Engraving Corp.*, 1 App. Div. 2d 170 (1st Dept., 1956). See also *Benton* v. *Kennedy-Van Saun Mfg. & Eng. Corporation*, 2 App. Div. 2d 27 (1st Dept., 1956); *Travelers Indemnity Company* v. *Unger*, 4 Misc. 2d 955 (S. Ct., Queens Co., 1956); *Green* v. *Time, Inc.*, 147 N. Y. S. 2d 828 (S. Ct., N. Y. Co., 1955), affirmed 1 App. Div. 2d 665 (1st Dept., 1955), affirmed 3 N. Y. 2d 732 (1957).

The essential elements of "prima facie tort" include the following:

(1) There must be an intent to injure plaintiff, at least to the extent of infliction of *wrongful* harm upon plaintiff without just cause or excuse. *Beardsley* v. *Kilmer*, 236 N. Y. 80 (1923); *Ruza* v. *Ruza*, 286 App. Div. 767 (1st Dept., 1955); *Advance Music Corporation* v. *American Tobacco Co.*, 296 N. Y. 79 (1946).

In *Ruza* v. *Ruza, supra*, Mr. Justice Breitel wrote:

"The key to the prima facie tort is the infliction of intentional harm, resulting in damage, without excuse or justification, by an act or a series of acts which would otherwise be lawful. The need for the doctrine of prima facie tort arises only because the specific acts relied upon—and which it is asserted caused the injury—are not, in the absence of the intention to harm, tortious, unlawful, and therefore, actionable. The remedy is invoked when the intention to harm, as distinguished from the intention merely to commit the act, is present, has motivated the action, and has caused the injury to plaintiff, all without excuse or justification." (p. 769)

In *Knapp Engraving Co. Inc.* v. *Keystone Photo Engraving Corp.*, 1 App. Div. 2d 170 (1st Dept., 1956), Mr. Justice Botein, now Presiding Justice of the First Department Appellate Division, wrote of prima facie tort:

> "It attempts to justify the omission of these conventional tort requirements on the ground that the counterclaim should be regarded as a 'prima facie tort'. A cause of action, however, must be judged by its allegations, not its label. A prima facie tort derives from the ancient form of action on the case, covering those situations where intentional harm has been inflicted, resulting in damage, by an act or series of acts which might otherwise be lawful and which do not fall within the categories of traditional tort actions (Aikens v. Wisconsin, 195 U. S. 194; Opera on Tour v. Weber, 285 N. Y. 348; American Guild of Musical Artists v. Petrillo, 286 N. Y. 226; Advance Music Corp. v. American Tobacco Co., 296 N. Y. 79; Brandt v. Winchell, 283 App. Div. 338, amended complaint dismissed 286 App. Div. 249)." (p. 172)

(2) Justification may be viewed as a neutralizing factor that overrides the intent to injure. What constitutes justification is a policy consideration.[1] In *Reinforce, Inc.* v. *Birney,* 308 N. Y. 164 (1954), Desmond, *J.* wrote:

> "* * * If the doers, by means not in themselves unlawful, of acts not in themselves unlawful, have any proper purpose to serve, they are not liable for the damage they cause (Peabody, Jr., & Co., v. Travelers Ins. Co., 240 N. Y. 511, 519; Al Raschid v. News Syndicate Co., 265 N. Y. 1). * * *" (p. 169)

---

[1] Recent Developments in the New York Law of Prima Facie Tort, 32 St. John's Law Review, 282, 288.

9b

In *Beardsley* v. *Kilmer,* 236 N. Y. 80 (1923) the concept of justification was expressed as follows:

"* * * The question how far one individual shall be restrained from doing acts which are inherently proper out of respect for the rights of others is bound to be a delicate one. The proposition that a man may not dig a well upon his own land or enter upon a lawful business is one to be advanced with considerable caution and the cases seem firmly to establish the rule that if he digs a well because he really wants the water or starts the business for personal advantage or gain his neighbor is without remedy however much he suffers, and even though the act may also have been tinged with animosity and malice." (pp. 89-90)

In *Brandt* v. *Winchell,* 3 N. Y. 2d 628 (1958), Chief Judge Conway stated:

"* * * The law is now settled in this State that, 'Even a lawful act done solely out of malice and illwill to injure another *may* be actionable.' (Al Raschid v. News Syndicate Co., 265 N. Y. 1, 4, emphasis supplied; see, also, Beardsley v. Kilmer, 236 N. Y. 80.) This is not to say that the present state of the law is that an act not otherwise tortious will, without exception become actionable when it is done with the blameworthy purpose of injuring another and such other is in fact injured. There are situations where for one of several reasons a court is constrained to ignore the wrongful motive of the actor. For example, a court may be prompted to disregard the actor's motive by reason of the paramount consideration of the public welfare. Accordingly, it may fairly be said that whenever the gist of an alleged cause of action (as here) is that an otherwise lawful act has become unlawful because the actor's motives were malevolent, the court is called upon to analyze and weigh the conflicting interests of the parties and of the public in order to determine which shall prevail." (pp. 634-635)

10b

(3) Damages, which must be specially pleaded. *Rager* v. *McCloskey,* 305 N. Y. 75 (1953); *Brandt* v. *Winchell,* 286 App. Div. 249 (1st Dept., 1955), affirmed 3 N. Y. 2d 628 (1958); *Faulk* v. *Aware, Inc.,* 3 Misc. 2d 833, 839 (S. Ct., N. Y. Co., 1956) affirmed without opinion 3 App. Div. 2d 703 (1st Dept., 1957).

In *Brandt* v. *Winchell, supra,* the Appellate Division, 1st Department, in a per curiam opinion stated:

> "* * * The amended complaint proceeds solely on the theory of prima facie tort. As we previously noted, damage is an essential element in a cause of action for prima facie tort and must be pleaded specially, for it consists of injury due to loss in plaintiff's occupation or business (see 283 App. Div. 338, 342)." (p. 250)

Although "the most conspicuous use of the prima facie tort doctrine has been to create new causes of action where the plaintiff's claim does not fall within a traditional tort category,"[2] as Mr. Justice Breitel said in *Ruza* v. *Ruza,* 286 App. Div. 767 (1st Dept., 1955): "A bad complaint is not made good by the blanket assertion that it relies on the doctrine of 'prima facie tort.'" (p. 769)

Plaintiffs, although not members of the Institute, seek to force it to follow certain prerequisites to publication of opinions of the Institute's Committee. Plaintiffs, having adhered to certain accounting procedures for several years, have recorded in "restricted earned surplus accounts" some $65,000,000, representing credits for payment of federal income taxes which may have to be paid in the future. Now, urge the plaintiffs, the Institute's Committee's opinion will or may be accepted by the Securities and Exchange Commission in rulings on financial statements.

The facts in the case of *Advance Music Corporation* v. *American Tobacco Co.,* 296 N. Y. 79 (1946) are basically different from those in the present case:

(1) There, the defendant misrepresented the nature of the survey of the popularity of the songs presented based on sales—a fact not an opinion.

---

[2] The Prima Facie Tort Doctrine, 52 Columbia Law Review 503, 512.

11b

(2) The defendant's acts and representations definitely and directly affected plaintiff's sales. A business interference resulted.

(3) Damages naturally flowing from the acts and misrepresentations of the defendant and causally affecting the sales of the plaintiff were set forth.

(4) No justification for the defendant's acts appeared.

Here, the communications which defendants intend to promulgate do not mention plaintiffs. The plaintiffs, like other business enterprises which may be affected, may, if they so elect, appear before the appropriate governmental body to sustain their own contentions. There is no misrepresentation, no fraud. The acts of the defendants can hardly be termed wanton. The purposes of the defendant Institute are adequate justification, if justification, indeed, be required, to permit the proposed communications. There is no adequate proof (even if the plaintiffs had any right to insist on the Committee procedures they mention) that the Institute's rules have been or are about to be violated. In fact, the contrary appears.

There is no allegation that the method of accounting proposed by defendants is inherently false or fraudulent. On the contrary, it is supported by respectable authority. Neither is there any allegation of special damages, except in the most general and speculative terms.

This action is not to prevent interference with plaintiff's contracts, their sales or their property. It seeks to delay the distribution of an adverse opinion relative to accounting procedures. True, it may ultimately affect plaintiffs' application for credit. However, such a result is collateral, not direct, an effect which incidentally flows from a justifiable act. The plaintiffs may have grievances, but they relate to the distribution of honest opinions, not facts. No threat of intentional, unjustifiable harm to plaintiffs' business rights or property exists.

This court has been unable to find any precedent under the doctrine of prima facie tort or otherwise for a preliminary or final injunction forbidding a group from publishing and distributing opinions under circumstances equivalent or even similar to these.

12b

Accordingly, the application for preliminary injunction must be denied and the complaint dismissed and summary judgment granted.

Settle order on notice.

RICHARD H. LEVET
United States District Judge

Dated: New York, N. Y.
May 20, 1959.

1c

APPENDIX C

Rule 12 of the Federal Rules of Civil Procedure.

"Rule 12. *Defense and Objections—When and How Presented—By Pleading on Motion—Motion for Judgment on Pleadings.*

* * * * *

(b) *How Presented.* Every defense, in law or fact, to a claim for relief in any pleading, whether a claim, counterclaim, cross-claim, or third-party claim, shall be asserted in the responsive pleading thereto if one is required, except that the following defenses may at the option of the pleader be made by motion: (1) lack of jurisdiction over the subject matter, (2) lack of jurisdiction over the person, (3) improper venue, (4) insufficiency of process, (5) insufficiency of service of process, (6) failure to state a claim upon which relief can be granted, (7) failure to join an indispensible party. A motion making any of these defenses shall be made before pleading if a further pleading is permitted. No defense or objection is waived by being joined with one or more other defenses or objections in a responsive pleading or motion. If a pleading sets forth a claim for relief to which the adverse party is not required to serve a responsive pleading, he may assert at the trial any defense in law or fact to that claim for relief. If, on a motion asserting the defense numbered (6) to dismiss for failure of the pleading to state a claim upon which relief can be granted, matters outside the pleading are presented to and not excluded by the court, the motion shall be treated as one for summary judgment and disposed of as provided in Rule 56, and all parties shall be given reasonable opportunity to present all material made pertinent to such a motion by Rule 56. [As amended Dec. 27, 1946, effective March 19, 1948.]"

* * * * *

Rule 56 of the Federal Rules of Civil Procedure.

"Rule 56. *Summary Judgment*

* * * * *

2c

(c) *Motion and Proceedings Thereon.* The motion shall be served at least 10 days before the time fixed for the hearing. The adverse party prior to the day of hearing may serve opposing affidavits. The judgment sought shall be rendered forthwith if the pleadings, depositions, and admissions on file, together with the affidavits, if any, show that there is no genuine issue as to any material fact and that the moving party is entitled to a judgment as a matter of law. * * *

* * * * *

(e) *Form of Affidavits; Further Testimony.* Supporting and opposing affidavits shall be made on personal knowledge, shall set forth such facts as would be admissible in evidence, and shall show affirmatively that the affiant is competent to testify to the matters stated therein. Sworn or certified copies of all papers or parts thereof referred to in an affidavit shall be attached thereto or served therewith. The court may permit affidavits to be supplemented or opposed by depositions or by further affidavits.

(f) *When Affidavits Are Unavailable.* Should it appear from the affidavits of a party opposing the motion that he cannot for reasons stated present by affidavit facts essential to justify his opposition, the court may refuse the application for judgment or may order a continuance to permit affidavits to be obtained or depositions to be taken or discovery to be had or may make such other order as is just."

* * * * *

1d

APPENDIX D

SUPREME COURT OF THE UNITED STATES
OCTOBER TERM, 1959.

Appalachian Power Company, Ohio Power Company and Indiana & Michigan Electric Company, Petitioners,

v.

American Institute of Certified Public Accountants, L. H. Penney, William W. Werntz and Carman G. Blough.

[July 7, 1959.]

MR. JUSTICE BRENNAN, Circuit Justice (temporarily assigned).

The petitioners apply for an order (1) staying the Mandate of the United States Court of Appeals for the Second Circuit on its judgment of June 17, 1959, affirming a summary judgment for respondents entered by the District Court for the Southern District of New York, and (2) restraining the respondents, pending the final determination of this action by this Court, from distributing to the members of the respondent American Institute of Certified Public Accountants or to any other members of the accounting profession a proposed letter dated April 15, 1959, or any other communication, to the effect that the respondent American Institute of Certified Public Accountants or its Committee on Accounting Procedure is of the opinion or recommends that a deferred tax account set up in recognition of the deferral of income taxes should not be credited to earned surplus or to any other account included in the stockholders' equity section of the balance sheet.

The petitioners, public utility companies which account for deferred taxes in the stockholders equity section of their balance sheets, brought this diversity suit in the District Court. They sought, in addition to other relief, an injunction against respondents promulgating or distributing said letter except upon compliance with certain specified procedures. An interim restraint was granted pending hearing on a motion for preliminary injunction. Respondents made a motion to dismiss the complaint under Rule 12(b) of the Federal Rules of Civil Procedure. Affidavits were filed by both sides. The District Court heard the motions together, denied the motion for a preliminary injunction and, treating the motion to dismiss, since affidavits of both sides were filed, as a motion for summary judgment under Rule 56 of the Federal Rules of Civil Procedure, entered summary judgment for the respondents. The District Court found that the letter of April 15 reflected the Committee's "honest opinions," that it was not "false or fraudulent" and that it could "hardly be termed wanton." The District Court held that, under such circumstances, the law of New York, which governs in this diversity case, does not provide a cause of action. The Court of Appeals unanimously affirmed.

The stay and temporary restraining order are sought by the petitioners upon allegations that respondents will distribute the letter, unless restrained, and this will cause petitioners irreparable injury and also render moot their proposed petition for certiorari, at least insofar as concerns their prayers for injunctive relief against such a distribution. Even assuming, however, the possibilities of irreparable injury and mootness, as claimed by the petitioners, I do not feel at liberty to grant their application unless in my judgment there is a prospect that the petition for certiorari which they propose to file will appear to at least four members of the Court to present questions which warrant our review.

I heard oral argument on this application and after consideration of the arguments made and the briefs filed, it is my judgment that the questions proposed to be presented in the petition for certiorari will not command four votes for review. The petitioners state that three contentions will be presented. One is that the District Court and the Court of Appeals erred in their conclusion as to the relevant state law. But this Court ordinarily accepts the determination of state law as found by the Court of Appeals, particularly when, as here, the same finding is made by the District Court, and no showing has been made to persuade me that such would

3d

not be the case here. The second contention is that the District Court, in treating respondent's motion to dismiss as a motion for summary judgment, erred in not following the requirement of Rule 12(b) that "all parties shall be given reasonable opportunity to present all material made pertinent to such motion [for summary judgment] by Rule 56." But ordinarily an application by a District Court of the Rules of Civil Procedure when affirmed by the Court of Appeals will not be reviewed by this Court. This is particularly true where, as here, the question is one that concerns the judgment of the District Judge in relation to a particular set of facts. And I do not find the conflict suggested by petitioners between the decision below and *Pacific American Fisheries* v. *Mullaney*, 191 F. 2d 137. That decision simply held that the District Court was incorrect in its conclusion as to the pertinent law, and that under the Court of Appeals' view of the law certain relevant facts were in dispute, so that the grant of summary judgment was improper. Finally, the petitioners suggest they will present in their petition for certiorari the question whether federal courts, in light of the First Amendment, are empowered to enjoin tortious communications. But the holdings below are that in the circumstances of this case the distribution by respondents of the proposed letter would not constitute a tortious act under New York law; therefore no First Amendment problem is involved.

The application is denied, since, in my judgment, none of the questions proposed to be presented in the petition for certiorari have the prospect of commanding four votes for review.

No. 388

Supreme Court of the United States

OCTOBER TERM, 1959

APPALACHIAN POWER COMPANY, OHIO POWER COMPANY
AND INDIANA & MICHIGAN ELECTRIC COMPANY,
Petitioners,

v.

AMERICAN INSTITUTE OF CERTIFIED PUBLIC ACCOUNT-
ANTS, L. H. PENNEY, WILLIAM W. WERNTZ AND
CARMAN G. BLOUGH, *Respondents*

---

*ON PETITION FOR A WRIT OF CERTIORARI TO THE UNITED
STATES COURT OF APPEALS FOR THE SECOND CIRCUIT*

**BRIEF OF RESPONDENTS AMERICAN INSTITUTE OF
CERTIFIED PUBLIC ACCOUNTANTS, ET AL.,
IN OPPOSITION**

HOWARD C. WESTWOOD,
FONTAINE C. BRADLEY,
STANLEY L. TEMKO,
ROBERT L. RANDALL,
   701 Union Trust Building,
   Washington 5, D. C.
      Attorneys for Respondents

COVINGTON & BURLING,
  Of Counsel

I N D E X

CITATIONS

Cases:

Miscellaneous:

Supreme Court of the United States

OCTOBER TERM, 1959

No. 388

APPALACHIAN POWER COMPANY, OHIO POWER COMPANY
AND INDIANA & MICHIGAN ELECTRIC COMPANY,
Petitioners,

v.

AMERICAN INSTITUTE OF CERTIFIED PUBLIC ACCOUNT-
ANTS, L. H. PENNEY, WILLIAM W. WERNTZ AND
CARMAN G. BLOUGH, *Respondents*

---

*ON PETITION FOR A WRIT OF CERTIORARI TO THE UNITED
STATES COURT OF APPEALS FOR THE SECOND CIRCUIT*

BRIEF OF RESPONDENTS AMERICAN INSTITUTE OF CERTIFIED PUBLIC ACCOUNTANTS, ET AL., IN OPPOSITION

In this case in which federal jurisdiction rests
solely on diversity of citizenship, petitioners are here
because of their disagreement with the holding below
that the conduct of respondents, the American Institute of Certified Public Accountants (hereafter
Institute) and three of its officials,[1] was not tortious

---

[1] The Institute, an incorporated body, is a non-profit, nationwide, professional society, membership in which is open to all
properly qualified certified public accountants and the purpose of

2

under the law of the State of New York. The Court of Appeals holding, of which review is sought, denied petitioners' claim that the circulation by respondents to the membership of the Institute of a letter expressing the opinion of the Institute's Committee on Accounting Procedure on an accounting question of general application and interest was a prima facie tort under New York law.

The District Court granted summary judgment in favor of respondents in an opinion examining in detail the applicable New York law (Petition, Appendix B). The Court of Appeals unanimously affirmed, stating that it agreed with the reasoned opinion of the District Court and holding that respondents' action involved no breach of duty owed by them to the petitioners (Petition, Appendix A). Mr. Justice Brennan, sitting as Circuit Justice, denied petitioners' application for a stay prohibiting the circulation of the letter pending action by this Court on a petition for writ of certiorari in an opinion in which he considered all of the contentions now advanced in the petition (Petition, Appendix D). The letter, circulation of which was prevented by petitioners for three months through interlocutory stays, was then distributed by the Institute to its members in July.

---

which is the furtherance of the ideals and principles of the accounting profession. The three individual respondents are the President of the Institute (Mr. L. H. Penney), the Chairman of the Institute's Committee on Accounting Procedure (Mr. William W. Werntz), and the Institute's Director of Research (Mr. Carman G. Blough).

3

STATEMENT

The background of the litigation is as follows: In the summer of 1958, the Institute's Committee on Accounting Procedure had issued "Accounting Research Bulletin No. 44 (Revised)," which related to the accounting treatment of liberalized depreciation for tax purposes (D.C. pp. 140-142a).[2] This Bulletin took no express position as to the proper treatment of "accounts for deferred taxes" on corporate balance sheets. In December of 1958, the Securities and Exchange Commission issued a "Notice of Intention to Announce Interpretation of Administrative Policy." (D.C. p. 159) This notice by the SEC set forth a proposed administrative policy that "accounts for deferred income taxes" should not be placed in the stockholders' equity portion of a balance sheet and that to do so would be considered deceptive to investors, and requested comments thereon. The proposed SEC policy was in accord with the position already taken by the Federal Power Commission and the Indiana State Public Service Commission (D.C. pp. 56-59). At public hearings held by the SEC pursuant to this notice, the Institute's Director of Research testified that the opinion letter here in question had been approved by the Committee on Accounting Procedure and was being prepared for distribution; and he read into the public record the significant portion of the letter (Petition, Appendix B p. 5b). The letter reads as follows:

---

[2] As noted in footnote 1 of the Petition, there is no printed record in this proceeding. For convenience of the Court, the system of record citation references suggested by the petitioners will be followed and the numbered pages of the certified record from the District Court will be referred to as "D.C. p.   " and those from that of the Court of Appeals as "C.A. p.   "

4

"AMERICAN INSTITUTE OF CERTIFIED
PUBLIC ACCOUNTANTS

"270 Madison Avenue,
New York 16, N. Y.

"April 15, 1959

"To the Members of the American
Institute of Certified Public Accountants

"Gentlemen:

"Question has been raised with respect to the intent of the committee on accounting procedure in using the phrase 'a deferred tax account' in Accounting Research Bulletin No. 44 (revised), *Declining-balance Depreciation,* to indicate the account to be credited for the amount of the deferred income tax (see paragraphs 4 and 5).

"The committee used the phrase in its ordinary connotation of an account to be shown in the balance sheet as a liability or a deferred credit. A provision in recognition of the deferral of income taxes, being required for the proper determination of net income, should not at the same time result in a credit to earned surplus or to any other account included in the stockholders' equity section of the balance sheet.

"Three of the twenty-one members of the committee, Messrs. Jennings, Powell and Staub, dissented to the issuance at this time of any letter interpreting Accounting Research Bulletin No. 44 (revised).

"COMMITTEE ON ACCOUNTING PROCEDURE

"By William W. Werntz, Chairman" [3]

---

[3] The Committee on Accounting Procedure approved the letter and its circulation to the members of the Institute by a favorable vote of 18 of its 21 members. Of the 18 members favorably voting, 16 had been members of the Committee when Bulletin No. 44 (Revised) was issued some months earlier, during 1958. These 16 constituted more than two-thirds of the members of the

5

As the letter was about to be circulated on April 15, 1959, petitioners filed a complaint seeking a judgment temporarily and permanently enjoining respondents from circulating the opinion letter "to the members of the Institute or to any members of the accountancy profession" and from adopting or issuing any statement similar to the opinion letter, unless and until the Institute had first:

"(a) Submitted a draft of the proposed letter to the persons to whom the exposure draft of Accounting Research Bulletin No. 44 was submitted.

"(b) Permitted such reasonable period of time, not less than 60 days, to have elapsed subsequent to said submission in order that such persons may have the opportunity of submitting for the consideration of the Committee their views and opinions.

"(c) Otherwise complied with the Institute's and the Committee's practices and procedures with respect to the publication of Accounting Research Bulletins." (D.C. pp. 12-13)

Each of the petitioner utilities carries in its balance sheets large sums (aggregating over $65,000,000 for the

Committee in office at that time. This plainly satisfied the requirement that the Committee act by a two-thirds majority of its members (Affidavit of Mr. William W. Werntz, Chairman of the Committee, Par. 11, and Ex. A, pp. 8-9, D. C. p. 56, 63a-64).

The Accounting Research Bulletins published by the Committee make clear that they represent *only* the opinions of the Committee, unless they have been specifically adopted by the Institute's membership. Neither by any law nor under the Institute's own rules do the statements have any authority beyond the force of their own reasoning. The Committee has discretion to work out its own procedures, except for the requirement that it act by a two-thirds majority, which it did here, and the requirement that the Committee may only presume to speak for itself (*id.*, Par. 6 and 11, and Ex. A, p. 9, D. C. p. 53, 56, 64).

6

three) in an account for deferred federal income taxes, which account appears in the stockholders' equity section of the balance sheet (D.C. p. 4). Petitioners asserted that if the opinion letter were circulated, the "prestige and authority of the . . . Committee" will cause accountants, financial institutions and governmental agencies to question such "continued inclusion of credits for deferred taxes in the earned surplus accounts" and that petitioners will therefore "be seriously interfered with in their dealings and relationships with such persons and institutions." (Complaint paragraph 29; affidavit of Mr. Donald C. Cook, a vice president of each of the petitioners, at paragraph 21, D.C. pp. 182-183)

As to the intent to injure, the complaint alleged merely that

> "30. The Institute and the Committee know that the foregoing [damage] will result . . . and intend that such . . . injury . . . shall occur. The actions of the defendants . . . are in wanton, reckless and wilful disregard of the said consequences of their proposed action" (D.C. pp. 11-12).

On the basis of the complaint and an accompanying affidavit, petitioners sought and obtained, without notice, from the District Court a temporary order restraining the circulation of the letter pending hearing and determination of an order to show cause why a preliminary injunction should not be issued (D.C. pp. 17-20). Respondents thereafter filed a cross-motion to dismiss for failure to state a claim on which relief could be granted (D.C. pp. 49-51). On May 6, the respondents served affidavits in opposition to the petitioners' application for an injunction, and later that day the parties exchanged briefs. A

7

reply affidavit by Mr. Cook, 28 pages in length with seven exhibits, was served upon the respondents late in the evening of May 6 (D.C. pp. 170-221). On May 7, the District Court held a hearing on the petitioners' application for preliminary injunction and the respondent's motion to dismiss. The petitioners' brief relied on Mr. Cook's affidavit in opposing the motion to dismiss; and in their argument on both motions petitioners did not differentiate between facts which came from the complaint and facts which came from affidavits.

On May 20, the District Court filed a full opinion, in which it concluded that because of the submission and consideration of matters beyond the pleadings, the motion to dismiss was to be treated as a motion for summary judgment under Rule 12(b) of the Federal Rules of Civil Procedure (D.C. pp. 222-236). The Court thereupon denied petitioners' application for preliminary injunction and granted summary judgment for respondents on the ground that no cause of action had been stated under New York law.

On May 25, counsel appeared before the District Court to settle the terms of the order. At no time during this hearing, which was approximately an hour-and-one-half in length, did petitioners suggest that they had any further material to offer in connection with summary judgment. The District Court granted petitioners' request for a stay only until the Court of Appeals could hear a motion for an injunction pending appeal (D.C. pp. 237-240).

Petitioners' motion in the Court of Appeals for such an injunction was set for argument on June 4.

8

On the preceding day, June 3, the parties exchanged voluminous briefs. Petitioners' brief raised for the first time the claim that they had been prejudiced by the District Court treating the case as being ripe for summary judgment. At the argument on June 4 the Court of Appeals determined, with the consent of the parties, that it would extend the injunction until its decision was handed down and that the case would be decided on the merits on the basis of oral argument and the submitted briefs (C.A. p. 1). On June 17, the Court of Appeals, in a unanimous per curiam decision, affirmed the judgment of the District Court and vacated its stay (C.A. pp. 14-16). On June 19, petitioners obtained a further stay pending an application to be made to and heard by a Justice of this Court not later than July 9 for a restraining order pending action by this Court on a petition for a writ of certiorari (C.A. pp. 24-26).

On July 7, Mr. Justice Brennan denied petitioners' application in an opinion which dealt explicitly with all the claims asserted in their petition and which concluded that none of these claims had the prospect of commanding four votes for review (Petition, Appendix D).

REASONS FOR DENYING THE WRIT

As the petition itself reveals, petitioners' basic claim, which they now seek to have reviewed here, is that:

"... the facts presented in the verified complaint established all of the elements of a prima facie tort under settled principles of New York law ...." (Petition, p. 4)

In other words, the petition rests on the claim that both the District Court and the Court of Appeals have

9

misapplied the New York doctrine of **prima facie tort** to the facts asserted by petitioners. This claim was fully considered by both courts below and properly resolved against petitioners. Even were this not so, however, a claimed misapplication of state law does not call for review by this Court.

The plain answer to petitioners' claim that the grant of summary judgment was improper is that, as the Court of Appeals found, petitioners were not denied the opportunity to present all relevant materials. At no time in the proceedings in the two courts below did plaintiffs ever indicate any fact not set out in their affidavits which could have changed the decision that under the applicable New York law they were not entitled to relief. Moreover, there is no conflict with the decision of any other Circuit.

I

THE DECISION OF THE COURT OF APPEALS ON A QUESTION OF NEW YORK LAW, UNANIMOUSLY AFFIRMING THE DISTRICT COURT, PRESENTS NO QUESTION WARRANTING REVIEW BY THIS COURT.

Petitioners contend that respondents are prima facie tortfeasors under the New York doctrine which provides for a cause of action "whenever one person [does] damage to another wilfully and intentionally, and without just cause or excuse." *Advance Music Corp.* v. *American Tobacco Co.*, 296 N.Y. 79, 70 N.E. 2d 401 (1946). It is the *Advance Music* case on which petitioners place their principal reliance.[4] The Dis-

_____

[4] Petitioners also rely on two labor cases in which the New York Court of Appeals found, respectively, that persuading members not to work for plaintiff employer or with members of a rival plaintiff organization was not justified as a lawful labor

10

trict Court, however, concluded, after an extensive review of the New York law, that neither the *Advance Music* case nor any other precedent would justify any injunctive or other relief against the respondents for their seeking to publish and distribute the views of the Institute's Committee. Before the Court of Appeals, petitioners again fully briefed and presented their claims under the New York law. The Court of Appeals, in its opinion affirming the judgment in favor of respondents, stated that it agreed with the District Court's decision on the substantive law of New York.

A question of state law does not, of course, merit review by this Court. As the Court has indicated on many occasions, in this area it defers to the decisions of the lower federal courts—skilled in the law of particular states—unless their conclusions are shown to lack a rational basis. As will be shown, the decisions of both the courts below, which unanimously concluded that petitioners have no claim against respondents, were the result of a reasonable and rational application of New York law.

With respect to the *Advance Music* case, as the District Court made clear, it like the other decisions advanced by petitioners is wide of the mark. In the *Advance Music* case the New York Court of Appeals reversed a decision dismissing a complaint· brought by a publisher of popular melodies against the sponsor, and its advertising agent, of a radio program known as "Your Hit Parade." The complaint alleged that the

objective. Opera on Tour, Inc. v. Weber, 285 N.Y. 348, 34 N.E. 2d 349 (1941) ; American Guild of Musical Artists, Inc. v. Petrillo, 286 N.Y. 226, 36 N.E. 2d 123 (1941). We need not elaborate upon the point that these cases, involving words and action specifically aimed solely at the plaintiffs concerned, have nothing to do with the present case.

11

program falsely represented to its large audience that it had ascertained, on the basis of volume of sales, the nine or ten most popular melodies each week, and the order of their sales popularity; that in fact no such ascertainment was made at all; that the plaintiff's melodies were consistently excluded from the list, without justification, or were given an unjustifiably low ranking; that this was done with intent to injure the plaintiff; and that the plaintiff had, indeed, been injured by a refusal of jobbers and others to distribute plaintiff's melodies to dealers because of their omission or low ranking on "Your Hit Parade."

The *Advance Music* case was thus a perfectly clear case of wanton misrepresentation of fact and came very close to a case of common-law unfair competition. The present case is completely different. As pointed out in the opinion of the District Court, the proposed letter of the Committee on Accounting Procedure is simply an expression of professional opinion on a general accounting question. Moreover, it is not alleged that the opinion is not honestly held by the members of the Committee who voted to issue the letter. In fact, as noted by the District Court, the Committee's view is supported by most respectable authority (Petition, Appendix B, p. 6b).

The breaking point of petitioners' case is the simple and obvious fact that the basis of prima facie tort is *malicious injury*—doing a harm malevolently for the sake of the harm as an end in itself and not merely as a means to another end legitimately desired. The doctrine has recently been so delimited by the New York Court of Appeals in *Reinforce, Inc.* v. *Birney,* 308 N.Y. 164, 124 N.E. 2d 104 (1954), a case which

12

petitioners do not mention. In that case the court held:

> "If the doers, by means not in themselves unlawful, of acts not in themselves unlawful, have any proper purpose to serve, they are not liable for the damage they cause [citing cases.] Unions, as well as everyone else, may claim the benefit of the settled rule that 'the genesis which will make a lawful act unlawful must be a malicious one unmixed with any other and exclusively directed to injury and damage of another' [citing cases]." 308 N.Y. at 169-170, 124 N.E. 2d at 106.

Moreover, as recognized by the New York Court of Appeals in the *Advance Music* case, a prima facie tort case does not arise where there is "justification" for the act of which complaint is made. Here the purposes of the Institute—those of a voluntary, professional association—are adequate justification, if justification be required, for the proposed communication.

II

THE TREATMENT OF THE CASE AS ONE FOR SUMMARY JUDGMENT UNDER RULE 12(b) WAS PROPER AND DOES NOT IN ANY WAY CONFLICT WITH A DECISION IN ANY OTHER CIRCUIT.

Rule 12(b) of the Federal Rules of Civil Procedure states that a District Court shall treat a motion to dismiss for failure to state a claim as a motion for summary judgment where matters outside the pleadings are before the court. It provides that in such circumstances all parties be given reasonable opportunity to present material pertinent to a motion for summary judgment.

13

Petitioner seeks to make out a conflict between the decision below and the decision in *Pacific American Fisheries, Inc.* v. *Mullaney,* 191 F. 2d 137 (9th Cir. 1951), on the propriety of entering summary judgment under Rule 12(b) in the circumstances of this case. There is no conflict.

The petition (pp. 10-11) discusses the *Pacific American Fisheries* case only by linking together widely separated sentences appearing at various places over three pages of the report of the opinion. This effort at plastic surgery fails to disclose what the decision was.

In the *Pacific American Fisheries* case, a non-resident fishing company had sued for injunction against enforcement of an Alaska fisheries tax which was greater for non-residents than for residents, and for a declaratory judgment of its invalidity. On a motion for temporary injunction, affidavits were filed. The District Court denied the motion on the ground that the facts did not show sufficient injury to warrant equity's interference with enforcement of a criminal statute (191 F. 2d at 139). Thereafter defendant—the Alaska Tax Commissioner—moved for judgment on the pleadings on the grounds that the statute had been held valid in a companion case recently decided by the Federal District Court in Alaska and that equity will not interfere with criminal prosecutions (*Ibid.*). On this motion the District Court entered summary judgment for the defendant, reciting that it had considered "matters outside of the pleadings," with a later minute entry explaining that there was no issue of fact "in view of the lack of power to grant injunctive relief." (*Id.* at 139-140).

14

The decision was reversed on appeal on the same day the same Court of Appeals reversed the decision in the companion case where the Federal District Court in Alaska had held the statute to be valid. *Anderson v. Mullaney,* 191 F. 2d 123 (9th Cir. 1951); *aff'd,* 342 U.S. 415.

The Court of Appeals held, first, that because the plaintiff had also sought declaratory relief, the mere showing that a case for injunction had not been made could not dispose of the case. (191 F. 2d at 140). Then, as to injunction, the Court held that, in view of its contemporaneous decision in the companion case, reversing the decision on which the lower court had relied, it would be most material to determine whether there was *in fact* a discriminatory burden on non-residents. (*Id.* at 141). Finally the Court held that "because of the importance of the issues presented in this suit" in no event should it have been disposed of by summary judgment. (*Id.* at 141).

Petitioners' case is not remotely similar. Here a motion for preliminary injunction, with voluminous affidavits—including petitioners' most exhaustive reply affidavit—and a motion to dismiss were briefed and argued together before the District Court. Both in briefs and in argument to the District Court the material inside the pleadings and the material outside the pleadings were mingled together. Then, when the Court in a full opinion rendered summary judgment, the parties met with the Court for approximately an hour and a half on the settlement of the order and on the question of an injunction pending appeal. At no time in this session with the Court was there the slightest hint by the petitioners

15

that they had anything further to present or that they complained of the summary judgment disposition of the case. This card was kept close to the chest until the petitioners made their argument in the Court of Appeals.

What was done here by the District Court was perfectly natural and normal in the circumstances. To countenance petitioners' argument would encourage poker playing with District Courts instead of the candor to which they are entitled. The Court of Appeals is well equipped to exercise supervision over questions of practice of this sort in its Districts. It was not impressed by petitioners' plea of prejudice and concluded that petitioners were not denied the opportunity to present all relevant materials.

In a slight variation of their claim, petitioners contend that the District Court in granting summary judgment decided controverted issues of fact. They are vague as to precisely what issues of fact they consider both material and controverted. This is as it must be, since, under the relevant New York law as applied by the courts below, there were no controverted issues of material fact. Petitioners claim that the District Court decided against them issues concerning respondents' intent in publishing the Committee's letter, concerning whether the characterization of the letter as interpretative of a prior bulletin was false, and concerning the actual effect of the Committee's opinions. The District Court's opinion makes plain that on its view of New York law the allegations of petitioners on their side of these issues were insufficient in law to sustain their claim. Therefore, they are not material facts.

16

The Court of Appeals has not misread Rule 12(b). It has not rendered a decision in conflict with that of any other Court of Appeals, and it has not sanctioned the use of the summary judgment procedure to decide material issues of fact.

III

THE DECISION BELOW PRESENTS NO QUESTION AS TO THE EQUITY POWERS OF THE FEDERAL JUDICIARY TO ENJOIN TORTIOUS SPEECH.

As a Parthian shot, petitioners proffer as a reason to justify review by this Court the claim that the decision below presents the question of whether a court of equity has the power to enjoin tortious speech by a professional organization. The decision below presents no such question. Both the District Court and the Court of Appeals rulings were based on the flat holdings that distribution of the letter of the Committee on Accounting Procedure was, as a matter of New York law, not a tortious act.

Although a basic question under the First Amendment would arise if a court were to sustain petitioners in their efforts to throttle the expression of opinion by a public service organization such as the respondent Institute, no such issue is presented here. The ruling below did not involve the question of whether tortious speech could or could not be enjoined. It was rather a carefully documented determination by the District Court and by a unanimous Court of Appeals that the action of the respondents in distributing the letter expressing the Committee's opinion was not a tortious act under the applicable New York law.

17

CONCLUSION

For the foregoing reasons, the petition for a w̄
of certiorari should be denied.

Respectfully submitted,

HOWARD C. WESTWOOD,
FONTAINE C. BRADLEY,
STANLEY L. TEMKO,
ROBERT L. RANDALL,
  701 Union Trust Building,
  Washington 5, D. C.
    Attorneys for Respondents

COVINGTON & BURLING,
  Of Counsel

September, 1959.

SUPREME COURT OF THE UNITED STATES

No. 388   October Term, 1959.

Appalachian Power Company, et al.,

Petitioners,

vs.

American Institute of Certified Public Accountants, et al.

On petition for writ of Certiorari to the United States Court of Appeals for the Second Circuit.

On consideration of the petition for a writ of certiorari herein to the United States Court of Appeals for the Second Circuit, it is ordered by this Court that the said petition be, and the same is hereby, denied.

November 9, 1959

UNITED STATES DISTRICT COURT
For the Southern District of New York

Appalachian Power Company, Ohio Power Company and Indiana & Michigan Electric Company, *Plaintiffs,* against American Institute of Certified Public Accountants, L. H. Penney, William W. Werntz and Carman G. Blough, *Defendants.*	Civil Action No. 145–161 ORDER ON JUDGMENT

Plaintiffs having appealed to the United States Court of Appeals for the Second Circuit from the judgment of this Court entered in this cause on May 25, 1959, and the Court of Appeals having affirmed such judgment on June 17, 1959, and plaintiffs' application for an order staying the mandate of the Court of Appeals having been denied by Mr. Justice Brennan of the Supreme Court of the United States, sitting as Circuit Justice, on July 7, 1959, and plaintiffs' petition for a writ of certiorari having been denied by the Supreme Court of the United States on November 9, 1959, and the mandate of the Court of Appeals having been issued and the judgment of the Court of Appeals having been received and filed in this Court;

Now, upon the mandate and judgment of the United States Court of Appeals for the Second Circuit, it is

ORDERED, ADJUDGED AND DECREED that the judgment of the United States Court of Appeals for the Second Circuit be and it is made the judgment of this Court.

Dated: New York, New York
    November 27, 1959.

/s/   RICHARD H. LEVET
U. S. D. J.

Judgment entered: November 27, 1959.

/s/ HERBERT A. CHARLSON
       Clerk

Agreed to:

/s/ SIMPSON THACHER & BARTLETT

      Simpson Thacher & Bartlett
      Attorneys for Plaintiffs
      120 Broadway
      New York 5, New York

UNITED STATES DISTRICT COURT
For the Southern District of New York

Appalachian Power Company,
Ohio Power Company and
Indiana & Michigan Electric Company,

Plaintiffs,

against

American Institute of Certified Public
Accountants, L. H. Penney, William W.
Werntz and Carman G. Blough,

Defendants.

NOTICE OF SETTLEMENT

Civil Action No. 145-161

S I R S:

PLEASE TAKE NOTICE that the within proposed order will be presented for settlement and signature to the Honorable Richard H. Levet, United States District Judge, at his Chambers at the United States Court House, Foley Square, New York, New York, on May 25, 1959 at 2:00 o'clock in the afternoon of that day.

Dated, New York, N.Y.
May 25, 1959

Yours, etc.,

SIMPSON THACHER & BARTLETT

By /s/ WHITNEY NORTH SEYMOUR
Member of the Firm

Attorneys for Plaintiffs,
Office and Post Office Address,
120 Broadway,
New York 5, N. Y.

TO:

MESSRS. HOWARD C. WESTWOOD, FONTAINE
C. BRADLEY and STANLEY L. TEMKO,
Attorneys for Defendants,
c/o American Institute of Certified Public Accountants,
270 Madison Avenue,
New York, N. Y.
      and
COVINGTON & BURLING,
Union Trust Building,
Washington, D.C.

UNITED STATES DISTRICT COURT

For the Southern District of New York

Appalachian Power Company,
Ohio Power Company and
Indiana & Michigan Electric Company,

    Plaintiffs,

  against

American Institute of Certified Public
Accountants, L. H. Penney, William W.
Werntz and Carman G. Blough,

    Defendants.

ORDER

Civil Action No. 145-161

A final order and judgment having been entered herein on May 25, 1959 denying plaintiffs' motion for an order, pursuant to Rule 65 of the Federal Rules of Civil Procedure, granting a preliminary injunction herein, granting defendants' motion for an order, pursuant to Rule 12(b) of the Federal Rules of Civil Procedure, dismissing the complaint herein on the ground that it fails to state a claim upon which relief can be granted and granting summary judgment in favor of defendants, and

Plaintiffs having filed a notice of appeal herein dated May 25, 1959 and having made application for an order, pursuant to Rule 62(c) of the Federal Rules of Civil Procedure, for an order granting an injunction pending the hearing and determination of said appeal,

NOW, upon the notice of appeal herein, the aforesaid order and judgment of this Court, and upon the complaint herein, duly verified on April 15, 1959, the affidavits of Robert O. Whitman and Donald C. Cook, duly sworn to on April 15 and May 6, 1959, respectively, submitted in support of plaintiffs' motion for a temporary injunction, the affidavits of F. Merrill Beatty and William W. Werntz, both duly sworn to on May 4, 1959, and the affidavit of George C. Christy, duly sworn to on May 6, 1959, all submitted in opposition to plaintiffs' said motion, and it appearing from the foregoing that the distribution of the letter and opinion proposed to be distributed by the defendants to the members of the defendant American Institute of Certified Public Accountants, or any other communication, to the effect that the defendant American Institute of Certified Public Accountants or its Committee on Accounting Procedure is of the opinion or recommends that charges made to income in recognition of the deferral of income taxes should not or may not, in accordance with generally accepted accounting principles be credited to earned surplus or to any other account included in the stockholders' equity section of the balance sheet, would cause the appeal herein to become moot insofar as review is sought of the denial of plaintiffs' application for a preliminary injunction, and the plaintiffs having given and filed the undertaking required by law in the sum of Five hundred ($500) dollars,

IT IS ORDERED THAT, pending the hearing of a motion to be made by plaintiffs in the Court of Appeals, Second Circuit, not later than June 1, 1959, for a stay pending the hearing and determination of plaintiffs' appeal herein from the order and judgment of the United States District Court of May 25, 1959, the defendants be and they are hereby enjoined and restrained from distributing to the members of the defendant American Institute of Certified Public Accountants or to any members of the accountancy profession, the aforesaid proposed letter or distributing any like statement to the aforesaid to the effect that the defendant American Institute of Certified Public Accountants or its Committee on Accounting Procedure is of the opinion or recommends that charges made to income in recognition of the deferral of income taxes should not or may not, in accordance with generally accepted accounting principles, be credited to earned surplus or to any other account included in the stockholders' equity section of the balance sheet.

Dated, May 25, 1959.   /s/ RICHARD H. LEVET
                                          United States District Judge

AT THE BREAST

THE FIRST IDEAL OF BEAUTY

The babe, emerging from its liquid bed,
Now lifts in gelid air its nodding head; . . .
Seeks with spread hands the bosom's velvet orbs,
With closing lips the milky fount absorbs;
And, as compress'd, the dulcet streams distill,
Drinks warmth and fragrance from the living rill; . . .
And learns, ere long, the perfect form confest,
Ideal beauty, from its mother's breast.

Anonymous, *New York Weekly Museum,* 1814

The first separation from my baby . . . w[as] very painful. . . . as the
baby was only half-weaned, it was necessary to have the milk drawn
from my breasts with a little machine. This was a ghastly experience for
me and caused me many tears. . . . often when I danced, the milk over-
flowed, running down my tunic, and causing me much embarrassment.
How difficult it is for a woman to have a career!

Isadora Duncan, *My Life,* 1927

. . . white people have assumed Samantha is not my child. This is curious to me, this inability to connect across skin tones. . . . So far no
one has accused me of child abduction, but I have been mistaken for
Samantha's nanny. . . . to be blunt, I don't like seeing black women caring for white children. It may be because I grew up in the South, where
black women once had no choice but to leave their own children and
suckle the offspring of others. The weight of that past . . . still stains
such pairings.

Kim McLarin, *New York Times Magazine,* 1998

Is there not something unseemly, in our society, about the spectacle
of a white woman mothering a black child? A white woman giving
totally to a black child; a black child totally and demandingly dependent
for everything, sustenance itself, from a white woman. The image of a
white woman suckling a black child; the image of a black child sucking
for its life from the bosom of a white woman. The utter interdependence of such an image; the merging it implies; the giving up of
boundary; the encompassing of other within self; the unbounded gener-
osity and interconnectedness of such an image.

Patricia J. Williams, *The Alchemy of Race and Rights,* 1991

TO MY FAMILY

come home from work [and she had worked long hours when her children were babies, with lots of breast-pumping], that baby will remember *who you are*."

These last statements intrigued me, perhaps because with my own son, I had felt somewhat fanatical too.[7] Can a mother be replaced so easily? What does it mean to think that your baby will forget *who you are*? Sociologist Sharon Hays answered such questions, which plagued the contemporary mothers she studied, by demonstrating that both employed and at-home mothers drew from, or were in dialogue with, the ideology of "intensive motherhood" (1996: esp. 145). Good mothers, in this view, not only put their children's needs first, but provide labor- and emotion-intensive care to protect them from a harsh, impersonal market-driven society. In this view, "children need" a prolonged period of protection and indulgence—and it must be provided by one, singularly focused mother. She must study each child's psychological, physical, and cognitive development and judge how to stimulate and enrich at just the right speed for the individual's age, stage, and temperament (1996: 54, 60, 78). Even if this mother is employed, according to Hays, she engages in arduous efforts to find and manage the proper substitute care (1996: 62). Employed and at-home mothers, in short, both see childrearing as their primary responsibility in life, and one that is ultimately theirs alone (1996: 108; also McMahon 1995).[8]

Hays's explanation of "intensive motherhood," though it reveals many of our unexamined but tenaciously held beliefs, metaphors, images, and practices, ignores an important dimension of modern motherhood. The physicality and sexuality involved in such intensively focused care have been of concern to all the twentieth-century experts on "children's needs." The behaviorists, early- and late-century maternalists, physicians, and Freudians (whom I discuss in the next chapter) all have emphasized the embodied aspects of the mother-child dyad, though they have not agreed on whether or how this physicality should be controlled, measured, encouraged, or repressed. There has been consensus, however, about the singularity of this dyad and the need for this attachment to have a special, exclusive character. Indeed, as I will point out in the next chapter, some experts liken the sensual tie between the mother and baby to the exclusivity of the monogamous marriage bond. And it is this norm or belief in

physical exclusivity that I suggest accounts for the "fanaticism" and fears of being forgotten or replaced expressed by late-twentieth-century white, professional mothers in the United States (e.g., Hays 1996: 145). I use the term *exclusive* rather than *intensive,* in this and ensuing chapters, to better describe this dominant ideology of motherhood. Interestingly, as I discuss in the following section, with all the tremendously rich feminist writing on motherhood, little attention has been paid to the specific, *inessential* historical meaning and organization of its physicality.

SO, WHY ANOTHER FEMINIST WRITING ON MOTHERHOOD?

Since the resurgence of the women's movement in the late 1960s, it seems that feminists have been obsessed with motherhood. Readers may wonder, as I often worried, whether there could be anything left to add. Novelists, memoirists, literary critics, and scholars across many disciplines have explored how motherhood, an activity and a relationship so immensely rewarding and enabling, could at the same time be so oppressive and disabling. Adrienne Rich brilliantly wrote that it was motherhood as institution which imposed the patriarchal entrapment, while motherhood as lived experience provided the former life-affirming, even liberatory qualities (1976). Like Rich, many have thought about how to retain these so valuable womanly experiences without reinforcing the institutional straitjacket, the seemingly "natural" gender arrangements, fixed and timeless, that have justified so much discrimination. In short, feminist ambivalence has centered on which to put first, "difference," the affirmation of women's "motherly" experiences, or "equality," the need for economic and political rights on a par with men's.[9]

These dilemmas of equality and difference are not new, as they stem from eighteenth-century discussions of the boundaries of citizenship. They do, however, need to be thought about in context; and in our political-economic era, which I return to in my concluding chapter, equality with and difference from men require rethinking. Feminist scholars have analyzed women's experiences of pregnancy and birth because of the thorny obstacles they pose to law and policy that would treat women no differently than men (e.g., Eisenstein 1988, Martin 1987, Oakley 1980, Vogel 1993, among many). Breast-

feeding, in contrast, has attracted little attention, perhaps because it seems a more optional aspect of motherhood. If an optional practice, however, it is an issue that is nearly impossible to avoid; readers will discover in chapters 4 and 5 that "breast is best" is a prescription most mothers contend with in some way.[10] Furthermore, as the Army pilot mother's story revealed, breastfeeding can pose even thornier obstacles to equal treatment. During pregnancy, most women have greater autonomy and freedom of movement than while nursing; and birth is simply a far shorter event. Because the lens on late-century breastfeeding reveals the collision of public and private concerns with the maternal body, I come to some different conclusions from other analysts of "body politics" and gender difference. Though many agree that putting gender difference first has been dangerous—the line between celebration and discrimination can be very slight—I suggest that mothers may need to strategically or tactically use this much-repudiated *essentialism*, if *they* can define when it is relevant.

Cultural feminists like Adrienne Rich, the gender "maximizers" who celebrated women's difference, have been most frequently found guilty of essentialism. As in the eighteenth and nineteenth centuries, *essence* meant this one inherent aspect of womanhood, motherhood, which by God or nature, made all women "woman." Most twentieth-century feminists, however, disagreed and, like Mary Wollstonecraft and John Stuart Mill and Harriet Taylor Mill in earlier centuries, they were gender "minimizers" who considered women more like men than different. The women's movement in the mid-twentieth century was, after all, most concerned with freeing women from the imperative *to* mother. Emerging from the profamily, pronatalist climate of the 1950s, most wanted to put equality first, break the claim of biology, and "denaturalize" nature. The equality approach was also pragmatic, modeled on the successes of the Civil Rights Movement, because most activists put access to male jobs and educational opportunities first.

This approach of seeking equal treatment and minimizing gender led to significant gains for women, but by the 1980s its limitations were also apparent. Access proved to be more difficult to gain than many had thought, and, where gained, was often not what feminists had bargained for. Many then saw more to the maximizing approach, because demanding similar treatment gained entry for a few, but left

public spheres, with their implicit male organization, unchanged. By the 1980s, even Gloria Steinem, glamorized feminist nonmother, had quipped: "We have become the men we wanted to marry" (Rothman 1989: 198). But to valorize motherhood shores up rather than tears down the old categories, contributing to their fixed, essential appearance.

Those who came to feminism from more radical Sixties movements, inspired by critiques of capitalism, also had been gender minimizers. Marxist and socialist feminists tended to categorize motherhood as merely unpaid work or "domestic labor" and painted the family as a "locus of struggle." Rather than with the valorizing terms of nurturance, care, and connectedness, they described women's experiences "in the [utilitarian] language of commodities and exchange." This picture was particularly criticized by women of color, who saw their families, and especially their mothers, in a warmer and more multishaded light.[11] By the 1980s, Marxists and socialists began to rethink their views, if not of capitalism, then of motherhood.[12] Ironically, the harsh political-economic changes of late-twentieth-century U.S. capitalism—the plant closings, corporate downsizings, and cutbacks in social provisions—on their own put a sharp end to the pronatalist climate.[13] Thus, feminists of many strands realized that "the right to bear and raise children without sacrificing one's health, one's sanity, or one's job, and without having to be a man's wife, will be a much more difficult right to gain than was the right *not* to have a child" (Van Allen 1990: 297, my emphasis).

In short, the "family *un*friendly" context of the Reagan and Bush presidencies and the new global economy threatened difference more than equality, and the authentic desire *to* mother replaced earlier concerns that women were being compelled or coerced into motherhood. The work of scholars such as Nancy Chodorow (1978), Carol Gilligan (1982), Barbara Katz Rothman (1989), and Sara Ruddick (1989, 1990) was widely influential, given a social world so lacking in care and mutual obligation. This mother-valorizing scholarship did not base woman's difference on God or nature, but it nonetheless gave a moral essentialism to exclusive motherhood. If this mother was produced by history and social location,[14] she nevertheless stood for all that was good, in opposition to the heartless profit-mongering of a world dominated by multinational corporations. And this goodness

AT THE BREAST

IDEOLOGIES OF BREASTFEEDING
AND MOTHERHOOD IN THE
CONTEMPORARY UNITED STATES

LINDA M. BLUM

BEACON PRESS   BOSTON

Beacon Press
25 Beacon Street
Boston, Massachusetts 02108-2892
www.beacon.org

Beacon Press books
are published under the auspices of
the Unitarian Universalist Association of Congregations.

Parts of this book have been previously published. Pieces of chapter 1 first appeared in the journal *Feminist Studies* 19 (1993): 291–311 as "Mothers, Babies, and Breastfeeding in Late Capitalist America: The Shifting Context of Feminist Theory." Material in chapter 3 appeared in the journal *Social Problems* 40(3) (1993): 285–300 as " 'Mother to Mother': A Maternalist Organization in Late Capitalist America," with second author Elizabeth A. Vandewater, used by permission of the University of California Press, and in *Qualitative Sociology* 16 (1993): 3–22 as "Mothers Construct Fathers: Destabilized Patriarchy in La Leche League," also with Elizabeth A. Vandewater, reprinted by permission of Plenum Publishing Corp. Material in chapter 5 appeared in *Gender & Society* 10 (1996): 199–211 as "Negotiating Independent Motherhood: Working-Class African American Women Talk About Marriage and Motherhood" and is reprinted by permission of Sage Publications, Inc.

05 04 03 02 01 00 99   8 7 6 5 4 3 2 1

This book is printed on recycled acid-free paper that contains at least 20 percent postconsumer waste and meets the uncoated paper ANSI / NISO specifications for permanence as revised in 1992.

Text design by Elizabeth Elsas
Composition by Wilsted & Taylor Publishing Services

Library of Congress Cataloging-in-Publication Data

Blum, Linda M.
    At the breast : ideologies of breastfeeding and motherhood in the contemporary
United States / Linda M. Blum.
        p.   cm.
    Includes bibliographical references and index.
    ISBN 0-8070-2140-7 (cloth)
        1. Motherhood—United States.   2. Mothers—United States.   3. Breastfeeding—
United States.   I. Title.
HQ759.B618   1999
306.874'3—dc21   98-46108

flicting meanings that emerge from collisions and meldings of cultural and corporeal bodies. That is, the body-as-text, planned and
meaningful, may disrupt the body-as-body, just as the corporeal
body's obduracy may disrupt the best-planned text. The media account, therefore, seems flattened: the lieutenant "[was] unable to
pump enough breast milk to feed her [daughter]" (Thompson 1997:
32). A more nuanced reading might point out that the lieutenant
(with/in her body) rejected the medical model in favor of a maternalist model of breastfeeding. The contemporary maternalist model
resists separating the embodied process—the mother with baby at the
breast—from its product, human milk. The maternalist model also
exalts motherhood and finds women's difference more valuable than
public equality.

WHAT ABOUT THE BABIES?
Readers may be surprised to have heard nothing up to now about infant's and children's needs, usually the main point of any conversation
about breastfeeding and, surely, of any conversation about motherhood. I am often reminded that my approach emphasizing the mother's side of the story may seem heretical to some. After all, two of the
strongest normative assumptions about contemporary motherhood
are that good mothers "naturally" put their "children's needs" first[5]
and that "children's needs" are fixed by "nature" and progressively
more knowable (Hays 1996, McMahon 1995). These assumptions
have been questioned by many feminist writers addressing heated issues like the effects of daycare or of fathers' parenting on children, but
they appear more fixed, more "in nature," with breastfeeding because
of its thick biological layers. A committed feminist and obstetrician,
whom I met socially, asked me how she could get her patients to
breastfeed more, how she could convey to them that breastfeeding is
so important for their babies that it's really "*not* a choice." She was incredulous when I replied that many women might want to know if it
helps prevent breast cancer.[6] And then I suggested perhaps she could
convince patients to give it a try because *they* might enjoy it (provided
she were available to help with problems). But, she insisted—against
my prioritizing of mothers' health and well-being—"I'm a fanatic for
breastfeeding. It's the best food *for the baby.*" As a mother herself, she
said: "It's the *one* thing you can do that no one else can. When you

using, promiscuous, or perhaps, at best, unwitting victims.[3] In this story, the cultural body and the corporeal body meld together and appear to be the same.

Perhaps, however, the appropriateness of public involvement in the breastfeeding story of the Army pilot mother, Emma Cuevas, is more questionable. There is no overriding question of infant health or survival, merely the mother's preference. Yet this story is, among other things, about confounding the gendered basis of citizenship and obligation to the body politic: women serve the nation through motherhood, and men, through the military. The lieutenant struck a male bargain by accepting publicly funded, highly skilled training in exchange for her service, yet when she became a mother, she reneged, expecting her motherhood to be equally valued. As one letter-writer joked, however, perhaps she should be allowed to resign if she repays taxpayers the estimated $500,000 spent on her military training (*Time* 1997: 31). She faced a difficult choice because, to be respected as a mother within the affluent middle-class, she should have properly "maximized" and perfected her child, which (stories like the one on intelligence instruct us) requires a commitment to breastfeed. In the current era, breastfeeding has become "the measure of the mother" (Maclean 1990: 52, 118, 164).

Scrutinizing these stories, however, reveals that "breastfeeding" points to more than one set of practices. The opening epigraphs to the book suggest how much practices have varied across history and social location. At present, breastfeeding can range from a six-week dose of "bonding" to an intense, several-year relationship. And, to add another layer of complexity, the body, in its stubborn physicality, sometimes defies plans for a particular interpretation. The recalcitrant, corporeal body, *and* its interaction with the individual's unconscious emotional life, do not always comply with conscious or cultural design.[4] The Army pilot and (*in*, or *with*) her body refused to comply with one increasingly popular interpretation of breastfeeding that equates it with large amounts of breast-pumping. The breast pump, in this medical model, seems to restore women's equality within male-workplace and public environments, with the milk she collects "standing in" for her and her motherly nature at home.

Readers, however, may first interpret this story as biological, as *if* breastfeeding had a fixed, obvious meaning rather than several con-

cause it provides a lens with which to sharpen our focus on the conflicts shaping and dividing women's lives in these postfeminist times.
Breastfeeding is, as British sociologist Pam Carter has written, a conversation about femininity (1995: 190). Because women are all "from
the mother half of humanity" (Snitow 1990: 35), we all are affected
by this standard, even if it is as potential mothers or as barren nonmothers. These conversations, moreover, like conversations about
abortion, genetic testing, fetal rights, teen pregnancy, and new reproductive technologies, are in part about the obligations of the maternal
body to the larger social body. Cultural historian Marilyn Yalom
notes that in the modern Western democracies breasts become "metonymically targetted" and symbolize the health of the body politic
(1997: 106).

Conversations that look "at the breast," therefore, are not private.
Motherhood and breastfeeding have been and continue to be public
matters. This public interest at first seems appropriate because of biological realities and actual concerns with health: primarily with infant
health and survival, but occasionally with pregnancy and maternal
health. I have learned to be cautious, however, in reading such *facts*.
Postmodern and poststructural scholars instruct us that bodily practices—despite their undeniable physicality—are always historical. In
other words, our meaning-making practices shape how we see, interpret, and treat the body (as well as external nature) and its *facts*; moreover, all 'knowledge' of the body develops in the context of particular power relations (Carter 1995: 216; also Foucault 1980, Riley 1983,
Soper 1995, among many). It is sometimes hard to see this plasticity in
our own culture, but think of the women who are able through rigorous training to pass the physical ability tests for police, fire-fighting,
and military training, physical capabilities once thought *factually, biologically* impossible for women.[2] This does not mean, however, that
breasts or bodies are infinitely malleable or plastic. Bodies do get sick,
suffer, and die. Yet the news stories about breastfeeding that I began
with, ostensibly about such biological facts as brain development and
HIV transmission, are also moral stories, cautionary tales, about maternal bodies and good or bad mothers, and the way they are 'read' in
the late twentieth century. Indeed, the HIV story is so powerful because it literally *and* metaphorically tells us which mothers have "dangerous" bodies—poor, Third World or U.S. women of color, drug-

CHAPTER I

"BREAST IS BEST"

Newsweek magazine announced, in its 1997 special issue on children, that breastfeeding may boost a child's intelligence (Glick 1997; also *New York Times* 1998b). But the *New York Times* warned of the dangers of HIV-infected mothers passing the virus to their infants through their milk (Meier 1997). And *Time* magazine told the story of a female Army pilot, Emma Cuevas, who asked to be released from the service to breastfeed her baby after her six-week maternity leave was up. She was denied this option, though experts on her behalf claimed a constitutional right to breastfeed and explained that the healthiest babies nurse until two (Thompson 1997). What is going on in these stories focusing on mothers' breasts? And what do they tell us about our dominant notions of good and bad mothers?

Letters in response to the story of the Army pilot mother (*Time* 1997: 31) reflected media "Mommy Wars," which pit employed, "masculinized" mothers against at-home mothers invoking women's different "nature."[1] This has been, however, an exaggerated divide, and it is just one of the emotionally charged questions represented within late-twentieth-century conversations about breastfeeding and motherhood. Others touch deep racial and class cleavages: Which women should mother? Whose babies will be valued? What social provisions do mothers need? And which mothers "deserve" provisioning? Still other explosive questions represent anxieties about mothers' bodies, their sexuality, and the physicality of feeding at the breast: Which women's bodies "deserve" to be seen as pure or trustworthy? Which women's bodies need to be controlled? And which women's bodies are cast as polluted and dangerous?

These questions are important *not* because breastfeeding, if chosen, is more than a brief interlude in a mother's life, but, rather, be-

CONTENTS

CONTENTS

"BREAST IS BEST"

Newsweek magazine announced, in its 1997 special issue on children, that breastfeeding may boost a child's intelligence (Glick 1997; also *New York Times* 1998b). But the *New York Times* warned of the dangers of HIV-infected mothers passing the virus to their infants through their milk (Meier 1997). And *Time* magazine told the story of a female Army pilot, Emma Cuevas, who asked to be released from the service to breastfeed her baby after her six-week maternity leave was up. She was denied this option, though experts on her behalf claimed a constitutional right to breastfeed and explained that the healthiest babies nurse until two (Thompson 1997). What is going on in these stories focusing on mothers' breasts? And what do they tell us about our dominant notions of good and bad mothers?

Letters in response to the story of the Army pilot mother (*Time* 1997: 31) reflected media "Mommy Wars," which pit employed, "masculinized" mothers against at-home mothers invoking women's different "nature."[1] This has been, however, an exaggerated divide, and it is just one of the emotionally charged questions represented within late-twentieth-century conversations about breastfeeding and motherhood. Others touch deep racial and class cleavages: Which women should mother? Whose babies will be valued? What social provisions do mothers need? And which mothers "deserve" provisioning? Still other explosive questions represent anxieties about mothers' bodies, their sexuality, and the physicality of feeding at the breast: Which women's bodies "deserve" to be seen as pure or trustworthy? Which women's bodies need to be controlled? And which women's bodies are cast as polluted and dangerous?

These questions are important *not* because breastfeeding, if chosen, is more than a brief interlude in a mother's life, but, rather, be-

cause it provides a lens with which to sharpen our focus on the conflicts shaping and dividing women's lives in these postfeminist times. Breastfeeding is, as British sociologist Pam Carter has written, a conversation about femininity (1995: 190). Because women are all "from the mother half of humanity" (Snitow 1990: 35), we all are affected by this standard, even if it is as potential mothers or as barren nonmothers. These conversations, moreover, like conversations about abortion, genetic testing, fetal rights, teen pregnancy, and new reproductive technologies, are in part about the obligations of the maternal body to the larger social body. Cultural historian Marilyn Yalom notes that in the modern Western democracies breasts become "metonymically targetted" and symbolize the health of the body politic (1997: 106).

Conversations that look "at the breast," therefore, are not private. Motherhood and breastfeeding have been and continue to be public matters. This public interest at first seems appropriate because of biological realities and actual concerns with health: primarily with infant health and survival, but occasionally with pregnancy and maternal health. I have learned to be cautious, however, in reading such *facts*. Postmodern and poststructural scholars instruct us that bodily practices—despite their undeniable physicality—are always historical. In other words, our meaning-making practices shape how we see, interpret, and treat the body (as well as external nature) and its *facts*; moreover, all 'knowledge' of the body develops in the context of particular power relations (Carter 1995: 216; also Foucault 1980, Riley 1983, Soper 1995, among many). It is sometimes hard to see this plasticity in our own culture, but think of the women who are able through rigorous training to pass the physical ability tests for police, fire-fighting, and military training, physical capabilities once thought *factually, biologically* impossible for women.[2] This does not mean, however, that breasts or bodies are infinitely malleable or plastic. Bodies do get sick, suffer, and die. Yet the news stories about breastfeeding that I began with, ostensibly about such biological facts as brain development and HIV transmission, are also moral stories, cautionary tales, about maternal bodies and good or bad mothers, and the way they are 'read' in the late twentieth century. Indeed, the HIV story is so powerful because it literally *and* metaphorically tells us which mothers have "dangerous" bodies—poor, Third World or U.S. women of color, drug-

using, promiscuous, or perhaps, at best, unwitting victims.[3] In this story, the cultural body and the corporeal body meld together and appear to be the same.

Perhaps, however, the appropriateness of public involvement in the breastfeeding story of the Army pilot mother, Emma Cuevas, is more questionable. There is no overriding question of infant health or survival, merely the mother's preference. Yet this story is, among other things, about confounding the gendered basis of citizenship and obligation to the body politic: women serve the nation through motherhood, and men, through the military. The lieutenant struck a male bargain by accepting publicly funded, highly skilled training in exchange for her service, yet when she became a mother, she reneged, expecting her motherhood to be equally valued. As one letter-writer joked, however, perhaps she should be allowed to resign if she repays taxpayers the estimated $500,000 spent on her military training (*Time* 1997: 31). She faced a difficult choice because, to be respected as a mother within the affluent middle-class, she should have properly "maximized" and perfected her child, which (stories like the one on intelligence instruct us) requires a commitment to breastfeed. In the current era, breastfeeding has become "the measure of the mother" (Maclean 1990: 52, 118, 164).

Scrutinizing these stories, however, reveals that "breastfeeding" points to more than one set of practices. The opening epigraphs to the book suggest how much practices have varied across history and social location. At present, breastfeeding can range from a six-week dose of "bonding" to an intense, several-year relationship. And, to add another layer of complexity, the body, in its stubborn physicality, sometimes defies plans for a particular interpretation. The recalcitrant, corporeal body, *and* its interaction with the individual's unconscious emotional life, do not always comply with conscious or cultural design.[4] The Army pilot and (*in*, or *with*) her body refused to comply with one increasingly popular interpretation of breastfeeding that equates it with large amounts of breast-pumping. The breast pump, in this medical model, seems to restore women's equality within male-workplace and public environments, with the milk she collects "standing in" for her and her motherly nature at home.

Readers, however, may first interpret this story as biological, as *if* breastfeeding had a fixed, obvious meaning rather than several con-

flicting meanings that emerge from collisions and meldings of cultural and corporeal bodies. That is, the body-as-text, planned and meaningful, may disrupt the body-as-body, just as the corporeal body's obduracy may disrupt the best-planned text. The media account, therefore, seems flattened: the lieutenant "[was] unable to pump enough breast milk to feed her [daughter]" (Thompson 1997: 32). A more nuanced reading might point out that the lieutenant (with/in her body) rejected the medical model in favor of a maternalist model of breastfeeding. The contemporary maternalist model resists separating the embodied process—the mother with baby at the breast—from its product, human milk. The maternalist model also exalts motherhood and finds women's difference more valuable than public equality.

WHAT ABOUT THE BABIES?

Readers may be surprised to have heard nothing up to now about infant's and children's needs, usually the main point of any conversation about breastfeeding and, surely, of any conversation about motherhood. I am often reminded that my approach emphasizing the mother's side of the story may seem heretical to some. After all, two of the strongest normative assumptions about contemporary motherhood are that good mothers "naturally" put their "children's needs" first[5] and that "children's needs" are fixed by "nature" and progressively more knowable (Hays 1996, McMahon 1995). These assumptions have been questioned by many feminist writers addressing heated issues like the effects of daycare or of fathers' parenting on children, but they appear more fixed, more "in nature," with breastfeeding because of its thick biological layers. A committed feminist and obstetrician, whom I met socially, asked me how she could get her patients to breastfeed more, how she could convey to them that breastfeeding is so important for their babies that it's really "*not* a choice." She was incredulous when I replied that many women might want to know if it helps prevent breast cancer.[6] And then I suggested perhaps she could convince patients to give it a try because *they* might enjoy it (provided she were available to help with problems). But, she insisted—against my prioritizing of mothers' health and well-being—"I'm a fanatic for breastfeeding. It's the best food *for the baby*." As a mother herself, she said: "It's the *one* thing you can do that no one else can. When you

Beacon Press
25 Beacon Street
Boston, Massachusetts 02108-2892
www.beacon.org

Beacon Press books
are published under the auspices of
the Unitarian Universalist Association of Congregations.

Parts of this book have been previously published. Pieces of chapter 1 first appeared in the journal *Feminist Studies* 19 (1993): 291–311 as "Mothers, Babies, and Breastfeeding in Late Capitalist America: The Shifting Context of Feminist Theory." Material in chapter 3 appeared in the journal *Social Problems* 40(3) (1993): 285–300 as "'Mother to Mother': A Maternalist Organization in Late Capitalist America," with second author Elizabeth A. Vandewater, used by permission of the University of California Press, and in *Qualitative Sociology* 16 (1993): 3–22 as "Mothers Construct Fathers: Destabilized Patriarchy in La Leche League," also with Elizabeth A. Vandewater, reprinted by permission of Plenum Publishing Corp. Material in chapter 5 appeared in *Gender & Society* 10 (1996): 199–211 as "Negotiating Independent Motherhood: Working-Class African American Women Talk About Marriage and Motherhood" and is reprinted by permission of Sage Publications, Inc.

05 04 03 02 01 00 99   8 7 6 5 4 3 2 1

Text design by Elizabeth Elsas
Composition by Wilsted & Taylor Publishing Services

Library of Congress Cataloging-in-Publication Data

Blum, Linda M.
    At the breast : ideologies of breastfeeding and motherhood in the contemporary
United States / Linda M. Blum.
        p.   cm.
    Includes bibliographical references and index.
    ISBN 0-8070-2140-7 (cloth)
        1. Motherhood—United States.   2. Mothers—United States.   3. Breastfeeding—
United States.   I. Title.
HQ759.B618   1999
306.874'3—dc21   98-46108

AT THE BREAST

IDEOLOGIES OF BREASTFEEDING
AND MOTHERHOOD IN THE
CONTEMPORARY UNITED STATES

LINDA M. BLUM

BEACON PRESS   BOSTON

public spheres, with their implicit male organization, unchanged. By the 1980s, even Gloria Steinem, glamorized feminist nonmother, had quipped: "We have become the men we wanted to marry" (Rothman 1989: 198). But to valorize motherhood shores up rather than tears down the old categories, contributing to their fixed, essential appearance.

Those who came to feminism from more radical Sixties movements, inspired by critiques of capitalism, also had been gender minimizers. Marxist and socialist feminists tended to categorize motherhood as merely unpaid work or "domestic labor" and painted the family as a "locus of struggle." Rather than with the valorizing terms of nurturance, care, and connectedness, they described women's experiences "in the [utilitarian] language of commodities and exchange." This picture was particularly criticized by women of color, who saw their families, and especially their mothers, in a warmer and more multishaded light.[11] By the 1980s, Marxists and socialists began to rethink their views, if not of capitalism, then of motherhood.[12] Ironically, the harsh political-economic changes of late-twentieth-century U.S. capitalism—the plant closings, corporate downsizings, and cutbacks in social provisions—on their own put a sharp end to the pronatalist climate.[13] Thus, feminists of many strands realized that "the right to bear and raise children without sacrificing one's health, one's sanity, or one's job, and without having to be a man's wife, will be a much more difficult right to gain than was the right *not* to have a child" (Van Allen 1990: 297, my emphasis).

In short, the "family *un*friendly" context of the Reagan and Bush presidencies and the new global economy threatened difference more than equality, and the authentic desire *to* mother replaced earlier concerns that women were being compelled or coerced into motherhood. The work of scholars such as Nancy Chodorow (1978), Carol Gilligan (1982), Barbara Katz Rothman (1989), and Sara Ruddick (1989, 1990) was widely influential, given a social world so lacking in care and mutual obligation. This mother-valorizing scholarship did not base woman's difference on God or nature, but it nonetheless gave a moral essentialism to exclusive motherhood. If this mother was produced by history and social location,[14] she nevertheless stood for all that was good, in opposition to the heartless profit-mongering of a world dominated by multinational corporations. And this goodness

feeding, in contrast, has attracted little attention, perhaps because it seems a more optional aspect of motherhood. If an optional practice, however, it is an issue that is nearly impossible to avoid; readers will discover in chapters 4 and 5 that "breast is best" is a prescription most mothers contend with in some way.[10] Furthermore, as the Army pilot mother's story revealed, breastfeeding can pose even thornier obstacles to equal treatment. During pregnancy, most women have greater autonomy and freedom of movement than while nursing; and birth is simply a far shorter event. Because the lens on late-century breastfeeding reveals the collision of public and private concerns with the maternal body, I come to some different conclusions from other analysts of "body politics" and gender difference. Though many agree that putting gender difference first has been dangerous—the line between celebration and discrimination can be very slight—I suggest that mothers may need to strategically or tactically use this much-repudiated *essentialism*, if *they* can define when it is relevant.

Cultural feminists like Adrienne Rich, the gender "maximizers" who celebrated women's difference, have been most frequently found guilty of essentialism. As in the eighteenth and nineteenth centuries, *essence* meant this one inherent aspect of womanhood, motherhood, which by God or nature, made all women "woman." Most twentieth-century feminists, however, disagreed and, like Mary Wollstonecraft and John Stuart Mill and Harriet Taylor Mill in earlier centuries, they were gender "minimizers" who considered women more like men than different. The women's movement in the mid-twentieth century was, after all, most concerned with freeing women from the imperative *to* mother. Emerging from the profamily, pronatalist climate of the 1950s, most wanted to put equality first, break the claim of biology, and "denaturalize" nature. The equality approach was also pragmatic, modeled on the successes of the Civil Rights Movement, because most activists put access to male jobs and educational opportunities first.

This approach of seeking equal treatment and minimizing gender led to significant gains for women, but by the 1980s its limitations were also apparent. Access proved to be more difficult to gain than many had thought, and, where gained, was often not what feminists had bargained for. Many then saw more to the maximizing approach, because demanding similar treatment gained entry for a few, but left

physical exclusivity that I suggest accounts for the "fanaticism" and fears of being forgotten or replaced expressed by late-twentieth-century white, professional mothers in the United States (e.g., Hays 1996: 145). I use the term *exclusive* rather than *intensive,* in this and ensuing chapters, to better describe this dominant ideology of motherhood. Interestingly, as I discuss in the following section, with all the tremendously rich feminist writing on motherhood, little attention has been paid to the specific, *inessential* historical meaning and organization of its physicality.

SO, WHY ANOTHER FEMINIST WRITING ON MOTHERHOOD?

Since the resurgence of the women's movement in the late 1960s, it seems that feminists have been obsessed with motherhood. Readers may wonder, as I often worried, whether there could be anything left to add. Novelists, memoirists, literary critics, and scholars across many disciplines have explored how motherhood, an activity and a relationship so immensely rewarding and enabling, could at the same time be so oppressive and disabling. Adrienne Rich brilliantly wrote that it was motherhood as institution which imposed the patriarchal entrapment, while motherhood as lived experience provided the former life-affirming, even liberatory qualities (1976). Like Rich, many have thought about how to retain these so valuable womanly experiences without reinforcing the institutional straitjacket, the seemingly "natural" gender arrangements, fixed and timeless, that have justified so much discrimination. In short, feminist ambivalence has centered on which to put first, "difference," the affirmation of women's "motherly" experiences, or "equality," the need for economic and political rights on a par with men's.[9]

These dilemmas of equality and difference are not new, as they stem from eighteenth-century discussions of the boundaries of citizenship. They do, however, need to be thought about in context; and in our political-economic era, which I return to in my concluding chapter, equality with and difference from men require rethinking. Feminist scholars have analyzed women's experiences of pregnancy and birth because of the thorny obstacles they pose to law and policy that would treat women no differently than men (e.g., Eisenstein 1988, Martin 1987, Oakley 1980, Vogel 1993, among many). Breast-

come home from work [and she had worked long hours when her children were babies, with lots of breast-pumping], that baby will remember *who you are*."

These last statements intrigued me, perhaps because with my own son, I had felt somewhat fanatical too.[7] Can a mother be replaced so easily? What does it mean to think that your baby will forget *who you are*? Sociologist Sharon Hays answered such questions, which plagued the contemporary mothers she studied, by demonstrating that both employed and at-home mothers drew from, or were in dialogue with, the ideology of "intensive motherhood" (1996: esp. 145). Good mothers, in this view, not only put their children's needs first, but provide labor- and emotion-intensive care to protect them from a harsh, impersonal market-driven society. In this view, "children need" a prolonged period of protection and indulgence—and it must be provided by one, singularly focused mother. She must study each child's psychological, physical, and cognitive development and judge how to stimulate and enrich at just the right speed for the individual's age, stage, and temperament (1996: 54, 60, 78). Even if this mother is employed, according to Hays, she engages in arduous efforts to find and manage the proper substitute care (1996: 62). Employed and at-home mothers, in short, both see childrearing as their primary responsibility in life, and one that is ultimately theirs alone (1996: 108; also McMahon 1995).[8]

Hays's explanation of "intensive motherhood," though it reveals many of our unexamined but tenaciously held beliefs, metaphors, images, and practices, ignores an important dimension of modern motherhood. The physicality and sexuality involved in such intensively focused care have been of concern to all the twentieth-century experts on "children's needs." The behaviorists, early- and late-century maternalists, physicians, and Freudians (whom I discuss in the next chapter) all have emphasized the embodied aspects of the mother-child dyad, though they have not agreed on whether or how this physicality should be controlled, measured, encouraged, or repressed. There has been consensus, however, about the singularity of this dyad and the need for this attachment to have a special, exclusive character. Indeed, as I will point out in the next chapter, some experts liken the sensual tie between the mother and baby to the exclusivity of the monogamous marriage bond. And it is this norm or belief in

AT THE BREAST

IDEOLOGIES OF BREASTFEEDING
AND MOTHERHOOD IN THE
CONTEMPORARY UNITED STATES

LINDA M. BLUM

BEACON PRESS   BOSTON

Beacon Press
25 Beacon Street
Boston, Massachusetts 02108-2892
www.beacon.org

Beacon Press books
are published under the auspices of
the Unitarian Universalist Association of Congregations.

Parts of this book have been previously published. Pieces of chapter 1 first appeared in the journal *Feminist Studies* 19 (1993): 291–311 as "Mothers, Babies, and Breastfeeding in Late Capitalist America: The Shifting Context of Feminist Theory." Material in chapter 3 appeared in the journal *Social Problems* 40(3) (1993): 285–300 as " 'Mother to Mother': A Maternalist Organization in Late Capitalist America," with second author Elizabeth A. Vandewater, used by permission of the University of California Press, and in *Qualitative Sociology* 16 (1993): 3–22 as "Mothers Construct Fathers: Destabilized Patriarchy in La Leche League," also with Elizabeth A. Vandewater, reprinted by permission of Plenum Publishing Corp. Material in chapter 5 appeared in *Gender & Society* 10 (1996): 199–211 as "Negotiating Independent Motherhood: Working-Class African American Women Talk About Marriage and Motherhood" and is reprinted by permission of Sage Publications, Inc.

05 04 03 02 01 00 99   8 7 6 5 4 3 2 1

This book is printed on recycled acid-free paper that contains at least 20 percent postconsumer waste and meets the uncoated paper ANSI/NISO specifications for permanence as revised in 1992.

Text design by Elizabeth Elsas
Composition by Wilsted & Taylor Publishing Services

Library of Congress Cataloging-in-Publication Data

Blum, Linda M.
    At the breast : ideologies of breastfeeding and motherhood in the contemporary
United States / Linda M. Blum.
        p.   cm.
    Includes bibliographical references and index.
    ISBN 0-8070-2140-7 (cloth)
    1. Motherhood—United States.   2. Mothers—United States.   3. Breastfeeding—
United States.   I. Title.
HQ759.B618   1999
306.874′3—dc21   98-46108

TO MY FAMILY

Kaplan 1994, Skocpol 1992, among many).[16] Because of this diver-
gence, literary critic Alice Adams notes, "motherhood seems to com-
prise mutually exclusive states—like light, motherhood can be observed as . . . wave or . . . particle . . . but never both at the same time"
(1995: 423).

Each side, the wave and particle, has strengths and limitations.
Focusing on particles, the ground of mothers' experiences, helped
to understand differences but made it harder to see the large historical context that shapes women's stories. Like biology or health *facts*
(as mentioned above), women's local stories do not have transparent
meanings and, taken on their own, may overplay differences between
women. The above-ground work on waves, in contrast, needs the local, the particular, because it cannot tell us how individual mothers
select from, reject, revise or negotiate with the available repertoire of
controlling images of motherhood. This work, taken on its own, runs
the risk of overplaying the influence of discourse, or these repertoires
that construct and control. It also may, in this sense, overplay similarities between women. What we need, as historian Ellen Ross (1995)
and anthropologist Nancy Scheper-Hughes (1992: 341) suggest, is a
"pragmatics of motherhood," a more rounded, realistic view of commonalities and differences (that are real but not essential) and their
practical consequences. This rounded view needs women's stories,
but framed knowledgeably, sympathetically in larger contexts; it is a
view of women as active subjects but subject to particular constraints
and conventions (Adams 1995, Ross 1995).

The reassertion and celebration of women's motherly difference
in the 1980s—the pure particle of light expressed in Rich's notion of
experience, Chodorow's relationality, Ruddick's maternal thinking,
Gilligan's ethic of care—is similarly at the core of maternalist visions
that I explore in the next two chapters. Although it is more hopeful to
cast this difference as a pure point of opposition to competitive masculine individualism and corporate capitalist heartlessness, it is more
accurate to say, as the 1990s focus on *differences* does, that no standpoint is so unified or so pure. Each can only be a place to start from,
to push and pull at the ambiguity and contradictions between and
within dominant representations. Motherly difference and maternalism, moreover, have tended to define their relationality, or caring, emotional connectedness, against "othered" women deemed less

and oppositionality was assumed to include all women in the same way: yet where were the nonwhite, nonwestern, nonheterosexual, nonbiological mothers? What of the nonmothers, or even mothers whose experiences deviated from this celebratory moment?[15]

Women of color kept trying to teach white feminists the lesson that the ideal of exclusive motherhood was racialized. This singular mother—with the irreplaceable physical, emotional, and moral responsibility for her pure, "priceless" child—was and continues to be a *white*, status- and class-enhancing project (Collins 1994, duCille 1994, among many). Exclusive motherhood had its origins in the idealized female domesticity of the eighteenth-century European middle-classes. Along with men's work ethic, women's childrearing justified their ascendancy and moral superiority over the "idle rich" and the unproductive, "parasitic" poor. This idealized domesticity also represented middle-class mothers' attempts to bolster their status as their economic contributions to the household diminished (Hays 1996, Ryan 1981). Women of color, however, repeatedly remind us that the white domestic ideal relied on slaves, indentured and nonindentured servants, wetnurses, laundresses—most of whom were nonwhite or immigrant women and were mothers themselves. Although this reliance declined in the mid-twentieth century, the use of low-paid women of color as daycare providers, house cleaners, babysitters, and nannies has again become common among affluent white couples (Glenn 1992, Rollins 1985, among many). Indeed the third epigraph I use to introduce the book emphasizes this racialized legacy.

In the 1990s, to grapple with these differences among women and mothers, feminist writing has diverged and gone toward experience or toward the institution. Many aim to recover the hidden mothers, to hear their long-silenced voices (Ross 1995: 402). This experience-valorizing work tends to gather the stories of differently located mothers, or to stay at a more grounded, particular level of analysis, but in either case to emphasize mothering as a verb, an activity, with mothers as subjects (e.g., McMahon 1995, Roiphe 1996, among many). In a divergent direction, others see mothers from far above the ground—*subject* to and *subjects* of dominant discourses or institutions. This work looks for the ways mothers have been imagined, projected, constructed, created, and controlled by the state, by science and literature, by the media and other authoritative sources (e.g., Eyer 1992,

and oppositionality was assumed to include all women in the same way: yet where were the nonwhite, nonwestern, nonheterosexual, nonbiological mothers? What of the nonmothers, or even mothers whose experiences deviated from this celebratory moment?[15]

Women of color kept trying to teach white feminists the lesson that the ideal of exclusive motherhood was racialized. This singular mother—with the irreplaceable physical, emotional, and moral responsibility for her pure, "priceless" child—was and continues to be a *white*, status- and class-enhancing project (Collins 1994, duCille 1994, among many). Exclusive motherhood had its origins in the idealized female domesticity of the eighteenth-century European middle-classes. Along with men's work ethic, women's childrearing justified their ascendancy and moral superiority over the "idle rich" and the unproductive, "parasitic" poor. This idealized domesticity also represented middle-class mothers' attempts to bolster their status as their economic contributions to the household diminished (Hays 1996, Ryan 1981). Women of color, however, repeatedly remind us that the white domestic ideal relied on slaves, indentured and nonindentured servants, wetnurses, laundresses—most of whom were nonwhite or immigrant women and were mothers themselves. Although this reliance declined in the mid-twentieth century, the use of low-paid women of color as daycare providers, house cleaners, babysitters, and nannies has again become common among affluent white couples (Glenn 1992, Rollins 1985, among many). Indeed the third epigraph I use to introduce the book emphasizes this racialized legacy.

In the 1990s, to grapple with these differences among women and mothers, feminist writing has diverged and gone toward experience or toward the institution. Many aim to recover the hidden mothers, to hear their long-silenced voices (Ross 1995: 402). This experience-valorizing work tends to gather the stories of differently located mothers, or to stay at a more grounded, particular level of analysis, but in either case to emphasize mothering as a verb, an activity, with mothers as subjects (e.g., McMahon 1995, Roiphe 1996, among many). In a divergent direction, others see mothers from far above the ground—*subject* to and *subjects* of dominant discourses or institutions. This work looks for the ways mothers have been imagined, projected, constructed, created, and controlled by the state, by science and literature, by the media and other authoritative sources (e.g., Eyer 1992,

Kaplan 1994, Skocpol 1992, among many).[16] Because of this diver-
gence, literary critic Alice Adams notes, "motherhood seems to com-
prise mutually exclusive states—like light, motherhood can be observed as . . . wave or . . . particle . . . but never both at the same time"
(1995: 423).

Each side, the wave and particle, has strengths and limitations.
Focusing on particles, the ground of mothers' experiences, helped
to understand differences but made it harder to see the large historical context that shapes women's stories. Like biology or health *facts*
(as mentioned above), women's local stories do not have transparent
meanings and, taken on their own, may overplay differences between
women. The above-ground work on waves, in contrast, needs the local, the particular, because it cannot tell us how individual mothers
select from, reject, revise or negotiate with the available repertoire of
controlling images of motherhood. This work, taken on its own, runs
the risk of overplaying the influence of discourse, or these repertoires
that construct and control. It also may, in this sense, overplay similarities between women. What we need, as historian Ellen Ross (1995)
and anthropologist Nancy Scheper-Hughes (1992: 341) suggest, is a
"pragmatics of motherhood," a more rounded, realistic view of commonalities and differences (that are real but not essential) and their
practical consequences. This rounded view needs women's stories,
but framed knowledgeably, sympathetically in larger contexts; it is a
view of women as active subjects but subject to particular constraints
and conventions (Adams 1995, Ross 1995).

The reassertion and celebration of women's motherly difference
in the 1980s—the pure particle of light expressed in Rich's notion of
experience, Chodorow's relationality, Ruddick's maternal thinking,
Gilligan's ethic of care—is similarly at the core of maternalist visions
that I explore in the next two chapters. Although it is more hopeful to
cast this difference as a pure point of opposition to competitive masculine individualism and corporate capitalist heartlessness, it is more
accurate to say, as the 1990s focus on *differences* does, that no standpoint is so unified or so pure. Each can only be a place to start from,
to push and pull at the ambiguity and contradictions between and
within dominant representations. Motherly difference and maternalism, moreover, have tended to define their relationality, or caring, emotional connectedness, against "othered" women deemed less

moral, less motherly, because of race, ethnic, and class divides. Looking at motherhood from this angle leaves less to celebrate.

A "pragmatics of motherhood" should also include the body, and women's interests, needs, and feelings for their own physicality and sexuality, their embodied health and well-being. The new writing and scholarship on the body has tended to be as divided as that on motherhood, by wave and particle, macro and micro; there are discursive constructions of subjects and histories of the body with authors looking down from high altitudes (Butler 1990, Foucault 1980, Laqueur 1990a), and there are grounded or subjective (or "subject-active") accounts of embodied experience that, for the most part, do not address the former (Davis-Floyd, Kahn, Kitzinger).[17] From the high altitudes, the maternal body, pregnancy, birth, and breastfeeding carry no essential meaning either positive or negative—this makes it easier for women to be free of biological claims, but in all the plasticity, it is harder to value *anything* or know what we aim for. On the latter experiential side, in contrast, while we know what to aim for, the body's goodness too easily veers back to the purity of difference, the singular essence of woman as reproductive body, as celebratory "biodance" with nature (Davis-Floyd 1992). Can we hold in view, at the same time, that women and mothers have valuable bodies and autonomous needs and wants, interests in bodily "power and pleasure" in other words (Yalom 1997: 272), and that the body is also always historically, politically, and culturally shaped?

This question and those I began the chapter with, looking at different mothers and at the maternal breast, and at the different shapes and values assigned maternal bodies, are woven through the next four empirical chapters of this book. Because I was interested in looking from the high altitudes and the ground, at the wave and particle of motherhood and breastfeeding, I went looking for both authoritative discourses and real mothers when I began this project in 1990. Because motherhood, however, is a class-marking (and making) and a racialized moral project, I purposely sought mothers at the ends of the spectrum of class and race and morality.[18] The second chapter details the historical emergence of exclusive motherhood in the United States, from the pitied $acred Mother of the early-twentieth-century immigrant working-class to today's affluent but disembodied Super-

mom, and the racialized class spectrum which configures beliefs about good and bad mothering, and breastfeeding, in changing social contexts. It also introduces the authoritative experts from the medical profession and the state who have generated specific prescriptions, and the forms of maternalism which have been in dialogue with or have attempted to reform these dominant models. Chapter 3 turns to late-twentieth-century maternalism in depth, examining how it emerged, how it has changed, and how it expresses its class-enhancing, racialized project. The white, married middle-class mothers drawn to maternalism find assurances that they are using the best, most "natural" methods of childrearing; these methods, shared by the "right" people, both demonstrate and instill in their children the proper "cultural capital" and "right" to affluence.[19] At the same time, I scrutinize maternalist "body politics," its thinking about and working with maternal bodies, because it provides, or at least suggests, a positive alternative to the disembodiment offered by the dominant medical model described in chapter 2. These mothers—with greater resources and unquestioned respectability—have a greater chance of finding breastfeeding an enjoyable, pleasure-enhancing experience, and also one that is relational and "different" in the best mother-valorizing, cultural-feminist sense.

Because, however, maternalist politics tend to be at the expense of other, less moral mothers, chapters 4 and 5 examine mothers at the other end of the spectrum. These chapters move far from the mothers in chapter 3, who would be considered highly reputable by state and medical authorities, to working-class mothers who might be cast as disreputable through the same lens. Many of the working-class mothers I spoke with rejected or failed at feeding their babies "at the breast." Chapter 4 looks at white working-class mothers whose bodies, from a dominant perspective, have long been considered suspect, or only safe if carefully supervised. That is, such mothers have been treated as if they can be taught to choose the "right" methods of childrearing and bodily self-discipline. The white working-class mothers I spoke with, though a small nonrandom group, indeed wanted to choose the right forms of childrearing, but without this public intrusion. Yet, despite their desires for class-enhancing motherhood—and their hopes of stability and upward mobility, at least for their children—most told their stories as failures. Their bodies and breasts were one key site of failure, but marriage—the legal tie to a

man required for a woman's children to be "legitimate" and her sexuality properly defined or contained, for her right to privacy itself—was another. The women's stories, put in the context of the hard, distressing circumstances they faced, reveal the lie of the "natural." "Natural" usually signals what is good, authentic, and untainted by social or human manipulation, and thus "natural" motherhood seems to belong outside the public realm. Public efforts to promote breastfeeding and supervise mothers confuse this distinction, as they draw on it, presenting a motherhood that requires no significant resources, that can be accomplished privately under any circumstances. Such efforts—motivated by the contradictory needs of state branches to control costs *and* suspect women, as well as to promote maternal and child health—have a mixed impact on working-class mothers and obviously can miss their most pressing needs.

Chapter 5 turns to African-American working-class mothers for whom the historical legacy of motherhood, maternal bodies, and breastfeeding are much different. Under slavery, African-American mothers labored like men, but were also "breeders" enriching the stock of plantation owners. Women's bodies were owned and available for sexual exploitation—and breasts, which sometimes suckled white babies, were examined like part of the livestock at auctions (Yalom 1997: 124–125). This focus on the Black breast erupted in a legendary historical moment when Sojourner Truth—the luminous antislavery and women's rights activist and former slave—spoke to a white audience. A group of proslavery men challenged her honor and claim to be a woman and demanded that she show her breast to the women in the audience. According to *The Liberator* (1858, cited in Painter 1996: 139),

> Sojourner told them that her breasts had suckled many a white babe, to the exclusion of her own offspring; that some of those white babies had grown [and] . . . although they had suckled her colored breasts, they were, in her estimation, far more manly than they (her persecutors) appeared to be; and she quietly asked them, as she disrobed her bosom, if they, too, wished to suck! . . . she told them that . . . it was not to her shame that she uncovered her breast before them, but to their shame.[20]

The African-American working-class mothers I spoke with did not speak directly of this legacy. It was, however, refracted through the meanings they attached to breastfeeding, as they primarily re-

jected the practice for the exposure of sexuality and the physicality or animal-like qualities it represented to them. Like white working-class mothers, they shared the stressful life circumstances that can make breastfeeding overwhelmingly burdensome or exhausting. They were, however, much less likely to be pained by guilt or regret about their bottlefeeding than the white mothers whom I met. Rather than seeing themselves as deficient, some used humor or irony to criticize the moralism of the "natural" and few used the term positively. After such a long history of oppression justified by their closeness to nature, their primitive, subhuman being, it makes sense that they would be wary of such ideologies. Nature rhetoric may at times glorify the "primitive," but it can easily be transposed. Black women early in the century, for instance, were assumed to be better breastfeeders than middle-class white mothers who were "too civilized"; but this led to improved (and expensive) breastmilk substitutes or "formulas" rather than improved healthcare, resources, or status for African-American mothers.[21]

The racialization of motherhood in the United States makes African-American working-class mothers, even today, more disreputable than white working-class mothers from the vantage point of state and medical authorities: I show in chapter 2 how they have been cast as "undeserving" because of the common lack of legalized marital ties and "legitimate" children, proof of their dangerous, out of control sexuality. As rates of nonmarital childbearing have begun to increase among white working-class women, some of these mothers sense the threat of falling into the more denigrated group. This language itself is revealing: "denigrate" means "to disparage, to defame or attack," but the word comes from the root for dark, or black, and literally means "to blacken." When feminist scholars write of the "denigration" of women's bodies, they signal this racialized class hierarchy, even if unknowingly (e.g., Martin 1987: 146).

DEFINING "WORKING CLASS"
At this point, I should stop and clarify what I mean by "working class," as so many dizzying debates have occurred about how to define and demarcate social class in the United States, where everyone supposedly thinks of themselves as middle class. In large part, this truism arose because of the gains made by organized labor in mid-century.

Workers (primarily white men) in the nation's biggest industries, such as auto and steel, could for the first time afford to purchase homes and new cars, take vacations, have their wives devote more time to motherhood and less to wage-earning than ever before and, in some cases, put their children through state or community colleges. Often when we refer to the blue-collar working class, it is this "settled," white group that comes to mind.[22]

But this is a group that has been shrinking fast in the political-economic restructuring of the last two decades.[23] I was particularly aware of this because I conducted the fieldwork for this project in the former industrial heartland of southeastern Michigan, home to the "Big Three" automakers. With all the plant closings and downsizings, the area had one of the highest rates of unemployment in the country in the 1980s; in the 1990s, the rise of the service economy had thrown many into the insecure, lower paid jobs savagely spoofed in Michael Moore's documentary *Roger and Me*.[24] For many, cobbling together resources to support a family meant turning to state social services, just as they began to be, somewhat paradoxically, cut back. The force of political-economic reorganization was especially reflected in a generational divide I found among the women I spoke with: most of the white women in chapter 4, and some of the African-Americans in chapter 5, had parents who had enjoyed high industrial wages and benefits and a nearly middle-class way of life. But they faced, in the 1990s, more difficult circumstances and were falling from "settled" to "hard" living.

BUT WHAT ABOUT MEN?
Intriguingly, the place of men in women's stories of embodied mothering was much larger than I had originally anticipated. I might have attributed this to the emotional significance of sexual relationships, but, after speaking with mothers of different race and class backgrounds, I realized that this explanation was too simple. Marriage and the legalized sexual tie to the father "legitimate" the mother as much as the child, I would now suggest, and are thus a key piece of exclusive motherhood. Fathers are never far from the picture, though the mother-baby dyad painted by prevailing images and assumptions is set apart. As one British (probreastfeeding but feminist-identified) author notes, *every* advice book assumes that nursing mothers have

a house and a husband (Palmer 1988: 300; my emphasis). Exclusive motherhood requires a manly provider to buy the house, but, as important, to provide legitimate social placement and generational ties in what is still a patriarchal society.

This aspect of exclusive motherhood (which can in one sense sound quite banal) came into sharper focus with the help of the many single mothers I met researching chapters 4 and 5. Social science, in contrast, has largely ignored the varied extralegal relationships of such single mothers. No authorized language exists to recognize, much less to honor, sexual relationships other than marriage, or its legal obverse, divorce, even as we enter the new millenium.[25] Like most sociologists, I had been operating with blinders, seeing only the presence or absence of marriage, and, consequently, I had to stand corrected (Blum and Deussen 1996).

In addition to deepening my notion of exclusive motherhood, I had to think more about the ways men have a stake in breastfeeding and mothers' bodies. As partners or husbands, they have claims to women's bodies, to their physicality and sexuality. According to scholar Carol Pateman, the marriage contract historically has been preeminently to grant men this right of sexual access and ownership (1988). Earlier, Rich coined the term "compulsory heterosexuality" to name and describe this male privilege, or male-centered sexuality (1980). These radical feminist insights reveal much that would otherwise go unexamined, even if we frame them less baldly. It is still true that women's sexuality is normatively oriented toward and displayed for men; and though women need not repudiate heterosexuality altogether, that compulsory aspect that has made us objects to be looked at (even to ourselves), that has made our bodies not first our own to revel or suffer within, does merit repudiation.[26] I use a revised notion of "compulsory heterosexuality" to capture these prevailing assumptions, beliefs, and practices that have put male desire and satisfaction first.[27]

Breastfeeding interacts with these prevailing expectations and assumptions about sexuality in complicated ways. While for some women breastfeeding may be an experience of autonomy and of reveling in one's body, others may, as sociologist Cindy Stearns found, "breastfeed in anticipation of and reaction to the male gaze" (1999: 21). And, of course, breastfeeding also adds the charged issue of cross-

Few things in life are this gentle.

It's how you caress your baby.
The way you softly sing a lullaby.
And the way you give your own milk, the perfect food.
Only you can give your baby gentle things like these.
But if the time should ever come when you need a formula, remember this.
Gerber understands just how delicate your baby's system is.
That's why Gerber® Baby Formula is patterned after your own milk.
To help your baby accept and digest it easily.
Talk to your doctor about Gerber® Baby Formula.
It's one of the gentle things you can give.

If it doesn't come from you, shouldn't it come from Gerber?

For breast-feeding information
call 1-800-421-4221
© 1992 Gerber Products Company

FIG. I.I   Breastfeeding's erotic tangle is suggested by this Gerber ad.

generational sensual ties. A recent popular magazine cover strikingly captured breastfeeding's erotic tangle: The December 1997 cover of *Redbook* depicted the actor Pierce Brosnan (who plays James Bond, Agent 007 in the movie series) posed with his second wife as she nursed their baby boy. He appeared to be holding or even clutching

her (with one hand on her shoulder and the other gripping her leg) as he gazed down at his son at his wife's largely revealed breast. Intriguingly, copy just to the side of their faces, but about another article, read: "How to Spark His Desire (Again & Again & Again)." Though *Redbook's* corporate policy prohibited reprinting this image, I include another more muted but typical depiction of breastfeeding and compulsory heterosexuality (see figure 1.1), this one from a formula ad. (It is paradoxical that ads for substitute milks are now the most common place that we see breastfeeding!) With the father in soft focus to the side of the nursing couple, the mother's wedding ring is very prominent.

Men's sexual claims, as I explore in the upcoming chapters, can conflict with the cross-generational claims of "children's needs" voiced by state and childrearing authorities. For mothers themselves, though, it is difficult to find a safe, much less autonomous, middle-ground. Breasts are exposed everywhere, in television, films, magazines, and constantly in advertising; yet nursing in public is only grudgingly condoned, and mothers have been harassed at restaurants, malls, and movie theaters for breastfeeding their babies (as I discuss in greater detail in chapter 4). Tellingly, when a midwife organization commissioned breastfeeding promotion posters for an ad campaign, complete with photos of mothers with babies at their breasts (but no fathers), they discovered they could not be used. Despite clever slogans such as "Fastfood outlets. Two convenient locations," or "Sometimes it's okay to suck up to the boss," the posters were deemed "offensive" and inappropriate for public display (Kotz 1996).

When I first began this project, I was resistant to seeing the centrality of sexuality. I wanted to explore everything but that, given the academic career pressures I was facing. Living in our late-twentieth-century world, however, makes this impossible, as I realized listening to the radio on my evening commute: "Women's Breasts! Is Bigger Better or Were the Eighties Breast-Obsessed? Why have we rejected the large chests and booming bustiers of the eighties? Tonight's Inside Story on *Entertainment Tonight*."

When I told women friends that I was pursuing this topic, they said it sounded fascinating but terrifying. But a colleague and warm-hearted mentor said it all: "It sounds okay. Just don't use the word 'breasts.'"

FROM $ACRED TO DISEMBODIED MOTHERHOOD
BREASTFEEDING WITH THE EXPERTS AND THE STATE

In the United States, maternal breastfeeding has long been advocated as a key to good mothering, womanly honor, and even to women's citizenship. Such prescriptive advice has been expressed in differing vocabularies, but the notion of breastfeeding as a mother's obligation to both her child and the larger social body extends from the colonial days, when nursing was a mother's sacred duty, through the eighteenth and nineteenth centuries, when it was considered a mother's civic duty to the growing republic, and finally, to twentieth-century public health campaigns that portray nursing as her contribution to U.S. global dominance. The mid-twentieth century break in which artificial feeding predominated, in fact, was only a brief hiatus, and, on scrutiny, it was more rather than less continuous with this history at the breast. By the 1970s, earlier sentiments in favor of "natural" mothering had resurged, though with new twists specific to conditions at the time. As we will see at the end of this chapter, this led to new controlling images (or nonimages) of the exclusive mother and the maternal body, which, ironically, tended to disembody her.

In this chapter, I detail the reshaping of exclusive motherhood as a class- and status-enhancing project of the white middle-class in different eras; though mothers retained exclusive responsibility for childrearing that was labor- and emotion-intensive, dominant public conversation about ostensibly private practices varied, particularly about the maternal body and its attachment to the child. I also show how these dominant conversations about maternal rights and obligations affected nonwhite, non-middle-class mothers.[1] Several impor-

tant sets of actors contributed to this assigning of moral meaning to
the practices of different kinds of mothers; though dominant actors
speak ostensibly as representatives of "children's needs," their rhetoric
signals that they deem nonwhite, nonaffluent women morally deficient. The first important actors are the professional experts: initially
people looked to the clergy and moral philosophers for guidance, but
by the twentieth century, medical practitioners had become the major authorities for the private realm. Within the medical profession,
moreover, psychiatrists, psychologists, and psychoanalysts emerged
with new specialties in child development. These experts interact
with a second set of dominant actors, from the state or the political
arena. It is in the interest of the nationstate, after all, for healthy mothers to supply the next generation of workers and citizens. And in the
twentieth century, public interest in the "fitness" of the nation became an explicit part of policy-making, with a racialized and classed
coding of population "quality" marking mothers' bodies. Finally, an
important ownership claim to mothers' bodies rests with men, as fathers, husbands, and heads of households; motherly obligations are,
and have been, constructed around such notions of male rights.

A QUICK BACKWARD GLANCE:
THE EIGHTEENTH AND NINETEENTH CENTURIES
Infant-feeding decisions directly affected infant mortality rates, and,
through this, the demographic structure and long-run viability of
societies; such "private" decisions were, therefore, thoroughly public (Golden 1996: 2).[2] Infants, furthermore, could only be fed at the
breast of the mother, at the breast of another lactating woman (wetnursing), or by "hand-feeding" or "dry nursing" with an "artificial"
food, usually diluted animal milk or a "pap" of flour, sugar, milk,
water, or tea. In early modern Europe, both church and state were
deeply involved in infant care, developing institutionalized systems of
wetnursing to care for abandoned and orphaned babies and for babies
whose mothers were too ill to nurse. Artisan mothers whose contributions to the family economy mitigated against breastfeeding also
used wetnurses, as did high-born women, who looked for "wholesome" farm wives or "ruddy cottager[s]" with whom to place their
babies.[3] High-born mothers were sometimes condemned for placing
their babies out to nurse, but twentieth-century analysts suggest im-

portant reasons why many may have done so: proscriptions against sexual relations during lactation interfered with husbands' conjugal rights; the contraceptive effect of lactation interfered with pressures to produce male heirs; and notions of beauty prized the "unused" bosom.[4] In fact, anthropologist Vanessa Maher suggests that the discouragement of maternal breastfeeding among wealthy women served to teach "them their place in the patriarchal system of kinship and property" (1992: 25).

In the United States, however, with little such wealth, Puritan ministers like Cotton Mather harshly criticized mothers who did not nurse their young (Treckel 1989). Harvard president and minister Benjamin Wadsworth, similarly, wrote that mothers who "reject that method of nourishing their children which God's wise bountiful Providence has provided" were "criminal and blame-worthy" (cited in Golden 1996: 12). Along with such exhortations, the lack of an established aristocracy made the use of wetnurses less common than in Europe, and church and state were little involved in such arrangements. Breastfeeding was probably, for most healthy, white mothers, an emotionally gratifying activity, described in women's letters as "so sweet an office" or "a great blessing and privilege" (McMillen 1990: 111, 120, also Hoffert 1989). Maternal breastfeeding, moreover, became almost an emblem of new democratic ideals, as images of "nature" were linked with equality, the rejection of decadent, aristocratic "culture," and the rising health and wealth of the middle class of the young nation.[5] Some mothers were unable, nonetheless, to fulfil this civic duty and were offered advice by religious and community leaders; but families made arrangements privately or informally and turned to physicians for help. Physicians meanwhile debated the merits of the two alternatives, wet or dry nursing. They knew that infant mortality was high with wetnursing, yet it was even higher with dry.[6] At the same time, families feared hiring wetnurses of questionable physical and moral fitness.

By the nineteenth century, the racialized class divisions between mothers and wetnurses, who, typically, were immigrants in the North and African-American slaves in the South, exacerbated these fears. African-American women, seen as "naturally" nurturant though denied their own mother-child bonds, were also cast as primitively oversexed and thereby polluted. Still, historians estimate that

perhaps 20 percent of plantation mistresses used black wetnurses to supplement or replace their own milk (McMillen 1990: 118).[7] In the North, where the racial placement of European immigrant groups, first from Ireland and Germany, later from Southern and Eastern Europe, was only later established as "white," wetnurses were seen as inferior and suspect.[8] Immigrant wetnurses were also increasingly recruited from the ranks of disreputable, unwed mothers rather than trusted farm wives of native or Anglo-European stock. (With urbanization, the latter were a rapidly declining group.) Physicians perceived the compromise of their professional authority involved in managing such intimate cross-class, cross-race relations, and, by the end of the century, they increasingly turned to artificial foods, renamed "scientific infant foods," when maternal breastfeeding failed. By the late nineteenth century, the germ theory of disease and Pasteur's discoveries about heating cow's milk had made bottlefeeding safer, and wetnursing consequently waned. By the start of the twentieth century, affluent mothers therefore preferred to negotiate infant-feeding according to a medical model, whether they used breast or bottle. Refashioned notions of mothers' duties were, however, no less moral than before and continued to be tied to the rising, white middle-class.

THE EARLY TWENTIETH CENTURY: MATERNALISTS AND BABY-SAVING

In the United States in the early twentieth century, the state became more explicitly involved in infant-care and feeding and the control of maternal bodies. As elite groups strove to make the country a world power, they saw domestic power relations and social order threatened by mass immigration. Concerns with population "quality" flared up over high infant mortality rates, the declining predominance of the Anglo-Saxon "race," and the physical "degeneration" bemoaned during World War I.[9] The state thus made gendered, raced bodies public issues: the push for military "fitness" targeted white (and potentially white) male bodies, but the improvement of population quality, to be achieved through "higher," "Americanized" mothering, targeted female bodies. Theodore Roosevelt exemplified this view when he likened motherhood to military service, each contributing to the vigor of the nation (Klaus 1993: 201). Mothers thus were

boarders, laundry, or piecework. Some Black mothers worked as fieldhands and by taking in work, but many were domestics in the homes of affluent whites.[12] Family economies required older children to watch the younger ones, perform household chores, and/or contribute to waged-work, and babies were sometimes neglected or brought into hazardous workplaces by necessity. U.S. maternalists, however, argued for the need to "educate, educate, educate" mothers to stop their waged-work (cited in Mink 1995: 68–69). In Europe, in contrast, welfare states provided day nurseries and cash maternity benefits in response to fears of depopulation (collection in Koven and Michel 1993).

Although U.S. maternalists recognized the larger causes of poverty, their approach nonetheless tended to hold poor mothers responsible. This contradiction is poignantly revealed in their use of the lithograph "$acred Motherhood." It depicts a haggard mother, bending over her sewing machine while she cradles her baby to her breast (see figure 2.1). She is clearly in a tenement, with other neglected children in the background.[13] Although protesting all-too-common "sweated" working conditions, use of the image underscored maternalists' aversion to the "unnatural" invasion of waged-work into the home, for exclusive motherhood was sacred only without the $ (see Boris 1985).

Along with this aversion to wage-earning, maternalist "baby-savers" condemned artificial feeding and irregular breastfeeding as causes of infant death and disease, and, linked closely with this, the consumption of "unAmerican" foods (Mink 1995: 58–59). Maternalists were right to make feeding a priority. Gastrointestinal ailments, easily prevented by breastfeeding and adequate sanitation, were responsible for as many as one-third of all infant deaths—and this figure was cut nearly in half by the campaign's education efforts. Moreover, artificial feeding was risky without sufficient money for pure milk and iceboxes, or the time to sterilize bottles and nipples and to heat and prepare formula (Ladd-Taylor 1994: 27, 88, 187).[14] Feeding advice, however, also implicitly blamed the mother. Reformers in the Children's Bureau regarded healthful breastfeeding as irreconcilable with wage work, in marked contrast to the European model of scheduling nursing breaks during the workday and putting nursing rooms in factories, as endorsed by the International Labor Organiza-

exhorted to breastfeed, for they became the conduit to national strength and global power (Mink 1995: 27–28, 58–62).

State policies of "race betterment" and public health promotion emerged in this nation-building climate, but from an uneasy alliance between eugenics followers, who wanted to control immigrants and nonwhites and their immutable, biological inferiority, and "race liberals," who wanted to promote their cultural assimilation—at least, those who were potentially "white" and could be reshaped to Anglo-American, middle-class norms (Klaus 1993: 201–202; Mink 1995). Educated, middle-class women became centrally involved in these social welfare efforts. Historians have labeled such women-reformers "maternalists" because, rather than claiming to be equal citizens with men, they used the rhetoric of gender difference, invoking women's motherly virtues, to gain a distinct voice as the defenders of children (Koven and Michel 1993; Skocpol 1992).[10] In fact, once they gained a foothold in the state, they made reducing the rates of infant death and disease, or "baby saving," their first national campaign.

Most U.S. maternalist reformers believed that mothers should be full-time homemakers to fully dependent children; the baby-saving campaign worked to discourage mothers' wage-earning as well as to prohibit child labor (Ladd-Taylor 1994). In contrast to European welfare states, U.S. maternalists did not strive for family or maternity allowances, fearing that such provisions, by removing the disciplining effect of the family's dependency on the father, might encourage men to abandon their families (as well as cause labor unrest).[11] U.S. maternalists strove to provide needy homemakers support from public funds, but only in selected, "worthy" cases of the father-provider's absence: "deserving" mothers in the early twentieth century were primarily white widows. But even with such strict limits, the Mothers' Pension programs never gained sufficient backing to fully fund the domestic ideal (Abramovitz 1988, Ladd-Taylor 1994; Mink 1995). Similar moral eligibility requirements, which disqualified most poor women of color and single or divorced mothers, continued under the enlarged federal New Deal program, Aid to Dependent Children (ADC, renamed Aid to Families with Dependent Children, AFDC, in the 1960s) (Abramovitz 1988, Mink 1995).

Many low-income mothers early in the century brought in family income, either by working in factories or sweatshops, or by taking in

exhorted to breastfeed, for they became the conduit to national strength and global power (Mink 1995: 27–28, 58–62).

State policies of "race betterment" and public health promotion emerged in this nation-building climate, but from an uneasy alliance between eugenics followers, who wanted to control immigrants and nonwhites and their immutable, biological inferiority, and "race liberals," who wanted to promote their cultural assimilation—at least, those who were potentially "white" and could be reshaped to Anglo-American, middle-class norms (Klaus 1993: 201–202; Mink 1995). Educated, middle-class women became centrally involved in these social welfare efforts. Historians have labeled such women-reformers "maternalists" because, rather than claiming to be equal citizens with men, they used the rhetoric of gender difference, invoking women's motherly virtues, to gain a distinct voice as the defenders of children (Koven and Michel 1993; Skocpol 1992).[10] In fact, once they gained a foothold in the state, they made reducing the rates of infant death and disease, or "baby saving," their first national campaign.

Most U.S. maternalist reformers believed that mothers should be full-time homemakers to fully dependent children; the baby-saving campaign worked to discourage mothers' wage-earning as well as to prohibit child labor (Ladd-Taylor 1994). In contrast to European welfare states, U.S. maternalists did not strive for family or maternity allowances, fearing that such provisions, by removing the disciplining effect of the family's dependency on the father, might encourage men to abandon their families (as well as cause labor unrest).[11] U.S. maternalists strove to provide needy homemakers support from public funds, but only in selected, "worthy" cases of the father-provider's absence: "deserving" mothers in the early twentieth century were primarily white widows. But even with such strict limits, the Mothers' Pension programs never gained sufficient backing to fully fund the domestic ideal (Abramovitz 1988, Ladd-Taylor 1994; Mink 1995). Similar moral eligibility requirements, which disqualified most poor women of color and single or divorced mothers, continued under the enlarged federal New Deal program, Aid to Dependent Children (ADC, renamed Aid to Families with Dependent Children, AFDC, in the 1960s) (Abramovitz 1988, Mink 1995).

Many low-income mothers early in the century brought in family income, either by working in factories or sweatshops, or by taking in

boarders, laundry, or piecework. Some Black mothers worked as fieldhands and by taking in work, but many were domestics in the homes of affluent whites.[12] Family economies required older children to watch the younger ones, perform household chores, and/or contribute to waged-work, and babies were sometimes neglected or brought into hazardous workplaces by necessity. U.S. maternalists, however, argued for the need to "educate, educate, educate" mothers to stop their waged-work (cited in Mink 1995: 68–69). In Europe, in contrast, welfare states provided day nurseries and cash maternity benefits in response to fears of depopulation (collection in Koven and Michel 1993).

Although U.S. maternalists recognized the larger causes of poverty, their approach nonetheless tended to hold poor mothers responsible. This contradiction is poignantly revealed in their use of the lithograph "$acred Motherhood." It depicts a haggard mother, bending over her sewing machine while she cradles her baby to her breast (see figure 2.1). She is clearly in a tenement, with other neglected children in the background.[13] Although protesting all-too-common "sweated" working conditions, use of the image underscored maternalists' aversion to the "unnatural" invasion of waged-work into the home, for exclusive motherhood was sacred only without the $ (see Boris 1985).

Along with this aversion to wage-earning, maternalist "babysavers" condemned artificial feeding and irregular breastfeeding as causes of infant death and disease, and, linked closely with this, the consumption of "unAmerican" foods (Mink 1995: 58–59). Maternalists were right to make feeding a priority. Gastrointestinal ailments, easily prevented by breastfeeding and adequate sanitation, were responsible for as many as one-third of all infant deaths—and this figure was cut nearly in half by the campaign's education efforts. Moreover, artificial feeding was risky without sufficient money for pure milk and iceboxes, or the time to sterilize bottles and nipples and to heat and prepare formula (Ladd-Taylor 1994: 27, 88, 187).[14] Feeding advice, however, also implicitly blamed the mother. Reformers in the Children's Bureau regarded healthful breastfeeding as irreconcilable with wage work, in marked contrast to the European model of scheduling nursing breaks during the workday and putting nursing rooms in factories, as endorsed by the International Labor Organiza-

tion (Klaus 1993: 195). The U.S. Children's Bureau listed requirements for nursing which were unrealistic for many homemakers, not
to mention $acred Mothers! Mothers were to sleep eight hours a
night, nap midday, exercise and take fresh air for an hour each morning and evening, and nurse on a strictly regular schedule (Mink 1995:
61). Feeding advice was also culturally biased, with the nursing
mother instructed to eat a "bland," i.e., American, diet, and to keep a
physical distance from her baby that was antithetical to many immigrant cultures.[15] Maternalists (following the child development and
medical experts of the time, who I come to in the next section)
stressed that mothers must avoid "excessive" cuddling and, according
to historian Molly Ladd-Taylor, expressed "misgivings about the sen-
suousness of their mother-child bond as well as about their diet"
(1994: 88).

The maternalist program in the United States, despite its limitations, laid down the terms for discussing society's obligation to provide for families, and raised the questions of who should mother, how
they should mother, and with what resources. Their fight to extend
domesticity to working-class, white-ethnic women did successfully
extend preventive health services to many urban dwellers. If infant
death and disease were high among the white working-class, however, conditions were worse among African-Americans. Ninety percent of African-Americans still lived in the South, where baby-saving
efforts rarely reached; in the North, de facto segregation excluded the
few Black families from receiving services. Historian Eileen Boris, in
fact, concludes that "within the word 'mother' . . . lurked the referent
'white'" (1993: 215).[16]

Within African-American communities, however, women from
the small middle-class organized as part of the Club movement for racial uplift and worked to save Black babies. Such Black maternalists
subverted racialized meanings by labeling themselves "pure mothers
for pure children." Although they had less aversion to wage-earning
mothers, their actions were similar to those of white reformers: they
set up clinics for children, hygiene classes for mothers, and milk stations to distribute safe, low-cost cow's milk (Boris 1993, Gordon
1991). Nonetheless, Black reformers were excluded from the foot-
holds of state power that the white maternalists had gained.

In the national baby-saving campaign African-Americans were
singled out and blamed for their own suffering. Black midwives, who

FIG. 2.1 "$acred Motherhood." This 1907 lithograph hung in the office of the president of the National Women's Trade Union League and was used as a postcard to solicit milk money for the infant children of strikers during the Chicago garment strike in 1910–1911. (From the Chicago Historical Society.)

FIG. 2.1   "$acred Motherhood." This 1907 lithograph hung in the office of
the president of the National Women's Trade Union League and was used as a
postcard to solicit milk money for the infant children of strikers during the
Chicago garment strike in 1910–1911. (From the Chicago Historical Society.)

tion (Klaus 1993: 195). The U.S. Children's Bureau listed requirements for nursing which were unrealistic for many homemakers, not
to mention $acred Mothers! Mothers were to sleep eight hours a
night, nap midday, exercise and take fresh air for an hour each morning and evening, and nurse on a strictly regular schedule (Mink 1995:
61). Feeding advice was also culturally biased, with the nursing
mother instructed to eat a "bland," i.e., American, diet, and to keep a
physical distance from her baby that was antithetical to many immigrant cultures.[15] Maternalists (following the child development and
medical experts of the time, who I come to in the next section)
stressed that mothers must avoid "excessive" cuddling and, according
to historian Molly Ladd-Taylor, expressed "misgivings about the sen-
suousness of their mother-child bond as well as about their diet"
(1994: 88).

The maternalist program in the United States, despite its limitations, laid down the terms for discussing society's obligation to provide for families, and raised the questions of who should mother, how
they should mother, and with what resources. Their fight to extend
domesticity to working-class, white-ethnic women did successfully
extend preventive health services to many urban dwellers. If infant
death and disease were high among the white working-class, however, conditions were worse among African-Americans. Ninety percent of African-Americans still lived in the South, where baby-saving
efforts rarely reached; in the North, de facto segregation excluded the
few Black families from receiving services. Historian Eileen Boris, in
fact, concludes that "within the word 'mother' . . . lurked the referent
'white'" (1993: 215).[16]

Within African-American communities, however, women from
the small middle-class organized as part of the Club movement for racial uplift and worked to save Black babies. Such Black maternalists
subverted racialized meanings by labeling themselves "pure mothers
for pure children." Although they had less aversion to wage-earning
mothers, their actions were similar to those of white reformers: they
set up clinics for children, hygiene classes for mothers, and milk stations to distribute safe, low-cost cow's milk (Boris 1993, Gordon
1991). Nonetheless, Black reformers were excluded from the foot-
holds of state power that the white maternalists had gained.

In the national baby-saving campaign African-Americans were
singled out and blamed for their own suffering. Black midwives, who

delivered most southern Black babies, were blamed for the high infant (and maternal) death rates, and ignorant mothers were blamed for turning to them rather than to medical science.[17] Although some public health physicians recognized the need for midwives in poor, rural communities underserved by the medical profession, others argued to eliminate them altogether. The 1925 meeting of the Southern Medical Association exemplified the latter view in its description of Black midwives as "filthy and ignorant and not far removed from the jungles of Africa, laden with its atmosphere of weird superstition and vodooism" (cited in Smith 1995: 125). National legislation implemented mandatory training and licensing, supervised by public health nurses who were overwhelmingly white. Like the Northern campaigns, teaching the necessity for sterile procedures was a legitimate goal, but other aspects of midwife training were more questionable. State-sponsored training prohibited traditional practices such as standing or squatting (rather than prone) birthing positions and the use of herbs. Furthermore, supervisors routinely invaded the privacy of midwives, inspecting not only their required, starched white uniforms, but their bags and sometimes their homes. Ladd-Taylor contends that "the obsessive attention to midwives' personal appearance suggests" that they were to be "symbolically cleansed of their race, their sexuality, and their motherhood" (1994: 183). A licensed midwife was also required to refer all but normal deliveries to medical doctors, and she could have her permit revoked for performing simple medical procedures such as digital cervical exams, syphilis tests, or abortions (Smith 1995: 125, 130–132). Such intrusive state regulation did save babies, but it also drove many midwives to quit or practice illegally (Smith 1995: 127–134; also Ladd-Taylor 1994: 177–184).[18]

White maternalist reformers, with their warnings about "excessive" cuddling and sensual infant-feeding, seemed to wish to cleanse the sexuality from poor mothers, as well as from Black midwives. Since eligibility for the Mothers' Pensions depended on the absence of a male breadwinner, recipients were required to refrain from sexual relationships, which were considered immoral by definition (Mink 1995: 38). Later, ADC continued the prohibition with its "man in the house" rules, which justified such practices as midnight home "visits" and other invasions of privacy (Abramovitz 1988: 323–325). This disciplining of maternal bodies was aptly described by Johnnie Tillmon, Black welfare rights activist: "In ordinary mar-

riage, sex is supposed to be for your husband. On AFDC you're not supposed to have any sex at all. You give up control over your body" (cited in Abramovitz 1988: 314).

The tendency to prohibit the sexual activity of poor mothers, which persists in the present demonization of welfare mothers, has continually hit African-American women the hardest. Most whites were little interested in saving the Black babies who threatened population "quality." And most whites did not grant legitimacy to African-American traditions of common-law marriage, taking the high numbers of "illegitimate" Black children as proof that their mothers cared less for them than for voracious sexual activity (Mink 1995: 38, 145).[19] Black maternalists, in contrast to white reformers, demonstrated less victim-blaming in their efforts to improve poor mothers' sexual morals. Although they shared white women's emphasis on sexual respectability as crucial to attaining middle-class status, Black maternalists blamed their people's immorality on the legacy of slavery and its destruction of marriage and motherhood. Moreover, they were as concerned with protecting women from rape and sexual exploitation as with punishing unwed mothers (Gordon 1991, Hine 1990, Ladd-Taylor 1994: 61).

The work of Black and white maternalists, along with public health providers, contributed to remarkable drops in the infant death and disease rates by 1930 (see note 18). And despite medical models nearly impossible to emulate, most mothers in all groups continued to breastfeed their infants. Although national statistics were not collected, those available from limited community studies indicate that between 85 and 90 percent of mothers breastfed their babies at birth in the first three decades of the century. Rural women were slightly more likely to nurse than urban women, and, while all mothers were nursing for shorter durations, urban mothers weaned earliest (Apple 1987: 152–154). In contrast to present patterns, African-American women seem to have been more likely to breastfeed before 1950. Hospital birth records from 1948 show the Southeast, where most Blacks still resided, with the highest rates of maternal breastfeeding (Apple 1987: 153), and retrospective surveys confirm that more Black mothers breastfed in the 1940s and '50s (Hendershot 1984: 598). This pattern may, somewhat perversely, have shaped dominant views that "primitive" women did not need medical assistance (Apple 1987: 73).

Medicine, Science, and White Middle-Class Mothers

Throughout the century, the medical profession has not acted merely to control motherhood. According to medical historian Rima Apple, physicians increasingly took over the supervision of infant-care and feeding for both humanitarian and self-interested motives.[20] If concerned with claiming new professional terrain, profits, and status, physicians were also legitimately concerned with infant death and disease, as well as with the safety of widely marketed patent infant-foods (1987: 24, 54–55).[21] The profession nonetheless built from traditions that had relegated breasts, lactation, normal birthing, and well-baby-care to women (nurses or midwives). Most relevant medical research and training had concerned only what to do when something went wrong, and, in terms of feeding, had focused only on imitating the contents of breastmilk. In fact, by the 1930s, discoveries in bacteriology, physiology, and nutrition had made it possible for medical researchers to improve their simulation of human milk substantially.[22]

Physicians, however, drew a primarily middle-class clientele; once they began to supervise infant-feeding, it became a large and lucrative part of family practice and pediatric medicine. If "primitive" mothers were "natural" breastfeeders, physicians worried that their clients, "civilized" mothers who lived under unnatural strains and had "highly developed nervous system[s]," were less suited to nursing (cited in Apple 1987: 73).[23] Thus, according to Apple, the profession took on the "responsibility to explain to a mother how to fulfil her nursing duty by regulating her life" (1987: 25, 36, 48, 76). The "regulatory" advice for middle-class mothers was similar to that offered to working-class mothers—exercise regularly in the fresh air, eat a bland diet, nurse on a strict schedule—but it emphasized the need to avoid becoming nervous, overwrought, or overcome with "fright, fatigue, grief, or passion" (1987: 110).[24]

Of course, middle-class mothers' advantages made it easier to adhere to breastfeeding advice and to "regulate" their babies' and their own bodies. They rarely faced financial pressures to seek paid work and usually lived in more comfortable, cleaner neighborhoods. Many middle-class mothers, however, were influenced to turn to bottles and formula by the prestige and authoritative weight of modern science, the growing confidence in artificial products, and the declining con-

fidence in breastmilk. Confidence in breastfeeding had been shaken by the discovery of such "problems" as newborn weight loss and the variability of mother's milk in quantity and quality. Physicians advised weighing infants before and after each nursing and offering regular supplemental bottles of formula, and soon began to regard the resulting failure of the mother's milk supply, and her eventual complete reliance on bottles, as inevitable (Apple 1987: 125–127). Whether breast or bottlefeeding, moreover, middle-class mothers came rapidly to believe that the "well baby" required regular medical attention. Although in the past devoted middle-class mothers had consulted clergy, kin, manuals, magazines, and, as a last resort, physicians, by the early twentieth century the physician's word was law (Apple 1987: 4, 144–145, 176; also McMillen 1990: 135–136).

Contemporary feminist scholars have been critical of this "medicalization" of birth and infancy. The rapid rise of hospital birthing, for instance, stripped women of control and subjected them to potentially harmful technological interventions.[25] There is ample evidence for blaming the patriarchal medical profession and, in the case of infant-feeding, their collusion with the burgeoning formula industry. Turn-of-the century physicians were already writing, "it is easier to control cows than women" (cited in Apple 1987: 56), and by the 1930s pediatric research was regularly funded by formula producers. Only those products, moreover, that received the American Medical Association's seal of approval could be widely advertised or distributed (Apple 1987: 48, 78–81). Hospitals (organized according to the results of sponsored research) sabotaged breastfeeding: they relied on strict feeding schedules, separated mothers and babies for long intervals, and regularly gave supplemental bottles. They sent mothers home with artificial feeding instructions, prepared bottles, and brand-name gifts (1987: 121, 126, 176). Few doctors understood that human milk is more easily digested than cow's milk, so that breastfed babies typically are hungry at frequent intervals. Furthermore, a mother's breastmilk "supply" is produced in response to the baby's "demand," or frequency and amount of suckling. Not surprisingly, "insufficient milk" quickly became the most prevalent reason for breastfeeding failure (Apple 1987: 128, 165). Finally, as hospitals sanitized and covered the mother's body and breasts and scrubbed her nipples, they conveyed that she and her body were not to be trusted.

This story is, however, more complex than capitalist-patriarchal collusion. The medical profession, as mentioned earlier, shared humanitarian concerns with maternalist reformers and was also acting in response to mothers' expressed needs. As sociologist Catherine Kohler Riessman has pointed out, elite women like the maternalists actively worked *for* medicalization (1983). They wanted freedom from the control biology extended over their lives, including pain-free, safe childbirth and birth control, and they saw medical science as an ally. As artificial infant-feeding became safer, the bottle was similarly an emblem of modernity, progress, and enhanced autonomy for affluent women in their maternal bodies. The advice literature suggests this, with breastfeeding mothers encouraged to give "relief" bottles to relax and enjoy "freedom" from the "very confining duties of nursing" (cited in Apple 1987: 56). Hospital routines, moreover, were intended mainly to prevent the spread of infection and allow mothers a respite from household responsibilities (Wertz and Wertz 1989: 155–158). Breastfeeding failure was largely an unintended consequence, and it is likely that both working- and middle-class mothers were grateful to have a safe alternative.[26]

Middle-class mothers, reformers, and pediatricians were also influenced or "medicalized" by another related science, the emerging field of child psychology. At the turn of the century, exclusive mothers already engaged in labor- and emotion-intensive childrearing, formed thousands of child study groups under the umbrella of, first, the National Mothers' Congress (later the PTA), and then, in the 1920s, of the ubiquitous *Parents* magazine.[27] Pediatricians seized on child development as an enhancement to their specialization (as they competed with family practitioners), and reformers saw the new science allied with their nation-building, family-strengthening efforts. The first influential child psychologists, L. Emmett Holt, G. Stanley Hall, and John Watson, were behaviorists, intent on making mothers give up their sentimental, indulgent caregiving in favor of rational discipline and "habit training." They believed that the child—a sort of neutral protoplasm or blank slate—needed strict regularity, in both daily activity and larger developmental tasks, according to standardized norms—and, of course, a mother trained to carry out this regime. The behaviorists reshaped norms of embodied attachment as they warned mothers against being "over solicitous" or rewarding

bad behavior (such as crying) by rocking or cuddling the baby (Hays 1996: 40). Some have seen the influence of industrial efficiency methods in this cold regime, while others point to a racialist or eugenic emphasis in obeying standardized "laws" of heredity (Eyer 1992: 100, Ehrenreich and English 1978: 184–187, Ladd-Taylor 1994: 46–49, Strathman 1984). There were also new elements of sexual restrictiveness in the early and demanding toilet training and strict disapproval of nudity, sex play, or masturbation (Breines 1992, Strathman 1984).

The middle-class mother of this era was in an exclusive mother-child dyad, but she was supervised closely by her doctor and was of course married to a good father-provider (this went almost without saying!). Like a well-informed technician, she also received a wealth of up-to-date information from the Children's Bureau, *Parents* magazine, the PTA, her child study group, and the hospital where she had given birth. She knew of the importance of fighting germs and feeding her family a vitamin-rich, "American" diet (Apple 1987: 118) and, most of all, of giving rational, measured love to her children (Hays 1996: 39–41). She was told repeatedly that breastmilk was best for babies, but that her body was *very unlikely* to be reliable. Bottles and formula, under careful medical supervision, were very nearly as good (Apple 1987: 165–166). By mid-century, a bottlefed baby was no longer an object of pity—and as L. Emmett Holt, Jr. wrote (in the revised edition of his father's manual): "a bottle mother may still be a perfect mother" (cited in Apple 1987: 3, 131).

MID-TWENTIETH-CENTURY MOTHERHOOD: SCIENCE AND ITS DISCONTENTS

The aftermath of the Depression and World War II brought changes in U.S. child-rearing ideals, but only modest criticism of the medical/behaviorist model. Hospital birthing, though "regimented, surgical, and lonely," was the overwhelmingly accepted norm (Eyer 1992: 159)—and, though about 40 percent of U.S. mothers still breastfed their babies (in hospital), both the initiation and duration of nursing were declining rapidly (Apple 1987: 153, Hendershot 1984). Breastfeeding became a low priority to the majority of physicians, child development experts, and state authorities in the postwar era. Yet, those influenced by British psychoanalysis and by postwar Chris-

tian familialism revived a sentimental view of this "natural" mother-child tie.

British psychoanalytic thought on mothering emerged from war-time work with orphan and refugee children,[28] but the notion that *any* separation of the young child from its mother would result in psychic damage was codified by psychiatrist John Bowlby. Bowlby's "attachment theory" appealed more than psychoanalysis, with its simple observations and animal study references. The psychoanalytic community objected to Bowlby's reductionism. Among other problems, he saw working mothers' daytime absence as a cause of maternal deprivation and lasting harm, similar to that of wartime loss.[29] Nonetheless, versions of Bowlby's theory have continued to dominate U.S. developmental psychology, and in the United Kingdom "Bowlbyism" became synonymous with a host of state policies enacted to keep mothers at home and out of waged-work (Eyer 1992: 50, 61–65, 73, also Riley 1983).

Although Bowlby primarily used breastfeeding as a metaphor for good mothering (Carter 1995: 57), many practitioners, like registered maternity-ward nurses, used his attachment theory to enforce it according to the rigid medical/behaviorist model. Of course, adding the imperative "to attach" to one's newborn to the fears of insufficient milk and "excessive" cuddling could hardly make mothers feel more nurturing (Eyer 1992: 41–42, 159; also Apple 1987). In the late '70s and '80s, Bowlby's work would fuel a similar "bonding craze," which made the first skin-to-skin, breast-to-mouth contact so critical that mothers feared disastrous consequences if they missed it (due to complications) or were not instantly enthralled (Eyer 1992: 13, 43). Another mid-century British expert, however, popularized "Bowlbyism" with a more humane, psychodynamic interpretation of breastfeeding.

D. W. Winnicott—psychoanalyst, pediatrician, author, and radio personality—was at once both more and less sympathetic to mothers. Although he reasonably wrote that most could be "good enough" mothers, he also maintained that extraordinary psychological capacities were required because each baby's most basic, charged, and conflictual task was to separate from the symbiosis with its mother (Chodorow 1978: 85, Eyer 1992: 64, 120, 141). Winnicott consequently saw breastfeeding as important and intense; he wrote that when the

infant has little sense of a separate self, the breast becomes the first object of fantasies of omnipotence, i.e., fantasies that s/he controls reality and, most important, the mother.[30] He acknowledged that this could be difficult for mothers, particularly as it evokes the mother's own inchoate feelings about early nurturance and feeding. Winnicott thus cautioned breastfeeding mothers to be mature, tolerant, and understanding (Friedman 1996: 478).[31]

The closest U.S. equivalent to Winnicott was Benjamin Spock, whose 1946 child-rearing manual was selling, by the end of that decade, one million copies per year. Spock, like Winnicott, was a pediatrician influenced by a Freudian approach, but it was more diluted than Winnicott's conflict-filled perspective (though perhaps less simplified than Bowlby's). Spock also emphasized the need for the exclusive dyad, because the mother's inherent sensitivity to her baby, her "instincts," were the very basis of good care (Eyer 1992: 126, 150; also Apple 1987: 119). He spoke against the restrictiveness of the behaviorists, earning the famous label as advocate of "permissive" parenting (Strathman 1984), though in truth his confidence in mothers' instincts was limited. He advised mothers to "follow the directions that your doctor gives you" (Spock 1957: 3) and to use firm "management" to keep children under "reasonable control" (1957: 1, 9, 45–49). From large-scale surveys during the 1950s, we also learn that most mothers combined "permissive" views pragmatically with the behaviorist practices they had grown up with (Breines 1992: 61–67).

Spock supported breastfeeding; yet, in contrast to Winnicott's emotion-laden account, his writing on the subject was informative but dry.[32] His discussion centered primarily on the almost inevitable insufficient milk and on weaning. He was silent on discouraging hospital regimens until the 1970s, though he noted that rooming-in, which I'll discuss in a moment, was "particularly handy" (1957), and the colored insert of ads and record-keeping pages in his manual contained no indication that *any* mother might breastfeed. (See figure 2.2.)[33] Spock also devoted a page, removed in later editions, to reassuring mothers that bottlefed babies were no less happy (1957: 67–68; also Apple 1987: 126),though he cautioned them to avoid the temptation to put the baby down with a propped bottle: "to hold her baby in her arms during bottle feedings . . . is the position that Nature intends" (1957: 117).

FIG. 2.2   Inserts from the 1957 Pocket Books edition of Dr. Spock's *Baby and Child Care*.

Along with Bowlby and Winnicott, Spock promulgated the mid-century prescription for mothers' civic duty, if not to breastfeed, then to mother with full-time "devotion to her baby" (Spock 1957: 67); such mothering, he implied, was necessary to shape well-adjusted members of society and prevent future world crises. Spock particularly counseled mothers on how to produce congenial, democratic citizens rather than "little dictators" with authoritarian, Nazi-like personalities (Eyer 1992: 126). And, the preeminent social scientist of the postwar years, Harvard's Talcott Parsons, agreed, calling exclusive motherhood a "functional necessity" to protect children (and men) from the harshness of the high productivity, market-driven public world. Parsons based this maternal assignment on biology and singled out breastfeeding (Parsons and Bales 1955). Some analysts, critical of his apology for the status quo, add that the demand for congeniality

came from the growing corporate world and its need for loyal "organization men" (e.g., Ehrenreich and English 1978, Strathman 1984). Others, however, emphasize less utilitarian motives for the postwar insistence on the mother's constant presence—and (for Winnicott and Parsons) on her available, empathic breasts. The mother's body may have offered a visceral, symbolic sense of protection from the human and technological horrors unleashed by fascism, the atom bomb, and the Cold War Soviet threat (e.g., May 1988). The return to "nature," with the child "naturally" entitled to a prolonged, carefree, innocent time also represents such desires to be sheltered from the "culture" men had produced (e.g., Strathman 1984).

Other lesser known members of the medical community also embraced this orientation. Edith Banfield Jackson, for example, another psychoanalytically trained pediatrician, struggled to reform hospital environments and became an early advocate of "rooming-in." To encourage breastfeeding, Jackson implemented hospital experiments with babies kept near their mothers and allowed to nurse on less rigid timetables.[34] She thought that babies returned to the "practice so old and natural" would be better adjusted, but also that strengthened mother-baby bonds would prevent such social ills as juvenile delinquency (Jackson 1947: 1, Stuart 1996). Later advocates of hospital reform similarly believed strengthened bonding would prevent child abuse and violent crime (Eyer 1992: 3–4, 186). But opposition to reform, to interference with several professional turfs, limited such mid-century experiments (Wertz and Wertz 1989).

The medical model of a sanitized and scrutinized, regulated, scheduled, and supplemented breast, which provided instant emotional "glue" as well, was difficult for mothers to attain or tolerate. Historian Rima Apple found in retrospective interviews that many did not reject breastfeeding, but felt deficient because they could not live up to (or with) this mechanistic, factorylike model (1987).[35] Rooming-in experiments were no panacea either: the hospital staff could be hostile or might simply fall back on the usual regimented practices, as in one instance, in which the mother of a fretful infant was told, "You have failed!"[36] In fact, in this climate, the number of women breastfeeding, already low in the hospital, fell quickly after discharge (Hendershot 1984: 596–597, Weiner 1994: 1365).

Other critics of the hospital environment sought to reform child-

birth itself. Interest in "natural" childbirth emerged from Catholic-based parents' groups that wanted to strengthen families to solve social ills, as well as from sympathetic physicians (Eyer 1992: 170–173).[37] Advocates used Christian rhetoric to describe birth as a woman's supreme spiritual fulfillment, a sublime event (Eyer 1992: 171). To be heavily drugged was to miss this and disrupt the most sensitive time, biologically and emotionally, for mother and baby to bond. Advocates for childbirth reform also wanted fathers to be present: this strengthened marriages, the important bedrock of exclusive motherhood. Natural childbirth advocates also enthused about breastfeeding and, like the psychoanalytically inclined, saw mother-baby bonding and breastfeeding as key to cultural betterment. One, for example, describing the placid infant at the breast and the contented, peaceful mother "giving herself to her beloved possession," wrote of such peacefulness extending to prevent future warfare (cited in Eyer 1992: 173, 171).

Inspired by such images, scattered breastfeeding support groups formed during the postwar years in different parts of the country. The most influential of these became La Leche League, which was first organized in 1956 in a Chicago suburb. Originally just seven white, middle-class, Catholic mothers who met through an ecumenical Christian family and social action organization, La Leche League grew fairly rapidly into a "mother-to-mother" network of self-help groups. By the latter part of the century, the League had become the major source of expertise on breastfeeding in the United States, and, according to one historian, it had replaced the Children's Bureau in promoting good mothering (Weiner 1994), though of course, it had no direct relation to the state. League founders also were active within the network of childbirth reformers and sympathetic physicians.[38] They challenged the medical model, but sought to persuade the medical community of the need for a voluntary organization to educate and support mothers. Like the early-century maternalists, the League's philosophy rests on women's gender difference and motherly authority, as in one of several mottos: "We speak for the baby." The organization incorporated ideas from the reform and psychoanalytic communities: natural childbirth, early bonding, exclusive and prolonged mother-child attachment through breastfeeding, and a child-centered family that respects each child's developmental timetable,

were best for the health and well-being of mother, child, and the larger social body. The maternalist practice of "complete" breast-feeding, in contrast to the severity and regimentation of the medical model, emphasized nursing flexibly and frequently according to the baby's demand, keeping as much physical contact as possible (never worrying about "excessive" cuddling), and following gradual, "baby-led" weaning. The philosophy of the child's prolonged inno-cent dependency extended to other practices as well, most notably toilet training and discipline. In warm, reassuring tones, the League describes this "good mothering through breastfeeding" as a "wom-anly art" that all mothers can learn and enjoy.

Sexuality and Breasts in the Postwar United States

The maternalist model put much greater trust in mothers than Dr. Spock did, but it still saw exclusive motherhood and breastfeeding as, by "nature," women's highest calling. In the meantime, however, fewer mothers were even attempting breastfeeding, with rates falling through the 1940s, '50s, and '60s. Maternal nursing hit an all-time low by 1970, with only some 20 percent of mothers nursing in-hospital, and very few, perhaps only 5 percent, continuing for several months (Hendershot 1984: 599–600, *Newsweek* 1970). In this "baby boom" era, more mothers were at home with more children, so fewer would have felt a conflict between breastfeeding and wage-earning. Bottles, however, meant that they could *get out*. It was easier to leave the baby, but also to be *out* in public with her, for with bottles, mothers could keep their breasts *out* of sight (see Carter 1995).

Nursing was doubly dangerous in this era, when breasts were sin-gled out and increasingly sexualized (Carter 1995: 124, 128). Breast-feeding threatened to expose the breasts to the heterosexual gaze, but also to compromise the object of that gaze, the stiff, uplifted breasts of Barbie, the fashion doll who so epitomized the era (Young 1990: 190; also NPR 1992b). Even Dr. Spock admitted, "Some women are hesitant to breastfeed because of the fear of what it may do to the shapeliness of their breasts, which is understandable in an age when this is considered so important" (1964: 18).[39] (See figure 2.3.) Dis-courses of sexuality, influenced by psychoanalysts and researchers like Alfred Kinsey, saw women as sexually desiring subjects. This ac-tive sexuality, however, was respectable, or well-adjusted, only if re-

FIG. 2.3
Ad for Maidenform bra, insert from the 1957
Pocket Books edition of Dr. Spock's *Baby and
Child Care.* The perfect "Barbie" breasts?

stricted within heterosexual marriage. Breasts in particular symbol-
ized this compulsory heterosexuality in the postwar years, with
women expected to conceal *and* display, and observe a complex code
of what could be seen, where, and by whom (Carter 1995: 52–53,
56, 59; also Breines 1992: 84–126). In fact, a 1957 survey report, *Patterns of Child Rearing*, recognized that the increasing avoidance of
breastfeeding indicated a discomfort about sex—though it implied
that individual mothers were to blame (1957, cited in Breines 1992:
64).[40]

Maternal nursing also became difficult because it seemed to violate husbands' ownership of their wives' breasts. In advice literature
breastfeeding is often likened to the marriage bond, and implicit then
is the notion that it is something like adultery, especially if enjoyed by
mother and baby. Many writers note that the husband will be understandably jealous, and, if they mention sexuality, tend to be preoccupied with when the mother resumes "normal" sexual relations with
him. Spock hints at this sexual angle, writing, "nursing becomes
definitely pleasurable for the mother," "[s]he and her baby are happy
in themselves," followed later by, "Quite a few fathers, including
some very good ones, object to breastfeeding—they can't help feeling
jealous" (1957: 63–64, 66). Penelope Leach, writing later in her popular book on baby care, also points to a sexual triangle: "your body is

ready and waiting for *him*. Your skin thrills to *his*" (cited in Hays 1996: 34, my emphasis), but she means *him,* the baby.

This *Parents* magazine mother's testimonial used the marriage metaphor yet ignored the implication of a sexual triangle: "Nursing is a sort of marriage, an intimate bond between two separate beings, and I wanted a private honeymoon so we could get to know each other" (Kanter 1972:68). What husband wouldn't be jealous!

Another article, from *Redbook*, acknowledged that breastfeeding was "sensually pleasurable" for mothers, "subtly similar" to orgasm. Fathers are described as initially jealous, but "[t]ime and again, we hear of a husband who [later] boasts to his co-workers about his nursing wife" (Rawlins 1968b: 44). Perhaps husbands brag about their wives' breasts because, through other men's admiration, they reassert their ownership and virility.[41]

Masters and Johnson, in their famous *Human Sexual Response*, investigated such preoccupations with breastfeeding and found that, as Spock implied, some mothers bottlefed because their husbands' objections were so strong (1966: 162). But the discovery that the small number of breastfeeding mothers in their study resumed marital sex faster than those bottlefeeding received greater attention. Although Masters and Johnson noted that resuming intercourse might sometimes stem from guilt (1966: 161–162),[42] popular advice celebrated the news: "Some studies show that a substantial number of women are more sexually active when breastfeeding than at any other time. This is good news for fathers . . . !" (Stanway and Stanway 1978, cited in Carter 1995: 138; also *Newsweek* 1970).

These deeper anxieties about violations of compulsory heterosexuality encourage strict mother-baby fidelity as a parallel or mirror reinforcing the mother-father monogamous sexual tie—and this parallel importantly supresses any suggestion of shared nursing. In the past, shared breastfeeding does not seem to have carried such anxieties—at least among lower social ranks in the United States and Europe. Formal records are lacking, but women's historians maintain that trusted kin and neighbors commonly cared for and nursed each other's nurslings (Fildes 1986, Golden 1996). In some nonwestern societies, moreover, shared nursing was so important that milk kinship was formalized in the law and restricted or structured marriage patterns as much as blood kinship (Khatib-Chahidi 1992).[43] In the twen-

tieth century United States, however, shared nursing had become unacceptable, as had wetnursing, its commercial counterpart. For a brief
time early in the century, shared nursing was replaced by the sale of
human milk through milk banks, which paid the lactating mothers.
This practice was quickly judged unacceptable, however, perhaps because of the exchange of a "sacred" fluid for cash, certainly not a way
to attract the best mothers (Golden 1996: 179–206). Milk banks became voluntary, charitable centers where primarily middle-class
mothers made donations when needed, but calls for human milk became extremely rare.[44] Formulas were improved and certainly easier
to get, but the increasing sexualization of breasts may have contributed in some small way. Breastmilk itself seems to have become sexualized, "dirty," and comparable to excretory fluids in recent constructions. Mothers, for example, who breastfeed in public spaces are
commonly relegated to bathrooms to nurse. And if they do not con-
fine themselves to bathrooms, they have sometimes been harassed or
cited for the overtly sexual charge of "indecent exposure" (I return to
this issue in the fourth chapter).

The few mentions I could find of shared nursing in popular literature were also revealing. In the only testimonial I came across, an
adoptive mother wrote that she struggled to relactate because nursing
her biological daughter had been "so pleasurable"; she looked for
"mothers who had babies they would let me nurse," but confessed
that when asking other mothers, she "felt like an obscene phone
caller" (Carlson 1973). The feminist "bible" *Our Bodies, Ourselves* (see
note 47) quickly mentions shared breastfeeding as a possibility (1992:
479), but ardent British breastfeeding advocate Gabrielle Palmer is the
only author I have read to treat the topic in its social context. She describes shared nursing as "a unique opportunity for solidarity and
friendship among women" and notes hearing of at least a few babysitting circles that included the practice. Palmer acknowledges the sexual anxieties this unleashes, as it violates the mother's fidelity to both
her baby and her husband. Palmer suggests that such embodied solidarity of women is perhaps easier for lesbian partners and can unleash
homophobic responses among others (1988: 138–139).[45]

Palmer stresses that most nursing mothers and their husbands "are
horrified by the idea of shared breastfeeding" (1988: 138). Although
La Leche League advises against it, they express their objection in the

neutral terms of health risks; intriguingly, members often develop playgroups and babysitting exchanges that would seem to invite shared nursing. Popular advice is permeated, however, by the monogamous imperative that reflects the marital tie on to the generational axis of the family. *New York* magazine explicitly tells readers that breastfeeding is "remarkably parallel to what happens when a man and woman make love"; "mother and infant develop an 'interactional harmony' that *locks* them together" (Marano 1979: 59–60, my emphasis; also Wesley 1982). More often, the exclusive embodied tie is described less sexually with the ubiquitous term "bond"—an embodied tie characterized as "powerful and lasting," "intimate," "profound," or even as "Nature's cement" (Brazelton 1985: xv, Brinkley and Charles 1980, Carro 1975, Clark 1978).[46]

THE LATE TWENTIETH CENTURY: A MACHIAVELLIAN PLOT?

In the late twentieth century two seemingly contradictory trends have reshaped mothering: the dramatic increase in mothers' wage-earning *and* the revival of breastfeeding prescriptions. These two trends 'work' through (and on) maternal bodies—bodies which have to *get out* into the public sphere, to seek autonomy, but also to engage in a most interdependent, private, and time-consuming act. In spite of this collision, both trends followed the resurgence of feminism, and this "second wave" of feminism, unlike the first, made workplace equality rather than difference a major goal. Many readers might now be reminded of Susan Faludi's influential book, *Backlash* (1991), which maintained that men found new ways to undermine these second-wave, feminist gains. It seems like a perfect Machiavellian plot: men, fearing their loss of control, revive breastfeeding prescriptions *just* as women start to become more autonomous. And women, who are trying to be good mothers, become stuck between marginal, contingent, part-time wage-earning and confining domesticity and remain economic dependents. Although this story makes for a tight, parsimonious explanation and it has some truth, it casts mothers too passively.

Mothers themselves are important actors—though of course their interests are far from uniform. It is true that at the height of the "baby boom" only 12 percent of mothers of preschool children were

out earning wages (1950 figure); but by the 1970s a changing economy and feminist goals had pushed, pulled, and inspired mothers, and
over 30 percent of those with preschoolers were employed (cited in
Eyer 1992: 122). Interestingly, state officials had so strongly assumed
that mothers with *infants* stayed home, that they did not count such
women separately until 1977, when they were astonished to find that,
of those with babies *one year old or under*, 32 percent were in the labor
force (Hayghe 1986). This rose dramatically in the next decade and
has remained high; in the 1990s slightly over half of mothers of infants were earning wages, many on a full-time basis. (See figure 2.4.)

In contrast to the idea of a patriachal plot against women, however, several left-wing movements were reviving breastfeeding with
little attention to the conflict this represented for working mothers.
And this revival occurred *prior to* breastfeeding's hegemonic medical
endorsement. First, feminists who had become active on reproductive rights moved to activism on women's health in general and
formed advocacy networks, women's clinics, and self-help groups.[47]
Clinics and self-help groups provided reciprocal, participatory care
and emphasized noninterventionist, "natural" healing techniques.
Because they saw medicine as part of male social control, activists, for

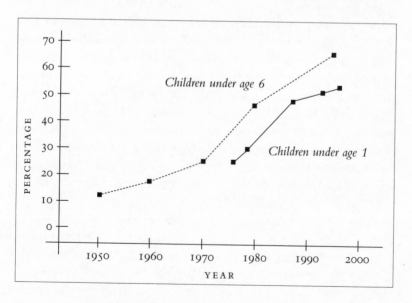

FIG. 2.4   Increase in mothers in the labor force with young children.

example, taught each other to perform pelvic exams and routine abortions (Zimmerman 1987). Maternalists in the early reform campaigns, and later in La Leche League, tried to build alliances with the powerful medical community, but feminist activists were more confrontational—and some were arrested for practicing medicine without a license (in one well-known case, for treating vaginal yeast infections with yogurt). These self-help groups, however, shared La Leche League's advocacy of natural childbirth and breastfeeding, as noted by a belittling American Medical Association editorial stating that "liberated" women "insist" on these practices despite the fact that "modern medicine has provided them with much less bothersome and painless alternatives" (1974, cited in Zimmerman 1987: 459).

The feminist health movement shared the "back to nature" ethos of the "counterculture" and the many social movements of the period (anti-Vietnam war, liberation movements of people of color and of gays and lesbians, environmentalism). Breastfeeding, in particular, was viewed through this social movement lens, as a 1970 *Newsweek* article announced: "the *hippies* seem to be in the forefront of a back-to-the-breast movement" (my emphasis). Breastfeeding also became politicized on a world scale through church and social movement activism pressing for corporate responsibility. In the 1970s church and university-based coalitions uncovered the corrupt practices of infant-formula producers selling to the Third World. The coalitions pressed corporations to change their policies and led the highly publicized boycott against Nestle, the Swiss-based multinational that dominated the two-billion-dollar world market.[48] Unlike maternalist baby-savers—who tackled similar public health problems—the Nestle boycott did not target mothers. Instead activists accused the multinationals of causing one million infant deaths per year through massive advertising and promotion efforts that discouraged breastfeeding (*Newsweek* 1978, 1981, Solomon 1981, Van Esterik 1989: 10–11, 77–78).[49]

The feminist health movement, the "hippies," and the Nestle boycott together added a subversive, anticapitalist interpretation to "natural" mothering. Although La Leche League and childbirth reform groups surged in numbers during the 1970s, the "subversives" formed an odd alliance with the founders and their Christian familialism. La Leche League, for example, would not take an official posi-

tion on the Nestle boycott (Van Esterik 1989: 78, 102), nor on feminist reproductive rights issues. Journalists, nonetheless, credit La Leche League activism for the rising popularity of breastfeeding; as one wrote, "[their] insistence that nature's way is best appeals to a generation weaned on ecology" (Solomon 1981: 100). The medical community, meanwhile, could not help but be influenced by this politicized consciousness, and contrary to the Machiavellian explanation, they were prodded into change by these larger social and cultural forces. Dr. Spock, for example, began to back the International Childbirth Education Association's calls for "family-centered" birthing (Eyer 1992: 163–164, 182). And members of the medical community protested when under the Reagan administration, the United States, alone among nations, refused to sign the World Health Organization's code for voluntary restriction of infant formula marketing—a code that had been years in the making (Mathews 1981, Solomon 1981).[50] Finally, in late 1978 the American Academy of Pediatrics (AAP) changed its official position to state that "human milk is superior to infant formulas"; they advised that, "newly discovered advantages" mean that "[i]deally, breast milk should be the only source of nutrients for the first four to six months" (Clark 1978).

This represented a switch from the mid-century advice that bottlefed babies could be just as happy and well-nourished. Beginning in the late 1970s, advice questioned the interchangeability of breast and bottle, emphasized the term "superior," and went to new lengths to paint the bottlefed baby as "an immunologic orphan, forced to fend for himself" (Marano 1979: 60, 56). But what were the "newly discovered advantages" that prompted such a change? Were these inflated to undermine feminist advances? Although when I began this research, I went looking for facts to prove that breastmilk either was or was not superior, I have since learned that there is no clear answer and no Machiavellian prince or Faludian conspiracy of men to blame. Anticorporate activists (many of whom were women) have been as likely to inflate the benefits of breastmilk as those interested in traditional femininity or family values.

Infant health and its relation to infant-feeding is a contested field of "facts," even in less developed societies where breastfeeding seems a transparent matter of life and death. In impoverished conditions,

breastfeeding is no panacea—and historically, in many instances breastfeeding has *declined* as infant health improved. Historian Rima Apple, for example, notes that infant deaths declined in the United States in the early twentieth century with improved living conditions, safer supplies of water and cow's milk, improved public sanitation, and better access to healthcare—and such changes masked the (less stark) negative effects of increased bottlefeeding (1987: 170–172). Similarly, in the contemporary Third World, though breastfeeding *is* optimal, the causes of infant death and disease are embedded in larger social problems.[51] The elite classes in developing nations tend to bottlefeed, and this has not proved hazardous. They do not, however, need to dilute the tins of formula or trade off which family members to feed; and most have access to healthcare, refrigeration, and clean water (Carter 1995: 65, Miller 1983: 36–58, Solomon 1981). Moreover, though it is true that malnourished mothers can produce some breastmilk, the common assumption that mother's milk is "free," or an extremely cheap "natural resource," is not (e.g., Andersen 1981; Ferguson 1998).[52] If inadequately fed, mothers' own bodies pay and can become severely depleted, with bones that "donate" their calcium, and blood, its iron (Chira 1993, Winick 1982).

On balance, it *is* safer for poor Third World mothers to feed their babies at the breast[53]—but it is problematic to single out breastfeeding if this ultimately only targets mothers. Even anthropologist Nancy Scheper-Hughes, who is exquisitely attuned to the local impoverishment caused by the global economy, makes this mistake. In asking why the poor mothers of Alto do Cruzeiro, a Brazilian shantytown, did not breastfeed when so many of their babies died, she assumed that breastmilk was "free." Although the mothers emphasized their poverty, and explained, "if we would feed them, they would make us sick and skinny and old" (1992: 325–326), she treats their words as *only* metaphoric. Scheper-Hughes considers the evidence for breastfeeding "so incontrovertible" as to warrant "draconian measures" coercive to mothers (1992: 317–318). Yet, in the past, when breastfeeding was the norm, she notes that many babies simply died later (of causes related to their families' lack of food).[54] The welfare of Third World *mothers*, anthropologist Vanessa Maher notes in sharp disagreement, has seldom been a concern of international breastfeeding advocates (1992).[55] In fact, suggestions that mothers receive food aid to

increase breastfeeding tend to come from population limitation advocates; the latter want to limit women's fertility (and breastfeeding can suppress ovulation) rather than value maternal health and volition for their own sake (e.g., *Science Digest* 1982).

Back Home, in the United States

Politicization of infant-feeding on a world-scale led activists to raise questions about class and race differences back home, where differences in rates of infant death and disease have remained pronounced. The Reagan administration's rejection of the WHO code angered African-American activists, who easily saw parallels between heavy-handed promotional efforts in the Third World and in U.S. inner-cities, home to our worst infant-health problems. Sympathetic physicians claimed that breastfed babies in the United States were ten times less likely to be hospitalized for serious illness than bottlefed babies, and that five thousand infants died annually from the "epidemic of formula misuse": as in the Third World, critics pointed to overdilution, lack of refrigeration, and contaminated water (Solomon 1981: 93, also Andersen 1981). Some questioned why breastfeeding rates were so much higher in private than in public hospitals (Wholey 1983). *Essence*, the African-American women's magazine, contained the most detailed indictment of the industry, its influence on hospital practices, and its lack of regulation (Reynolds 1982).

Critics were correct to note that the race differential in infant death rates has persisted, even as overall death rates declined. African-American babies are *still* twice as likely to die as white babies, although rates are at an all-time low.[56] At the same time, the rates of breastfeeding in the 1990s are lower among African-American mothers. As I discuss in chapter 5, African-American women, long exploited by their identification with "nature," may have a different response to contemporary "nature-endorsing" rhetoric and may reject an ideology so associated with white women. In the late 1980s, over half of white mothers breastfed at birth, but only about one-quarter of Black mothers did (Ryan et al. 1991). Even after state promotion efforts in the 1990s, the race differential remained: some 64 percent of white mothers breastfed at birth, compared to 37 percent of Black mothers (Ross Labs 1996).[57] A class-dimension interacts with the racial one: low-income white babies are more likely to get sick and

die than affluent white babies, but still less likely than Black babies (Hummer 1993).[58] Similarly, the low-income white baby is less likely to receive breastmilk than the affluent white baby, but still more so than the Black baby (Kurinij et al. 1988, Ryan et al. 1991, Ross Labs 1996).[59] As in discussions of less developed nations, however, it is a mistake to single out breastfeeding.

Recent state breastfeeding promotion efforts, however, do just that. The *Healthy People 2000* objectives established by the U.S. Department of Health and Human Services made improving breastfeeding rates a national priority, and, late in 1997, the American Academy of Pediatrics increased their recommendation for breastfeeding from four-to-six months to at least one year.[60] These state efforts target the behavior of individual mothers yet are pervaded by mixed messages. On one hand, current health education models are part of the attack on social provision and make infant death and disease, like other health problems, appear to be the result of ignorant or bad individual choices, in this case by mothers (Carter 1995: 60). Even before the current welfare "reform"—the Personal Responsibility and Work Opportunity Reconciliation Act of 1996—funds for maternal and child health had been slashed (WAC 1993: 40). Whereas the baby-saving reformers lobbied for increased public resources for mothers, now it seems to be assumed that mothers need little more than to be told over and over to feed at the breast. But, on the other hand, one of the few resources government provides to poor and near poor mothers is free formula, distributed through WIC, the Special Supplemental Food Program for Women, Infants, and Children. This program, intended precisely to reduce infant death and disease, purchases some $400 million per year of artificial infant food; and, while nursing mothers can get extra food vouchers, the formula is ubiquitous (Creager 1991, GAO 1993).[61]

BUT WHAT *DOES* BREASTFEEDING DO?

The American Academy of Pediatrics (AAP) now recommends breastfeeding more strongly than ever (1997), though the cautions from their detailed 1984 Task Force Assessment still concern scientists. In the earlier report, the AAP emphasized the difficulties of isolating breastfeeding from the confounding social factors within which it is embedded, and concluded that infant-health benefits in advanced societies were likely modest (AAP 1984: 580). Medical sci-

ence has long known that human milk is more easily digested by infants than other milks, and that the composition of water, proteins,
sugars, fats, and mineral salts differs; and the protection from gastrointestinal infection and diarrheal disease has long been recognized. In
the 1970s the "living" immunological properties first came to light
that explained how this protection works and how human milk responds to pathogens. According to advocates like La Leche League,
human milk therefore cannot be artificially duplicated. Scientific understanding, however, of breastmilk's bioactive properties has been
rapidly advancing.[62] Numerous studies show how antibodies work,
how respiratory and ear infections as well as allergies are also prevented by breastfeeding (AAP 1997). Moreover, discoveries about
long-chain lipids or fatty acids, hormones, enzymes, the antimicro-
bial effects of complex sugars, and other biologically active protective
agents are accumulating (Newburg and Street 1997). While this all
prompted the AAP to strengthen its endorsement of breastfeeding, it
is still true, as its 1984 report noted, that most of the problems it prevents no longer pose serious health risks in this country and that most
formula-fed babies thrive.

Other, more dramatic claims for infant-health benefits, however,
suggest links between artificial feeding and Sudden Infant Death Syndrome,[63] ulcerative colitis, Crohn's disease, type-1 diabetes, liver and
kidney problems, some types of cancer, even autoimmune diseases
(Minchin 1989: 10, 29, 310). Scientists explain though, that such protective mechanisms of breastfeeding, which work in interaction with
many other factors, are not well understood, and those protecting
"against chronic diseases later in life are hardly understood at all"
(Newburg and Street 1997: 198; also AAP 1997). Some advocates
blame multinational capital and its sponsorship of research for this
lack of knowledge. Most research, in fact, does continue to be funded
by formula producers, and one top manufacturer contributed large
sums for the 1984 AAP Task Force study (Quick 1997, Van Esterik
1989: 143, 196). Advocates contend that research methods systematically *under*estimate the benefits of breastfeeding; most notably, the
"breastfed" measure—"fed *any* breastmilk, ever"—includes many
children fed some, or even lots of, formula. Anticorporate advocates
also complain that incidents of formula contamination or deficiency
receive little attention, although in one four-year period (1982–86)
they uncovered at least sixteen major problems (Palmer 1988: 273–

274). Formula does tend to be treated as a pristine, "manmade" substance, while fears of environmental pollutants contaminating human milk receive serious public attention.[64]

The latest claims for breastfeeding's benefits are even less scientifically established: breastfeeding may slightly heighten I.Q. and visual acuity (Horwood and Fergusson 1998, Glick 1997, NPR 1992a); it may condition the body to better process fats and cholesterol and prevent obesity (deMauro 1991, LLLI 1987: 154), or even teach the baby to enjoy a more varied, healthful diet (Shapiro 1997); and, finally, it may enhance facial, dental, and speech development (Eiger and Olds 1987: 25, LLLI 1987: 370–372). These most recent claims speak to less serious health issues than earlier concerns about infectious and chronic disease. Furthermore, researchers are again concerned that claims could be spurious; for example, mothers in New Zealand, whose breastfed children scored slightly higher on I.Q. tests, were older, better educated, and wealthier (*New York Times* 1998b). The exhortation that "breast is best," in light of such small, unverified claims, may represent new kinds of middle-class anxieties about children as much as rational health-enhancing advice. With the U.S. economy changing and most middle-class children expecting *not* to be financially better-off than their parents, such anxieties may have provoked a new maximizing view of "child-centered" child-rearing. This could explain the desires for perfect, priceless children that seem expressed in breastfeeding advice and trends, as well as in genetic testing trends, educational competitiveness, and popular culture (see Hays 1996, Zelizer 1985).[65] In terms of breastfeeding, the new cultural imperatives imply that certainly no good mother would deny her child optimal health and longevity, and that the best mothers will do all they can to maximize their children's intelligence and beauty. Even one advocate wrote: "[I]n reality much of this [increased breastfeeding] has occurred among well-educated . . . women seeking optimal outcome for the few well-planned and carefully-engineered pregnancies they will experience" (Lawrence 1988: 267).[66]

BUT WHAT ABOUT MOM?
Research and advice literature each pay less attention to maternal health and breastfeeding. Assumptions of maternal altruism run high,

and mothers particularly curious about the effects of breastfeeding on their bodies are likely to meet with frustration. The structure of medical subfields is part of the problem: obstetricians deliver babies, and, after delivery, mothers deal primarily with pediatricians. Neither specialty is trained to knowledgeably treat breastfeeding mothers.[67] Some mothers find help from sympathetic nurses, or from the new paraprofessional specialists, lactation consultants; but few hospitals employ full-time consultants or have sufficient numbers of knowledgeable nurses, and the costs to see consultants privately can be prohibitive.[68]

Advice to mothers typically mentions a few ostensible health benefits, but also instructs that youthful, slim bodies are culturally required. One popular manual features under the bold subtitle "Good for Your Figure" that breastfeeding speeds the contraction of the uterus back to prepregnancy size (something never achieved fully by bottlefeeding mothers) and burns extra calories so that mothers can enjoy gradual weight loss without dieting (Eiger and Olds 1987: 29). Dr. Spock devotes most of his discussion of maternal health to "the mother's figure," cautioning that breast sagging occurs mainly from excessive weight gain: "You certainly don't have to . . . get fat in order to make milk." If a nursing mother feels unwell, Spock counsels, she may be a "worrisome" or insecure person, "[o]r *least likely of all*, she may be in poor physical health" (1985: 107, 109, my emphasis).[69]

Advice on maternal benefits also speaks of the lactational hormones, prolactin and oxytocin, believed to trigger tranquility and contentedness that spontaneously make for better mothering (Eiger and Olds 1987: 27, 40, LLLI 1987: 12, 88); these hormones are also related to sensual or sexual pleasure, something ignored or only fleetingly mentioned by many authors (except Eiger and Olds 1987: 19, 191–196). Another benefit frequently cited is the contraceptive effect, as hormonal changes tend to suppress ovulation if a mother nurses without supplements (Eiger and Olds 1987: 30–31, 202), but this effect varies widely and may be of benefit mainly to those religiously committed to "natural" family planning.

Many women, in my experience, want to know if breastfeeding helps prevent breast cancer, an important question, as the disease now touches one of eight women (Love 1995). Unfortunately, there has been less research than we would like and little conclusive evidence

(Love 1995: 37). This may be because women's health research has been a low funding priority (though recent political activism has helped to change this), or because breastfeeding is seen as a mother's duty to her child rather than something she should pursue in self-interest; or perhaps it simply stems from the complexity of the disease itself. But the advice literature, if it mentions this question at all, tends to subtly exaggerate the possible benefit (except Eiger and Olds 1987: 249–250). La Leche League's manual, for example, cautions that "answers are still being sought," yet it details a number of cross-cultural comparisons and studies which suggest a preventive link (1991: 381–382, also Kitzinger 1987: 142).[70] Recent research also suggests that breastfeeding may decrease a mother's risk of ovarian cancer (Whittemore et al. 1992); and this complex finding will be similarly taken out of context (e.g., Quick 1997).

It is ironic that maternal malnourishment is not seen as a problem for the Third World, yet nursing mothers back home are advised, "you need to pay close attention to your own nutrition" (Karlsrud and Shultz 1993a). Whether this reflects our maximizing middle-class orientation or our ethnocentrism, U.S. mothers are expected to follow quite detailed directions (e.g., Eiger and Olds 1987: 79–88, Spock 1985: 112–113) and to vigilantly monitor themselves and allow themselves to be monitored. They must not only consume the proper proteins, fats, and carbohydrates, but refrain from smoking and consuming alcohol, caffeine, or "recreational drugs" (LLLI 1987: 235). Like the early-century reformers' emphasis on regulation, this suggests that maternal bodies cannot be trusted and that breastmilk is only as "pure" as the mother who produces it (Carter 1995: 68).

AT LAST, THE DISEMBODIED MOTHER

Although combining wage-earning with mothering and breastfeeding was a concern early in the century, the question loomed large again in the 1980s and '90s as the majority of mothers, even mothers of infants, even middle-class mothers, began returning to the workplace (as shown in figure 2.4). The maternalists in La Leche League, who I discuss at length in the next chapter, struggle with the issue because they continue to see physically tied mothering as basic to women's identity, to their difference from men, and to young children's needs. The predominant medical model, however, stretches the

meaning of exclusive mothering; it borrows from the popularized feminist rhetoric of equality with men and "having it all," and views the solution, as in the title of this educational pamphlet: "The Best of Both Worlds: A Guide for the Working, Breast-Feeding Mother" (Ross Labs 1984). (See figure 2.5.)[71] One pamphlet takes the language of equality so far that it uses the gender-neutral term "parenting" to describe the extra effort of combining career and breastfeeding (Mead Johnson 1986: 4), while another advises mothers to "Dress for Success *and* Breastfeeding" (Mead Johnson 1990: 27).

Many in the medical community express concern that the modern workplace is hardly "baby-friendly" (NPR 1992a, AAP 1997); however, they use their authority to recommend little in the way of workplace or public policy reforms. Instead, the medical profession solves the wage-earning/breastfeeding dilemma by glibly advising mothers to use breast pumps.[72] An employed mother, in other words, can feed her baby at the breast at home, but she should collect her milk and keep up her supply by using a pump (or expressing milk by hand) during worktime. In fact, the AAP's recent statement prioritizing longer breastfeeding mentions only the need for employers to provide space and time for breast-pumping (1997: 1037). The AAP fails to mention options that would allow mothers more time with their infants (as the army pilot in the first chapter desired), such as increasing (and funding) the Family and Medical Leave Act, which now provides just twelve weeks of *un*paid leave. The AAP also might advocate for more on- and near-site nurseries, which are scarce, but instead it stresses the need for health insurance to cover breast-pump rentals and lactation consultant fees. Major press coverage responding to the AAP's recommendations also focused almost exclusively on breast-pumping (e.g., Foreman 1998, Sepah 1998, Slade 1997).

This change in the authoritative prescription for the disciplining of maternal bodies redefines breastfeeding. What had once seemed—and still does in the maternalist model—a deeply embodied and interdependent act, likened to the marital sex act, has fast become something that can occur without the mother being physically present, if she follows the new regulatory regime. Psychoanalyst Michelle Friedman points out that the breastmilk takes on a fetishized quality when it is so often emphasized apart from, and as equivalent to, the embodied, relational practice (1996: 484). Through this fetish, the

The Best
Of Both Worlds
A Guide for the Working,
Breast-Feeding Mother

FIG. 2.5   A pamphlet cover from formula–maker Ross Laboratories.

mother is disembodied, as if she *is* the milk; by providing this milk, she still qualifies as an exclusive mother, *as if* mother and baby are still monogamous and physically tied. Some maternalists are troubled that the working mother is not with her baby for much of the day, as perhaps are some who believe in traditional "family values." But I am more struck by the lack of attention to mothers, as if nothing *really* different were being endorsed. The mother in her body, her pleasures and needs, satisfactions and pains, have been largely erased.

Breast pumps began to be patented in the nineteenth century, though improvised devices as well as techniques of hand expression had certainly long been used. Isadora Duncan was ahead of her time, since pumps had been used to stimulate the milk supply *only if the baby could not* owing to weakness, illness, prematurity, or other crisis.[73] The new regularized, fetishized "breastfeeding"—something largely between mother and pump, and pumped milk and baby—is exemplified in the widespread advertising of pumps. Many of the ads show neither baby nor mother, just the apparatus itself, as in this example, which juxtaposes the high-tech image with the name, "The Nurture III" (see figure 2.6). Other names are telling: the Evenflo Natural Mother, Gerber's Precious Care, Healthteam's Gentle Expressions (Owen 1988). We can see the need for workplace privacy in the "Nurture III" ad's copy: it's *small*, it's *quiet*, it's *portable*.[74] Others emphasize privacy and the mother's status, like "The Commuter," which comes concealed in its own briefcase (Schewel 1991). Another ad is more blunt about workplace priorities: "More Milk, Less Time," softened only in the small print: "Naturally, with a little help from a friend" (figure 2.7). Another declares its apparatus to be "revolutionary" (figure 2.8); while the most fetishized puts the mother back in the frame where she appears to be having a sensual relationship with the pump, the Sof-Touch Ultra, while the baby is elsewhere (figure 2.9), or she is with her baby but the ad is for formula (figure 2.10).

Popular advice is now pervaded by the medical model and its reliance on the breast pump at work. Authors and experts proclaim "it's easy" (Parks 1993) or even that it's a "modern woman's dream" (Foreman 1998). Yet, at the same time, women are reminded that pumping does not empty the breast as completely as the baby (as Isadora Duncan discovered on stage); that "a bustling office environment inhibits 'let-down,'" the reflex that allows the milk to flow (Mauk 1984); and that exhaustion can lead to breast infections (Barr 1990). Mothers are

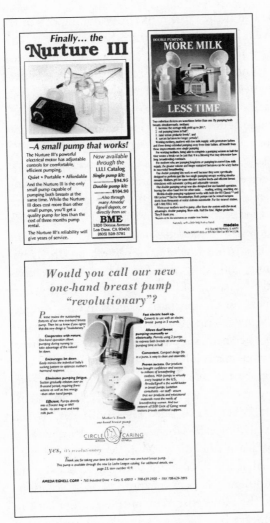

FIG. 2.6
The "Nurture III" pump.

FIG. 2.7
"More Milk, Less Time."

FIG. 2.8
A "revolutionary" pump.

urged to practice pumping during their maternity leave; to bring pictures and baby clothes, even play soft music and sip wine, to stimulate let-down at work; all during their "uninterrupted" thirty-minute breaks, even if they must use the "ladies' lounge" (Mauk 1984). Other heroic suggestions are to nurse frequently through the night to keep up the milk supply and satisfy the baby (e.g., Barr 1990, Mead Johnson 1990: 8), to pump on airplanes while on business trips (cabin pressure makes this "easy") (Katz 1980), or even, when your schedule gets hectic, to pump while stuck in traffic (Paterno 1992, also Slade 1997).

FIG. 2.9
The Evenflo "Sof-Touch Ultra." When we see the mother's body, the sensual relationship is displaced on to the pump.

FIG. 2.10
In this Gerber ad the sensual relationship is not displaced, but the ad is for formula.

The ads and advice tend to skirt the issue of the workplace environment itself. Although some acknowledge that limited maternity leaves and inhospitable workplaces make breastfeeding seem "unmanageable," good mothers know that "with careful planning" these apparent barriers can be overcome (Mauk 1984). Feminist scholars emphasize that the advanced capitalist employer—especially one which is "lean and mean"—wants unencumbered workers, workers free from the intrusion of "private" caregiving responsibilities or recalcitrant physical needs, whether those be from muscle fatigue or disabilities, or from pregnancy or engorged breasts (Acker 1990, Martin 1987). Some economists differ, arguing that women continue to prefer the low-paying jobs where women are concentrated because they better accommodate such "womanly" needs, offering ease of job exit and entry, part-time options, flexible schedules, lax supervision, generous break time, and less taxing work (summarized in Glass 1990). Such options, if they existed, might facilitate breastfeeding, or at least breast-pumping, in the absence of on- or near-site nurseries or truly generous leaves. Sociological research has found, however, in contrast to this imaginary workplace, that most of the jobs that are predominantly women's are actually *less* flexible, offer less break time, and require working faster, harder, and longer than many male fields (Glass and Camarigg 1992). Maternalists thus may be right to worry about what this workplace does to mothers and mothering.

Instead, expert advice along the medical model presents a new Supermom. In the popularized feminist rhetoric of "juggling multiple roles," she chooses to meet her baby's needs and keep her "freedom"; she can "balance" work and breastfeeding (e.g., Mason and Ingersoll 1986: 94–95). She can pump in a parking lot, a supply closet, a bathroom stall, or on the freeway. Although compromising the century-long emphasis on exclusive mothering as the mother's full-time physical presence, this breastfeeding Supermom testifies: "I have a lot less guilt leaving this baby *that I'm nursing* than I did leaving my other baby, who was bottlefed" (Ross Labs 1984: 13, my emphasis). This Supermom, of course, also keeps herself attractive and slim: she won't fill up on "empty calories" (Ross Labs 1984: 11), and perhaps breastfeeding is part of her "postpartum weight-loss plan" (*Parents* 1992). She is exemplified by this model mother, from the fashion show at a medical conference promoting breastfeeding:

Representing the United States is "Janice Newton," an all-American mother, who nurses her daughter, works full-time as a computer programmer, and makes time to run, swim, and bike regularly. "Janice" is sporting red running shorts with her . . . Triathalon shirt commemorating the event in which she took first place . . . last month. Her daughters, eight-month-old "Kathy" and twenty-two-month-old "April," are in matching . . . overalls.[75]

This career-breastfeeding Supermom seems to transcend recalcitrant embodied needs, wants, or desires. Certainly she cannot follow the early or mid-century regimen prescribed to nursing mothers, with all its time for sleep; nor would "Janice" likely have time for the fifteen-minute relaxation interludes Dr. Spock advised before each nursing to ease the let-down reflex (see 1957: 70). We haven't been told, but we can easily guess at "Janice's" racialized class location and just as easily assume that she is married and employs an immigrant nanny (who may also be a mother). She has, however, solved the dilemma posed by being at once exclusive and irreplaceable *but* replaced—at least during her hours working and working-out. She has the "lock" of the breastmilk, "Nature's cement," to "bond" her children to her, even if she has to rely on a breast pump to collect much of it.[76] (See figure 2.11.) And her feelings about this activity—whether of discomfort, inconvenience, distaste, or acceptance—are of no concern, for her milk is "something no one else can give [the baby]" (Spock 1985: 105; also Eiger and Olds 1987: 18). Moreover, any negative feelings about pumping might be resolved by new technological innovations—a new pumping vest has just been patented that allows working mothers to remain at their desks "while the vest works discreetly" (Chatrand 1996). In the end, the rewards for the mechanistic pumping are the few times when she can actually nurse her daughter "in the flesh," for, as several popular manuals (and my obstetrician-acquaintance in the first chapter) put it, this "remind[s] the baby who the real mother is!" (Eiger and Olds 1987: 169, also Brazelton 1985: xv, 73, Ross Labs 1984: 3).

The kind of disembodiment that Super-breastfeeding-career moms like "Janice" experience, in which the maternal body and embodied experience are devalued and all but erased, is similar to the erasure of the pregnant maternal body analyzed by feminist scholars. New technology such as fetal monitoring and ultrasound imaging has

The Pumping Free™ Kit
#87016*

Designed to provide exceptional convenience for busy mothers, with hands-free double pumping. When fastened onto Medela's nursing bras, this unique product allows mothers to connect to a Medela electric breastpump and pump both breasts simultaneously, leaving both hands completely free.

Isis, Helena, and Pumping Free are trademarks of Medela, Inc.   *Patent Pending
Lycra is a registered trademark of Du Pont.

FIG. 2.11
"*Pumping Free.*" The mother becomes to herself body-less.

the effect of removing the mother and her body from the picture, in every sense of the word. Studies of birthing in the 1990s find that obstetricians, nurses, and other attendants literally turn their backs to laboring women in order to stare at the monitor screen; as one mother described, "I got the weirdest feeling that *it* was having the baby, not me" (from Davis-Floyd 1992: 107, also Martin 1987: 145–146). Mothers and their bodies, or mothers *in* their bodies, also disappear from obstetric textbooks (Martin 1987: 147) and from books, photographs, and films depicting pregnancy (now depicted as fetal development) and childbirth (Adams 1993, Carter 1995: 145, Kaplan 1994, Petchesky 1987). This erasure of the maternal body also invites new forms of social control, as evidenced in fetal endangerment or fetal rights cases (Daniels 1993). For the disembodied mother, her body is not her own—but more than that, she is treated, and pressed to treat herself, as if body-less.

Breastfeeding in twentieth-century United States takes us from the $acred to the Disembodied Mother, hand-in-hand with experts and

the state. The promotion of breastfeeding has been fairly consistent through the century, although authoritative exhortations have been louder in some periods than others. Also, exhortations have been full of mixed messages for mothers, who certainly, as I detail later, have not simply internalized these prescriptions. Through the 1950s U.S. mothers were subject to increased medical control and definition, whether they were breast or bottlefeeding. They were told that breast was best, that the "fitness" and "vigor," or later, the "adjustment," of the nation were at stake,[77] as well as their children's health and well-being. In this sense it was best to be closer to nature, for if a mother were too civilized and nervous in temperament, it could be dangerous to breastfeed, or her breasts might simply fail. In this case, however, the white, middle-class, expert-guided mother was reassured that bottles were perfectly fine. Yet, at the same time, African-American mothers deemed closer to nature, natural breeders and breastfeeders, were cast as too polluted to cross the color-line to respectable or honorable motherhood—and their babies too inferior to contribute to nation-building.

Maternalist reformers and public health professionals, through branches of the state, reached out to save the babies of those mothers who were potentially white, who could be taught respectability. And, in some ways, it was the bodies and breasts of such immigrant and working-class mothers which were the most marked or visible in the early twentieth century. Their sexuality was also suspect and has been persistently used to divide those who were "deserving" of public support from those who were unworthy and polluting. The suspect sexuality of such women, particularly if they were breastfeeding, also collided with the favored "habit training" and disciplined, measured love children were said to need.

The shifts over time in the notion of *what children need* reveal many things. Pronouncements about "children's needs" might express a particular group's interests for power and economic gain, as well as humanitarian concerns or historically provoked anxieties. Thus in the aftermath of World War II, "children's needs" for exclusive mothering and empathic breasts signaled the consolidation of the medical profession's power, but also of particular racialized class and gender relations. These class relations are sometimes referred to by sociologists as "Fordist," shorthand for the fact that white, male workers employed in large, unionized industries such as the auto industry had gained decent earnings and access for the first time to middle-class

family arrangements and exclusive mothering. But, against this new-found postwar security, "children's needs" also signaled the threat of new technologies of genocide. In our era, perhaps we can't yet discern the entire configuration "children's needs" represents. I have suggested that for the white, middle-class the disembodied mother's exclusivity, her fetishized presence and the cement of her breastmilk, speak to new insecurities of a new, yet-to-be discerned world order. But, clearly, there are also worries about racialized class and gender relations at home in the postindustrial, "postfeminist" and "post-Fordist" era, which I turn to in the ensuing chapters.

Even from this rather limited history, we see that "breastfeeding," like "children's needs," has been and can be organized in varied ways, with differing compatibilities and incompatibilities with mothers' waged-work, as well as with dominant discourses of sexuality. In the next three chapters, I look in detail at the varied practices and meanings of breastfeeding to contemporary mothers, beginning with some of those who are most reputable from the dominant standpoint of experts and state officials, the mothers attracted to the contemporary maternalism of La Leche League.

CHAPTER 3

"MOTHER TO MOTHER"
IN LA LECHE LEAGUE

The major alternative to the mechanistic, cold, and, finally, disembodied mother offered by medical authority in the late twentieth
century has been and continues to be offered by La Leche League. As
a women's voluntary organization, La Leche League is run by and for
mothers to promote a "philosophy" of "good mothering through
breastfeeding" that values mothers' exclusive embodied presence.[1]
The League is larger than many readers might guess, but it has been
the subject of surprisingly little analysis in its over forty-year history.
This lack appears in marked contrast to the large amount of writing
circulated by the organization itself. My purpose here is not to provide the comprehensive history that the organization deserves,[2] but
to emphasize how the League's philosophy differs from the medical
model and, despite some important changes, continues to emphasize
an embodied, relational view of motherhood that appeals to some
mothers, even in our late-twentieth-century gender-egalitarian milieu. I also examine how La Leche League's maternalism, like its fore-
mother in the early twentieth century, both meshes and competes
with feminism and, as much as the medical model, represents a racialized class-enhancing project for white middle-class women.

THE ORGANIZATION

La Leche League was founded in the United States in the celebrated
domesticity of the 1950s by seven white, middle-class mothers, all
Catholic, who met through an ecumenical Christian family-social
action organization. Like others in the post–World War II childbirth
reform community, they were committed to "natural" childbirth,

long-term (or extended), on-demand breastfeeding, and large families. The seven "Founding Mothers" came together with the
"dream" of "finding a way to help those women [i.e., other like-
minded mothers] experience the joy and deep fulfillment of breastfeeding" (LLLI 1987: 385–386). The organization grew quickly from
these founding mothers with their mimeographed materials: the first
edition of the group's manual, *The Womanly Art of Breastfeeding,* was
published in 1958 and sold 17,000 copies; between 1963 and 1981,
the second edition sold over one million copies. Also, by 1981, the
League had a central office with paid staff, some 4,000 active local
groups, and some 60,000 subscribers to a monthly newsletter (Halonen and Mohrbacher 1987: xvii, LLLI 1981: 343–346). Ten years later
the organization claimed to be second in size only to Alcoholics
Anonymous among U.S. self-help groups (*Brighton Argus* 1991).[3] This
success has been attributed both to the organization's support for
breastfeeding and to the respite it offers from the isolation of middle-
class mothering (Merrill 1987, Weiner 1994).

Like Alcoholics Anonymous, the League's primary activities offer
mutual support: local leaders run monthly drop-in meetings, give
phone support, and offer individual counseling. Leaders are unpaid
volunteers, breastfeeding or formerly breastfeeding mothers who
"have been there," but who have also been through a screening and
accreditation process (Merrill 1987). The drop-in groups follow a rotating, four-part series of topics or curriculum established by the
founders,[4] but the discussions are informal and range widely to meet
the needs of the mothers who attend, with their babies and small children in tow. Local groups also run small lending libraries of League
materials and often develop extracurricular activities, toddler playgroups, family potlucks, picnics, etc. The national level offers regional and state conferences throughout the year targeting members
and professional healthcare groups. In addition, La Leche League runs
a national "hot line," publishes numerous books and pamphlets, gath-
ers information on breastfeeding, and accredits leaders. By 1991, the
group counted some 28,000 past and present leaders (LLLI 1991: 392).

EMBODIED MOTHERHOOD
In marked contrast to the medical model analyzed in the last chapter,
La Leche League's philosophy of mothering emphasizes the need of

the child for the mother's presence, and the need of both mother and baby for an intimate, physical relationship—needs that are best and "naturally" fulfilled through breastfeeding.[5] Their interpretation of breastfeeding thus differs from the mechanistic medical model, which emphasizes a disembodied product, breastmilk, and a disembodied laborer-producer, the mother, who requires external regulation or labor control. The League has advocated instead "complete" breastfeeding in which breastfeeding is a relational process, and one in which mother and baby take their cues and habits reciprocally, from each other rather than from outside experts. Complete breastfeeding therefore includes minimal separation from the baby, few supplemental bottles (if any), and feeding on the baby's demand, even if very frequent and/or irregular.[6] Ideally, from this point of view, mothers should rely as little as possible on substitutes for the bodily comfort they provide—this includes bottles and pacifiers, but also playpens and carriages, as League mothers prefer slings and carriers that keep the baby on the mother's body and at or near the breast.

La Leche League does not specify a definite end to this complete relationship. Instead, the organization recommends that weaning be a gradual, "child-led" process that can continue well into toddlerhood, into the third or even fourth year. The mother, rather than the pediatrician, is considered the best judge of her own child's needs in this gradual process. The League, like other pronatalist mid-century reform groups, assumed that the child was an inherently innocent being, that his or her intense dependence on the mother was also innate and would gradually lessen with the child's own inner-directed growth, and that, likewise, the mother's devotion to her child was "natural." This returned authority to mothers and honored their caregiving at a time when most middle-class, white women remained in the home. From the contemporary perspective of much of the white middle-class, which places a high value on women's success in the workplace (e.g., Hochschild 1997), it can seem, in contrast, frighteningly all-consuming. As one of the League's founding mothers wrote: "The needs of their babies are not only for mother's milk, or mother's breast, but for *all of her*" (White 1987; my emphasis).

La Leche League, in addition to its promotion of complete breastfeeding, has represented a grassroots effort to speak from and reshape women's embodied experiences, which had been so degraded

by medicine and hospital birthing. The League in this respect anticipated feminist self-help health movements of the 1970s, and, in fact,
the League became larger than these more explicitly politicized efforts in later decades (Weiner notes this as well, 1993, 1994). Because
"embodiedness" itself, as discussed in chapter 1, is such a complex in-
tertwining of cultural and biological realities, the League represents
a significant historical case: here mothers have attempted to recraft or
revise the text, the cultural reading of their corporeal selves, in what
is the crux of femininity, motherhood.

In my view, the League's creation of a "body" of mother-centered
expertise and revision of the maternal body is at least as important as
the philosophy of childrearing they promulgate. League groups share
expertise on breastfeeding as a physiological, relational, and cultural
experience, and while they do voice their moral authority in terms of
children's needs, mothers' points of view and bodies receive at least as
much attention, if not more. In group meetings, mothers' needs and
wants receive time and attention, and group expertise is devoted to
making these experiences empowering and pleasurable. Mothers
need to be bodily present for their babies, but their bodies need to
work and feel good for "the woman in the body" as well;[7] if self-
abnegation was admired (such as mothers who endured painful nipples or sleepless nights), such altruism was also named and treated as
avoidable, with the help of the organization's collective knowledge.
In spite of all its talk of the fixity of exclusive motherhood in "nature," League practice tells another story, of a body "unfixed." This
"unfixed" body could be less objectified, less for others, and could be
lived in, savored, and enjoyed. League founders have called the group
very "radical" for its time (Weiner 1994: 1371), and, to me, this respect for the "unfixed" experiences of the body continues to be its
most radical contribution.

The Body That Works

The message of embodiment found in the League works on at least
two levels. Generally the more threatening message of pleasure and
sensuality is only gently hinted at, with the more acceptable and
louder stance an affirming notion of the mother's body as one that
works and is beautiful in its functionality. In the meetings I attended
there was lots of talk about the body and "down-to-earth" problem-
solving, in addition to the unusual visibility of so many women nurs-

ing. The talk and problem-solving offered mother-to-mother expertise in much the way that feminist self-help health groups have: that is, with "warmth and caring" (LLLI 1987: 386), without monetary fees, and from those who have or have had similar experiences.

At one meeting I attended, much time was spent preparing the one very pregnant mother for her anticipated Caesarean delivery. Several leaders discussed their own experiences with Caesarean deliveries and how to deal with the problems of pain, needed medications, and breastfeeding while you recover from the surgery. To cheer on the expectant mother, one went on at some length, saying, "I did everything wrong, everything you can do. But still I managed to breastfeed." The talk was detailed and immodest, focused on how to handle not just painkilling drugs, but sore stomachs and nipples, plugged breast ducts and breast infections. Motherly martyrdom was definitely not endorsed, with one leader recounting her fear of pain and need for medications, and others recommending lots of physical assistance from husbands, (grand)mothers, and even hired "doulas" or baby nurses.

Generally, if there was not someone at a meeting with a similar body problem, leaders made great efforts to provide phone numbers to put mothers in touch with others who had shared the experience. I later met women who identified themselves as VBACs, vaginal births after Caesareans, and mothers who had had midwife-supported home births or other alternative births, for whom the League was their most important referral and support network. Referrals to alternative medical providers were always local and informal—so that the organization was not infringing on professional medicine—but the contacts, and the "mother to mother" support, were vital to members who felt their bodies had been misused or traumatized by medical professionals. As League mother Pam White recounted:[8]

> With my Caesareans, I didn't know better. I [had] believed every doctor. [But] when we decided to have another baby . . . I started reading. And I ran into a friend, and unknown to me, she had become a La Leche leader, and we started talking . . . and she asked if I wanted to be contacted by a La Leche leader in our area. . . . It just made a lot of sense, the things she was saying, it whet my thirst for learning . . . It had never dawned on me until then, how *unnecessary* my second Caesarean was. . . . It got me into a different set of knowledge that I had never had my hands on before . . . Then it started *really bothering* me. I wanted a VBAC *really bad!*

Another long-time leader, Marg Walters, told a similar story:

> At that point, I had had one miscarriage . . . and going to League, I switched doctors and hospitals and went to the one place in town where fathers were permitted. League mothers, that was my referral source for much of my health care from then on. They really knew who was good and who was supportive . . . it was excellent.[9]

At another meeting I attended, talk about the body was somewhat less prominent, but discussion time was spent encouraging a mother who was losing too much weight and whose baby seemed to require her (the mother's) rather severe dietary restriction.[10] Time was also spent discussing recent medical prohibitions against alcohol and caffeine that call for complete abstention, from the point of conception on through pregnancy and breastfeeding. Sociologist Elizabeth Armstrong contends these medical protocols, particularly in the required warning labels on all alcoholic beverages, create a "cult of purity" for contemporary middle-class mothers (1997). The League tends to reject such alarmist prohibitions, as they are based on only the most extreme scientific facts or cases and treat mothers as if they are the antagonists of their babies.[11] One League mother (Liz Davenport) later explained the hypocrisy when mothers must be pure, but doctors feel free to expose newborns to unnecessary or invasive procedures: "I gave birth standing up. I had no drugs, no fetal monitoring." But, she continued, "the second my son came out, it seemed like they wanted to find something wrong with him. They x-rayed him very thoroughly for no reason . . . it was *completely* unnecessary. So they risked cancer in his future and it pisses me off, it *really does,* because you go to so much work to not drink caffeine, to *not* do this and *not* do that! And you are just so careful!"

In addition, and in contrast to the prevailing obsession with slimness, League leaders encourage mothers to nourish themselves, even to treat and indulge themselves. In one meeting we talked about ice cream—and for the mother with the highly sensitive newborn, about "Rice Dream." And in a later individual conversation Liz Davenport described how she let her body change and become more rounded (and this over two years since her child's birth): "I have a completely different look now physically than I did before. I weighed twenty pounds less." "I used to run all the time, I ran *all the time,* that was how

I controlled my weight . . . but, it's funny. I'm more laid back and it's like I don't really care, and I just do something with my son instead."

Sociologist Ann Oakley has detailed how the medical model, by its narrow focus on individual *maternal* behaviors, like alcohol and caffeine consumption or weight control and exercise, conceal the much larger role of social factors in determining infant-child health (1992). Even smoking, which exemplifies the notion of a bad individual choice, turns out to be *much* more dangerous for babies of low-income mothers than for the babies of the affluent (1992: 320–25). Yet the medical model repeatedly comes to harsher judgments against working-class mothers, blaming them for their poor choices and failing to analyze their behavior or their children's health in context (an issue I return to in the next chapter). Even the babies of mothers addicted to crack-cocaine have fared reasonably well compared to the dire fates and social disasters predicted by medical professionals (Begley 1997a). With the white middle class, suspicions of maternal bodies are still present, if weaker; after all, on the label of every bottle of beer and wine the Surgeon General emphasizes the need for expectant mothers' abstinence *before* the dangers of drunk driving (Armstrong 1997). Thus, even affluent, white mothers seek reassurance that their judgments are reasonable and their bodies do not easily harm.

Although La Leche League meetings are not as "hands on" as feminist self-help groups that performed pelvic exams and abortions (Zimmerman 1987: 456–459), the League's twenty-four-hour phone counseling serves a similar purpose. Leaders counsel mothers with problems nursing premature, ill, and disabled infants (Andrews 1991), and they suggest effective treatments for common complaints such as sore or bleeding nipples, breast infections, and fussy, restless babies. They may visit the mother and provide "hands on" assistance if they suspect that the baby is not latching on to the breast properly, an underlying cause for a range of problems.[12] League leaders, like feminist activists, aim to give women greater knowledge of their bodies (as Pam White had explained). They tread lightly, however, when it comes to actually prescribing or treating, as this can constitute practicing medicine without a license, a legal violation used in the 1970s to harass feminist activists (Zimmerman 1987: 459). To prescribe, moreover, violates the League's notion of "mother to mother" sup-

port, which should (as leaders explain) "empower the mother to make her own choices." Though this is similar to feminist goals for nondominating interactions (Zimmerman 1987: 456), the League probably would be less than fully supportive if a mother chose to abandon breastfeeding when confronted with problems. To be fair, however, this varies greatly; as some leaders do say, "*any* breastfeeding is great."

League counseling also works against widely held beliefs that *many* women are *physically* unable to nurse their babies. The two most commonly cited physical factors for this failure, insufficient milk and inverted nipples, actually have little direct relation to biology (that is, in a static or monocausal sense) (Van Esterik 1989: 126–29). La Leche leaders consider a range of social and psychological factors inter-twined with—even constructing, shaping—the physical body-as-body, and, in this practice, they move well beyond notions of fixed, essential femininity. Leaders will question the mother's household situation, whether she has good practical and emotional support, and disentangle remediable, unfixed physical problems, for example, en-gorgement that temporarily flattens or inverts the nipples. Leaders treat varied breast sizes and shapes as normal and suggest methods to ease babies' latch-on even if the mother has less prominent nipples. They also often suggest that the husband take over housework while the mother stays in bed with the baby, enjoying unscheduled sleeping and suckling, eating and drinking liberally. Rather than a fixed bio-logical trait, insufficient milk is caused by exhaustion, anxiety, infre-quent suckling, and a less nourished mother, all mutable conditions of cultural bodies.

Because of its positive, enabling body-work, feminist health groups developed some respect for the League, though it was at first only grudging. According to historian Lynn Weiner, the first issue of *Our Bodies, Ourselves* by the Boston Women's Health Book Collective recommended the League only "if you can get past the sickening stuff about a woman's role is to bear and raise kids" (1971: 111); the second edition was already more positive, saying that the League "will give you facts and confidence" but with a "philosophy different from ours" (1976: 312; Weiner 1994: 1377). In contrast, the twenty-fifth anniversary edition recommended seeking the League's assistance and expertise at least seven separate times, each without hesitation

(BWHBC 1992: 479–487). The feminist manual, indeed, advises consulting La Leche League "rather than relying on pediatricians," who are rarely "experienced and/or supportive enough of breast-feeding to be really helpful" (1992: 479).[13]

The League model of confidence in the maternal body rejects or at least revises the dominant medical metaphors analyzed cogently by anthropologist Emily Martin, of women's bodily processes as failed production, with female bodily secretions seen as evidence of waste and degeneration (1987).[14] If in Martin's terms the League does not represent full resistance because new key metaphors are lacking, it does make possible more positive experiences by rewriting the pro-duction metaphors. The words "use" and "useful" thus were com-mon in women's recounting of their changed body images. At one meeting, for example, a leader's remarks exemplified this positive no-tion of useful, productive, and positive maternal embodiment. She was a slight woman and acknowledged that she had long been dis-satisfied with her small breasts. Because it is such a common myth that small breasts are inadequate—another supposed fixed, biological cause of a mother's inability to nurse or to satisfy a baby's appetite, as well as to satisfy an adult male appetite as objects of the heterosexual gaze—she emphasized how transforming the experience of breast-feeding her two children had been: "I did not feel so good about my body before nursing. I feel my breasts have a *use* now and I have much more confidence in my body. My breasts are not just there for men!"

Later another mother told me in our one-to-one conversation: "The first La Leche meeting that I went to, a woman was talking about how her body image totally changed when she started breast-feeding, and she came to have a more positive image of her body. And I remember thinking, 'Wow! She's echoing my sentiments exactly.'"

According to this mother, we experience our breasts predomi-nantly as sex objects, objects to be looked at, and they almost never look right: "Our society is so moody in the way that breasts are viewed, and that's always bothered me. I really enjoy looking at my breasts as having *a use*. I like that a lot. . . . I would change the whole way society views a woman's body!"

Among the La Leche mothers I spoke with, fully half made em-

phatic comments that they felt more relaxed with, respectful of, or happier with their bodies since breastfeeding and becoming involved in the League.[15] One mother, Mary Vincent, spoke lightly: "[Breastfeeding] adds a sense of *usefulness* to your body. Your body's just a little shell. You hang around with it, you say 'yuck' at it once in a while because you don't like the shape of it. It's nice to give it a sense of purpose."

But another, Nicole Strickler, whose words I return to later in this chapter, spoke more eloquently: "Overall I think the nursing relationship has enhanced my sexuality in the sense of making me feel more comfortable and that my body is more valuable and beautiful in a way that I had not realized before."[16]

MOTHERING AND FATHERING

The exclusivity of embodied mothering and "complete" breastfeeding of course has implications, and limitations, for the place of fathers in childrearing. La Leche League has always emphasized the need for the father's involvement and particularly (as Marg Walters had recalled) for his support in childbirth. Originally the curriculum for League groups (of four rotating topics) included a meeting for fathers; however, this quickly became optional, with regular groups just for mothers and babies. Fathers have been welcome at conferences, where some panels are specifically aimed at them.[17] In addition, League publications devote space to "the Manly Art of Fathering."[18] The group, in its early days, cautioned fathers not to become too work-focused and, according to historian Weiner, prescribed a more domestic role for fathers than the dominant "organization man" of that postwar era (1994: 1373). Still, the League veered little from the ideal expressed by sociologist Talcott Parsons and other mid-century family experts.[19] The "Father as Provider and Protector," as the 1963 League manual depicted him, was outside (and above) the mother-baby dyad.[20] "For some time," it stated, "the baby's only need will be for the loving care of its mother" (LLLI 1963: 111), though wives needed encouragement (and occasional help with the dishes). By the 1980s, fatherhood was less clearly differentiated: "Husband and Wife [Become] a Parenting Team" and "Fathers Get Involved" (201, 195) the 1987 manual proclaimed while cautioning, "[i]n language that is irrefutable, biology makes it clear that the mother-baby relationship is primary" (195).

Such reinforcement of essential gender difference has become less coherent over time, but the League remains ambivalent about the entrance of fathers into exclusive, embodied mothering. This kind of divided, contradictory statement, for instance, is typical: "Although mothers do indeed have a *hormonal* head start . . . I believe fathers also have *natural* nurturing abilities" (LLLI 1987: 194; my emphasis).[21] League mothers I met found it hard to reconcile these conflicting scripts. Equality-inspired "parenting" became something of a media "buzzword" in the 1980s and '90s, as for example, with the 1987 launch of the magazine *Parenting*, which is "geared toward a more upscale" audience, to the "urban, dual-income family," compared to the more traditional *Parents* (Katz and Katz 1992: 256). The very term, however, detracts from the maternalist recognition of women's invisible caregiving and of breastfeeding itself.[22]

Psychologists who study and endorse shared-parenting, interestingly, caution against breastfeeding. Diane Ehrensaft found that among her group of equality-oriented mothers, a significant number stopped breastfeeding very early owing to resentments and anxieties aroused by its physical exclusivity (1990a: 37). Similarly, Cowan and Cowan counsel against complete breastfeeding as it discourages fathers' involvement (Cowan and Cowan 1992: 103–104). Nevertheless, at the statewide conference of the League which I attended, the organization's usual logo of mother with baby-at-the-breast was modified to include a triad of father, mother, and baby, with tee shirts that read "Parenting—a Proud Profession." League mothers I spoke with sometimes described attempts to draw fathers further into "parenting," but most also held on to a belief in a "natural" maternal advantage that recognized and honored their care:[23]

> Only a mother can give what a child needs, nobody else can, not even a father. A father can give almost as close, but only a mother can give what they really need.

> I hate to make gross generalizations that all women are just naturally more nurturing. But, I think, for the most part, that women *are* more nurturing than men.

> I think biologically men are just *not* as tuned in about little kids. Even a "Mr. Mom."

A member testimonial in the League magazine also exemplifies this desire to valorize mothers and maternal bodies: "Just a year ago I

thought that mothers and fathers were equally qualified to take care of infants . . . [but] [a]ny woman who is awake and aware during the birth of her child and who feeds the child from the substance of her own body cannot believe that her feelings for the child are the same as the father's" (Tamm, 1987).

Interestingly, late-century feminists have also become divided on such issues of how, or whether, to honor mothers and their corpo-reality. Such divisions were exacerbated by controversial surrogate mother cases, which so discounted the birth mothers' embodied experiences while overvaluing fathers' rights of ownership of the "child-product" (see Rothman 1989). In reaction, some feminists turned back to biological arguments, striking similar maternalist chords to the League's philosophy. They felt, according to one ana-lyst, a "desperate need to find a secure and defensible basis on which to reassert mothers' claims" against the dominance of fathers (Stan-worth 1990: 298). Others, however, feared the return of essentializing arguments based on women's biology and stuck doggedly to the need for egalitarian, noncorporeal claims and the goals of shared parenting (debate summarized in Rapping 1990). In this feminist debate, cul-tural and corporeal bodies tangle and collide, much as they do in the League's maternalist philosophy.

WORKING BODIES AND MOTHERS WHO WORK

One of the largest challenges faced by La Leche League has been the turn among white, middle-class mothers since the 1970s to wage-work outside the home. Because embodied motherhood emphasized being physically present, it was hard for the organization to accept new norms and practices. According to sociologist Laurel Richard-son, who studied La Leche League in the 1970s, many groups at that time ignored the existence of mothers working outside the home.[24] League publications contained some glimpses, with negative nods to feminism. In 1977, for example, one newsletter piece was entitled "Liberated as a Mother": "Feminists may be right when they strive for 'equal pay for equal work' and for better job opportunities for women. But as women gain self-esteem, they should take pride in the things only women can do . . . it's time we stop apologizing for being 'just a mother' " (in Halonen and Mohrbacher 1987: 20).[25]

By the 1980s, as significantly more mothers of young children

were out in the paid workforce, the question of how the organization should handle "working" mothers loomed larger. The third version of *The Womanly Art of Breastfeeding*, published in 1981, tackled the problem in print for the first time. One chapter asked: "Are You Thinking of Going Back to Work?" (LLLI 1981: 55) and endorsed mothers' needs for "a healthy sense of self-esteem, achievement, and self-confidence" (1981: 57); yet it recommended only very part-time or in-home wage-earning and cited child development experts of the Bowlbyist persuasion: "prolonged maternal separations cause distress to the child" (1981: 57–63). Later, buried in a chapter on "special circumstances" along with illness and disability, came this advice: "Our plea to any mother who is thinking about taking an outside job is, 'if at all possible, don't'" (1981: 271).

Rebecca Cross, a long-time League leader, explained that, like this old manual, leaders had been instructed to discourage women from returning to work. The organization had suggested leaders use questions like: "Have you thought of what your baby needs?" Leaders were also to steer the conversation, if mothers mentioned economic need, to suggestions for supplementing family income from home. Such moralistic questioning was, however, at odds with the objective of "mother-to-mother" warmth and support, as another longtime League leader explained. Gerry Kemp, a leader since about 1970, recalled:

> In the very, very beginning I would hear them [working mothers] talk and I would say, "no, no that's not right." I wanted to say things I had no business saying to them, to beg them to please stay home with that baby because I know what it means to the baby and I know my reality. But they [the leaders] knew, of course, that it wasn't going to be helpful to this mom to beg her to stay home.

Gerry explained that they began to merely ask, "Can you stay home a little longer?" and then to focus solely on breastfeeding, saying, "Come to our meetings to meet others who are doing it and they'll give you a lot of good tips. You'll need our support so please come." Rebecca Cross said similarly: "We do what we can" to "see that the baby is breastfed as much as possible when the mother *is* there." She added that she had never followed the more intolerant instructions: "I can remember getting into a big discussion and I said

'That's not the usual way that you counsel someone . . . how can we change our method of counseling when a woman calls just because she's going to work? It just doesn't seem right.'"

Gerry Kemp and Rebecca Cross each also rejected the authoritative approach because of its similarity to the medical model. Rebecca saw her purpose as encouraging the mother "to realize that she's the one in control . . . as opposed to telling her what to do . . . to make that woman feel good about the decision she's making and feel good about herself."

Gerry, in our separate conversation, said: "If your purpose is to give the baby back to the mother and to instill in her the confidence of her own [decisions], then you can't replace her doctor and say: 'Listen to ME!'"

Historian Weiner writes that by the mid-1980s the League's inclusion of working mothers was inconsistent, with at least some groups welcoming them; a 1984 survey found groups for working mothers in at least five states (1994: 1379). Many leaders, according to Rebecca Cross, moved from being "offend[ed]" to a "general softening," while those hardened against employed mothers eventually left the organization. Gerry Kemp stayed, and, like the national organization, came to downplay the distinction itself: "the mothering effort is there, and we are more sisters than not."

Such a "softening" certainly made sense when over half of the mothers of infants were returning to the workplace nationwide (and the percentage of the League's main constituency of white middle-class mothers was even higher). It also, however, led to greater incoherence in the core ideal of "good mothering through breastfeeding."[26] Take, for example, the League publication *Of Cradles and Careers: A Guide to Reshaping Your Job to Include a Baby in Your Life* (Lowman 1984). Its title sounds an approving note and it includes nonjudgmental statements that echo a feminist rhetoric of self-determination: "Our respect for the uniqueness of each individual woman includes recognizing that it is each woman's right to determine what is best for herself and her family" (1984: 248).[27] Yet this awkward embrace of a plurality of choices is contradicted a surprising number of times. Just two pages later, the author writes that to put a baby on the "back burner" to pursue a career is "to tamper with one of the most fundamental and basic elements of human *nature*" (1984:

251; my emphasis). But the book's emphasis on workplace change surprises yet again. The many anecdotes or vignettes about mothers negotiating longer maternity leaves, flexible schedules, job-sharing, and on-site care options, as well as those bringing lawsuits against recalcitrant employers (some with League assistance), suggest that it might be the social context for mothering that most requires attention.

The 1987 fourth edition of *The Womanly Art of Breastfeeding* had been further "softened" from the 1981 edition, with a new chapter of practical advice for employed nursing mothers. Embodied motherhood was blurred by advice on expressing, pumping, and storing breastmilk, and on how to find substitute caregivers. Featured stories began to recognize economic need: "I knew I had *no choice* but to return to work shortly after Laura's birth, although I would have dearly loved to stay home with her" (LLLI 1987: 162, my emphasis; 1991 same). The next chapter, however, is entitled "Making a Choice," and it shows a lurking, harder intolerance. It includes boldface headings such as "Separation Brings Anxiety" and "Does it Pay to Work?" which instruct that women's "choices" in favor of employment may be misguided (1987: 179, 181; 1991 same). As in *Cradles and Careers*, the League's stance becomes most incoherent with the term "choice," which is so crucial a measure of both middle-class and feminist self-determination.

I found just one League mother among those I met who spoke more coherently and negatively against employed mothers. Jane Lensky nonetheless carefully distinguished between her role as a League representative and her own views as a mother of four: "I accept as a La Leche League leader, when I'm wearing that hat, I accept each mom 'where she's at.' My personal feelings can be a little bit different. And La Leche League allows you to do that. We just don't pronounce that at meetings. But I don't like it that moms go back to work."[28]

Recently accredited leaders were more tolerant though less coherent than Jane Lensky. Liz Davenport spoke thoughtfully in our several-hour interview-conversation about her own experiences. She had initially intended to continue her career in high-income real-estate sales after her first child's birth. In her account of events, she had changed her mind only at the very last minute: "I did love my job . . . it was a conflict the whole time I was pregnant." But finally, she stated,

Nursing really influenced me because you do have those hormones that kick in, and when that baby cries, that baby is crying for *you.* So, yes, I guess I am very strongly opinionated about [using other caregivers]! But you know, I have friends that do it, and I think their daycare arrangements are great, and I think their children are nice. I'm not trying to condemn people who do it differently . . . I'm not for martyring women and making them stay home and be miserable!

With this tension between two core tenets—to provide nonjudgmental, "mother to mother" support ("to support the mother where she's at") and to be the moral voice that "speak[s] for the baby" as well as for "those [maternal] hormones"—Liz Davenport explained her own uneasy balance: "They [employed mothers] want me to tell them that it will be okay for their baby. . . . And they want me to tell them what they're doing is the right thing. . . . But I obviously don't feel it's the right thing for *me* . . . [though the League] wants to encourage them, they're definitely not applauding."

The youngest leader I met, Rory Gerardo, was also the most positive about wage-earning mothers. In her late twenties, Rory identified herself as an employed mother, though this was on a flexible, freelance basis: "I don't know exactly [how many] but I know that some of the mothers do work. I know I do. I didn't advertise the fact, but everybody in my group knows that I am [employed] . . . it would have been out of line for them to question it because I do believe in mother-baby togetherness, and I try to do that as much as I can."[29]

Rory became a League leader just as the official position, that employed mothers should *not* be leaders, became controversial.[30] Gerry Kemp remembered several big arguments, with much at stake, for leaders were the role models, the model mothers:

Did that hit the fan! . . . If you're going to be a leader and you are going to represent this organization, you have to buy these concepts. That's fair isn't it? It doesn't matter if it's moms coming to you for help. You just help them and love them to pieces. But if you're *representing* us, you have to buy all this packaged stuff.

After a "big blow-up" over this issue, the national organization did revise one of its ten "concepts," the core slogans that condense the League's philosophy and guide its leaders (Merrill 1987: 226–227). From "the baby needs the mother's presence early and often," according to Gerry Kemp, the concept was changed to "the baby's need

for mother remains as intense, even though the mother's needs may be different." "We call it the working mom concept," she told me. Gerry also explained, "If you want to be a leader, you have to believe that moms and babies have to be together when the babies are small. Do you have to *do* it? Yes, at least for a while." Rory Gerardo acknowledged to me that when she applied she had minimized her employment because the League role model was to have "no regularly scheduled separations from her baby," but one year after being accredited, Rory increased her employed hours to between twenty and thirty each week. League officials in the 1990s well might approve, however, knowing the details and having vaguer definitions of "regularly scheduled" and the age of the "baby": Rory Gerardo's son was nearly three when she increased her hours; he was cared for by his grandmothers during her fluctuating work hours; and he played quietly or napped while she completed paperwork at home. Rory planned to cut back if she had another baby, which she went on to do, having her second child, a girl, about a year and a half after our initial meeting.

League officials, at least at regional and state levels, likely remained familiar with Rory's situation through on-going communication, leader gatherings, and conferences, but the most thorough scrutiny of role models does occur during the initial leader application process. That process begins with a recommendation from the local group. Counseling and staffing the phone lines are labor-intensive and unpaid, so leaders usually are in need of good prospects, though, ironically, such volunteer work itself competes with a baby's needs. Although some mothers like Marg Walters took the initiative to suggest becoming leaders, others like Liz Davenport were flattered when it was suggested to them. These prospects, either way, become "core" mothers who attend meetings and the evaluations that follow,[31] and take on other group chores (serving as treasurer or librarian, running fund-raising garage or bake sales, etc.) until they have been attending and breastfeeding their babies successfully for one year. Certification then involves individual scrutiny, as the applicant writes up a long account of her marriage, pregnancy, birth, and breastfeeding experiences, and her philosophy of mothering, as well as any past and present paid-work experiences. She is asked to provide reactions to books from the League catalog and to correspond with a regional leader, who screens to be sure the applicant agrees with League tenets. Prospects are also screened for personal troubles that might affect their ca-

pacity to support others. If the regional leader is satisfied, the applicant goes on to learn counseling techniques and to research the most
common questions. This training emphasizes both practical information about the body and the empathic listening skills for "mother
to mother" support.[32]

MOTHERHOOD AS A CLASS-ENHANCING PROJECT
The Struggling and Secure Middle Class
As in earlier historical eras, motherhood for the middle class, and the
aspiring middle class, has an aspect that is bound up with status or cultural capital production. Mothering in the best expert-advised fashion demonstrates membership and reinforces class boundaries against
those both above and below.[33] In the era of rising industry, for instance, the middle class wanted boundaries from both the "idle rich"
and the "ignorant" or "unproductive" lower classes; they wanted
their children to be instilled with self-discipline and to acquire the
proper "upstanding" demeanor to ensure their future success through
hard work (see Hays 1996). Since the '50s, rather than focusing on discipline, class-enhancing mothering has focused on the attentive promotion of the child's inner-life (so-called "permissive parenting") as
well as on the display of the husband-father's achievements, talents,
and efforts. Contemporary anxieties as we approach the year 2000
may strengthen desires for boundaries and status produced *against* others. The boundaries between middle-class mothers' attentiveness and
rich and poor mothers' busyness outside the home have eroded, or
even reversed, and may no longer serve as reassurance of middle class
membership or of a secure future for one's children.

Some League mothers expressed confusion about just what to do.
Two whom I spoke with exemplified the conflict for those less se-
curely middle class. Each had assumed that they would be quickly
back to work after their babies were born, and this was not merely an
economic matter but one of "choice." They were, after all, college-
educated women with many years in the workforce and careers they
really cared about. But each found that combining embodied motherhood with work outside the home was more than they had bargained for. It was certainly much more difficult than all the glib advice
they had consumed (like that described in the previous chapter). Teresa Jankowski recounted: "When [my daughter] was three months
old I was going to go back part time, that was my big plan . . . And I

tried to go back . . . I went three weeks and . . . I was just torn apart! So I went three weeks and then quit for two years!"

Employment conditions threatened breastfeeding in the case of each of these mothers. Teresa, a medical technician, explained that she worked: "patient, patient, patient, one right after the other," with no breaks in which to express or pump milk. After three weeks of painful engorgement back at work, her milk supply dropped off sharply, and she quit her job rather than risk having "insufficient milk." There was, therefore, a literal aspect to Teresa's claim of being "torn apart": in addition to the physical pain of engorgement (which can be intense), working conditions threatened her breastfeeding relationship. One League-sponsored survey of 567 employed breastfeeding mothers found, in fact, that 85 percent expressed milk during the working day, many up to three times per day.[34] In contrast, most women's work environments, like Teresa's, do not offer the flexibility and time needed for regular pumping (e.g., Glass 1990; Glass and Camarigg 1992). Although mothers' attempts to breast*feed* at work— with the baby brought in—have been problematic, with harassment, job dismissals, and lawsuits (Lowman 1984, also see Bonavoglia 1983), sometimes employers also refuse to allow breast-*pumping* (see Foreman 1998).

Even for Kay Chavez, a professional with greater workplace autonomy and a more generous maternity leave, the spatial and temporal distances between home and work directly conflicted with a baby who wanted frequent, round-the-clock nursing:

> Because I was gone 11 hours a day (with my commute), I decided that I wouldn't go back to work . . . I just wasn't going to be gone away that long . . . They give you six months maternity leave and they hold your position for you. And then you have to come back. I had requested an extension and they said no. And then I asked if I could go to work part time, and they said no. And so then I said, "Well, I guess I am not coming back."[35]

When I met Kay and Teresa, it was about two and a half years later, and each was still breastfeeding and attending League meetings. Kay had weaned her first daughter but had gone on to have a second, and was breastfeeding at home full time. Teresa was nursing her toddler and had just returned to part-time work after her short-lived early attempt. In fact, the two had become friends through the League, and

Teresa had turned to Kay for childcare; such exchanges, I learned, were not uncommon among League mothers.[36] Kay was also fairly relaxed about Teresa's choice and commented, "I'm pretty much 'live and let live.'"[37]

Another daycare-providing League mother, Pam White, expressed a more negative evaluation of this exchange. Though Pam declared that she enjoyed earning money (she laughed happily about "my little paycheck"), she also stated that caring for her neighbor's son (just two days a week) compromised her own embodied mothering (of her daughter) and was hard on the boy. "I feel it's not fair for him to watch someone else nursing when his mommy's gone."[38] Interestingly, Pam, who had had only a high-school education and low-status jobs, might have been seeking greater status from her mothering than Kay was, as she lacked other sources. She spoke of deeply regretting her earlier mothering style (a more controlling style associated with the working class) before she began breastfeeding and joined the League; she also felt that at least one of her Caesarean sections had been unnecessary and blamed herself for her lack of knowledge. She ended our conversation by bringing up feelings of low self-esteem that had recently led her to seek professional psychotherapy.

Paradoxically, Teresa Jankowski, the out-of-the-home mother of the three, was the most intolerant and relied on a stricter interpretation of the crucial middle-class measure of "choice."

> I would not enforce my opinion on others as far as whether they should stay home. . . . I would just encourage her to read and investigate because there are things that help you stay at home that are not always out-in-front to people these days in the mad rush to the money-bank.

Though the 1990s League supports mothers "where they're at," Teresa invokes a stronger status boundary between herself and mothers who "rush to the money-bank" and, according to another League tenet, fail to "put people before things." Employed mothers, from Teresa's perspective, only think they lack "choice" because of their inability to resist a rampant consumerist culture.[39] Like the League itself, Teresa ignores the dramatically widened gap between the cost of living and the breadwinning wages of many men.

League publications still advise ways to cut expenses so that the husband-father's can be the sole "family wage": "natural foods" are more wholesome and cheaper; mothers can bake from "scratch" and

have a vegetable garden; they can buy at garage sales, or even move to smaller homes or become childcare providers. The "Home Business Section" of the League's magazine continues to offer free advertising space to support mothers' small income-generating endeavors, and booths at the state conventions sell such handicrafts. Some mothers believed, as one told me, "So much of what I see of two-income families, it's to get so many extras they don't really need!" Teresa Jankowski was thus understandably defensive about her lack of "choice" and the reality of her family's economic constraints. When I spoke with her in her home, as at the meetings where I first met her, she struggled to make clear that she *had tried* to follow League advice. She had joined a food co-op and had baked her own bread. Still she exclaimed: "it's *really* just financial need, we have pressing financial need!"

Teresa's defensiveness, however, was multilayered and confused. It stemmed from the League's blindness to economic change,[40] but it also stemmed from her resentment of (and the often popular prejudice against) affluent, employed mothers; if they have the "choice" to remain at home but don't, then they are *selfish*.[41] Indeed, even routine jobs offer women an escape from domestic isolation and the symbolic value of (as Pam White quipped) "my little paycheck." Teresa, in fact, wanted these selfish intangibles, though she expressed great status-anxiety and could ill afford to compromise her class-enhancing mothering. With her blue-collar husband's earnings dropping to $30,000, the family was going into debt—yet beyond earnings, Teresa spoke of how deeply she had identified as a "career person." Full-time motherhood with the intensity of on-demand breastfeeding, had been, she stated, "a very big shock."[42] At one meeting, as mothers shared what was most surprising about becoming a mother, Teresa had boomed out: "How hard it was to figure out who I was!" In spite of these longings for autonomy, however, Teresa emphasized exclusive mothering: "I think in the League there's a deep commitment to putting the child first . . . and I need to go back and be reminded and supported. [League meetings] are like a shot in the arm. . . . And that all ties in with my struggle of working or not working and my image of myself as a mother."

Teresa's feelings about her husband were also mixed up in these class-based resentments and anxieties, and epitomize one outcome of the large-scale economic restructuring occurring in the United States: "I grew up with a lot of nice things, and it's real hard because

of the man I married that I have had to do with a lot less . . . [I had] that idea, you know, that the husband is supposed to bring home *all* the bacon."

Teresa went on to tell me that the couple faced "serious marital problems." Their modest ranch home seemed to display this, with its large but unfinished addition. When I arrived for our appointment, I complimented her on the remodeling and remarked that it would be impressive when completed. She snickered because the project had dragged on for years, awaiting her husband's attention and requiring his increased earnings.

Kay Chavez's white-collar husband earned about $40,000 annually, and, in contrast to the Jankowskis' debt, the Chavez family was able to manage from "paycheck to paycheck."[43] Kay, however, expected she would need to work outside the home at some not-too-distant point, for her part-time daycare earnings were minimal. Kay spoke of day-to-day financial worries: "When I get back from shopping he'll say, 'Did we really need these cookies?'" "Anytime we ever have a fight, it's always about money!" At the same time, status was also a sensitive issue, for Kay's husband chafed when she gave their daughters "used" toys purchased at garage sales. In fact, such shared, sharply mixed feelings about class-enhancing motherhood, status-anxiety, and economic constraints, had drawn Kay to Teresa: "I went to this meeting and poured my heart out . . . We're having difficulty, not only with nursing, but I was in shock! What had I done? . . . I had been working my whole life and all of a sudden I am tied down to this little baby! . . . The room was quiet, but then Teresa spoke of feeling the same."

Even quite affluent League mothers, like Liz Davenport, whose husband earned $100,000 annually (the high-end outlier of those I met), found full-time, breastfeeding motherhood to require a new identity that was far from any romanticized image:

> It's like if you're forced to be in a room with somebody for a long period of time, you either kill each other, or you end up probably getting this bond. I think that . . . motherhood . . . it's indoctrination by fire, with the whole purpose that you're forced to forge a strong connection with this kid.

Many La Leche mothers shared this less-than-romantic image. One mother of two commented in our conversation: "Women have returned to the workforce in greater numbers because it's more fun.

I'm trying to think what the last fun day I had was!" Such a view does combat the devaluation of women's private caregiving—but it also reinforces the "selfish" image of the mother who goes out into the public world.[44]

In spite of some mothers' resentments, most of the League mothers I met expressed more "prochoice" views and did not condemn others to elevate their maternal status. Like Kay Chavez, they seemed to reject judging other mothers simply on the basis of employment outside the home.[45] As Rebecca Cross, one of the long-time leaders, aptly explained: "If a woman *needs* to go back to work, she needs to go back, for *any reason*. Who's to say I wouldn't be doing the same thing if I were her? . . . La Leche League still believes that mothers and babies should be together, but we live in the real world."

Mommy Wars and Cautionary Tales

I found it intriguing that women in situations as disparate as those of Liz Davenport, comfortable and secure on her husband's income, and Teresa Jankowski, struggling to cover car and house payments, could find a shared haven in the League. Though all would be considered middle class,[46] those above and below the group's halfway mark (that is, the median, which was about $45,000 in annual family income) evidenced pronounced differences. All the families owned their own homes, an important benchmark, but they varied from a mobile home, to modest ranch homes in need of repairs, to large new, designer homes with gleaming cathedral ceilings. Also, some mothers spoke of having paid domestic help, while others had little beyond occasional assistance from family members. Although I did not ask directly, I would speculate that the secure versus struggling families differed in their ratio of debt to savings and the extent of any family "safety net." In spite of these divides, however, in the League the two groups of mothers had forged a tentative alliance.

For struggling mothers, League maternalism offered solace for dampened aspirations, while sharing with the secure mothers the same escape from domestic isolation and reassurance of a superior method of childrearing. Anne Held, a struggling college-educated mother of two young girls, expressed such feelings as we sat in her cozy living room. Her husband had only a two-year degree and earnings similar to Teresa's husband. Recently she had begun to work some evenings to earn a little extra and to get *out*:

> When I was home [with my first baby], I counted the days until the next
> meeting . . . Like one of the big things was not working at all . . . Even
> though there's days when I think "God, I wish I had a job!" . . . The
> women that I knew through the League . . . they were all giving up in-
> come too. I mean, none of us have a whole lot, we live from paycheck to
> paycheck, and sometimes we don't even make it. . . . We all have this com-
> mon bond because we just don't have the same kinds of material things.

Though Anne seems to speak *only* for the struggling middle class,
affluent women spoke in a similar way and included themselves in the
"bond" against an overly consumerist culture. Liz Davenport spoke,
for example, of her own transition out of the paid work force: "You're
not bringing home that paycheck, and then you can't say, 'Well, let's
go off and have a vacation.' You're using coupons for the first time in
your life, that kind of thing. It's a real change!" Ignoring such substantial differences in husbands' earnings might seem to trivialize the
strains felt by struggling League mothers. Nonetheless, I found such
talk quite common. Gerry Kemp also had a high-earning husband
who decided to take a "less stressful" job, "sacrificing" an income of
$95,000 for a $65,000 annual salary. Although she still had over twice
the household income of Teresa or Anne, Gerry commented:

> We've got to get beyond the money! I mean, when a mom goes out and
> they buy a house premised on two $40,000 incomes, she says "I have no
> choice." So you said living in [the better suburb] is more important than
> being with your kids! We've had people in our group who sell their
> houses in the suburbs, buy this little dinky house . . . when they realized
> the baby was coming. We're all consuming so much, and we assume that's
> our God-given right! . . . We [*sic*] just changed jobs, so we don't have that
> kind of income either . . . so I'm just using all my old skills that I had
> grown rusty with.

Sometimes in meetings when the incipient resentment of struggling mothers threatened to disrupt (that is, *because* their struggles
were not distinctly recognized), leaders diffused this with their "up-
beat" response. Leaders are instructed in the training process to repeat
or restate what a mother has said so that she feels heard while highlighting something encouraging and positive. In one meeting I attended, several mothers, clearly in secure homes with professional
spouses, shared tips for getting dads to help with night feedings and to

bond with their babies. Then Cathy Seeley, whose husband worked most nights—and who, I learned when I visited, lived in a mobile home park—broke in: "My husband is into that *Great Provider* thing! So he took a second job so that I can stay home . . . But I wish he was home for *me*, and to hold this little one [their two-month-old son] so I could have *five minutes* to myself! [Sometimes] he does take our older boy, like to wash his car and that kind of stuff. *But . . .*"

At this point, the leader (Rory Gerardo) broke in. She quickly redirected Cathy's palpable anger with the positive, even perky response: "So he gives you space to mother?" Surely, however, Cathy's anger had been provoked by the affluent mothers who spoke of having providers *and* teammates in their more comfortable mothering spaces.[47]

La Leche leaders also diffuse incipient hostility between struggling and secure middle-class mothers by aiming it at targets outside group boundaries. They redraw the basis for in-group solidarity, and at the same time help themselves to be receptive and encouraging to mothers who come to the League. Although this is not a conscious strategy, possible "Mom versus Mom" or "Mommy Wars" resentments about which mothers "really" need paychecks are diffused when the worst mothers, the truly bad mothers, are placed outside the League entirely.[48] Most of the leaders I spoke with told cautionary tales of the "Bad Yuppie Mothers" who embrace their careers, work long hours, use extensive daycare, and, worst of all, do not breastfeed. This "Bad Yuppie Mother," a mythlike "antimother" (see Tsing 1990), would never seek their maternalist support.

In Jane Lensky's telling of the cautionary tale, the redirection of class-based resentment outside the League was obvious. With her husband earning just slightly more than Anne's, the family clung to their quaint farmhouse. But it was increasingly encroached on by subdivisions of new, more expensive homes.

> There are some very dedicated women who really, *really* believe in La Leche League philosophy, but for some reason, *have to* work outside the home . . . But I would never like to see a mom who lives over here [pointing across the street] in these new homes and goes to work every day just to pay for the house . . . they must have a lot bigger house than I do! I wouldn't *choose to* live there if I couldn't afford it on my husband's salary!

Later in our conversation, Jane crucially added this emblematic story of her sister-in-law:

> She was never there when her children were young, she worked all the time. She did not believe in getting up with her child at night. They were all bottle-fed, and . . . she would put four bottles of Tang in the corners of the crib, and turn on her radio, and sleep through it all . . . And these children have monumental problems!

Leaders who were quite affluent, from their husbands' salaries alone, used a similar tactic to Jane's, praising employed mothers who had sought out the League, but describing the Bad Yuppie Mothers who reject the group and its philosophy of embodied motherhood. Liz Davenport praised women who had come to their group who "had worked since the child was six weeks old who are success stories because they nurse their babies at night . . . and to me that is fantastic . . . these women should be given gold medals." Yet when she spoke of "Tracy," her "ex-friend" from her previous fast-track life in real-estate sales, her tone was very different:

> They have their cars, they have their house, they have their kid. . . . I finally asked Tracy, "You went away the last four weekends, and you leave your child at daycare all day, and you use a babysitter many weeknights, so when do you spend time with your child?" She said, "I can't help it . . . we need to get away because she just drives us nuts," which answered my question, you know!

What finally made "Tracy" the emblematic antimother, however, was her disgust with breastfeeding and its embodied, intimate aspect: "Tracy had never nursed. . . . My son hit nine months and she came over and she looked at me and said 'Are you going to nurse until he goes off to college?'"

Trish Kreiser, another League leader of the upper-middle class, also carefully distinguished between employed League mothers and the Bad Mothers who are out there.

> We had a woman I thought worked it out so well! She has two twelve-hour shifts when her husband is home with the baby so she doesn't have to worry about any caregiver, and then she has four nights off . . . it's great . . . There's another who's going back to work four hours a day and her baby's tiny, only nine weeks old, and she's terrified. We had to give her a lot

of reassurance, and I suggested she go to an evening meeting because you'll meet more of the working moms there. We've had a few who have worked full-time and breastfed, and that's worked out great—you just have to work a little harder at it.

Trish, interestingly, had used breast pumps extensively when her own son was born prematurely, and offered employed mothers support for their efforts to pump during the workday. But later in our conversation, her encouraging tone changed:

> I'm pretty negative to people who just want to dump their kids off and go to work eight hours a day. I have a cousin who's like that. She's the epitome of the yuppie. They live in a real expensive house and they drive expensive cars and they've got the Rolex watches . . . And she will sit there in her office and talk to you on the phone and say: "I just feel like I'm missing [my daughter's] growing up." She's got this Mexican maid that doesn't even speak English, she's taking care of the kid . . . Even when she's not working, she's off doing something.

In contrast to such "Bad Mothers," the three League mothers I spoke with who were fully sharing breadwinners were, like the "success stories" the leaders described, very committed breastfeeders. Two (Mary Vincent and Debra Milstein) used breast pumps extensively and rushed home to nurse each evening. The third (Marg Walters) had remained at home for over two years, and then had continued nursing nights and weekends until her child was four. These atypical League mothers might be accepted as "really" needing full-time paychecks with husbands earning in the $20,000 to $30,000 range, but actually each seemed happily career-identified. Both Debra and Marg felt overwhelmingly positive toward the League, with Marg continuing as a part-time leader, and Debra commenting, "It's a wonderful organization . . . I am with it a hundred percent [because] it's just like the Baby League!" Only Mary Vincent, a professional educator, expressed some hesitation. Though she credited the League with bringing her the wonderful experience of long-term nursing, she complained that as a "working mother," "I feel like a minority."[49]

According to historian Weiner, the League has been concerned that mothers like Mary might feel marginalized. National officials have cautioned against "overzealous," "holier than thou" attitudes,

and, as early as 1968, some stated that the working or bottlefeeding mother was not "beyond the pale" (Weiner 1994: 1373).[50] Thirty years later—with the normalization of maternal employment—this caution is taken deeply to heart. Yet, as the leaders' storytelling indicates, some mothers are still "beyond the pale": those who work extensively outside the home *and* bottlefeed, thus rejecting the League's belief in the embodied, physical exclusivity of the mother-baby relationship. Indeed, the cautionary tales have perhaps become more extreme as once clearly marked boundaries between good and bad mothers have blurred, and many mothers who work also want well-working bodies. As a result, the "Bad Mother" not only works outside the home, she sleeps when her babies cry in the night. She withholds mother's milk and offers only Tang. She leaves her child with "strangers" and is almost never home. She engages in "conspicuous consumption"—the cars, the Rolexes—and treats her child as merely another high-status possession. The Bad Yuppie Mother in this sense inverts (or even perverts) the status-enhancing devotion to and investment in the child's inner life. League mothers can approve of some range of differences among women, but they deplore mothers who literally reject the embodied intimacy as well as the intensive attention-giving. Bad Yuppie Mother stories may be read as condemning employed, nonbreastfeeding mothers; but I think they should also be read more subtly, as complex tales of middle-class anxieties and tensions, and of the tug of war between the maternal body-as-body and as symbolic class-enhancing resource.

PUBLIC AND PRIVATE MOTHERHOOD
Drawing the Boundary

Although the privacy of motherhood and the maternal body are often assumed among the contemporary white middle class, their public-ness becomes visible when controversies arise over who can or should be encouraged to mother, with what resources or technologies, and whether women (and which women) may gain greater autonomy over their reproductive choices. In the early part of the century, maternalist reformers were centrally involved in such issues and assumed both that motherhood should be a public concern—with those in the white middle class setting a model for the assimilation of the less fortunate—and that the public and the state needed the involvement of

those model mothers. As one leading reformer wrote: "Home is not contained within the four walls of an individual home. Home is the community. The city full of people is the Family . . . And badly do the Home and Family . . . need their mother."[51]

The present-day maternalists in La Leche League, who equally value women's motherly virtues, have a more limited notion of extending those virtues into the public world. They place a firm boundary around activism to promote "good mothering through breast-feeding" and prohibit any other public voice. The organization in fact requires leaders to have a single-issue focus and respect this distinction. As one leader told me, "the League is very careful to stay out of politics."

Though La Leche League's maternalistic philosophy is more restricted or privatized than the maternalism of the reformers in the early twentieth century, it shares a similar uneasy relation to feminism and feminist movements.[52] League mothers do see themselves as critics of U.S. culture, its cold focus on money and consumption, and its devaluation of care and nurture; and, in this sense, League maternalism meshes with strands of feminist discourse, most notably the cultural feminism of Carol Gilligan (1982). At the same time, many League mothers reject identification with feminism and see it as competing rather than meshing with maternalism:

> I'm not sure they [feminists] really did all that much because I still pretty much believe in the traditional . . . [but] I really think that we're moving in a sad direction in this country. Production is nice, but . . . some little infant is not going to care whether there's a new bomber being built! So I'd like to see more women in politics . . . but then I have this conflict with myself, well, do I think Mom should be home with the kids?

> When you say feminist, my first reaction is real negative, which is unusual coming from [me]. I've always been in a men's working environment [engineering] and I'm sure that some of that was made easier because of the quote-unquote feminist movement . . . but I think the feminist movement tends to be trying to be like men.

> I was very pro the feminist movement before I got pregnant . . . [but] I disagree with the women's movement because it has devalued mothering, it devalued raising human beings . . . we have a society which is dehumanized, we value the work ethic over the mothering ethic.

Gerry Kemp, one of the long-time leaders I spoke with, was unusual in seeing only a deep compatibility between feminism and maternalism.[53] Unlike subsequent generations, her initial activism in La
Leche developed in the context of the Sixties' social movements:

> I was marching against the [Vietnam] war, I was boycotting grapes, and I
> was doing La Leche League. I was just vital. And people would say,
> "Aren't you bored being at home?" . . . [but] my husband called *me* for
> the news . . . I was a charter subscriber to *Ms. Magazine,* and I belonged to
> NOW right from the beginning. All of this was so exciting! . . . I did *not*
> take that as being representative of the feminist movement, that which
> seemed to say "You aren't worth anything unless you are getting an out-
> side paycheck." I felt that it was not liberation to adopt the male value
> system.

Outside of this social movement context, only Nicole Strickler, a
younger mother and leader, identified herself as a feminist, and she
was more critical than Gerry Kemp. Nicole saw the League as a better
form of activism, closer to the real needs of women and children:

> I consider myself a really strong feminist, more since I have been a
> mother, believe it or not . . . [but] the feminist movement has failed
> women because it has not allowed us to be successful at things that are
> ours.

I then asked her, "But you still identify yourself as a feminist?"
"Yeah, I just think we haven't gone far enough!"
Nicole was also the only League mother I spoke with who identified with politics and with being political in the 1990s (when even
Gerry Kemp's activism had faded). She had recently volunteered to
lead League groups in an inner-city area and observed that this "outreach" had not been particularly successful: "I feel more politicized in
my League efforts . . . [but] one of the most admirable things about
the League [its single-issue focus] is also one of the most frustrating
. . . Stronger action needs to be taken [for low-income mothers]!"

Clearly, more mothers like Gerry and Nicole were involved in La
Leche League twenty-five or thirty years ago, when the League appealed to the broader "return to nature" ethos and alternative movement culture (see chapter 2). According to historian Weiner, however, the belief in breastfeeding's singular importance kept the League
from broadening its agenda when new members wanted to bring in

environmental politics, home schooling, and abortion politics; from the organization's point of view, such issues threatened to dilute their message and make some mothers feel unwelcome (1994: 1375).[54] La Leche League restricted its public agenda to such an extent that it *even* stayed out of the Nestle boycott against unscrupulous corporate promotion of infant formula and discouragement of breastfeeding in the Third World. Anthropologist Van Esterik notes that the Canadian League refused to display brochures of the major boycott group, INFACT, at its conferences, and that in the United States the INFACT mailing list showed just one local La Leche group (1989: 102, 78).

Some League women I spoke with still had Sixties-influenced interests in home schooling, homeopathy, and environmental politics,[55] but, as I observed at meetings, these interests provoked others' irritation. Though some local groups allowed mothers to air such views at "extracurricular" meetings, at regular meetings they were to restrain themselves and make clear that their views were not the organization's. And if a mother was seen as unable to exercise restraint, she was discouraged from applying for leadership. Anne Held, for example, had been involved in her local group for four years and was committed to complete breastfeeding, yet she told me she could not become a leader. She felt the leaders did not sufficiently appreciate her critical views of the U.S. medical and food industries, nor her advocacy of vegan diets, homeopathic and herbal remedies, or her strong belief in home birthing.

Although the League's desire to stay out of such fringe issues may be understandable, the lack of support for family policies in the context of widespread work/family conflict surprised me. Maternalist reform policies in Western Europe, after all, have included generous maternity (and sometimes, paternity) leave policies with income replacement, family allowances or mothers' pensions, publicly subsidized childcare, on- or near-site workplace nurseries, workplace flexibility, breastfeeding breaks, and "mothers' hours" programs. Intriguingly, though the early-century maternalist agenda in the United States was limited to public health and mothers' pensions, European-style expansive reforms were endorsed in the League's book *Of Cradles and Careers* (Lowman 1984). Such family policies appear straightforward for an organization devoted to "good mothering through breastfeeding" and extend easily from the League's moral rhetoric: "we speak for the baby" and "the baby's need for the mother

remains intense", might powerfully voice such demands, while "put people before things" might be an excellent slogan for increased public and corporate funding. Such reforms, moreover, were spoken of with enthusiasm by League mothers when I asked individually.[56] Historian Weiner finds mention of policies like mothers' pensions in the League as far back as 1979 (1994: 1379), yet, to date, the organization has taken no formal political stance. It has assisted, however, in some individual lawsuits against employers (see LLLI 1986, Lofton and Gotsch 1983). Perhaps the lack of League identification with the women's movement discourages more formal action, since this would invite alliances with explicitly feminist groups. Also, the League's lack of public maternalism may reflect its middle-class standpoint, as those public policies which now most strictly enforce mother-baby separation involve the welfare "reform" that targets poor mothers.

Blurring the Boundary

Despite its emphasis on privatized motherhood, there have been moments when La Leche League became formally involved in public disputes. These have been moments in which grave threats to embodied mothering and the physicality of breastfeeding flared up. It may be that the group can more easily speak when public intrusions on private mothering appear as singular events rather than persistent, embedded social problems.

The League became overtly public during a singular environmental crisis, for instance. In 1976–77 in the state of Michigan, PBB (polybrominated biphenyl), a highly toxic fire retardant that had accidentally contaminated animal feed, was discovered to have entered the food chain and, as a result, human milk. PBB was found in the milk of 90 percent of the mothers tested, despite the earlier destruction of contaminated cattle and chickens, millions of tainted eggs, and thousands of gallons of cow's milk. Alarms were also sounded because PCB, a related toxic from industrial dumping, was discovered in breastmilk along with the PBB. Reports on the safety of breastfeeding were ambiguous and conflicted: officials admitted a lack of knowledge but advised nursing mothers to continue.[57] At least one "recognized national authority on PBB," however, denounced the recommendation and cited the potential role of the compound as a carcinogen (Chen and Bullard 1976).[58] The League was called on by the press, and, through their phone lines, by many distraught moth-

ers. The organization took a reassuring stance, that the benefits of nursing outweighed the risks. This may have been foolish, representing their blind faith in the importance of breastfeeding and the maternal body; but it can also be interpreted as a resistive, critical stance, as a public affirmation that mothers' bodies were not the main cause of harm or the primary danger. During the crisis, the League's size in the state increased rapidly, and their suggestion that cow-milk formulas were unlikely to be pristine seemed to come from clear-sightedness rather than blindness. After all, the press reported that only 9 of 140 mothers tested (about 6.5 percent) were found to have PBB levels *higher* than those allowed in cow's milk.[59] Gerry Kemp, the long-time leader, recounted:

> When PBB hit, oh God! PBB hit like a, just like a brick wall. And here they were saying, "that means our whole city is contaminated, it is dangerous for mothers to nurse." Well, you know, as a bunch of liberated, intelligent people that La Leche people are, we go, "wait a minute! Are you saying that Battle Creek where Gerber is made is not contaminated? That's cattle country."[60]

La Leche League in the last decade has also become formally involved in a very different, ostensibly private issue, that of divorce. The organization became involved when mothers facing awards of paternal or joint custody, or even liberal visitation that threatened their breastfeeding relationships, came to them for help.[61] One national leader explained why they established the Legal Associates Program:

> It's just horrendous! We think that there should be visitation, but this should be short, frequent visits until the child is older. They say it's all about allowing the baby to bond with the father, but these children don't have a strong bond with the father! And if the child is grieving for the mother, how can it have a relationship with the father?

Thus, while the League maintained that it was solely a single-issue organization, it began to coordinate legal referrals, expert witnesses, case documentation, phone advising, sample agreements, and information on the internet for mothers in divorce suits.[62] Such involvement clearly blurs the distinction between private and public motherhood and reveals the sharp limits to rhetoric endorsing involved fathers and "parenting." Interestingly, maternalists come closer to recent feminist views on this more embedded and on-going issue. To

both groups, the push for the father's greater involvement has had un-
foreseen negative consequences, including a climate that increasingly
favors fathers' rights in divorce.[63] This climate helps mask a more
grim reality of "deadbeat dads" and fathers' absence after divorce, and
the "myriad of father problems," including violence, abuse, and incest, that often cause marital breakdown (Ruddick 1990). Perhaps a
feminist-maternalist alliance for new legal standards, based on caregiving and the critical scrutiny of fathers' involvement, might be possible (see Ehrensaft 1990b, Fineman 1995, Rothman 1989).[64]

Although the League's involvement in divorce is on-going, it has
not as yet grown from assistance in individual cases to a formal political agenda or push for state action. Seeing a very different kind of
public intrusion, in what is overwhelmingly a father rather than a
mother problem, La Leche League in the 1990s did challenge state
officials on a one-time basis. The case of single-mother Denise Perrigo directly confronted the regulation of maternal bodies and enforced norms of compulsory heterosexuality elaborated in chapter 2.
Denise Perrigo, according to press accounts, was alarmed at her sexual arousal when nursing her two-and-a-half-year-old daughter; she
called a community volunteer center and asked to be put in contact
with La Leche League. Instead, on hearing of sexual arousal, she was
put through to the local rape crisis center, where counselors heard this
as sexual abuse. Rape crisis counselors then contacted the county's
sexual abuse "hot line," which dispatched local police; the police
arrested Perrigo, and her child was placed in foster care. Criminal
charges referred to inappropriate "mouth to breast" contact, but press
coverage cast Ms. Perrigo as a victim of the "national hysteria" over
incest (*Washington Times* 1992, also Davidowitz 1992) (here the press
masks a father problem as a genderless "hysteria"). Though the criminal charges were dropped, social services filed charges of sexual abuse
and neglect with the family court and Perrigo was allowed only
biweekly supervised visits with her daughter during an almost one-
year separation (Ryckman 1992). La Leche League assisted Perrigo
through this ordeal by providing expert testimony and lawyer referrals, as well as local leaders' emotional support. The League's magazine also reassured its members that Perrigo's feelings of sexual arousal
were "normal, natural" (*New Beginnings*, March-April 1992, 34). The
member magazine, however, claimed that "[i]n actuality none of the
[remaining] charges were directly related to breastfeeding" (*New Be-*

ginnings, May-June 1992, 83–86) when something closer to the opposite was true. The family court focused on Perrigo's suspect sexuality,
specifically discussed her failure to wean and her supposed involvement with a married man, and "much [was made] of the fact [that]
Perrigo is a single mother" (Ryckman 1992). The League defended
long-term nursing rather than Perrigo *per se*, but their Web page now
features information on coping with social service caseworkers. It
states: "Yes, there is a very small risk that extended breastfeeding can
result in or complicate a false report of abuse or neglect" (Baldwin
1997: 3), thus the League advises *never* confiding in unfamiliar professionals who may interpret their "attached parenting" as "pathological" (*New Beginnings*, May-June 1992, 83).

Private Bodies, Public Bodies, Bodies That Enjoy
The sense of self expressed in the feeling that one's body is useful and
working well is clearly related to a positive sense of sexuality and desirability, as the earlier discussion and comments of League mothers
in this chapter suggested. The League's defense of autonomous maternal sexuality is, however, more vague than their public support of
Denise Perrigo might indicate. Examining their literature and talking with League mothers, I noticed contradictory views of maternal
sexuality and ambivalence about to whom women's bodies and breasts
ultimately belong.

League leaders and mothers worry about the organization's repu-
tation. The assumptions revealed in the Perrigo case, that mothers
might breastfeed for their own "pathological" pleasures, would seem
to indicate good reasons for this. One leader explained, for example,
that they don't want to be seen as "running around nursing five- and
six-year-olds" or as mothers who were "going to go on Phil Donahue
and make a laughing-stock of League." Another recounted these intrusive comments from friends and relatives: "Six months is a good
cut-off time because women who *do it* longer than that have a problem. You know there is something wrong with women who nurse
longer than that!" Nursing mothers in Masters and Johnson's famous
study (discussed in the previous chapter) seemed to have had similar
worries, as the sexologists reported they returned to "normal" marital
sex to relieve "fears of perverted sexual interest" in their babies
(1966: 162).

Despite these concerns, and a national average for breastfeeding

that is far less than six months, League writings gently endorse breast-feeding's pleasures. The most recent version of *The Womanly Art* features this statement, for example: "Breastfeeding is intended to be a pleasurable experience for a mother. A woman who breastfeeds with pride and satisfaction is aware that breastfeeding is a sensual experience. She also knows that this is a perfectly healthy and normal aspect of her sexuality" (LLLI 1991: 387).

Another example can be found in the League book specifically endorsing long-term nursing: "We have so sterilized and idealized nursing in our minds that many of us have lost sight of the fact that breastfeeding is a sensual behavior for both mother and baby. . . . Despite what our Puritan background may shout at us from inside our heads, it is not bad for something to feel good" (Bumgarner 1982: 41). The author also mentions that breastfeeding can bring sexual arousal and, on rare occasions, orgasm (42) and notes: "There is nothing to worry about . . . but rather much to be enjoyed" (42).

League mothers I spoke with tended, however, to divide the sensual from the sexual. For example, Mary Vincent recounted how much she liked to return from her workplace at the end of the day, "lie down, and enjoy a long slow nursing" with her baby; but she kept this distinct from our discussion of sexuality and body image. Other mothers tied breastfeeding to positive feelings about their bodies and desirability, but at the same time, felt less sexually available to their husbands. Anne Held spoke of feeling empowered in her body after experiencing a home birth and "complete" breastfeeding, and described the pleasing physical intimacy she shared with her two daughters, but she told me bluntly,

> The sex issue was a real issue for me and my husband after having the kids. I'm just not interested, and I really feel that I'm giving so much of my physical being all day long with nursing, with carrying children around, that by the time my husband comes home . . . I just want to be all alone . . . I don't want to have anyone touching me, or you know, that's when I get possessive of my body. So that has been difficult for us and I think it's difficult for a lot of women . . . Everybody's afraid to admit that you aren't interested in sex . . . because all the magazines have told them that you're supposed to be having sex every night.

Several other mothers spoke of making their breasts "off limits" to their husbands. One leader nursing a toddler (Trish Kreiser) com-

mented that while she felt much more relaxed with her body, "it's gotten to the point where if [my husband] touches my breasts, I instantly go like this [flinching] because I just don't want it." Though in describing breastfeeding Nicole Strickler recounted that the "holding and cuddling and nursing" created a special "sweetness" and "contentedness," she also discussed this sense of flinching, which League writings call being "touched out" (LLLI 1987: 117):

> Sometimes there is a conflict. And I really feel physically violated, especially when my son paws at me; I mean, I just can't express it any other way. . . . Then of course, at the end of the day when my husband gets a little romantic, I just feel like, "Don't touch me!" Or at least, leave my breasts alone.

Yet Nicole went on to explain that while her body was less available to her husband and at times too much so to her babies, her own, autonomous sense of her body was still much more positive. As I noted earlier, Nicole felt that nursing two babies had "enhanced [her] sexuality," as she became more "comfortable" with her body, and it became in her own eyes "more valuable and beautiful." Obviously Nicole would not have spoken in my more academic terms of resisting compulsory heterosexuality or its normative male gaze. She expressed such ideas, nonetheless, in her own, nonacademic words: "You know," she told me emphatically, "we are not there just for *Playboy!*"

La Leche League's positive notion of maternal embodiment and sexuality, however, is rooted in a procreative rather than feminist model, as it stems from the Christian familialism of the founders. Maternal sexual pleasure is defended as functional for the species' survival, as intended by nature's, and thus God's, design. Intercourse, orgasm, and lactation are described as physiologically similar, with the release of the pleasure-inducing hormones prolactin and oxytocin.[65] The League manual states that "Breastfeeding is the completion of a woman's sexual cycle" (LLLI 1991: 117), and the member magazine that, "the human race would not have survived if breastfeeding was not enjoyable for mothers" (*New Beginnings*, March–April 1992, 34).

This biological defense does not, however, go far enough to create a safe place for mothers' enjoyment against the dominant experts. Most child development experts of the twentieth century have argued for the control or repression of maternal sexuality; indeed, for some in the psychoanalytic tradition, the repression itself creates

motherliness through the channeling or redirecting of active libido. Constructions of the child's sexuality have varied, but the "good mother" consistently has been the neutral stimulator of the baby's eroticism and not a pleasure-seeking subject of her own.[66] Psychologist Susan (Contratto) Weisskopf criticizes both this dominant model and "naturalized," maternalist views like the League's. Together, she writes, they create an exaggerated dichotomy with a dangerously repressed mother on one side and a dangerously *over*sexed one on the other. Both sides deny mothers' autonomy, the "goodness" of autonomous desires and ordinary enjoyment.[67] And, according to Weisskopf, they do little to help us unravel the "considerable confusion over what constitute harmful erotic interactions with children" (1980: 780–781).

Certainly the Perrigo case touched off such confusion. Weisskopf argues that "breastfeeding is an area which, perhaps *more than any other*," provokes this collision of maternal bodies, sex, and danger (1980: 778; my emphasis). Also, in my view Denise Perrigo added to the perception of danger by violating compulsory heterosexuality: her body and sexuality became public because she was unmarried and they were not claimed by a rightful private owner. The League, in fact, may have distanced itself from the case because Perrigo was unmarried, for their maternalism seldom challenges the marriage imperative.[68] In their writings I found very occasional mentions of single mothers, but these were presented sadly, as anything but normal. The assumption of a husband's presence also pervaded meetings (see Merrill 1987: 226–227), as when leader Rory Gerardo asked without knowing the new mothers in attendance: "Anyone have suggestions on the dads?"

The League may hope to protect the embodied mother from charges of "perversion" and public scrutiny, but it does not always protect her from self-abnegation, with her body consigned to others within the private realm. In the past, according to sociologists Gorham and Andrews, the League espoused patriarchal notions of men's rights over their wives' bodies and assumed men would have difficulty supporting breastfeeding: while they encouraged wives to try persuasion and "clever" ways to change their husbands' minds, they advised women not to contradict a husband's wishes (1990: 250).[69] As longtime leader Gerry Kemp told me: "The dads. Oh, that's the *big* change

from twenty years ago! I can't tell you how many people would say, 'I want to nurse but my husband really doesn't want me to,' 'My husband says I'm nursing too much.' And my husband *this* and my husband *that!*"

League women indeed may have been influenced by feminist rhetoric of bodily self-determination in the past twenty years. Such pro-choice rhetoric, for instance, was clear in Nicole Strickler's account of an argument with her husband:

> I was five months pregnant . . . and he happened to casually mention, "Well have you given any thought to whether you are going to breastfeed or bottlefeed the baby?" And I looked in shock . . . [breastfeeding, at that point] struck me as a really repulsive idea . . . But he said, "Well, look, it's your body." And I said, "That's right, *it is!*" . . . I was real adamant about MY body and MY choice.[70]

Yet a self-abnegating voice was also present in Nicole's account, in her description of "tandem nursing" both a three-year-old son, who "paws at me," and a several-months-old infant. Anne Held's story also sounded double voiced, as she resisted the objectifying "magazine gaze" (see Young 1990) yet also spoke of "giving so much of my physical being all day long" that her body belonged to her daughters. League writings on sexuality are also somewhat double voiced, though, as I discussed earlier, group practices work against martyrdom. At times the writings endorse a Madonna-like self-sacrifice, as the manual advises in its section on marital sex: "It isn't fair to put your husband and children in competition with each other for your time and affection. Whoever has the greatest need at the time for love and affection receives it" (LLLI 1987 and 1991: 118). At other times, however, writings about sex encourage self-determination: "[you] need to have the final say over the use of your body" (Bumgarner 1982: 75).

ABSENCES ARE PRESENCES
Compulsory Heterosexuality

Philosophers point out that "nature-endorsing" positions (that speak *as if* endorsed by nature) like League maternalism employ a moral absolutism because they lay claim to the purest, most authentic identity and cast others as "unnatural," or worse, as "crimes against nature" (e.g., Soper 1995). Some of this moral absolutism in the League's dis-

course was visible (or audible) in the "Bad Yuppie Mother" stories discussed earlier. Other identities, however, were far less visible—and they created absences (or silences) so telling that I consider them presences.[71] The most telling absence is that of lesbian voices.

In all the League literature I studied, I did not find a single mention of a nonheterosexual mother.[72] The sole mention of nonheterosexual identities was concerned only with the normalcy of the breastfed child. The author of the League book on extended nursing, in a section on sexual development, dispels the "myth" that long-term nursing, especially of a boy, will "make" him homosexual. Although the author is not overtly condemning, her rhetorical questions suggest that homosexuality requires an explanation: "Do we have more homosexuality in our early-weaning society? Or do we have factors unrelated to weaning patterns that contribute to homosexuality? Or is there merely something in the sexual mores we have developed that makes us worry about these things while other societies may take them as variations on the normal?" She then invokes an odd (and white, Anglo-Saxon Protestant-centered) historical example: "the valiant and virile Englishmen who defeated the Spanish Armada in 1588 were nursed for three years." Girls are not ignored in the discussion but are clearly of less concern (no historical nostalgia here). The author assures the reader, nonetheless, that there is no evidence of continuing attachment to female bodies in adulthood: "[E]xperience with now grown-up girls who nursed long and eagerly . . . has just not borne this out" (Bumgarner 1982: 40–41).

None of the League mothers I spoke with revealed a lesbian identity or same-sex partnership; and, while some could be closeted, all were in legal marriages with men when I met them.[73] I did speak with one long-time leader, Marg Walters, who brought up the topic without my prodding. Marg had worked with lesbian couples using insemination in her capacity as a paid healthcare professional. What explained her rapid assertion, "I have no problem with it at all"? Would Rory Gerardo have said something like this if in response to her query, "How about the dads?", a mother had said, "My son has no dad, but he's got two moms"? A League mother who read a draft of this chapter told me: "Once a lesbian mother did self-identify at a meeting I attended. There was a long moment of silence, and then her question was answered respectfully," but she didn't come again. Marg

also chuckled, with a certain air of superiority, that the League slogan about "supporting mothers where they're at" would not extend so far. Most leaders she had known "would have had a problem with it." When I asked if she thought the organization might change, as it had toward employed mothers, she was very skeptical:

> I have a friend who's gay who had a baby . . . and I was her support [in labor and delivery]. She breastfed but did not make contact with La Leche League. I didn't recommend it because just knowing what the values were [in the League], they weren't what she needed. She needed support, but she didn't need La Leche.

Surprisingly, anthropologist Ellen Lewin found in a study of lesbian mothers that they relied heavily on nature-endorsing discourse to negotiate motherhood "in a difficult world" (1994: 350). Although Lewin's group differed in terms of their "routes" to motherhood, whether through prior marriage, male partners, adoption, or donor insemination, she found that they spoke in strikingly conventional and essentialized terms. Moreover, most felt, according to Lewin, that motherhood was the most essential aspect of their identity, and they had weak ties to, or even resentment of, lesbian communities of non-mothers (1994, 1990). Lewin contends that because homosexuality has long been considered a "crime against nature," it is partially subversive to claim this right to feminine normalcy (1994). Not wholly unlike League mothers, lesbian mothers speak within the existing cultural vocabulary and use the moral resource "nature" provides.[74]

Whiteness

Another telling absence in the largely white, middle-class world of La Leche League is that of women of color. By this I mean that the League perspective is seldom seen as partial or privileged, and their view is assumed to be a universal rather than a racialized one. The whiteness of La Leche League, then, is more than the lack of non-white members but also the absence of the standpoints and identities of women of color who are mothers.

I was aware during my field research that few League mothers were women of color, and I frequently questioned leaders about the lack of diversity. Eventually, I was referred to Betty Jackson, the one African-American leader whose name several others could recall.

Betty and her family were also among the very few people of color at the state convention I attended (in a region with a large Black population.) Although Betty Jackson had been a League leader for fourteen years, when I asked if there had been other minority mothers, she emphatically replied: "I was the only one, and I still am!"[75]

Betty was a middle-class mother of three, who lived in a predominantly white suburb, a location on which she told me her civil-servant husband had insisted. Although she described herself as shy and deferential to her husband, she had forged an impressive League career leading outreach efforts to the nearby Black urban community. She explained that this was always her main motivation to continue with the League. These efforts were initially to train white leaders who would enter Black middle-class areas, a somewhat more comfortable goal. But with the push from one dynamic African-American leader at the national office, middle-class outreach was abandoned in favor of a focus on low-income groups. Together the two Black League leaders led efforts to train low-income, nonwhite mothers as peer counselors out of their concern with high rates of infant mortality.

Because infant mortality reflects large-scale problems of poverty, I was surprised that Betty did not speak of frustration with the League's narrow emphasis on promoting breastfeeding and its lack of a larger antipoverty agenda. Even if every low-income baby were breastfed, this would be no panacea.[76] As a college-educated mother, however, who had nursed three babies for a total of nine years of her adult life, she embraced the League's self-help framework and exclusive motherhood philosophy. Her attitude and experience—reaching across classes to offer a form of self-help—suggested parallels to early-century Black maternalism, when educated African-American women performed such community uplift work. Yet La Leche League—in sharp contrast to the early-century white maternalist reform movement—demonstrates a surprising lack of action for low-income mothers and the enhanced social provisions they need to nurture their children. The group, though purporting to "speak for the babies," has had little to say about the tragic numbers reared in poverty. It does provide a base for the individual efforts of leaders like Betty Jackson, and others who sometimes volunteer to help within the WIC programs for low-income mothers (discussed in chapter 4). Overall, however, La Leche League leaves such actions on the periph-

ery. It does not directly address the high infant mortality rates publicized by groups like the Children's Defense Fund or the National Urban League, which primarily represent nonwhite standpoints.[77]

Another important aspect of La Leche League's racialization is the "naturalizing" of difference and inferiority with which white mothers imbue their view of paid caregivers. Recall most explicitly Trish Kreiser, affluent at-home mother and leader, who said of her cousin, the Bad Yuppie Mother: "She's got this Mexican maid that doesn't even speak English, she's taking care of the kid." Other mothers did not use such clearly racial terms but used the word "stranger," as in, "I don't want a *stranger* raising my child," to mark the "otherness" of domestic workers. Sociologist Sharon Hays also found that affluent white mothers told cautionary tales about children left with Spanish-speaking nannies (1996: 88),[78] and upscale magazines like *Parenting* include additional examples (e.g., Eisenberg and Murkoff 1997). Multiracial feminist scholars instruct us, however, that the relief from household or reproductive labor has been a defining criterion of racialized class categories and white privilege throughout U.S. history (Glenn 1992, 1994, among many). Affluent white women were entitled to exploit "inferior" women of color or immigrants, whose own motherhood was effaced; it was only in the mid-twentieth century that the actuality of exclusive maternal care (rather than the talk of it) became a status-enhancing boundary (Hays 1996: 35–36). In our contemporary era, this boundary is more blurry and clearly less reassuring.

Paradoxically, though the Spanish-speaking nanny is a worrisome "stranger," the name of the League itself comes from the Spanish language. The founding mothers turned to their religion and named the (officially nonsectarian) group after a Florida shrine to the Virgin Mother: "Nuestra Señora de la Leche y Buen Parto" ("Our Lady of Happy Delivery and Plentiful Milk") (LLLI 1987: 387). For the seven white Midwesterners, this may have been simply a deeply beloved symbol of motherhood—yet the use of Spanish signals more, for it "exoticizes" this symbolic mother and her racialized difference.[79] As one founding mother recounted, thinking back to the early days, "you didn't mention 'breast' in print unless you were talking about Jean Harlow" (Weiner 1994: 1360).[80] To use instead an "exotic," Latina mother to stand for breastfeeding and "natural" motherhood (to

make her the "native") was to invoke religious purity, but also to reinforce the taboo character of maternal embodiment and sexuality for
the "civilized." Even with our enlightened post-1970s rhetoric of
multiculturalism and diversity, "La Leche" remains a "strange" name:
as Liz Davenport told me, "I could never remember the name of it. I
thought it was the *weirdest* name."[81]

La Leche League and its philosophy of motherhood represent a complex, multifaceted construction. Both meshing and competing with
strands of modern feminism, the League's maternalism valorizes feminine difference and caregiving. By rejecting most action in the public
sphere and the label "political," however, the League keeps its boundaries distinct, unlike the early-twentieth-century maternalism that
emphasized public reform and feminine political activism. League
activists feel, though, that theirs is an alternative morality, one that is
perhaps even more pertinent today with the United States becoming
increasingly "lean and mean" and "family *un*friendly." Yet the privatized, self-help approach masks the extent to which good mothering is
inherently public—a point to be explored in the next two chapters.
    Like the few other contemporary feminist scholars who have
looked in some depth at La Leche League, I was at first preoccupied
with the conflict that mothers' participation in the workforce seemed
to present. In fact, however, the "softening" and blurring of boundaries between "good" and "bad" mothers over the last two decades
have made many middle-class mothers' work/family compromises
more acceptable, even commendable when linked to breastfeeding.
Though I had earlier written that the League risked pitting mothers
against each other like the media-touted "Mommy Wars" (Blum
with Vandewater 1993a), I now see this as a relatively small divide
among those who are white, middle class, and married.[82] More sa-
lient, in my view, are the League's body politics and the ways they attempt to reshape maternal embodiment and sexuality. If the group's
practices do less to challenge the assumption that sexuality must be
contained within marriage, they do combat the excessive commodification of the breast as object for the marketing gaze. At the same
time, the League's practices emphasize positive metaphors of production and use of the breast, the lived experience of the woman for
whom breasts are part of embodiment, and the revision of cultural
images of dangerous maternal bodies.

Feminist analysts of women's self-help groups debate whether they represent a positive challenge to women's subordination. Though such groups are currently proliferating, and doubtless express important forms of collective identity-making, it is less clear that they transform unequal gender arrangements. Sociologist Verta Taylor, who studied postpartum depression groups, comes down strongly for the positive, transformative potential of women's self-help, and found the PPD movement, in particular, to be challenging normative scripts for motherhood (1996). Yet the PPD movement's explicit aim to medicalize depression and reinscribe exclusive motherhood as the *normal biological* response to childbirth confound her optimism.[83] Other analysts of women's self-help groups are less sanguine, though they focus primarily on "twelve-step" rather than mothers' groups. Both Wendy Kaminer (1992) and Elayne Rapping (1996) find that such self-help groups encourage passivity and individual accommodation rather than positive social transformation. Such an interpretation is compatible with my view of the League's emphasis on privatized motherhood and its admonition to its most active members (in the words of one) "to not mix causes." It would be less apt, however, if the League began to advocate for national family policies.

Finally, though, it was the absences in the League that loomed largest in my mind. Analysts of women's self-help organizations note their primarily white, middle-class make-up (and Taylor adds that PPD groups consist mainly of *married*, white, middle-class mothers), yet they do not let these absences become presences with something more to tell. In the next two chapters, as I turn to mothers close to the bottom of the status hierarchy, the presence of compulsory heterosexuality and racialized class relations will speak volumes.

"TO EDUCATE AND PERSUADE"

WHITE WORKING-CLASS, RESPECTABLE MOTHERS

It was a major insight of U.S. family studies in the mid-twentieth century that working-class parents, which primarily meant mothers, differed in their childrearing practices from middle-class parents. Scholars argued that middle-class parents attended to the child's inner dynamics and sense of self-direction, while working-class parents strove for outer respectability and conformity (e.g., Bronfenbrenner 1958, Kohn 1963, among many); similar studies in the U.K. also argued that middle-class mothers were more "psychology conscious" (Newson and Newson 1963, cited in Carter 1995: 57–58). Such differences tended to characterize the working-class mother as "lagging behind." Nonetheless, the basic insight that child-rearing practices are contextually specific, that mothers respond to specific material conditions as well as larger cultural values, remains helpful and is recapitulated, without the middle-class bias, in recent feminist scholarship on motherhood and diversity (e.g., Glenn, Chang, and Forcey 1994). Even with the mid-century bias, Melvin Kohn cogently noted: "middle-class parents . . . [are] able to take for granted the respectability that is still problematic for working-class parents" (1963: 239). Kohn made this comment during a period of U.S. industrial affluence; in our postindustrial era, respectability—which the *American Heritage Dictionary* defines as the meriting of sufficient esteem, from appropriate, conventional behavior and a presentable appearance, to be accorded privacy and boundaries from unwanted interference (1992: 1536–1537)—may be even harder to come by. In this chapter, I explore how these larger changes have affected white working-class mothers confronted with middle-class parenting norms, which now include the exhortation to breastfeed.

From the stories of a small number of white, working-class mothers, I also learned how crucial marriage remains for respectability. Marriage was simply taken for granted by La Leche League mothers: even the "Bad Yuppie Mothers" were married. But, for the white working-class mothers I spoke with in a deindustrializing region of the upper Midwest, the availability of Manly Providers and Protectors was rapidly diminishing. If I began with a simple, materialist tale, in which economic change explained everything, the stories of the mothers soon led me to a more complex view of their negotiations with the men in their lives.

On a practical level, these mothers had much in common with the African-American mothers I discuss in the next chapter. Yet in their struggles to be good and respectable mothers, they were deeply engaged with white middle-class ideals of exclusivity. Although many ended up bottlefeeding, this was an emotionally costly outcome, for they shared the notion that "breast is best." Public health officials express concern with low rates of breastfeeding among lower-income groups, and they tend to cast such bottlefeeding mothers as irrational, but the stories of the women show that the reasons breastfeeding fails are more socially embedded (and thus out of their control) than the individualized health framework captures. In the latter half of the chapter, I turn to these embedded factors and discuss the demands of heterosexuality and the public interest in maternal bodies, crucial influences on the "choices" mothers make.

MEN, MARRIAGE, AND MOTHERHOOD

By 1990 southeastern Michigan had been transformed by General Motors' disinvestment and downsizing.[1] The plant closings and layoffs, like those in many other regions, were "celebrated" in popular culture through the narratives of working-class men, in the mournful songs of Bruce Springsteen, the blistering humor of Michael Moore's film *Roger and Me*, the sardonic essays of factory "Rivethead" Ben Hamper. Although these stories of dishonored working men are poignant, I wondered why there were no popular stories from the women, the wives, girlfriends, and daughters of these men, whose way of life was just as shaken.[2] I met and spoke with white working-class mothers in two locations: most were drawn from clients at a public family medicine clinic in Flint, one of two in the city accepting

Medicaid, while others were service employees, cleaners, and food service workers, at a large regional hospital. This chapter is based on a close reading of interview-conversations with twenty-seven mothers from these locations (for details, see appendix B).

Many of these working-class mothers told angry, resentful stories, stories about male partners who had "pulled the rug out from under" their hopes and expectations. A majority had fathers who were shop-rats (factory workers in the auto plants or related industries) and they had expected motherhood to include marriage to such a Manly Provider. Family life was so connected with the industry that General Motors was nicknamed "Mother Motors, the breast that feeds Flint" (Christian 1998). In their parents' generation—the last good years for U.S. industry—if a woman got pregnant, her boyfriend got a unionized plant job and, with his stable, nearly middle-class earnings, the couple would marry. In the era of deindustrialization, many working-class men have little such "manliness" to offer, and these mothers told stories of feeling cheated, of mothering in anger and, sometimes, hardship. Although there were some varied notes in their stories, I begin with two that sounded this shared theme.

Ricki Gorsany was a twenty-three-year-old with a three-month-old daughter. When we spoke, she fought back tears and repeatedly told me that raising a child was not something a person should have to do alone. She confided that she was having terrible conflicts with her boyfriend that had begun during her pregnancy. In her words, "He tried every trick possible to get me to have an abortion!" Ricki was enraged; with a Catholic background, and having had an earlier abortion, she was adamant that she wanted to "settle down."[3] After all, when her mother had become pregnant at seventeen, her father had found good-paying work as a mechanic, and the couple had married and eventually raised three children. Ricki found herself, in contrast, unmarried, on welfare, and remarkably isolated in her small apartment. Her boyfriend remained in his parents' home, working part time in a restaurant and bar; he visited Ricki and the baby and occasionally gave them a little cash. Ricki told me how "bitter" she felt: "He is so immature, he's so irresponsible! . . . It's absolutely ridiculous that he won't settle down. . . . He doesn't understand anything, anything of what he put me through!" She finally concluded: "I just don't see any reason why he couldn't marry me!" Ricki grasped at threads

of hope: he had gone through Lamaze classes with her, he was taking classes at the local community college, and perhaps if she weren't "so mean" and didn't expect to "change him overnight," he might yet marry her.[4]

Demographic research confirms the dramatic generational shift which Ricki observed in her family. Through the 1970s marriage was still the overwhelming "solution" to unplanned pregnancies for young white women like Ricki's mother, for in the postwar United States a whole set of laws and state policies targeting white, single women who became (or might become) pregnant had tied "true motherhood" to marriage. Most white unwed mothers were urged to give their babies up for adoption, and the law defined a "suitable home" only as one headed by a married couple (Solinger 1994: 290–295). In the past two decades, however, premarital sex has become increasingly common, and marriage far less so—the birthrate for single (never-married) white women has increased dramatically, as has the number of women keeping their children.[5] Scholars now tell us that "the link between marriage and childbearing has become more tenuous for everyone" (Furstenberg 1991: 131), and the "out-of-wedlock" distinction carries less stigma. Yet the loss of status troubled most of the white single mothers I spoke with, as it did Ricki, who wanted the respect, and the practical and emotional support, of being a man's wife.

Melody Jenksman was like Ricki Gorsany in that her anger toward her child's father was palpable. She differed though, for, in her proud telling, she had married before her son was conceived.[6] Yet, unlike her father, who put in twenty-seven years at General Motors, her husband was only sporadically employed and had dropped out of the local community college. The couple fought continually over money and were forced to rely on state aid to cover their son's birth and medical care. Indeed, Melody claimed that *had she not* wanted children, "I would be definitely single. I was never going to marry because husbands are just a pain in the butt!" Melody told a cautionary tale of unwed motherhood when telling of her husband's previous girlfriend, the mother of her stepson. She portrayed this woman as so irresponsible and unmotherly that it was left to Melody to deal with the serious emotional problems she had caused in her son.[7] The importance Melody places on marriage is striking next to the grim pic-

ture of it she paints. Indeed, her parents' marriage was also troubled and they eventually divorced. As she put it, "My dad was a *good* provider. He was never home. He worked nights and went to school during the day . . . But he provided."

How crucial marriage was for motherhood came up again and again in the women's stories. Two unwed mothers expressed this imperative in different ways. Louise Welt was committed to full-time mothering despite her reliance on state aid. Although insisting she did not want to be married to her long-term partner and the father of her two children, I noticed that she wore wedding rings, a very obvious gold band and diamond engagement set, on the ring finger of her left hand. When I asked, she vigorously rationalized: she had inherited them from a great-aunt, she really deserved them, they didn't fit over the knuckles of her other fingers, and she never took them off for fear of theft. Clearly she desired at least the "cover" of legal marriage.

Selene Lavry also lived with the father of her children and was a full-time at-home mother, but rather than state aid, the family relied on the father's salary as manager of a strip-mall retail store. Like Ricki and Melody (and most of the mothers in this chapter) Selene had a father who was a Manly Provider: he had worked his way up from the shopfloor to plant management. If the label "manager" was shared, however, by her father and her partner, it hardly offered Selene a middle-class life. The family lived in a mobile home park, and, like Cathy Seeley's husband in the previous chapter, her partner had taken on a second job when they needed extras.[8] Nonetheless, Selene described herself like an exemplary League mother, following the labor-intensive, budget-stretching practices advised for the struggling middle class: baking, canning (her family "never had storebought food" she explained), even learning to cut hair. Also, although she had failed to breastfeed successfully (a story I'll come back to), she dedicated herself to full-time mothering, explaining: "Oh, I just can't leave them, not for very long. We do everything together. . . . I don't think you can justify staying home with your children unless you spend the time with them."

Selene remained unwed, however, and, in her account, this was the major complaint in an otherwise contented life. In fact, she had concealed her pregnancies from her own large family, and in our conversation she skirted the reasons the couple remained unwed. But she

emphatically stated: "I am *going* to get married. I will be married before [the older daughter] goes to school because I will never do *that* to her," "*that*" meaning burden her children with the stigma of being "illegitimate." Interestingly, Selene did not measure herself against other unwed mothers, but against the neglectful mothers in her trailer park, saying, for instance, "I'll look outside and I'll be the only mother out there with my kids." In effect, she used the intense dedication to full-time mothering to compensate for her unwed status, but without that crucial missing piece, as she herself indicates, she falls short of exclusive motherhood.

About half of the mothers I spoke with for this chapter were committed to full-time motherhood—and, like Louise Welt, they followed this practice even if they lacked a breadwinner and their decisions defied rational, economic thinking. Marcy Herdon in fact had earned breadwinning wages; in ten years in a male factory job, she had out-earned both her ex- and present husbands, who were only seasonally employed. She quit her plant job, nonetheless, when expecting her first child, explaining, "We both felt real committed for me to be home with the kids." Marcy spoke like a League mother: "We just don't feel there's any sense in having someone else raise our kids when we have a *choice*"—but the threshold for choice-making was scaled down drastically, and the couple's decision was financially dubious. The Herdons had been living for several years with a low and fluctuating income, no health insurance (state Medicaid covered the children), and assistance from a food bank during difficult months. Marcy described their situation as "evolving," but not toward her reentry into the workforce, as she was deeply invested in exclusive mothering and breastfeeding (a story I'll return to). Rather, she pinned her hopes on her husband and, comparing him to her upwardly mobile, self-made father, explained, "my husband, he's learning how to do that."[9]

The stories these white working-class mothers told suggest that the association of marriage and "true motherhood" constructed by the postwar state and economy has been culturally cemented and is difficult for white women to undo on an individual level. Despite the lack of male breadwinning jobs, women clung to their marriages, or to their hopes of being married in the future, rather than moving to more autonomous or woman-centered family strategies (such as

those I examine in the next chapter). Their stories depicted many good or "good enough" partnerships and even a few Involved Dads, but they also included the myriad "father problems" Sara Ruddick has described in questioning the new ideal of the involved father (1990): absent fathers who worked very long hours, or, if living separately, seldom visited their children or paid child support; fathers with serious alcohol and drug problems, or fathers who were addicted to gambling; and, in two extreme cases, ex-husbands who had stolen their children.

BODIES, BREASTS, AND BABIES

Public health and state welfare officials tend to target the bodies, breasts, and babies of working-class mothers, especially those of questionable respectability, and evaluate such mothers in light of increased risks for low-birthweight babies, low rates of breastfeeding, and other health problems. To state officials, it is always puzzling why more such mothers are not in compliance with accepted pre- and postnatal health regimens and thus with proper maternal behavior. "Answers" often rest on questionable assumptions, not simply of middle-class mothers' superior knowledge and motivation, but of a lost past of "natural" motherhood. Recent scholarship, however, emphasizes that nature may never have been purely "natural."[10] For example, while feeding customs have varied, mothers have long relied on multiple methods, using supplemental "paps" and foods, and formal and informal wet-nursing arrangements, along with maternal nursing. Moreover, as historian Ellen Ross demonstrates, beyond its "natural" role as physical nourishment, food has played a large symbolic role in class struggles, boundary making, and conflicts over mothers' respectability (1993).[11]

Foods, methods of feeding, and maternal nursing, not surprisingly, mattered greatly to the white working-class mothers I spoke with in southern Michigan. Whether or not they succeeded, they were engaged with breastfeeding as an ideal and a measure of the good mother, for working-class mothers take pride in feeding their families well (DeVault 1991, Ross 1993). Overall, the white women I met were much less critical of the imperative to breastfeed than the African-American working-class mothers in the next chapter (though of course I spoke with only a small number), even though

this acceptance caused a good deal of emotional, and at times, physical pain. They expressed the reasons they wanted to breastfeed in maternalist or motherly terms, if less elaborated than those of La Leche League mothers. Many said, like one mother, "I figured it's the natural way" (Maggie Thulin) and spoke of the desired closeness and bonding. Others added health benefits to the "motherly" benefits, listing immunological and allergy-preventing properties, saying for example, "my first daughter never had a drop of formula [and] she has rarely been sick in her life" (Donna Howerly). Some simply emphasized that they wanted to do the best they possibly could for their babies.

Why do so many then end up bottlefeeding? As Pam Carter cogently points out in a study of British working-class mothers, infant-feeding decisions are affected by cultural dictates and public health information, but also by mothers' health, financial and family circumstances, and complex needs for privacy and bodily autonomy (1995: 104). Also, an element of contingency enters the working-class mothers' stories, with unpredictable life events upsetting their plans and intentions to breastfeed. Such women's lives, as Carter also underscores, do not easily lend themselves to the controlled and planned decision-making that public health frameworks value (1995: 101).

BODIES THAT FAIL

Many of the mothers in this chapter did not achieve "good mothering through breastfeeding," though it cannot be attributed to a lack of desire or effort on their part. In fact, only five of the mothers had never wanted to breastfeed; but even of those with more positive breastfeeding stories, only a few felt entirely successful. Moreover, about half of the mothers told their stories as failures, and these stories were often quite wrenching narratives of failed bodies.[12]

For Ricki Gorsany, the first working-class mother introduced in this chapter, failing at breastfeeding added to her sense of being cheated out of respectability. In other words, she connected her failed maternal body very tightly to her unmarried status. Ricki had engaged in rational planning during her pregnancy, reading health pamphlets and popular advice books, and attending childbirth classes. And she had started out breastfeeding in-hospital and for several days at home. Within a week, however, the stitches from her episiotomy

became infected, requiring antibiotic treatment that, according to her physician, precluded breastfeeding. Ricki was advised to pump her breasts while using formula and bottles and to try nursing again after the infection cleared in three weeks. With nursing barely established, to continue would have meant round-the-clock pumping at about three-hour intervals, and this for three weeks. Ricki burst out, telling me: "You know, it was too hard for me to have to do that! Do her bottles, clean the episiotomy a hundred times a day, take your sitz baths! There was just too much for me to do already, and I just couldn't do it all alone." Ricki stressed that if she had had a husband, this outcome might not have been so sad: "I cried so hard. The night, after they came in and they gave me the antibiotic, and I couldn't breastfeed anymore, I just cried. I just wanted to be close to her." Quantitative research has found that having a supportive husband is very predictive of breastfeeding among white mothers, whereas, among Mexican-American mothers, the mother's mother is most important, and, among African-American mothers, a close friend is (Baranowski et al. 1983). Ricki emphasized, in contrast, that she felt very alone, that her body had failed and she had failed at being close to her baby *because* of her boyfriend's failings. Missing a Manly Provider, she seemed to cling resentfully to that absence rather than trying to find other sources of emotional and practical support. She would be an exclusive mother or else![13]

Later Ricki confessed to other motherly failings: she not only turned to bottles, but sometimes resorted to propping them so that she was not holding her daughter during feedings: "Sometimes I just prop the bottle, which I know I shouldn't. But if I have something that I'm trying to do, I can't sit there. Plus I try to make up for it. I try to pay as much attention to her as I possibly can." Again, Ricki related this failing to her lack of a husband: "It's just hard. Because I can't count on anybody but myself." Propping is, as Ricki has gleaned from all the advice literature, an ever-present temptation, but one to be resisted. *Parents* magazine articles repeat that bottlefeeding is acceptable *only* when mothers take the time to make feedings "a haven of cuddling" (Salmon 1992b: 142; also McCall 1982: 74). Dr. Spock cautions against propping, using the words Ricki echoed, that the "busy" parent must "make it up to the baby" (1985: 167); he also includes avoiding propping under the good mothering tips in "How to be nat-

ural" (1985: 7–8). Another expert states that babies "get the warmth and security of close bodily contact" only "by being held for *every* feeding instead of being put down with a propped bottle" (Olds 1980: 50, my emphasis), and *Redbook* adds *every* feeding, for the *entire* feeding (Winick 1982b: 115). It seems that without breastfeeding's "iron-clad" guarantee of attachment (*Parents* 1970: 112), experts fear that mothers will *de*tach and *un*bond from their babies.[14]

Medical literature also cites health problems from propping. Propping can lead to overfeeding and subsequent tendencies to obesity, to tooth decay from the pooling of sugary liquid in the mouth, to choking and ear infection (Mead Johnson 1990: 23).[15] One author, in *Working Mother* magazine, is even more extreme, stating that propped bottles can cause babies to aspirate milk into their lungs, leading to pneumonia or even death! (Keuffner 1991: 72). Researchers suggest, moreover, that low-income single white mothers like Ricki rely on "inappropriate feeding practices" more than others (Kaste and Gift 1995), reinforcing the stereotype from authoritative standpoints that they are suspect or of questionable respectability.[16]

Melody Jenksman, the second angry mother we met in this chapter, also had problems caring for her newborn, although she had a husband. In fact, she described herself as having had a "bad case of postpartum blues" that had lasted for about three months. She also began breastfeeding but, like Ricki Gorsany, was able to continue for only a brief time, ten days in her case. She reported having extended crying jags, while the baby was very colicky and was projectile vomiting: "I'm crying all the time. [The baby] could sense that something was wrong with Mama. Plus . . . I mean, my child was sick. And all these nurses were telling me 'It's okay honey; babies spit up.'"

According to Melody, she was told that her son was allergic to her breastmilk and that she must stop nursing. To her confusion, however, after her baby had been on formula for a week, she was told she might start nursing him again. This suggestion struck her as outrageous, as she had just endured a week's pain from engorgement to let her milk supply dry up, and she was given no reassurance that the baby would not have the same strong allergic reaction. She told me that next time (she hopes to have one or two more children), she would not even attempt to breastfeed for fear of harming her baby and going through a similar ordeal. Yet, Melody also angrily defended herself and the

workings of her body. She emphasized that her son was a "big healthy baby," weighing nine pounds, eight ounces (in a clinic setting in which battling low birthweight was a major objective). Nonetheless, she ended on a more defeated note:

> At first it [breastfeeding] was great. I can't explain the feeling, but at first it was really great. [But then,] I felt like useless, if I couldn't nurse my baby, I was a flop as a mother. I carried this child inside me for nine months and nourished him, and now that he's breathing life, I can't nourish him anymore! I felt very incomplete.

Selene Lavry also told a wrenching story of failed breastfeeding. With both her daughters she had started to nurse and had done so for three days (in-hospital and at home), when she was told to stop because of infant jaundice. "They said they weren't sure if it was caused by me." She went on to explain what happened:

> They said the minute she was better, I could try again. So I came down everyday to o.b. [the obstetrics ward] and pumped my breasts. But . . . there was nothing left. I was so devastated that she was in the hospital that I couldn't eat, I couldn't do anything. I never left her room except to go down there to pump. Which I did faithfully, every few hours . . . it really tore me up. [I] was just pumping nothing but blood!

These upsetting stories indicate the need for an alternative, maternalist or feminist, perspective to defend mothers' bodies. La Leche League activists would contest the "facts" and revise these stories of failed or dangerous bodies, as the problems resemble those mothers often bring to the League. In cases like Ricki's, the League manual counsels that antibiotics be switched, as some are acceptable while nursing (although these are not the "wide-spectrum" antibiotics that some physicians prefer) (LLLI 1987: 140; also Kitzinger 1987: 111, 145, 147).[17] In cases like Selene's, infant jaundice, which affects approximately half of all newborns, provides the reason for suspicion of the mother's milk. This is such a common misconception that the League repeatedly prints correctives to inform mothers that *frequent* breastfeeding is more a *cure* than a *cause* (LLLI 1987: 286–290; Minami 1991, 46).[18]

Both Ricki and Selene accepted the medical interpretation of their failed bodies, but Melody was more ambivalent about the medi-

cal diagnosis she received: while she thought her depression had probably harmed her baby, she was also angry that healthcare providers
were slow to take her account seriously. She also wondered if her milk
was the only problem, because the ordeal went on for another two
months. While the baby initially did a little better on formula, and
was put on a more expensive soybean-based product, he did not settle
down until a medication supplying a digestive enzyme was added.[19]

La Leche League publications again provide alternative information that recasts failed maternal bodies: they contend that a baby can
never be allergic to its mother's milk and suggest that with cases of
colic, cow's milk consumed by the mother is often the culprit (1987:
102–103, 363–367; also Eiger and Olds 1987: 90; Kitzinger is emphatic on the point, 1987: 29–30). Both La Leche League and feminist health activists agree that with *any* problems, medical advice to
mothers is typically the same, to *stop* breastfeeding (BWHC 1992: 479
fn.; Weiner 1994). Even if, as in these stories, mothers are then advised
to resume, interrupting breastfeeding in the early days makes this
difficult (both in terms of the mother's milk supply and the baby's
ability to latch on); moreover, most mothers are unable to develop the
confidence (without extensive, positive, hands-on support) to work
with their bodies and their babies in such a very short time.

WHY DO WORKING-CLASS MOTHERS "FAIL"?

Middle-class mothers, of course, are not free from such problems.
They also struggle with jaundiced or colicky babies, their own recov-
eries from childbirth, and worries about the adequacy of their milk
supply. Middle-class mothers, however, are more likely to surmount
these problems and are more likely to both initiate and continue
breastfeeding (GAO 1993, Kurinij et al. 1988, Ryan et al. 1991; also
Maclean 1990). Is this because working-class women lack good health
information, and thus "lag behind" educated middle-class mothers,
as the public health research (like that just cited) so often assumes? Or,
are they more easily swayed by advertising and media representations
of bottlefeeding, or by a nagging mother-in-law, another common
assumption of breastfeeding promotion campaigns?[20] Or, do they
place a lower value on health-promoting behaviors, another common
social science explanation (e.g., Starbird 1991)?

British sociologist Carter disagrees vigorously with all such as-

sumptions and claims that public health discussions misconstrue the experiences and needs of working-class mothers. I found, as she did in the U. K., that the working-class mothers I spoke with knew that "breast is best" and did not "lag behind" in their knowledge of medical facts. The distress felt by the women who told stories of failure also indicates the seriousness with which they take medical or health-promotion information. Moreover, these stories indicate that health-care professionals not only advise women *to* breastfeed, but often advise, or even order them, *to stop*. Finally, the several women who struggled despite unsupportive health professionals and disapproving relatives to attempt breastfeeding suggest that working-class mothers have the same motivations that middle-class mothers do.

So why do working-class mothers breastfeed less? Carter explains that there is no one answer, but rather a set of contextual, socially embedded factors (1995: 104, 136). These include issues I have already touched on, like the mother's health, competing demands on her time and energy, and the health of her household (physically, financially, emotionally); there are also issues of bodies, privacy, and sexuality that I discuss later in this chapter. One of the five mothers in this chapter's interview group who rejected breastfeeding may have best summed up the effect of these factors when she explained, "Breastfeeding is best for the baby, it's just *not* the best thing for me."

In addition to missing this socially embedded context in which mothers feed their infants, public health discussions greatly oversimplify the bottle versus breast decision, presenting it as a one-time, either/or choice between absolutes. In fact, many mothers try both, if not simultaneously, then over time. Most of the white working-class mothers I spoke with (22 out of 27, or about 80 percent) had attempted to breastfeed at least some of their children, but then needed to supplement or wean for a variety of reasons. Yet if, as in most large-scale surveys, they are counted as "breastfeeders" because, like Selene, Ricki, or Melody, they gave any breastmilk at all, their understanding of an experience of failure (and rapid resort to bottlefeeding) is misconstrued.[21]

Reasons for breastfeeding failure remain greatly oversimplified in longitudinal studies that track mothers over time (see Carter 1995: 79). The use of biological explanations, like the most often cited "insufficient milk" or "sore nipples," misses how stressful life events in-

tervene in mothering and entangle biological and social cause-and-effect. Mothers who told me their stories experienced health problems, or crises with children and other family members; and because their lives were hard or "under-resourced" (Oakley 1992), they felt impelled to wean. Eleanor Hoch's complicated stories illustrate this entanglement: she weaned her first baby at two months—after mixing breast and bottle "fifty-fifty"—owing to her own health crisis (physicians "suggested" that she stop). At that time her husband was only sporadically employed, and they were forced to move in with her in-laws. She weaned her second baby at three months because she felt that her milk was drying up from the stress of divorcing her husband and finding another home. At the time of our interview, she was pumping breastmilk for her third baby, just three weeks old, because after the interruption for jaundice treatment, he would not latch on to the breast. With blisters from pumping every four hours, her supply was dwindling and she was giving more supplemental formula, but she still hoped to continue a little longer. She was now living as a single mother on welfare. The infant-feeding decisions of working-class mothers like Eleanor Hoch are rational or "sensible" when the multiple, stressful demands in their lives—and the need to get at least some of these demands (quite literally) off their bodies—are considered (Carter 1995: 86–105, 126–127).

Is there a meaningful divide between the failed breastfeeding stories of mothers like Ricki, Melody, Selene, and Eleanor, and the successful breastfeeding stories I look at in the next section? Or do mothers simply make their own eclectic, idiosyncratic assessments? Maclean studied over one hundred Canadian breastfeeding mothers, primarily middle-class and presumably white (since she does not mention race or ethnicity) and observed a distinct pattern: mothers who weaned prior to four months expressed a sense of "inadequacy and guilt," were "distressed," and repeatedly used the term "failure," whereas those who weaned after four months expressed enjoyment and said that the rewards outweighed the difficulties (1990: 111–144). Maclean attributes this to the influence of the infant-feeding recommendations of the Canadian Pediatric Society (nearly identical to those in the United States, discussed in chapter 2) and the minimum standard for maternity leave (which is four weeks longer than the U.S. standard of twelve weeks and includes income replacement). The in-

fant's stage of development is also an influence: after the first three months, as babies become more responsive and settle into more predictable sleeping and eating patterns, caring for them generally becomes less demanding and more rewarding.[22] Because Maclean included mainly affluent mothers, however, just 16 percent of her sample told stories of failed bodies (1990: 14, 112). I found, somewhat differently, that while the four-month divide was meaningful, less privileged women also evaluated whether the circumstances surrounding weaning were under their control: thus one woman at the low end judged two months of nursing very positively (Frances Mieran); and another, who made it to the four-month threshold but weaned because of a sudden health problem, told a story of failure and felt compelled to explain why she breastfed only "for a little while" (Delia Duncan). Unfortunately though, the sense of control and of having made self-determined choices may itself be largely a class privilege.

As I indicated earlier, a maternalist perspective might help working-class mothers by contesting "facts" that hold their bodies and mothering suspect: clearly, when facing distressing circumstances, it is preferable to receive positive, supportive information. If the mother then decided to wean, she might feel a greater sense of control, feel better about her body, and be better prepared to negotiate the birth of subsequent children. Might she, however, also feel increased guilt for weaning and thus falling short of motherly ideals? Sympathetic healthcare providers may be aware of this double-bind: at the public clinic which was one of my field sites, two women staff members recounted that too many mothers they had known were convinced of breastfeeding's importance but then felt like failures when it didn't work out—and even concluded that they were not good mothers. So, over the years, out of genuine concern that mothers facing difficult circumstances not be "overloaded with guilt," the clinic actually offered less information and breastfeeding support. One insightfully commented that they risked patronizing working-class mothers either way, whether they advised them to breastfeed *or* if they backed off from information they routinely provided to more privileged mothers.

Maclean also suggests that maternalism offers a mixed package. While some of the advantaged mothers she studied established sup-

portive, "collegial relations" with physicians, many "relied heavily" on La Leche League (1990: 157–171, 196–197), but a few
who weaned early complained that the League was "too pro-
breastfeeding" and provoked guilt (1990: 197). La Leche League leaders do see mothers' lives more holistically and, in this sense, understand the multiple, embedded causes of "insufficient milk" or "sore
nipples." Yet, because they are largely unable to recognize their own
class standpoint, they might tend to judge working-class mothers
harshly. My conversations with working-class mothers, however,
suggest that social distance mainly precludes this risk, for about 70
percent of them had never even heard of La Leche League (19 out of
27). Of those few who had (8 out of the 27, about 30 percent), all were
fairly positive, but they had had little contact with the organization.
Only two mothers actually sought out the League's support—one
through phone counseling and one who became an active member (I
recount their stories in the next section). Two others had read the
League's manual. Despite the group's outreach efforts, only Eleanor
Hoch had attended a talk given by a League leader at the local WIC
office (WIC is the federal Special Supplemental Nutrition Program
for Women, Infants and Children).[23]

Simone de Beauvoir argued in the 1940s that one defining discourse of femininity was that women's bodies were not good enough,
never good enough (in Carter 1995: 148, 159). For most of the
women in the small group of white working-class mothers I spoke
with infant-feeding was one more unfortunate instance of this. But in
some cases, because like Ricki Gorsany or Selene Lavry their mothering lacked its "legitimate" social placement and respectability, it became a crucially confirming one. Middle-class mothers also feel guilt,
distress, even desperation when their breasts fail, yet their greater resources and more controllable lives greatly reduce the chances of such
a confidence-breaking experience.

BODIES THAT WORK

Were the mothers with successful breastfeeding stories different?
Their circumstances may have been somewhat more fortunate: most
were married or in stable partnerships at the time of our conversations, and this social support can be an important buffer against stress.
(Of course, Selene and Melody's stories suggest that this is no guaran-

tee of breastfeeding success.) Some exposure to maternalist discourse may help, for these were, for the most part, the women who had heard of La Leche League (all who had heard of the League, except Eleanor Hoch, told successful breastfeeding stories; and most of those who told positive stories had had knowledge of the League).[24] The mothers' stories, however, are complicated and dynamic, and they differ only in degree from those of mothers who told negative stories.

At least four of the mothers with positive stories had succeeded after attempts with previous babies had failed. Recall Marcy Herdon, the married mother who had quit her plant job for full-time motherhood despite the family's financial hardship. For Marcy, breastfeeding was crucial to good mothering. She explained that with her first baby, she "did have a commitment" to breastfeed because of the "closeness," the "bond," which is "just really special," but health problems intervened, and when her son was four months old she had to be hospitalized for a week and undergo minor surgery. She had hoped to resume nursing and pumped her breasts during that week, even with considerable pain from the surgical incision; however, her milk diminished. Pumping is never as effective as an infant suckling, and illness and the separation itself created additional distress. When she returned home, her son's need to nurse every hour around-the-clock became too much for her. Although constant stimulation should increase the milk supply, she was exhausted, and, in her account, the baby began to reject the breast. Thus, after a frantic week, Marcy stopped breastfeeding because of what could be labeled "insufficient milk."

With her second baby, Marcy was even more determined to breastfeed. When we spoke, she was still nursing at seven months, and because she had overcome chronic mastitis (breast infections), it had not been easy. She described spending many days feeling "very, very ill," and this was with the primary responsibility for two children under three. Although her doctor told Marcy to quit nursing (as did her mother-in-law), she sought out the League's "mother-to-mother" support because she so wanted to succeed and she suspected that her physician's "facts" were wrong. Marcy never attended League meetings, but she had read *The Womanly Art of Breastfeeding* (so she knew that continued nursing usually helps clear infected ducts), and she relied on phone support from the League to get through the mastitis.

She told me that League leaders were "very, very helpful, very compassionate." She was sure that, as a result, her bond with her daughter was "even deeper" than the connection she had with her son.[25]

Lissa Mooney was also a married, full-time mother reliant on limited state assistance because her husband was unable to find stable, breadwinning jobs. She was also the only working-class mother I met who actually became a La Leche League member. Along with identifying herself as a League member, she intriguingly described herself as a feminist and a "very liberal," "hippie-type person"; she also spoke proudly of having a small portion of Native American ancestry.[26] In her account, she developed some of this alternative, countercultural self-definition from very negative experiences with hospital care and her failure to nurse her first baby. He was slightly premature, jaundiced, and sleepy from the painkillers she regretted taking during labor. She explained how she failed: "I was twenty years old and pretty naive. I let the hospital staff push me around . . . They finally said, 'Just put him on formula, he's not going to nurse,' and I believed them." Lissa attributed her son's challenging or difficult personality to her early failed mothering, as well as his health problems: "He's had chronic ear and respiratory infections and digestive problems, milk allergy, and I think it's all bottle-related!"

In her second pregnancy, Lissa recalled, "I said, I'm going to nurse this child no matter what! And when it turned out to be twins, everybody thought I was crazy, but I did it anyway." After "reading every book from the library on breastfeeding," she began by pumping her breasts for three weeks while the premature babies, too immature to suckle, remained in the intensive care nursery. Lissa fortunately had the help of an intensive-care nurse—a La Leche member herself—to finally get the twins started nursing. She then successfully breastfed both girls completely for fifteen months (with supplemental foods after six months but no formula). Lissa was convinced that there was a great difference between bottlefeeding and breastfeeding: "Because I nursed them I'm more attuned to their desires, and when they babble at me, I know what they're saying. With [her first child], I didn't understand what he needed from me. I reared the twins better and they are happier, more relaxed children. And it made me a mellower person."

Lissa Mooney credited the League for her improved mothering.

She had become an active League mother and, after attending the sets of monthly meetings, even took referral calls from mothers of twins and "premies" with whom she would share her experiences and lend support. After weaning, she kept in touch with her former leaders, but rejected their encouragement to pursue leader accreditation. When I asked why, she retorted, because "it takes money to be a leader." Although thus implicitly aware of the League's class-standpoint, Lissa still found more support there than in other groups for mothers, in particular, "Mothers of Multiples":

> They don't allow your children to come. And when you're nursing that's impossible! It's supposed to be a support group, but they never talk about their kids. They spend their time doing charity drives. And they're basically suburban housewives with nothing else to do. The thing I liked about the League was that I could take my children with me and they have the approach to parenting that I subscribe to. With League, they give you more. And they had more in common.

Although Lissa may have entered motherhood with a more politicized, alternative identity than the other mothers in this chapter, her experiences with the League seem to have enhanced this positive sense of difference. Lissa expressed, among this group of working-class mothers, a uniquely positive sense of her body, for example. Some of the mothers in this chapter were preoccupied, or even overwhelmed, by their sense of having a failed body. But even those who had the proud sense of a well-working body were preoccupied with their weight, their slack and stretched muscles. Marcy Herdon, despite her success at nursing and overcoming mastitis, had remarked: "I don't feel good about my body right now at all!" Lissa, in contrast, said immediately, "I liked being pregnant and I liked my body when I was nursing. . . . I think the pregnant and nursing body is beautiful." The only other mother to express anything close to Lissa's positive body image was Frances Mieran, who, like Lissa, had successfully nursed twins (in addition to several earlier babies); but she had had no contact with the League.[27]

I have primarily observed these breastfeeding success stories through a positive lens, but they indeed have less positive facets. White working-class mothers may feel particularly vulnerable to expert advice when they have experienced downward mobility and

have less settled and respectable lives than their parents. Family sociologist Melvin Kohn noted even thirty years ago (when chances for respectable, settled lives for the white working-class were good) that some working-class parents become very anxious to follow expert advice, for it seems "a sort of handbook to the middle class" (1963: 234), and perhaps this is even more so today: good mothering may represent one of the only available routes to status. Breastfeeding may also allow mothers a limited way to surpass their parents: Lissa, for example, emphasized that her stably employed father thought breastfeeding was "barbaric" and that her mother, who had submitted to his will, was "*not* a very excellent role model." And Marcy, who had reconciled with her upwardly mobile parents after several years' estrangement, explained with some air of self-satisfaction that her mother knew nothing about breastfeeding.[28]

PRIVATE BODIES, PUBLIC BODIES

Contemporary public health officials acknowledge that the loss of modesty and embarassment occasioned by breastfeeding—especially when outside the home—are an important reason that many mothers reject the "breast is best" imperative.[29] Indeed, historian Janet Golden confirms that as early as the nineteenth century public breastfeeding in the United States had become clearly unacceptable (though this had not always been the case). Mothers became subject to mixed messages that linger to this day (if modified by the lens of medical science): while it was considered immoral not to breastfeed, mothers faced great pressure to keep the nursing breast out of sight (1996). Paradoxically, most contemporary breastfeeding advice emphasizes the ease of nursing in public, or, as La Leche League asserts, mothers can nurse "discreetly" in nearly any location.[30] This infant-feeding advice holds mothers accountable and makes managing the maternal body each woman's individual responsibility. One popular book, for example, states: "As *women themselves* accept the *naturalness* and the *respectability* of breastfeeding, societal acceptance of public nursing will keep apace" (Eiger and Olds 1987: 163; emphasis added).

The repetition of newsworthy cases of mothers being censured for public breastfeeding, however, reveals that societal acceptance has not kept apace. Yet women, *themselves,* have filed complaints, gone to court, even protested in public "suck-in's" when stopped from

breastfeeding at public swimming pools (in Long Island in 1977; again in New Jersey in 1993), in restaurants (in Dubuque in 1981; again in Albany in 1994), and even in their own parked cars (in St. Louis in 1981; again in Connecticut in 1996).[31] Workplace cases have been especially problematic: a Florida teacher, an Iowa firefighter, and a Hollywood actress have all sued for the right to nurse during breaks, in private spaces, but at their employment sites (Bonavoglia 1983; Henig 1979; Lowman 1984: 102, 226–227). La Leche League documented that about 10 percent of the calls they received for legal help concerned public breastfeeding, while another large number stemmed from workplace problems (LLLI 1986: 3).[32] The courts declared nearly twenty years ago that "the Constitution protects from excessive state interference a woman's decision respecting breastfeeding her child," but while likening the breastfeeding relation to marriage in this privacy, no explicit right to nurse in public was stated (cited in LLLI 1986: 7). At present, according to La Leche League's Web page, just fourteen states have passed legislation to specifically make public breastfeeding "decent." When proposed, such legislation is often met with hostility and ridicule, as it was recently in New Hampshire where it died in committee.[33]

What gives the force to this modern taboo? According to several feminist scholars, public breastfeeding disturbs because it violates what I termed compulsory heterosexuality.[34] In other words, while women's bodies are expected to be sexual and to be displayed, they are expected to signal only sexual availability to men. This body can and should now be an active, desiring body rather than merely a passive sex object, as was the case in earlier eras, but the feminine body is coded *for* men. Breastfeeding threatens the lateral, erotic male-female tie by invoking the generational tie in which eroticism is taboo. Moreover, breasts alone become the focus of this normative heterosexuality, at least in many Western cultures. As discourses of sexuality became increasingly visual through the twentieth century, the construction of femininity became more about managing the body to be looked at, and the breasts' appearance seem to stand in for this complexity of bodily practices and disciplining (Young 1990). Breasts also signal the conflict of feminine extremes: the "good" maternal body and the "bad" sexual body, the Madonna and the whore (Carter 1995: 154). After all, we are surrounded in contemporary society, even

bombarded, by visual representations of breasts, "the sine qua non of female attractiveness" and the "bodily focus for the policing of women" (Carter 1995: 152, 154). Women today can't appear *unattractive,* but neither can they flaunt their breasts; they must enjoy "the male gaze" but vigilantly manage the scrutiny of their breasts, displaying just the right size (even if this calls for surgical manipulation) and for just the right viewers. Above all, women must keep the heterosexual body strictly separate from the maternal body, although in daily life they continually collide. As one popular writer quipped after a nursing mother was asked to leave a movie theater, "patrons could see a whole lot more of the female form [up on the screen] than what's revealed during a breastfeeding" (Quindlen 1994).

The need for public vigilance and bodily privacy influences mothers' infant-feeding decisions, as the research literature grudgingly admits (see Carter 1995: 135). Maclean found that the majority of the middle-class mothers she interviewed thought in great detail about where, and in front of whom, it was appropriate to breastfeed (1990: 83–94). Privacy is also a favorite topic at La Leche League meetings, where mothers exchange tips on the best places to nurse, discuss the awkwardness of nursing in front of in-laws, and practice nursing discreetly. Neither medical nor maternalist advice literature, however, has recognized that privacy is a more difficult issue for working-class mothers, as feminine bodies are sexualized and suspect along race and class lines.

Privacy is more difficult for working-class mothers because physical space itself may be lacking. Carter, for example, found that crowded, chaotic households encouraged bottlefeeding among working-class women because maternal and sexual bodies collide even within the "private" sphere of the home, as women negotiate the ownership of their bodies and breasts with husbands and boyfriends (Carter 1995: 108, 128). The need for privacy was an important part of the stories of the working-class mothers I spoke with, and two of the women with positive breastfeeding stories spoke of how they had to manage privacy according to their husband's definitions. After she spoke in detail of how much she had enjoyed nursing her babies (even saying "it was a hundred percent easier" than bottlefeeding), I asked Frances Mieran why she had weaned her first three children at two months. She replied: "My husband would want me to

start going here or there with him. It was just more convenient not to have to go into another room or a bathroom or whatever to breast-feed." Similarly, Shandra Canaly had trouble negotiating privacy with her husband: "I wasn't uncomfortable about it. He was, he was real uncomfortable. He didn't want me to even sit there and feed the baby, even with something to cover my shoulder. I always had to be alone, just go in the other room: 'Don't do that in here, go in there!'"

For the five mothers who had rejected breastfeeding, the difficulties of managing these public/private divides loomed large. Their comments, like those of Frances and Shandra, point to the lack of privacy that makes breastfeeding more disturbing if it is more likely to be seen:

> I wouldn't sit there and breastfeed in front of somebody, not even my mom and dad. My husband, okay. But nobody else. (Theresa Long)

> To be out in public and have to breastfeed, you know, that is supposed to be something beautiful, out of nature. But I don't think I ever could have done that! (Louise Welt)

> I thought about breastfeeding, but I'm just not the type of person that could go out in public and show it all. (Gena Hardesty)

Their words suggest the extremes of the feminine that breasts stand for: a particular "type of person" will "go out in public and show it all," the whore, whereas for the Madonna, breastfeeding is "something beautiful, out of nature." This dichotomy is difficult for all women, but for working-class women, respectability and the right to privacy are already too vulnerable, too questionable to risk mismanaging breastfeeding. A fragile respectability often can rest on keeping the body under control, a control fraught with the threat of public or state intrusion if it should lapse (Carter 1995: 118).

Respectability has long been racialized in the United States in a way that particularly targets mothers like the ones in this chapter: the white (or potentially white) working-class mothers measured by state officials against those considered "rough" or disreputable.[35] In the United States, as in Western Europe, motherhood became increasingly public and subject to state control as part of nation-building and imperialism in the late nineteenth and early twentieth centuries. Such efforts were concerned with building a superior, white "nation," with population growth and "quality," and with avoiding the

feared "race suicide." White working-class women's reproduction, if less safe than the middle-class, was still in the public interest. This racialized divide in reproductive politics was evident in debates over protective labor legislation and the design of welfare programs, in campaigns to reduce infant mortality, and in discourses of infant feeding.[36]

Although it was considered virtuous, even patriotic, to breastfeed, mothers confronted, and still confront, many conflicting messages. In the nineteenth century, for example, mothers faced racialized stereotypes such as the fat Irish or coarse German nurse (Golden 1996: 152, 137–138). Breastfeeding thus signaled a closeness to "nature" and the low social status, the animal-like, polluting bodies of inferior, non-white races. In the early twentieth century, laws in some parts of the country actually made breastfeeding mandatory for the disreputable unwed mothers in public maternity homes, ostensibly to reduce infant mortality rates (Solinger 1994: 288, 306 n. 3).[37] Finally, two similar headline cases underscore the class context in which mothers' lactating bodies are viewed: In the first, "well-to-do" mothers whose "zeal" to breastfeed led to their children's dehydration, brain damage, and, in at least two cases, death, were cast as "well-meaning," as "perfectionists" who suffered from a "yuppie syndrome" caused by the "power" of the "breastfeeding movement." No public, state action was taken against the mothers: according to the *Wall Street Journal*, "the problem is the fault ultimately of the medical profession" (Helliker 1994). In sharp contrast, a single mother "who supported herself and her children on welfare" was charged with criminally negligent homicide because her six-week-old breastfed baby starved to death. According to the *New York Times*, she was the second such mother to be charged (in the New York City area) in an eight-month period. Though both women had tried to take their babies for routine checkups, each had been turned away because of their inability to pay. Of the more recently arrested mother, the reporter opined: "She left the clinic, never to return." Both mothers await trials and possible sentences of up to four years in prison (Swarms 1998).[38]

The vulnerability of the mothers I spoke with was demonstrated less dramatically by their everyday dealings with the welfare system and, for some, with one local arm of state social services, the public health clinic.[39] Clinic staff spoke of their clients with a mix of suspicion and genuine concern, but efforts to prevent low-birthweight ba-

bies led to many petty invasions of privacy. Pregnant women were told to keep detailed food diaries, and staff members routinely phoned women who missed appointments; they also required clients to fill out a *non*anonymous questionnaire on their "substance abuse behaviors" and inquired into family and household relations to determine eligibility for state assistance and subsidized clinic counseling. In our conversations, staff members recognized sympathetically that negotiations with boyfriends' and husbands' sense of sexual ownership, taboos against public display, and the clinic's continued monitoring of their behavior all discourage breastfeeding. Yet the intrusive practices signaled their suspicion of the mothers' ability to keep their bodies under control.

The suspicion of working-class mothers' sexuality has been, as mentioned, an important element in their vulnerability. Golden, for example, documents fears of wetnurses' sexuality in the nineteenth century; sexual arousal was believed to contaminate breastmilk, to be toxic, and to pass the nurse's bad character on to the nursling (1996: 65–66, 151). The reticence of the contemporary mothers I met to speak of the pleasures of breastfeeding may reflect their sense of vulnerability, of their need for vigilance. Carter came to similar conclusions, arguing that the language of sensuality is less available to working-class mothers, who rely rather on the language of motherliness (1995: 142). So, for example, mothers told me:

> My babies, I would take them in bed with me. I especially liked the time I spent with the babies, and holding them close. (Frances Mieran)

> I really did enjoy nursing him. I cried when he quit, I cried for two days because I was just so close to him. (Roma Anderson)

> I could just lay her next to me and we could both fall asleep while she was nursing, which was really nice. I liked everything about it. (Donna Howerly)

> She's real close to me. And when she's eating and, you know, she'll like pat me, and she'll rub her hand on me. And she's always looking at me. She's real happy, and it makes you feel good. (Polly Strathern)

Considering this talk of "motherly" pleasures along with the sexual coding of the breast also suggests that the fact of incest, a most disturbed blurring of the sexual and maternal bodies, and of lateral and

generational family axes, lurks beneath breastfeeding. Child sexual abuse and incest were long seen as problems specific to the working class (Gordon 1989). And if more the problem of working-class men, the responsibility to moderate and manage the bodies in the (often overcrowded) household lay with the respectable mother. This was somewhat evident among the women I spoke with, in their talk of breastfeeding and privacy (see Carter 1995: 114–115). But the disapproval of extended nursing also indicated the mothers' sense of responsibility and need for vigilance over bodily boundaries.[40] From a maternalist perspective, their notions of proper weaning may be overly restrictive and rigid. Yet affluent, white mothers, with their less suspect bodies, have a greater luxury to indulge in "weaning gradually, with love." Donna Howerly's cautionary story was typical: "My sister-in-law just weaned her daughter at two and a half. But with a toddler at two, they can remember things, so I'd rather have weaned them before they can remember it. And my husband, he was going: 'That's wrong!' "

Polly Strathern was still nursing her ten-month-old but knew she would stop soon: "My mother keeps telling me she's too old to be breastfed . . . and my sister-in-law, she's like, 'How can you do that?' Like she'll say, 'My child's not going to be as spoiled as hell!' " Such remarks suggest that respectable mothers must also manage the child's desires.

The case of Denise Perrigo discussed in the last chapter also testifies to the suspicion of incest in working-class mothers' extended breastfeeding—and of the vulnerability to state intrusion of those lacking in class privilege and the protection of heterosexual marriage. (Perrigo was the single mother charged with child abuse after she called a social service help-line to ask if arousal while nursing her two-and-a-half-year-old was normal.) Perrigo's sensual pleasure was more disturbed, and more disturbing of the public interest, than depictions of privileged white women's "motherliness" are deemed. Perrigo, while white, was not married or employed and, with her child beyond the innocence of infancy, she had failed to manage and contain her own adult sexuality. Thus the state saw fit to remove the child from her custody, blurring another divide, that between protecting the child and disciplining the mother (see Abramovitz 1988: 168).[41]

WORKING BODIES, WORKING MOTHERS

For those mothers working outside the home, managing breastfeeding and the privacy in space and time it requires are obviously even more complicated. The advanced capitalist workplace requires a tricky vigilance. In the past, working-class jobs treated the body as machine, as Taylorist-influenced management sought to control workers' every movement. Embodied needs—hunger, thirst, fatigue, pain, and sexuality—were strictly relegated to the private sphere. When white women, the future mothers of the nation, entered the workplace, it complicated this public/private divide but created a rationale for extensive job segregation. By the postindustrial era, however, much had changed. With so many women in the workplace, and service jobs requiring bodies, work becomes another "heterosexualized" space, where women's bodies must signal availability and attractiveness to men (although women can also be penalized and harassed through this sexualization).[42] It is not surprising that women might hesitate to combine breastfeeding, and the collision of the maternal and heterosexual body, within such an environment.

If a mother in this work environment does try to keep breastfeeding, she typically has to rely on a relatively new apparatus, the breast pump.[43] This is ironic considering breastfeeding's "naturalness" and all the advice that has cast it as "a vote . . . against technology" (Kanter 1972: 32): in our era, breastfeeding has its own technology, just as bottlefeeding has had its weights, measures, and sterilization equipment. Some form of pump has been around for at least the last century; when wet-nursing declined, cities established human milk banks where milk was bought and sold, or, later, donated (Golden 1996: 198–203). Also, mothers long improvised, using jars and bottles, if not to return to work, to empty engorged or infected breasts (see Kitzinger 1987: 127–128). Isadora Duncan wrote of her "ghastly experience" with a "little machine" some fifty years ago,[44] but little else has been written on mothers' views of this technology, which now includes manual, battery-powered, and electric versions with single or double-pumping.[45] Yet the promotion and advertising of pumps, even in La Leche League publications, have become widespread, and pumps pervade the recent advice literature.[46] Furthermore, for the working-class mothers I spoke with, the apparatus was a major, even definitional, part of the experience and of all that they associated with

breastfeeding. No doubt this is also true for many contemporary middle-class mothers, though highly educated mothers are more likely to have the (atypical) workplace autonomy that this practice requires.[47]

Donna Howerly had the most positive experience using breast pumps on the job, in part because she had one of the highest status jobs among this group. Donna had remained at home for nine months while nursing her first baby; but after her second was born, she needed to return to work as a medical assistant after just eight weeks' unpaid leave. She was determined, nonetheless, to provide the "best way," the "perfect food for the child": "I was at the point where I'd look at bottles on babies and feel sorry for them, like their mother was depriving them."

As Donna recounted, the use of the apparatus is neither obvious nor appealing, and she had never tried one with her first baby. Donna explained:

> My sister-in-law worked and nursed her child, and she was really encouraging me to do it. And she talked about how to pump. She didn't exactly show me how, but she would describe it. And a lot of things I didn't know, like how much you were supposed to be getting, and how to freeze it.

Donna kept to a regimen of pumping during her break times, with extra pumping before and after work, for four and a half months.[48] About all that pumping, she said: "It wasn't always fun! It was sometimes a chore. But I felt better that I was trying to breastfeed. Ten years from now I'm not going to care how hard it was for a few months."

Some mothers told very different stories about breast pumps. Louise Welt's strong feelings about privacy (noted in the last section), and against using breast pumps, made her one of the few to rely completely on bottles: "The breast pump—it was nothing that I would want to do! I saw [my sister] when she had to pump it just so she could go somewhere. It didn't look like fun to me!"

Kath Gardiner briefly tried to combine breastfeeding and working, but, unlike Donna Howerly, found she could not pump an adequate amount:[49] "I was pumping out bottles, and then we also had formula as a back-up, but she wouldn't take the formula. So because I was trying to nurse her [after two months] I quit." For Karen Mathis, it was not the technique but the workplace that made pumping impos-

sible. While Donna Howerly worked in a small office with a "really understanding boss," Karen worked as an assistant manager for a fast food outlet.[50] She cobbled together eight weeks of partially paid leave after her son's birth, but then returned to a fifty-hour week of hectic and varying shifts. Thinking about what it would have been like to try to pump during a shift, Karen concluded:

> They probably would have given me a few minute breaks, but there's so many kids [to supervise] and so much action. And dealing with the customers, I could have been in pain, because there might not be time when I needed to pump. And I would have had to find a way to refrigerate it.

Karen was also worried about her breasts leaking at work: "I thought about having to change bras all the time and wear those nursing pads, and I just preferred not to, because if I was leaking at work, it would be like, 'Let's go home' because I don't want anyone to see me."

Painful engorgement and leaking are common in the early weeks or months of breastfeeding; they are good examples of Connell's notion of the body's recalcitrance (1995), the ways the body can "act back" and refuse to be ignored despite the demands of a job or the need for privacy. Although both engorged and leaking breasts can be managed by diligently pumping (when separated from the baby), this is impossible if private time and space are lacking. Donna Howerly's autonomy on the job was unusual, as was her employer's supportiveness of her need for privacy. As discussed in the last chapter, even some of the middle-class mothers in La Leche League were unable to find such support. And popular writing occasionally mentions privileged "corporate mothers" who need to hide their breast pumps at work, a need corporate marketers seem well aware of (see figure 4.1) (Brown 1993; also Eiger and Olds 1987: 185).

The mother presented in the "typical weekday in the life" in one popular advice book points to the extremes envisioned for working mothers with working bodies. The authors describe "Charlotte," an executive at a Wall Street investment banking firm who is married and has both an infant and a toddler. She pumps her breasts in the women's bathroom three times during the work day, having somehow gained the proficiency to accomplish this in just ten minutes—a remarkable feat when most women need two or three times this much time.[51] (Somehow this also goes unnoticed by colleagues, clients, and superiors.) This "typical" working mother, like the model mother in

FIG. 4.1 The pump is concealed for the successful, high-status career woman. "Pump in Style," Medela.

chapter 2, also finds time to work-out each evening—even though her infant will nurse five or six times between 6:00 P.M. and 6:00 A.M., and her three-year-old will want at least some attention. Luckily, she "has vast reserves of energy" (Eiger and Olds 1987: 182–184).

Most recently, a few large corporate employers have begun to assist mothers' pumping in the workplace. *Ms.* magazine, for example, reported that the CIGNA health care and financial services corporation offers its female employees "discreet" pumping centers complete with electric pumps and "private storage systems."[52] And the *Boston Globe* reported that Hancock Insurance provides a similarly equipped "mothers' room" (Foreman 1998). Florida state legislation in 1994 mandated that such programs be designed for state employees, and Texas followed suit in 1995 (Baldwin and Friedman 1997). In 1998, in fact, Representative Carolyn Maloney (of New York) introduced a bill to provide tax incentives to employers to rent breast pumps and to provide space and as much as an hour's paid break-time daily for nursing mothers.[53] As one consultant explained, "[Companies] see it as a real low-cost way to help working moms" (cited in Foreman 1998). Clearly, such pumping stations would be much cheaper than maternalist reforms like the extended, paid leaves common in Western Europe or the on-site nurseries favored by many of the La Leche League mothers I spoke with.

With, however, breast-*pumping* policies in short supply and the workplace a "heterosexualized" space, many mothers may *not* want to pump at work. The pump may still be a major part of their breastfeeding experience at home or in the hospital. This was, for example, an important part of Selene Lavery's and Eleanor Hoch's stories, and it can be a central part of the experience for mothers of premature babies, as it was for Lissa Mooney (and for Trish Kreiser in chapter 3).[54] Karen Mathis had relied on the pump from the start, when her baby failed to latch on properly to the breast. Like several other mothers I spoke with for this chapter, Karen felt that she must at least provide some breastmilk, and, in a twist from dominant advice, she pumped her breasts *until* she returned to work. Such experiences, however, are far from pleasurable or senuous. In fact, Karen expressed a good bit of resentment and guilt:

> I thought I *had to* breastfeed. Everybody was pushing me, saying, "It's *natural*, it's what the mother *should* do." So I just felt pressured into it. Then

with my son, it was difficult. I was impatient, so I would resort to giving him a bottle, and then he did not want to breastfeed again. For weeks I pumped and fed him through the bottle because I couldn't get him to want to breastfeed. And I thought, "Well, I'm giving him my milk." Like I said, it's what I thought I had to do.

Part of the pressure Karen felt to breastfeed came from the state, specifically through the local WIC office. According to Karen, the WIC staffer had made an example of her own experience of nursing for two years (which Karen found "a shocker"). Such breastfeeding promotional practices were not new, but they increased in the 1990s, as new government directives and the Healthy People 2000 plan aimed to increase breastfeeding among low-income mothers. Promotion in Southeastern Michigan increased in the year after my fieldwork, with funds for training peer counselors, "past or current WIC recipients who [would] educate and persuade other WIC recipients to breast-feed." Also, as one local newspaper account remarked, mothers were to receive t-shirts, infant car seats, and other gifts: "the longer they breastfeed, the more valuable the gift" (Strobe 1991). Similar or even more extensive promotion efforts have been implemented in Massachusetts, with state and federal funds. Deborah Krauter, WIC Statewide Breastfeeding Coordinator, whom I spoke with in 1997, emphasized that women need to be educated, supported, and encouraged to breastfeed. To that end, Massachusetts WIC fills its waiting rooms with pamphlets, posters, and videos and provides nutrition and peer counseling, breastfeeding support groups, incentive food packages (with a "regular breastfeeding package" of milk, cheese, juice, eggs, dried beans or peanut butter, and extra tuna and carrots for those who take no supplemental formula), and many "little freebies": water bottles, stickers, pins, magnets, baby t-shirts, sippy cups for mothers who go six months . . . games, raffles, and parties for World Breastfeeding Week. (See figure 4.2.) Another innovation—because more low-income mothers are employed or must work to receive state assistance—is the provision of breast pumps, with some states spending about 10 percent of their allocated promotional funds to buy them (GAO 1993).[55] Research suggests that these efforts "to educate and persuade" are effective in getting more mothers to initiate breastfeeding, if not to continue (Brent et al. 1995, Schwartz et al. 1995); and Krauter observed that, in seven years,

FIG. 4.2   Some of the materials from Massachusetts WIC's efforts to promote breastfeeding.

Nhửng điêu bạn sẽ gặp phải và bạn phải làm

- Tốt hơn hết là nên cho con bạn bú sửa mẹ trong 4 - 6 tuần đầu. Như vậy sẽ làm cho cơ thể bạn tạo nhiều sửa mẹ hơn.

- 4 - 6 tuần sau, bạn có thể cho con bạn bú một bình sửa mẹ hay sửa hộp (sửa mẹ là tốt nhất). Bạn cùng có thể cho con bạn bú sửa mẹ bằng ly, muống hay ống bơm thuốc nhỏ mắt.

- Nếu bạn trở lại sở làm hay trường học, bạn có thể cho con bú khi bạn ở nhà. Người giữ trẻ có thể cho con bạn bú sửa mẹ của bạn vắt ra khi bạn đi khỏi. Xin liên lạc với nhân viên chương trình WIC của bạn, nếu bạn muốn biết về việc hút hay vắt sửa mẹ và làm thế nào để dự trữ sửa mẹ.

(Cho con bạn nằm bên hông bạn) Kiểu ấm bên hông

Graphics on positions used by permission of Medela, Inc.
VIETNAMESE "Breastfeeding: Getting Started"
Massachusetts WIC Program
WIC Multicultural Task Force   1/29/97
Breastfeeding Promotion Task Force   WIC Form #91

Tips For Breastfeeding:

- Nurse your baby often - about 10 times a day

- Take care of yourself -

  * Rest when your baby sleeps

  * Let others help with housework

  * Eat healthy meals and snacks

  * Drink lots of fluids

- Trust yourself - if your baby seems hungry, go ahead and nurse

- Relax and enjoy your baby

- And remember - WIC CARES! Let us know how things are going.

BREASTFED IS BEST FED!

MA WIC 10/93

the percentage breastfeeding (not initiating, but at any one point in time) has gone from just under 16 percent to 23 percent of postpartum enrolled mothers in her state.

Paralleling turn-of-the-century campaigns, the state's interest in maternal bodies is both instrumental and symbolic, oriented to potential cost savings and to the nation's health.[56] And for low-income mothers, as Karen Mathis indicated, the effects are decidedly mixed. Carter rightly notes, on the negative side, that breastfeeding promotion fits well with our era's massive attack on welfare expenditures and reinterpretation of health as a private rather than public responsibility (1995: 61–62). Indeed, she writes of such campaigns: "There is a constant assumption that [working-class and Third World] women have [only] to be told *again and again* of the benefits of breastfeeding" (1995: 67, my emphasis). Though some research finds that bottlefeeding mothers get the "breast is best" message (Lawrence 1988), state officials and researchers *still* assume that more education is needed. Deborah Krauter shows this ambivalence: "I think most people know that breastfeeding is best . . . the knowledge is out there . . . but a woman who is low-income doesn't have as much education and may not really understand as much the health benefits." An author in *Ms.* magazine even advocated "a massive educational campaign" to "convince individual women" to breastfeed, though without acknowledging the class and race implications (Quick 1997: 35). And most recently, breastfeeding promotion coincides not only with "ending welfare as we know it," but with specific threats to the federal WIC budget (*New York Times* 1997b, c, NPR 1998).

The two major recommendations of a government report on the current WIC efforts to promote breastfeeding underscore that, for mothers, the promotion can be both controlling and helpful. The first, in a liberal "Americanizing" vein, aims to increase the dissemination of non-English language educational materials. Presumably immigrant women must be told at least as repeatedly as other low-income mothers of breastfeeding's advantages. According to Deborah Krauter, Massachusetts WIC strives to reach nineteen different ethnic and language groups, with staff trained to work with different cultural traditions, to "help the mother" with beliefs that may prevent breastfeeding.[57] Ms. Krauter's words indicate that well-intended outreach might still be problematic:

Southeast Asian women come to the U.S. and see bottles as the American way . . . they see formula as having value and feel they're losing out monetarily if they don't take the formula [from WIC] . . . A lot of cultures believe it sours the milk if they get angry . . . So they stop breastfeeding . . . Then some believe colostrum is bad.[58] They like, throw it away. And it's the best, full of immunoglobulins . . . it's liquid gold! And we're horrified that they throw it away! . . . [But w]e try not to say "You're bad for believing that," "How could you possibly believe that?" . . . We try to work with the traditions but try to change people's beliefs.

The second major recommendation emphasizes the need for strict "guidance" for "situations when breastfeeding is *not* recommended" (GAO 1993: 8; my emphasis). Some of these "situations"— cancer chemotherapy, use of certain prescription medications, or a high exposure to environmental contaminants (which in fact is class and race-linked, though many contaminants are found at higher levels in water, cow's milk, and formula than in human milk[59])—are relatively unstigmatized. But the list emphasizes those that stamp mothers as individually out-of-control, "disreputable": drug and alcohol abuse, HIV-positive status, even cigarette smoking (GAO 1993: 14– 15, 8–9). This seemingly obvious presentation of medical contraindications treats suspect mothers punitively by flattening ambiguous facts, particularly when drug and alcohol abuse are *not* class-linked. Evidence for HIV transmission, in fact, is equivocal;[60] the dangers of maternal smoking, and even of drug and alcohol use, have often been exaggerated (Begley 1997a, Daniels 1993; also Oakley 1992, Tsing 1990); and few public health campaigns have made treatment programs for substance-abusing mothers a major goal (see Chavkin 1991). Furthermore, this emphasis on extremes leads quickly to the "cult of purity" mentioned in chapter 3. It paradoxically undercuts other WIC efforts to provide mothers with more realistic, supportive advice such as what middle- or upper-income women (and, sometimes, lower-income women) find in La Leche League.[61]

CONVENIENCE?

For overworked working mothers, doesn't breastfeeding simply increase overwork at home and on the job? Actually the practice is widely touted as more "convenient" in advice literature, with no mixing of formula, no sterilizing and heating of bottles, no running

to the kitchen for the midnight feeds. Most add that breastfeeding is more portable: with no equipment to lug around, just pick up the baby and go. The cost-savings, finally, is also seen as part of breast-feeding's convenience (although Eiger and Olds highlight this under benefits for fathers!)(1987: 212, 29–30; also Spock 1985: 105).[62] Yet "convenience" is a relative evaluation that makes no sense out of context. Mothers pointed out to me, for example, that breastfeeding is hardly portable if you're lugging a pump, bottles to collect breastmilk, and extra nursing bras and pads. Moreover, some mothers were offended by talk of cost-savings as part of infant-feeding decisions, thinking that a mother does what is right and best for her child despite the cost. Karen Mathis brought this up, but also pointed out that cost/benefit evaluations differ for low-income mothers: "My cousin is breastfeeding because of the affordability. That's a good idea, but I know I'm on WIC, so I get formula free. It's so convenient. Plus, I didn't even want cost to be a consideration."

Another mother (Maggie Thulin) had said: "My boyfriend just thinks, 'Oh, you're going to breastfeed because it's cheaper.' But I don't feel that way!" She supplied instead: "It was better for them. Plus, I figured that was the natural way."

State policies create different incentives for low-income mothers, if one considers "cost" as the rationality of the choice in the broadest terms. WIC still provides free formula, which, given the increasing stinginess of government policies, can be one of the major "family allowances" many mothers receive. In fact, even breastfeeding mothers utilize this resource; since the promotional efforts of the 1990s have increased maternal nursing, lots of formula is used as a supplement (GAO 1993). WIC was criticized in the past for promoting formula and discouraging breastfeeding, which led to the new emphasis on food vouchers and all the "freebies" for nursing mothers.[63] Still, formula, as the Southeast Asian women in Massachusetts realized, is the more tangible resource offered by the state.

Additional "private" factors may make bottlefeeding a "rational" choice for overworked working-class mothers. Many mothers mentioned that they can get help with bottlefeeding, particularly from husbands and boyfriends. And this can be an important exchange if male partners are not taking on other, less pleasant tasks at home (also Carter 1995: 124–127). Only Donna Howerly told me of the oppo-

site, happy exchange: with the "excuse" that she had to nurse the baby, her husband would have to cook, clean, and tend to their other child. Help with bottlefeeding also enables mothers to get more sleep and go out more easily, as it removes or at least distances the burden of infant-care from their bodies. It also leaves mothers free of monitoring, free to eat, drink, smoke, and even take birth control pills —without worrying about harming the baby or provoking the disapproval of state social service and healthcare providers. Deborah Krauter, of Massachusetts WIC, again was very illuminating:

> DK: As breastfeeding promoters, we say, "Oh, breastfeeding is so much easier, there's nothing to it. It's *so* much more convenient!"
>
> AD: But is that really true?[64]
>
> DK: Well, for a mom that's on the bus and her baby's crying, it may be more of a hassle to breastfeed, because she's got to pull up her shirt and maybe be exposed and feel embarassed and all of that. So in *her* feeling it may not be more convenient. Or it means that *she* has to feed her baby, and she's feeling more tied down. And if she's bottlefeeding . . . she can go out and . . . know that her baby is going to be well fed. So our perception as professionals isn't necessarily what the women we're working with perceive.

What has become of respectable motherhood among the white working-class? Mothers whom I met suggest that, cheated out of Manly Providers and of the financial stability enjoyed by their parents, they still want the status, support, and protection offered by legal, heterosexual marriage. Breastfeeding may loom large as mothers anxious to do the right thing become more vulnerable to authoritative advice, or simply want to feel they have succeeded in at least that aspect of mothering. Ironically, public health frameworks draw the opposite conclusion and see continual needs to "educate and persuade." They miss the stressful life circumstances and inadequate "mother to mother" support that make breastfeeding difficult and mothers' bodies likely to "fail." Moreover, strict taboos to keep nursing out of sight, and maternal and sexual bodies distinct, make breastfeeding especially problematic for working-class mothers. Middle-class mothers experience some of these difficulties, for women of all classes are affected by the greater sexualization of breasts and bodies in the late twentieth century. Middle-class mothers, how-

ever, have greater control of time, space, and resources, and their respectability is woven into their class position, particularly if they are married, so that their bodies are much less liable to harsh judgments and public surveillance (see Carter 1995: 206).

The state promotion of breastfeeding and targeting of low-income mothers thus raises basic questions of women's interests: Can breastfeeding be something genuinely good for mothers? Or are efforts to "educate and persuade" mainly coercive? Carter found that among working-class mothers in the U.K., the meaning of state intrusion in baby care was complex and, for some, quite negative. One mother put this brilliantly in describing a conflict with a home health visitor: "I told her not to come back and she told me the baby belonged to the state" (Carter 1995: 168). Others, however, expressed positive feelings about health or social service staff who were "ordinary" mothers and took their worries seriously (1995: 172–175). Few of the women I spoke with for this chapter mentioned feeling pressured or coerced to breastfeed. Although it is possible that such feelings will increase with the new government campaigns, it may depend on the extent to which the programs are sympathetically women-centered or more "democratic" in their approach (which poses fascinating questions for other researchers to pursue).[65]

For this small group of white working-class women, the desire to breastfeed was tightly linked with the desire to be a good and respectable mother, and thus was more all-encompassing than can rightly be understood as acquiesence to state authorities. But, of course, state actions contribute to the production and reinforcement of such norms. To advocate more positive support and encouragement for mothers who genuinely want to breastfeed is, therefore, problematic: although it is surely more positive to succeed than to fail, assertions of such "genuine" wants or "authentic" interests always risk romanticizing motherhood and placing women back in the straitjacket of biology. Breastfeeding *can* be a positive experience for mothers, and one that challenges confining norms of femininity, in the sensual, relational pleasures and the enjoyment and confidence in the well-working body. However, simply to breastfeed does not guarantee such an outcome, as many of the stories in this chapter illustrate, because no bodily practice carries inherent, invariable meaning. Some feminist scholars have thought about the ways women can strategi-

cally use biology and claims of "natural" sex differences: this might be a strategy, for example, to reduce working-class mothers' over-work, to argue for longer (paid) maternity leaves, or to generally chal-lenge the low social value of caregiving (e.g., Martin 1987, Young 1990). The danger, of course, is in how to keep such provisional, stra-tegic claims of difference from sliding back into entrapping founda-tional assertions of women's inherent "nature," so vividly illustrated in La Leche League's maternalism. I will take up this important ques-tion in the final chapter.

In the next chapter, I explore the stories of African-American working-class mothers and find more forms of resistance to dominant norms of motherhood. The white mothers in this chapter, for the most part, were very engaged with dominant ideals of motherhood: if they challenged them, it was mainly through what Martin termed "laments" (1987). Such expressions of sadness acknowledge that things could have been different, but they are not resistance in the sense of oppositional consciousness. For a few of the white mothers, resisting dominant advice and state intrusion may represent assertions of autonomy, but this, too, is a theme I will discuss in more detail in the next chapter.

CHAPTER 5

"TO TAKE THEIR OWN INDEPENDENCE"

AFRICAN-AMERICAN WORKING-CLASS MOTHERS

If family studies scholars had cast the white working-class mother as lagging behind the psychologically attentive middle-class mother, they had placed Black mothers even further behind, lost in a "tangle of pathology" (Rainwater and Yancey 1967). From the Moynihan report's emphasis on overly strong Black "matriarchs" who emasculate their men (1965) to current stereotypes of dependent welfare queens and teen mothers (e.g., Murray 1993), scholars and policy-makers have assumed that strengthening the Black family required the assertion of male family headship. These public discussions also have assumed that Black mothers draw only from white discourses that make legal marriage the basis of legitimizing the dyadic mother-child relationship, ignoring African-Americans' distinct historical legacy. Centuries of slavery and racist exploitation led African-American mothers to develop community-based alternatives to exclusive motherhood, as well as distinct meanings and inflections within the institution of marriage, which, if desirable, has not been a prerequisite of motherhood.

African-American mothers, furthermore, face a particular legacy of embodied exploitation, in which their sexuality and reproduction were appropriated by white men or demonized as dangerous and out of control. Although some Black women were caregivers for white children, and were then seen as "naturally" maternal, their own children were neglected, even sent or sold away. Breastfeeding, in which the Black baby was denied its mother's milk as she nursed the white infant, is a particularly charged symbol, at once metaphoric and lit-

eral, of these historic relations. In this chapter, I explore such resonances with some contemporary African-American working-class
mothers. I found that the mothers I spoke with drew from alternative
discourses of independent mothering and were less engaged with,
and less pained by, norms of exclusive motherhood than the white
working-class mothers of the last chapter. They also largely rejected
breastfeeding, but for reasons much more complex than have been
typically understood. Their stories share similarities with those of the
white working-class mothers, yet go beyond them to reveal a critical,
resistive stance toward racialized norms and practices. I also found,
and begin the chapter with, the more optional, yet positive notions of
male partnerships and marriages that were part of the independent
motherhood ideal.

MEN AND INDEPENDENT MOTHERING

With the help of two colleagues, I collected interview-conversations
with twenty-six African-American mothers in southeastern Michigan.[1] Half of the mothers were recruited from the urban public family practice clinic discussed in chapter 4, and the others were service
employees at a large hospital: nurses' aides, cleaners, and food service
workers (see appendix B for details). Although the women were similar to the white working-class mothers in lacking good male providers, their responses, and how they connected their partnerships
to their mothering, were notably different. The stories they told evidenced more flexible expectations of men, other bases of emotional
and practical support, and the detachment of motherhood from marriage so repudiated in current policy debates. If this, on the one hand,
reflects historical conditions in which both mothers and fathers have
been necessary breadwinners, it also reflects racialized law and policy
that constructed Black motherhood and reproduction as less socially
valued, less in the public interest, than white motherhood.

Rickie Solinger has furthered our understanding of this racialized
legacy. She demonstrated that in the post–World War II era marriage
came to define "true motherhood" for white women only, to promote the relinquishing of the highly valued, adoptable babies of
white unwed mothers (1994: 209). Such white women could also
be rehabilitated through marriage, the other common "solution" to
the problem of teen pregnancies. Black unwed mothers, in contrast,

were expected to keep their unmarketable children, and there was little incentive to marry, for they could never be "rehabilitated" in any case. As Joyce Ladner points out, however, no notion of illegitimacy has existed in the Black community, with its long tradition of common-law marriage and the high value assigned to children (1971: 217–218). Thus, if allowed more space for maternal sentiment, African-American mothers were excluded from the respectable motherhood of white, married women. And public concern was, as it continues to be, not so much with whether these mothers were married, but with who pays the cost of raising their children.[2]

Most of the mothers I spoke with for this chapter were unmarried but had long-term male partners. The stories they told about these relationships occasionally echoed the liberal side of current debates about the Black family; that is, that women do not want to marry when men lack manly breadwinning jobs (e.g., Wilson 1996). These policy debates always assume a kind of marital rationality; namely, that, given manly providers, women want to marry and it is in their interest to do so. Sharona Daniels may have felt this way; she had four children, and her partner (the father of the younger two, who lived in the household) wanted to marry her. She explained that it was difficult to refuse, but she did not want to be legally tied to someone who was not a good provider:

> Once you get those papers on each other, you're his and he's yours. That's the way I look at it. [But] it's hard to bring up the subject [she mimics in an exaggerated way]: "Well, I don't want to marry you because you don't have a job!" You know, I kind of hint around what I'm trying to say to him. It makes him feel bad. He wants to get married.

Sharona, however, was unusual in emphasizing marriage and these (male) economic obstacles; only one other mother told such a story. And Sharona had conflicting feelings, drawing her toward marriage. She recounted, for example, that her partner was "so good" about the housework and childcare that even with four little ones "I can lay up in bed in the morning!" "I think [she mimics again] 'Well, he ain't got no job. Why would you want to marry him?' But then if you put six or seven years in with somebody . . . You know, it's like a total war in my mind."

For other mothers, marriage itself was a much less dominant

theme. They spoke of autonomous hopes and goals, and, despite good partnerships, most spoke of wanting better jobs and public entitlements to support their children. None told stories like the mothers of the last chapter, pinning their hopes for the future on their partner's paycheck and willingness to marry. Jenny Johnston, for example, was thirty-one years old and the mother of three girls. Although she and her partner had been together for fifteen years and he was stably employed in construction, she was content to live single. In her discussion of the future, Jenny spoke happily of her upcoming transfer from the local community college to a four-year college and of her hopes for a career: "I would like to be working and supporting my family and having a job that I truly loved, plus including my children in that, and they would be all happy and everything. That would be my fantasy."

Jenny, in fact, told a cautionary tale about the harm a bad mother can do that was remarkably similar to Melody Jenksman's story in the previous chapter, except that marriage's place in it was reversed. Both cautionary tales centered on a child from their partners' previous relationships. Each emphasized how damaged the child was and blamed the self-centered, immature mother. For Melody the bad white mother's unmarried status explained everything. For Jenny, keeping mothering distinct from any partnership, precisely by not marrying, showed far greater maturity. The bad mother actually had been married (to Jenny's partner) when she had her child; she was subsequently divorced and became determined to find a better husband, causing too many disruptions and too much emotional preoccupation with her own love life. According to Jenny, "The child's mother has been married several times and it has messed the child up. It truly has."[3]

Jenny's account of her life was rich with detail about each of her daughters. Even as a single mother who had struggled to support her family on welfare and to stay in school, she clearly took deep pleasure in her mothering. When I asked how it was to have a new baby again with her third daughter, she quickly responded: "She's the joy of my life!" Although very content to remain unwed, Jenny pleasurably boasted about what a good father her partner was. "When I had my first two, I didn't have to do anything for those kids. Nothing. He would feed them, dress them, he would get up with them during the night. [She laughed a little.] [The new baby] is the first one that I have taken care of!"

Deb Childers was similarly uninterested in marriage though she and the father of her infant son had been together for six years. "Everybody keeps asking me when we're going to get married. No, right now, I'm not thinking about it, and he's not either." Both Deb and her partner were in vocational training programs, but in contrast to many of the white working-class mothers, she emphasized, "When I get married I want him to be on his feet. And I want to be on *my feet*." Later Deb explained further: "I'm the type of person, I don't want to depend on nobody. I grew up under my mother's standards [a divorced single mother]. She never depended on nobody, so I know I don't want to." As for her mothering, Deb, like Jenny, saw her partnership separately, and, while she felt it would last, she stressed, "you know, my son can have a nice life even if I'm with his father or without his father."

In contrast to most of the mothers in the previous chapter, these women spoke of wanting their independence, as both an economic and noneconomic aspect of relationships with male partners. One maintained, for example, "Every woman needs her own money so she can take care of her children" (Kerry Williams); and another said, "I want a better job before we get married. I just want it to be my *own* money!" (Sherri Riley). Others (like Jenny Johnston and Deb Childers) spoke of a more emotional "space" that kept the partnership outside of the primary relation of mother and children. In fact, many of the women did not live with their long-term partners and explained that, as one put it, "he comes by every now and then and stays a while, but he doesn't live with us" (Thea Carpenter). Another mother, who had lived with her partner at one time, stated (to correct the interviewer's query): "It was always *my* place" (Ramona Matthews). Clarice Wilcox answered my question about how often her partner came by laughingly, "Too much. Every day. I really don't want him to be up under me every day." Finally, Cynthia Good told me how much better she and her partner got along since they had stopped living together. She characterized herself, at twenty-nine with a full-time job and a young daughter, as a "homebody," but without contradiction as just "not ready for marriage."

The few married women I spoke with for this chapter told stories that were also about independence and expressed similar themes of marriage as nonimperative and distinct from motherhood.[4] Most of the married mothers, in fact, had married long after having children.

Katie Bagins, for example, was in a shared-breadwinning marriage when I met her, but she had spent eight years as a single mother before marrying. She explained that, even with a full-time job and a young son, she had just not wanted to be "tied down" and had spent years in a friendship with the man she later finally married. Another married mother, Joy Barkeley, married after her first child was two years old. She worked full-time and out-earned her partner, who she described as sometimes threatened but overall "pretty cool." "I've always been independent, and I just felt like that's part of everyone, to take their own independence. And I didn't think that just because we had a child that we needed to get married."[5]

Social Support and Networks
As many writers point out, African-American working-class mothers "take their own independence" with the significant support of kin and friendship networks. In this sense, "independence" is really an interdependence or a community-based standard. The fact that for most, or possibly all, of the mothers in this chapter raising children was not an individual undertaking contrasts notably with the isolation of many of the white working-class mothers discussed in the previous chapter. Good mothering was not defined by exclusivity, by the mother's singular, irreplaceable presence, as it was for so many of the white mothers. Black feminist scholars note that the honor and responsibility for children tend to be shared as, "Vesting one person with full responsibility for mothering a child may not be wise or possible" (Collins 1990: 119). Among the white working-class mothers I spoke with, about half were committed to full-time mothering, and many of the others were still committed to the ideal of exclusive mothering. Among the African-American working-class mothers I met, however, even those with infants said *no* when asked whether they preferred to be at home full-time; and they spoke of shared childrearing as positive and normal.

Jenny Johnston had found caring for her first two girls, born just a year apart, exhausting: "Oh my God! It was hell, let me tell you!" Her parents, however, were able to care for the babies so that she could return to school: "Their grandfather, he was crazy about them. They were a handful, but it was really fine."

Thea Carpenter shared the care of her baby and two younger sis-

ters with her mother, a swing or evening shift worker: "I get along pretty good because I have two younger sisters. They like to come over and help me out. I keep them while my mother is at work. She gets off at eleven, so some nights they end up spending the night." Her mother reciprocated on her days off: "She will call for him, 'Bring him over, let me keep him for the day, let you get a break.' And I say okay. I will be glad enough."

Yvonda Wagner's tearful story illuminates similarities and differences between these white and Black working-class mothers. Yvonda and Ricky Gorsany of chapter 4 were both young mothers who told of being emotionally overwrought, stuck in turbulent relationships with partners who would not commit to them.[6] Both resorted unhappily to AFDC to support themselves and their babies, though before the pregnancies, they had been working steadily. As Yvonda lamented, "This was nothing like I thought it was going to be." Ricky Gorsany, however, was so preoccupied with whether or not her boyfriend would marry her that she failed to seek out alternative practical or emotional support, and she was living a very isolated life alone with her baby. In contrast, Yvonda was trying to end the relationship with her baby's father (though she feared his angry retaliation), and she was completing the vocational program she had begun while pregnant.[7] Although her network was riven with the problems of hard, poverty-stricken lives, she and her baby were able to live with her best friend and count on the shared caregiving of her grandmother, great-aunt, and father. Of her independent mothering, Yvonda concluded: "I'm the only one who graduated [high school] of all three of my sisters. And if I never get married, I will be working. So my baby won't never be on ADC again. When he gets old enough, you know, he'll be proud of me."

Shared child-rearing was not just regarded as a necessity for economic survival, to accommodate mothers' school and work schedules, but was also valued for its own sake and was not seen as competing with or detracting from the mother-child relationship. Ramona Matthews, for example, wanted her children to be mothered by her sister and aunts so that they would grow up as she had, surrounded by kin: "My whole family is from here, so we're extremely close. I went to school with at least five cousins at all times." Katie Bagins valued and sustained shared mothering relationships even after her marriage

because her three children had special loving ties to her mother and aunt. Finally, Janet Tadison praised the care her son received from her sister, who kept the boy each week while Janet worked swing shift. "She's the kind of person, she gets along with young kids, she thrives on it. My patience is not as good as hers."

Interestingly, according to sociologist Ann Oakley, most research investigating the relation of social support to overall health and well-being has been "heavily weighted by 'maritalist' assumptions" that assumed marriage to be synonymous with support itself. The poorer pregnancy outcomes of unwed mothers thus were often explained by their "lack" of social support, although "[J]ust what it was about the marital relationship that was supposed to give pregnant women support (money? housing? moral support? affection? help with housework? access to a wider kin group? etc.)" was never clearly defined (1992: 36). Oakley worries that the political appeal of "social support" as a "quick fix," and a private, nongovernmental one, will blind us to the multiple, socially embedded causes of the problems working-class mothers face—married or not (Oakley 1992: 326). This is a particularly apt worry in the context of recent "reforms" of the welfare state and public entitlements.

Mothers and Children, With and Against the State
The stories told by these African-American working-class mothers also differed from those of white mothers in their emphasis on mothers' rights to public entitlements "to take their own independence" as they rear their children. In contrast, the white mothers of the last chapter emphasized negotiations with male partners, and instead of "taking their independence" most seemed to prefer *dependence* on men. Although most used (or had used) some form of state assistance for their children, they were reticent about their dealings with social services, which few saw as a credit to respectable motherhood.[8] Although sharing care, the Black working-class mothers I spoke with were often intensively managing their children's daily lives and were particularly adept at dealing with school systems, a stereotypically middle-class activity. Sharona Daniels, for instance, carefully explained to me the complex magnet school system with which she had worked to place her two older daughters in schools for the gifted. Historically, however, most forms of public assistance (including public

schools) treated white and Black mothers very differently. Provisions for low-income families were miserly, but some impoverished white mothers were defined as "fit and worthy" homemakers who deserved assistance, if with careful monitoring and supervision (as discussed in chapter 2).[9] African-American mothers were largely denied benefits through selective application of rules that cast them as unworthy or unfit.[10] This exclusion changed little until African-Americans mounted grass-roots and legal challenges in the 1960s, which, along with demographic and political changes, led to a dramatic expansion in the welfare rolls.[11] Sadly, the inclusion of Black families, though they were never a majority, exacerbated the stigma, provoked racist backlashes in public opinion, and increasingly led to treating all welfare mothers as "undeserving" (Abramovitz 1988: 326–336). Clearly this stigma only worsened in ensuing decades, and children's genuine needs were increasingly ignored as welfare was increasingly coded "Black." According to legal scholar Dorothy Roberts: "The powerful Western image of childhood innocence does not seem to benefit Black children. Black children are born guilty . . . criminals, crackheads, and welfare cheats waiting to happen" (1997: 21).

The African-American mothers in this chapter who had used public assistance spoke of the extensive skills needed to combat such stereotypes and struggle for their children. Yet most were nothing like the stereotype of the mother for whom welfare is a way of life. Research documents that this stereotype is accurate for only a small number of recipients; about 70 percent receive aid for two years or less (e.g., Ellwood and Bane 1994). Most used assistance to return to school or supplement meager workplace benefits. Even one single mother (Kerry Williams) who had *not* used state assistance was critical of (racialized) stereotypes:

> A lot of people are complaining, like one woman who works here, "just because people have kids, do you think we should have to pay *our* taxes!" I hate to hear people talk like that! I pay taxes and I never complained about people on welfare. Everybody doesn't abuse the system. People use it to help, so they can be better in their life. Like a lot use that money to go back to school, for themselves and their kids.

Several working mothers who had used AFDC to supplement or extend minimal (largely unpaid) maternity leave benefits were also

critical of stingy public support for mothers. If African-American babies are not seen, in dominant views, as innocents in need of nurture and protection, mothers themselves feel differently. Of those I met, many fought for extended time at home, some for as much as a year, and expressed the belief that babies are particularly vulnerable before they can talk. Janet Tadison, for instance, was angry that there was no real support for extended time with her new baby before returning to her hospital service job:

> I went to social service and they tell me I have to sell my car. And I said "I only need this help for a couple of months. What happens when I go back to work?" And they was like, "That's not our problem." I worked all these years, and I need a little help now and they said no. So basically I got Medicaid but that's all. I was shocked!

Elise Brown's story also exemplifies independent Black mothers' critical response to the public devaluation of their children. A single mother with a stable employment history,[12] Elise also went to social services to get at least some income replacement while at home for her second son's early months. At the time we spoke, her baby was six months old, and she described her situation without stigma: "My household, it's very healthy and happy." When I asked if there was anything that she wished to change, the contrast with the white working-class mothers was striking: Elise did not mention marriage or improved job options for her partner, but instead burst out with the need for enhanced public entitlements for childrearing: "More help with daycare! Definitely, because it's not affordable at all! The government can kind of help you with ADC. They pay some of the cost. But if you're making maybe $6, $7, or $8 an hour, there really is no help in there!"

Elise Brown, like many of the mothers in this chapter, also was aware of inequities in public entitlements and, thus, had a sense of which children were valued: "The help I have seen is for, I would say, the upper middle-class families . . . At the bank [where she had worked], they came up with a program of tax deferment [for dependent care], but it wouldn't benefit making what *I* made! And I was like, 'If you're making *that much*, you're not actually having that much problem with the cost.' "

For the Black mothers in this chapter, a mother's duty to care for

her children was shared with valued kin and "other mothers" (Collins 1990), although their sense of young children's need for time and nurture was similar to that of the white mothers.[13] These Black mothers, however, emphasized that caregiving within the African-American community should receive more public support. Black women's magazines, though more directed to the Black middle-class, also evidence this critical, divergent norm. *Essence* articles, for example, depict family diversity, defend single mothers, and argue for public entitlements, whereas mainstream white magazines like *Parents,* as well as the maternalist publications from La Leche League, still largely assume that childrearing occurs within the private confines of married-couple families.[14]

Though the Black mothers argued for more state support, some of their stories reveal the punitive costs that, at present, come with even the most meager public resources. Bernice Gooden, a hospital cleaner, struggled to support two children with health and behavioral problems. She told of tough times when she had been laid off or forced to work reduced hours because of on-the-job injuries. Her stories were studded with negotiations with different state agencies, though also with help from kin.[15] Two incidents particularly highlight Bernice's vulnerability, caught between the need for assistance and the desire to avoid state intrusion.[16] In the first, Bernice described her utter devastation when she discovered that her toddler son had been physically abused by his caregiver, an older neighbor. Although ready to "just quit and stay home" and "try to survive with social services as long as I could," Bernice was able to call on family from out of state who kept her children while she arranged other care.[17] She did not feel, however, that she could press charges against the caregiver for fear of involving state authorities. In the second incident, Bernice felt her maternal "fitness" might be seen as even more questionable:

> My daughter [a thirteen-year-old], she got in trouble at school this year. Her attitude was terrible. I was constantly up at the school. I was afraid that if I didn't go, *the state would snatch her out of here.* Her behavior was so bad. And I think they attribute it to the home.[18]

Bernice was really caught in a double-bind, unable to afford to miss so many hours of work as her family's provider, and afraid that her

mothering would be judged negatively by school and social service officials. Working-class, single, Black mothers with few sources of respectability, are easily judged inadequate, and questions of "proper" disciplinary methods are important to state authorities. Sociologist Sharon Hays recounts that a Black-Latina working-class mother she interviewed was charged with abuse and her children (temporarily) removed because of her use of spanking (1996: 84), though some experts argue that harsh or rigid discipline makes sense when rearing children for difficult and racist environments (e.g., Ogbu 1985). At the same time, Bernice might have been as easily charged with neglect if she relied on middle-class "psychologized" disciplinary methods and these were ineffective.[19] Ross's study of the U.K. suggests that harsh disciplinary methods were in part more common among "disreputable" mothers *because* they were so vulnerable to state scrutiny and, ultimately, to the loss of custody of their children. Early-century British maternalists, like La Leche mothers today, opposed physical punishment, but vulnerable working-class mothers needed and may continue to need presentable children (Ross 1993: 147–152, 197), though of course not all resort to corporal punishment.[20]

Shawn Lawrence told an even more desperate story than Bernice Gooden of rearing children in tough times. A single mother with five children, Shawn's settled life was torn apart when her long-term partner was sent to prison. Suddenly, in her account, gang members threatened her home, caseworkers threatened to remove her children (because of the gang activity), and she was evicted and forced to move to a shelter. Although Shawn might be easily stereotyped as a "welfare queen," the ostensibly lazy mother who has more babies just to fatten her monthly check (Lubiano 1992, Roberts 1997: 17–18), her story was more complex. She was close to completing a two-year college degree, and she described her partner, the father of all five children, in far more positive terms than many use to describe their legal husbands and providers. She had found, moreover, a shelter that allowed long-term family residence, and she spoke, even under these terrible circumstances, of deeply pleasurable times with her children. Shawn also had a critical awareness, cutting through dominant stereotypes, of why poor mothers face such hard times, of how the state exacerbates their troubles. She spoke so emotionally of mothers she knew in her neighborhood and at the shelter to also defend her own actions:

I feel like they should get more help for women. Because I am sure they love their kids. I am sure they provided and were really good mothers to their children. Right now, I think they feel that they are all alone. A lot of them want help, but they are afraid. So they don't say anything, and then the problem gets worse, and then when it gets worse, that's when the system wants to step in and do something about it. And take your kids away. You see, before it gets worse, and she is out crying for help, she can't get no help! It just makes me mad that way. They should be trying to help all the time, before it gets to that point.

Although in the last chapter I discussed how white working-class mothers are also vulnerable to state intrusion, *if* they maintain their respectability, particularly by remaining married, their privacy is less apt to be violated. White working-class women told stories of petty intrusions and sometimes of a sense of surveillance, but none spoke of deeper vulnerabilities, of fears for survival or of having their children "snatched" away by the state (although two told of having children "snatched" by their fathers). Mothers have long been deterred from seeking public assistance by the threat, veiled or explicit, of separation from their children. Policy-makers and social service workers have also used that threat to discipline and disqualify those on the rolls. Because Black mothers were seen as the most undeserving of the poor, they have been particularly vulnerable to this threat (Abramovitz 1988). In the contemporary United States, such fears are not groundless. Although there are doubtless abused, neglected children helped by child protection policies, punitive pressures for child removal have also increased with the increasingly stigmatized view of welfare mothers and strident antidrug campaigns. Both Bernice Gooden and Shawn Lawrence were vulnerable: each needed state assistance but had partners who were involved with drugs. (Though this feeds the stereotype of the "disreputable" Black mother, remember that six white mothers in the previous chapter spoke of partners and husbands with serious substance abuse problems.[21]) A drug-using partner poses a considerable risk when the number of poor mothers sent to prison and separated from their children for drug-related crimes, including possession, has been increasing dramatically—particularly as both prosecution and sentencing of nonwhites continues to be overwhelmingly more punitive than for whites. (African-American women are currently seven times more likely to be imprisoned than

white women.) Several feminist researchers, in fact, concluded that "the War on Drugs" is really being waged against low-income minority mothers.[22]

BABIES, BREASTS, AND BODIES
Similar to White Mothers . . .

Living within a racist society, African-American mothers may not be able to view childhood as the same "protected, carefree" time depicted by Anglo-American cultural norms (Ladner 1971: 44–47). But they strive to be good mothers, nonetheless, drawing their sense of what this means from dominant white discourses, Black community traditions, and their own personal histories.[23] Because of these interwoven strands, there are important similarities in the infant-feeding stories of the African-American and the white working-class mothers I spoke with—but the contrast in their responses to dominant mothering prescriptions is also notable. National surveys on breast versus bottlefeeding give us only a very superficial account of such similarities and differences (as discussed earlier), indicating that African-American working-class mothers are among those least likely to breastfeed.[24] It would be misleading, however, to conclude that the experiences of white and Black working-class mothers are *only* different.

In the previous chapter the predominant story told by the white working-class mothers was of failed breastfeeding and failed bodies. Because for them breastfeeding represents a mother's moral duty, these stories contained a good deal of emotional anguish. In contrast, very few of the African-American mothers told such stories (only three, in fact, while two told successful breastfeeding stories). Most (twenty-one mothers) rejected breastfeeding, but because Black women are often "bicultural" and aware of the "norms of whiteness,"[25] they still had quite a bit to say about the topic. And a signficant amount of what they had to say sounded the same themes expressed by the white working-class mothers I had spoken with.

Again, as in the previous chapter, the lack of breastfeeding among this population is considered a matter of public health concern, and it is one goal of the U.S. Surgeon General's Healthy People 2000 campaign to raise both rates and durations. Officials voice particular concern for low rates among African-Americans because of higher rates

of infant mortality and morbidity. Yet the public health framework can individualize these problems, casting them as a result of poorly made choices by immature or ignorant mothers.[26] The framework, as in the previous chapter, misunderstands mothers' own stories, and, in this case, an even more complicated reality than that faced by white "under-resourced" mothers (term from Oakley 1992). To begin with, public health frameworks ignore that health care itself is racially discriminatory, with Blacks receiving less and worse care than whites overall, and even white low-income women receiving better, more respectful care than similarly situated Black women (Kilborn 1998, Martin 1987: 152–155).[27]

Like the white working-class mothers in the previous chapter, however, the mothers in this chapter did not lack adequate information about infant-feeding and care. Education "to tell them over and over" of breastfeeding's benefits would have been just as unlikely to address their needs. Many mothers in this chapter told how they had read pamphlets and heard from their healthcare providers that breastmilk was the best thing for the baby. Clarice Wilcox, who bottlefed her baby, recalled, "I'd come into my doctor's office, and they'd give me some pamphlets to read, and most of the time, it was about breastfeeding." And Sherri Riley, who also rejected breastfeeding, quipped that it was "all everybody talked about!" Andrea Bronson was a bit more assertive and sure of her decision: "The doctors said that breastmilk was the best, but I told them I didn't want to. They tried to talk me into it, but they couldn't. They gave me a videotape and papers, but I didn't want to breastfeed!"

The Black mothers who rejected exhortations to breastfeed, seemed, in their telling, to be relatively free of the emotional anguish many of the white mothers expressed. In fact, as sociologist Carter suggested, rejecting medical advice may enhance some mothers' feelings of autonomy and well-being (1995).[28] Much of the mothers' discussion, however, was similar to that of the white mothers; they spoke of difficult life circumstances and a lack of the time, space, and health that would help make breastfeeding a positive experience. This raises the question again of whether some mothers are better off rejecting breastfeeding—like these Black mothers—than feeling that they have failed at their motherly duty.

Pat Sampson, Yvonda Wagner, and Dena Vaws were the three

women whose stories were most like the narratives of failure in the previous chapter. With her last child, Pat told of multiple sources of stress: the newborn required a blood transfusion and remained in the hospital for several weeks. Pat herself required minor surgery and was unable to pump to maintain her milk supply. At the same time, she was coping with a five-year-old with serious behavioral problems and feeling financial pressure to return to her full-time hospital service job. Dena Vaws felt she had failed in the hospital when she was "so nervous" that she could not get her baby to latch on to the breast. Pregnant with her next child during the interview-conversation, she was planning to try again to nurse—but she was coping with the recent death of her husband in a tragic accident. She said sadly: "I was going to go to this breastfeeding class. I go to the midwives and they are like, 'Well, go to this class.' But I am not into the little family thing now because my mate is not here."[29]

Yvonda Wagner expressed the most emotional anguish of the three women. Speaking through tears during this part of our conversation, she again reminded me of Ricki Gorsany (as she had earlier, since both had partners who were unwilling to make a commitment). Yvonda, like Ricki, struggled with fears of parenting alone. When I asked about bottlefeeding, she began crying quietly and gave a long "lament":

> I used to get so depressed. It was just so hard to go through that pregnancy all by myself. I was going through a lot, and I couldn't eat much at all. And I need to drink sometimes so I could go to sleep. So I chose to bottlefeed. I wasn't in good condition. I kept praying that my baby would be a normal baby. And when I had him, they said he was a normal baby, but he was jaundiced. That was because I was drinking alcohol, and I cried about that because I did it to him. Even though I was going to breastfeed, you have to eat right, you know? But I think you get closer to your baby when you breastfeed. I believe that if I would have been married and didn't have a lot of the stress and pressure on my mind, I would breastfeed.

In this moving account, Yvonda expresses the same blaming of her body, the failed, even dangerous maternal body, the body that does harm, that so many of the women in the previous chapter expressed. She also appears guilt-laden, and this for behavior that seems equivocal—not eating right, drinking alcohol—since her baby was of normal birthweight, and jaundice occurs in almost half of all births.[30]

Like many of the white working-class mothers, Yvonda seems to have internalized cultural notions of her suspect body.

Most of the African-American mothers, however, showed a detachment from these harsh, negative judgments, a detachment that protected them from the anguish described by Ricki and Yvonda. These mothers rejected breastfeeding, showing varying degrees of resistance or oppositional consciousness to external control of the body, though often they coped with chronic health problems aggravated (or even caused) by working-class environments: asthma, lupus, and injuries from physically demanding jobs.[31] This perhaps made it difficult for them to view their bodies *very* positively as well-working bodies; but, again, the overwhelming number did not express the tears, pain and "laments" heard in the previous chapter.

Concerns with negotiating workplace, school, and hectic households, and with their overwork as working-class mothers, played a major role in the Black mothers' rejection of breastfeeding. Much like the white working-class mothers' stories (but in sharp contrast to popular advice), Black mothers I spoke with depicted breastfeeding as burdensome, while bottlefeeding allowed others to help. Indeed, Shawn Lawrence, with her very hard life, described the pleasure her older daughters took in feeding the new baby and commented: "Breastmilk is better than canned milk. But the bottle was more convenient for me. I always bottlefed because it was more convenient." Some mothers received help from their partners (as Shawn did before his incarceration), who were more likely to feed the baby than to take over less enjoyable chores. (Shawn recounted laughingly how her partner would never change dirty diapers!) Two single mothers with demanding lives, Kerry Williams and Bernice Gooden, each spoke of bottlefeeding (in slightly self-mocking tones) as "the easy way out," words that may make them sound like negligent, selfish mothers. Yet each returned to strenuous hospital service work (Kerry as a nurses' aide and Bernice as a custodian) after just two or three months' leave—despite complicated births and health problems, as well as trying "father problems" with partners who were absent or abusive.[32] Such "father problems" were shared by some of the unhappy mothers in the previous chapter who "failed" at breastfeeding. With these multiple sources of stress, Kerry and Bernice received extensive help from kin and neighbors—and each probably made the best, most "rational" infant-feeding decision under the circumstances.

In addition to the overwork of under-resourced mothers, the shared childrearing arrangements valued by African-American mothers seem to mitigate against breastfeeding—though of course shared care and breastfeeding are not inherently incompatible. It is a particularly specific cultural construction (particular to class and race relations of the late-twentieth-century United States) that has tied breastfeeding to norms of white, middle-class exclusively dyadic mothering.[33] The association with exclusive care, nonetheless, may *seem* inherent because breastfeeding is at once so saturated with this meaning while considered a purely *natural* act. Several Black mothers ruminated on the special attachment or bond breastfeeding ostensibly creates. Andrea Bronson, who shared the care of her two children with her mother-in-law, thought of the bond in mainly negative terms: "When they breastfeed, they get really attached. I didn't want that hassle, especially with me going back to work. I want my babies to be attached, but not *that* attached."

Jenny Johnston was more ambivalent than Andrea Bronson and tried to sort out the positives and negatives in our long, fascinating conversation about breastfeeding. Jenny, if you recall, was a single mother struggling to finish college who supported her children with sporadic part-time work, work-study jobs, and AFDC (which was mainly a transfer of child support payments made by her long-term partner). She explained that with her three children, she "was just not into it [breastfeeding] like I should have been" and recalled that her sister and friend, who had breastfed their babies, each said "Oh shame on you!" She recounted many reasons for preferring to bottlefeed. Breastfeeding, she said, "that's more geared for a person that's going to stay home with the baby," whereas she had shared care with her parents. Jenny mentioned, however, that she had regrets. She felt it might be *natural* for babies if not mothers to breastfeed: "It seems as though babies are born with the instinct. They always turned toward my breasts. They would put their hands down my blouse and pat, and go to sleep like that." Jenny also worried about bonding:

> You know, I hear about people, women, who breastfeed, and it furthers a really strong bond between mother and child. And I'm not trying to minimize that I'm not close to my children, but I think probably we could be closer. I don't have any regrets as far as anything else but that part . . . Maybe I should have, maybe I should have breastfed all of them.

When I pressed her to explain further, Jenny did not enlarge on her regret, but instead developed an insightful critique of how controlling, "expert" norms of motherhood work on women:

> My girlfriend who has breastfed all of her kids, I am not saying that her children and her are any closer than mine are to me. But you can look at other people and see things. I mean, you might be *not perfect*, but you might be just fine. But you can look at someone else and say, "Well, gosh, I wish I was like that." Because of insecurities, you know? I guess I have a lot of insecurities. It has a lot to do with our situation, how we're living. I wish a lot of times that I could do more for my children than I can right at the present time. But, you know, it has a lot to do with insecurity.

Finally, Sharona Daniels, another single mother in a long-term partnership, brought up the issue of fathers and bonding. "They say breastfeeding is supposed to bring you closer or some kind of bonding. But bottlefeeding, it was bonding, because when I fed them, I had a chance to hold them and talk to them. And their father, he did most of the night feeding. And you know, it's a bonding there also!" This critique of exclusive mothering points to the problem that the white, middle-class mothers involved in La Leche League mentioned, a core dilemma in the maternalist discourse: the mothers want Involved Dads, but exclusive mothering and "complete" breastfeeding may preclude or constrain the father's involvement.[34]

Deeper issues of gendered, classed, and raced bodies, control of such bodies, of their sexuality and reproduction, are ultimately as central to understanding mothers' infant-feeding stories and decisions as their work and family arrangements.[35] Although most of the African-American mothers gave multiple reasons for rejecting breastfeeding, nearly all touched on the public/private divide, the need for vigilance in keeping their suspect bodies private, and of how severely breastfeeding violates that privacy. The thought of public exposure was very troubling, as in the following comments:

> My aunt breastfed. And she would be out, out in public, and that baby would get to crying, and she would actually pull them out. And I just thought that was a disgrace! (Shawn Lawrence)

> I didn't want to be out in public and have to, you know, whip it out. (Deb Childers)

I said naah, uh-uh [to breastfeeding]. If you go out and the baby wants milk, you gotta do this and you gotta do that, you know. (Bernice Gooden)

Clarice Wilcox had the most to say on the topic of public exposure:

> My uncle's wife, she breastfed all three of her children. She was like, she would just start breastfeeding in front of us. And I always thought that she shouldn't expose herself in public like that. That was one of the reasons why I really don't want to breastfeed. . . . I was thinking that I'd never be able to, in front of people, regardless of if it's my family or not. Just be able to, you know, have everybody looking at my breasts.

In addition, many of the mothers mentioned breast pumps and how unpleasant, even distasteful, it would be to rely on one. Andrea Bronson touched on this issue, "All that pumping—*no!* I know it's good to breastfeed, but I wouldn't recommend it." Clarice Wilcox, like mothers in this and the previous chapter, was also put off by the thought of using an apparatus to control her breasts in order to be able to go out without her baby. She had watched her aunt use the device, yet she described it awkwardly:

> I don't know the name of it, but she'll use it to put it on your breast, and then you put the other end on a bottle, and you drain the milk into there. You kind of pump a couple of times and then the milk goes into there. It kind of, well, I don't know—it just seemed like a lot of work. It seemed like it would leave your breasts sore too.

Even Dena Vaws, who wanted to breastfeed the child she was expecting soon, seemed uncomfortable with the idea of relying on a breast pump to negotiate public spaces. She grimaced as she spoke of going back to work (which she expected to do six to eight weeks after the birth):

> Well, you get embarrassed thinking about it. You think, okay, I want to be able to continue to do this for a while, but I don't want to leak everywhere. I guess you have to take a pump to work. I don't know! I mean like, I leak already [she was nearing the end of her pregnancy]. But, what do you do? I mean, do people take a pump to work and pump milk at work? [She laughed.] Put it in the refrigerator?[36]

Like some (though not all) of the mothers in chapter 4, neither of the two Black women who told successful breastfeeding stories were willing to negotiate breastfeeding once they had gone back to work. Just like Dena, each was concerned with engorgement, leaking, and the need to pump. These are all ways that the recalcitrant body, the body that cannot always be kept under control or out of sight, might violate the dictate that the maternal body be invisible on the job. Katie Bagins had had a bad experience before returning to work, when she left her baby to attend a family funeral: "I had the pump, which helped, but my milk built up so fast. Even at the funeral, I was leaking!" In regard to returning to work, she said: "I didn't want to stop, but I know I didn't have time to go pump milk. And I just couldn't see myself saving this milk and taking it home. There's refrigerators, but I would feel funny putting breastmilk in there. It's not private."

Ramona Matthews actually did try briefly with her first baby to continue nursing after returning from maternity leave. But she did not try to use a breast pump because "it was too hectic" and, consequently, painful engorgement "literally made me cry, it hurt really bad." Even when the pain stopped, according to Ramona, the leaking continued, so within two weeks she completely weaned the baby. In addition, Ramona recounted that her mother, who shared the care of the baby, did not want to touch bottles of breastmilk. "My mom was like, 'I'm not gonna use that kind of milk in a bottle!' You have to warm it up, and she was like, 'AAAh!'"

But Different From . . .

There were similar threads in the stories of the Black and white working-class mothers I spoke with—both groups knew that "breast is best" but many decided (or ended up) bottlefeeding because of stressful lives, health problems, and the difficulties of nursing in public. There were, however, also notable differences. African-American mothers' experiences are refracted through the distinct historical lens of slavery and race hatred, which casts particular meanings on women's bodies. Black women have represented the most essentialized "other" of all groups to white Americans, their sexual and reproductive bodies cast as dangerous and impossible to rehabilitate. African-American mothers, in this sense, could never attain the respectability in the eyes of state authorities that white working-class

mothers struggled for, and their children could never attain the sacred, priceless character of white children.

Although the mothers in this chapter did not speak directly of this legacy, and perhaps few think about it in their everyday lives, it lurks beneath the surface of their words nonetheless.[37] My conversations with this group of mothers suggest that, because of the continuing, or even intensified demonization of their racialized bodies, African-American working-class mothers at the present time find greater autonomy, and some escape from this weight of external controls and judgments on their bodies, by resisting prescriptions to breastfeed. The epigraphs to my book from contemporary Black women authors, as well as the story of Sojourner Truth, show that the legacy of slavery clearly casts different meaning on African-American women's breasts and their public exposure, as on the meaning of privacy itself.[38]

The exploitation of Black women's bodies, their lack of privacy, also continues in the present. The media sensationalizes cases like that of Tawana Brawley, reminding all that Black women's bodies are still dangerously over-sexed and are ultimately not their own.[39] And emotional debates about welfare "dependence" focus a host of "diffuse cultural anxieties" about postindustrial economic, social, and family changes on to the demonized bodies of Black women (Fraser and Gordon 1994: 314). The welfare debates reinvoke old arguments of biological inferiority and conflate them with new elements, as in the media panic over dangerous mothers' drug "dependency" and the "epidemic" of crack babies.[40] Philosopher Nancy Fraser and historian Linda Gordon remind us of past Vice President Dan Quayle's infamous words: "Our inner cities are filled with children having children, with people who are dependent on drugs and the narcotic of welfare" (1994: 327).[41] In a sense, these demonized, "dependent" maternal bodies conceal anxieties from which white mothers, beginning to fall through the cracks of respectability, may no longer be able to clearly differentiate themselves. In the United States, white ethnic groups struggling for respectable working-class or sometimes even middle-class membership have constructed status against others (often unintentionally shoring up antagonisms created by powerful employers and state officials): the slave, the "undeserving" poor, the welfare mother, and the "rough," "hard-living" worker (see Fraser and Gordon 1994: 318).[42]

The white working-class mothers in chapter 4 struggled for respectability by practicing vigilance over their suspect bodies. Although they believed that breastfeeding should be private, fewer rejected it before at least attempting to negotiate where and in front of whom it could be visible (compared to the mothers I spoke to for this chapter). The white working-class mothers believed that maternal and sexual bodies should not be blurred, spoke of breastfeeding in terms of motherly rather than sensual pleasure, and were worried about husbands' and partners' ownership claims to their breasts and sexual bodies. All of these corporeal issues and divides, so difficult for white mothers with class vulnerability, are so much more difficult for racialized "others" with inescapably "disreputable" bodies. It is thus unsurprising, and perhaps even quite rational, that Black mothers reject breastfeeding.

The African-American mothers' stories most clearly differed from white mothers, and perhaps most alluded to the history of their demonized bodies, when they rejected the "animal-like" aspects of nursing. Interestingly, its animal-like aspects were occasionally spoken of very positively by La Leche mothers, whose respectability and virtue were secure; one said she learned from watching her cat with its kittens, and another told of visiting the zoo and defending the evolutionary superiority of "complete" breastfeeding by comparison to other mammals.[43] Elise Brown's feelings were typical of the Black working-class mothers, however. She was very negative about breastfeeding and told me of her stepmother's counsel: "She said the person that would actually give their baby breastmilk, they should do it through a bottle rather than feed the baby off the chest. She feels we're like animals if we have to nurse our kids like that."

LaKeisha Howard was also emphatically negative: "I just don't like it. You know how dogs, like they are all sucking on their mothers? I would feel like a dog or something, or a cat. I just couldn't do it!"

Other mothers only hinted at the animal-like sexuality attributed to African-Americans and mixed up with breasts and breastfeeding. Marcine Sanderson blurted out while laughing (perhaps intending to playfully shock), "I didn't want nobody taking from my boobs!" Thea Carpenter also laughed and used sexual slang when recounting how she had once seen her aunt breastfeeding: "I did think it was kind of gross, like, there's a baby *doing it!*"

In popular advice written within Black communities, I also saw a

different response to the blurring of sexual and maternal bodies that breastfeeding has come to represent. Whereas white mainstream magazines quickly nod approvingly at the sexuality and sensuality of breastfeeding (framing it as safely contained in heterosexual marriage), Black advice was largely silent on the topic (though one *Essence* article did add to the standard advice, "On top of that, it's fun to nurse" [Stewart and Stewart 1971]). The only mention I uncovered of sexuality was a notable article in the *Black Collegian*, which responded with vehement disapproval to the suggestion in a mainstream magazine that nursing could be arousing. The author wrote, this is "just as mis-directed as an adult who finds kissing a small child sexually arousing."[44] When a La Leche League representative suggested that some women are unusually sensual, the author concluded abruptly: "I choose to label it wrong . . ." (Hamilton 1979: 86).[45] Here the legacy of slavery may also create an imperative to keep Black children as well as mothers from any association with animality. The dehumanization of Black children, after all, legitimated the denial of maternal bonds and of the nurture accorded white children, as it allowed the violent disciplining of children and their separation from parents (Roberts 1997).

White working-class mothers, who also worried about their vulnerable right to privacy, did not have to worry about their children in the same way. Interestingly, they also did not speak of the distinct visibility of breastmilk itself, of bottles of their breastmilk, as a source of anxiety (although some spoke of fears of visible leaking). Yet, Dena Vaws, Katie Bagins, and Ramona Matthews each spoke of this with distinct anxiety, in addition to their anxiety over the problems of pumping in the workplace (quoted above). Were they worried their bodily fluids were (or others might see them as) "soiled" or "dirty" compared to the neutral safety of formula? Or were they primarily expressing their more intense need to reinforce boundaries of bodily integrity and privacy? Sarah Raygrove, who worked as a hospital custodian, had rejected breastfeeding with her two children but importantly noted that the white women she saw at work seemed able to handle these visible violations. Working in the intensive care nursery, she had often walked in on mothers pumping, especially white women professionals and mothers of premature and sick babies in the nursery: "A lot of them breastfeed. I hardly ever see them *not*. The

freezer is just *full* of breastmilk!" she exclaimed, and continued: "My head nurse just got back from maternity leave, and she does it *a lot* . . . [but] it would be *too much* for me."

Both Southern slavery and Western eugenic traditions linked the animality of breastfeeding among the "darker races" to the purity of white womanhood. In the slave system, this link was direct: "Not only did the southern white woman push sex out of her life as a shameful thing . . . she also gave her children to 'Black mammies' to suckle and nurture, because, according to the myth of sacred white womanhood, the white woman was above such 'nasty' things . . ." (Hernton, cited in Ladner 1971: 281).

Although historians are divided on the extent to which wealthy Southerners actually used slave wetnurses, a tradition clearly existed justifying the practice. The wealthiest may have preferred white women, but only if needed, for even in the South maternal breast-feeding was advocated as a mother's sacred duty.[46] There are, however, many indications of cross-race nursing, from the writings of traveling Northerners ("shocked and fascinated" by the sight) to the narratives of former slaves collected by the Works Progress Administration in the 1930s.[47] Some contend that the tradition continued well past Emancipation, though, on the whole, the practice of wetnursing rapidly diminished (Golden 1996: 72, 25–27; also Apple 1987).[48] Even as late as 1917, a panel of the American Medical Association's Section on the Diseases of Children debated the link between race, ethnicity, and quality of mother's milk, with participants expressing divergent views about the quality of African-American mothers' milk (cited in Golden 1996: 192).

In our era, the emotional resonance of this racialized legacy continues. In the 1960s the editor of *Ebony* magazine—addressing an affluent Black readership—praised Black womanhood by recalling the slave woman who "bore children" "for lecherous white slave owners and young whites feeling their first need of a woman." "She also nursed the children of her mistress," he continued, and the twentieth-century Black mother is "still the mammy to many a wealthy white woman's child" (*Ebony* 1966). More recently, novelists Toni Morrison and Sherley Ann Williams have specifically explored slavery through the idiom of maternal love and breastfeeding, and each has used cross-race breastfeeding as a powerful metaphor

for African-American women's experiences as "both mother and mother-dispossessed" (Spillers, cited in Davies 1991: 48). Sadly, cross-race breastfeeding's continuing power to "shock and fascinate" (to paraphrase historian Janet Golden) was demonstrated in the 1990s in the "United Colors of Benetton" campaign, which violated many boundaries. One ad in particular depicted a white baby at the breast of a Black woman, blurring the maternal and sexual bodies and directly evoking the pain of African-American history, all to sell sweaters. (See figure 6.1.) Although Benetton's worldwide advertising manager said, "We believe our advertising needs to shock," after advice from the co-founder of *Essence*, the African-American women's magazine, the ad was used only in Europe (Graham 1989). If the intent had been to shock but also to disrupt in a more positive direction, Benetton might have listened to Black feminists Sherley Ann Williams and Patricia Williams, who each imagine the emancipatory possibilities of white mothers feeding Black babies at their breasts.[49]

Obviously, in the United States eugenic traditions feared and repudiated such intimate cross-race contact, while the slave system had exploited it. Eugenics followers, as well as other nativists and jingoists (Mink 1995), campaigned against miscegenation and contamination by the "darker races" and saw high mortality and morbidity rates among African-Americans as evidence of their inferior, degenerate character (Smith 1995: 37). Eugenic politics made maternal breastfeeding a patriotic duty for the future of the white nation, a common thread in U.S. and Western European late-nineteenth and early-twentieth-century public health and child welfare campaigns (Koven and Michel 1993, Mink 1995).[50] Some governments provided incentives to encourage mothers to nurse (such as the WIC efforts discussed in chapter 4), but the extreme was found in Nazi Germany, where "Aryan" mothers were required to breastfeed for the Fatherland.[51]

With such resonances, African-American movements might have been expected to develop a counterdiscourse or counternationalism exhorting Black mothers to breastfeed *against* the state and white nation. In the early twentieth century, grass-roots health movements did voice concern for the survival of the Black race. However, focused on "racial uplift," these organizations were nonconfrontational and primarily conducted educational campaigns within the community stressing hygiene (Smith 1995). To a greater extent, Black nation-

alist movements of the 1970s suggested a counterdiscourse. Activists linked abortion rights movements of white middle-class feminists with ongoing sterilization abuse, in which many poor women of color were sterilized without their full consent when seeking publicly funded health care. Black nationalists, rightly outraged, condemned all family planning and birth control programs, labeling them "racial genocide" programs, although this caused some tension with militant Black women who claimed the right to reproductive self-determination.[52]

Some Black nationalism, embracing breastfeeding to nurture and build the African-American community, can be detected in advice literature written by and for Black communities. Such advice notes the higher risks of low birthweight and of infant mortality and morbidity for African-Americans and demonstrates a critical perspective that is missing from mainstream parenting advice. Articles in *Essence* have mentioned the need for "sisters" to breastfeed (Oliver 1984) and have castigated the formula industry not only for their scandalous practices in the Third World, but for discouraging "thousands of women—especially low-income and minority women" from nursing in the United States (Reynolds 1982).[53] One article even spoke literally of breastfeeding for "Mother Africa" (Powell and Wogu 1985). Finally, another provided a critical, Black nationalist view of the PBB scare in Michigan, a scare which was of great concern to La Leche League (see chapter 3). The author, a Black nursing mother, concluded—like the League—that the environment must be cleaned rather than mothers' bodies targeted: "As Black people we have a battle, a difficult and unrelenting struggle, to obtain our rightful position on this planet. When we can finally walk this earth with dignity as free men and women with free, beautiful children, I want the walk to be worth it" (Hanible 1978).

African-American childrearing manuals also sound such counternationalist themes and mention that through breastfeeding and this "physical contact with a Black body" Black children can develop a healthy sense of self (Hopson and Hopson 1990: 110).

I found, though, such counternationalist maternalism to be only occasional. In the Black popular literature, most infant-feeding advice was little different from the white mainstream of *Parents* magazine or Dr. Spock.[54] Articles advise that breastfeeding is "The Natural

Way" and that it's easy to combine breastfeeding and working; they recommend breast pumps, repeat that you can nurse discreetly in public, and refer readers to La Leche League. Like the white parenting magazines, the authors of advice to Black mothers write that, with breastfeeding, you will bond better, improve the baby's health, enjoy the "convenience," and regain your figure quickly, but you should worry if your husband is "jealous."[55] One *Essence* article goes so far as to echo the public health literature: the author complains that Black mothers who do not breastfeed must be unaware of the benefits—or, he reasons, they must lack maturity and the proper "emotional equilibrium."[56] He warns of the dangerous maternal body, for even if, aware of the health benefits, the mother lacks the right emotions: "You will either fail to produce an adequate quantity of milk, or your child, sensing your anxiety, will become irritable, vomit frequently or experience stomach cramps called colic" (Robinson 1978a).

This last author, like the public health approach in general, ignores what I found striking: most mothers I spoke with worried terribly about harming their babies, whether bottle- or breastfeeding, as they also worried about losing their sexual attractiveness. Indeed, the health perspective trivializes larger gendered problems surrounding the scrutiny and sexualization of women's bodies. Few women of any color feel that they look good *enough* or have the right sized or shaped breasts; and in the current hyperbolic antidrug climate, all worry about what a Diet Coke, a cigarette, or even their bad moods might do to their babies. Many seem to feel that it is only safe to breastfeed with a *perfect* body. Mothers in this chapter told of rejecting breastfeeding because their breasts were too small or too large—and several feared that nursing makes your breasts sag. But these fears were expressed by white mothers as well, and they seemed to be incredibly widespread, if the number of exhortations regarding breast size and shape in the advice literature, both Black and white, were any indication.[57] Some mothers, white and Black, also maintained that they did not have the required "patience" or the proper emotional state to breastfeed.[58] Such gendered body (and mind-body) politics pose difficulties for all mothers—although for some white, affluent, married mothers like those in La Leche League, breastfeeding can provide an escape, a limited form of resistance, because their bodies are safe, protected, and highly respectable from the perspective of dominant

ideologies. For others, particularly the working-class mothers in this and the last chapter, breastfeeding is very problematic, for reasons that should be taken seriously.[59]

A counternationalist rhetoric to breastfeed against the state might take Black mothers' needs or interests more seriously, as in some ways the fight against sterilization abuse did. Yet, as with other pronatalist discourses that target mothers' bodies for the nation, such rhetoric and reforms pose contradictions for women. Historically such efforts typically led to (some) enhanced resources and entitlements (for some mothers), but only along with enhanced surveillance and reduced autonomy for the mothers (e.g., Koven and Michel 1993, Mink 1995, Roberts 1997). Rather than any such collective maternalist (but nonfeminist) resistance from African-American women, I find a great deal of individual resistance in the mothers' stories.[60] Anthropologist Emily Martin thinks of oppositional consciousness on a scale or continuum (leading up to collective acts) including, at the low end, the laments heard in the previous chapter, which express "grief, pain, or unhappiness" and may "go with a conviction that things could be changed" (1987: 184). But the Black mothers I spoke with were more likely to express opposition combining aspects rated higher on Martin's scale, including "nonaction" (for example, rejecting advice perceived to be against their interests), "sabotage" (acting specifically against the advice, although keeping this hidden), and "resistance" (rejecting advice and saying so, openly refusing to act as recommended) (1987: 185–187).

Many women's stories involved forms of "nonaction" and "sabotage," kinds of resistance which reject the continued body monitoring that breastfeeding entails. This was an assertion of autonomy—a kind of protection against or defiance of victim-blaming external judgments—that was missing from most of the white women's stories. Joy Barkeley, for example, defiantly stated the reasons that she didn't breastfeed: "I knew I was going to smoke. And I knew I was going to have me a glass of wine." Similarly, Elise Brown thought it was too much to "make sure I was eating the right foods and the other things you have to watch out for," especially after being careful through her pregnancy. Family clinic staff promoted breastfeeding during prenatal visits, but Elise confided, "I told Bonnie [the prenatal educator] that I'd think about it, [but] I didn't very much. I

just couldn't see myself breastfeeding." Quite simply, these women wanted the state off their bodies—as several women stated emphatically, after all the external monitoring during pregnancy, they wanted their bodies back for themselves!

The mothers in this chapter also used "nonaction" to resist infant-feeding advice and spoke in terms of race difference to accomplish this. This strategic use of race, of categorical difference, may be the best way to protect from the ubiquity of individual criticism in our mother-blaming culture. As sociologist Pam Carter has noted, mothers' infant-feeding stories have a defensive quality and sound as if they are constructed to fend off such criticism (1995). In my interview-conversations for this chapter, this quality came through, although the mothers' stories became more complex and varied the longer I listened. Elise Brown, for example, told of her stepmother's view that breastfeeding is animal-like, of her exercise class where nursing mothers complained of soreness and leaking ("It didn't give me a really great impression," she had laughed), and of her dislike of continued body monitoring. Finally, she added categorical race difference: "I wasn't actually around a lot of people that breastfed. I haven't seen anyone, actually, sitting back, trying to recall. I guess now you don't find too many Black women that do." Joy Barkeley, after her "sabotage" remarks about cigarettes and wine, thought of how her mother's breastfeeding a generation ago "was not a factor" influencing her own or her sisters' decisions: "I don't know why it is that Black women don't breastfeed anymore, but I must say, I have noticed that."

Several mothers' remarks went further—they not only used race difference to defend their "nonaction" but criticized white practices and values. In Martin's terms, they may remain at the level of "sabotage" because it is unclear that they voiced their critique to medical, workplace, or state authorities, or to any white women other than in our interview-conversations. Their critique, however, is penetrating, and, considering that the interviewers with whom they spoke (myself, and Peggy Kahn and Theresa Deussen) are noticeably white, I would raise their remarks to the level of "resistance." (I return to the complexity of white women interviewing Black women in appendix B.)

LaKeisha Howard and Kerry Williams met for interview-conversations separately, but they were friends who worked together in the hospital sterilizing and processing surgical instruments. Each

had a lot to say about the white women they knew who worked as registered nurses.[61] LaKeisha, after emphatically rejecting the animal-like quality of breastfeeding, immediately thought: "That's the thing that's strange—all the nurses just love it." She laughed with gentle amusement when telling about the white women: "They are all into that, breastfeeding and *natural*, and saving their milk. They put it in the freezer! They go pump, and they must have had to pump like every two or three hours! Oh god, they get all wet and have to change clothes."

LaKeisha spoke insightfully about many themes: the invasion of privacy, the difficulty in the workplace, the reliance on the unappealing apparatus, the recalcitrance of the body, and the visibility of the breastmilk. More than that, she revealed the irony of calling all this *natural*. She elaborated, invoking the boundary problems between maternal and heterosexual bodies:

> I think the reason why some of them do it is to lose their weight. By breastfeeding, you lose a lot of calories. I think this one lady got addicted! [She laughed.] One of the nurses got addicted, and she got a second baby, and now both of them are still breastfeeding. And the one boy is two! He might be off of her by now, but she got addicted.

LaKeisha's inversion of the popular language of addiction, to target the white nursing mother rather than the "disreputable" Black mother, is also an important stategic use of race.[62]

Kerry Williams similarly spoke to many important themes. On the public/private divide in the workplace: "A lot of the [white] nurses do. They go pump their breasts right up there on the [obstetrics] unit, put it in the refrigerator! Sometimes I start to go in and they say, 'Kerry, I'm pumping right now, can you come back?'"

Kerry Williams's use of humor also emphasized the particularity and *unnaturalness* of white women's mothering, as in the following conversation:

> KW: The Labor and Delivery nurses, we talk a lot and stuff. And they are into this. Like this one lady, she was going to use cloth diapers, and breastfeed. And what else? She's not going to circumcise her baby! I thought, "My god! that was gross."
>
> TD: So this was a white woman, telling you she was going to use cloth diapers and all?
>
> KW: Yes, oh yes. And I was thinking, "Why??? When they got Pampers

in the store?" [She laughed.] For some reason, I noticed that the white women don't circumcise their sons, and they breastfeed *a lot*. And Black women just do it the other way. That's true.

TD: [laughing] That holds for me too. I mean, my son is not circumcised and I breastfed. And I used cloth diapers.

After further interchange about diapers, and about circumcisions, Kerry continued: "Me and LaKeisha, we just think it's hilarious when they talk . . . The nurses are always talking about [mimicking], 'Oh, they're getting this wonderful milk.' I'm like, 'They can survive on the other type too.'"

LaKeisha Howard and Kerry Williams used irony and humor to critically replace the presumed *universality* of "natural" motherhood with its actual cultural (raced and classed) and historical specificity. Indeed, the humor "works" because their observations reveal how fetishized, and even technologically mediated, such practices are in the contemporary United States. Other Black mothers in our small group shared their sense that claims to the "naturalness" of breastfeeding were funny, a distinct humor missing in white women's stories. Dena Vaws, who spoke of wanting to nurse, laughed ruefully as she thought of her deceased husband: "He was into 'This is *natural*, this is *natural*,' you know, 'Let's go run around the block.'"

TD: Yeah, I saw that he was quite the athlete [admiring photos].

DV: Yeah. And breastfeeding, that was just the natural thing, that was what you were supposed to do. But I tried, and the baby, he was looking up at me like, 'What?' with a look on his face. And my breasts, they're out to here [gesturing], and I'm shoving it up to him. It wasn't *natural* to me!

Finally, Elise Brown, with many reasons to reject breastfeeding advice, including categorical race difference, quipped, "The *natural* thing to me was to bottlefeed."

"To take their own independence" has many meanings for these African-American mothers. Though each had her own story to tell, the mothers in this chapter shared narratives in which the pain and power of Black motherhood were intertwined. As literary critic Carole Boyce Davies has emphasized about writings on Black motherhood, "painful rememberings" and "liberating narratives" need to "interrupt each other's dominance" because either story taken alone is too limiting and defining (1991: 56, 53). Thus these African-

American mothers emphasized taking their independence from male partners, with marriage pleasurable but nonimperative. Experiences with partners were often postive, with tales of long-term "Involved Dads," but some shared the kinds of "father problems" described by several white mothers in the previous chapter. Black working-class mothers also told of taking their independence by relying on kin and community for emotional and practical support; yet shared childrearing was not sufficient by itself, and most had received state social services as well. If this was sometimes painful and demeaning, mothers protected themselves with a critical view of welfare as rightful entitlement, crucial for their mothering. (Because the 1996 "reforms" of the welfare system are so drastic, it will be important for other researchers to track how such mothers fare and what new narratives they may shape.)

The mothers in this chapter also take their independence by rejecting resonances of the historical legacies that threaten to entrap and define their bodies. In other words, in varied ways, the African-American mothers distance themselves from notions of exclusive and respectable motherhood, which have been defined by (or against) their embodied "otherness"—whether as inferior, closer-to-nature "mammy"; super-strong, emasculating "matriarch"; or oversexed, impulse-driven, "welfare queen." To assert autonomy from these oppressive readings, and to resist increased external monitoring by and vulnerability to state health and social service authorities, most of the mothers reject dominant prescriptions to breastfeed. Their own "readings" of dominant discourses of motherhood, however, were subtle and perceptive, full of insights into the "unnaturalness" of contemporary white motherhood. If they use different vocabularies, they may share a postmodern feminist "body politics"—in this instance, an awareness that maternal breastfeeding carries no inherent, "natural" meaning, that it is always located where historically specific, culturally articulated interests and power relations collide with the recalcitrance of the body. In the next and final chapter, I will further explore what such a "body politics" might look like, and what the oppositional consciousness in Black mothers' stories can contribute, as I return to the themes of equality, similarity, and embodied differences.

CHAPTER 6

TWENTY-FIRST-CENTURY
VIRTUAL MOTHERS
OR ROUNDED MOTHERS?

Breast milk is not nature to the culture of Nestle's formula.

Donna J. Haraway

She is an unruly woman, actively making a spectacle of herself . . .
leaking, projecting, shooting, secreting milk, transgressing the
boundaries of her body. Hundreds of years have passed and we are still
engaged in a struggle for the interpretive power over our bodies.

Lynn Randolph

I began this book by asking questions about the contemporary meanings of breastfeeding and moral politics of motherhood. Readers, I
hope, can now see how a conversation about breastfeeding opens up
a much larger conversation about femininity and caregiving, about
maternal bodies and sexual bodies, about the body's public obligations and women's private wants and needs. Thinking about bodies
also means thinking about "good" mothers with "nurturing," white,
affluent bodies, and "bad" mothers with "dangerous," dark, impoverished bodies, because ideologies of motherhood are read through existing social relations, relations of power and inequality. While some
mothers engage in status-enhancing efforts against disparaged "others," which tend to reinforce existing racialized class inequalities,
some develop their own "readings" and challenge dominant norms
of exclusive motherhood, of the mother who is married and cares for
her children with intensive attention and dyadic bonding. As one of
the insightful, independent mothers in the last chapter suggested,
however, it is hard to feel confident in those challenges when mothers
who lack the "house and husband" assumed by advice books are insecure about the ways they may shortchange their children.

With some mothers now literally or metaphorically "denigrated" by those pushing to dismantle the welfare system, today's moral politics of motherhood have taken a particularly stingy and divisive turn. Two interrelated needs, therefore, are clearly the most pressing for the twenty-first century: as is much discussed by feminists of all strands, there is a pressing need to value caregiving with public resources, to treat it as a basis for social entitlement. Those caring for the old, the ill and disabled, for infants and children, must be considered worthy of resources without having to disparage an "othered," "undeserving" group for moral justification. But less widely discussed, and more complicated, is the need to value mothers' embodied well-being, in pregnancy, birth, and breastfeeding.

Because feminists have struggled to free women to determine their own reproductive and embodied destinies, this argument in favor of corporeal motherhood may seem like a reactionary throwback (a danger of which I have been keenly aware). Those scholars and writers in the mother-valorizing strand who have emphasized women's difference and the special value of pregnancy and birth also face this risk. They, however, have seldom moved from relationality to pleasure or dealt with the complexities of maternal sexuality.[1] To suggest that breastfeeding might be in a woman's interest as a uniquely relational experience—an argument we might extrapolate from this perspective—risks being a throwback, and, furthermore, risks imposing the singular perspective of those with the safest, most trusted bodies, and thereby ignoring the cultural construction of embodied experience. There is no one *true, unmediated* pleasure. Breastfeeding, in actuality, is as likely to represent an oppressive aspect of social control and disciplining of the body as the sensuous, relational interlude that I had envisioned. Because of the layering of meanings, it is easy to turn to the other extreme and conclude that feminists should *not* favor feeding at the breast, and would do better to improve bottlefeeding conditions, as left-wing women's groups have at some historical points demanded.[2] But much depends on *which* bodies are in question.

Literary critic Barbara Christian has written that U.S. mothers are denied their autonomy and complexity as human beings because only sacrifices count as evidence of "goodness" (1994). This dictate of maternal selflessness combined with the privileging of men's sexual

needs means that women must split their maternal bodies, which belong to their babies, from their sexual bodies, which belong to their husbands. Although the rare author suggests pleasurable, sexual aspects of giving birth (e.g., Kitzinger 1987), this likely strikes most in contemporary cultures as bizarre. Only breasts so immediately signal female sexuality and threaten to blur the social organization of male privilege in feeding at the breast (Carter 1995, Weisskopf 1980, Young 1990). This is why, as I have shown, current discourses of breastfeeding place the child's needs in the forefront, and, at best, merely hint at the mother's pleasure.[3] Breastfeeding norms are, as anthropologist Vanessa Maher writes, always so much more than just for children's health or even psychology; they are part of the political and symbolic systems organizing gender relations and sexuality (1992: 4–5). Given this, to enjoyably breastfeed could be a subversive act: as Maher and her coauthors found, breastfeeding can be a route to a more self-determined sense of the body, an alternative to male representations. Yet it is just as likely to represent a capitulation, with the maternal self and body vigilantly disciplining the sexual body, or with both being subject to external surveillance.

To sort out this dilemma of pleasure and discipline, I examined the context and the particular historical conditions of breastfeeding in the United States. In the early twentieth century, breastfeeding, like reproduction itself, became implicated in the growing nationalism; strained by immigration and tense racialized class relations, state public health and social welfare programs created a hierarchy of good and bad mothers. White, middle-class mothers and their "pure," "civilized" bodies became the standard for European ethnic and immigrant women; but African-American mothers were largely ignored by the assimilationist efforts of "baby-saving" campaigns. State officials, medical and child development experts, corporate producers of artificial milks, as well as elite mothers, contributed to these discourses of "children's needs"—and interests in profit, authority, and political power were mixed with genuine humanitarian concerns to lower the rates of death and disease among children. Thus, the health advice itself was contradictory: giving the breast was the duty of every mother for the vigor of the country; but anxieties about race, the containment of "suspect" mothers' sexuality, and privileged women's desires for enlarged public roles led to the medical endorse-

ment of bottlefeeding as an equally good alternative, at least, for mothers of value to the nation, if supervised by their physicians.

By the late twentieth century, though mixed messages about breastfeeding were still rampant, the practice was deemed medically, and thus once again morally, superior. Two partially distinct interpretations of breastfeeding practices had developed, however: a medical and a maternalist model. The medical model contained remnants of regimented habit training from behaviorist psychology, together with the factory production metaphors that pervaded medical science. By the 1970s the medical model also incorporated (or deformed) imperatives that mother and baby "bond" as part of this reproductive assembly line. A new controlling image emerged from this amalgam by the 1980s, a breastfeeding-wage-earning Supermom, who is, paradoxically, free from any embodied constraints or wants. She is treated, and treats herself, as nearly body-less, and so can be endlessly self-disciplining. For medical and state authorities, the early-twentieth-century wage-earning mother was, like the $acred Mother, a tragic figure, a poor, immigrant mother who needed help to assimilate to "healthful American" living. But the current breastfeeding-wage-earning mother is affluent, thin and toned, and white, and is held up for others to admire. The $acred Mother may have held her baby at her breast while she performed sweated labor, but she could never be an ideal mother who enhanced her family's status. In contrast, today's Disembodied Supermom gets medical approval to carry her breast pump to work, and, through her milk, to maintain her claim to exclusive, class-enhancing motherhood.

Ideologies of motherhood still contribute to and justify racialized class relations, but the divide between wage-earning and motherhood no longer maps on to a clear moral hierarchy. In fact, as wage-earning has become the norm for white middle-class mothers, anxieties about class-enhancing mothering may have increased.[4] In this atmosphere, the production of breastmilk moves to center stage. Middle-class white mothers, in the medical model, can seize on their milk as "the measure of the mother." What was advocated early in the century in an effort to "save" babies is now promoted in an effort to maximize and perfect them. Perhaps every extra I.Q. point, vocabulary word, and physically enhancing feature is needed to compete in the flexible, "postFordist" United States. As the nation becomes more internally

diverse and incorporates more nonEuropean immigrant groups, as it also seeks to dominate a new global order, the (Euro) white middle and working classes face new threats of displacement.[5] Such concerns with population "quality" encoded in the racialized politics of welfare "reform" and debates about immigration, like early-century discourses, play out on women's and mothers' bodies.

A response to this medical model is contained in the maternalism of La Leche League. La Leche League's rejection of the regimentation and overarching technical discourse of the medical model was also a reaction to the technical horrors unleashed by World War II. But the hope for a warmer, better-adjusted world was not linked to any feminist vision, and the connection of private and public, of motherhood to social reform, was much vaguer than it had been for the original maternalist reformers. The early maternalists furthered racialized class divisions when they promulgated a narrow standard of the "deserving" mother, but they tied mothering to public provision and entitlement in a way that contemporary maternalists have not.

La Leche League's vision of "good mothering through breast-feeding" was originally tied to postwar Christian familialism, but it became less coherent over time. First, a generation of mothers influenced by the 1960s social movements came into the organization, adding new critical, anticapitalist meanings to breastfeeding and "natural" mothering. And, by the end of the 1980s, wage-earning mothers—once considered antithetical to League maternalists— were increasingly welcomed. (Thus the divide between medical and maternal models does not reflect the media-hyped "Mommy Wars" between employed and at-home mothers.) Other precepts of the organization's maternalist philosophy, however, remained relatively constant. Both the body politics that arose against the mechanistic, authoritative model of medical science, and the status-enhancement of the white, middle-class that carried over from it, remain central features. In a fascinating paradox, contemporary maternalism thus *is* involved in politics—though the group believes itself to be apart from the public arena.

BODY POLITICS

La Leche League offered a practice based on the positive embodiment of mothers as it quietly challenged the disembodied medical model.

In the collective setting, women shared their experiences, supported the importance of caregiving, and encouraged each other to enjoy the physicality of the nursing relationship, to enjoy their well-working or even sensual bodies. The counseling and group meetings allowed mothers to recast the body's "failings" as normal, remediable events, to learn about variability in women's bodies, and to acquire their own women-centered expertise. The League offered mothers the recognition of experiences of the body in breastfeeding that were pleasurable, relational, yet partially autonomous of men and compulsory heterosexuality. Women might experience corporeality from the inside, with their babies and their own mindful bodies—with power and pleasure more autonomously derived than from being looked at by men or medical practitioners, or from having that gaze mirrored in images and objects of consumer society.[6] The League's embodied mothers also might collectively establish some safe point for themselves, between or outside the dangerously oversexed—dangerously repressed dichotomy. It might be a place to find, as Marilyn Yalom has quipped (paraphrasing Freud), that "[s]ometimes a breast is just a breast" (1997: 158).[7]

Perhaps in the late-twentieth-century United States, this alternative body politics is particularly needed. Women, as feminist authors have pointed out, are increasingly subject, and subject themselves, to intense regimes of bodily discipline and manipulation in pursuit of nearly unobtainable visual ideals, and the preoccupation with being *looked at* reaches down to girls at younger and younger ages (e.g., Bordo 1989, 1990, Brumberg 1997, Wolf 1991, Young 1990). In addition to eating disorders, dangerous diet pills, and the massive industry devoted to slimness, much of this attention has focused on breasts. The Wonderbra and other devices for "bust development" continue to earn billions, while many go to greater extremes. An estimated two million women had silicone implant surgery to enlarge and "uplift" (Yalom 1997) until the Food and Drug Administration banned cosmetic silicone implants in 1992 in response to numerous complaints and lawsuits.[8] Common side effects included painful hardening of the scar tissue and interference with cancer detection, as well as the uncertain risk that leakage of silicone might contribute to serious autoimmune disorders (see Yalom 1997: 237–238). Women also risked being unable to breastfeed; even those who still could risked harming

their babies and literally becoming dangerous mothers, as researchers found a link between silicone leaking into the breastmilk and serious infant esophageal disease (Hilts 1994, Levine and Ilowite 1994). Only the saline implants have been available for cosmetic surgery since 1992, to rapidly increased demand (Gilbert 1998a). Saline-filled implants, however, still use a silicone envelope whose long-term safety has not been demonstrated, and they too can cause scarring and impede mammography (Bonavoglia 1996). With such surgery, as with the smaller but still significant number of breast reduction surgeries, women risk complete or partial loss of the sensitivity of the nipple, but in the preoccupation with being *looked at,* this risk is seldom discussed.[9]

In the same way that equality-oriented rhetoric helped to create the disembodied mother of the medical model, the body politics of popular strands of feminism have not been of great help against these harmful technologies and disciplining practices. The equality-oriented "bodies" rhetorically constructed for reproductive rights battles extended vocabularies of classic property rights, of "property in one's person," to women's right to self-possession or self-sovereignty. To have such ownership is to have freedom of *choice* and control over the body, secure against others' claims. Such a body politics continues to be crucially important to challenge abortion restrictions, sterilization abuse, fetal rights claims, and different forms of forced sex like marital and date rape. It does little, however, to break with the dichotomy of mind *over* body, of the mind as rational actor which transcends the body's needs. The body-as-property lends itself well to selling techniques of body manipulation—after all, why not *exercise* your right to *choose* your body's design (see Bordo 1990; also Turner 1996)? The body-as-property becomes a hard, detachable, "thing-like" object, separate and split off from the self.[10]

Other feminist scholars extend these criticisms of liberal property-rights-in-the-body to the global capitalist marketing of women's bodies and body parts, claiming that the rhetoric encourages the sex trade, pornography industry, surrogacy, mail-order brides, even the right to buy and sell human organs and gametes. Some suggest dropping the property language (Pateman 1988), while others favor redefining it from oppositional standpoints, standpoints of disowned groups, for example (Petchesky 1995, Williams 1991). These

are important suggestions to which I am sympathetic, but they may not do enough to address the latest in body disciplining and manipulating. Just as it is unclear how property ownership applies to material on the World Wide Web, it is unclear what rights we have over bodies in virtual space: bodies disappear as selves engage in cybersex, rely on artificial intelligence, and utilize "assisted reproductive technologies."[11] We manipulate and remanipulate, in seemingly endless flexibility, this twenty-first-century body, which sociologist Bryan Turner says is both "dismembered" and made "fluid" by the new high-tech, global environment (1996: 15, 21). Turner, along with several feminist analysts, contends that an epochal shift is occurring in how we think, speak, and construct bodies because of this large-scale social transformation (Clarke 1995, Haraway 1997, Martin 1992).[12]

Newspaper accounts of the tragic death of a young ballet dancer underscore just how troubling such a new "flexible specialization," or global production metaphor for the body, can be when it collides with the corporeal body. A twenty-two-year-old dancer, Heidi Guenther, was instructed to drop five pounds after her body was scrutinized as a criterion for artistic advancement; the balletic "gaze" is like an exaggerated version of the heterosexual gaze (e.g., Diesenhouse 1997, Dunning 1997). When she had lost the weight, she was promoted and told, "Please do not get too thin," but she continued to drop weight and, though "not emaciated," suddenly died of heart failure. At her death she weighed just ninety-three pounds (Temin 1997, Terry 1997). It is as if she were to sit at a computer keyboard and redesign her virtual body according to the slightest shifts in market demand[13]—with no felt connection between that artificial mind conveying data and the virtual body being produced. As Haraway writes, the woman in the maternal body in the twenty-first century may be the woman at such a keyboard whose body is merely a "data structure" for the perfect designer baby; for the imperfect, simply hit the "delete" key (1997: 187, 186). She does not add (but well might have) that this twenty-first-century mother will return to the workstation with the super-efficiency "no hands" breastpump depicted in chapter 2, or if she fails to be sufficiently "flexibly specific," she can purchase genetically engineered animal milk (see Crouch 1995).[14] Caught in this extreme of medical technoscience and body-less bod-

ies, League maternalism offers a partial escape. Although it reverts to nature and at times makes women's biology *the* answer, the League practice provides at least a glimpse of a woman in a mindful body who can speak back to medical or technoscientific authority. Unfortunately, she is a very specific and privileged woman.

CLASS POLITICS MEET BODY POLITICS

The stories of the white working-class mothers in chapter 4, like the young ballet dancer's story, further highlight the need for new ways to live in and with our bodies and for metaphors that don't inflict the harm of factory or global production models. The majority of the white working-class mothers I spoke with told painful stories of breastfeeding failure, of bodies which were inadequate, which failed to produce that perfect food. They exemplified what the medical model, with its mind-*over*-matter, body-as-property, body-as-visual-object view, implies: "The value we attach to the self depends on the body's capacity to do its performing and representing. When it fails, we fail; our bodies, ourselves" (Frank 1990: 141). If they escaped the public, medical disciplining and surveillance breastfeeding invited, they did this mainly by accepting a negative assessment of their body-as-property and their mind-as-manager.

Most of the white working-class mothers, not surprisingly, told complicated stories involving some breast *and* bottlefeeding, stories that fit neither medical nor maternalist ideals for exclusive motherhood. In these stories mothers described grasping at class-enhancing practices such as breastfeeding, but they required "a house and a husband" as well, requirements that most acknowledged they could not attain. At best, they clung to what they could provide, whether that was some breastmilk or their presence at home full-time, to defend against feelings of inadequacy. Only one mother, whose household income was closest to the middle class and whose workplace circumstances were unusually favorable, was able to approximate the medical ideal of disembodied Supermom and exemplary breast-pumper. At the same time, only a few had heard of La Leche League and its alternative ideal. Yet, in their "under-resourced" situations, filled with unpredictable and stressful events, they might have benefited from a maternalism that defended their suspect, vulnerable bodies. They suffered from medical indictments that they produced insufficient or

harmful milk—or that they should have been able to handle breast-pumping and myriad interruptions of feeding at the breast. The working-class mothers' stories instead portray breastmilk as a luxury that they can seldom, or only fortuitously, provide. Even more than middle-class mothers, they need collective efforts to recast their physicality in positive, woman-centered terms.

For working-class mothers, however, the private embodied act of feeding at the breast is linked intimately to the state. Such mothers will not easily be able to recast their bodies if there are no public resources to lessen stress, improve well-being, and support their caregiving.[15] But La Leche League's maternalism veers close to arguing against such support, and it fails to challenge growing sentiment against women having children they cannot support alone. The early maternalist reformers made a partial challenge to this kind of privatizing of motherhood, but contemporary maternalism has retreated from formal politics. Maternalism would best serve low-income mothers by making their working conditions a public responsibility and arguing that children flourish where mothers as well as other caregivers flourish.[16]

Such mother-centered collective efforts, though, cannot occur when the state and maternalist discourse reinforce compulsory heterosexuality. If even the "Bad Yuppie Mother" was married, then growing numbers of single, never-married, and nonheterosexual mothers are almost "unspeakable." Maternalism in the United States, in both its early and contemporary versions, has been a class-marking project, a demonstration of cultural capital and a measure of social distance from "bad" mothers. It has been, also, about sexual respectability, as only mothers whose sexuality was owned and contained by husbands and heads of households could claim moral authority. Sociologist Lisa Brush similarly concluded, "[M]aternalist claims . . . about 'good mothers' . . . [meant] above all sexually respectable mothers," i.e., heterosexual and married ones (1996: 450, 447). Maternalists did not support feminist efforts to legalize birth control or abortion, or women's sexual and reproductive autonomy. This dominant notion of maternal virtue has led philosopher Iris Young to observe: "[the "good" mother] cannot be giving if she is wanting, desiring" (Young 1990: 199; also Weisskopf 1980).[17]

Low-income mothers suffer most directly from this repressive

maternal ideal, since, for much of the century, state policies made "respectability" a major criterion for receiving public assistance. This is currently being revived, as low-income single mothers are increasingly required to establish paternity for their children. In one "model" state, all unmarried mothers are contacted to submit information on the "alleged father," but only mothers who need public assistance can be punished for "noncooperation." So "class condition[s] the state's intrusiveness" and the surveillance of mothers' sexuality; yet only heterosexual marriage offers complete protection (Monson 1997: 292).[18]

Despite all the shortcomings of maternalist politics, working-class mothers still might benefit from something like La Leche League. Lisa Brush also has noted that maternalism is "alluring" because it potentially can shame the public into treating mothers as persons (1996). Working-class mothers, however, would need to make it a maternalism of their own, to counter the tendency toward defining the "good" mother *against* some despised, distanced other.[19] Some effective strategy is sorely needed for working-class mothers to argue for public provision, to defend their physicality and autonomous sexuality, and, as in the case of Denise Perrigo (discussed in chapters 3 and 4) arrested and separated from her daughter for one year, their right to breastfeed pleasurably, with "passionate attachment" (Ruddick 1990, in a slightly different context).

The working-class white mothers I spoke with, however, if they did succeed in nursing for a time, did not often experience it as "passionate attachment." Rather the experience was mixed and, even if welcomed, also represented a chore in generally overburdened lives. Breastfeeding also was difficult for mothers with little control of space outside, or even sometimes inside, their homes. With more vulnerable sexual respectability, their breasts particularly violated boundaries between properly repressed maternal bodies and sexually desirable, desiring bodies. Thus breastfeeding was difficult to navigate in public, and even in private with husbands or boyfriends. Understanding what such violations mean to vulnerable mothers is as key to explaining declines in contemporary breastfeeding as mothers' increased wage-earning. Anthropologist Vanessa Maher argues similarly: "It is difficult to imagine how a woman who tries so hard *not* to appear to breastfeed . . . is going to manage it at all" (1992: 14, 16–17; my emphasis).

Feminist Partial Solutions?

If late-twentieth-century maternalism has implied that all the problems of the world can be solved on the bodies, and at the breasts, of
individual mothers, many feminist scholars have endorsed shared parenting with male partners, husbands, and fathers as at least a partial solution to this overwhelming burden.[20] Nancy Chodorow's 1978 book
was one of the most influential to advocate such shared care; yet more
recent scholars have followed her argument. Sharon Hays, for instance, writes that only when men participate equally in caregiving
will care itself be socially valued (1996: 177), and R. W. Connell sees
transformative potential if fathers "re-embody" their masculinity
through the tactile, sensual pleasures of cuddling and rocking babies
(1995: 233). While Chodorow and Hays did not explicitly challenge
heterosexual assumptions, Connell envisions men being primary
caregivers under diverse arrangements (also Rothman 1989). Other
researchers, however, uncovered many problems in the actuality of
shared parenting.

Few found, for one thing, that couples advocating sharing really
practiced it. Rosanna Hertz found one typical pattern, like the night-
marish antimother of La Leche League leaders: rather than share,
affluent couples ("Bad Yuppie Parents") paid "other" women to take
over (1986). Barbara Katz Rothman, similarly, argued that affluent
career mothers now share the distanced position of the Freudian father, and that the paid caregiver has become the primary love object
of the young child (1989). Even Chodorow is rethinking her earlier
position on men's potential for care, as she remarked that we can't leg-
islate or engineer subjectivity.[21]

With couples in which the men have actually been involved in
infant and child care, researchers have given little attention to breastfeeding and women's corporeal difference. Three who paid fleeting
attention found overly anxious women who tended to give up nursing
very quickly (Cowan and Cowan 1990, Ehrensaft 1990a). Interestingly, this anxiety and forfeiture of the physicality of breastfeeding is
treated as an afterthought and a footnote, an altogether trivial issue in
the progress to equality. Sociologist Robbie Pfeufer Kahn is alone in
taking feminists to task for ignoring this forfeit (1989a, b). I found,
however, that even mothers drawn to La Leche League and its exalted
notions of difference felt ambivalent about excluding fathers and had
been influenced by feminist ideals for greater male parenting (though

the group is less ambivalent when divorce threatens to place the father before the breastfeeding mother-baby dyad). Other research, however, which does not consider breastfeeding as even an afterthought, has found that when men parent, they tend to take over pleasures such as playing with and bathing children; women are left the "dirty work," the diapers, laundry, and dishes (e.g., Biernat and Wortman 1991, Hochschild 1989, Segal 1990). Must women be disembodied, I wonder, for men to become, in Connell's term, re-embodied? And is the adamant "need" to breastfeed felt by many white mothers also a partial resistance to this usurpation by fathers?

More dangerous than this usurping of pleasure, however, is the potential for physical harm to mothers and children from an uncritical embrace of the ideal of the involved father (Ehrensaft 1990b, Ruddick 1990). Stories recounted in these chapters by both white and Black working-class mothers remind of the serious risks when mothers and children are unprotected: stories of abuse, kidnapping, stalking, and of women afraid to leave their children alone with alcohol or drug-abusing fathers.[22] Shared parenting, moreover, is all too compatible with the new zeal of the state and conservative political officials to promote fathers' involvement and demonize single mothers. Thus many unwed mothers now have little protection from fathers whose involvement is unwanted or potentially dangerous. At paternity hearings, for instance, single mothers can claim a "good cause" exemption (to declaring the father) if they fear for their own or their child's safety. Yet nationally, fewer than 1 percent of low-income single mothers have successfully done so, a frightening figure considering the rates of serious "father problems." "Alleged fathers" also are routinely asked if they object to the mother having custody and if they want visitation, again promoting the father's involvement when it may be ill-advised.[23] Finally, on a less frightening but still serious note, all the emphasis on shared parenting and the father's involvement tends to devalue alternatives that many women already rely on, including "shared parenting" with women kin, lesbian partners, and friends.

RACIALIZED MOTHERHOOD

The African-American working-class mothers I spoke with told other kinds of instructive stories, stories that more openly contested

the privatization of motherhood and the lack of public support than those of white working-class mothers did. African-American working-class mothers also challenge the *exclusionary* basis of exclusive motherhood and its apotheosis in contemporary maternalism. Exclusive motherhood, in other words, fails in both class and race terms to recognize its own specific, "special" point of view; it does not truly respect mothers without "husbands and homes," and, like even the shared parenting ideal, it fails to valorize woman-centered shared care, particularly what has been traditional in working-class African-American communities. The stories of African-American working-class mothers, moreover, instruct us that the meanings of the maternal body are specific, that "breastfeeding" represents "special" points of view, refracted through prisms of historical difference.

Most public health efforts to promote breastfeeding, even the most well-meaning, have ignored the meanings of *not breastfeeding* for African-American working-class mothers. Marked historically as "breeders," their breasts part of the "livestock," such mothers were the "primitives" whose bodies were bought, sold, and exploited by white men. Even in the twentieth century, stereotypes of Black women's "oversexed nature" have continued to underlie the meagerness of public resources and the intrusions of state surveillance. African-American working-class mothers, thus, spoke with intense feeling to reject the animality of breastfeeding and the exposure of such sexualized body parts. Importantly, they use irony and humor against the two-faced moralism of the "nature" rhetoric that they hear from authoritative discourses and white women—"nature" may be used to exalt white mothers, but it has overwhelmingly been used to dehumanize African Americans.

Consequently, La Leche League maternalism, like its predecessor, has even less to offer African-American mothers than the white working-class mothers of chapter 4. White working-class mothers remain at least potentially eligible recruits to Anglo-American, middle-class norms. Arising with eugenics movements to better the "American" race, maternalism has continually promoted its claims of virtue at others' expense—rarely reflecting on the assumptions involved in this sorting or categorizing. Even the famous first-wave feminist Charlotte Perkins Gilman—who, along with many suffragists, worked with the maternalists to enlarge female citizenship—en-

dorsed eugenics and selective breeding to cultivate "roses" rather than "tumbleweeds." Perkins Gilman, like many of the Progressive-era reformers, believed European immigrant groups were at lower stages of development, unsuited to democracy. She saw African-Americans, however, as even lower, as suited to a compulsory, militaristic industrial corps—a disturbing suggestion after centuries of slavery (Lanser 1989: 426–430).[24]

The immediacy of the legacy of slavery and its marking of women's bodies to contemporary African-Americans was brought home to me by an incident that occurred at the University of Michigan in the early 1990s. Faculty from an interdisciplinary program, The Center for the Study of Social Transformation (CSST), chose to use the Benetton breastfeeding ad as the centerpiece of their cultural studies conference poster (see figure 6.1). The CSST group was led by highly esteemed white men from history, anthropology, and sociology departments, though it had originally included several noted white women. The core CSST faculty came together as a group of left-wing scholars engaged with postmodern/poststructural theories of culture and a sense that Marxism and class analysis were no longer as helpful to understand our rapidly changing, globalizing, hybridizing world. As a group, CSST had looked at some feminist and critical race scholarship, though this was not its main emphasis.[25]

When the Benetton poster for the CSST conference appeared in the hallways, the University's Women of Color Task Force, a group primarily consisting of staff women, sent a distressed query. Faculty organizers therefore opened the conference with a very brief explanation, saying they used the ad, "to generate controversy and intellectual discussion," though they had probably thought Benetton would be the object of any controversy that arose: I think the audience of left-wing cultural studies scholars was presumed to *already* share a critique of the ad series and its hip, commodified transgressions of obviously tabooed race and gender boundaries. The response of the Women of Color Task Force, however, was poignant, direct, and personal rather than hip and theoretical, written and read by Ms. Monica S. Johnson:

> On behalf of the Women of Color Task Force, I would like to say that the slide [of another ad in Benetton's "race" series] with the people handcuffed together [a Black man and white man] would not have hurt as

FIG. 6.1   The poster for a cultural studies conference held by the Center for the Study of Social Transformation (CSST), which used the Benetton ad (University of Michigan, October 1993).

much. I'm from a generation where I was fortunate enough to know my grandparents, who remembered things like this. And when I saw that, it hurt. . . . I'm angry that this was used on the campus where I work and I'm supposed to be a part of the team. . . . [Members of the Task Force] hope . . . to discuss images of women of color—of women, period—that are used to generate discussion, intellectual discussion . . . I hope your conference is worth the pain I feel.[26]

Unfortunately, the eloquent response of the Women of Color Task Force received little further attention. Though I was listening intently, it was several years before I could write this section and realize that it should honor Monica Johnson's voice. When I began this project, I had been loathe to make sexuality a central focus, but I also had not thought enough about the racialized meanings that make sexual objectification so much more dehumanizing for women of color. Indeed, I recall that I merely sputtered when I first saw the CSST-Benetton poster: "There's so much wrong with that I don't know where to start!" I was struck by the layers and layers of objectifying gazes, from the "hip" ad agency, to the "hip" faculty analyzing the "hip" ads, to the "hip" audience for the "hip" faculty, all staring, "shocked and fascinated" by this Black woman with a white infant at her bared breasts. I was, I think now, too preoccupied with my own, very white experience of the public/private divide to see what this might mean to a Black woman, that such an image was conceived to sell sweaters, that it was combined with a slogan to unite the races, and that it was used again to attract attention to an academic conference by those who profess to know, to sympathize, to understand about oppression.

When I first began this project, because of my own resistances, I had made work/family conflict and wage-earning *versus* breastfeeding *the* problem—and I saw a neater class divide in policy remedies, just as I had in earlier research on women in the workplace (Blum 1991). (That is, affluent women more clearly benefited from equality-oriented access and nondiscrimination policies, whereas working- and even many middle-class mothers need more generous difference-oriented provisions, like European maternalist benefits, though of course, optimally, women should have both.[27]) So, because I had pushed sexuality out of the picture, resources for women to genuinely choose interludes of difference, policies for equality *and* difference, appeared *the* solution to the breastfeeding problem.

First-wave feminism, after all, "was full of [such] double aims" with women honored as equal *and* different, as citizens *and* mothers—if not yet as honorable wage-earners *and* mothers (Cott 1987). And sociologist Lise Vogel, who prefers the term "differential consideration" for such extensions of equality across difference, sees the potential for "differential consideration" in the language of the Family Medical Leave Act because it endorses comparability across childbirth, adoption, and family illness, as well as across diverse families (1993). Such "comparable needs" solutions are now fairly well agreed on by feminist scholars,[28] but of course, as Vogel emphasizes, the right terminology or best metaphor will not suffice. The biggest barriers remain the political power to define relevant differences and to gain more than minimal or stingy, unpaid options. In the present U.S. political context, it seems unlikely that policies will venture much beyond the model of temporary disabilities (of the corporeal body). Funding for *paid* family leaves could at least address the periodic flare-ups of lupus and asthma, the torn or strained muscles, and other chronic problems of those with demanding lives in physically demanding jobs. Any such policy, however, fits less well for life events without explicit physiological justification. Ideally, "special" needs should be extended so far that "neediness" becomes the norm and "care" is defined less biologically and more humanely. Army Lieutenant Emma Cuevas wanted time for extended breastfeeding rather than breast-pumping, and as I heard from the working-class mothers I met, others wanted an extended time to spend with a new baby, to deal with an older child's school problems, or even to grieve over a loved one's death.[29] These "special" needs of cultural bodies will be very difficult to justify.

The stories of African-American working-class mothers, particularly when put in historical context, make the "class-ed" equality/difference problem and its solution in "differential consideration," workplace-focused policies more questionable, because this has not been an approach that truly addresses racialized dimensions of difference, the body, or women's sexuality. Between the super-exploitation of African-American women as cheap labor and "breeders," their "natural" aptitude to care for white women's homes and children, and their continual erasure from the category of "deserving" mothers, African-American women have rarely been treated as "equal" or "different" in any positive sense. Rather than the stingy

supports like Mothers' Pensions available to poor, but respectable white mothers, Black mothers were offered only a "mean, and motherhood-denying equality" for much of the twentieth century (Vogel 1993). Amid the assaults on public spending, maternalist arguments fail to challenge racialized stereotypes and, in the ways analyzed earlier, even contribute to their persistence. Similarly, neither maternalist nor feminist visions defend today's other racialized, "denigrated" mothers: the undocumented immigrants, mainly Latinas, hired to care for white children while their own are increasingly considered unworthy of any public resources (Haraway 1997: 190), and the "transnational mothers" whose children, partly because of such measures, must be left behind in the "mother" country (Hondagneu-Sotelo and Avila 1997).[30]

Beyond new models and metaphors, we need coalitions of "disreputable" and "denigrated" mothers who can seize maternalism and force its moral authority to speak for them. From such mothers, demands of their *rights* to be with their babies and to determine their own mothering arrangements, form a powerful call for justice and certainly have a different connotation than affluent white mothers ensnared in romantic, sentimental views. "Special" needs for interludes of "difference" must be defined, therefore, from the point of view of the "disreputable," of the wholly "undeserving." Breastfeeding may or may not even make it on to the list(s) of such coalitions, for, as my analysis has shown, we cannot assume some true, positive meaning, some purity of experience, in the maternal body or at the breast. And as the Women of Color Task Force at the University of Michigan enlightened us, there is still pain in the historical meaning of the breast and body, which some African-American mothers may wish to avoid in the face of continuing objectifying representations.

PARTIAL ANSWERS, ENDLESS QUESTIONS

Can breastfeeding be in women's interests in the twenty-first century? I have shown through these chapters that there is *no one* answer and no position free of danger. To nurse our babies at the breast may offer a way to revalue our bodies and force a public reevaluation of caregiving—*or*—at the same time, it may represent acquiescence to dominant regimes of self-sacrifice, overwork, and surveillance. It can blur into a disembodied regime and threaten an overriding sense of

failure. Bottlefeeding can thus be empowering, a refusal to be tied to our biology, to always be marked by gender and race, to always be vulnerable to oversexualization. But, at the same time, it can represent capitulation to inhumane public and workplace demands, to compulsory heterosexuality, to letting external forces interpret our embodied choices.

Unfortunately, of the few self-identified feminists who have looked "at the breast" and breastfeeding, most have assumed that there is one true meaning, outside of these dilemmas and paradoxes. This truth may be an ultimate rejection of patriarchal capitalism (Palmer 1988, Van Esterik 1989), or even more, as in Pfeufer Kahn's notion of breastfeeding as also the site of our pure spiritual, "maialogical" strength (1989a, 1995). Philosopher Iris Young writes of the "eroticization" of breastfeeding (1990: 199) and her notion of mothers' autonomous pleasure comes closer to my own. Young presumes, however, that a positive experience, a nonthreatening, nondangerous eroticism and relational experience, is an almost *inevitable* outcome of nursing at the breast. Varied responses seem only intelligible, in her view, on an individual, psychological level. Though she writes, "I do not mean to romanticize motherhood" (1990: 199), she sees no sociologically or historically intelligible variations between women.[31]

Sociologists Pam Carter (1995) and Jane Gordon (1989)[32] raise the possibility of coercion by state and medical authorities and see the power relations of breastfeeding, relations that threaten to transform any possible pleasures. They importantly call into question any assumption of one true, fixed meaning of the maternal body. Neither, however, posits anything beyond a simple mapping on to the equality/difference divide. In their view, in other words, to bottlefeed is to be equal, to be out of the home, to gain access to male public space, and to resist medical and state intrusion—but it is also, in resisting difference, to miss a *potentially* positive womanly experience. Conversely, in their views, to breastfeed is to be tied to the specificity of the body, with all its allure, but with all the attendant risks of "naturalizing" gender and inviting male power over the body. Yet this mapping, clarifying some dilemmas in contemporary mothering and *unfixing* the meaning of the maternal body, still misses much.

In the contemporary United States, we can no longer map the bottle on to equality, and the breast, to difference. Advice to rely on

breast pumps is now ubiquitous, and because so many mothers reenter the workplace within a few weeks or months of giving birth (or face other reasons to be apart from their babies), this causes a significant blurring of equal and different, of bottle and breast, of technology and nature, and finally, of medical and maternalist visions. La Leche League has become a major source of advice on breast-pumping, to the chagrin of some older leaders, and will likely face increased "demand" from white, professional women in the twenty-first century. It becomes increasingly difficult to hold on to a pure notion of difference, just as the League philosophy of "good mothering" becomes less coherent. State public health officials, moreover, find blurred categories for many (primarily white) low-income mothers, as their promotional efforts lead to a new norm of techno-bodies: many WIC mothers use a bit of feeding at the breast, some breast-pumping, and lots of "supplemental" formula (GAO: 1993). Such blurred conceptions of "breastfeeding" represent neither the purely positive womanliness of difference—or the scientific sterility and privacy of equality.

I chose the chapter epigraph from theorist Donna Haraway because her work most exemplifies this kind of postmodern blurring, confusion about bodies, and the complexity of the relation of "natural" and "man-made" as we reach the second millennium and move to twenty-first-century mothering (1997). The cultural and corporeal merge, collide, twist, turn, and feed each other; they cannot be sorted into the truth and ultimate goodness of the "natural" and the false, ultimately oppressive realm of the "man-made." The final chapter epigraph, by painter Lynn Randolph, appears in Haraway's book, along with her many vivid images. I chose it to underscore my notion of "body politics." Breastfeeding does not have inherent truth, but meanings determined out of power relations, various disciplining practices, and conflicting needs and interests, which are inherently political. Our goal as feminists should be, as Randolph so well expresses it, to gain interpretive power over our embodied experiences, to define our own embodied wants and desires. To do this, to resist, we need to disrupt dominant metaphors and apparently fixed, seamless meanings that preempt discussion, as well as to promote institutional change (see also Bordo 1989, 1990: 167, Connell 1995: 48). I hope this book, in its questioning, contributes to such a process. For it matters what "breastfeeding" will mean in the twenty-first century,

just as it has in the past. Will "breastfeeding" mean six to twelve weeks of a heated rush to perfectly "bond"? Or will it mean overwork, and little privacy, a sort of feminist "dystopia"—like Atwood's *A Hand-maid's Tale*—of data processors, food service workers, and nurses' aides all lined up for their breast-pumping breaks?[33] Will authorities continue to see Black mothers as in need of education? Or will African-American mothers defend their own, alternative representations of Black bodies?

It matters whether women in the twenty-first century will have greater genuine freedom in infant-feeding choices and in determining their own mothering arrangements. But infant-feeding questions, as this diverse group of scholars all implies, are about citizenship, national and global politics, and as such the meaning of the maternal body should not be seen as the periphery of scholarship. The question of which mothers, and as a result which babies, will flourish, of whether we continue to encourage the privileged to their "intensely cultivated" while the many are as "weeds," will be fundamental to social justice (Haraway 1997: 204). Whether bottle- or breastfeeding, or some hybridized combination using genetically engineered animal milks, I hope for a twenty-first century of flourishing, rounded, multishaded mothers.

APPENDIX A

Statement of Ms. Monica Johnson for the University of Michigan, Women of Color Task Force

This statement was written in response to the Center for the Study of Social Transformation's use of Benetton's cross-race breastfeeding ad for its 1993 "Culture Conference" (Personal communication with the author, October 1997).

It's harder than I thought it would be to attempt to put something in writing because I hurt and I get angry. When I saw that poster it hurt—and it hurts even now.

It was my birthday; I chose to work. It was a good day, but then I entered the LS&A [Letters, Science & Arts] Building and saw this advertisement. My thoughts were: "What in the world? A Black breast giving suck to a white baby?" My chest tightened up; I was sick. This poster was offensive to me as a Black woman, descendant of a runaway slave. I'm from a generation where I was fortunate to know my grandparents, who experienced things like this; and memories shared by my grandfather flooded me. I had heard stories of Black slave fathers walking in on the white overseer raping a child or perhaps his wife. When the slave tried to defend his family, he was either beaten within an inch of his life, killed, or sold off. The system of slavery in America was the worst in history, the family structure was constantly destroyed. The men, women, and children were listed as property, the same as the livestock, and many times were treated worse. The child in this picture could have been a by-product of violence. So could the woman. If she was not raped, she was still being exploited as the "nanny" suckling the white master's/lady's child. Her child would go hungry until the young master or mistress was satisfied (she could only pray she had milk left over).

What was the point of the poster: culture? Whose? . . . In discussing this poster with the CSST program staff, it was clear to me that they did not understand what I felt or what I meant. Even if I were a white woman, this

poster would offend me for other reasons—for instance, the display of a woman's bared breast. Why was this necessary? What about men's privates—are they not also a part of the culture? . . . I understand the purpose of the conference. I understand what the organizer said about stirring up interest and controversy, but I can't deal with it because of this pain. I am not an educator, nor am I an anthropologist, so the subtleties of generating academic interest are meaningless to me . . . I am angry that this was used on the campus where I work and I'm supposed to be part of the team, where the president [of the university] has an agenda for diversity and for women. The goal is to create a unversity climate that fosters the success of women, drawing upon the strength of our diversity.

The speakers at the introduction of the conference explained the rationale for the use of this particular poster instead of the one with two men (Black and white) handcuffed together: it was to cause "controversy," to generate the process. Instead it brought pain and anger.

This far removed from the conference, I am still troubled that many learned men would utilize such an image to generate discussion. When will we get to the place where we are aware of the feelings of others?

APPENDIX B: METHODOLOGY

SOME "META-METHOD" COMMENTS:
THOUGHTS ABOUT WHAT I DID

My research for *At the Breast* spanned a seven-year period, from 1990 to 1997. During that time, I used several research approaches and qualitative strategies to gain clarity and understanding of such a complex and contradictory topic. I also began to explore the interdisciplinary worlds of cultural and women's studies during this research and moved across epistemological divides between these realms and and my "home" discipline, sociology. In this appendix, I clarify my path through the empirical research, but, to start, I briefly locate myself at these epistemological crossroads.[1]

Like any critical, qualitative sociologist, I was familiar with the usual criticisms of fieldwork and its unrepresentative, overly subjective words and stories—and, like others who study women's words and stories, I knew well the refrain that such research was peripheral to the discipline. Other criticisms arose when I entered the interdisciplinary arena, flush with postmodern and multicultural insights in 1990. An ethnographic approach to "human subjects"—particularly across differences of class, race, status, family choice, and, sometimes, age—had come to seem naive and atheoretical. Interdisciplinary scholars saw the aims of feminist ethnographers to recover women's experiences and "give voice to the voiceless" as dangerously full of unequal power relations and the potential for exploitation. In their terms, "giving voice" too often became "speaking for others" (Alcoff 1991–92, duCille 1994). Thus, instead of being cast to the disciplinary periphery, in interdisciplinary waters, I was cast back to the dishonored mainstream, to mindless empiricism. As British scholar Michelle Barrett observed, "the social sciences have lost their purchase within [interdisciplinary] feminism and the rising star lies with the arts, humanities, and philosophy" (1992: 204).

The interdisciplinarian already in the business of linguistic and literary analysis questions the fieldworker's reliance on people's stories as real, true reflections of coherent experience. Words and stories, even from living, speaking people, perhaps are better or more fully treated as also text, as discursively

constituted representations, as within language, as utterances of fragmented subjects—and all this even if the words and stories come from subjects on the privileged margins. Do such important literary insights, however, with renewed attention given to the ubiquity of power (who are we to give voice? to make the subordinate's standpoint intelligible?), mean that ethnography or research with human subjects is fatally flawed? At least one provocative theorist thinks so, as she declared "the end of ethnography," arguing that, as a genre, it is too entrapped in modernist desires for mastery and control (Clough 1992, 1993).[2]

As I confronted old and new epistemological challenges, I felt truly caught. Sociology in the United States, as Michael Burawoy has written, has been preoccupied with debating research technique to the exclusion of epistemology and the additional literary questions of representation (1998). In my research for *At the Breast*, at times I felt this disciplinary preoccupation and the need to defend my qualitative approach against the standardized questionnaire and the random sample (a preoccupation reflected in the remainder of this appendix). At other moments, however, I wanted to defend sociology and talking with others as valuable endeavors, as similar to yet different from literary or textual deconstruction. Talking with living subjects, in living interactions, means that those subjects can talk back. There is always the possibility that people will say something unexpected, something that challenges the identities or assumptions of both researcher and researched. Even if that possibility is seldom fully realized, like a good clinical exchange, the dialogue can have creative moments in which *what can be said* or understood is itself enlarged. Interdisciplinary insights can help the qualitative sociologist, because people use language, metaphor, genre, and their stories are, in important ways, not seamless. Sociological dialogue differs from textual analysis, however, in that (as in clinical work) we aim to reflect on the "seams" together with the storytellers themselves. Rather than giving up on such conversations altogether because of the ubiquity of power asymmetries, sociologists can use the unrelenting postmodern/ multicultural challenge to improve our attentiveness and tentativeness. That is, our interviews and conversations in the field, and our representations of them, improve (or become less partial) with the willingness to hesitate, to reflect on what may have been misheard or misunderstood, and to stand corrected (see Blum and Deussen 1996; DeVault 1995; Haraway 1997: 191, 198–99).[3]

WHAT I DID

Because I set out to examine dominant knowledges of mothers, babies, and breastfeeding, I turned first to medical discourse; from there to La Leche League, the mother-to-mother group endorsing breastfeeding from outside the medical arena; and finally to the popular advice literature which constantly relies on medical discourse but often also refers to La Leche League. To understand medical discourse, I systematically read the various pronouncements of the American Academy of Pediatrics on infant-feeding, the organization's 1984 Task Force report on the issue, and key research articles comparing breast- and bottlefeeding in such authoritative journals as *Pediatrics* and the *Journal of the American Medical Association*. I supplemented this with a formal interview with a pediatrician and specialist in maternal and child health, then at the University of Michigan, Ann Arbor, Department of Public Health.[4]

To explore La Leche League, however, and its maternalist ideology, I emphasized my preferred methods of field research and informal interview-dialogues. To that end, in the spring and summer of 1990, I attended meetings as a participant observer. In the ensuing months, I conducted intensive one-on-one interviews while also reading systematically from League publications. My own son's birth (of course) had prompted my first thoughts about such a project, but, with another book to complete, I did not finally begin the fieldwork until my son was nearly a year old. At that point, he was only partially breastfed so I approached the group with curiosity and some trepidation. Although the instructor of my childbirth class had portrayed the League as very accepting, the community activist who cut my hair had snorted, "They're like breastfeed or DIE!" My mother added interesting historical dimensions: she associated La Leche League with a bohemian lifestyle and wished she'd known of the group when she had had babies. I formally sought the organization's approval—though, informally, I worried that my less-than-exclusive mothering and careerist intentions would meet with disapproval. At the first meeting I ventured in alone while my son napped at his daycare, and I was looked at somewhat warily. I did not repeat that mistake and afterwards always brought my son along; this made it difficult to take field notes, but was as delightful as that energetic, curious but not-yet-walking stage with a young child can be. Yet, during long summer days home with him, I also felt the isolation that brings some mothers to the group, and thus became sensitized to another dimension of the organization.

In all, I attended seven League meetings, which included visits to three

different local groups in the southeastern Michigan region. Though one of the groups drew from a primarily affluent area, the other two drew from mixed neighborhoods with modest, older homes and apartments and some newer subdivisions. As I discussed in detail in chapter 3, the mothers at these meetings were nearly all white and middle class; as other research on the League concurs, the League is a white, middle-class organization. I also attended a statewide League convention (in that case, more as observer than participant) with my husband and son in tow, and dispatched my husband to take field notes during the "Dads Only" sessions; finally, my research assistant Elizabeth A. Vandewater (in 1991–92) made several calls to the League's national office for information.

Much of my understanding of the League rests on the twenty-four one-on-one interview-conversations I had with League mothers, twenty of whom I met at the local meetings. The additional four interview-conversations were with long-time leaders to whom I was referred. The total included twenty-three interviews with white women and one with an African-American mother, to whom I was referred after I repeatedly asked about women of color in the organization. All of the women were in "intact" marriages, though two were married to men who had been previously married.[5] Most were middle class with nice homes, which I was able to visit in all but two cases.[6] Their annual family incomes ranged from $30,000 to the high-end outlier of $100,000, with the median about $45,000, substantially above the national average for families in the early 1990s.[7] Our long conversations, averaging two hours, covered their families, their education and work backgrounds and aspirations, their experiences of pregnancy, birth, breastfeeding, and childrearing, and how they had reached their decision to breastfeed, as well as why and how they had been drawn to the League. We also talked about their views of feminism. Some of these interview-conversations challenged any easy preconceptions on either side of the researcher/researched divide: one non- or even antifeminist mother seemed reluctant to end a long conversation in which we had gone over and over her "conversion" story (to exclusive at-home mothering) and explored its incoherent moments; she thanked me effusively for trying to write a book about such experiences, but I felt guilty and duplicitous, as if I were misrepresenting myself to exploit her confidences. So I gently countered to remind her that I was leaving my own son in substitute care to do this work. She laughed, likely because she *had* put that out of her mind while enjoying my clinical listening; but then she concluded, "I'm still glad that it is some-

one like you!" While I was sitting with another mother, a leader, in her kitchen, she began using her League counseling techniques on me after we had spoken at great length of her life and transformation to a "complete breastfeeding" mother: "Why do you think you have decided to do this project? What are you working out?" I surprised both of us when I burst out that breastfeeding was one of the most intensely ambivalent experiences of my life, an insight that had not fully crystallized before this exchange.

Rather than send drafts to the twenty-four women I had spoken with, I used other strategies to validate my interpretations of La Leche League's maternalist ideology. A League mother in the Boston area read a lengthy draft, attended a research presentation, and generously gave detailed written and verbal responses. I also had e-mail conversations with three League leaders in New England, two of whom attended other presentations of this work and gave me their feedback. Some qualitative sociologists do solicit participants' responses to their written texts (e.g., Liebow 1993, Stacey 1990), though others provide only transcripts or tapes rather than their interpretive analysis (e.g., Edwards 1990). Joan Acker and her colleagues concluded that it was not possible to be truly reciprocal, as the researcher still decides where to end the interaction and how to represent it (Acker, Barry, and Esseveld 1996). Like them, I was reluctant to share my interpretations with those whom I expected to disagree, and with those to whom, in some sense, I had already let my disagreements be known (as in the two exchanges with League mothers above).[8]

My reading of League publications included two years of the bimonthly members' magazine (1990–92); four editions of the League manual, *The Womanly Art of Breastfeeding* (LLLI 1963, 1981, 1987, 1991); numerous pamphlets; a published collection from past member magazines (Halonen and Mohrbacher 1987); and League books on long-term breastfeeding (Bumgarner 1982), working mothers (Dana and Price 1987, Lowman 1984), at-home mothers (Cahill 1983, Cardozo 1986), and fathers (Sears 1983).[9]

Finally, to complete my understanding of dominant knowledges, I examined popular advice literature. With the help of two undergraduate students, I gathered magazine articles on breastfeeding over a thirty-year period from a list we put together of large-circulation general-interest, women's, and parenting magazines (see appendix C).[10] The greatest number of articles came from *Parents* magazine, the oldest and largest magazine directed to mothers (Katz and Katz 1992: 256). I included top popular advice books on baby care by pediatricians Spock and Brazelton and by childbirth educators

Kitzinger and Hotchner; and I relied on Sharon Hays' perceptive analysis of
1990s popular televised expert, Penelope Leach (Hays 1996). Interestingly,
Hays points out that 97 percent of U.S. mothers surveyed had read at least one
childcare book, and Dr. Spock's six editions alone have sold forty million
copies (1996: 51). Finally, I included *The Complete Book of Breastfeeding* (Eiger
and Olds 1972, 1987), whose authors write for *Parents* magazine and refer
readers to their book, and its very similar British counterpart *Breast Is Best*
(Stanway and Stanway 1978). This facet of my research most clearly followed
the interdisciplinary vein of cultural studies.

When my scrutiny of these authoritative texts was underway and fieldwork
with the League complete, I wanted to speak with mothers who were less influenced by dominant ideologies and who might even resist them. It was less
clear how to purposively set out to find such women. As one senior colleague
of mine astutely observed: "It's too bad there isn't an *anti*-breastfeeding group
you could study. Then your methodology would be perfect!"

I decided, however, not to directly pursue mothers who were bottlefeeding. Instead, I pursued working-class and low-income mothers historically
outside of dominant prescriptions for motherhood; such prescriptions have
largely been addressed (by the state, by professional experts, and by affluent
mothers) to the middle class and to others deemed able to assimilate. In fact, I
learned that this was a somewhat circular social or cultural process: dominant
prescriptions have been drawn, at least in part, to create boundaries of respectability from low-income, nonwhite "othered" mothers. At any rate, I
decided to compare, in particular, African-American and white working-
class mothers, more likely in the 1990s to have children outside of legal
marriage and less likely on average to breastfeed than the middle class. Public health and demographic research find that income, education, race, and
marital status are strong predictors of who breastfeeds, but the discussion
of why "less advantaged" mothers do not comply with the "breast is best"
imperative struck me as overly abstract, arrogant, and sometimes mother-
blaming.

In the summer of 1991, I therefore conducted fieldwork in an urban
family practice clinic where the main clients were women seeking pre- and
postnatal care and care for their young children. According to the staff, 99
percent of their clients were lower-income and 60 percent were on welfare.
They also reported that 65 percent were white and 35 percent African-
American. By "hanging around" I was able to observe staff interactions, in-

take groups for the expectant mothers, and a few one-on-one sessions between clients and the prenatal educator.[11] I also perused the various pamphlets and videos available to the expectant and new mothers, but it was difficult to interact with mothers as they hurried in and out for their appointments, often with sick children. I decided therefore to solicit volunteers for interview-conversations with me at separately scheduled times.[12]

By the end of the summer, I had conducted thirty-four interviews in all. These were very valuable and had some wonderful exchanges, but they also contained limitations that worried me. First, I had only ten interview-dialogues with African-American mothers, a problem for my purposes as well as a problem noted for qualitative research in general (Cannon et al. 1988). Second, because I conducted the interviews in the clinic, in whatever exam rooms or offices were vacant, I may have suffered a loss of rapport. I was already divided from these mothers by social class and education, sometimes by age, race, and marital status. I tried to distinguish myself from the clinic staff by bringing my son's toys for the mothers' children to play with, by introducing myself without a title, and by emphasizing that I was *not* a health-care provider. It was, however, probably never fully possible to keep myself separate, particularly because the issues of infant care and feeding I asked about are so authoritatively "owned" by the medical profession.[13] Moreover, as British sociologist Pam Carter has written, low-income mothers become so used to surveillance by state authorities (from welfare caseworkers to school personnel), that talking with a researcher can seem just another occasion in which they have to explain themselves (1995: 211). Finally, I felt these interviews might be limited because most of the families at the clinic lacked a steady breadwinner, at least at the time I met them, so I wondered if stably employed breadwinning mothers would differ substantially.

To address these limitations, I devised another strategy. With Theresa Deussen, my graduate assistant in 1993–94, and then later with my colleague, Professor Peggy Kahn, I gathered more interviews in the summers of 1994 and 1995 from the low-status service employees at a large hospital in the region. These women were recruited more informally, from workers we met hanging around the cafeteria and the union office; we then "snowballed" to coworkers, friends, or kin also employed at the hospital. Our clear status as outsiders in their workplace was more conducive to developing rapport, if initially more awkward for me; and our conversations, in their homes or in quiet corners of the large cafeteria, once even in a car, occurred outside of an institutional context like the clinic. Also, there was a chance for more re-

peated contact: women would see or chat with us again as we were hanging around, some would continue an interview over more than one lunch break, others we would talk to again by phone, one woman even brought her kids by on a morning off. With this strategy I collected nineteen more interviews, sixteen with African-American mothers.[14]

The question then of how to treat interviews gathered from the two distinct sites was a difficult one. In the end, I decided to pool the two groups because they overlapped considerably, something which is very consistent with national poverty research: that is, many families move between the poor and near-poor over time. Clinic mothers and hospital workers shared comparable educational levels: most had completed high school or even some community college credits. And though the hospital workers were better off, with earnings of about $15,000 to $16,000 per year (clinic mothers averaged only $9,000 to $10,000 from earnings and government aid) the hospital workers still earned well below U.S. medians. If their households lacked another stable income, even the "breadwinning" mothers who earned the highest wages told stories of struggling to find adequate housing, transportation, child and health care that were similar to those of the offically poor clinic mothers. Moreover, as national studies of poverty have found, many mothers from both the clinic and the hospital told of alternating between periods of employment and periods on government assistance (this was for multiple reasons, as I discussed in chapters 4 and 5). A one-time "snapshot" of two distinct class groups would, therefore, have greatly oversimplified their lives over time.

Moreover, the image of a "working class" better off than either group of mothers I met is itself being eroded by the deindustrializing economy. Good-paying jobs for those without higher degrees have been shrinking in number, reflected in the deterioration of earnings of high-school educated men (e.g., Kuttner 1992). In the Michigan region, the reliance on the auto industry and its related products made the problem more acute, and a picture of settled working-class families with lives very distant from those of the near-poor is becoming a hazy memory. This is particularly true of younger generations now raising children, for they lacked the chance to acquire the seniority in industry which protected some of their elders. Mothers at the clinic and those employed at the hospital lacked options for true breadwinning employment, paying a decent family wage, as did their male partners.

My group of interviews of working-class mothers for chapters 4 and 5 thus included:

	Family Practice Clinic	Hospital Workers	Total
WHITE	24	3	27
BLACK	10	16	26
			53

What may stand out in this table is the very small number of white hospital-working mothers I included. Logically, this might make my emphasis on racialized discourses of motherhood shaky—perhaps just an artifact of the skewed groups. That is, I may have overstated the difference race makes (or *under*stated the difference breadwinning makes) because so many more African-American mothers I spoke with were stably employed. The independence or autonomy from men that I assert is more characteristic of African-American working-class mothers might also seem to be an artifact of the skewed groups. Both are, however, consistent with theory and research by African-American scholars, and with the research at the same hospital site conducted by Theresa Deussen for her dissertation (1996). Also, I was immersed in the stories of other white mothers employed at the hospital but ultimately excluded many of them because their children were older and their memories of infancy and feeding choices had faded.[15] Finally, I reiterate that, as I had to learn, my "snapshot" of lives obscured the fact that most mothers had moved in and out of employment over time.

Some readers may still be unhappy with this flaw in my research design, and I can only reiterate that my work is suggestive, small-scale, and exploratory—concerned with extending theory, as most qualitative projects are. It also does not follow a tidy design comparing mothers by race and class, in sociologists' terms a "two by two" or "four cell" design. Rather, I set out to study prescriptive discourses or dominant knowledges and their reception by those closest to and furthest from them. Still, because the mothers drawn to La Leche League and its ideal of exclusive mothering were primarily from the white middle class, my omission of Black middle-class mothers may be problematic. Surely Black middle-class mothers have important similarities with and differences from the groups of mothers I spoke with. Although not originally intended to fill this gap, my reading of magazines partially addressed it. I found in my search of general periodical guides that Black periodicals were not well indexed;[16] I turned to the *Guide to Black Periodical Literature* and a cover-to-cover search of *Essence*, the African-American women's magazine with the largest circulation, for materials which probably reach a primarily college-educated audience. These texts suggested that Black

middle-class mothers draw from both dominant and alternative knowledges, and may sometimes resist white ideologies. These questions, however, deserve a book of their own.

My largely dichotomous treatment of race in this project, as a Black/white comparison, is also problematic. Race and ethnic groupings are more dynamic and diverse, as I have only touched on briefly. The fact that one of the white mothers I met at La Leche League was married to a Mexican-American, or that two of the clinic mothers who counted themselves as white mentioned grandparents who were part Native American, begins to illustrate the complex and nondichotomous character of U.S. racial formations.[17]

Interdisciplinary readers may be more bothered by another issue: how I, a white middle-class researcher, can claim to understand and even partially represent the stories of working-class African-American mothers. Black literary scholars Hazel Carby (1982) and Ann duCille (1994) worry about such intrusions, with Carby instructing white feminist researchers to study racism among white women and duCille finding no truly respectful model for taking up the words of Black women without taking over (also Alcoff 1991–92). White feminist researchers Barrett and McIntosh agree, and write that though theories need to be inclusive, we should leave the empirical work to be carried out by Blacks (1985). In contrast, I have tried (as I've mentioned) to draw increased attention to problems in cross-race dialogues, to reflexively scrutinize the interactions and their limitations, but not to give up; it seemed worse to exclude Black women because I was white than to attempt imperfect or hesitant dialogue (Edwards 1990; also Anderson and Jack 1991, DeVault 1995, Riessman 1987).

In fact, I learned most from those facets of African-American women's stories which I had the most trouble hearing. I have written elsewhere of learning that, particularly with respect to African Americans, assumptions of "marital rationality" make it difficult to hear of or to honor important extralegal relationships (Blum and Deussen 1996).[18] I add here that I also learned most from being made very uncomfortable. The stories and laughter of African-American working-class mothers willing to speak with me (as well as with Deussen and Kahn) often revealed my arrogance and conformity to dominant knowledges. Nonetheless, the twenty-six mothers were very willing to participate, and, perhaps because we elicited participation mainly by approaching women in person, we did not meet with the hostility discussed by Rosalind Edwards (1990). When I carefully reviewed the tran-

scripts of these interviews, I found that other differences and similarities also seemed to matter in gaining rapport. Age, for instance, stuck out, and, perhaps due to my own bias, my conversations with younger mothers did not go as well and were usually shorter. Some of the older mothers, moreover, evidenced seemingly little feeling of inhibition with me; though perhaps they would have had a different conversation with a woman of color. Even in the relative formality of the clinic, for instance, Jenny Johnston (who was in her early thirties, as was I, at the time), twice broke in to establish our commonalities, to reverse roles, and perhaps to get more of her needs met. The second of these exchanges was lengthier, but of course our interactions were not truly reciprocal, and as the following exchange indicates, I kept the upper hand:

JJ: I don't know what I am going to do [when she returns to school] as far as A. [her baby] is concerned. Now I have used daycare [centers] but my children were older. I have never put my children in daycare as young as A. is. . . . My grandmother [who took care of her older children as infants] is getting up in years, she's sixty-eight years old, she has arthritis. And to take care of an infant, it takes a lot, you know? So some days, A. will have to be in a daycare. . . . Do you have your son in a daycare?

LB: Kind of. He is with a mom who has a license for her home. I guess they can have six [kids] but she has not had that many.

JJ: And he likes it?

LB: Yes, it worked out surprisingly well. I didn't know what I was going to do either. We don't have family around, so we interviewed different sitters. You know, it just is really hard to tell.

JJ: Yes it is! Especially like you say, when you don't have anyone to fall back on. I know exactly what you mean by that. So did you go back to work after you had him, or how did you handle that part?

LB: Well, it was kind of mixed. I had him in the summer, but then I took the next semester off from teaching. But I was doing some writing . . . then, like at six months, I was teaching again.

JJ: Oh that's good! Was it hard leaving him?

LB: [Laughing] This is supposed to be your interview!

JJ: [Laughing also] Yeah I know [but then quiet waiting for me to answer].

LB: I guess it was mixed. Somedays it was, some it wasn't. My job is a lot more flexible in hours than a lot of jobs, so this is kind of an advantage. . . . But sometimes it's hard. . . . Now let me ask you a couple of other things.

APPENDIX C

Mass Circulation Magazine Articles, 1963–1993

As I discuss in appendix B: Methodology, this list was generated by a search of the *Readers' Guide to Periodical Literature* for articles on breastfeeding in mass circulation, general, family, women's, or health magazines. I included magazines that were published over all or most of the thirty-year span (based on Katz and Katz 1992). (I did not include *Parenting,* for instance, because it began publishing only in 1987, but I did include *Working Mother* and *Working Woman,* which originated a decade earlier.) It may interest readers to know that, because breastfeeding had become so uncommon, it was not a distinct subject heading prior to volume 28, March 1968 to February 1969. I also added a list generated from searching the *Index to Black Periodicals* and a cover-to-cover search of *Essence,* the magazine for African-American women.

Abbott, Leandra Henneman. 1975. "The Day-Care Dilemma." *Essence* March, 14.

Adams, J. 1982. "Second Thoughts on Motherhood." *Essence* May, 82.

Aladro, B. 1982. "200 Women Nursed My Baby." *Good Housekeeping* May, 48.

Almond, A. M. 1974. "Is Breastfeeding Right for You?" *Parents* April, 29–31.

Andersen, K. 1981. "Battle of the Bottle." *Time* June 1, 26.

Baker, G. 1963. "Breast or Bottle?" *Redbook* August, 28.

Baker, S. 1986. "A Guide to Breastfeeding." *Good Housekeeping* September, 110.

Barr, Amy Biber. 1990. "Breastfeeding Can Work for Working Mothers." *Working Mother* July, 62–66.

Bartholomew, C. 1967. "How Breast-feeding Can Get You Out of Practically Anything You Don't Want To Do." *Ladies Home Journal* October, 36.

Birchfield, M. 1964. "How to Succeed as a Nursing Mother." *Parents* May, 40–41.

Black, R. 1992. "Bottle-feeding Basics." *Working Mother* September, 76.

Bonavoglia, A. 1983. "Decent Exposure?" *Ms.* July, 106–107.

Bonds, C. A. 1973. "Initiation into Parenthood." *Essence* September, 58.

Brazelton, T. B. 1981. "Why Shouldn't You Force Your Baby to Eat." *Redbook* May, 60.

Brinkley, B., and P. Charles. 1980. "Breast-feeding: The Natural Way." *Essence* January, 46.

Brothers, J. 1964. "On Being a Woman." *Good Housekeeping* February, 32.

Campbell, Barbara. 1976. "Art of Mothering." *Essence* May, 50.

Carlson, R. 1973. "Why Nursing a Baby Means Love to Me." *Redbook* December, 59–60.

Carrington, B., and F. Bush. 1979. "Mother-to-Be, Baby-to-Be." *Essence* May, 84.

Carro, G. 1978. "Is It Safe to Breastfeed?" *Ladies Home Journal* March, 32.

Carro, G. 1975. "Is Breast Best?" *Ladies Home Journal* October, 24.

Chan, J. 1977. "Getting Your Baby Off to a Good Start." *McCall's* November, 83.

Cherry, S. H. 1991. "Deciding Whether to Breast-Feed." *Parents* September, 175.

Chou, J. S. 1991. "When Baby Wants What's on Your Plate." *McCall's* March, 40.

Clark, M. 1978. "Back to the Breast." *Newsweek* November 6, 92.

Cochran, W. D. 1974. "Demand Feeding vs Schedule Feeding." *Redbook* March, 86.

Cooper, J. 1983. "The First Meal." *Parents* January, 44.

Cranch, G. S., and S. F. Trien. 1977. "Breast or Bottle: Which Way Is Best for You?" *Parents* October, 49–51.

Davidowitz, E. 1992. "The Breast-feeding Taboo." *Redbook* July, 92–95.

Dobrish, C. M. 1972. "I Preferred Bottle Feeding." *Parents* June 33.

Eaton, A. P. 1991. "Breast-feeding Your Baby." *Good Housekeeping* September, 162.

Ebony. 1991. "High-Profile Working Mothers." September, 60.

Ebony. 1966. "The Negro Woman." August, 25.

Echewa, T. O. 1981. "Mothering: African Sexual Attitudes." *Essence* January, 54.

Essence. 1989. "Mothering." September, 108.

Essence. 1984. "Mothering." March, 20.

Essence. 1980. "Breasts, More Than Symbols." January, 42.

Essence. 1980. "Breast Self-Examination." January, 46.

Essence. 1979. "Children and Allergies." December, 50.

Falconer, B. 1971. "Milk Bank Thrives." *McCall's* October, 50.

Feinstein, P. 1970. "Advice from a Nursing Mother." *Redbook* November, 12–13.

Ferdinand, Daphne, and Taylor Kwa Salaam. 1979. "Breast Is Best." *Black Collegian* May/June, 82.

Filstrup, J. M. 1980. "Art of Breast Feeding." *Redbook* February, 48.

Fontana, V. J. 1979. "Feeding Problems." *Parents* October, 86.

Givens, R. 1980. "Remember the Woman Firefighter in Iowa?" *Ms.* September, 25.

Good Housekeeping. 1980. "Facts About Baby Food." February, 176.

Good Housekeeping. 1977. "Baby Food." September, 238.

Good Housekeeping. 1966. "What's New in Feeding Babies." May, 175.

Good Housekeeping. 1963. "Why Women May Fail in Breastfeeding." August, 140.

Greenspan, E. 1980. "Why Babies Eat Funny." *Parents* August, 74–76.

Gregg, S. 1980. "Into the Mouths of Babes." *Essence* April, 66.

Hamilton, Connie. 1979. "Breastfeeding: A Sensual, a Sexual, or a Nurturing Experience." *Black Collegian* May/June, 86.

Hanible, P. 1978. "Bringing It Down Front." *Essence* May, 156.

Hatcher, Cindie Watkin. 1982. "On Responsible Black Parenting." *Essence* June, 128.

Hazelton, L. 1981. "Who's Minding the Children." *Essence* April, 61.

Henig, R. M. 1979. "Case for Mother's Milk." *New York Times Magazine* July 8, 40.

Hillard, P. A. 1988. "Suppressing Breast Milk." *Parents* October, 202.

Homan, W. E. 1971. "Mother's Milk or Other Milk?" *New York Times Magazine* June 6, 75 (and "Discussion" July 4, 15).

Jet. 1988. "Doctor Makes Mock Baby Breast Feeder for Dads." January 4, 44.

Jet. 1986. "Health Officials Urge New Moms to Breast-feed Baby." September 29, 29.

Jet. 1985. "70% of Modern Mothers Breast Feed Their Young." July 22, 29.

Johnson, Victoria L. 1978. "Working and Pregnant: What Can You Expect." *Essence* September, 32.

Kagan, J. 1978. "Advice for Nursing Mothers." *McCall's* March, 44.

Kanner, B. 1986. "Into the Mouths of Babies." *New York* November 17, 27.

Kanter, E. 1972. "I Chose to Nurse My Baby." *Parents* June, 32.

Karlsrud, K., and D. Schultz. 1993a. "Is Milk Enough?" *Parents* December, 84–86.

Karlsrud, K., and D. Schultz. 1993b. "Newsflash: He's Starting Solids!" *Parents* November, 156–158.

Karlsrud, K., and D. Schultz. 1991. "Weaning from the Breast." *Parents* October, 158.

Karlsrud, K., and D. Schultz. 1988. "Breastfeeding for Beginners." *Parents* March, 156.

Katz, S. 1980. "Yes, You Can Keep on Nursing Your Child After You Go to Work." *Glamour* November, 170.

Keiser, M. B. 1964. "Today's Research for Babies' Future." *Parents* November, 20.

Kueffner, S. H. 1991. "The Well-Fed Baby." *Working Mother* June, 70.

Ladies Home Journal. 1975. "Is the Breast Best?" October, 24.

Lainson, S. 1983. "The Erotic Factor." *Ms.* February, 66.

Lehrer, S. 1975. "Breast-feeding and Immunity." *Harper's Bazaar* July, 50.

Levine, K. 1987. "Breast-feeding and Working." *Parents* December 64.

MacCallum, L. 1987. "Breast-feeding and Sore Nipples." *Glamour* May, 252.

MacCallum, L. 1982. "Comfortable Positions for Nursing." *Glamour* November, 78.

Marano, H. 1979. "Breast or Bottle: New Evidence in an Old Debate." *New York* October 29, 56–60.

Margolies, M., and H. La Barre. 1978. "Gift of Life." *Ladies Home Journal* December, 98.

Mathews, T. 1981. "Breast vs. Bottle: World Health Organization Vote." *Newsweek* June 1, 54–55.

Mauk, S. 1984. "Breast-feeding and Work." *Working Woman* April, 43–44.

McCall, R. B. 1987. "Breastfeeding: The Father Factor." *Parents* June 182.

McCall, R. B. 1982. "Starting Solids." *Parents* September, 88.

McCall, R. B. 1980. "Intricate Process of Nursing." *Parents* February, 78.

McCall's. 1986. "Nursing Your Adopted Baby." October, 76–77.

McCall's. 1984. "Decent Exposure?" February, 18.

Moore, Linda Wright. 1988. "Parenting: Pleasures and Pains." *Essence* December, 54.

Morgenstern, D. 1979. "New Benefits from Breast Milk." *McCall's* May, 68.

Mosher, L. 1981. "I Nursed My Adopted Baby." *Good Housekeeping* July, 86.

Ms. 1975. "Hooked on Weaning: Excerpts from *The Baby Viva.*" April, 51–54 (and "Discussion" August, 6).

Mullings, Betty. 1976. "Dispelling the Myth of the Single Parent." *Essence* July, 25.

Nelson, Jill. 1988. "Mothering: Children's Rights, 1988." *Essence* March, 96.

Newsweek. 1986. "Gerber Balks at Recall." March 17, 48.

Newsweek. 1986. "Beech-Nut: The Case of the Ersatz Apple Juice." Nov. 17, 66.

Newsweek. 1981. "United Nations: The Breast vs. the Bottle." June 1, 54.

Newsweek. 1978. "Campus Crunch: Boycott of Nestle Products Over Controversial Baby Formula." November 27, 115.

Newsweek. 1975. "Nursing-Bottle Mouth." August 4, 64.

Newsweek. 1973. "Adopt and Breastfeed." August 13, 45.

Newsweek. 1970. "Return to Breast-feeding?" January 12, 62–63.

Niefert, M. R. 1990. "Ask Dr. Mom." *McCall's* January, 69.

Norment, Lynn. 1989. "The Trials and Triumphs of Working Mothers." *Ebony* September, 38–45.

Olds, S. W. 1980. "25 Vital Questions and Answers." *Parents* January 86.

Oliver, S. S. 1984. "Why Breast-feed Your Baby?" *Essence* September, 153.

Osborne, Gwendolyn E. 1977. "Motherhood in the Black Community." *Crisis* December, 479.

Panter, G. G. 1981. "Breast-feeding Problems and Concerns." *Parents* August 76.

Panter, G. G. 1979. "Obvious and Not So Obvious Drugs in Breast Milk." *Parents* January, 37.

Parents. 1992. "Breast-feeding and Weight Loss." February, 126.

Parents. 1970. "Happy Mother's Guide to Successful Nursing." February, 52–53.

Parks, P. L. 1993. "How to Breast-feed—and Work." *Essence* February, 110.

Patrick, M. 1990. "A Feed Your Baby Quiz." *Essence* March, 104.

Pickhardt, T. 1983. "Coping with First Baby Blues." *Essence* February, 112.

Pomeranz, V. E., and D. Schultz. 1987. "Breast Versus Bottle." *Parents* February, 144.

Pomeranz, V. E., and D. Schultz. 1986. "Weaning Your Baby." *Parents* April, 150.

Pomeranz, V. E., and D. Schultz. 1980. "From Hand to Mouth." *Parents* May, 92.

Pomeranz, V. E., and D. Schultz. 1979. "Solid Foods." *Parents* April, 76.

Powell, Ronald, and K. M. Wogu. 1985. "I Returned to Ethiopia to Breast-feed Dying Babies." *Essence* December, 112.

Prevention. 1993. "Turning Sour on Exercise: Effects on Lactic Acid Levels in Breast Milk." August, 20.

Prevention. 1991. "Yogurt for Tots: Cure for Infant Diarrhea." May, 17.

Prevention. 1986. "Breastfeeding and the Pill: Do They Mix?" November, 124.

Princess Grace of Monaco. 1971. "Why Mothers Should Breastfeed Their Babies." *Ladies Home Journal* August, 56.

Pryor, K. 1963. "They Teach the Joys of Breast-feeding." *Reader's Digest* May, 103–106.

Raphael, D. 1970. "When Mothers Need Mothering." *New York Times Magazine* February 8, 67.

Rawlins, C. M., with D. Z. Meilach. 1968a. "Technique of Nursing." *Redbook* October, 59–60.

Rawlins, C. M., with D. Z. Meilach. 1968b. "Should You Nurse Your Baby?" *Redbook* July, 44.

Reuben, D. 1971. "Breastfeeding." *McCall's* May, 64.

Reynolds, B. A. 1982. "Breast or Bottle: The Right to Choose." *Essence* June, 27.

Ricci, C. 1988. "The Breast-Milk Test." *Parents* August, 79.

Robinson, Lawrence D. 1978a. "Breastfeeding: Nurturing the Natural Way." *Essence* November, 41.

Robinson, Lawrence D. 1978b. "First Lessons in Love." *Essence* October.

Robinson, Lawrence D. 1975. "Working and Mothering." *Essence* December, 33.

Sackett, W. W., Jr. 1963. "Are We Drinking Too Much Milk?" *Science Digest* April, 19–25.

Salmon, D. K. 1992a. "Starting Solids." *Parents* May, 117–118.

Salmon, D. K. 1992b. "Breast & Bottle Feeding." *Parents* September, 141–142.

Salmon, D. K. 1991. "In Search of the Burp." *Working Mother* April, 66.

Samons, W. A. H., and T. B. Brazelton. 1978. "Food Facts for Babies." *Parents* March, 38–39.

Scarupa, Harriet Jackson. 1976. "Speaking of Mothering." *Essence* May, 60.

Schildkraut, M. L. 1979. "What We Know Now About Mother's Milk." *Good Housekeeping* June, 245.

Science Digest. 1982. "Natural Birth Control." January, 100.

Science Digest. 1980. "Bottle-fed Baby Phase Fades as More Mothers Take Over." July, 76–81.

Science Digest. 1976. "Breasts, Not Bottles." May, 21–23.

Science Digest. 1975. "DDT and Mother's Milk." April, 14.

Science Digest. 1967. "Feed Baby Fashionably: Breastfeeding." December, 70–71.

Scott, R. B. 1974. "Is Breastfeeding Obsolete?" *Journal of the National Medical Association* 66 (September): 446–447.

Seligmann, J. 1977. "Tanka Syndrome: Effects of Nursing Babies on One Side Only." *Newsweek* September 12, 52.

Simon, N. 1984. "Why Breast-feed?" *Parents* May, 66–70.

Solomon, S. 1981. "Controversy Over Infant Formulas." *New York Times Magazine* December 6, 92.

Spock, B., and M. B. Rothenberg. 1992. "Into the Mouths of Babes." *Redbook* January, 116–118.

Spock, B. 1983. "The Way Kids Eat." *Redbook* August, 24.

Spock, B. 1983. "Dr. Spock Answers Your Questions About Parenting." *Redbook* January, 20.

Spock, B. 1977. "What Mothers Should Know About Breast feeding and Weaning." *Redbook* September 22.

Spock, B. 1976. "What Parents Should Know About Their Infants' Diets." *Redbook* September, 24.

Spock, B. 1976. "At What Age Should a Baby Be Weaned?" *Redbook* February, 40.

Spock, B. 1964. "Difficulties in Breast Feeding." *Redbook* June, 16.

Spock, B. 1963. "Why Some Babies Become Too Attached to Their Bottles." *Ladies Home Journal* September, 21.

Stewart, C., and S. Stewart. 1971. "More Love to the Once, and Convenience Too." *Essence* April, 5.

Stone, E. 1983. "A Feminist Fad?" *Ms.* February, 68.

Sunley, E. 1963. "Your Baby Doesn't Need a Clock." *Parents* March, 52–53.

Taylor, Susan. 1975. "About Breasts: Straight Facts on Breasts, Bras, and You." *Essence* February, 60.

Time. 1968. "Back to the Breast: La Leche League International." July 19, 53.

Time. 1965. "To Nurse or Not to Nurse?" April 23, 68.

Time. 1963. "Baby's New Bottle." June 7, 52.

Trien, S. F. 1977. "When It's Time for a Bottle." *Parents* October, 51.

Wesley, V. W. 1982. "Breast-feeding Is Still Best for Baby—and You!" *Essence* September, 127.

Wessel, M. A. 1980. "When You Can't Breastfeed." *Parents* June, 34.

Wessel, M. A. 1978. "Why Does That Baby Have Spaghetti in His Hair?" *Parents* October, 70–71.

Wessel, M. A. 1972. "Weaning Made Easy." *Parents* December, 40–41.

Wessel, M. A. 1965. "Breastfeeding Made Easy." *Parents* November, 70–71.

Wholey, J. 1983. "Breast-beating: Low Percentage of Breast-fed Babies in New York City." *New York* October 31, 84–86.

Wilding, S., and J. Winters. 1977. "The Pride of a Single Parent." *Essence* May, 58.

Williams, D. C. 1987a. "Working and Breastfeeding." *Essence* April, 96.

Williams, D. C. 1987b. "Mothering: A Guide to the Love, Care, and Well-Being of Our Children." *Essence* March, 94.

Winick, M. 1982a. "What Every Young Mother Should Know About Feeding Her Baby." *Redbook* May, 36.

Winick, M. 1982b. "Breast or Bottle—or Both?" *Redbook* February, 25.

Yarrow, L. 1983. "But Will It Keep?" *Parents* April, 76–77.

Yarrow, L. 1979. "Breast-feeding: The New Etiquette." *Parents* September, 46–48.

Zevin, D. 1987. "Breast Milk Express." *Health* May, 16.

Zimmerman, D. R. 1985. "50 Fascinating Facts About Mother's Milk." *Good Housekeeping* April, 84.

NOTES

1. "Breast Is Best"

1. Thus one letter-writer sees the lieutenant as a "whiner" who "embarrass[es] military women everywhere with her drivel," as the other praises her "selflessness and courage" (*Time* 1997: 31). On "Mommy Wars" see J. Block (1990), Bryant (1997), and Jackman (1991); also Hays (1996) and Hochschild (1997).

2. Other examples come from high-tech birthing. Ultrasound imaging, genetic testing, and fetal monitoring are represented as scientific innovations that get us closer to the biological *truth*, but they actually offer little in terms of improved treatment options and may do harm in some cases. Robbie Davis-Floyd points out that these practices constitute *rituals* rather than the *truths* of the body that we *believe* them to be (1992; also Rapp 1990).

3. In the last, best-case representation of the "polluted" mother, I think of the HIV-infected mothers at both the 1995 Democratic and Republican national conventions, who were white middle-class victims.

4. Without specific reference to breastfeeding, this point has been insightfully made by sociologist R. W. Connell (1995: 45–66).

5. In the case of mothers of infants, this entails discerning the infant's needs, not always an easy task, as by definition *infant* means "unable to speak" (Pear 1997).

6. This question, which I discuss in the next chapter, frequently has come up when I have given talks.

7. Though because I was not institu-

tionally compelled to do so, I worked shorter hours, and, as readers may discern from the following chapters, I was never so proficient at, or fond of, breast-pumping.

8. If all mothers do not follow this model, as hegemonic, it does shape the terms of discussion. Mothers feel they must negotiate with and respond to it, particularly to justify aspects they reject (Hays 1996: 72–76).

9. Many have written on this equality/difference dilemma. Two of the most accessible are Snitow (1990) and Vogel (1993).

10. "Breast Is Best" originated as a catch-phrase from the title of a very influential and popular British advice book (Stanway and Stanway 1978).

11. This more rounded perspective was expressed by many African-American women, in novels by Toni Morrison (1973, 1987), Alice Walker (1976), Sherley Anne Williams (1986), and in analysis by Patricia Hill Collins (1990) and Walker (1983), among many.

12. Thus, Nancy Folbre and Heidi Hartmann wrote in criticism of their earlier views, "the Hobbesian metaphor is wrong" (1988). The first two phrases in the paragraph are from Hartmann's earlier writings (1981), and the third comes from Barbara Ehrenreich (1990). Alison Jaggar and William McBride also added that the Marxist feminist preoccupation with productive (waged) *versus* reproductive (unpaid household) labor was "invidious and male-biased" and cast women's child-rearing as inherently less creative, less fully

human, less "history-making" than men's work (1985).

13. Peck and Senderowitz note that the term "pronatalism" was originally used by demographers for policies, adopted in response to falling national or regional population trends, that were intended to encourage women to have more babies. Feminists later took up the term because of concern for the effects of such social forces, exalting motherhood, on women's self-determination (1974: 1–6; also see Riley 1983: 151).

14. Gender difference was explained by social location, either emphasizing day-to-day caregiving practices and the orientation they produced (Rothman, Ruddick), or emphasizing early, unconscious processes of identity formation and psychological development (Chodorow, Gilligan).

15. Several also find a cohort effect to this shift to mother-valorizing perspectives: a largely white, middle-class, daughter-defined movement in the sixties and seventies changed as (white) feminists aged and many became mothers (Hirsch 1989, Ross 1995).

16. The use of the term "discourse" points to an important but dense epistemological dialogue in feminist theory. Many influenced by poststructural/postmodern theories prefer the term "discourse" to the earlier term from Marxism, "ideology," to describe the bodies of knowledge, structures of meaning, categories, beliefs, values, metaphors, and norms, that link power and social practice. To those who prefer "discourse," "ideology" implies a reductive model in which "representations" can be separated from the "realities" of people's experiences, and then can be found true or false. To postmoderns, categories of knowledge *produce* realities. The poststructural/postmodern model is not that far, however, from critical Marxist notions of hegemonic and counterhegemonic ideologies existing in a complex web of power rela-

tions. Therefore, I use the terms interchangeably.

In terms more specific to this project, it is also helpful to limit the relativism that some find in postmodernism and its multiple truths. While the limits of discursive abilities to construct and reconstruct the body are not known, there must be some definite, physical limits; "the slipping and sliding can only go so far" (Frank 1990: 160).

17. Also see Catherine MacKinnon's pointed, but ahistorical response to masculinist, macro-discursive histories of sexualities (1991).

18. In other words, I do not speak of some typical or average mother. And I do not aim to cover all groups or differing racial, ethnic and class combinations. See appendix B for details of my methodology.

19. "Cultural capital" refers to the intergenerational transmission of power in forms less tangible, and more accessible to the middle-class, than the stocks, bonds, and trust funds of the wealthy: education, knowledge of high culture, language, and the arts, as well as what some term "symbolic capital"—the right presentation of self, demeanor, attitudes, emotions, and embodied appearance. Cultural capital naturalizes class inequality so that its persistence over time appears to be fair, the legitimate outcome of individual traits and accomplishments rather than the result of the advantages class confers (Frank 1990: 155; also Lamont 1992).

20. This story has been retold and revised many times for many purposes, but what remains constant, according to biographer Nell Irvin Painter, is that Truth's proud response inverted the image of the slave auction and shamed the manliness of her harassers. Truth, Painter explains, herself revised her life story to make it more politically effective; it was unlikely that she had literally suckled white babies on the small farm in New

York where she had been a slave. It was true, however, that serving as a wetnurse was an experience shared by a significant number of unheard, unrepresented slave mothers in the South (Painter 1996: 141).

21. The now common usage of the term "formula" rather than "artificial human milk" or "human milk substitute" is instructive. It points to the power of corporate producers to use the discourse of modern science to displace the "natural" mother, a theme expanded in chapter 2 (also see Palmer 1988: 174–175).

Another good example of the ambivalent "nature" rhetoric is found in contemporary struggles for gay and lesbian rights. On the one hand, "nature" can be invoked to justify what *is*: since sexual diversity exists, it is *natural*. It should be left alone, it is not something we should tamper with. On the other hand, this libertarian evaluation is as likely to be transposed: sex is *naturally* for reproduction of the species, so homosexuality is a crime against *nature* (see Phelan 1993).

22. Several sociological classics described this group, including Berger's study of auto workers in suburbia (1968). The changes caused by political-economic restructuring and the distinction between "settled" and "hard" living are well summarized in Stacey (1990).

23. In brief, restructuring has meant that fewer men earn breadwinning wages and women's wage-earning has become increasingly important for families. In addition to the rise of the global economy, national political trends caused these shifts. The Reagan and Bush administrations encouraged the assault on organized labor, the movement of capital out of basic industry, and the tax breaks that resulted in a greater split between "haves" and "have-nots." For more detailed analysis see Kuttner (1992), Newman (1988), *New York Times* (1996), among many.

24. These included working at a fast-food outlet, as a freelance color consul-

tant, or starting a home-based business selling rabbit meat.

25. The term "cohabiting" misses most, if not all, of these important relationships (see Blum and Deussen 1996).

26. Radical feminist Catherine MacKinnon argues similarly: "The object is allowed to desire, if she desires to be an object" (1994: 274); though, even more than Rich, she defines all sex under patriarchy as forced.

27. An undergraduate at the University of New Hampshire was getting at this when, after examining magazines for an assignment, she mused, "you would think that lesbianism was something invented for men's entertainment."

2. From $acred to Disembodied Motherhood

1. Such mothers certainly do not necessarily internalize such controlling or dominant prescriptions, but readers must be patient, for this becomes a major focus only later in the book.

2. This section draws heavily from historian Janet Golden (1996).

3. Benjamin Rush, cited in Golden (1996): 17, n. 21. Urban institutions such as foundling hospitals, where numbers of poor women wetnursed abandoned babies, were clearly unhealthy and had very high rates of infant mortality. So the positive, healthful denotation of rural life was an apt one.

4. According to historian Valerie Fildes, the proscription against sexual activity was stronger in Catholic than in Protestant countries, leading to larger, more institutionalized systems of wetnursing (1986: 105, 121, 152–167; on husbands' claims and beauty ideals, see Yalom 1997: 107, 105).

5. Maternal breastfeeding and "natural" childrearing became a part of democratic ideals by the mid-eighteenth century. The importance of virtuous

mothers for the raising of democratic citizens was promulgated by Rousseau in his popular novel *Emile* (1762) (although it was later revealed that he was raised by a wetnurse and abandoned his five children to a foundling hospital), and by physician William Cadogan in the widely read *An Essay Upon Nursing, and the Management of Children from Their Birth to Three Years of Age* (1748) (Golden 1996: 13–15, also Carter 1995: 35–36, 40; Yalom 1997: 105–123).

6. Prior to the invention of rubber nipples in the 1840s (Hoffert 1989: 148), some "pap boats" made of soft pewter had high lead contents. Gloves, animal skins, and teats were used, but they were easily contaminated with harmful bacteria. The foods also were far less nutritious and digestible than human milk and were easily contaminated as well (Golden 1996: 17).

7. Historians and Black scholars debate the extent of this practice but agree that it occurred. As with northern wetnursing, the record is obscure because of the lack of institutionalization. Much supplemental wetnursing was likely informal, between kin and trusted neighbors, or, perhaps, between servants/slaves and their mistresses. See Golden 1996, McMillen 1990.

8. Regionally, other "nonwhite" groups included Mexican Americans, Native Americans, and Asian Americans, whose "whiteness" is at times still fluid and class-linked. See Mink 1995: 9, 12, in addition to Golden 1996. Critical race theory has contributed the notion that racial categories are politically and culturally constructed (e.g., Frankenberg 1993; Omi and Winant 1986; Roediger 1991).

9. Infant mortality rates were much higher for nonwhites than whites, but all mothers shared the fear of death. In 1915, 99 white babies per every 1,000 live births died in their first year; but fully 181 out of 1,000 nonwhite babies died. Stated differently, about 10 percent of white babies and nearly 20 percent of babies of color died (Ladd-Taylor 1994: 18–19, 35 n.5).

At the same time, large numbers of young men failed their army physicals, and this was attributed to race and ethnicity rather than poverty (Ladd-Taylor 1994: 89; Mink 1995: 58).

10. The term is also used as the female version of "patronize" to underscore the unequal power relations between women reformers and their poor clients. The literature on the gendered welfare state, the key role played by these women reformers, and their class and race politics, is now vast.

11. This gendered form of labor control was key to securing an acquiescent work force, but maternalist objectives were not always so complementary with the interests of industrial capitalists (May 1985).

12. Ladd-Taylor cites a number of studies showing, for example, that in Philadelphia 44 percent of Black mothers and 19 percent of white mothers went out to work, and that, in another city, some 67 percent of Italian immigrant mothers with infants took in boarders (1994: 29–30).

13. Luther Bradley, a *Chicago Tribune* artist, made the lithograph for the city's Industrial Exhibit of 1907, but a framed print hung in the office of Margaret Dreier Robins during her tenure as president of the National Women's Trade Union League from 1907 to 1922 (Payne 1988: 118). The NWTUL printed the image on postcards to raise funds for milk for women strikers' children during the great Chicago garment strike of 1910–1911 (Payne 1988: 118, 134; also Boris 1985, 1993). See Ladd-Taylor (1994) on the different organizations that made up the maternalist reform network.

14. Bottlefed babies were three times more likely to die in their first month than breastfed infants (Ladd-Taylor 1994: 27). Some reformers did start milk stations to distribute pure cow's milk at a slight discount in immigrant neighbor-

hoods, but this occurred only in some cities, and the main emphasis in the national campaign was on maternal breastfeeding (Mink 1995: 61). By comparison, breastfeeding became explictly contested in Germany, where the state provided premiums for breastfeeding mothers at child welfare clinics, but the left-wing League for the Protection of Mothers argued for safer bottled (cow's) milk (Yalom 1997: 128, 140).

15. Also see historian Ellen Ross's study of working-class mothers in turn-of-the-century London, for whom feeding schedules and physical distance were practical difficulties (1993: 138–140, 144).

16. Historians debate the intentions of the early-century maternalists. At best, they were constrained from forging alliances with Black communities by the rapid erosion of popular and political support for their programs. At worst, they judged Blacks to be less assimilable than European immigrants and prepared the latter to claim white privilege by reinforcing the color line that excluded Black mothers (Abramovitz 1988, Gordon 1991, Klaus 1993, Ladd-Taylor 1994: 55–63, 88, Mink 1995: 116–120).

17. Although immigrant mothers also relied on midwives, in the urban areas where most resided, this practice diminished rapidly. By the 1910s, for example, Northern community studies found about 40 percent of foreign-born mothers using midwives, but a study of rural Mississippi found that close to 90 percent of Black mothers had midwife deliveries. By comparison, Anglo middle-class mothers were overwhelmingly attended by physicians (about 90 percent of the Northern and close to 80 percent of the Southern white mothers used physicians) (Ladd-Taylor 1994: 23). By 1930, just 15 percent of all births were attended by lay midwives; and 80 percent of those licensed to practice midwifery were Southern Blacks (Smith 1995: 119).

18. Infant death rates did drop among African-Americans between 1910 and

1930, so the campaign could be considered a success. However, the racial differential persisted. Over the period:
For Blacks: rates fell from 181 per 1,000 live births to 100 per 1,000.
For whites: rates fell from 99 per 1,000 live births to 60 per 1,000.
(Figures from Ladd-Taylor 1994: 33. On maternal/child health among Native and Mexican-Americans see Ladd-Taylor 1994: 180–184.)

19. Dominant whites' desires to control and punish African-Americans' sexuality may explain the prohibition against midwives performing abortions and treating veneral disease as much as the ostensible need of the state to respect physicians' professional jurisdiction (see Smith 1995: 75).

20. This section draws heavily from Apple (1987).

21. Physicians only gradually came to have confidence in prepared, marketed infant foods as compared to individually prescribed or supervised (and mother-prepared) "formulas." This story is told in detail by Apple (1987).

22. Furthermore, physicians' overall confidence in artificial feeding grew. By the 1920s, studies began to show that medically supervised infant-feeding, whether by breast or bottle, had comparable results, with hygiene and medical care the most decisive factors in infants' health. (Of course, this begged the question of who could obtain medical care and decent hygenic conditions.) With "discoveries" that breastmilk seemed to lack vitamins C and D (begging the question of the mothers' nutritional status), physicians became even quicker to recommend artificial feeding and supplements to breastmilk in the 1930s, and artificial feeding came to appear as good or better—and more reliable than—human milk.

23. This was associated with urbanization and an accompanying nostalgia for "the olden days when every mother nursed her baby as a matter of course, and

strong, sturdy men and women grew from this gentle, capable motherhood which reared large families in the comparative shelter of rural or semi-populous towns" (1909, cited in Apple 1987: 140).

24. All mothers were similarly urged to maintain medical supervision of their babies and of their feeding methods. Middle-class mothers received this from private physicians, and working-class and poor mothers through the maternalist clinics, but the advice was also disseminated from the state. Mothers of all classes relied on the Children's Bureau's widely circulated pamplet *Infant Care*. First written in 1914, the pamphlet (in subsequent editions) was distributed to some 34 million mothers by 1955 (Apple 1987: 117; also see Ladd-Taylor 1994 on its popularity).

25. In 1900, less than 5 percent of women had hospital births. By 1920, just under 20 percent of mothers did—and these were mainly white, affluent, and urban women. By 1940, this was up to 55 percent (75 percent of whom were urban-dwellers); by 1950, 88 percent, and by the 1970s, 99 percent of U.S. mothers had hospital births (Leavitt 1986: 172; Wertz and Wertz 1989: 133).

26. Riessman thinks that "there has tended to be a 'fit' between medicine's interest in expanding its jurisdiction and the [expressed] need[s] of women," though the results paradoxically have tended to leave women with less authority over their bodies (1983: 14; also Ladd-Taylor 1994: 189) Verta Taylor's study of the postpartum depression self-help movement provides an illuminating contemporary example of this paradox in controlling motherhood and maternal bodies (1996). Primarily white, middle-class mothers have actively sought *to* have their experience medicalized, thus leading to treatments for distressed mothers; but psychiatrists become the arbiters of the experience, and cultural ideals of exclusive motherhood are "normalized" as the standard of health.

27. *Parents* magazine began publishing to educate mothers in the childrearing methods advocated by this new science. The magazine was initially funded by the Laura Spelman Rockefeller Memorial Foundation, as part of the package that funded the first academic child study centers at Yale, Columbia, and the Universities of Iowa and Minnesota (Strathman 1984: 11).

28. This work, begun by Anna Freud, complemented her father's theory of the "normal," mature woman's fulfillment in motherhood (she desires babies to compensate for the lack of a penis), and of the baby's primary love for the mother; but it extends this to stress the child's need for her full-time, exclusive love, and it de-emphasizes Freud's focus on later Oedipal conflicts with the father. The significant work of Melanie Klein also fits in this tradition, focusing on the pre-Oedipal mother-baby relationship (see Chodorow 1978, 1994).

29. Many objected to Bowlby's use of animal research. Others pointed out that attachment ratings were gross distinctions based on culturally biased notions of appropriate behavior. Moreover, attachment was measured only by gauging the mother's responsiveness, with no measures for the infant's temperament, or the responsiveness of other caregivers, the father, or family members (Eyer 1992).

30. Winnicott also followed Melanie Klein, who was particularly focused on the mother's breasts as objects for the infant, of both its love and hate. Curiously, few psychoanalysts have been interested in studying mothers' side of the breastfeeding experience, even those recent feminists who are committed to theorizing maternal subjectivity (but see Friedman 1996).

31. Feminist psychoanalyst and sociologist Nancy Chodorow characterized this general dynamic, but without reference to breastfeeding. The mother is completely taken for granted when providing "good enough" care, but, when failing to satisfy,

she brings on the infant's intense rage; she must empathize with her enraged infant by regressing, but she must simultaneously remain adult (1978: 84, 87).

32. According to historian Lynn Weiner, in the postwar years, individual public health physicians and women's club activists continued to quietly promote breastfeeding and urge the Children's Bureau to collect data and publicize findings supporting it (1994: 1367).

33. I examined the 1957 edition, in the Pocket Books version. In the insert, there were four ads for bottle-feeding supplies (one complete with the *Parents* magazine and *Good Housekeeping* seals of approval) and none for such accoutrements of breastfeeding. Similarly, there is one record page for "Notes on Formula," with a drawing of baby with bottle at the top, but none for "Notes on Nursing" among the pages for recording weight, growth, innoculations and illnesses, "firsts," and the five pages for "Questions for the Doctor" (1957, insert at 308).

34. While mainly focused on infant development, Jackson did at least briefly consider the mother's point of view. She wrote in *Parents* magazine that rooming-in provided a warmer, more peaceful atmosphere for the mother, who should have time to rest, get to know her infant, and arrive home "confident that she could care for her baby" (1947: 4).

35. Novelist Mary McCarthy's account of a new mother's (Priss Crockett's) sense of inadequacy in *The Group* (1963) captures the mid-century experience: " 'the most natural thing in the world' . . . was completely unnatural, strained, and false . . . and right now, in the nursery, a baby's voice was rising to tell her so. . . . It was making a natural request, in this day and age; it was asking for a bottle" (cited in Apple 1987: 162).

36. Gail Wasserman, personal communication, April 1997.

37. A similar trend developed in Britain, sparked by the publication of obstetrician Grantley Dick-Read's *Childbirth*

Without Fear (1933 in the U.K., U.S. ed. 1944, cited in Eyer 1992: 207, n. 2). By the 1950s, this led to the formation of the National Childbirth Trust, also by white, middle-class, Christian parents (Carter 1995: 58).

38. In fact, the husband of one founding mother was a sympathetic obstetrician who favored natural childbirth. Gregory White saw several of the founding mothers as patients, supplied the name for the organization (see next chapter for discussion of the name's origin and racial subtext), and became an adviser to the group along with his mentor, a public health physician and Chicago-area commissioner (Weiner 1994: 1360, 1367).

39. Another typical advice article, aptly entitled "Why Women May Fail in Breast Feeding," listed both the fear that the breasts will become pendulous and the inconvenience of needing so much privacy (*Good Housekeeping* 1963: 140).

40. The "sexual revolution" that occurred with the birth control pill only heightened this complexity, for too much display or autonomous desire were still dangerous (Carter 1995: 149–153).

41. For a psychiatrist urging that mental health experts try to modify husbands' negative reactions, including unconscious jealousy and sexual frustration, see Waletzky 1979.

42. Masters and Johnson wrote that six of twenty-four nursing mothers expressed guilt over their arousal during nursing and "were anxious to relieve concepts or fears of perverted sexual interest by reconstituting their normal marital relationships as quickly as possible" (1966: 162). Typical advice to mothers encouraged this resumption of compulsory heterosexuality: "let your husband play with your breasts as he did before" (Stanway and Stanway, cited in Carter 1995: 138). Surprisingly, even feminist magazine *Ms.* echoed such advice (Lainson 1983).

43. In Islamic law one cannot marry the kin of the milk mother; and because potential marriage partners may not mix

in daily life, this actually extends the range of cross-gender social relationships (Khatib-Chahidi 1992: 113).

44. On the history of milk banks, see Golden 1996: 179–206; for testimonials on the use of donated human milk, see Aladro 1982, Falconer 1971, Margolies and La Barre 1978.

45. Philosopher Iris Young has made similar observations about lesbian, breastfeeding mothers. She sees the pleasurably nursing lesbian mother (even if she isn't sharing the nursing with her partner) as doubly displacing her erotic relations away from men, and thus as the "ultimate affront" to what I term compulsory heterosexuality (1990: 198). As the mother of a daughter, however, Young fails to note that the crossgenerational tie for mothers nursing sons is, if no less gratifying, in some sense male-oriented.

46. A few psychoanalytic scholars have seen cultural associations between breasts and penis as markers of gender and sexuality. Both give "sacred" fluids, are hormonally sensitive, become erect, penetrate, and evoke "primordial" unity with the mother. Both are powerful sources of pride and vulnerability, of pleasure and anxiety, especially as they become objects of intense meaning-making fantasies (Deutsch in Friedman 1996). Breastfeeding advocates sometimes use this parallel (less psychoanalytically) in witty 'genderbending' to criticize the factory-like medical model. They ask, would we have young men attempt their first sexual intercourse in a hospital, watched by experts, with an artificial penis close by (Palmer 1988: 29–30)? Would we instruct men to scrub the penis to toughen it up beforehand (Kitzinger 1987: 42)? And, would we, in the end, insist that artificial insemination was really more reliable (Van Esterik 1989: 98)?

47. The veritable "bible" of the movement became the bestselling Boston Women's Health Collective's book, Our

Bodies, Ourselves (1971 orig. ed., Taylor 1996: 93).

48. In the 1990s, the figure was higher and was estimated to reach $4 billion per year (Palmer 1988: 6). By the 1960s, the U.S. market was dominated by two corporations: Bristol-Meyers (makers of Enfamil), and Abbot Laboratories (owners of Ross Labs' Similac and Isomil) (Miller 1983: 4). Carnation, which has a small market share in the United States, is owned by Nestle.

49. Routine promotional practices included the use of saleswomen dressed as nurses to distribute samples (along with free bottles) and "enticements" for rural health officers who would promote the products. The Nestle boycott dated from 1977 to 1984, but actions began earlier and grew from the many church and university-based study groups in Canada, the United States, and other countries (see Chetley 1986 for a comprehensive account; Miller 1983 for a less sympathetic view).

50. There is little doubt that multinational formula producers need vigilant regulation. Nearly a decade after the Nestle boycott was officially halted, the United Nation's Children's Fund and the World Health Organization launched a new campaign to discourage the stillwidespread distribution of formula samples (NPR 1992a, also deMauro 1991, New York Times 1998a). Also, in the United States, the Federal Trade Commission investigated complaints (from consumers and state welfare officials) of price-fixing after prices increased six times faster than for cow's milk (Meier 1991a, b).

51. The science examining multiple causes of infant morbidity and mortality has been surprisingly weak (Millman 1985).

52. From the infant's perspective, a poorly nourished mother may be acceptable. Research suggests that breastmilk's composition remains relatively constant

even if the mother's diet becomes inadequate, but that its quantity diminishes (Winick 1982, World Health Organization, cited in Carter 1995: 67–68). Palmer, as an ardent pro-breastfeeder and corporate critic, argues that the risk of mothers becoming depleted is overstated (1988: 73).

53. Indications that the HIV virus can be passed to infants through mothers' milk makes this risk-to-benefit assessment even more difficult; but the United Nations still recommends breastfeeding in developing nations, home to 90 percent of the world's AIDS cases, because of the much larger problems with artificial feeding (Lerner 1998, Meier 1997). Some scientists, moreover, read the data on HIV transmission through breastmilk as inconclusive. The odds of transmission may depend to a large degree on when the mother became infected; also, human milk is known to contain proteins that can block the virus receptor and prevent infection (Newburg and Street 1997).

54. Some Nestle boycotters also pursued a less publicized strategy: to develop low-cost, easily prepared, indigenous weaning mixes from local grains and legumes (Solomon 1981).

55. Maher and Scheper-Hughes do agree that the shift from breast to bottle represents women's efforts to transfer more costs of reproduction to men. The rise of cash economies in many developing nations has made fathers' purchase of infant formula an important symbol of family headship, but the two anthropologists differ in weighing the material versus symbolic aspects of this gender transfer. In poor urban communities in the United States, like those I discuss in chapters 4 and 5, mothers can obtain formula through public assistance, and Pampers have become the material-symbolic currency of fatherhood.

56. By the 1990s, overall infant mortality had dropped to about 10 deaths per 1,000 births. For whites, the rate was just over 8 in 1,000, but among African-Americans it was 2.2 times higher, at just over 18 per 1,000 (Hogue and Hargraves 1993, Hummer 1993). (See note 18 for historical comparisons.)

57. Data from Massachusetts also indicate that when the category "Black" is disaggregated, rates for African-American mothers may be lower, as for instance West Indian, Haitian, and Cape Verdean mothers have higher rates (Massachusetts WIC Program, 1997).

58. Public health experts attribute this race differential to maternal health but are perplexed that it cannot be explained by income, education, or access to health care; it is therefore labeled "the paradox of the well-off Black mother" (Hummer 1993).

59. Breastfeeding rates for Hispanic mothers have fallen between those of white and African-American mothers but are converging to those of white mothers in the 1990s (Ross Labs 1996) (though even more than the category "Black," "Hispanic" conceals ethnic and national differences). Native American mothers in the past decade have had breastfeeding rates similar to those of Hispanic mothers, though with higher rates for duration than other racial/ethnic categories (DHHS 1990).

60. On the AAP, see *Pediatrics* 1997. The DHHS has two breastfeeding objectives: to raise initiation of breastfeeding to 75 percent of mothers and to raise duration to 50 percent of mothers at six months. In contrast, current rates stand at just 60 percent of all mothers initiating breastfeeding, with only 18.5 percent continuing up to six months (and, of those, few breastfeed without formula supplementation). Among "at risk" (poor and near poor) mothers in 1992, 39 percent initiated breastfeeding, but only 10 percent were still nursing at six months (and of these, only 5.5 percent were exclusively breastfeeding) (GAO 1993).

61. Recently, this program, which can

not even cover all those eligible for it, has been threatened with further budget-slashing (see *New York Times* 1997a, b).

62. Scientists liken breastmilk to blood, another "living" fluid that responds to pathogens in the environment by producing proteins that fight infection (LLLI 1992: 352–353; Newburg and Street 1997). *Science Digest* reported that breastmik was found to contain more of the responsible white blood cells than blood itself (Winter 1980). Researchers have made progress toward artificially duplicating blood, though this has mainly been red blood cells (Feder 1994). But, it is surely not possible to predict technological limits in this era of high-tech medicine; in fact, scientists recently conducted experiments adding human nucleotides, the building blocks of genes, to infant formulas and successfully increased some infant immune-system responses (Gilbert 1998b, Pickering et al. 1998).

63. The British medical journal *Lancet* notes that the evidence of a relation between formula and SIDS is equivocal (editorial 1994, 344: 1239).

64. For a discussion of formula contamination see Kitzinger 1987: 140–141, Minchin 1989: 247, Palmer 1988: 53, Van Esterik 1989: 195–196. Public fears of breastmilk contamination have arisen over radioactive residues from nuclear testing and accidents, and from pesticide and industrial chemical residues (e.g., Pollack 1997, and see chapter 3). The latter breastmilk contaminants were described in scary terms in the AAP assessment, while formula was described as merely causing a "few nutritional problems"; no mention was made that the same environmental pollutants are found in cow's milk (Miller and Chopra 1984: 643, 640–643). Advice literature conveys some of the scary messages, with a not-very-convincing reassurance that, because scientists do not know what levels are safe, mothers should generally keep breastfeeding (Carro 1978, Eiger and Olds 1987: 45, Hanible 1978, Ricci 1988).

65. The "maximizing" child-centeredness of Yuppie (young, urban, professional) parents was taken to extremes in the 1980s by the Better Baby Institute and satirized in movies like "Baby Boom" and "Parenthood" (Hays 1996: 58). It is currently evident in the media attention given to "discoveries" of the benefits of exposure to speech and vocabulary during the first year of life (e.g., Begley 1997b).

66. I easily fit this description myself.

67. In a survey of recently trained obstetricians, pediatricians, and family medicine practitioners, less than 20 percent had had experience in teaching breastfeeding techniques, and over 50 percent responded incorrectly to common questions about treating a breast abscess. Although 90 percent endorsed the idea of physicians promoting breastfeeding, half rated themselves ineffective in counseling breastfeeding mothers (Freed et al. 1995).

68. Lactation consultants go through a certification process and typically enter the field through two routes: from (paid) registered nursing or from (unpaid) La Leche League activism. They work independently and through hospitals, but as of 1990 there were only some 1500 nationwide. It can be expensive for a woman to turn to such consultants; insurance companies only reimburse about half the time (Bates 1990, Freed 1993).

69. Many magazine articles only mention the benefits to the infant's health (e.g., Cherry 1991, Pomeranz 1987, Salmon 1992b); others mention maternal health very briefly (e.g., Karlsrud 1993a, Simon 1984), or concentrate on breastfeeding as "nature's own postpartum weight-loss plan" (*Parents* 1992: 126).

70. The problems with cross-cultural studies, like the studies of breast vs bottlefed infants, are the large number of confounding factors that might explain lower cancer rates: environmental hazards, diet, life stresses, etc. Recently, better controlled studies have found that the younger a mother is, and the longer she

breastfeeds, the more she reduces her risk of *pre*menopausal breast cancer. However, to see a substantial reduction, a mother must be under twenty and nurse for six months; researchers found *no* evidence that nursing prevents the disease after menopause, when the overwhelming number of cases occur (Newcomb et al. 1994). Dr. Susan Love, breast cancer specialist, also mentions a Chinese study which found that *nine* consecutive years of breastfeeding led to a lower incidence of breast cancer, a finding that is not very useful for women in our culture (1995: 37). Readers should know that regular exercise and a low-fat, high-fiber diet are also known preventive factors (Brody 1997, Love 1995), but the entire research framework may overindividualize risk and understand it through dominant gender ideology (Yadlon 1997).

71. Ironically, such pamphlets are prepared by formula companies and are widely available in medical offices, hospitals, and clinics. They are laden with mixed messages.

72. The formula companies which distribute educational pamphlets are also happy to sell you breast pumps: "the Ross/Faultless Deluxe Breast Pump System, is widely recommended" (Ross Labs 1985: 7). And of course, "If you find that you can't express enough breast milk to feed your baby," they are happy to sell you their formula products (Mead Johnson 1990: 23). "Breast milk is the best milk for feeding throughout the first year of life. The next best choice is infant formula, such as Similac" (Ross Labs 1987: 26).

73. Remarkably little has been written on the history or use of this apparatus (discussed in chapters 3, 4, and 5). I thank Colleen Manning Owen, R.N., for providing a copy of her typescript paper and patent search. Owen notes that the first U.S. patent was issued in 1830, listed under "Surgery Inventions or Discoveries" and described as "Milk, Apparatus for drawing from the breasts of women."

Between 1830 and 1918, there were an additional twenty-eight patents for breast pumps (including just one issued to a woman); but this was followed by a hiatus of over fifty years before patents were again issued in the 1970s. Today there are over forty different pumps available, with several improvements in safety and comfort devised by women inventors. Also, the electric pumps once affordable only to hospitals became available as rentals in 1975 (Owen 1988).

74. According to Owen, the first portable electric unit which could pump both breasts simultaneously (speeding the milk flow) was invented by a woman in the 1980s. Importantly, it was small, light, quiet, and was designed to be concealed in a Samsonite makeup case (1988).

75. I have changed the names of this all-American family (National Center for Education on Maternal and Child Health 1985: 7). I also should clarify that "Janice's" exercise regime is only an easy target because it is portrayed as so extreme; women's desires for physical fitness, to build endurance and strength, certainly can represent (or be a route to, even if unintended) a more autonomous and positive sense of the body and enjoyment of the activity itself, rather than just an obsession with slimness and heterosexual attractiveness. Interestingly, however, research indicates that very strenuous exercise by nursing mothers increases lactic acid levels and sours breastmilk. In one study, babies rejected milk they were offered within 90 minutes of their mothers' workout (*Prevention* 1993). (Also see Carey et al. 1997 who found no increase in lactic acid with exercise of moderate intensity.)

76. In his book for working mothers, Brazelton is quite explicit that the prototypical professional mother, who desperately desires to, should keep up breastfeeding after her return to work. His story about the working-class mother is, in contrast, much different; she rejects the intimacy of breastfeeding and feels she

should save her strength. Although he
expresses sadness over this, he rightly
points to the lack of social provision as the
cause (1985: 73, 98–99).

77. In the most recent "millennial"
rhetoric expressed in the Healthy People
2000 plan and the new AAP statement, it
may be the economic health of the nation
which is at stake, as much emphasis is
placed on dollars saved by breastfeeding.

3. "Mother to Mother" in
La Leche League

1. I use quotation marks to indicate that
these are important phrases used widely
by the League.

2. But see Weiner 1994 for a start.

3. The League also reports members in
some forty-eight countries (LLLI 1991:
392), but most are in North America and
it remains largely based in the United
States.

4. The four topics are (i) the advantages of breastfeeding, a topic aimed
mainly at expectant mothers; (ii) getting
started with the new breastfed baby and
fitting the new baby into the family; (iii)
the "art of breastfeeding" and solving
problems; (iv) and finally, "weaning
gently, with love" and using nutritious
"whole foods" (see Merrill 1987: 226).

5. According to feminist scholars Gorham and Andrews, "natural" is one of
the most frequently used words in the
League's literature (1990: 247).

6. Anthropologist Ann V. Millard finds
that medical advice has dropped the
explicit talk of rigorous feeding schedules, dating from the influence of behav-
iorism early in the century when it was
believed necessary to discipline the baby.
Themes of scheduling and regularity,
however, still pervade the breastfeeding
advice, but now with a physiological
rather than moral justification (1990).

7. To use anthropologist Emily Martin's felicitous title (1987).

8. The names of the mothers have

been changed to protect their confiden-
tiality.

9. A student reported to me that, while
studying abroad, her French La Leche
League group also (informally) gave referrals to abortion providers (University of
Michigan, March 1991).

10. The baby had a bad reaction to his
mother's milk when she consumed dairy
products, a common problem I discuss in
chapter 4, but also when she consumed
wheat and peanut products.

11. See Armstrong 1997; even in the
extreme case of fetal alcohol syndrome, it
is not clear that alcohol alone is the terato-
gen or causal factor; on caffeine, see LLLI
1991: 231–232; also, Love 1995: 40–41.

12. I noted in chapter 2, as have many
journalists, that the medical professional
offers little help with such common problems. A 1968 *Time* magazine article on La
Leche League, for example, commented,
"Most obstetricians could not care
less. . . . Most pediatricians have been
inadequately trained" (1968: 53).

13. Weiner finds parallels to the publishing history of the League's manual
twenty years earlier. Both *The Womanly
Art of Breastfeeding* and *Our Bodies, Ourselves* began as "kitchen table" efforts to
make medical knowledge accessible to
women (1994: 1362, n. 9).

14. Although the League has long
challenged the medical profession, it has
also worked to influence and educate
healthcare providers. From the beginning
the group consulted with physicians and
held workshops and conferences for the
medical community. Early attention in
the popular press, such as a 1963 *Reader's
Digest* article, indicates that physicians
were never monolithically opposed to the
League's efforts (Pryor 1963, also Weiner
1994: 1376). However, see one pediatrician's attack on the League (also as a
"defender of the child") which appeared
in the *New York Times Magazine* (Homan
1971).

15. Merrill also suggests this among
the group she studied (1987: 237).

16. While twelve mothers spoke of having very positive body images after breastfeeding, seven had mixed responses, with five mostly negative. The latter mothers expressed concern that their bodies had changed and that they had failed to achieve their ideal weight. Maclean, a Canadian researcher, also found that prevailing cultural ideals for women's bodies, particularly for extreme slimness, can make the breastfeeding experience less positive for some women (1990). Although the cultural-body and body-body are deeply entangled, some facts are more-or-less clear: lactation does speed uterine contractions and the body's return to its prepregnancy shape; it also burns extra calories. The lactation process, however, is enhanced by some body fat, which can slow progress toward thinness.

17. I observed a substantial number of men at the conference I attended in 1991, perhaps one-third of those attending.

18. This is a chapter title in *The Womanly Art of Breastfeeding*; the member magazine features a "Focus on Fathers" column, and a favorite League author, Dr. William Sears, wrote *Becoming a Father* (1983), which was published by the League.

19. The "organization man" was the name coined by sociologist William H. Whyte (1956) for the burgeoning number of white-collar employees, who were loyal, conforming, and placed organizational demands first in exchange for employment security and predictable career ladders. Talcott Parsons was the influential postwar sociologist whose framework was taken up by many family experts (see chapter 2) and who was attacked by feminist Betty Friedan (1963); he argued that the nuclear family with male breadwinner and female homemaker was imperative for the functional socialization of children and stabilization of adult personality (Parsons and Bales 1955).

20. A cartoon depicts the "manly art": the father stands firmly "protecting" his wife, as she is seated in a chair with baby at her breast, from two obviously critical, female "busybodies."

21. Both 1981 and 1987 editions of the manual featured photos of nurturing, expressive fathers with babies in their arms. A more formal coding of *Becoming a Father* also found divided messages, with a nearly equivalent number of vignettes portraying fathers as shared-parenting partners and, conversely, as the secondary Providers and Protectors (see Blum and Vandewater 1993b).

22. Studies find that expectations of fathers are changing (with feminist challenges and economic contractions), but that even the new Involved Dad leaves Mom with the major responsibility. And when fathers do participate, they tend to take over pleasurable activities, like Kay Chavez's husband (in this chapter) who takes his girls to Gymboree (Biernat and Wortman 1991, Hochschild 1989, 1997, Wright et al. 1992, also Segal 1990: 33–35). I termed this family arrangement "destabilized patriarchy" (Blum and Vandewater 1993b), though Connell labels it "moderniz[ed] patriarchy" (1995: 139). On the one hand, League mothers resist their maternal valor and pleasure being usurped by men. Yet, on the other hand, the League contributes to the modernizing project by promoting a modestly reformed, role-sharing family, with men still dominant.

23. I found just two families in which the fathers did as much infant care as mothers. And only a few mothers challenged this asymmetry.

24. Personal communication, April 1991.

25. The 1983 publication of *The Heart Has Its Own Reasons*, written by a founder of the League, provided further defense for those who were "just mothers" (Cahill 1983).

26. The national organization now helps all mothers "where they are at," as Gerry Kemp explained: "We are obligated to help moms who are working and not

judge them. . . . The organization just has [this] to say, 'Mothers who come to us, we want to help.' "

27. In the margin next to this sentence, the boldface heading reads: "What works well in one woman's life may not work at all in another woman's life" (Lowman 1984: 248).

28. Jane also saw a long-term goal and hoped that if she hid her feelings employed mothers might return with a subsequent child and *then* be ready to remain at home. I noticed more open intolerance toward maternal employment at the state conference, an event oriented to League "insiders." Gerry Kemp disagreed with my interpretation, however, saying that I had merely been seeing generational differences, with conferences geared to honoring the original activists, now grandmothers or great-grandmothers.

29. Of twenty-four League participants I spoke with, volunteers drawn from daytime meetings, over half did at least some work for pay: three were fully sharing breadwinners, six had regular part-time jobs, and one was a full-time graduate student. Seven mothers identified themselves as at-home mothers but worked occasionally, or regularly, though for less than 10 hours per week. Only seven were truly exclusive mothers, neither in school nor working to earn money, and four of them were La Leche leaders with volunteer careers (Liz Davenport, Jane Lensky, Gerry Kemp, and Trish Kreiser).

30. Rebecca Cross remembered that she was scrutinized during the leader-accreditation process (in the late 1970s) because of her summer job at a children's camp: "they had a real hard time with that because I was *working* . . . so I had to explain that my children [were] with me all day."

31. These evaluation meetings indicate how seriously the League takes its "process" goals of providing practical advice with "warmth and caring." After each open meeting, leaders and core mothers review the group process and how they handled questions and group facilitation. Leader Rebecca Cross explained:

When you evaluate how a meeting's gone, you worry a lot . . . we worry about a new mother coming if she's going to be turned off with the older children nursing . . . The same thing with working mothers . . . We try to keep the discussion going where someone says something positive and encouraging . . . a League meeting may seem unstructured, but they're really not. We're really trying to meet the needs of a lot of people that are there at all different levels of needs and expectations.

32. Two leaders shared their applications with me.

33. Many sociologists have analyzed the importance of status or social esteem for the maintenance of class privilege; in the new cultural studies, the term becomes nearly synonymous with "cultural capital." Members of the middle class draw invisible moral boundaries, marking superior ways of life, to justify and protect their economic advantages (Lamont 1992).

34. Some health professionals endorse what is called "minimal" breastfeeding to avoid the need to pump or express milk: the baby is given formula during the work-day and nurses when the mother is home. Because, however, breastfeeding works on a supply and demand basis, "minimal" nursing and infrequent emptying of the breasts can threaten supply in the early months. Auerbach and Gus (1984) found that before four or five months, pumping at work was critical to success (also Foreman 1998).

35. Kay had also investigated daycare centers and found only two that would take six-month-old infants. Each had a waiting list.

36. A League mother who read an early draft of this chapter suggested that

local groups have become referral networks for home daycare providers. I met three mothers who babysat part-time; and another three reported that they found their care providers in the League. I also observed a League leader who began a home daycare when her children entered school.

37. The League endorses home daycare for mothers who need to supplement family income (see Lowman 1984), but sociologist Margaret Nelson found many sources of conflict with mothering, as well as between client and provider mothers (1990).

38. This expression of exclusivity or monogamy is quite fascinating, and is much as I characterized advice literature in the previous chapter. Pam White recounted an incident in which, because she had such "deep feelings" for her neighbor's son, she was "ready to nurse him." The young boy had cut his foot, was quite distressed, and was sobbing for his mother, yet Pam explained, "There was nothing I could do for him." "It just reinforced for me how much, by God, I'm going to be the one that's here when she [her daughter] needs me and not someone else."

39. Historian Lynn Weiner points out that the "people before things" slogan had a less mother-blaming history. Originally, like Betty Friedan's critique of the homemaker as head consumer, it criticized the mid-century emphasis on the display of wife and home. In place of Friedan's solution in careers, the League asserted that intensive attention to children and deep affectional ties were more important than suburban, upward mobility and "conspicuous consumption" (1994: 1372).

40. Both popular and academic analysts have focused attention on the squeezed middle class because their presence marks the significance of long-term economic restructuring and the decline in well-paid male jobs (Kuttner 1992, Newman 1988, *New York Times* 1996).

41. I revised this chapter in the fall of 1997, when this prejudice had been reinflamed by the "Nanny Murder" trial of British au pair Louise Woodward, charged with murdering the infant son of an affluent physician couple in a Boston suburb (Bryant 1997).

42. She also gave me a copy of a favorite book, *The Shock of Motherhood* by Beppie Harrison (New York: Scribners 1986).

43. Teresa identified as of Eastern European heritage, while Kay Chavez, who was white Euro-American, had married a Mexican-American and adopted his surname.

44. Sociologists Gorham and Andrews contend that League mothers worried about their "selfishness" in depriving their families of income (1990). Although my interpretation seems at odds, both may be apt, for women today may be vulnerable to either criticism. As Hays concludes (1996), no group ever gets motherhood completely right, whether they are perceived as shortchanging their families of paid or unpaid efforts.

45. I did not bring my son on the one-on-one interviews, but many of the women had seen me at meetings with him, undercutting my image as a professional researcher. Jane Lensky, for instance, had hesitated, "I know you work outside of the home. I hope I don't offend you."

46. Four women had husbands in blue-collar jobs and might better be considered working class. However, all four of the women had some college education, and two with degrees were employed in professional jobs themselves. One family had combined earnings well above the group median because of the wife's profession.

47. As indicated in note 46, I place Cathy Seeley in the struggling middle class despite her husband's blue-collar jobs. A white woman who worked part time in an office job, she had a two-year college degree. Perhaps what I characterize as today's struggling middle class seems closer to the mid-century settled or secure

working class; but current economic restructuring sorts such families differently and their providers often have jobs that fail to pay a family wage. Cathy's husband, for instance, worked in a small, nonunion plant and in a service job at night (see chapters 1 and 4 and appendix B).

48. On "Mommy Wars" see Block 1990, Bryant 1997, Jackman 1991; also Hochschild 1997.

49. Nonetheless, Mary Vincent had attended during both her pregnancies and maternity leaves.

50. Gorham and Andrews (1990) and Merrill (1987) might disagree.

51. Rheta Childe Dorr, 1910, cited in Mink 1995: 11.

52. Historian Ladd-Taylor examines the relation early in the century (1994).

53. All the League mothers I met expressed support for workplace rights, which have become so taken for granted in the postfeminist era (Stacey 1990). Few blamed feminism for the proliferation of Bad Yuppie Mothers, but only four pointed to the political-economic context instead.

54. Indeed, two long-time leaders (Gerry Kemp and Marg Walters) each reported that the fights between "Sixties' movement types" and "Bible bangers" (evangelical Christians) over the League's rejection of corporal punishment had been much larger than any tensions about maternal employment. "People left in *droves* over that one," Gerry explained. Corporal punishment is at odds with the League's core concept that discipline should be accomplished only through "loving guidance" coupled with respect for each child's individual nature (Merrill 1987: 227). The League's position on discipline is class- or status-enhancing in two senses: it is consistent with the most up-to-date expert advice and encourages traits associated with success and high occupational achievement (see Straus 1994).

55. I found in my interview-conversations that opinions on abortion were actually quite varied.

56. Only three mothers spoke against publicly subsidized daycare, which can be a sensitive topic for those dedicated to mother-baby exclusivity. Eight women spoke of the need to increase public provision for childcare, and many more were in favor of on-site care. Others were more vehement for allowances or tax incentives to reward at-home parents, intriguingly similar to some feminist suggestions for caregiver allowances (Mink 1995).

57. See Bullard 1976a,b, *Detroit News* 1976a, b. The League was specifically cited in Carro 1978 and Chen and Bullard 1976.

58. Sociologist Barrie Thorne shared a personal recollection: "The PBB scandal was going full blast in 1977 when our second child was born." She recalled that her frozen milk sample, sent by overnight bus to the state testing lab, was found with detectable levels. "The pediatrician said, 'we don't know what this means.' . . . I gave up breastfeeding, it worried me so. The PBB scare *is* still scary; you can imagine how it felt . . . thinking about my new-mother's milk, what should be the most benign of substances, as poison" (personal communication, 1996).

59. PCB levels ran higher, but the average level found was still below the level allowed in cow's milk. Moreover, similar levels had been found by the Environmental Protection Agency in other states (*Detroit News* 1976b). Contaminants such as lead, mercury, arsenic, cadmium, and strontium-90 are typically found at higher levels in water, cow's milk, and formula than in human milk (IOM 1991, WHO 1990).

60. For other environmental crises in which alarms were raised about breast-milk, see Kitzinger 1987: 140–43. La Leche League, in failing to draw connections to systematic environmental problems, may be drawing racialized as well as

public/private boundaries (a topic I return to at the chapter's end). Environmental pollutants disproportionately harm nonwhite mothers who live and work amid hazards many whites can afford to avoid. Nuclear waste and dioxin, for instance, have been dumped near Native American-owned land, and high levels of PCBs in breastmilk have been found in Native mothers, like the Mohawk living near the St. Lawrence River, long polluted by General Motors (Baumgardner 1998).

61. The League reports, for a surveyed period in the 1980s, that divorce was the single largest reason for calls seeking legal assistance; it far outnumbered calls about extending maternity leaves or being harassed for nursing in public, a topic I come to in chapter 4 (LLLI 1986: 3).

62. See Baldwin and Friedman 1997, LLLI 1986, Lofton and Gotsch 1983, *New Beginnings* March-April 1992: 46 and May-June 1991: 87, Trimm-Harrison 1991.

63. Although the number of contested custody suits is small, fathers win in approximately two-thirds of cases (Ehrensaft 1990b: 74, n. 29). Moreover, numerous agreements are made on the basis of partially coerced conditions because of men's threats and mothers' vulnerability (Lewin 1990; Stanworth 1990).

64. The League's nature-endorsing deployment of biology might thwart such alliances, however; feminists have been divided on such discursive politics, as they have on the issue of surrogate mothers.

65. This functional, biological similarity has been argued most vigorously by Niles Newton, the physiological psychologist whose expertise is often cited by the League. The League does not share Newton's emphasis on the sexuality of childbirth, nor the inferences she drew from laboratory research on mice. Although writings from Newton are available through the League, other League authors tend to see the effect of social attitudes on human sexuality as at least as significant as hormones (e.g., Bumgarner 1982: 72).

66. Early in the century, children's sexuality was seen as far less innocent than in more contemporary views, in which the child's eroticism is viewed positively and is biologized as "natural" (though the mother's is not).

67. Though each extreme denies the normalcy of nonmothers, Weisskopf makes it clear that the maternalist view is not on a par with authoritative discourses, whose requirement of sexual repression poses the greater problem for mothers. In this respect, the League's use of "nature" in defense of maternal sexuality might be considered counterhegemonic (see Soper 1995).

68. It is also revealing to compare the treatment of Perrigo with that of Deborah Norville, the television morning show host, who was subjected to harsh criticism for the sensual nursing photo published in *People* magazine in 1991. Norville, a married, white celebrity, depicted with her infant son, was not attacked as harming her child but only for an overly revealing or exhibitionist act (Davidowitz 1992). Perrigo's case, in contrast, had several more dangerous aspects: she was single, nursed beyond infancy, and admitted her arousal rather than exhibiting it for the normative male gaze. Another fact perhaps compounds Perrigo's violations of compulsory heterosexuality: Perrigo nursed a daughter, while Norville, a son.

69. This male aversion to breastfeeding, with the loss of access to the wife's body, may have long historical roots in Catholicism. At least one historian has argued that in early modern Europe, Catholic countries institutionalized wetnursing more thoroughly than Protestant countries because their taboos against lactating women having intercourse (which were relaxed in Protestantism) contradicted husbands' conjugal rights (Fildes 1986: 105, 121, 152-167).

70. Also Nicole's earlier talk, of feeling "violated," may stem from other feminist vocabularies of bodily self-determination such as those against rape, pornography, and violence against women.

71. I thank Bunting fellow Alex Chasin for this phrase.

72. In contrast, other subordinate maternal identities, low-income, single, and nonwhite, all received token attention.

73. Although I believe this represents the League's overall make-up and traditional family bias, my participants were not drawn randomly (see appendix B for details).

74. Rhetorical claims to nature are so powerful that, as Lewin points out, lesbian mothers renamed what had been called "artificial" insemination, "donor" insemination, or just, insemination, "in an effort to downplay the implication that there was anything intrinsically 'unnatural' about this way of getting pregnant" (1994: 352–53).

75. Historian Weiner notes briefly that there appear to have been few women of color in the League through its forty years: photos and letters in publications identified token African-American, Asian, and Hispanic members, but a 1970 survey found that the majority were white, middle class, and native born (1994: 1363). I examined pictures in 1987 and 1991 editions of *The Womanly Art* and found similarly that only a small number (about 10 percent) clearly depicted people of color, while another small group (about 15 percent) were ambiguous. Admittedly, racial membership, as a trait of cultural bodies, is not always visible. Nonetheless, the overwhelming majority of pictures (nearly 75 percent) depicted white or pale-skinned mothers, fathers, and children.

76. Personal communication with Lewis Margolis, M.D., M.P.H., specialist in maternal-child health, University of Michigan, December 1990.

77. The League also fails to recognize the nonexclusive mothering traditional to African-American mothers. I treat this important alternative script in depth in chapter 5. Betty Jackson illustrates, however, that middle-class Black mothers may draw from both dominant and nondominant scripts. Though she drew from exclusive motherhood, she was closer to the working-class African-American mothers in her dislike of economic dependence, telling me that she had never gotten used to "ha[ving] to get my money from my husband."

78. Hays, however, treated this solely as an aspect of class difference and failed to examine its racialized basis.

79. I thank Lorena Chambers, graduate fellow, University of Michigan, Differences Between Women, 1994–95, for this insight.

80. Outside the specificity of race relations in the United States, however, some groups have named themselves in their own languages, as the Australian Nursing Mothers' Association, or, in the U.K., the Association of Breastfeeding Mothers (listed in Kitzinger 1987: 209–10).

81. A young white mother in my childbirth class consistently mispronounced the name, referring to the League as "La Leech," suggesting a most unappealing image.

82. Researchers tell us that the life-course has changed and most white mothers combine roles over time (e.g., Vandenheuvel 1997).

83. There are fascinating parallels between La Leche League and the postpartum depression movement, as each represents white, married, middle-class mothers collectively negotiating exclusive motherhood. Both struggle over ownership of maternal bodies and tensions between presumptions of essential maternal care and harm (Taylor 1996: 3). And they share the tendency to be trivialized compared to male forms of association, though research estimates that far more

U.S. women, as many as 45 percent, have been involved in self-help groups (cited in Taylor 1996: 8).

4. "To Educate and Persuade"

1. About 40 percent of U.S. auto employment had been located in southeastern Michigan, but some 30,000 (of 70,000) industrial jobs in Flint, one of the cities in the industrial triangle, were lost in the 1980s. Unemployment was about three times the national average when I interviewed mothers in 1991 (Hoffman et al. 1991; Lord and Price 1992).

2. Moore and Hamper received national media attention: the Phil Donahue Show broadcast two segments from Flint on Moore's film (Lord and Price 1992) and Hamper was featured on "Sixty Minutes" (Hamper 1991). The *New York Times Book Review* judged Moore and Hamper the two "Dantes" of this dying way of life (Klinkenborg 1991: 8). Their stories exclude women or objectify them, typical of the masculine discourse of shopfloor culture (see Collinson 1992).

3. This earlier pregnancy was with a previous boyfriend, who "had already left a girl with a six-month-old baby."

4. Ricki framed her story, a lament for the lack of a husband, with a comparison of her own (reduced) circumstances to her mother's, but this ignored the many indications that (as expressed in the mournful masculine narratives of Hamper and Springsteen) these families were often unhappy. Ricki herself mentioned a troubled past, her mother's at times "hyper" and "abusive" behavior, and her resulting months in a foster home as a teenager.

5. In 1975, 75 percent of all births to white teenagers (mainly aged seventeen or older) were to married mothers (Furstenberg 1991: 130). Between 1955 and 1988, the "out-of-wedlock" birth rate for white teens quadrupled, so that by 1988

over half of births to white teens were to single mothers (Furstenberg 1991: 131). Also, the birth rate for white unmarried women between twenty and thirty-four doubled during the 1980s (Bumpass and McLanahan 1989: 279). The reported shortage of white, adoptable babies speaks to changed norms in which most unwed mothers now keep their children.

6. Of the 27 white working-class mothers I met, 12 were married (44 percent), and 15 were unmarried (56 percent, though a few were divorced rather than never married). Only 4 of the 12 married mothers told of being married before they became pregnant.

7. Melody described the boy by saying "he's just like his mother. He lies all the time." Although Melody married and then conceived a child, the bad mother became pregnant and had a child from "a relationship that lasted only about three months!" Furthermore, according to Melody, her stepson only received help in the summer months, when he lived with Melody and her husband, because she took him to a psychiatric social worker, a practice the boy's mother wouldn't "even hear of!"

8. Selene reported that he earned about $25,000 annually (this was in 1991), quite a bit below the national median.

9. Marcy's father, as the industrial economy flourished, had moved from the shopfloor to the top layer of plant management and had attained an engineering degree. She recalled that money was tight growing up, but her parents were now in the secure middle or upper-middle class.

10. On breastfeeding, the most important works are by sociologist Pam Carter (1995) and historian Janet Golden (1996). On birthing, the literature is now vast (Davis-Floyd 1992; Riessman 1983, among many).

11. Ross documents that in turn-of-the-century London, working-class mothers struggled to serve food "properly" as a sign of respectability: they cre-

ated a boundary from the "rough" lives of the dependent poor by serving hot meals and Sunday dinners, with milk for children and meat for the head of the household. Feeding one's family well, keeping them "full," was a source of pride for mothers scrutinized by school and health officials and maternalist reformers (1993: 28–33).

12. Their stories were not easily categorized. For example, at least four mothers had failed at breastfeeding with one or some of their children but succeeded with others. Of the twenty-seven mothers, nine told mainly positive breastfeeding stories, twelve told stories that were primarily negative, and one was evenly mixed. Just five had never desired to breastfeed and never attempted it, although even one of these five was sufficiently influenced by dominant discourses of motherhood to give nursing a half-hearted and very abbreviated try with one of her three children.

13. Ricki stated quickly, dismissively, that her mother was too busy with her own job and family; that her friends did not have children, or their children were already school-age. In contrast, the African-American mothers I discuss in the next chapter, as part of their rejection of exclusive motherhood and the breastfeeding imperative, relied on kin and friendship networks and did not express such feelings of terrible isolation. Interestingly, the League mothers in chapter 3, who, if I had asked in a structured way, might have stated that their husbands were their major source of support, found positive alternative support within the League itself; and many did mention the isolation they had felt before joining.

14. See appendices B and C on my reading of popular advice literature. Other breastfeeding advocates have referred to propping as "a tragedy" and blame corporate producers of baby bottles for developing products with handles

(Palmer 1988: 138–139, Van Esterik 1989: 167–171).

15. Summarized in Armstrong 1993: 6. On tooth decay, see Kaste and Gift 1995.

16. Kaste and Gift found statistically significant differences only in terms of income, education, and ethnicity (with Hispanic mothers most likely to feed "inappropriately"); bottle-propping was more prevalent among single mothers, but the difference was not statistically significant in their sample. Another study, which included only low-income mothers, found whites far more likely to prop than Black mothers (78 compared to 44 percent) (McLorg and Bryant 1989), a finding that might be explained by Black mothers' greater alternative sources of social support.

17. Feminist health advocates in *Our Bodies, Ourselves* briefly offer similar advice to nursing mothers, that medications can generally be substituted, or dosages lowered, so that breastfeeding can continue. They also recommend seeking support from La Leche League (BWHBC 1992: 479). In addition to this different interpretation of biological causality, the League's counseling approach would certainly have touched on Ricki's great need for social-emotional support.

18. Jaundice occurs as the newborn's excess red blood cells are broken down, as the blood supply adapts to the oxygen-rich life outside the uterus. A residual product, bilirubin, the yellow-colored bile pigment, can build up as the immature liver does not excrete it efficiently. Because, in rare cases, this can lead to brain damage, it is important to speed the excretion, commonly by keeping the infant under "bili-lights." According to maternalist sources, along with the light treatment, frequent breastfeeding resolves the problem more effectively than the common use of water (Kitzinger 1987: 64; LLLI 1987: 286–290). Other breastfeeding experts note that substances in the breastmilk have been shown to aggravate

jaundice in only 1 percent of cases and, even in these, with no serious consequences (Eiger and Olds 1987: 237). Maternalist advocates suspect that the high incidence of jaundice is related to the induction of labor and use of epidural anesthesia (Kitzinger 1987: 63).

19. Melody, unfortunately, was not aware of either the allergenic properties of cow's milk or soy products (see Kitzinger 1987: 29). At least five other mothers in this chapter had children who ended up on soy products, and several had problems with those as well.

20. One study found that "ego maturity" was the strongest predictor of breastfeeding among low-income mothers. "Women with more ego maturity may breast-feed because of increased feelings of empathy or nurturance or because they are more attuned to current health advisories and able to deviate from community norms to adopt breastfeeding practices more characteristic of the white middle class" (Jacobson et al. 1991: 728).

21. See Minchin 1989 for critique of the measures; also Carter 1995: 73–74. Balsamo et al., in a small-scale study in Turin, Italy, also found that when mothers had to resort to bottles shortly after leaving the hospital, their stories were "tales of real desperation" (1992: 68).

22. U.S. popular authority T. Berry Brazelton argues that infant development should be the basis of any humane maternity policy, and he often argues for leaves of *at least* four months (1985). In his book of working mother stories, the one working-class mother notably does *not* breastfeed because she feels like "a workhorse first, and a mother second" (1985: 98).

23. This suggests a limited effectiveness for the outreach strategies of leaders such as Betty Jackson or Nicole Strickler (see chapter 3).

24. But this exposure to a maternalist discourse may be an effect (of some other factor) rather than directly causal.

25. These stories also underscore how unfair it is to dismiss mothers' physical complaints. Cultural beliefs such as those mentioned in chapter 2, that breastfeeding drains the mother's energy, or that the breastfeeding infant "eats a part of the mother" (Fishman et al. 1988, Weller and Dungy 1986), are more than the superstitions or neuroses of uneducated women. For women whose lives are already stressful, lactation may represent a *real* conflict between the needs of mother and baby (see Maher 1992); historian Ellen Ross noted, for instance, that in London at the turn of the century it was common to see a thriving breastfed child and a wasting mother (1993: 142).

26. Lissa recounted that a great-grandmother was perhaps one-fourth Native American, but no relatives that she knew of had kept any tribal affiliation.

27. Although Frances weaned her twins at four and a half months (compared to Lissa's at fifteen months), this had been her self-determined goal. In a large, fairly chaotic household, she got much-needed help with bottlefeeding from her teenaged daughters.

28. Lissa's father, like those of most of the women in this chapter, had been a "shoprat" and a good provider. Recall that Marcy's more exceptional father had moved from shopfloor to top plant-management.

29. Interview with Deborah Krauter, Massachusetts WIC Statewide Breastfeeding Coordinator, July 1997. Also, see Armstrong 1993.

30. Although Ann Landers wrote that mothers should not nurse in front of guests even in their own homes, this is cited by breastfeeding advocates as the old, prudish advice (cited in Eiger and Olds 1987: 162).

31. Mothers can still be charged with indecent exposure in the majority of states. See the following newspaper and magazine accounts of mothers being harassed: Brown 1993, Chira 1993, Henig

1979, Gillam 1995, *McCall's* 1984: 18, Nieves 1996, Quindlen 1994, Yarrow 1979.

32. But the greatest number of complaints dealt with divorce and custody and visitation issues (see chapter 3).

33. See Gronvaldt 1997; also Kelleher 1997, Warren 1997 on California's ultimately successful passage. The information on New Hampshire is also from a personal communication from Dr. Kathleen Kendall-Tackett, March 1998. According to Deborah Krauter, Massachusetts WIC Statewide Breastfeeding Coordinator, Massachusetts has no legislation, so public breastfeeding falls under "lewd and lascivious" behavior if a woman is cited, as one had recently been for nursing in a North Hampton courtroom (interview, July 1997).

34. Although they do not use the term, my analysis is compatible with those of Carter (1995), Maher (1992), Stearns (1999), and Young (1990); also Weisskopf (1980).

35. As discussed in chapter 2, the boundaries of racial categories in the United States have not been static, and many European immigrant groups were not clearly "white" in the nineteenth century. But clearly some groups, mainly African-Americans, were treated by dominant classes as beyond eligibility (except in individual cases of "passing").

36. See Carter 1995: 46–47, 118, 161–162; also Abramovitz 1988, Mink 1995, among many.

37. It is not surprising that by the early twentieth century, increasing numbers of white mothers were opting out, turning to artificial "formulas," and weaning earlier (see chapter 2).

38. Just as this book went to press, charges were dropped against both low-income mothers, owing to the protests of middle-class breastfeeding advocates (Bernstein 1998).

In another headline case, few defended the breastfeeding mother. The mother, characterized as having "no job" and "little income except her welfare checks," was tried for murder, convicted of child endangerment, and sentenced to a six-year prison term. She had snorted methamphetamine, which allegedly "poisoned" her breastmilk and caused the death of her two-month-old infant (*Los Angeles Times* 1994a and b; *New York Times* 1994). The biological evidence, however, was equivocal; the child exhibited none of the major symptoms of methamphetamine poisoning, and only a miniscule amount of the drug was found in his system. In fact, physicians who had testified as expert witnesses for the defense protested the decision in a letter to the *Journal of the American Medical Association* that alluded to the class bias in such harsh punishment (see Ariagno et al. 1995 and reply, Green 1996; on fetal endangerment, its class and racialized basis, see Daniels 1993).

39. A large literature now speaks to the issue of how state welfare both assists and controls low-income women (see chapter 2).

40. Extended breastfeeding's threat of incest and child abuse stands in marked contrast to the often-assumed preventive effect of early nursing (at least on child abuse) (Carter 1995: 64, Eyer 1992). Historically, extended breastfeeding by working-class mothers may have been particularly disreputable, as in Ellen Ross's discussion of Jewish mothers in East London criticized by health officials for prolonged breastfeeding (1993: 142).

41. Also, Perrigo's sensuality was her own rather than, as in photos of 'celebrity' nursing mothers, constructed for the viewer and the male, heterosexual gaze. See Davidowitz 1992.

42. British sociologists Hearn and Parkin (1987) have most extensively developed this analysis of sexuality in the workplace. I have presented a complicated historical analysis in very schematic terms.

43. As mentioned in previous chapters,

one survey of 567 working mothers found that 86 percent either hand-expressed or pumped their breasts during the work day, some as many as three times per day (Auerbach and Gus 1984).

44. See the second epigraph with which I began the book.

45. Carter does not include any discussion of breast-pumping among the women she interviewed, who gave birth before 1980 (1995), and, while the use of pumps may have been more unusual before the recent increase in the number of mothers of infants in the work force, Maclean writes almost nothing on the subject in a contemporary study (1990).

46. While medical discourse now typically encourages reliance on breast pumps, maternalist discourse is ambivalent. *Mothering,* a very small-circulation magazine, restricts advertising because "advertising breast pumps can give new mothers the impression that these are necessary to successful breastfeeding." Yet one mother wrote that both she and her La Leche leader were confused by the magazine's policy (1991: 30). In contrast, Kitzinger includes photos of mothers using each type of pump in her large-format photo-based advice book (1989: 136–139). And mainstream magazines, like *Parents,* discuss the pros and cons of the various types (e.g., Salmon 1992b).

47. But sufficient autonomy is not always the case for college-educated mothers, as the story of Teresa Jankowski in chapter 3 illustrated. Two public relations professionals and two researchers at the University of New Hampshire (who work together and take turns pumping) recently shared their stories with me, highlighting that for women in professional-level jobs, breast-pumping may be a positive option. The *New York Times'* recent coverage, however, featured women physicians who chose to pump their breasts contrasted to a secretary who "chose" not to (Slade 1997).

48. When the baby was over six months old, Donna (Howerly) decided to stop pumping, have her caregivers use supplemental foods and formula, and nurse only when at home.

49. Achieving the milk "letdown" with a pump can be difficult, as the reflex relies on a complex mind-body interaction. The advice literature (as discussed in chapter 2) is fairly glib, at most suggesting that women can train themselves with a little practice.

50. On the routinized labor process in fast food, see Leidner 1993.

51. Just carrying the pump around—presumably one of the more efficient, but larger electric types if she can pump so quickly—and setting it up and cleaning it takes some time. Most advice literature recommends that mothers allow about thirty minutes, since the milk letdown reflex can be inhibited by tension (see Mead Johnson 1990: 18). Time, however, is an acknowledged concern, and double-pumping can be faster (e.g., Zevin 1987).

52. With over two hundred work sites, when a center is no longer needed, it "close[s] shop and [is] move[d] to another site" (Sepah 1998).

53. The bill is HR 3531. As of October 26, 1998, it was pending (personal communication with Congresswoman Maloney's office and congressional Web site).

54. Pumping in order to lactate is also an important experience for some adoptive mothers (see Olson 1992, *McCall's* 1986, Mosher 1981, *Newsweek* 1973).

55. Recommendations in the Healthy People 2000 report include simply giving pumps to all WIC and Medicaid breastfeeding mothers; allowing pumps to be purchased with food stamps; and requiring all federal government employers to provide new mothers with breast-pumping rooms, as CIGNA and Hancock Insurance have done (GAO 1993: Appendix VI).

56. Data on actual and projected cost

savings are mixed, particularly because
many WIC mothers now appear to be
mixing breast and bottle rather than
exclusively breastfeeding (GAO 1993:
Appendix V); the AAP estimates larger
national savings in infant health care as
opposed to narrowly in reduced WIC
budgets (1997) but they ignore provisions
for mothers recommended by many WIC
directors, such as increased maternal food
supplements, lactation consultant services,
and breast pumps (GAO 1993: Appendix VI).

57. See Class 4 module of the Massachusetts WIC program for peer counselor
training on cultural considerations.

58. Colostrum is the premilk or first
milk produced for the newborn.

59. See IOM 1991, WHO 1990.

60. Even the WIC oversight report
admits confusion: The World Health
Organization recommends that HIV-
positive mothers in less developed nations
should breastfeed, but the U.S. Centers
for Disease Control has taken the opposite stance (GAO 1993: 8; see p. 229
n. 53).

61. In the Massachusetts WIC peer
counselor training, for instance, two of
five sessions stressed that mothers do not
have to be perfect. Public health research
has found that if mothers feel they cannot
eat junk food or have an occasional beer,
cigarette, or cup of coffee, they are more
likely to reject breastfeeding (e.g., Lawrence 1988). In some states (though not
Massachusetts) WIC programs use La
Leche League leaders to assist in peer
counselor training (GAO 1993).

62. Eiger and Olds also highlight
breastfeeding's portability in the chapter
"Especially for Fathers," noting that "the
father is usually the one who carries all
the paraphernalia" (1987: 212).

63. Pregnant and lactating women are
targeted for this food aid, while exclusively bottlefeeding mothers are a low priority and under tight funding may receive
little or nothing except for their eligible
children (GAO 1993).

64. Though I spoke with Deborah
Krauter in phone conversations, this face-
to-face interview was conducted by Amelia Dunlop, my research assistant in the
summer of 1997.

65. For the question of whether my
research was seen as part of this state
intrusion, see appendix B. Middle-class
professional women have often been those
who work in the lower levels of state
bureaucracies and check up on working-
class women (Carter 1995: 211).

5. "To Take Their Own Independence"

1. My colleague-collaborators were Dr.
Theresa Deussen and Professor Peggy
Kahn.

2. Even after *Roe vs. Wade* legalized
abortion, this racial difference persisted.
In the late 1970s, while 90 percent of
white single, pregnant women either had
abortions or got married, 90 percent of
Black single, pregnant women kept their
babies and remained single (*The Crisis*
1977).

3. After their divorce, according to
Jenny, the ex-wife would repeatedly "just
drop the child off on" her partner. That
child "was back and forth, back and
forth." When she remarried, this pattern
of emotional inattentiveness became
worse.

4. There were six mothers among the
twenty-six who were married at the time
of the interview-conversations. An additional mother was a recent widow (Dena
Vaws), and one was divorced (Elise
Brown); the remaining eighteen mothers
had never been married.

5. Joy Barkeley's story reminded me of
Marcy Herdon, the white mother in the
previous chapter, who, in contrast, quit
her higher-paying job and relinquished
this independence from her husband as a
serious part of her maternal duty. Joy's
discussion of marriage was more light-
hearted; indeed she joked that her second
son, born after the couple had married,

was angry not to have been in the wedding pictures like his older brother.

6. Both Yvonda and Ricky were in their early twenties and were high school graduates; both had been steadily employed since graduation, but only in low-paying food service jobs.

7. Yvonda Wagner even told of how she hoped to marry, although, unlike Ricki, she now wanted to "find somebody" who wouldn't "be always hurting me all the time."

8. Between the two groups of mothers, the numbers using state assistance were similar: of the Black mothers in this chapter, eight relied fully on assistance (although some of the money was child support payments collected from the fathers by the state); thirteen relied on limited forms of aid (just Medicaid or food stamps, or a childcare subsidy) or relied on welfare for a very limited period of time (using AFDC for a maternity leave); and five had not received any public assistance. Of the white mothers in the last chapter, ten relied fully on aid (again, often partially subsidized by the fathers' child support); twelve had relied on assistance in a limited form or for a limited period; and five had never received public assistance. Only two of the twenty-two white mothers who had used public aid voiced any of the critical, entitled sentiments expressed by the African-American mothers (Tori Reynolds, Devanna Smith). Most said little, emphasizing their male partners' or husbands' job prospects; one spoke of feeling guilty (Delia Duncan).

9. Because the boundaries of "whiteness" are cultural and political rather than biological, some groups have been in a "gray" area and had to struggle for white privilege. Historian Abramovitz notes, for example, that, in 1922, Mexican, Italian, and Czechoslovakian mothers received smaller pensions than Anglo-American mothers, while most Black mothers were denied assistance (1988: 201).

10. Most Black mothers were disqualified and deemed "employable," or their homes were deemed morally "unsuitable" (often, because of "illegitimate" children). African-American mothers thus were pushed into low-wage work, mainly as agricultural or domestic workers. Prior to the creation of ADC, they were only 3 percent of Mothers' Pension recipients, even less in many regions; in the Depression, ADC rolls overrepresented white, widowed mothers; African-American mothers did not increase on the rolls substantially until the 1960s (Abramovitz 1988: 201, 381). Black mothers have remained at similar proportions since that time, stabilized at somewhat under half (e.g., in 1995, 39.2 percent of AFDC mothers were Black, while 55.2 percent were white) (Sherman 1996: 104).

11. Among other changes, the proportion of widows declined as proportions of divorced, separated, and never-married mothers in the welfare population increased (Abramovitz 1988, Piven and Cloward 1971).

12. Elise Brown was the only mother in this chapter to receive a four-year college degree, which she earned by attending the local branch of the state university at night. She supplemented her income through the army reserve, and reported earning about $14,000 from her bank job, with a total of about $20,000 per year from the army supplement. Among Black women at that time, these were above average earnings (NCPE 1989), as women of color suffer from the most severe pay inequities (NCPE 1993–94). At the time we spoke, she was soon to begin training for a new job in military recruitment.

13. Concepts of childhood may diverge from the middle-class at older ages, beyond babyhood, but much of this has been analyzed in terms of class alone. Scholars maintain that, as children get older, working-class parents become less indulgent than those in the middle-class; their concerns shift from self-development to survival skills and the

need to see hardworking role models, to be presentable to state authorities, and (at least in the past) to accept hardship with forbearance (e.g., Hays 1996: 84–88, Ross 1993: 128, 146–152). There are similarities across class, however, in parents' sense of attentiveness and time, as my earlier discussion of Sharona Daniels' dealings with her school system indicated.

14. See especially the following articles in *Essence*: Abbott 1975, Mullings 1976, Scarupa 1976, Wilding and Winters 1977, Moore 1988, Nelson 1988. For details on my reading of Black periodicals, see appendix B.

15. Bernice Gooden exemplified the extensive survival skills these mothers developed. She spoke of receiving WIC assistance, of getting her son into the Headstart program, and of her extensive dealings with Worker's Compensation. She also mentioned a section 8 housing subsidy for which she had been on a waiting list for two years. Finally, she knew exactly how little she would receive if she were to quit work and be eligible for AFDC, an "option" that threatened with each family crisis. Such skillful negotiation with state agencies is itself a form of intensive mothering.

16. Another single mother, Sherri Riley, who had used AFDC to get through a medical crisis, expressed this vulnerability aptly: "They just pry in your business too much!"

17. This is again in contrast to many of the white mothers of chapter 4, who tended to lack such social support and faced difficulties in isolation. One stressed white mother with two children, who also worked in the hospital, told of going through ten babysitters in the months after she and her husband split up (Anna Brooks). Bernice also looked to state entitlements, as this is when she enrolled her son in Headstart.

18. Throughout this account, Bernice repeated phrases like, "I must just be a strong woman because of the things I went through!" and, "I thank the Lord for making me as strong as I am sometimes." This "strength" arises from the need to swallow the pain of raising children in a racist society. Byllye Avery, founder of the Black Women's National Health Project, captured this painful part of independent mothering: "If one more person says to me that Black women are strong, I am going to scream in their face" (Avery 1990: 6). In the same collection, writer Opal Palmer Adisa noted that strength masks oppression: "We know that the image of the strong Black woman is a mask we wear that brings us closer to madness" (1990: 13; also sociologist Joyce Ladner 1971: 30–31).

19. Some mothers also worry that they can be charged with neglect for leaving children at home alone, for example, because their job shift starts before the school bus arrives. As one said, "I know it's illegal."

20. Ross argues that community standards in the United Kingdom in the early twentieth century ensured that acceptable punishments did not do physical harm (1993: 150–151). But in the United States the legacy of slavery, and its reliance on state-authorized physical abuse and violence to discipline Black people (see Roberts 1997), makes authoritative judgments against parental spanking, or harshness by otherwise loving mothers, tragically ironic.

21. In Bernice's case, this was an ex-partner, the father of one of her children. She was no longer involved with him, but he had been in the home to visit his child. In chapter 4, both Delia Duncan's and Marcy Herdon's ex-husbands had been imprisoned for drug-related crimes; and Devanna Smith's alcoholic ex-husband had stolen their son.

22. Eighty percent of women in prison are mothers, over 90 percent had only poverty-level incomes, and 60 percent have been convicted of drug-related crimes, most of which are nonviolent (WAC 1993: 46–47). In fact, 35 percent are in prison for drug possession alone.

With mandatory sentencing, there is no judicial discretion to place mothers in possession of small amounts of drugs on probation, as was done in the past. On racial differences in prosecution and sentencing, see Bloom 1997, Roberts 1997. Roberts also argues that medical professionals who report poor Black mothers rarely report middle-class or white patients, even pregnant women addicted to alcohol, pills, or even crack.

23. As Ladner instructively repeats throughout her ethnographic study, there is no singular Black woman or mother, though shared oppression and history lead to some shared values and aspirations (1971: 33, 44–47, 174–175). In this chapter, I do not mean to suggest that all African-American working-class mothers conform to a singular model; even among my small group of similarly situated mothers, there are, of course, important differences.

24. See discussion in chapter 2. Currently just over 60 percent of white mothers breastfeed at birth compared to slightly over 30 percent of Black mothers. Race and class do interact, but race alone explains more of the difference in breastfeeding rates according to demographers (e.g., Armstrong 1993).

25. This argument is eloquently made by several Black feminists; see Julia Boyd 1990: 231. Sociologist Ladner traces the origin of the theory to W. E. B. DuBois's notion of "twoness" (1971: 279).

26. See chapter 2 on higher infant mortality and morbidity rates among African-Americans.

27. At the public family practice clinic where I met ten of these mothers, both the current and past prenatal educators on the staff were white women with public health backgrounds from the Peace Corps who had worked in Africa. In conversations with me both said that they were probably "more hands off" in dealing with African-American mothers.

28. Sociologist Jane Gordon suggests that to skeptical mothers breastfeeding

"facts" may seem another health fad (1989)—hardly to be trusted when they come and go so quickly, like megadoses of vitamin C or oat bran. More importantly, among contemporary Black women, widespread abuses of surgical sterilization (something I return to at the end of this chapter) and of the contraceptives Norplant and Depo Provera make for suspicious attitudes toward public medical care (Roberts 1997).

29. In spite of her grief, Dena did ask Theresa Deussen (who conducted this interview-dialogue) many questions about breastfeeding. They had a long conversation about the midwives, the classes, and how to deal with pumping and leaking in the workplace. When Theresa recontacted Dena some months later, she thanked her for tips on reusable cloth nursing pads.

30. In our conversation, I did try sympathetically (acknowledging how very difficult the pregnancy was for her) to ask how much she drank; she explained that it wasn't every night, but perhaps every few, that she would have "a big jar of Champale." Although this is not optimal for infant health, internalizing the blame and even hysteria from absolutist public health messages certainly is *not* health-enhancing, and, in Yvonda's case, it made for an even more stressful pregnancy. Furthermore, like smoking, the effect of alcohol on the fetus may be explained by the mother's overall health, and thus, her income (Roberts 1997: 158, 335 n. 34).

31. Among other differences, the number of health problems of the white and Black working-class mothers, children, and kin that threaded through their stories made for a striking contrast to the La Leche League mothers of chapter 3. On higher rates of lupus, see Jones 1990, and on the socioeconomic causes of health problems, see Davis 1990. On the environmental causes of asthma among the urban poor, see Nossiter 1995.

32. Kerry's partner developed a drug problem and, consequently, serious

financial problems. With one young child and another on the way, she was forced to move in with her parents. She then gave birth very prematurely, and while this may or may not have been related to the stress she was under, she spoke of her partner's lack of support during the baby's long, frightening stay in the intensive care unit.

Bernice had a child with each of two (ex)partners, neither of whom was reliably present. With the second birth, she faced complications from a Caesarean delivery and had a hard recovery. In addition, the father of this child, who had shared care with her in the early years, had recently begun to stalk and physically threaten her.

33. The association of breastfeeding with exclusive mothering also stems from gender arrangements in which men have the privilege to reject childcare and household tasks that are dirty, demeaning, or simply not much fun.

34. Also, as I pointed out in the second chapter, feminist psychologists interested in egalitarian, shared parenting also see problems with breastfeeding if it keeps the father outside the mother-child dyad.

35. To some extent, of course, these are not separable issues, with bodily control a problem for the workplace, and even in the home, as developed in the last chapter.

36. As mentioned in note 29, trying to follow feminist notions of reciprocity in the interview dialogues, Theresa Deussen did respond with some of her own experiences as a working and breastfeeding mother.

37. It seeps into awareness on some level; as sociologist Joyce Ladner found, young adolescent girls knew that white meant pure and Black meant dirty (1971: 81).

38. Under slavery, after all, Black women had no right to privacy or bodily integrity, as well as no legitimated relation to their children, who were the property of the white slaveowner (Roberts 1997).

39. Tawana Brawley is the young African-American woman over whose body competing stories have been told, one of a brutal gang rape by white men, the other of an out-of-control, oversexed teen, who lied to cover her own behavior, or perhaps was too dumb to speak for herself (see Williams 1990, also Haygood 1997).

40. See Roberts 1997. Senator Carol Moseley-Braun, in the welfare debates, felt compelled to contest biological notions by stating, "Poverty is not a genetic issue" (cited in Sherman 1996: 104).

41. In fact, Black mothers like those whose stories I attempt to tell have to be extremely hardworking, resourceful, and self-controlled to deal with difficult life circumstances and such demeaning stereotypes. As Black feminists instruct, Black motherhood rests on long traditions that value waged work, educational achievement, and community caregiving and activism (Collins 1990, 1994; Ladner 1971; among many). In public debate, however, if Black women are "independent," as the mothers in this chapter see themselves, this is deemed excessive (e.g., Moynihan 1965, Rainwater and Yancey 1967). According to Fraser and Gordon, Black mothers are demonized as "pathologically independent with respect to men and pathologically dependent with respect to government" (1994: 327).

42. There is another, closely related story to be told about current tendencies to demonize immigrant, Latina women. I mentioned this in chapter 3, but it is also worth noting that one white working-class mother in chapter 4 asserted her respectability by distinguishing herself from such an "other," recounting how she *had* to take her son from the babysitter "when he started talking Mexican!"

43. Anthropologists Balsamo et al., however, indicate that these affluent white mothers may falsely essentialize other mammals and, again, romanticize "nature"; they cite primate studies find-

ing that female monkeys and lemurs are often (naturally) negligent about breastfeeding their young (1992: 64).

44. The overall stance of the article was pro-breastfeeding and included the standard advice. Interestingly, diverging from mainstream parenting magazines, it was followed by a defense of the Nestle formula boycott. See Hamilton 1979, and Ferdinand and Salaam 1979.

45. The whole question of whether or not Blacks should depict the sensuality or seductiveness of Black women, given this historical legacy, is a troubling one within the Black community. It has recently been the topic of debate among Black artists (see Marriott 1997).

46. Paradoxically, because of the extent of cross-race contact, including wetnursing, views of the inheritability of character "modernized" more rapidly in the South than in the North, where belief in character transmission through breastmilk remained strong (Golden 1996).

47. The historical record is ambiguous as to whether white babies actually received mothers' milk denied to Black slave infants. Shaw argues that slave-owners had a heavy investment in their labor supply and its reproduction, so at times they allowed slave mothers nursing breaks (to nurse their own babies) and supplemented their diets (1994: 238–239). Fox-Genovese maintains that there were even instances in which white plantation mistresses nursed Black slave infants (cited in Golden 1996: 73). Surely, however, Black babies seen as labor supply or live-stock were not valued in the way that white babies were (Roberts 1997). Golden, moreover, discusses many cases of Northern wetnursing in which a poor (often immigrant) baby's life was traded for that of a rich (Anglo) baby (1996: 97–128).

48. Booker T. Washington may have been referring to wetnursing in the following speech delivered in 1914: "When food is being prepared, the Negro touches the white man's life; when food is being served, the Negro woman touches the white man's life; when children are being nursed, the Negro woman touches the white man's life; when clothes are being laundered, the Negro woman touches the white man's life. . . . Disease knows no color line" (cited in Smith 1995: 42); the phrase could also refer, however, to the more general care of young children.

49. See Davies 1991, for a discussion of this theme in S. Williams's novel *Dessa Rose.* (See also P. Williams 1991, part of which I've used as the fourth epigraph to this book.) Interestingly, Davies misses one facet of the cross-race breastfeeding in *Dessa Rose*: in many non-Western societies, such as those under Islamic law, the white mistress's nursing Dessa's Black son would make him "milk kin" with the mistress's baby daughter, and thus would prohibit a later adult sexual tie between the two children. In this reading, cross-race breastfeeding is more complex: while disrupting white supremacy, it also prohibits miscegenation. (See p. 227 n. 43.)

50. Many reformists leading such campaigns were, however, more liberal and believed immigrants and African-Americans could assimilate to Anglo-American cultural norms. Although they stressed environmental factors rather than the immutability of biology, progressive reformers shared the unquestioned assumption of Anglo-American superiority with followers of eugenics (Ladd-Taylor 1994, Mink 1995, Roberts 1997).

51. Breastmilk production under the Nazis was periodically checked to ensure compliance (Sichterman, cited in Yalom 1997: 140). See Klaus 1993: 207, on breastfeeding bonuses in France in the interwar years.

52. In the 1930s compulsory sterilization of the "unfit" was advocated by the American Eugenics Society, spurring the passage of legislation in at least twenty-six states. Southern states used the technique primarily against Black mothers. In the 1970s, further abuse came to light when

Black women brought lawsuits against several states. Other women of color, primarily Native American and Puerto Rican, were targets of sterilization policies (Davis 1983: 202–221, Ladner 1971: 253–254, Roberts 1997: 89–101).

53. One author even notes that Blacks are more prone to cow's-milk allergies than whites, with breastfeeding the "ideal solution" (Robinson 1978a).

54. The specificity of Black motherhood visible in this popular literature lies primarily with the defense of family diversity, of single and working mothers, and of public assistance as entitlement, as discussed in the first part of this chapter.

55. From *Essence*: Parks 1993, Patrick 1990, Williams 1987a, Oliver 1984, Pickhardt 1983, Wesley 1982, Brinkley and Charles 1980, Carrington and Bush 1979, Johnson 1978, Robinson 1978a, Stewart and Stewart 1971. See also the section on breastfeeding in Villarosa 1994. Although an article on African sexual attitudes mentioned the acceptance of nudity and openness around birthing, there was no mention of breastfeeding (Echewa 1981). In *Jet* 1985, 1986 "Health" items briefly noted the advantages of mother's milk; in 1988 it featured an odd piece on "the Baby Bonder," a device that allowed dads to simulate breastfeeding by wearing a bib with two bottles attached. The only mention I uncovered in *Ebony*, directed to a very affluent group (and, like *Jet*, not specifically for women) reminded me of "Charlotte," the high-status, super-breastfeeding-career-mother from the white advice literature discussed in the previous chapter; it depicted actress Vanessa Bell Calloway, who worked and breast-fed by bringing her housekeeper along (1991: 64).

56. The author does acknowledge that some mothers who cannot afford a healthful diet should not breastfeed because they will be overly depleted—but he fails to recommend enhanced public entitlements (Robinson 1978a).

57. Advice literature repeated over and over that you can breastfeed no matter what your breast size, that nursing doesn't cause breasts to sag, that if your breasts were already overly large, the swelled size from nursing was only temporary, etc. I was tempted to read such repeated advice—it really, really, really won't make your breasts sag—subversively, thinking you "doth protest too much!"

58. I tried to get Jenny Johnston to explain this to me: "To breastfeed, you shouldn't have anything else on your mind. You know what I'm saying? There shouldn't be anything else on your mind. And I was sitting there, and true enough, with bottlefeeding, I would have to sit there and take the time too. But I can be thinking about a million things at once and I'm not focused on what I am doing." I had less trouble understanding her concern with mental or emotional perfection after I came across passages like these in a maternalist advice book: "The mother who just plonks her baby down on her lap, plugs in the nipple and feeds while staring at the TV screen or glancing through a magazine is missing a great deal . . . if she does it habitually . . . the experience is impoverished for the baby. . . . So we cannot take it for granted that the woman who breastfeeds interacts with her baby in a satisfying way" (Kitzinger 1987: 164, 167).

59. Some conjecture that Black culture partly protects African-American women from these gendered body politics by providing positive alternatives. *Essence*, for example, has a counterhegemonic stance and presents diverse images of Black women, including those who are older or heavier and those with full African features (Chambers 1995); also see Harris 1990, Jefferson 1997, and Thompson 1994 on the different ways in which Black women are affected by hegemonic white definitions and depictions of beauty.

60. There have been and continue to be important forms of collective action around related issues of Black mothers' needs, for example, in the 1960s, the

National Welfare Rights Organization (see Ladner 1971: 176, Roberts 1997: 100, 207) and, at present, the Black Women's Health Project and the Birthing Project, which helps poor women get adequate prenatal care and other needed resources through one-on-one support (Ryan 1997, Villarosa 1994, White 1990).

61. On aggregate, while there are high concentrations of women of color in lower-paid healthcare jobs like nurses' aids and orderlies, white women make up 86.5 percent of registered nurses, African-American women constitute 9 percent, and Asian-American women 4.6 percent (from Reskin and Padavic 1994: Table 4.2).

62. According to legal scholar Dorothy Roberts, crack addiction has been errone-ously seen as confined to the Black com-munity, so the language of addiction becomes, to the dominant white culture, a code for "Black mothers' depravity" (1997: 159). As a result, the mothers pros-ecuted are primarily Black. Increased drug testing of newborns has meant that "more and more agencies snatch drug-exposed babies from their mothers imme-diately after birth" with no knowledge of the extent of drug use, of any harm to the infant, or of the mother's competence as a caregiver (1997: 160). (Also, to reiterate from chapter 2: mother's drug use cer-tainly is harmful, but the extent of harm has been wildly exaggerated, as well as racialized.)

6. Twenty-First-Century Mothers

1. Some maternalist breastfeeding advo-cates come close (e.g., Kitzinger, New-ton), but they tend to collapse women's sexuality into physiological reproduction itself, seeing sexual fulfillment, birth, and lactation as equivalent and ignoring the many cultural and individual differences between women.

2. In pre-Nazi Germany, while the state provided premiums at child welfare clinics for breastfeeding, the feminist League for the Protection of Mothers campaigned for more milk stations and the distribution of safer bottled cow's milk (Yalom 1997: 128, 140).

3. Some advice literature tells of mothers finding enjoyment by accident or surprise—suggesting its intentional pur-suit, like the active pursuit of sexuality outside of heterosexual marriage, is more morally dubious than being passively *swept away.*

4. Although I do not agree completely with her argument, Hochschild suggests that something similar occurs with employed mothers wanting guidance and reassurance (1997).

5. One observer has suggested that notions of childhood and children's needs again are being fundamentally reconceived, as they were in the late eigh-teenth century, such that we are shifting from childhood seen as a time of protec-tion to childhood as a time of preparation (Winn 1983). Whether, however, the changes will be this fundamental remains to be seen.

6. Cross-cultural analysis highlights the way that compulsory heterosexuality has been closely tied to commodification, the process that puts everything into the "cash nexus" to buy and sell in advanced capitalist economies. Anthropologist Lila Abu-Lughod found that young Bedouin women exposed to urban ways of life turned to Western (hetero)sexualized femininity as resistance to the system of arranged marriages and kin alliances. Their resistance made the isolated male-female couple predominant and encour-aged commodified standards of attrac-tiveness oriented to the male gaze (Abu-Lughod 1990). According to Vanessa Maher, such cultural changes toward compulsory heterosexuality are associated with declining breastfeeding, as women and their breasts are *looked at* and belong to the husband, and maternal-kin ties and maternal-child ties are de-emphasized in relation to the conjugal tie (1992: 10–15).

7. By this I mean that the breast can become an integrated part of the body image, of a whole rather than fragmented, objectified, or fetishized sense of corporeal self, that enjoyment in the physicality of breastfeeding and infant-care should be expectable and "no big deal." Weisskopf calls this "everyday enjoyment" (1980). I do not mean that some timeless truth lies in the breast, above and beyond human meaning-making processes.

8. Sociologist Wini Breines notes that millions of "falsies" were sold in the immediate postwar years (1992: 99), but Dr. Susan Love reports that before silicone, "Some surgeons experimented with paraffin injections, with fairly awful results" (1995: 47–48).

9. The debate on the safety of silicone implants revealed the depth of visual breast-obsession in the United States. A government advisory panel found that the 80 percent of women with purely cosmetic reasons for the surgery suffered from a sense of physical deformity *just as strong* as the 20 percent receiving the devices after breast cancer surgery (Hilts 1991). Many still protest the federal ban on the devices (see Yalom 1997: 236–239), though according to the American Society of Plastic and Reconstructive Surgeons, they are still being studied in a small number of clinical trials (June 1998, personal communication). Though Yalom takes a neutral stance, philosopher Iris Young is quite critical of augmentation surgery (presumably, regardless of the substance implanted) and reports that women are not sufficiently warned of possible consequences, particularly of loss of sensitivity (1990). In studying media reports on these issues, I found, as Young suggested, that there was *no* mention of this risk to women's pleasure.

Yalom also notes cross-cultural differences in visual ideals. In Brazil, upper-class families wanting to display their social distance from the lower classes and the Black population offer their daughters

breast reduction surgery! This is fairly unpopular in the United States but, nonetheless, in 1992 alone nearly forty thousand women underwent such surgery (1997: 236, 238).

10. Emily Martin finds that, in fact, these are the dominant modes in which women talk about their bodies (1987: 76–78).

11. "Assisted reproductive technologies" include a range of medical practices, notably in vitro fertilization and its new more complex variations, gamete intrafallopian transfer, zygote intrafallopian transfer, and intracytoplasmic sperm injection. These also include sperm banks, egg donation, embryo freezing, and surrogacy (Hodder 1997).

12. This transformation includes, most prominently, the new global economy. Haraway and Martin agree that it brings a disorienting compression of time and space as international capital flows respond ever-more rapidly to changes in specific market niches. In addition to changing forms of labor control and how such control disciplines bodies, this affects "technoscience" and helps "to render a kind of aesthetic or architecture for our bodies" (Martin 1992: 126; Haraway 1997: 12–14). Clarke applies this most clearly to reproduction, saying we are shifting from "modern" notions of birth *control* to "postmodern" notions of genetic *design* and manipulation (1995).

13. Although Haraway observes that disembodiment is a false problem, I do not find her suggestion of scrutinizing "ontologically confusing *bodies*, and the practices that produce specific embodiment" too far from my critique of disembodied motherhood as a very located ideology. Furthermore, I do not see the embodied motherhood offered by La Leche League as a foundational truth, but as a very located ideology, an actually-existing form of partial resistance of the type she advocates exploring.

14. Crouch worries that biotechnol-

ogy industries that are engineering cows with human genes to mimic human milk and produce new pharmaceuticals will further lead us to a medicalized world of male control over women, to even "a world of motherless machines, a world without women" (1995: 32). Like Haraway, I would not go so far but agree that the research funds might be far better spent on direct support for maternal health and well-being (Haraway 1997: 308–309, n. 46).

15. Obviously there are many needed resources: subsidized child and elder care, universal family or caregiver allowances, family leaves with income-replacement, access to better housing, transportation, job training and education (see Mink 1995: 174–191, among many). Also, to support breastfeeding, on- or near-worksite nurseries, and flexible, nontoxic workplaces are needed. In the United States today, however, this is a utopian wish-list. In fact, the recent embrace of health insurance plans for children of the working-poor, plans which leave parents uninsured, highlights the disregard for working-poor parents' (disproportionately mothers') physical being (Fein 1997).

16. Even in cases of the most vilified, public policies generally do better to address the mother's needs, to improve her circumstances, than to assert adversarial claims such as "fetal rights" (Daniels 1993, Roberts 1997, Williams 1991: 183–185). After birth, the question of children's interests is more complex, but see the insightful, balanced assessment of legal scholar Dorothy Roberts (1997: 160). In the sociological literature, "children's needs" are a topic of debate. Sharon Hays contends that family life has become increasingly child-centered (1996), but Arlie Hochschild sees parents who Taylorize their caregiving, falsely minimize their children's needs, and make their "home" in the workplace (1997). I see more of the first in La Leche League's

maternalism, and more of the second in the medical Supermom, and see both as largely middle-class preoccupations. But, with Lisa Brush, I agree that appeals to "children's needs" should be made with extreme caution because they have so often invited demonization of mothers, making them shoulder the blame for larger social ills (1996). Historian Ellen Ross found, in fact, that in Western Europe negative images of mothers generally led to fewer public resources being allocated for caregiving and for children (1993: 201, 220–221).

17. Anthropologist Ellen Lewin observed that in some regions of the country, as gay rights become more accepted, there may be a further distinction between "good" and "bad" queers, with "good" lesbians being those who are white, middle-class mothers in committed parterships, and "bad queers" being those who are not parents and who continue to be "promiscuous" (Brandeis University, Conference on Mothering and Family Diversity, April 13, 1997). Whether exclusive motherhood will stretch to include such "good queers," and whether this is a liberatory, emancipatory change or largely a cooptative one (that is, still embedded in and reinforcing racialized class and male-dominated inequalities) will depend largely on movements and their political strategies and capacities.

18. State employees question mothers' sexual activity and fidelity, but the privacy of "alleged fathers" is accorded greater respect (Monson 1997). This is further indication of our national "policy" of compulsory heterosexuality, though it is challenged by the increasing number of single mothers who do not declare paternity for their children (NPR 1998).

19. If not, it risks exploiting race/ethnic antagonisms, or even newly refined distinctions as in note 17 above.

20. Of course shared parenting fails to challenge middle-class lines of public and

private to argue for the resources that many families, even if sharing parenting, need.

21. Conference on Mothering and Family Diversity, April 13, 1997, Brandeis University.

22. Such problems obviously cross class lines and occur in affluent homes; but mothers would not be likely to turn to a group like La Leche League for support in such cases of "disreputable" parenting. I also do not mean to imply that all mothers are saints.

23. Monson 1997: 291, 294 n. 7; also Ehrensaft 1990b, Ruddick 1990. Furthermore, National Public Radio reported that low-income single mothers, routinely pushed to declare paternity in the hospital after giving birth, are not informed of such possibly serious consequences (NPR 1998).

24. Intriguingly, like an exaggerated version of the maternalist baby-saving in which elite white women knew best, Gilman wrote of a utopia in which those selected for biological motherhood would breastfeed but turn childrearing over completely to experts (Ladd-Taylor 1994: 111).

25. At least in my view, as a previous member and interested on-looker.

26. Ms. Johnson later enlarged her statement and I include it (with minor editing) as appendix A.

27. Cynthia Cockburn made a very similar argument about women in the United Kingdom, finding that only the "high flyers" benefited from equal employment measures (1991).

28. See, among many, Carter 1995: 229, Fraser 1989, Minow 1990, Pateman 1988, Young 1990: 114–137.

29. At the hospital where I met many of the working-class mothers, service workers were allowed three paid days off for a death in the family. Though three days may be too few, it was also left to supervisors to define "family."

30. As we heard in chapters 3 and 4,

many white mothers also seem to suspect that such "foreign" women may in some way harm their children (also see Eisenberg and Murkoff 1997: 62).

31. Her description, nonetheless, of her own experience is lovely, as she "crossed a forbidden river" from "stiff," "efficient and gentle" "mother work" in the early weeks, to "pleasure" (1990: 199).

32. I have discussed Carter's research in earlier chapters, but I should note that Gordon's fascinating article examines aggregate data on the Finnish case. Gordon suggests that extensive state and medical promotion of breastfeeding (lengthened maternity leaves, provision of breast pumps in the hospital to all new mothers, etc.), possibly restricts women's freedom and self-determined choices.

33. As discussed in chapter 4, lactation consultants and pump manufacturers are trying to develop this market niche. Infant-development expert Brazelton recommends pumping in *Working and Caring*, his advice book for wage-earning mothers. Though he notes that the few firms providing mothers with near- or on-site care so that they can actually get to their babies during breastfeeding breaks find that "mothers' productivity increases dramatically," he does not make clear whether pumping breaks would accomplish the same good business outcome (1985: 19). This lack of clarity exemplifies precisely the blurring moves toward the disembodied, virtual mother.

Appendix B. **Methodology**

1. Many of these ideas were developed with Andrea Press (Blum and Press 1996).

2. Many sociologists have thought about the power relations between researcher and researched in the moments of interaction. If I understand Clough's argument, however, we have thought less about the textual conventions and genres employed in representing the research and

of the inevitable difference of interests between researcher and researched.

3. Paradoxically, some feminist philosophers call for such situated knowledges, for research on local or specific subjectivities, yet they pay little (or no) attention to the critical, qualitative sociology that continually tries to produce such knowledge (e.g., Haraway 1988, 1997; Martin 1994, Phelan 1991). Such calls from the "high ground" of theory and abstraction seem loath to lower themselves to the "local" where field researchers inevitably make messy, flawed compromises with relations of power and authority.

4. Dr. Lew Margolis, M.D., M.P.H., December 1990. My comprehension of medical research was also greatly assisted by my sister-Bunting fellow, Dr. Joan Butterton of Harvard Medical School and Massachusetts General Hospital.

5. The mothers were young, however, ranging in age from twenty-six to thirty-five, so they may yet experience divorce firsthand.

6. I interviewed two leaders from an urban center at their church retreat near my home.

7. The national average for families was $35,500 at that time (Kilborn 1992).

8. I also faced practical problems: by the time I could write this book, nearly seven years had passed since my dialogues with these mothers, and I had relocated to another state. One professional writer suggested an entirely instrumental, careerist approach to the ostensible reciprocity of feminist methods, that I only recontact those mothers who might have the best stories to add.

9. Elizabeth A. Vandewater valiantly sampled and coded this material for me in terms of beliefs about fathers' involvement with babies and about mothers' employment. She used an episodic or vignette method, which organized the large numbers of anecdotal stories in these publications by themes (see Blum and Vandewater 1993a,b). For this book,

however, I often went back to the texts themselves.

10. We had initially intended to draw a sample of articles, but because in some years there were few or none, we ended up gathering the entire population of articles which appeared in the largest magazines.

11. I conducted an open-ended interview with both former and present Prenatal Educators, a full-time staff position that required a bachelor's degree in a related field. Intriguingly, each woman who had held the position had also worked in maternal and child health in the Peace Corps in Africa.

12. I limited eligible mothers to those over eighteen, with children one year or younger.

13. I would say things like, "I teach in Ann Arbor" and "I'm not a medical person" to create some sign of being an "outsider."

14. These jobs employed disproportionate numbers of women of color (in 1995, 68 percent of the service workers were nonwhite; 34 percent were women of color). I had to relax the rule I used at the clinic to include only those with children one year or younger, but I included only those with preschool children.

15. Although some studies of women's experiences of infant-feeding have used retrospective stories going back many years (Apple 1987, Carter 1995), I wanted to rely on recent, vivid experiences. My larger analysis was informed, however, by the eleven interviews with white mothers employed at the hospital which I ultimately decided not to use.

16. I am grateful to reference librarian Lynn Westbrook, who first suggested this and provided strategies to work around it.

17. I also ignored regional differences in breastfeeding practices, a potentially interesting question beyond the scope of this project. Breastfeeding rates by the latter quarter of the twentieth century no longer differed between rural and urban

areas, but some regional variations remain. Rates have been lower in the South and higher in the West, though the same race and class patterns hold for all regions. Few demographic studies offer much explanation other than to suggest that a different milieu or different population compositions account for the variation. Elizabeth Armstrong, for example, suggests that the higher proportion of Blacks in the South, and of Hispanics and whites in the West, may explain the different incidence rates (1993). This topic is better examined through skilled quantitative analysis.

18. In one interview, we (Theresa Deussen and I) literally inserted the word "husband" after the mother had stated that she and her partner had never married. In another interview, gaps and misunderstandings abounded as at least eight different terms were supplied to try to correctly capture the meaning of an extralegal relationship.

BIBLIOGRAPHY

AAP. 1997. American Academy of Pediatrics, Work Group on Breastfeeding. "Breastfeeding and the Use of Human Milk." *Pediatrics* 100: 1035–1039.

AAP. 1984. American Academy of Pediatrics, Report of the Task Force on the Assessment of the Scientific Evidence Relating to Infant-Feeding Practices and Infant Health. Supplement to *Pediatrics* 74.

Abramovitz, Mimi. 1988. *Regulating the Lives of Women: Social Welfare Policy from Colonial Times to the Present*. Boston: South End Press.

Abu-Lughod, Lila. 1990. "The Romance of Resistance." *American Ethnologist* 17: 41–55.

Acker, Joan, Kate Barry, and Joke Esseveld. 1996. "Objectivity and Truth: Problems in Doing Feminist Research." In *Feminism and Social Change*, edited by Heidi Gottfried. Urbana: University of Illinois Press.

Acker, Joan. 1990. "Hierarchies, Jobs, Bodies." *Gender & Society* 4: 139–158.

Adams, Alice. 1995. "Maternal Bonds: Recent Literature on Mothering." *Signs* 20: 414–427.

Adams, Alice. 1993. "Out of the Womb: The Future of the Uterine Metaphor." *Feminist Studies* 19: 269–289.

Adisa, Opal Palmer. 1990. "Rocking in the Sun Light: Stress and Black Women." In *The Black Women's Health Book: Speaking for Ourselves*, edited by Evelyn C. White. Seattle: Seal Press.

Alcoff, Linda. 1991–92. "The Problem of Speaking For Others." *Cultural Critique* 20: 5–32.

Anderson, Kathryn, and Dana C. Jack. 1991. "Learning to Listen." In *Women's Words*, edited by Sherna Berger Gluck and Daphne Patai. New York: Routledge.

Andrews, Florence Kellner. 1991. "Controlling Motherhood: Observations on the Culture of La Leche League." *Canadian Review of Sociology and Anthropology* 28(1): 84–98.

Apple, Rima D. 1987. *Mothers & Medicine: A Social History of Infant Feeding 1890–1950*. Madison, WI: University of Wisconsin Press.

Ariagno, Ronald, Steven B. Karch, Robert Middleberg, Boyd G. Stephens, Marie Valdes-Dapena. 1995. "Methamphetamine Ingestion by a Breastfeeding Mother and Her Infant's Death." Letter to the editor. *Journal of the American Medical Association* 274: 215.

Armstrong, Elizabeth M. 1997. "Diagnosing Moral Disorder: The Discovery and Evolution of Fetal Alcohol Syndrome." Talk given to the Department of Sociology, University of New Hampshire, December 9.

Armstrong, Elizabeth M. 1994. "The Impact of WIC on the Infant Feeding Deci-

sions of Poor Women: Evidence from the National Longitudinal Survey of Youth." Paper presented at the annual meeting of the Population Association of America, Miami.

Armstrong, Elizabeth M. 1993. "Breastfeeding Among Disadvantaged Women in the U.S." Paper presented at the International Sociological Association, Intercongress Seminar, Montreal.

Atwood, Margaret. 1986. *A Handmaid's Tale*. Boston: Houghton Mifflin.

Auerbach, Kathleen, and Elizabeth Gus. 1984. "Maternal Employment and Breastfeeding." *American Journal of Diseases of Children* 138: 958–960.

Avery, Byllye Y. 1990. "Breathing Life Into Ourselves." In *The Black Women's Health Book: Speaking for Ourselves*, edited by Evelyn C. White. Seattle: Seal Press.

Baldwin, Elizabeth N. 1997. "Extended Breastfeeding and the Law." http://www.lalecheleague.org/LawExtended.html

Baldwin, Elizabeth N., and Kenneth A. Friedman. 1997. "Is Breastfeeding Really a Visitation Issue?" http://www.lalecheleague.org/LawVisitation.html

Balsamo, Franca, Gisella De Mari, Vanessa Maher, and Rosalba Serini. 1992. "Production and Pleasure: Research on Breast-feeding in Turin." In *The Anthropology of Breastfeeding*, edited by Vanessa Maher. Oxford: Berg.

Baranowski, Tom, David E. Bee, David K. Rassin, C. Joan Richardson, Judy P. Brown, Nancy Guenther, and Philip R. Nader. 1983. "Social Support, Social Influence, Ethnicity and the Breastfeeding Decision." *Social Science Medicine* 17: 1599–1611.

Barrett, Michele. 1992. "Words and Things: Materialism and Method in Contemporary Feminist Analysis." In *Destabilizing Theory*, edited by Michele Barrett and Anne Phillips. Stanford, CA: Stanford University Press.

Barrett, Michele, and Mary McIntosh. 1985. "Ethnocentrism and Socialist Feminism." *Feminist Review* 20: 23–45.

Bates, Betsy. 1990. "Experts Give Mothers and Nature a Hand." *Los Angeles Times*, October 18, J-15.

Baumgardner, Jennifer. 1998. "Women of the Year: Indigo Girls and Winona LaDuke." *Ms.*, January/February, 63–65.

Begley, Sharon. 1997a. "Hope for 'Snow Babies': A Mother's Cocaine Use May Not Doom Her Child After All." *Newsweek*, September 29, 62–64.

Begley, Sharon. 1997b. "How to Build a Baby's Brain." *Newsweek Special Issue*, Spring/Summer, 28–32.

Berger, Bennett M. 1968. *Working-Class Suburb*. Berkeley: University of California Press.

Bernstein, Nina. 1998. "Charges Dropped for Mother Whose Baby Starved to Death." *New York Times*, July 16, A-28.

Biernat, Monica, and Camille Wortman. 1991. "Sharing of Home Responsibilities Between Professionally Employed Women and Their Husbands." *Journal of Personality and Social Psychology* 60: 844–860.

Block, Joyce. 1990. "What's Behind the Mommy Wars?" *Working Mother*, October, 74–79.

Bloom, Barbara. 1997. "Population Explosion: Who are the women in prison and what are they doing there?" *Women's Review of Books*, July, 6–7.

Blum, Linda M., and Theresa Deussen. 1996. "Negotiating Independent Motherhood." *Gender & Society* 10: 199–211.

Blum, Linda M., and Andrea L. Press. 1996. "What Can We Hear after Postmodernism?" Paper presented at the annual meeting of the American Sociological Association, New York. (Forthcoming in *Across Disciplines and Beyond Boundaries: Tracking American Cultural Studies,* edited by Mary Vavrus and Catherine Warren. Urbana: University of Illinois Press.)

Blum, Linda M. 1993. "Mothers, Babies, and Breastfeeding in Late Capitalist America." *Feminist Studies* 19: 291–311.

Blum, Linda M., with Elizabeth A. Vandewater. 1993a. " 'Mother to Mother.' " *Social Problems* 40: 285–300.

Blum, Linda M., and Elizabeth A. Vandewater. 1993b. "Mothers Construct Fathers." *Qualitative Sociology* 16: 3–22.

Blum, Linda M. 1991. *Between Feminism and Labor.* Berkeley: University of California Press.

Bonavoglia, Angela. 1996. "Beauty and the Breast: Alternatives." *Ms.,* March/April, 58.

Bonavoglia, Angela. 1983. "Decent Exposure?" *Ms.,* July, 106–107.

Bordo, Susan. 1990. " 'Material Girl' ": The Effacements of Postmodern Culture." *Michigan Quarterly Review* 29(4): 653–677.

Bordo, Susan. 1989. "The Body and the Reproduction of Femininity." In *Gender/ Body/Knowledge,* edited by Alison Jaggar and Susan Bordo. New Brunswick, NJ: Rutgers University Press.

Boris, Eileen. 1985. "Regulating Industrial Homework: The Triumph of 'Sacred Motherhood.' " *Journal of American History* 71: 745–763.

Boris, Eileen. 1993. "The Power of Motherhood: Black and White Activist Women Redefine the 'Political.' " In *Mothers of a New World,* edited by Seth Koven and Sonya Michel. New York: Routledge.

Boyd, Julia A. 1990. "Ethnic and Cultural Diversity in Feminist Therapy." In *The Black Women's Health Book: Speaking for Ourselves,* edited by Evelyn C. White. Seattle: Seal Press.

Brazelton, T. Berry. 1985. *Working and Caring.* Reading, MA: Addison-Wesley.

Breines, Wini. 1992. *Young, White, and Miserable: Growing Up Female in the Fifties.* Boston: Beacon Press.

Brent, Nancy B., Beverly Redd, April Dworetz, Frank D'Amico, and J. Joseph Greenberg. 1995. "Breast-feeding in a Low-Income Population." *Archives of Pediatric and Adolescent Medicine* 149: 798–803.

Brighton Argus. 1991. "La Leche League sets meeting for September." (Brighton, Michigan) August 14, A-7.

Brody, Jane E. 1997. "Personal Health: What is a woman to do to avoid breast cancer? Plenty, new studies suggest." *New York Times,* May 7, 12-C.

Bronfenbrenner, Urie. 1958. "Socialization and Social Class through Time and

Space." In *Readings in Social Psychology,* edited by Eleanor E. Maccoby, Theodore M. Newcomb, and Eugene L. Hartley. New York: Henry Holt.

Brown, Patricia Leigh. 1993. "Nursing Strategies for Busy Mothers." *New York
Times,* March 11, B-1.

Brumberg, Joan Jacobs. 1997. *The Body Project.* New York: Random House.

Brush, Lisa D. 1996. "Love, Toil, and Trouble: Motherhood and Feminist Politics."
Signs 21: 429–454.

Bryant, Adam. 1997. "In case of mothers vs. work, plenty of judges." *New York
Times,* November 16, A-10.

Bullard, George. 1976a. "PBB is found in milk of 22 nursing mothers." *Detroit
News,* August 20, A-1.

Bullard, George. 1976b. "Insurance sought for tests of PBB in mothers' milk."
Detroit News, October 16, 1976, A-6.

Bumgarner, Norma Jane. 1982. *Mothering Your Nursing Toddler.* Franklin Park, IL: La
Leche League International.

Bumpass, Larry, and Sara McLanahan. 1989. "Unmarried Motherhood: Recent
Trends, Composition, and Black-White Differences." *Demography* 26: 279–284.

Burawoy, Michael. 1998. "The Extended Case Method." *Sociological Theory* 16: 4–
33.

Burros, Marian. 1990. "Eating Well: What infants eat in the first months is critical,
and some formulas may be deficient." *New York Times,* October 10, B-5.

Butler, Judith. 1990. *Gender Trouble.* New York: Routledge.

BWHBC (Boston Women's Health Book Collective). 1992, 1976, 1971. *Our Bodies,
Ourselves.* New York: Touchstone.

Cahill, Mary Ann. 1983. *The Heart Has Its Own Reasons.* Franklin Park, IL: La
Leche League International.

Cannon, Lyn Weber, Elizabeth Higginbotham, and Marianne A. Leung. 1988.
"Race and Class Bias in Qualitative Research on Women." *Gender & Society* 2:
449–462.

Carby, Hazel. 1982. "White Women Listen!" In *The Empire Strikes Back,* edited by
the Centre for Contemporary Cultural Studies. London: Hutchinson.

Cardozo, Arlene Rossen. 1986. *Sequencing.* New York: Collier.

Carey, Gale B., Timothey J. Quinn, and Susan E. Goodwin. 1997. "Breast Milk
Composition After Exercise of Different Intensities." *Journal of Human Lactation* 13(2): 115–120.

Carter, Pam. 1995. *Feminism, Breasts and Breast-feeding.* New York: St. Martin's Press.

Chalmers, B., O. J. Ransome, and A. Herman. 1990. "Working While Breast Feeding Among Coloured Women." *Psychological Reports* 67: 1123–1128.

Chambers, Veronica. 1995. "The Essence of *Essence.*" *New York Times Magazine,*
June 18, 24–27.

Chartrand, Sabra. 1996. "Patents: A special vest can take the place of hand-held
pumps for breast-feeding mothers." *New York Times,* December 2, D-2.

Chavkin, Wendy. 1991. "Mandatory Treatment for Drug Use During Pregnancy."
Journal of the American Medical Association 266: 1556.

Chen, Edwin. 1976. "PBB burial snafu sets off state row." *Detroit News*, October 13, B-2.

Chen, Edwin, and George Bullard. 1976. "No Facts Yet on PBB, PCB in breast milk." *Detroit News,* August 21, A-3.

Chetley, A. 1986. *The Politics of Baby Food.* London: Frances Pinter.

Chira, Susan. 1993. "Nursing Becomes a Feminist Battlefield." *New York Times,* October 10, E-6.

Chodorow, Nancy. 1994. *Femininities, Masculinities, Sexualities.* Lexington, KY: University of Kentucky Press.

Chodorow, Nancy. 1978. *The Reproduction of Mothering.* Berkeley: University of California Press.

Christian, Barbara. 1994. "An Angle of Seeing." In *Mothering: Ideology, Experience, and Agency,* edited by Evelyn Nakano Glenn, Grace Chang, and Linda Rennie Forcey. New York: Routledge.

Christian, Nichole M. 1998. "City G. M. Built Looks Ahead Warily." *New York Times,* June 15, A-12.

Clarke, Adele. 1995. "Modernity, Postmodernity, and Reproductive Processes, 1890–1990." In *Cyborg Handbook,* edited by C. H. Gray, H. Figueroa-Sarriera, and S. Mentor. New York: Routledge.

Clough, Patricia T. 1993. "On the Brink of Deconstructing Sociology." *Sociological Quarterly* 34: 169–182.

Clough, Patricia T. 1992. *The End(s) of Ethnography.* New York: Sage.

Cockburn, Cynthia. 1991. *In the Way of Women.* Ithaca: Cornell Industrial and Labor Relations Press.

Collins, Patricia Hill. 1994. "Shifting the Center." In *Mothering: Ideology, Experience, and Agency,* edited by Evelyn Nakano Glenn, Grace Chang, and Linda Rennie Forcey. New York: Routledge.

Collins, Patricia Hill. 1990. *Black Feminist Thought.* New York: Routledge.

Collinson, David L. 1992. *Managing the Shopfloor.* Berlin: Walter de Gruyter.

Connell, R. W. 1995. *Masculinities.* Berkeley: University of California Press.

Cott, Nancy. 1987. *The Grounding of Modern Feminism.* New Haven: Yale University Press.

Cowan, Philip A., and Carolyn Pape Cowan. 1992. *When Partners Become Parents.* New York: Basic.

Creager, Ellen. 1991. "Breast-feeding has reached a dry spell among new mothers." *Detroit Free Press,* October 9, F-1.

Crouch, Martha L. 1995. "Like Mother Used to Make?" *The Women's Review of Books* 12 (February): 31–32.

Dana, Nancy, and Anne Price. 1987. *The Working Woman's Guide to Breastfeeding.* New York: Meadowbrook.

Daniels, Cynthia R. 1993. *At Women's Expense.* Cambridge: Harvard University Press.

Davidowitz, Esther. 1992. "The Breast-Feeding Taboo." *Redbook,* July, 92–95.

Davies, Carole Boyce. 1991. "Mother Right/Write Revisited: *Beloved* and *Dessa*

Rose and the Construction of Motherhood in Black Women's Fiction." In *Narrating Mothers*, edited by Brenda O. Daly and Maureen Reddy. Knoxville: University of Tennessee Press.

Davis, Angela Y. 1990. "Sick and Tired of Being Sick and Tired." In *The Black Women's Health Book: Speaking for Ourselves*, edited by Evelyn C. White. Seattle: Seal Press.

Davis, Angela Y. 1983. *Women, Race and Class*. New York: Vintage.

Davis-Floyd, Robbie E. 1992. *Birth as an American Rite of Passage*. Berkeley: University of California Press.

deMauro, Lisa. 1991. "Beating the Bottle." *New York Times*, September 21, A-13.

Detroit News. 1976a. "State pushes PBB probe of breast milk." August 27, B-2.

Detroit News. 1976b. "Breast milk tests show toxic PBB." October 13, B-2.

Deussen, Theresa Lynn. 1996. *Postindustrial Parenthood*. Ph.D. Dissertation, University of Michigan, Ann Arbor, Department of Sociology.

DeVault, Marjorie. 1995. "Ethnicity and Expertise: Racial-Ethnic Knowledge in Sociological Research." *Gender & Society* 9: 612–631.

DeVault, Marjorie. 1991. *Feeding the Family*. Chicago: University of Chicago Press.

DHHS (U.S. Department of Health and Human Services). 1990. *Healthy People 2000: National Health Promotion and Disease Prevention Objectives—Nutrition Priority Area*. Public Health Service. Nutrition Today, November/December. U.S. Government Printing Office, Publication No. 017–001–00474.

Diesenhouse, Susan. 1997. "In a Darwinian World of Weight Control." *New York Times*, October 12.

duCille, Ann. 1994. "The Occult of True Black Womanhood." *Signs* 19: 591–629.

Duncan, Isadora. 1927. *My Life*. New York: Horace Liveright.

Dunning, Jennifer. 1997. "Pursuing Perfection, Dancing With Death: Eating Disorders Haunt Ballerinas." *New York Times*, July 16, 1-B.

Edwards, Rosalind. 1990. "Connecting Methods and Epistemology: A White Woman Interviewing Black Women." *Women's Studies International Forum* 13: 477–490.

Ehrenreich, Barbara. 1990. "Life Without Father." In *Women, Class, and the Feminist Imagination*, edited by Karen Hansen and Ilene Philipson. Philadelphia: Temple University Press.

Ehrenreich, Barbara, and Deidre English. 1978. *For Her Own Good*. Garden City, NY: Anchor Press.

Ehrensaft, Diane. 1990a. *Parenting Together*. Urbana: University of Illinois Press.

Ehrensaft, Diane. 1990b. "Feminists Fight (for) Fathers." *Socialist Review* 20: 57–80.

Eiger, Marvin S., and Sally Wendkos Olds. 1972, 1987. *The Complete Book of Breastfeeding*. New York: Workman.

Eisenberg, Arlene, and Heidi E. Murkoff. 1997. "What to Expect: Bilingual Babies." *Parenting*, September, 62.

Eisenstein, Zillah R. 1988. *The Female Body and the Law*. Berkeley: University of California Press.

Ellwood, D. T., and M. J. Bane. 1994. *From Rhetoric to Reform*. Cambridge: Harvard University Press.

Eyer, Diane E. 1992. *Mother-Infant Bonding: A Scientific Fiction.* New Haven: Yale University Press.

Faludi, Susan. 1991. *Backlash.* New York: Anchor.

Feder, Barnaby J. 1994. "Race for Artificial Blood Heats Up." *New York Times*, February 14, D-1.

Fein, Esther B. 1997. "New York Health Insurance Plan for Children Draws Wide Attention." *New York Times*, April 27, A-33.

Ferguson, Laura. 1998. "A Natural Resource: Mother's Milk." *Tuftonia, Magazine of Tufts University*, Spring, 14–15, 46.

Fildes, Valerie. 1986. *Breasts, Bottles, and Babies: A History of Infant Feeding.* Edinburgh: Edinburgh University Press.

Fineman, Martha. 1995. *The Neutered Mother, The Sexual Family, and Other Twentieth-Century Tragedies.* New York: Routledge.

Fishman, C., R. Evans, and E. Jenks. 1988. "Warm Bodies, Cool Milk." *Social Science and Medicine* 26: 1125–1132.

Folbre, Nancy, and Heidi I. Hartmann. 1988. "The Rhetoric of Self-Interest." In *The Consequences of Economic Rhetoric*, edited by Arjo Klamer, Donald McCloskey, and Robert Solow. Cambridge: Cambridge University Press.

Foreman, Judy. 1998. "Space for Working Mothers: Health Sense." *Boston Globe*, January 5, C-1.

Foucault, Michel. 1980. *An Introduction*, vol. 1 of *The History of Sexuality.* New York: Vintage.

Frank, Arthur W. 1990. "Bringing Bodies Back In." *Theory, Culture & Society* 7: 131–162.

Frankenberg, Ruth. 1993. *White Women, Race Matters.* Minneapolis, MN: University of Minnesota Press.

Fraser, Nancy, and Linda Gordon. 1994. "A Genealogy of Dependency." *Signs* 18: 1–43.

Fraser, Nancy. 1989. *Unruly Practices.* Minneapolis: University of Minnesota Press.

Freed, Gary L. 1993. "Breast-feeding: Time to Teach What We Preach." *Journal of the American Medical Association* 269: 243–245.

Freed, Gary L., Sarah J. Clark, James Sorenson, Jacob A. Lohr, Robert Cefalo, and Peter Curtis. 1995. "National Assessment of Physicians' Breast-feeding Knowledge, Attitudes, Training, and Experience." *Journal of the American Medical Association* 273: 472–476.

Friedan, Betty. 1963. *The Feminine Mystique.* New York: Dell.

Friedman, Michelle E. 1996. "Mother's Milk." *Psychoanalytic Study of the Child* 5: 475–490.

Furstenberg, Frank R. 1991. "As the Pendulum Swings: Teenage Childbearing and Social Concern." *Family Relations* 40: 127–138.

GAO (U.S. General Accounting Office). 1993. *Breastfeeding: WIC's Efforts to Promote Breastfeeding Have Increased; Report to Congressional Requestors*, December 16, Washington D.C.

Gilbert, Susan. 1998a. "Gauging the Risk Factors in the Search for a Perfect Face." *New York Times*, special section on Women's Health, June 21.

Gilbert, Susan. 1998b. "Additive Bolsters Baby Formula, But Study Favors Breast-Feeding." *New York Times*, February 3, C-8.

Gilligan, Carol. 1982. *In a Different Voice*. Cambridge, MA: Harvard University Press.

Glass, Jennifer. 1990. "The Impact of Occupational Segregation on Working Conditions." *Social Forces* 68: 779–796.

Glass, Jennifer, and Valerie Camarigg. 1992. "Gender, Parenthood, and Job Family Compatibility." *American Journal of Sociology* 98: 131–151.

Glenn, Evelyn Nakano, Grace Chang, and Linda Rennie Forcey, editors. 1994. *Mothering: Ideology, Experience, and Agency*. New York: Routledge.

Glenn, Evelyn Nakano. 1994. "Social Constructions of Mothering: A Thematic Overview." In *Mothering: Ideology, Experience, and Agency*. Evelyn Nakano Glenn, Grace Chang, and Linda Rennie Forcey, editors. New York: Routledge.

Glenn, Evelyn Nakano. 1992. "From Servitude to Service Work: Historical Continuities in the Racial Division of Paid Reproductive Labor." *Signs* 12: 309–336.

Glick, Daniel. 1997. "Rooting for Intelligence." *Newsweek* special issue, Spring/Summer, 32.

Golden, Janet. 1996. *A Social History of Wet Nursing in America: From Breast to Bottle*. Cambridge: Cambridge University Press.

Gordon, Jane. 1989. "'Choosing' to Breastfeed: Some Feminist Questions." *Resources for Feminist Research* 18: 10–12.

Gordon, Linda. 1991. "Black and White Visions of Welfare: Women's Welfare Activism, 1890–1945." *Journal of American History* (September): 559–590.

Gordon, Linda. 1988. *Heroes of Their Own Lives*. New York: Viking.

Gorham, Deborah, and Florence Kellner Andrews. 1990. "The La Leche League: A Feminist Perspective." In *Delivering Motherhood*, edited by Katherine Arnup, Andree Levesque, and Ruth Roach Pierson. New York: Routledge.

Graham, Judith. 1989. "Benetton 'colors' the race issue." *Advertising Age* (September 11) 60 (39): 3.

Green, Lisa S. 1996. "The Prosecution Responds." Letter to the editor. *Journal of the American Medical Association* 275: 183.

Gronvaldt, Claudia Moore. 1997. "We don't need a breast-feed law." *The Exeter News* (New Hampshire), December 9, 5.

Halonen, Virginia, and Nancy Mohrbacher. 1987. *Learning a Loving Way of Life*. Franklin Park, IL: La Leche League International.

Hamper, Ben. 1991. *Rivethead*. New York: Time Warner.

Haraway, Donna J. 1997. *Modest_Witness@Second_Millennium*. New York: Routledge.

Haraway, Donna J. 1988. "Situated Knowledges." *Feminist Studies* 14: 575–599.

Harris, Angela. 1990. "Race and Essentialism in Feminist Legal Theory." *Stanford Law Review* 42: 581–616.

Hartmann, Heidi I. 1981. "The Family as a Locus of Gender, Class, and Political Struggle." *Signs* 6: 366–394.

Hayghe, Howard V., and Suzanne M. Bianchi. 1994. "Married mothers' work pat-
    terns." *Monthly Labor Review* (June): 24–30.

Hayghe, Howard V. 1986. "Rise in Mothers' Labor Force Activity Includes Those
    With Infants." *Monthly Labor Review* (February): 43–45.

Haygood, Will. 1997. "In the Shadows of Doubt." *Boston Globe*, February 16, A-1.

Hays, Sharon. 1996. *The Cultural Contradictions of Motherhood*. New Haven: Yale
    University Press.

Hearn, J., and W. Parkin. 1987. *"Sex" at "Work."* Brighton, UK: Wheatsheaf.

Helliker, Kevin. 1994. "Dying for Milk: Some Mothers, Trying in Vain to Breast-
    Feed, Starve Their Infants." *Wall Street Journal*, July 22, A-1.

Hendershot, Gerry E. 1984. "Domestic Review: Trends in Breastfeeding." *Pediat-
    rics* 74: 591–602.

Hertz, Rosanna. 1986. *More Equal Than Others*. Berkeley: University of California
    Press.

Hilts, Philip J. 1994. "Risks Found in Nursing Infants of Implant Recipients." *New
    York Times,* January 19, 7-B.

Hilts, Philip J. 1991. "F.D.A. Panel Cites Need to Keep Breast Implants." *New York
    Times*, November 15, A-8.

Hine, Darlene Clark. 1990. "Rape and the Inner Lives of Black Women in the Mid-
    dle West." In *Unequal Sisters*, edited by Ellen Carol DuBois and Vicki L. Ruiz.
    New York: Routledge.

Hirsch, Marianne. 1989. *The Mother/Daughter Plot*. Bloomington, IN: Indiana Uni-
    versity Press.

Hochschild, Arlie Russell. 1997. *The Time Bind*. New York: Metropolitan.

Hochschild, Arlie Russell. 1989. *The Second Shift*. New York: Viking.

Hodder, Harbour Fraser. 1997. "The New Fertility." *Harvard Magazine,* November-
    December, 54–64, 97–99.

Hoffert, Sylvia D. 1989. *Private Matters: American Attitudes toward Childbearing and
    Infant Nurture in the Urban North, 1800–1860*. Urbana: University of Illinois
    Press.

Hoffman, William S., Patricia Carpentier-Alting, Duane Thomas, V. Lee Hamil-
    ton, and Clifford L. Broman. 1991. "Initial Impact of Plant Closings on Auto-
    mobile Workers and Their Families." *Families in Society, Journal of Contemporary
    Human Services* 72: 103–107.

Hogue, Carol J. Rowland, and Martha A. Hargraves. 1993. "Class, Race, and Infant
    Mortality in the United States." *American Journal of Public Health* 83: 9–11.

Hondagneu-Sotelo, Pierrette, and Ernestine Avila. 1997. " 'I'm Here but I'm
    There': The Meanings of Latina Transnational Motherhood." *Gender & Society*
    11: 548–571.

Hopson, Darlene Powell, and Derek S. Hopson. 1990. *Different and Wonderful: Rais-
    ing Black Children in a Race-Conscious Society*. New York: Prentice Hall.

Horwood, L. John, and David M. Fergusson. 1998. "Breastfeeding and Later Cogni-
    tive and Academic Outcomes." *Pediatrics* 101(1): E91-E97.

Hummer, Robert A. 1993. "Racial Differentials in Infant Mortality in the U.S."
    Social Forces 72: 529–554.

IOM (Institute of Medicine). 1991. *Nutrition During Lactation*. Washington, D.C.: National Academy Press.

Jackman, Jean. 1991. "The Mommy Wars." *Ann Arbor News,* January 13, D-1, 3.

Jackson, Edith Banfield. 1947. "Mothers and Babies Together." *Parents* (October), 4.

Jacobson, Sandra W., Joseph L. Jacobson, and Karen F. Frye. 1991. "Incidence and Correlates of Breast-feeding in Socioeconomically Disadvantaged Women." *Pediatrics* 88: 728–736.

Jaggar, Alison, and William McBride. 1985. " 'Reproduction' as Male Ideology." *Women's Studies International Forum* 8: 185–196.

JAMA. 1996. "*People v Henderson*: The Prosecution Responds." Letters. *Journal of the American Medical Association* 275: 183–184.

JAMA. 1995. "Methamphetamine Ingestion by a Breast-feeding Mother and Her Infant's Death: *People v Henderson*." Letters. *Journal of the American Medical Association* 274: 215.

Jefferson, Margo. 1997. "Looking at What Black Looks Like." *New York Times*, June 11, B-1.

Jones, Vida Labrie. 1990. "Lupus and Black Women." In *The Black Women's Health Book: Speaking for Ourselves*, edited by Evelyn C. White. Seattle: Seal Press.

Kahn, Robbie Pfeufer. 1995. *Bearing Meaning*. Urbana: University of Illinois Press.

Kahn, Robbie Pfeufer. 1989a. "Mother's Milk: The 'Moment of Nurture' Revisited." *Resources for Feminist Research* 18: 29–36.

Kahn, Robbie Pfeufer. 1989b. "Women and Time in Childbirth and During Lactation." In *Taking Our Time: Feminist Perspectives on Temporality*, edited by F. J. Forman and C. Sowton. Oxford: Pergamon.

Kaminer, Wendy. 1992. *I'm Dysfunctional, You're Dysfunctional*. Reading, MA: Addison-Wesley.

Kaplan, E. Ann. 1994. "Look Who's Talking Indeed." In *Mothering: Ideology, Experience, and Agency*, edited by Evelyn Nakano Glenn, Grace Chang, and Linda Rennie Forcey. New York: Routledge.

Kaste, Linda M., and Helen C. Gift. 1995. "Inappropriate Infant Bottle Feeding." *Archives of Pediatric and Adolescent Medicine* 149: 786–791.

Katz, Bill, and Linda Sternberg Katz. 1992. *Magazines for Libraries*, 7th ed. New Providence, NJ: R. R. Bowker.

Kelleher, Kathleen. 1997. "It's Legal, So Why Isn't It Accepted?" *Los Angeles Times*, July 28, E-1.

Khatib-Chahidi, Jane. 1992. "Milk Kinship in Shi'ite Islamic Iran." In *The Anthropology of Breastfeeding*, edited by Vanessa Maher. Oxford: Berg.

Kilborn, Peter T. 1998. "Health Gap Grows, With Black Americans Trailing Whites, Studies Say." *New York Times*, January 26, A-16.

Kilborn, Peter T. 1992. "The Middle Class Feels Betrayed, But Maybe Not Enough to Rebel." *New York Times* January 12, D-1.

Kitzinger, Sheila. 1989. *Breastfeeding Your Baby*. New York: Knopf.

Kitzinger, Sheila. 1987. *The Experience of Breastfeeding*. London: Penguin.

Klaus, Alisa. 1993. "Depopulation and Race Suicide: Maternalism and Pronatalist

Ideologies in France and the United States." In *Mothers of a New World*, edited by Seth Koven and Sonya Michel. New York: Routledge.

Klinkenborg, Verlyn. 1991. "Balled and Chained to General Motors." *New York Times Book Review*, August 18, 8.

Kohn, Melvin L. 1963. "Social Class and Parent-Child Relationships: An Interpretation." *American Journal of Sociology* 68: 471–480.

Kotz, Pete. 1996. "Not for Public Consumption: When are breasts obscene?" *Utne Reader* (July-August): 68.

Koven, Seth, and Sonya Michel, editors. 1993. *Mothers of a New World*. New York: Routledge.

Kurinij, Natalie, Patricia H. Shiono, and George G. Rhoads. 1988. "Breast-Feeding Incidence and Duration in Black and White Women." *Pediatrics* 81: 365–371.

Kuttner, Robert. 1992. "An Economics for Democrats." *American Prospect* 8: 25–27.

LLLI. 1963, 1981, 1987, 1991. *The Womanly Art of Breastfeeding*. Franklin Park, IL: La Leche League International.

LLLI. 1986. "Breastfeeding Rights Packet." Franklin Park, IL: La Leche League International, Reprint No. 78.

Ladd-Taylor, Molly. 1994. *Mother-Work: Women, Child Welfare, and the State, 1890–1930*. Urbana: University of Illinois Press.

Ladner, Joyce A. 1971 (1995 ed.) *Tomorrow's Tomorrow: The Black Woman*. Lincoln: University of Nebraska Press.

Lamont, Michele. 1992. *Money, Morals, and Manners*. Chicago: University of Chicago Press.

Lanser, Susan S. 1989. "Feminist Criticism, 'The Yellow Wallpaper,' and the Politics of Color in America." *Feminist Studies* 15: 415–441.

Laqueur, Thomas. 1990a. *Making Sex: Body and Gender from Greeks to Freud*. Cambridge: Harvard University Press.

Laqueur, Thomas. 1990b. "The Facts of Fatherhood." In *Conflicts in Feminism*, edited by Marianne Hirsch and Evelyn Fox Keller. New York: Routledge.

Lawrence, Ruth A. 1988. "Major Influences in Promoting Breastfeeding: US Perspectives. In *Programmes to Promote Breastfeeding*, edited by D. B. Jelliffe and E. F. P. Jelliffe. Oxford: Oxford University Press.

Leavitt, Judith Walzer. 1986. *Brought to Bed*. New York: Oxford University Press.

Leidner, Robin. 1993. *Fast Food, Fast Talk*. Berkeley: University of California Press.

Lerner, Sharon. 1998. "Striking a Balance as AIDS Enters the Formula Fray." *Ms.*, March/April, 14–21.

Levine, Jeremiah J., and Norman T. Ilowite. 1994. "Sclerodermalike Esophageal Disease in Children Breast-fed by Mothers with Silicone Breast Implants." *Journal of the American Medical Association*, 271: 213–216.

Lewin, Ellen. 1994. "Negotiating Lesbian Motherhood." In *Motherhood: Ideology, Experience, and Agency*, edited by Evelyn Nakano Glenn, Grace Chang, and Linda Rennie Forcey. New York: Routledge.

Lewin, Ellen. 1990. "Claims to Motherhood." In *Uncertain Terms*, edited by Faye Ginsburg and Anna Lowenhaupt Tsing. Boston: Beacon.

Liebow, Elliot. 1993. *Tell Them Who I Am*. New York: Free Press.

Lofton, Mary, and Gwen Gotsch. 1983. "Legal Rights of Breastfeeding Mothers: USA Scene." Franklin Park, IL: La Leche League International, Reprint No. 59.

Lord, George, and Albert C. Price. 1992. "Growth Ideology in a Period of Decline: Deindustrialization and Restructuring, Flint Style." *Social Problems* 39: 155–169.

Los Angeles Times. 1995. "Panel Rejects Bill Establishing Right to Breast-Feed in Public." March 31, A-26.

Los Angeles Times. 1994a. "Drug-Using Mother Convicted After 2-Month-Old Son Dies." September 11, A-13.

Los Angeles Times. 1994b. "Breast Milk Trial Deadlocks." August 9, A-19.

Love, Susan M., with Karen Lindsey. 1995. *Dr. Susan Love's Breast Book*. Reading, MA: Addison-Wesley.

Lowman, Kaye. 1984. *Of Cradles and Careers: A Guide to Reshaping Your Job to Include a Baby in Your Life*. Franklin Park, IL: La Leche League International.

Lubiano, Wahneema. 1992. "Black Ladies, Welfare Queens, and State Minstrels." In *Race-ing Justice, En-gendering Power*, edited by Toni Morrison. New York: Pantheon.

Lucas, A., R. Morley, T. J. Cole, G. Lister, and C. Leeson-Payne. 1992. "Breast Milk and Subsequent Intelligence Quotient in Children Born Preterm." *Lancet* 339: 261–264.

MacKinnon, Catherine. 1994. "Sexuality." In *Theorizing Feminism*, edited by Anne C. Herrmann and Abigail J. Stewart. Boulder, CO: Westview Press.

MacKinnon, Catherine. 1991. "Does Sexuality Have a History?" *Michigan Quarterly Review* 30: 1–11.

Maclean, Heather. 1990. *Women's Experience of Breastfeeding*. Toronto: University of Toronto Press.

Maher, Vanessa, ed. 1992. *The Anthropology of Breast-Feeding: Natural Law or Social Construct*. Oxford: Berg.

Marriott, Michel. 1997. "Black Erotica Challenges Black Tradition." *New York Times*, June 1, 41.

Martin, Emily. 1992. "The End of the Body?" *American Ethnologist* 19: 121–138.

Martin, Emily. 1987. *The Woman in the Body*. Boston: Beacon.

Martin, Jane Roland. 1994. "Methodological Essentialism, False Difference, and Other Dangerous Traps." *Signs* 19: 630–657.

Mason, Diane, and Diane Ingersoll. 1986. *Breastfeeding and the Working Mother*. New York: St. Martins.

Massachusetts WIC Program. 1997. "Breastfeeding Rates." Available from Debra Krauter, Statewide Breastfeeding Coordinator, Boston, MA.

Masters, William H., and Virginia E. Johnson. 1966. *Human Sexual Response*. Boston: Little, Brown and Company.

May, Elaine Tyler. 1988. *Homeward Bound: American Families in the Cold War Era*. New York: Basic.

May, Martha. 1985. "Bread Before Roses." In *Women, Work, and Protest,* edited by Ruth Milkman. New York: Routledge & Kegan Paul.

McCarthy, Mary. 1963. *The Group.* New York: Harcourt, Brace, and World.

McLarin, Kim. 1998. "Lives: Primary Colors." *New York Times Magazine,* May 24, 58.

McLorg, P., and C. A. Bryant. 1989. "Influence of Social Network Members and Health Care Professionals on Infant Feeding Practices of Economically Disadvantaged Mothers." *Medical Anthropology* 10: 265–278.

McMahon, Martha. 1995. *Engendering Motherhood: Identity and Self-Transformation in Women's Lives.* New York: Guilford Press.

McMillen, Sally G. 1990. *Motherhood in the Old South.* Baton Rouge: Louisiana State University Press.

Mead Johnson. 1990, 1986. *The Breastfeeding Guide for Working Mothers.* Evansville, IN.

Meier, Barry. 1997. "In War Against AIDS, Battle Over Baby Formula Reignites." *New York Times,* June 8, A-1.

Meier, Barry. 1991a. "Doctors Oppose Infant-Formula Ads." *San Francisco Chronicle,* January 2, B-3.

Meier, Barry. 1991b. "F.T.C. Re-Emerges as a Watchdog on Prices." *New York Times,* January 28, A-1.

Merrill, Elizabeth Bryant. 1987. "Learning How to Mother." *Anthropology & Education Quarterly* 18: 222–240.

Millard, Ann V. 1990. "The Place of the Clock in Pediatric Advice." *Social Science Medicine* 31: 211–221.

Miller, Fred D., Jr. 1983. *Out of the Mouths of Babes: The Infant Formula Controversy.* Bowling Green, OH: Social Philosophy and Policy Center, Bowling Green State University.

Miller, Sanford, and Joginder Chopra. 1984. "Problems with Human Milk and Infant Formulas." *Pediatrics* 74: 629–647.

Millman, Sara. 1985. "Breastfeeding and Infant Mortality: Untangling the Complex Web of Causality." *Sociological Quarterly* 26: 65–79.

Minami, Judy. 1991. "Finding a Doctor For Your Baby." *New Beginnings,* March/ April, 45–46. La Leche League International.

Minchin, Maureen. 1989. *Breastfeeding Matters.* Sydney, Australia: Alma Publications, Allen & Unwin.

Mink, Gwendolyn. 1995. *The Wages of Motherhood: Inequality in the Welfare State, 1917–1942.* Ithaca: Cornell University Press.

Minow, Martha. 1990. *Making All the Difference.* Ithaca: Cornell University Press.

Monson, Renee A. 1997. "State-ing Sex and Gender: Collecting Information from Mothers and Fathers in Paternity Cases." *Gender & Society* 11: 279–295.

Morrison, Toni. 1987. *Beloved.* New York: Knopf.

Morrison, Toni. 1973. *Sula.* New York: Knopf.

Mothering. 1991. "Your Letters." Summer, 14ff.

Moynihan, Daniel Patrick. 1965. *The Negro Family: The Case for National Action.* Washington, D.C.: U.S. Department of Labor.

Murray, Charles. 1993. "The Coming White Underclass." *Wall Street Journal*, October 29, A-14.

NCPE (National Committee on Pay Equity). 1993–94. "Face the Facts: About Wage Discrimination and Equal Pay." Washington, D.C.

NCPE (National Committee on Pay Equity). 1989. "Fact File." *Newsnotes* 10: 10.

NPR (National Public Radio). 1998. Report on WIC funding debate in Congress. *Weekend Edition*, June 14.

NPR (National Public Radio). 1996. "The Politics of Breastfeeding." *Talk of the Nation*, January 17.

NPR (National Public Radio). 1992a. Interview with James Grant, Executive Director of the United Nations Children's Fund. *Morning Edition*, March 9.

NPR (National Public Radio). 1992b. Report on silicone breast implants. *Morning Edition*, April 17.

National Center for Education on Maternal and Child Health. 1985. *Breastfeeding and Women Today: Conference Proceedings*. Washington, D.C.

Nelson, Margaret K. 1990. *Negotiated Care*. Philadelphia: Temple University Press.

New Beginnings: La Leche League's Breastfeeding Journal (bimonthly members' magazine). Vol. 6 (4 July-August 1990) to Vol. 9 (3 May-June 1992).

Newburg, David S., and Jacqueline M. Street. 1997. "Bioactive Materials in Human Milk." *Nutrition Today* 32: 191–201.

Newcomb, Polly A., Barry E. Storer, Matthew P. Longnecker, Robert Mittendorf, E. Robert Greenberg, Richard Clapp, Kenneth P. Burke, Walter C. Willett, and Brian MacMahon. 1994. "Lactation and a Reduced Risk of Premenopausal Breast Cancer." *New England Journal of Medicine* 330: 81–87.

Newman, Katherine S. 1988. *Falling From Grace*. New York: Free Press.

New Scientist. 1987. "Powdered Milk Nips Breastfeeding in the Bud." February 5, 26.

Newton, Niles. 1955. *Maternal Emotions*. New York: Paul B. Hoeber, Inc.

New York Times. 1998a. "Infant-Formula Makers Said to Violate Code." April 11, A-6.

New York Times. 1998b. "Breast-Feeding Is Tied to Brain Power." January 6, C-4.

New York Times. 1997a. "Fed-up Mother Prompts a Bill on the Right to Nurse in Public." February 16, A-47.

New York Times. 1997b. "Protecting Infant Nutrition." Editorial, April 24, A-34.

New York Times. 1997c. "Feeding Children Well Saves U.S. Money." Letters, April 27, A-14.

New York Times. 1996. "The Downsizing of America" (a series of seven articles). March 3–10, A-1.

New York Times. 1994. "A Mother's Drug Use, an Infant's Death and Then a Conviction." September 11, A-36.

Nieves, Evelyn. 1996. "Public Furor Over Nursing Baby In a Car." *New York Times*, September 15, A-45.

Nossiter, Adam. 1995. "Asthma Common and on the Rise in the Crowded South Bronx." *New York Times*, September 5, A-1.

Oakley, Ann. 1992. *Social Support and Motherhood*. Oxford: Blackwell.

Oakley, Ann. 1981. "Interviewing Women: A Contradiction in Terms?" In *Doing Feminist Research*, edited by Helen Roberts. London: Routledge & Kegan Paul.

Oakley, Ann. 1980. *Women Confined: Towards a Sociology of Childbirth*. Oxford: Martin Robertson.

Ogbu, John U. 1985. "A Cultural Ecology of Competence Among Inner-City Blacks." In *Beginnings: The Social and Affective Development of Black Children*, edited by M. Spencer, G. Kerse-Brookins, and W. R. Allen. Hillsdale, NJ: Erlbaum.

Olson, Robin May. 1992. "Adoptive Moms Nurture Bonds by Breast-Feeding Babies." *Los Angeles Times*, March, 25, E-3.

Omi, Michael, and Howard Winant. 1986. *Racial Formation in the United States*. New York: Routledge.

Owen, Colleen Manning. 1988. "Some Discoveries about Women and Breast Pumps," and "A Patent Search of the Breast Pump." Unpublished typescripts from the author, Concord, MA.

Painter, Nell Irvin. 1996. *Sojourner Truth: A Life, A Symbol*. New York: Norton.

Palmer, Gabrielle. 1988. *The Politics of Breastfeeding*. London: Pandora Press.

Parsons, Talcott, and Robert Bales. 1955. *Family, Socialization, and Interaction Process*. Glencoe, IL: Free Press.

Pateman, Carole. 1988. *The Sexual Contract*. Cambridge, UK: Polity Press.

Paterno, Susan. 1992. "Nursing at Work: Secrets for Breastfeeding Away from Home, Express Yourself." *Parenting*, February, 43.

Payne, Elizabeth Anne. 1988. *Reform, Labor, and Feminism: Margaret Dreier Robins and the Women's Trade Union League*. Urbana: University of Illinois Press.

Pear, Robert. 1997. "Greasy Kid Stuff: Washington Kidnaps Dick and Jane." *New York Times*, June 15, E-1.

Peck, Ellen, and Judith Senderowitz, editors. 1974. *Pronatalism*. New York: Thomas Y. Crowell.

People. 1991. "Today's Latest Coo." March 25, 67–70.

Petchesky, Rosalind Pollack. 1995. "The Body as Property: A Feminist Re-Vision." In *Conceiving the New World Order: The Global Politics of Reproduction*, edited by Faye Ginsburg and Rayna Rapp. Berkeley: University of California Press.

Petchesky, Rosalind Pollack. 1987. "Fetal Images." *Feminist Studies* 13: 263–292.

Phelan, Shane. 1993. "(Be)coming Out." *Signs* 18: 765–790.

Phelan, Shane. 1991. "Specificity." *Differences* 3: 145–160.

Pickering, L. K., D. M. Granoff, J. R. Erickson, M. L. Masor, C. T. Cordle, J. P. Schaller, T. R. Winship, C. L. Paule, M. D. Hilty. 1998. "Modulation of the Immune System by Human Milk and Infant Formula Containing Nucleotides." *Pediatrics* 101(2): 242–249.

Piven, Frances Fox, and Richard Cloward. 1971. *Regulating the Poor*. New York: Random House.

Pollack, Andrew. 1997. "In Japan's Burnt Trash, Dioxin Threat." *New York Times*, April 27, A-10.

Quick, Barbara. 1997. "Breast Milk: It Does a Body Good." *Ms.*, January/February, 32–35.

Quindlen, Anna. 1994. "It Took Protests to Win Right to Feed Babies in Public." *Los Angeles Daily Journal*, May 27, A-22.

Rainwater, Lee, and William L. Yancey. 1967. *The Moynihan Report and the Politics of Controversy.* Cambridge: MIT Press.

Randolph, Lynn. 1993. "The Ilusas (Deluded Women): Representation of Women Who Are Out of Bounds." Paper delivered at the Bunting Institute of Radcliffe College, Cambridge, MA, November 30.

Rapp, Rayna. 1990. "Constructing Amniocentesis." In *Uncertain Terms*, edited by Faye Ginsburg and Anna Lowenhaupt Tsing. Boston: Beacon.

Rapping, Elayne. 1996. *The Culture of Recovery: Making Sense of the Self-Help Movement in Women's Lives.* Boston: Beacon.

Rapping, Elayne. 1990. "The Future of Motherhood." In *Women, Class, and the Feminist Imagination*, edited by Karen Hansen and Ilene Philipson. Philadelphia: Temple University Press.

Reskin, Barbara, and Irene Padavic. 1994. *Women and Men at Work.* Thousand Oaks, CA: Pine Forge Press.

Rich, Adrienne. 1980. "Compulsory Heterosexuality and Lesbian Existence." *Signs* 631–657.

Rich, Adrienne. 1976. *Of Woman Born: Motherhood as Experience and Institution.* New York: Bantam.

Riessman, Catherine Kohler. 1987. "When Gender Is Not Enough." *Gender & Society* 1: 172–207.

Riessman, Catherine Kohler. 1983. "Women and Medicalization." *Social Policy* 14: 3–18.

Riley, Denise. 1983. *War in the Nursery.* London: Virago.

Roberts, Dorothy. 1997. *Killing the Black Body.* New York: Pantheon.

Roediger, David R. 1991. *The Wages of Whiteness.* London: Verso.

Roiphe, Anne. 1996. *Fruitful: A Real Mother in the Modern World.* Boston: Houghton Mifflin.

Rollins, Judith. 1985. *Between Women: Domestics and Their Employers.* Philadelphia: Temple University Press.

Ross, Ellen. 1995. "New Thoughts on 'the Oldest Vocation.'" *Signs* 20: 397–413.

Ross, Ellen. 1993. *Love and Toil: Motherhood in Outcast London, 1870–1918.* New York: Oxford University Press.

Ross Labs. 1996. *Updated Breastfeeding Trends, 1987–1995.* Unpublished, December. Available from La Leche League International.

Ross Labs. 1987. *Breastfeeding: Feeding Your Baby "The Natural Way."* Columbus, OH: Division of Abbott Laboratories.

Ross Labs. 1985. *Supplemental Feeding: What Breastfeeding Mothers Ask.* Columbus, OH: Division of Abbott Laboratories.

Ross Labs. 1984. *The Best of Both Worlds: A Guide for the Working, Breast-feeding Mother.* Columbus, OH: Division of Abbott Laboratories.

Rothman, Barbara Katz. 1989. *Recreating Motherhood.* New York: Norton.

Ruddick, Sara. 1990. "Thinking about Fathers." In *Conflicts in Feminism,* edited by Marianne Hirsch and Evelyn Fox Keller. New York: Routledge.

Ruddick, Sara. 1989. *Maternal Thinking.* Boston: Beacon.

Ryan, Alan S., David Rush, Fritz W. Kreiger, and Gregory E. Lewandowski. 1991. "Recent Declines in Breast-Feeding in the United States, 1984 Through 1988." *Pediatrics* 88: 719–727.

Ryan, Mary. 1981. *The Cradle of the Middle Class.* New York: Cambridge University Press.

Ryan, Michael. 1997. "'That Baby Is Loved.'" *Parade,* March 9, 8–9.

Ryckman, Lisa Levitt. 1992. "A Simple Question Leads Mom to Jail." *Chicago Tribune,* February 9, I-16.

Scheper-Hughes, Nancy. 1992. *Death Without Weeping.* Berkeley: University of California Press.

Schewel, Susan. 1991. "Combining Breastfeeding and Employment: Is This the Best of Both Worlds?" Unpublished typescript from the author, University of Pennsylvania, School of Nursing.

Schwartz, J. Brad, Barry M. Popkin, Janet Tognetti, and Namvar Zohoori. 1995. "Does WIC Participation Improve Breast-Feeding Practices?" *American Journal of Public Health* 85: 729–731.

Sears, William. 1983. *Becoming a Father.* Franklin Park, IL: La Leche League International.

Segal, Lynne. 1990. *Slow Motion: Changing Masculinities, Changing Men.* New Brunswick, NJ: Rutgers University Press.

Sepah, Torang. 1998. "Work Notes." *Ms.,* January/February, 44.

Shapiro, Laura. 1997. "Beyond an Apple a Day." *Newsweek* Special Issue, Spring/Summer, 52–56.

Shaw, Stephanie. 1994. "Mothering Under Slavery in the Antebellum South." In *Mothering: Ideology, Experience, and Agency,* edited by Evelyn Nakano Glenn, Grace Chang, and Linda Rennie Forcey. New York: Routledge.

Sherman, Gordon M. 1996. "Welfare Reform and Its Impacts on Social Security." *Southern Business and Economic Journal* 19: 90–109.

Skocpol, Theda. 1992. *Protecting Soldiers and Mothers.* Cambridge: Harvard University Press.

Slade, Margot. 1997. "Have Pump, Will Travel: Combining Breast-feeding and a Career." *New York Times,* December 27, BU-12.

Smith, Susan L. 1995. *Sick and Tired of Being Sick and Tired: Black Women's Health Activism in America, 1890–1950.* Philadelphia: University of Pennsylvania Press.

Snitow, Ann. 1990. "A Gender Diary." In *Conflicts in Feminism,* edited by Marianne Hirsch and Evelyn Fox Keller. New York: Routledge.

Solinger, Rickie. 1994. "Race and 'Value': Black and White Illegitimate Babies, 1945–1965." In *Mothering: Ideology, Experience, and Agency,* edited by Evelyn Nakano Glenn, Grace Chang, and Linda Rennie Forcey. New York: Routledge.

Soper, Kate. 1995. *What Is Nature?* Oxford: Blackwell.

Spock, Benjamin. 1957, 1985. *Baby and Child Care.* New York: Pocket Books.

Stacey, Judith. 1990. *Brave New Families.* New York: Basic.

Stanway, P., and A. Stanway. 1978. *Breast Is Best.* London: Pan.

Stanworth, Michelle. 1990. In *Birth Pangs: Conflicts in Feminism,* edited by Marianne Hirsch and Evelyn Fox Keller. New York: Routledge.

Starbird, Ellen H. 1991. "Comparison of Influences on Breastfeeding Initiation of Firstborn Children, 1960–69 vs 1970–79." *Social Science Medicine* 33: 627–634.

Stearns, Cindy A. 1999. "Breastfeeding and the Good Maternal Body." *Gender & Society* (in press).

Strathman, Terry. 1984. "From the Quotidian to the Utopian." *Berkeley Journal of Sociology* 29: 1–34.

Straus, Murray A. 1994. *Beating the Devil Out of Them.* New York: Lexington.

Strobe, Mike. 1991. "Poor Moms Targeted in Grant to Promote Breast-feeding." *Flint Journal,* October 10, B-4.

Stuart, Ann Elisabeth F. 1996. "Edith B. Jackson and the Rooming-In Project: Changing the Hospital Birthing Experience." Unpublished typescript from the author, Radcliffe College.

Swarns, Rachel L. 1998. "Grieving Mother Is Charged in Baby Daughter's Starvation." *New York Times,* May 29, A-20.

Tamm, Merike. 1987. "And then came Aleksander." In *Learning a Loving Way of Life,* edited by Virginia Halonen and Nancy Mohrbacher. Franklin Park, IL: La Leche League International.

Taylor, Verta. 1996. *Rock-A-By Baby: Feminism, Self-Help, and Postpartum Depression.* New York: Routledge.

Temin, Christine. 1997. "The Body of the Ballet." *Boston Globe,* August 17, 1-N.

Terry, Sara. 1997. "A Ballet Dancer, So Very Thin, Dies and the Questions Begin." *New York Times,* July 11, 13-A.

Thompson, Becky W. 1994. *A Hunger So Wide and So Deep.* Minneapolis: University of Minnesota Press.

Thompson, Mark. 1997. "A Call to Nurse." *Time,* February 24, 32.

Time. 1997. "Breast-Feeding Army Pilot." Letters, March 24, 31.

Treckel, Paula A. 1989. "Breastfeeding and Maternal Sexuality in Colonial America." *Journal of Interdisciplinary History* 20: 25-51.

Trimm-Harrison, Mary. 1991. "A Time of Turmoil." *New Beginnings* (September-October) 8(5): 153–154.

Tsing, Anna Lowenhaupt. 1990. "Monster Stories." In *Uncertain Terms,* edited by Faye Ginsburg and Anna Lowenhaupt Tsing. Boston: Beacon.

Turner, Bryan S. 1996. *The Body and Society.* London: Sage.

Van Allen, Judith. 1990. "Capitalism Without Patriarchy." In *Women, Class, and the Feminist Imagination,* edited by Karen Hansen and Ilene Philipson. Philadelphia: Temple University Press.

Vandenheuvel, Audrey. 1997. "Women's Roles After First Birth." *Gender & Society* 11: 357–368.

Van Esterik, Penny. 1989. *Beyond the Breast-Bottle Controversy.* New Brunswick, NJ: Rutgers University Press.

Vanzi, Max. 1997. "Assembly O.k.'s Right to Breast-Feed in Public." *Los Angeles Times,* July 1, 18-A.

Villarosa, Linda, editor. 1994. *Body & Soul: The Black Women's Guide to Physical and Emotional Well-Being.* New York: Harper Perennial.

Vogel, Lise. 1993. *Mothers on the Job.* New Brunswick: Rutgers University Press.

WAC (Women's Action Coalition). 1993. *WAC Stats: The Facts About Women.* New York: The New Press.

Waletzky, Lucy R. 1979. "Husbands' Problems With Breast-Feeding." *American Journal of Orthopsychiatry* 49: 349–352.

Walker, Alice. 1983. *In Search of Our Mothers' Gardens.* New York: Harcourt Brace Jovanovich.

Walker, Alice. 1976. *Meridian.* New York: Harcourt Brace Jovanovich.

Warren, Jennifer. 1997. "Wilson Signs Bill on Right to Breast-Feed." *Los Angeles Times,* July 15, A-12.

Washington Times. 1992. "Mother and Child Reunion." January 28, F-21.

Weiner, Lynn Y. 1994. "Reconstructing Motherhood: The La Leche League in Postwar America." *Journal of American History* 80: 1357–1381.

Weiner, Lynn Y. 1993. "Maternalism as a Paradigm." *Journal of Women's History* 5: 96–98.

Weisskopf, Susan (Contratto). 1980. "Maternal Sexuality and Asexual Motherhood." *Signs* 5: 766–782.

Weller, S. C., and C. I. Dungy. 1986. "Personal Preferences and Ethnic Variations Among Anglo and Hispanic Breast and Bottle Feeders." *Social Science and Medicine* 23: 539–548.

Wertz, Richard W., and Dorothy L. Wertz. 1989. *Lying In: A History of Childbirth in America.* New Haven: Yale University Press.

White, Evelyn C., editor. 1990. *The Black Women's Health Book: Speaking for Ourselves.* Seattle: Seal Press.

White, Mary. 1987. "A Worthwhile Career." In *Learning a Loving Way of Life,* edited by Virginia Halonen and Nancy Mohrbachen. Franklin Park, IL: La Leche League International.

Whittemore, Alice S., Robin Harris, Jacqueline Intyre, and the Collaborative Ovarian Cancer Group. 1992. "Characteristics Relating to Ovarian Cancer Risk: Collaborative Analysis of 12 US Case-Controlled Studies." *American Journal of Epidemiology* 136: 1184–1203.

WHO (World Health Organization). 1990. *Infant Feeding: The Physiological Basis.* Supplement to *Bulletin of the World Health Organization* 67.

Whyte, William H. 1956. *The Organization Man.* New York: Simon and Schuster.

Williams, K. Malaika. 1990. "The Best Foot Forward: A Black Woman Deals with Diabetes." In *The Black Women's Health Book: Speaking for Ourselves,* edited by Evelyn C. White. Seattle: Seal Press.

Williams, Patricia J. 1991. *The Alchemy of Race and Rights.* Cambridge: Harvard University Press.

Williams, Sherley Anne. 1986. *Dessa Rose*. New York: William Morrow.

Wilson, William Julius. 1996. *When Work Disappears*. New York: Knopf.

Winn, Marie. 1983. *Children Without Childhood*. New York: Pantheon.

Wolf, Naomi. 1991. *The Beauty Myth*. William Morrow.

Wright, Erik O., K. Shire, S. Hwang, M. Dolan, and J. Baxter. 1992. "The Non-effects of Class on the Gender Division of Labor in the Home. *Gender & Society* 6: 252–282.

Yadlon, Susan. 1997. "Skinny Women and Good Mothers." *Feminist Studies* 23: 645–677.

Yalom, Marilyn. 1997. *A History of the Breast*. New York: Knopf.

Young, Iris Marion. 1990. *Throwing Like a Girl and Other Essays in Feminist Philosophy and Social Theory*. Bloomington: Indiana University Press.

Zelizer, Viviana A. 1985. *Pricing the Priceless Child*. Princeton, NJ: Princeton University Press.

Zimmerman, Mary K. 1987. "The Women's Health Movement." In *Analyzing Gender*, edited by Beth B. Hess and Myra Marx Ferree. Newbury Park, CA: Sage.

Zola, Irving Kenneth. 1972. "Medicine as an Institution of Social Control." *Sociological Review* 20: 487–504.

ACKNOWLEDGMENTS

Many people have my deepest thanks. For help near the start: Julia Adams, Renee Anspach, Susan Contratto Weisskopf, Linda Frankel, Peggy Kahn, Lew Margolis, Ruth Milkman, Jeff Paige, David Pingitore, Patricia Smith, Judith Stacey, and Abby Stewart. For help at the start and finish: Barrie Thorne. For keeping me going: Julia Adams, Michael Burawoy, Peggy Kahn, and Andrea Press. For their interest when I was in the doldrums: Arlene Kaplan Daniels and Verta Taylor. For research assistance and much more: Elizabeth A. Vandewater, Theresa Deussen, Mary Moroschan, Natalie Bennett, Ann Elisabeth Stuart, and Amelia Dunlop. For their wonderful editorial skills: Amy Caldwell and Susan Meigs. For lending pieces of their expertise and experience: Jane Hassinger, Vicki Honeyman, Monica Johnson, Kathleen Kendall-Tackett, Debra Krauter, Colleen Manning Owen, Marcie Richardson, Rachel Stark, Gail Wasserman, and Lynn Westbrook; and Lorena Chambers, Andrea Hunter and the other fellows of the Differences Between Women Program at the University of Michigan, 1994-95. For sharing their shimmering brilliance: the sister-fellows at the Bunting Institute of Radcliffe College 1996-97, especially Paula Bennett, Alex Chasin, Celeste Goodridge, Farah Griffin, Janis Kapler, Elizabeth King, Julia Scher, and, most especially, Joan Butterton and Jane Kamensky. For my mother, for all the clippings. For all the women who shared their stories with me. And finally, for my husband and son, for their passionate attachment.

I gratefully acknowledge funded support from the University of Michigan Rackham Faculty and Research Partnership Awards, the American Sociological Association/National Science Foundation Fund for the Advancement of the Discipline Award, and the Bunting Fellowship at Radcliffe College.

INDEX

Page numbers appear in italic for illustrations.

erhood," 24, 25, 26, 183; science and,
32–38; sexuality, 38–42. *See also*
motherhood
Scheper-Hughes, Nancy, 10, 46
science, 29–38; hospital birthing, 30, 32;
psychoanalysis, 32–34; psychology,
child, 31–33. *See also* medical model
sexuality, 1, 5, 11, 38–42, 181, 199;
African-American women, 13–14;
African-American working-class
mothers, 147, 167, 168, 169–70, 174,
193, 196; disembodied motherhood,
61; La Leche League, 66, 71–72, 96–
101, 106; men, role of, 16–18, 182,
189; sacred motherhood, 27–28, 51;
white working-class mothers, 128,
132, 133. *See also* compulsory heterosexuality; homosexuality; sexualization of breasts
sexualization of breasts, 38–41, 144, 185.
See also sexuality
shared child-rearing, 153
shared nursing, 40–42
shared parenting, 191–92
silicone implant surgery, 185–86
social issues, 3, 12, 19, 44, 69, 92; African-
American working-class mothers, 152,
154, 168
Solinger, Rickie, 148
Southern Medical Association, 27
Spock, Benjamin, 34–35, 38–39, 45, 51,
59, 116
state influences, 141, 145, 167–68, 175,
183, 199, 200; legislation, 138; policies,
190; regulation, 27, 61, 143, 176; social
services, 179; support, 154, 157
Stearns, Cindy, 16
Steinem, Gloria, 8
sterilization, 173, 186
Sudden Infant Death Syndrome (SIDS),
49
support groups, 37, 43–44, 107, 185. *See
also* La Leche League
surrogate mothers, 74

Taylor, Verta, 107
Third World, 46, 47, 52, 93
Tillmon, Johnnie, 27
Time, 1
Truth, Sojourner, 13, 168
Turner, Bryan, 187

United Colors of Benetton, 172, 194–96,
202–3. *See also* advertising; corporate
influences
University of Michigan, 194
U.S. Children's Bureau, 24, 26, 32, 37
U.S. Department of Health and Human
Services, 48

vaginal births after Caesareans (VBAC),
67
Van Esterik, Penny, 93
Vogel, Lise, 197

Wadsworth, Benjamin, 21
wage-earning mothers, 52–62, 74–80, 81,
134–46, 183; African-American
working-class mothers, 167, 176–77;
"Bad Mothers," 89–90, 150; breast
pumps, 134–39; Mommy Wars, 1, 85–
90; promotion, breastfeeding, 139–46;
sacred motherhood, 24, 42; white
working-class mothers, 128, 134
Wall Street Journal, 131
Watson, John, 31
Weiner, Lynn, 70, 72, 76, 89–90, 92–93,
94
Weisskopf, Susan (Contratto), 100
welfare reform, 48, 184. *See also* state
influences
wetnursing, 20, 21, 22, 41
Williams, Patricia, 172
Williams, Sherley Ann, 171, 172
Winnicott, D. W., 33–34
Wollstonecraft, Mary, 7
Womanly Art of Breastfeeding, The, 64, 75,
77, 98, 124
Women, Infants and Children (WIC), 48,
104, 123, 139, 141, 143, 200
Women of Color Task Force, 194, 196,
202–3
Working Mother, 117
working mothers. *See* wage-earning
mothers
Works Progress Administration, 171
World Health Organization, 45, 47
World Wide Web, 187

Yalom, Marilyn, 2, 185
Young, Iris, 189, 199